ETHNIC STRATIFICATION AND ECONOMIC INEQUALITY AROUND THE WORLD

While global inequalities have had popular as well as academic attention for years, in recent years the developed world has suddenly woken up to the rising inequality within wealthy nations, particularly in the United States. So far, explanations for this growing inequality have focused on changes in the global economy and its impact within nations. Max Haller has written a well-researched and timely book showing how inequality within nations is more complex and involves differences in racial stratification as well as economic changes.

Harold Kerbo, California Polytechnic State University, USA

Max Haller's work is commendable for its comparative perspective, comprehensive coverage and wealth of empirical data, deftness of analysis and for its historically-sensitive approach. Refreshingly, the volume goes beyond arm-chair theorizing about inequality and offers, on the basis of a vast and carefully-marshalled array of empirical data, some valuable suggestions for reducing levels of inequality between and within nations and mitigating the suffering and hardships of excluded and marginalized groups in society.

A. R. Momin, University of Mumbai, India

T0304074

Ethnic Stratification and Economic Inequality around the World

The End of Exploitation and Exclusion?

MAX HALLER

in collaboration with ANJA EDER
both at the University of Graz, Austria

Routledge
Taylor & Francis Group

LONDON AND NEW YORK

First published 2015 by Ashgate Publishing

Published 2016 by Routledge
2 Park Square, Milton Park, Abingdon, Oxon OX14 4RN
711 Third Avenue, New York, NY 10017, USA

First issued in paperback 2017

Routledge is an imprint of the Taylor & Francis Group, an informa business

British Library Cataloguing in Publication Data
A catalogue record for this book is available from the British Library

Library of Congress Cataloging-in-Publication Data
Haller, Max, Dr.
Ethnic stratification and economic inequality around the world : the end of exploitation and exclusion? / by Max Haller in collaboration with Anja Eder.
  pages cm
Includes bibliographical references and index.
ISBN 978-1-4094-4952-2 (hardback) – ISBN 978-1-4094-4953-9 (ebook) – ISBN 978-1-4724-0193-9 (epub) 1. Income distribution. 2. Equality. 3. Ethnic groups. 4. Social classes. I. Eder, Anja. II. Title.
HC79.I5H35 2014
339.2'2089–dc23

2014018335

ISBN 13: 978-1-138-30647-9 (pbk)
ISBN 13: 978-1-4094-4952-2 (hbk)

Contents

List of Figures

List of Tables

Preface

The Problem

In 2009, worldwide there were 1.9 billion poor people who had to live with less than one Dollar per day. Extreme poverty, daily hunger, afflicted 40 million.[1] GNP per capita, adjusted for purchasing power, was 52,000 Dollar in the United States, 43,000 in West European countries like Austria, Netherlands and Sweden, but only 3,900 in India and 550 in Burundi and Eritrea. At the same time, over 10 million persons owned more than one million Dollars worldwide, and 1,200 persons were billionaires, owning one billion (one thousand million dollars). It is obvious to ascribe these extreme differences to global injustices, privileges and discriminations. Yet, 70% of the poor do not live in the poorest countries of the world but in those with a middle income seen in global terms. 643,000 millionaires live in China whose GNP per capita is 9,000 Dollars, in Brazil 165,000.[2] The list of the super-rich of this world is headed in 2012 by a Mexican; among the twenty two richest billionaires there is one Chinese and one Indian. Global inequality, the difference between the mean incomes between the richest and the poorest countries of the world, is blatant and the rich countries of the global North could and certainly should do much more to alleviate poverty in the South. However, this is a task which cannot be solved by the North or at the global level alone. The central thesis of this book is that inequality within nation states is at least as large, if not larger, than that between the rich and poor ones; widespread poverty and massive inequality exists also within nations. What is particularly important: It is mainly at the level of the nation state that inequality and poverty can be tackled in political terms. Even some poor nations have been able to reduce or contain their internal poverty and inequality in a significant way; in others, strong economic growth has indeed reduced poverty but it has also increased internal inequality. To understand why this is so is not only a task for politics, it is also an eminent task of comparative social science. My argument is that it has received, by far, too little attention and that only partial explanations have been provided for it.

This book seeks to make a contribution to understanding this problem. It is the result of a long-standing work which began some five years ago. It resulted from three principal areas of interest of mine, namely social inequality, stratification and mobility; ethnic and national identity and relations; and European macro-regional integration. A significant part of the book was elaborated during my stay as a visiting researcher at the Wissenschaftszentrum Berlin für Sozialforschung (Germany) in the Winter Term 2008/09. There, I profited a lot from discussions with Jens Alber and Ulrich Kohler at the Department 'Inequality and Social Integration'. Many critical and helpful responses from presenting draft papers and lectures at conferences and invited lectures helped me to elaborate the basic ideas. They include the following lectures: 'The state and the interaction between class and ethnic stratification. Explaining world-wide differences in income inequality', Department of Sociology, University of Minnesota, Minneapolis (22 April 2008); 'Patterns of ethnic stratification and their consequences for inequality within the different countries of the world', Department of Sociology, Kharkiv National University, Ukraine (November 11, 2008); 'Die sozialen Klassen im ethnisch heterogenen Milieu. Zur Erklärung der ökonomischen Ungleichheit im weltweiten Vergleich', Lecture Series 'Global Sociology', University of Graz (5 May 2009); 'Why Empires build Walls. Sociological considerations about the new Iron Curtain between Africa and Europe (and between the South and North in general)', Department of Anthropology and Sociology, Universidade Estadual Paulista (UNESP), Sao Paolo, Brazil (27 April 2011); 'Why is economic inequality so high in Africa? A theory of ethnic stratification', St. Augustine University, Mwanza, Tanzania (3 February 2012); 'Ethnic class stratification and economic

---

1   Data reported by the President of the World Bank, Robert Zoellick, at the UN-Summit Conference on the state of the attainment of the Millennium goals, New York, September 2010.
2   See the annual World Wealth Reports: https://www.worldwealthreport.com/.

inequality. A global comparative analysis', Vienna Institute of Demography, Austrian Academy of Sciences (3 July 2012); 'Glaring Inequality. The Heritage of Slavery from the Perspective of Historical and Comparative Sociology', Conference of the British Sociological Association, Theory Study Group, Birmingham (11–12 July 2011); 'Extreme ökonomische Ungleichheit in der Welt von heute – ein Erbe historischer und Resultat moderner Formen von Sklaverei', University of Salzburg, Lecture Series 'Human Trafficking' (23 May 2013); 'Ethnic stratification and income inequality. The legacy of slavery'. Annual Meeting of the American Sociological Association, New York (10–13 August 2013) 'Ethnic stratification and income inequality around the world. The Legacy of Slavery', Department of Development Studies, University of Vienna (16 October 2013).

An overview on the main theses has been published under the title 'Die sozialen Klassen im ethnisch homogenen Milieu. Ein soziologischer Ansatz zur Erklärung der Einkommensverteilung in den Ländern der Welt', Discussion Paper of the WZB Berlin (SP I 2011), July 2011. A part of Chapter 5 has been published with the title 'Why empires build walls. The new Iron Curtain between the South and North' in Alberto Gasparini & Eliezer Ben-David, eds., *The Walls between Conflict and Peace*, Leiden/Boston, Brill (in print).

Content Overview

The book is structured in two parts, corresponding to the Weberian idea that a sociological explanation should employ two approaches, a quantitative-causal statistical approach and a qualitative approach based on *Verstehen* (understanding) of individual action and employing a historical-typological approach to the analysis of institutions. The first part of the book delineates the problem, defines the basic concepts, develops a theoretical background and concrete hypotheses, and tests these in a quantitative way using a newly created aggregate data file. In the second part of the book, a typology of different systems of ethnic stratification is developed. Then, a dozen particular types of such systems are sketched out and for each of them one or a few specific countries representing them are described in more detail, using historical knowledge and actual social scientific research. In the latter regard, individual-level data on income inequality and attitudes toward inequality and ethnic-national issues are re-analysed.

Chapter 1 starts with a demonstration of the huge cross-national differences in national income distributions. It argues that this issue must remain central for economics and sociology today contrary to the thesis of some theorists of globalization which argue that today the overall differences between nations should be the main focus of research. An overview on economic and sociological research on national patterns of income inequality shows that only a few researchers have investigated this important topic.

Chapter 2 starts with the argument that the international differences in income inequalities within countries must to be explained as an interaction process between class formation, social stratification and ethnic differentiation. The latter process and its interaction with social stratification has seldom been in the focus of the relevant scientific literature; the main tendency was to consider only one of these processes as crucial and the others as dependent on this one. For Marxists, class differences are basic, while theorists of ethnic conflict tend to neglect class-based interests and processes. It is then shown that a considerable proportion of present-day societies are characterized by high levels of internal ethnic differentiation; the distribution of the countries by this dimension corresponds in surprisingly strong way to that according income inequality, thus giving a first hint toward the close connection between the two phenomena.

In Chapter 3, the three concepts of class formation, social stratification and ethnic differentiation are specified and their interdependence is outlined. Then, a series of concrete, testable hypotheses are developed. It is argued that class societies in the full sense have emerged only in ethnically homogeneous societies, and that ethnic homogeneity is one of the main reasons why these societies have always been quite equal. Ethnic heterogeneity leads not only to higher overall economic inequality but also to an increase of the privileges of the upper classes, and a stronger deprivation of the lower classes. Then, it is argued that the most pervasive effect on income inequality comes from historical ethno-class exploitation in its most extreme form, that is, from slavery. This aspect, despite its high relevance in nearly all societies of the past, is very seldom recognized; it is discussed, therefore, in more detail in a sociological-historical excursus. Then, two further macro-level aspects highly relevant for income distribution are introduced. One of them is the type of the political system; it is hypothesized that a democratic system, a federal constitution and a welfare state are able to reduce inequality in a significant way. The other aspect is secular and religious ideologies of equality and inequality. Although their effect cannot be grasped in a quantitative way, they nevertheless have been and still are important for the historical evolution and the present-day shape of the patterns of ethnic stratification. This is particularly so if ideology and political system coincide as it was the case in the former Communist societies of East Europe or if a religious world view and the system of ethnic stratification are closely intertwined, as it is the case in India.

In Chapter 4, these hypotheses are submitted to an empirical test in two forms. A new aggregate data file was created which includes about 130 countries of the world and some new variables (e.g. ethno-class exploitation) were developed particularly for this analysis. These data are first analysed through a quantitative multivariate analysis which allows the estimation of the linear effects of the independent factors. Here, we find that both ethnic differentiation and ethno-class exploitation are connected with higher income inequality, but that the effect of the first dimension disappears when we introduce the variables related to the political system. The effect of historical ethno-class exploitation, however, persists in all models. Inequality of land distribution turns out as an additional important determinant of income inequality; it is closely interrelated, however, with ethno-class exploitation. Very strong positive effects on a more equal income distribution come also from the political system if it was Communist in former times, and from a strong welfare state; the effect of a federal constitution is also significant, but weaker. In a second kind of analysis, Fuzzy Set Analysis, a variant of Qualitative Comparative Analysis, we investigate the interaction between these different independent factors. This method is a significant complement to linear regression because it enables us to grasp also the interaction effects between ethnic differentiation, class situation and characteristics of the political system. Thus, we can investigate directly the central hypotheses about interaction effects postulated in Chapter 4. It could be shown, in particular, that ethnic heterogeneity or fractionalization as well as some political variables which were not significant in the regression analysis, turned out as important factors in combination with other variables.

The second part of the book starts with the development of a typology of systems of ethnic differentiation and stratification in Chapter 5. Four principal strategies are distinguished here: First, a state can try to preserve or restore its ethnic homogeneity. Here, again different methods can be used: A more or less total isolation from the outer world; an encapsulation of internal minorities and their separation from the rest of society; an assimilation of minorities to the majority; and, finally, minorities who are living more or less in circumscribed territory may try to secede from their mother state in order to establish their own, more homogeneous nation state. A second type of strategies uses the control of ethnic heterogeneity as a consequence of immigration processes: In this case, a selective immigration policy can be applied, accepting certain categories of immigrants (e.g., those from similar cultural areas or those with high skills) and excluding others. A third strategy is the establishment of ethnically based systems of socio-economic exploitation, particularly in the forms of slavery and Apartheid. The fourth strategy encompasses the establishment of political systems by a specific ethnie (ethno-nations) or the domination of specific ethnic groups over others; if such a system is also legitimized in religious terms we can speak of an ethnic theocracy. Economic inequality, by and large, is smallest in ethnically homogeneous societies, intermediate in societies which try to control ethnic heterogeneity by selective immigration and integration policies, and very high in systems of ethno-class domination and in ethno-nations and ethnocracies.

In Chapters 6 to 12, some of the most significant examples of such types of societies are analysed in detail, showing how economic inequality has developed in recent times and what the role of ethnic stratification (or its absence) was therein. In Chapter 6, two countries are analysed which are very different in many socio-cultural and political terms, but surprisingly similar both in terms of ethnic homogeneity and a low level of economic inequality, namely Sweden and Japan. It is shown that ethnic homogeneity was an aim clearly aspired to by the governments of these countries, not the least in order to preserve a low level of inequality. The strategies used toward these aims were quite different: In Sweden, it was the establishment of a strong welfare state, in Japan it was a more indirect socio-economic policy of securing an adequate income level of all groups of the population, particularly of the farmers.

A history of Communism has turned out as one of the main determinants of a considerable level of economic equality in Chapter 4. Ethnic-national differentiations were considered as only secondary phenomena by Marxism and Communism; thus it was of high interest to investigate their role in the history and fate of

Communist societies. Comparing the developments in Eastern Europe and in China in Chapter 7, it is shown that in the first group of countries, ethnic-national differentiations and divisions played a highly significant role. In the last instance, they contributed to the collapse of the two multinational states of Yugoslavia and the Soviet Union, and the Communist system. That such a system persists in China may be due not the least to its internal ethnic homogeneity, but also to the acceptance of elements of market liberalism which, on their side, contributed to a massive increase of economic inequality in recent times.

A very different case is India, which is discussed in Chapter 8. India, one of the two most populous countries of the world, is also one of the most heterogeneous in terms of ethnic differentiation. From the viewpoint of the central thesis of this book, at first sight this is highly surprising and appears as an apparent contrary evidence because its degree of economic inequality is relatively moderate. Four reasons were given for this fact: First, the unique stratification system of India in the form of castes which focused on vertical hierarchies and social distance mechanisms, but was not a system of direct exploitation; its federalism which combines unity and diversity in a unique way; its 'socialist' democratic system which includes significant mechanisms of central redistribution; and its socio-cultural value system of multi-communitarianism which emphasizes recognition of differences, respect of others and a communal division of living spaces and resources.

In the next three Chapters, two sub-continents are analysed and discussed which show the highest degrees of economic inequality worldwide. The one is Latin America, the other Sub-Saharan Africa. The patterns of ethnic stratification in Latin America and particularly in Brazil are analysed in Chapter 9. These patterns are rather unique: In contrast to the Dutch, British and French colonizers, the Portuguese were ready to intermix with the native Indian population as well as with the imported slaves from Africa. As a consequence, no open race discrimination did emerge as in most other countries where whites were living together with blacks and other natives. As a result, new 'national' races are emerging in these countries. Yet, behind the façade of a seeming equality between people of different color a hidden discrimination persists. A specific 'coloured class' structure did emerge, involving a close interdependence between colour and ethnicity on the one side and class situation and social status on the other side. Its present shape, including the extreme levels of civil violence in Latin America, can be understood only if one takes into consideration the pre-history of one of the most brutal forms of slavery on this continent.

Slavery was also very important for Sub-Saharan Africa, the other highly unequal macro-region. It includes three quite different sub-regions: (1) The southernmost part, comprising the Republic of South Africa and its immediate neighbour states; (2) the countries lying between this region and the Sahara (formerly also called 'Black Africa'), comprising the bulk (about 80 %) of the population of Africa; and (3) North Africa with its relatively homogeneous, predominant Arab-Muslim population. Slavery has played a very important role in Africa South of the Sahara, with a very different history in the southern and central parts. In Central Sub-Saharan Africa, analysed in Chapter 10, slavery was known from ancient times but was less violent and cruel than in other parts of the old world. However, with the advent of the European colonizers, it took on a new form which led to a devastation of the continent in physical, social and moral terms: Millions of people were captured and displaced toward the Americas and, within Africa, new aggressive political regimes emerged which cooperated with the European slave traders. In addition, the colonizers created new states which often united dozens, even hundreds of smaller ethnic communities into large and very heterogeneous states. Given the lack of experience with democratic procedures and reliable public services, in many of the new states soon bloody fights broke out between those ethnic groups which were able to grasp state power and those without influence. In these conflicts and wars, also traditional African patterns of politics, including the central role of 'Big Man', were revived. In recent times, there are promising signs of a decline of violent civil wars and considerable economic growth in many countries. However, the degree of economic inequality remains blatant. One of the main reasons is the privileges of the urban population, many of them working in the public sector, and the masses of the poor population living on the outskirts of the exploding urban agglomerates and on the countryside.

In southern Africa, a very different historical trajectory from the history of colonialism toward present-day societies has taken place. Here, the Dutch and British colonizers were able to develop the immense natural resources of the country in a very productive way, so that the Republic of South Africa today constitutes the most advanced national economy in Africa. This remarkable achievement, shown in Chapter 11, however, was connected with a peculiar and efficient form of ethno-class exploitation. It was developed after the abolishment of slavery, forced by the British and only reluctantly accepted by the *Afrikaans* (formerly called *Boers*). They introduced a unique system of exploitation of the blacks in the form of Apartheid, which allowed economic exploitation but established a strict separation in terms of settlement and private intercourse, and dispossessed the Africans of most political rights. After the abolition of this system in the 1990s, the social and political rights of whites and blacks have been adapted and many black Africans were able to get access to public jobs and political offices. However, as it is shown in this Chapter, the pervasive economic discrimination of the mass of blacks continues and so does ethno-class economic discrimination. A parallel shorter analysis is carried out for the United States which also had a long period of slavery and, later on, a period of race segregation in public spaces. Here, it is shown that blacks still are experiencing a significant economic discrimination and that economic inequality is higher in the southern US-states; both facts are clearly related to the history and experience of slavery.

In Chapter 12, a country rather unique in terms of ethno-class stratification is investigated, namely Israel. This is the only state on the world today which defines itself clearly in ethnic terms, as the nation of all Jews around the world. The history and present-day position of this state in terms of socio-economic development is a final proof of the immense power of ethnic and national identification: Within half a century, the Jews were able to build up from close to scratch a well-functioning, economically prosperous and democratic modern state which far outperforms all neighbour states. This remarkable achievement, however, had also a dark side which encumbers the young state with a heavy mortgage: It was achieved with the use of military violence and by the expulsion of hundreds of thousands of Palestinians living on the state's territory in former times. In addition, the living space of the remaining Palestinians is extremely restricted; one part of them is settling in a small, highly densely populated territory, the Gaza Strip, the other one in the West Bank, a territory cut into pieces by Israeli settlements and streets. A concomitant of the highly dense relations between Israel, the Palestinians and all its neighbour states was that economic inequality within Israeli society increased massively. This was due, on the one side, to new privileges of the upper classes (comprising an alliance between the political, military and business elites) and, on the other side, a discrimination of the Arab citizens of Israel and of Jewish immigrants from Arab countries and, more recently, from the countries of the former Soviet Union. The Chapter concludes with a discussion of the prospects for a reconciliation between the Jewish and Arabs within Israel and the state of Israel, Palestine and the neighbour Arab states.

The final Chapter 13 resumes the discussion in Chapter 5 where different types of social exclusion and ethno-class formation have been elaborated but looks at this issue from a positive, future-orientated perspective. It asks which kind of political changes and reforms appear as practicable given the pervasive ethno-class inequalities in many countries and macro-regions around the world. Such reforms, it is argued should not aim only at deprived ethnic groups, but come to grips with the close interaction between ethnic and class privilege and discrimination. Four main strategies are elaborated. In the case of a relatively large ethnic minority, living on a closed territory, secession from a larger mother state could be an option; this secession however would have to occur in a way which does not overpower the new minorities and which is acceptable for the state as a whole. A second strategy is the strengthening of federal structures which empower ethnic minorities within a state to preserve their cultural and political autonomy and to participate fully in economic development and the territorial-regional distribution of state resources. The third type of political strategies refers to particularly deprived ethnic groups and ethno-classes within some states. It is argued that such policies should be based on two principles: They should not aim toward specific ethnic minorities but toward an improvement of the situation of all deprived lower classes which as a rule include also members of other ethnic minorities and also of the societal majority. They should also not be imposed from above, by experts and politicians, but should aim toward the empowerment of the involved deprived minorities. Worldwide experiences have shown that measures imposed from above or from outside – including established development aid – have no long-lasting effect concerning the improving of the situation of the deprived groups and classes. Three main strategies of empowerment are proposed: The implementation of an egalitarian educational policy; a comprehensive urban and regional planning and development; and the development of new models of welfare states which are suited to the particular situation in which the poorest nations – particularly in South Asia and Sub-Saharan Africa – find themselves today. In these regions and countries, most of the people have no formal employment contract, and the resources of the governments are extremely limited given the dimension of the problems of poverty. It is mainly private social networks of help and support which enable the poor to survive. It is the power of these networks which a new model of welfare state for the South should strengthen and support.

In the last section of this chapter the new international processes of migration are investigated, particularly as they affect the social structure in the rich countries of the North. It is asked which of them lead to the emergence of new minorities within a nation state and which would be able to improve the situation of deprived ethno-classes. In general, the vast processes of international migration are continuously creating new ethnic minorities within the receiving countries. It is argued, however, that migration politics can influence significantly the socio-economic situation of immigrants. Four models are distinguished which have quite different effects: The model which aims to bring home co-ethnics; a liberal laissez-faire model; the Gastarbeiter model; and a selective immigration policy, favouring the immigration of highly skilled, but excluding that of unwanted people. Each of these models is evaluated shortly in terms of its human rights and its potential socio-economic effects.

Acknowledgements

The work on this book has been supported immensely by discussions with many colleagues and their critical readings of draft versions of the text. At my Department of Sociology at the University of Graz, most helpful were comments by Franz Höllinger, Bernadette Müller, and Markus Hadler (now Macquarie University Sidney), and the members of the research group 'Comparative social research and historical sociology', Helmut Kuzmics, Dieter Reicher, and Sabine Haring. Very useful comments on several chapters of the book have been provided by Klaus Eder (Berlin), Walter Müller (Mannheim), Hermann Strasser (Duisburg), Patrick Ziltener (Zürich), Harold Kerbo (California Polytechnic State University) and Joachim Savelsberg (University of Minnesota). Detailed comments on single chapters have been given by Elena Samarski (London School of Economics), Gad Yair (Hebrew University of Jerusalem), Heribert Adam (Simon Fraser University, Canada), Alejandro Cunat (University of Vienna), Anthony Löwstedt (Webster University, Vienna), Michael Mann (University of California, Los Angeles), A.R. Momin (University of Mumbai), Patrick Neveling (University of Berne), Mirko Petric and Inga Tomic-Koludrovic (University of Zadar, Croatia), Reinhard Stockmann (University of the Saarland, Saarbrücken), and Göran Therborn (Prof. em. University of Cambridge). Also the decade-long cooperation with the members of the *International Social Survey Programme* (ISSP) from all over the world was extremely challenging and helped me to break away from a Western- or parochial European-centred view of inequality. I am also very grateful to Ashgate, the publisher of this volume which accepted a much longer manuscript than foreseen in the contract. Neil Jordan, Senior Commissioning editor, was always ready to provide advises how to proceed in my work, and patient in tolerating my overrunning the agreed deadlines; Matthew Irving carefully prepared the proofs. Vice-Rector Peter Scherrer from the University of Graz granted a small financial support for collecting the data on the new variable ethno-class 'exploitation' and for the finishing the manuscript; Gerd Kaup and Manuel Weichinger assisted me in this work. Sandra Kofler prepared the indices; Edith Lanser assisted in the proof-reading. Finally, I would like to express my gratitude to Gabriele Strohmeier who typed across the years most accurately and diligently the many versions of the manuscript and controlled the bibliography on completeness. It goes without saying that I am alone responsible for all the theses proposed, data analyses and findings reported in this book.

PART I
The Problem, Theory and
Quantitative Statistical Analysis

Worldwide Differences in National Structures of Economic Inequality. Some Basic Facts and Their View in Economics and Sociology

Introduction

In this chapter, first some basic data are shown concerning the existence of huge international differences in intra-national income distributions. Then, it is argued that this aspect of inequality – income distribution within countries – has not lost its relevance in the age of globalization. In the next section, the relevant levels of analysis for income inequality are discussed; in particular, intra-national inequality is distinguished from other forms of income inequality at the world level. Finally, the main strands of thinking about international differences concerning inequality within nations in economics and sociology are presented and discussed. We will see that this highly relevant issue is strongly underexposed in both these academic disciplines.

A World of Equal and Unequal Nation-states

In 2005, the West African state Namibia had a Gini coefficient of income inequality of 74.3; a value of 100 in this index implies that the whole national income would go exclusively to the highest income group, one of 0 that all persons or groups earn the same. In Namibia, only 4.4 percent of gross national income (14 billion$) went to the lowest 40 per cent of the population, but 64.5 per cent to those 10 per cent who had the highest incomes: 800,000 Namibians got 616,000$ all together, that is less than 1$ per head, but 200,000 got 9 billion or 70,000$ per head![1] With these figures, Namibia is the most unequal among about 139 countries in the world for which reliable data on income distribution are available (see Table 1.1). Namibia is a small and poor country with about 2 million inhabitants. Incredible degrees of economic inequality, however, can be observed also in large and more advanced societies. Brazil, with over 190 million inhabitants and a surface of 8.5 million square miles, the fifth largest state in the world, has a Gini coefficient of 58; here, the lowest 40 per cent get 8.8 per cent of total national income, the highest 10 per cent however 45.8 per cent. Brazil cannot be considered as being a real latecomer of industrialization; it enjoys now over 200 years of continuous, independent existence as a nation-state; less than 10 per cent of its population are employed in agriculture. Similar extreme levels of economic inequality exist in the Republic of South Africa, the most developed state in Africa with about 50 million inhabitants. These are not 'small' inequalities compared with the 'large global inequalities', those between the rich and the poor countries as some theorists of globalization argue. If one looks at these patterns, one is not distracted from the misery of the world, as Ulrich Beck (2002: 56) writes – quite the contrary. Compared with the countries mentioned at the beginning, even the United States, from European eyes a paradigmatic example of an unequal society, looks a relatively egalitarian country.

On the other side of the income inequality continuum in the world, we find Sweden (and other Scandinavian countries). Here, the Gini coefficient is 25; the lowest 40 per cent get 23.1 per cent of the national income, and the highest tenth, 22.2 per cent. Swedish politicians and social scientists are proud of this considerable equality and attribute it to a consistent and generation-enduring policy of social democratic redistribution (Korpi 1983; Olson 1986; Korpi and Palme 1989; Esping-Andersen 1990; Therborn 1995). However, comparable low degrees of economic equality have been achieved also in other European countries

---

1 These and the following numbers in this section are taken from *World Development Indicators* (2006), Table 2.8. According the CIA World Factbook, Namibia's Gini coefficient is 70.7.

without long-standing social-democratic governments and explicit policies of redistribution, such as Austria, Slovenia or the Netherlands. The same is true for the largest and economically most powerful EU member state, Germany. The welfare state of this country – as seen from Swedish eyes – is conservative and 'ugly' (Manow 2002), cementing traditional class- and status-related inequalities between occupational groups. Nevertheless, Germany has a Gini coefficient of only 28. But even more surprising is the fact that Japan, a 127-million people country in the Far East with only a rudimentary welfare state, has an astonishing low degree of economic inequality, according to some sources as low as that of Sweden.[2] Even India, a huge subcontinent and internally probably the most heterogeneous country on earth, has a Gini coefficient of only 32.5, comparable to that of France (see also Deaton and Drèze 2002; Borooah et al. 2006)

International data on income distribution certainly are afflicted with serious methodological problems (see Menard 1986; Smeeding et al. 1990; Atkinson and Bourguignon 2000b; Atkinson and Brandolini 2001; Milanovic 2005; Brandolini and Smeeding 2008). They may be particularly inaccurate in countries with a large sector of agriculture and subsistence economy, in extremely big and population-rich countries like India or China, and in less developed countries with an under-developed infrastructure for statistical records and surveys. In addition, the Gini index does not capture differences well at the margins of income distribution, that is, the very low and the very high incomes (Nollmann 2006).[3] Often, there exist considerable differences between findings from Gini indices and those from deciles, that is, percentages of the whole income in a society which people at the lower and the upper end of the income distribution get (Brandolini and Smeeding 2008). However, the enormous differences and the rank order between the countries and country groups, as shown before, are not affected seriously by these problems. The data presented in Table 1.1 are supported by other sets of data that show similar figures and relations (see, for example, Hoover 1989). For some countries we have data for more points in time which also confirm the figures presented here. Where significant changes have been going on over time, we will come back to them in the chapters on the single countries or groups of countries in Part II of this book. The validity of the data presented here is also confirmed by the fact that neighbouring countries with similar social structures and political institutions typically are located near to each other, thus forming 'families of nations' (Haller 1990; Castles 1993): this fact suggests to developing typology of systems of stratification. The development of such a typology is a central aspect of this book (see Chapters 5 and 6). Let us have a closer look at the patterns of income distribution in the different countries from this point of view:

Table 1.1 shows that nearly all European and many Asiatic countries are located in the lower part of the income inequality continuum (with Gini coefficients up to about 35.0). Most Latin American and African countries are placed in the upper part, as inequality is much higher here in comparison with the rest of the world (Gini coefficients 40 to 60). Three of the largest countries of the world, the United States, Russia and China, are in the upper middle; India is a clear exception in this regard with its lower value. Most Central and West European and three of the New-World countries outside Europe (Canada, Australia and New Zealand) as well as some North African and Asiatic countries are placed somewhat below, in the upper half of countries with a relatively egalitarian income distribution.

I have already mentioned one other aspect of economic inequality, that between the countries. World inequality taking countries as units has increased continuously between 1960 (Gini about 47) and 200 (Gini about 54); since then, it decreased a little bit. If we do not take the countries, but all individuals of the world as the basic units, we can speak of *global inequality*. This dimension of inequality has significantly increased since the onset of industrialization in the 18th and 19th centuries; countries and regions outside Europe fell behind Europe and its 'offshoots' in North America and the Far East (Milanovic 2002, 2005, 2007; Firebaugh 2003). Since the 1960s, however, it decreased slightly, due to the strong economic growth of China and other East Asian countries. Nevertheless, today, the poorest countries (which include the two most populous countries of the world, China and India) are worlds apart from rich European, North American and Far East

---

2   According to the Wikipedia Encyclopaedia, Japan had a Gini Index of 24.9 in 1993 (these data are based on the UNDP Report 2004). This was the second-lowest level of inequality in the world, practically identical with that of Sweden (see http://de.wikipedia.org, 9.4.2008).

3   In my regression analysis of income distribution at the aggregate level in Chapter 4, I will therefore include also deciles at the lower and upper ends.

Table 1.1 Income inequality in 139 countries of the world (Gini coefficients, 1997–2003)*

	Western Europe	Eastern Europe	America, Australia, New Zealand	Africa	Asia
60				74.3 Namibia (64.4)	
				63.2 Lesotho (63.2)	
				63.0 Botswana (48)	
				62.9 Sierra Leone	
				61.3 Central Africa	
			60.1 Bolivia (54.4)	60.9 Swaziland (50)	
			59.0 Haiti (55)	57.8 South Africa (62.8)	
			58.8 Brazil (51)		
			58.6 Colombia (56.6)		
			57.8 Paraguay		
			57.1 Chile (52)		
55			55.6 Panama		
			55.1 Guatemala		
			54.0 Puerto Rico		54.0 Thailand (46.5)
			53.8 Honduras		
			52.8 Argentina (46)		
			Peru		
			52.4 El Salvador	50.5 Mali, Niger	
			52.3 Nicaragua	50.3 Malawi (44.1)	
			51.7 Dominican Rep.	50.2 Gambia	
			50.9 Papua New Guin.	50.1 Zimbabwe	
50			49.5 Mexico (52.8)	47.5 Madagaskar	48.2 Malaysia (45.3)
			49.4 Costa Rica	47.0 Guinea-Bissau	
				44.8 Rwanda	47.2 Nepal
				44.6 Cameroon (51)	46.7 Philippines, Armenia, Nepal
				Côte d'Ivoire	43.4 Hongkong
		43.6 Turkey (43.0)	44.9 Uruguay	43.7 Nigeria (48)	43.0 Iran
			44.1 Venezuela	43.0 Uganda (49)	42.5 Singapore (46.3)
			43.7 Ecuador (57.5)	42.5 Kenia (53)	42.0 Thailand (44.9)
45			43.1 Nicaragua	42.4 Burundi	
				42.1 Zambia (55)	
				41.3 Senegal	
				40.8 Ghana	40.4 Cambodia (43.6)
				40.3 Guinea	

Table 1.1 *Concluded*

	Western Europe	Eastern Europe	America, Australia, New Zealand	Africa	Asia
40	38.7 Portugal (35.4)	40.4 Georgia 39.9 Russia (42.0) 39.0 Macedonia	40.8 USA (37.0) 40.3 Trinidad & Tobago	39.8 Tunisia 39.5 Burkina Faso (58) Morocco 39.6 Mozambique 39.0 Mauritania	41.2 Iran 39.2 Israel (37.4) 38.8 Jordan 38.3 Iraq 44.7 China (38.4)
		37.7 Latvia	37.9 Jamaica		37.0 Vietnam
35	36.0 Italy (30.3) UK (34) 34.7 Spain 34.3 Greece, Ireland (31.2) 33.7 Switzerl. (27.8) 33.0 Belgium (29.7)	36.0 Lithuania 35.8 Estonia 35.1 Serbia 34.7 Poland 33.2 Moldova (40.1)	36.2 New Zealand 35.2 Australia (30.5)	36.5 Benin 35.4 Ethiopia 35.2 Algeria 34.6 Tansania (36.7) 34.4 Egypt	34.7 Indonesia (38) 34.6 Laos 33.9 Kazakhstan 33.6 Azerbaijan 33.4 Yemen 33.3 Armenia 33.3 Sri Lank
30	32.7 France (27.2) 30.9 Netherlands 29.1 Austria (26) 28.3 Germany (27.5)	31.0 Romania 29.7 Belarus 29.2 Bulgaria 29.0 Croatia (34) 28.4 Slovenia 28.2 Albania 28.1 Ukraine (38.9)	32.6 Canada (31.0)		32.6 Tajikistan 32.5 India (33.2) 32.4 Taiwan 31.8 Bangladesh (37.5) Mongolia 31.6 Rep. Korea (33.6) 30.9 Belarus 30.6 Pakistan 30.3 Kyrgyz Rep. (42) Mongolia 28.6 Turkmenistan
25	26.9 Finland 26.7 Luxembourg 25.8 Norway (31.2) 25.0 Sweden (26.2) 24.7 Denmark (32.2)	26.9 Hungary 26.1 Bosnia-Herz. 25.8 Slovakia 25.4 Czech R. (26)			26.8 Uzbekistan (39.7) 24.7 Japan (31.1)
n	17	21	28	36	37

N = 123; *Source*: World Bank (2006); Solt (2009). For large countries and for those with extreme values, within parentheses the mean values for available years 1996–2004 are also reported. * For a few countries the data are older.

nations. The main reason for the increasing gulf between these two groups of countries was industrialization; because it led to an unprecedented increase in productivity and income, all regions of the world which did not experience the Industrial Revolution in the 19th and early 20th century dropped back.

Present-day worldwide inequality from the global point of view is historically unparalleled: 15 per cent of the world population, about 1 billion people, have 30,000$ per head and year at their disposal and control 80 per cent of world production; on the other side, about a billion people must survive on about 93$ per year and person (Pogge 2007: 132). Thus, global inequality is extreme, both from the absolute and the relative perspective; for a typical individual person or family in the poor part of world, is an everyday experience.

The Socio-economic and Political Relevance of Equality and Inequality Within Nation-states

How can we explain these amazing facts and differences? Economic inequality within societies is a central aspect of their class structure; research on both phenomena has always been considered as a central task of sociology (Carlsson 1968; Dahrendorf 1974b: 353; Collins 1975: 38), and even of social philosophy of the modern age (Rousseau 1967 [1754]; Tocqueville 1945 [1835]). The distribution of income is also an eminent economic, social and political problem. Extreme inequality is connected with many other aspects of socio-economic deprivation, such as unemployment and poverty (Wade 2007), and it leads to many kinds of social problems such as reduced life expectancy, family break-ups, social violence and political instability (Sagan 1987; Bourguignon and Morrisson 2002; Jencks 2002; Ali 2010; Ziegler 2011). Most authors found also that it delays economic growth (Persson and Tabellini 1994; Hewlett 1997; Aghion et al. 1999; Eicher and Turnovsky 2003; Kerbo 2006; Wade 2007).

A comprehensive analysis of the negative societal effects of economic inequality has been carried out by epidemiologists Kate Pickett and Richard Wilkinson (2009). They have shown strong correlations between inequality of income distribution in about two dozen developed countries and a number of social and psychological problems; psychic diseases, adiposis, alcoholism, interpersonal distrust, crime and violence are more frequent the more unequal income distribution of a country is.[4] In all these regards, the Scandinavian countries and Japan perform best, the United States worst – corresponding exactly to the data in Table 1.1. Pickett and Wilkinson (2009: 50ff.) present plausible explanations for these relationships: in very inegalitarian societies, everybody is exposed more frequently to social comparisons producing stress; people in lower social classes are more frequently depreciated and degraded and – as a consequence – they develop feelings of inferiority. We will show how this happens particularly in former slave societies, such as Brazil (see Chapter 9). Similar observations have been made again and again by psychologists and sociologists since the seminal writings of Alexis de Tocqueville (1945 [1835]) and Alfred Adler 1972 [1912]; for recent works see Scheff 1990; Sennett and Cobb 1972; Botton 2004). High inequality has negative effects also on members of better situated social groups and classes. In very unequal societies, members of the middle classes are afflicted by *Statusangst* (fear of losing status), members of upper classes suffer from the high level of general societal mistrust, insecurity and violence. In the developing world today (but even in some parts of the United States), it is a normal sight that the settlements and villas of the rich are encircled by huge walls with barbwire on top, with guards watching over the house day and night; and children are brought to school by drivers in cabs with bulletproof windows. Even 'private' social institutions, like marriage and the family, are negatively affected by extreme economic inequality in a country. The anthropological perspective shows that polygamy is more frequent where there is less equally distributed wealth, while in equal societies monogamist marriage patterns prevail (Kanazawa and Still 1999). The subordination and exploitation of women is closely related to general patterns of inequality and exploitation (see several contributions in Devine and Waters 2004; Coates 2004). A recent German study shows that inequality in happiness between the people of a country is affected significantly by income inequality (Delhey and Kohler 2011); the same has been shown for Latin America (Graham and Felton 2005). Frederick Solt (2008) has shown in a cross-national comparison that

---

4   The analyses of Pickett and Wilkinson, however, are limited from the methodological point of view: Most of their analyses are carried out only at the aggregate level of countries, they compare only advanced countries and they mostly neglect the ethnic factor.

higher income inequality depresses political interest, the frequency of political discussions and participation in elections among lower and middle social strata. This fact is particularly relevant for an explanation of the quiescence of people in the highly unequal societies of Latin America and Sub-Saharan Africa.

In the less developed and poor countries of the South, socio-economic inequality is a far greater problem than in the rich North (for a comprehensive view of it see Myrdal 1980 [1944]). The large armies of very poor people and particularly the least protected, stateless migrants constitute a vast, disposable reservoir for human trafficking and exploitation under slave-like conditions (Bales 2004; Batstone 2008: 16; see also Chapter 13). Societies with high and increasing inequality seem to slip into a *circulus vitiosus*: the rich are less and less willing to pay taxes (which are needed for public services and transfers) and try to elude tax duties altogether (huge amounts of money are transferred from poor countries to countries with hard currencies or tax heavens); governments whose members often come from the circles of the rich reduce taxes which again leads to a deficit in state revenues (Wade 2007: 117). Kerbo (2006: 116ff.) argues that two factors stood behind the secret of the dynamic economic development in Japan and South East Asia: a lesser economic inequality in the population as a whole, and a strong state with coherent elites which were motivated and able to further national interests.

Before going on to a discussion of social scientific approaches to the issue of international differences in income distribution, we have to discuss some problems of definition and measurement; however, we should note also some aspects qualifying the relevance of income inequality as an indicator for quality of life and well-being. A first aspect concerns the fact that a higher level of inequality does not always indicate more deprivation or discrimination. An increase in income inequality at the level of personal income can occur also as a consequence of an increasing proportion of women who are working; many of them are employed on a part-time basis. If they are living with a partner who is also employed, this might increase household income, however. Thus, we have to distinguish clearly between income distribution at the individual and at the household level. A second aspect concerns the relation between income and quality of life. A main rationale for the new concept of 'quality of life' and the related extended social indicators research was the fact that economic indications such as GDP per head were insufficient to measure 'real' quality of life. As a consequence, both in science and politics, new concepts and indicators have been developed, such as the Human Development Index (HDI) which combines mean life expectancy, educational level and income of a country. Another broad area of research is that on subjective well-being (SWB) and life happiness. This research also shows that the level of income is relevant for subjective well-being both at the level of individuals and of societies as a whole. However, after a certain level of income has been reached, its effect on SWB is declining (see, for example, Frey and Stutzer 2002). However, there are some groups of nations in which SWB is significantly higher than one could expect given their level of development (Haller and Hadler 2004, 2006). In Chapter 9 it will be shown that such inconsistencies which are particularly evident, as in the case of Latin America, can be explained better by taking into consideration the aspect of ethnic stratification. A third aspect concerns the fact that socio-economic inequality from the sociological perspective includes not only economic aspects, but also issues of social participation, social status and prestige, and lifestyles in general. My basic assumption in this regard is, however, that: (1) income is a central determinant of life chance in all spheres, and (2) the use of data on income inequality enables us to compare many countries in a methodologically rigorous and substantively very fruitful way. (I will come back to this issue later in this section.)

Contexts and Measures to Grasp Economic Inequality

When speaking about inequality at the world level we have to distinguish, first of all, between the distribution of individual incomes and the distribution of mean incomes at the aggregate or country level; based on this distinction, three ways to measure international income inequality exist as I have already indicated before (See also Milanovic 2005, 2007). If we compare the mean incomes of different countries, we speak of *international inequality*. This is done if poor and rich countries are contrasted with each other. If we look at income distribution within countries, we refer to the incomes of persons or households; we speak here of *intra-national inequality*. This is the central perspective of this book. The person- or household-related perspective can be applied also to the world as a whole; in this case, we speak of *global inequality*. From this point of view, we can see, for instance, that the poorest segment of the French population is richer than 72 per cent of the world population; the Gini coefficient of global inequality is about 62 to 66 (Milanovic 2007: 39ff.; Sutcliffe 2007: 68). Thus, it corresponds to that of the countries with the highest levels of intra-national inequality, such as Brazil or South Africa. In this sense, we can also speak about a stratification of nations in the present-day world (Gakuru 2002).

Recent research pertinent to these issues has shown that international inequality, inequality between nations, has been increasing strongly since about 1800; this aspect covers the larger part of worldwide inequality. Thus, it is justified to claim that today also international and global inequality must be considered seriously and that it is inadequate to analyse only inequalities within the single nation-states (Beck 2002; Kreckel 1992, 2008; Cohen and Kennedy 2007; Bayer et al. 2008; Berger and Weiß 2008). However, it would mean throwing out the child with the bathwater if analysis of intra-national inequalities is neglected because of this new aspect (Schwinn 2008: 27). The most convincing argument for this thesis has been proposed by Glenn Firebaugh (2003): he argues and supports with much data that in the middle of the 20th century a decisive second turning point was attained. Up to this time, inequality between nations was rising, but since then it has been declining; inequality within nations, however, remains stable or is even increasing in many countries (see also Harrison and Bluestone 1998; Katz 1999; Goesling 2001; Kreckel 1992; Milanovic 2005; Nollmann 2006; Dollar 2007; Berthold and Brunner 2010; Greve 2010; Brand 2011). A main reason for this reversal of the earlier trend is the recent, rapid industrialization and growth in large countries such as China and India which decreases their distance from the rich countries, but increases their internal inequality. As a consequence of these trends, global inequality will also drop – contrary to wide-spread assumptions (see also Berger 2005).

From these facts and trends, a clear conclusion emerges concerning research on intra-national income inequality: The nation-state has not lost its relevance as a context for the analysis of economic inequality – quite the contrary. Nation-states remain the decisive units for the production and reproduction of income not only because most relevant data are available on this level, but also because it is mainly at the national level where the relevant actions and decisions in relation to income distribution are taking place (Firebaugh 2003: 11; Therborn 2006b: 41). These actions and the resulting huge international differences are also produced by particular national industrial characteristics, typical forms of interest organizations and industrial relations and by political processes (Müller and Schindler 2008). Even at the global level it is not the international institutions proper (such as the UNO, the World Bank, the WTO and so on) which make most decisions; they have little power and their measures often even enforce global inequalities (Stiglitz 2004). Rather, it is the direct and indirect influence and actions of the governments of the large and powerful nation-states or communities of nations capable of action, such as the European Union as well as those of the large multinational companies, which are decisive (Chomsky 1993; Perkins 2004; Stiglitz 2004; Reich 2008: 221). Firebaugh (2003: 18, 205) concludes, therefore, in accordance with other authors (Haller and Hadler 2004/05; Greve 2010), that it would be largley mistaken to veer off nation-states as units of analysis. The result of the increasing integration of national economies with the world 'is not so much a globalized world (where national differences virtually disappear) but rather a more internationalized one …' (Weiss 1998: 187). Firebaugh argues that those authors who assume a further increase of global inequality make the same basic error as many actors in the crime movies of Sherlock Holmes, namely to theorize before a critical scrutiny of facts.[5]

Firebaugh (2003: 185ff.) enumerates six reasons for the decreasing inequality between and the increasing inequality within the nations of the world today. The first two are of a singular or transitory nature: the breakdown of the Communist regimes in East Europe and the population explosion in the Third World. The

---

5 It seems to me that theorizing without data is a tendency typical of German sociology. Among the numerous contributions to two recent volumes on the comparative analysis of income (Bayer et al., eds, *Transnationale Ungleichheitsforschung* 2008, and Berger and Weiß, eds, *Transnationalisierung sozialer Ungleichheit*, 2008) only a small number contain empirical data and – if they do so – only for illustrative purposes. It seems, moreover, that the 'container-model' of sociology much critized by U. Beck is more a straw man than a reality; the most famous classical sociological studies (for example, Durkheim, *Suicide*; Weber, *Protestant Ethic*) have been comparative; a strong focus on comparison is evident also in more recent research on stratification and mobility, welfare states and so on.

four other causes are: the industrialization of the Third World; the growth of the tertiary sector which is internally differentiated into productive high-income and marginal and precarious low-income sub-sectors; the convergence of national economic and political institutions; and the proliferation of new technologies, which are independent of geographic locations and reduce international mobility barriers. In addition, we can assume that the extreme inequality within some of the poorest countries of the world (particularly in Sub-Saharan Africa) is one of the reasons for their retarded economic growth.

It is also obvious that the relation between ethnic-national differences and income distributions must be analysed within the framework of national or state societies. It is possible to speak of ethnic diversity and of minorities only in a national context in which several ethnic groups exist whereby often one is dominant over the others; however, it is also possible that new processes of 'trans-nationalization' have some effects on the relative situation of minorities within a nation-state (Pries 2010). The image of Black Africans could become more positive among the youth as a consequence of the fact that several of their most favourite soccer stars (and, maybe, some female models and actors) are Black. Further, it could be that processes of trans-nationalization enforce ethnic segregation. If Turkish men and women who work in Central Europe return regularly and often even re-migrate to their native country, this could reduce their interest in becoming integrated into their host society (these issues will be taken up again in Chapter 13, pp. 362–70). The relevance of trans-nationalization processes comes to the fore also if government heads visiting foreign countries appeal to their compatriots living in these countries not to strike off their native culture but to contribute to the development of their countries of origin.

An additional methodological aspect must be noted here, concerning international comparisons of income inequality. We must distinguish also between overall inequality in a country, the relative privilege of the well-to-do and the relative deprivation of the lower and poor social classes. The United States, for instance, is different to France or Germany not only in its general higher level of overall income inequality but also in these two aspects: in the USA, the lower classes are more deprived, while the upper classes are not more privileged than in France or Germany (Haller 1987; Raffalovich 1999). A central thesis of this book stipulates that deprivation and exploitation of the lower classes is much more probable and easy if they are distinct from other social strata also in ethnic terms. Likewise, the economic and political elites of a country will be the more powerful and privileged the more homogeneous they are in social and cultural terms. Thus, we have to distinguish clearly between three aspects of income inequality: (1) overall income inequality, as it is captured, for instance, by the Gini index; (2) the relative privilege of the upper classes; and (3) the relative deprivation of the lower classes. The latter two aspects will be captured in Chapter 4 by deciles, that is, by the proportions of the whole income of a country which go to the lowest 40 per cent, and to the highest 10 per cent of income receivers.

How Economics and Sociology have Dealt with the Problem of International Differences in Intra-national Income Inequalities

How far have the problems of international differences in economic inequality been dealt with by economics and sociology, the two social scientific disciplines which could be considered as being mainly in charge of them? A glance at relevant sociological monographs and textbooks is disappointing. The enormous differences in inequality within and between different societies have hardly been noticed, or explained – there are a few exceptions though, such as Glenn Firebaugh (see also Therborn 2006b: 2–3). One reason for this situation may be that sociologists think the discipline of economics is responsible for investigating this topic. Economic approaches doubtless are important in this regard. Let us first have a short look at them, therefore.

In the economic literature it is difficult to find theories and explanations for international differences in national income distributions. The central variables considered by economists are structures of labour demand and supply (also in connection with population growth) and the endowment of the employable population with human capital. These facts certainly play an important role in every country of the world (for an overview see Neal and Rosen 2000). It is hard to see, however, how they could explain the huge differences in income distribution as shown in Table 1.1. In a very interesting comparison between Brazil and South Africa, economist David Lam (1999) investigates the role of schooling for income inequality. Using large-scale household surveys, he finds that South Africa has considerably lower schooling inequality than Brazil and that schooling in fact explains a large part of earnings (together with age over 40 per cent of the variance). However, South Africa's lower schooling inequality has not in itself an equalizing effect on earnings inequality. He concludes that there may be 'an important element of inertia in the evolution of schooling distributions on income distributions in developing countries' (Lam 1999: 22). A similar point was made 30 years ago by the Austrian economist E. and M. Streissler (1981: 91) who argued that a main characteristic of income inequality over time is the dependence of distribution at a given time from the distribution at the foregoing period; income distribution can be interpreted from this point of view as a time-dependent process of diffusion, even as a coincidental meander. I would suggest that it is exactly the underlying ethnic stratification which explains both the high inequality of schooling and that of earnings in the two countries mentioned before. Seen from this perspective, the 'explanation' of income inequality by inequality of schooling is not really an explanation but only the demonstration of the fact that both these two aspects of stratification are closely related to each other. There are at least two recent papers by economists who look at international differences in intra-national inequality from a broader, comparative perspective. Angeles (2007) and Engerman and Sokoloff (2005) show that colonialism has had a long-lasting impact on higher economic inequality; this is particularly so if colonialism brought into a country a number of European settlers which was considerable but still smaller than the local population. Due to their higher skill and technical resources, these colonies were able to exploit the native population.

There are some additional problems associated with economic explanations of income inequality. Although there exist different paradigms within these explanations,[6] one could say that the dominant economic explanations in general exhibit some of the problems discussed below (see also Arndt 1979; Bunge 1998: 100–154; Weiss 2002; Bögenhold 2010, Haller 2014).

First, they typically start from the basic model of perfect competition – even if they consider monopolistic tendencies (for examples of such models see Stiglitz 1969; Galor and Zeira 1993; for critical views Lydall 1979: 2ff.; Atkinson and Bourguignon 2000a: 7). But in regard to the central aspect considered in this book – that of ethnic differentiations in a society – the assumption is fully unrealistic that labour power, like all other factors of production, is homogeneous and mobile; that the price of labour power, the wages, levels off into an equilibrium state; that education and knowledge are factors accessible to everybody in the same way. Micro-economic, individualistic models and explanations, which exclude structural framework conditions like segmentation of labour markets, the patterns of industrial relations and political pre-conditions for the formation of wages and prices and so on, obviously are inadequate for the explanation of the existing huge international differences. It is typical from this point of view that one of the few leading economists who also has written some important sociological essays, Joseph Schumpeter explicitly excludes ethnic differentiation when speaking about social classes (Schumpeter 1953 [1927]).

A second relevant characteristic of most economic approaches is their individualism and subjectivism (for critical views of this aspect by economists see Arndt 1979; Klanberg 1981: 19) A basic problem of all theories which want to explain income distribution out of the distribution of individual human capital is the fact that the distributions of the two diverge significantly (Rivlin 1981: 279; Bohnet 1999: 121ff.). While individual abilities exhibit a normal distribution, the distribution of incomes is log-normal and askew toward the right: the number of income recipients becomes lower the higher the income is (few people are rich, even fewer very rich). Also the assumption of individual utility functions on whose basis people decide where and how much they work (and earn) is far from reality in many countries and situations because of societal restrictions and because many people do not have clear utility functions (Kleinewefers 2008: 278ff.). This assumption is fully escapist in developing societies where often only 20 per cent to 30 per cent of all adults have a regular full-time job at all. In these studies (approaches), problems of business cycles (connected with unemployment

6   Klanberg (1981: 13–14) distinguishes three paradigms: (1) those which aim toward universal explanations and laws (including human capital theories); these theories tend to be deterministic; (2) open, multi-factor theories which only represent ordered enumerations of relevant factors and are not really systematic explanatory theories. In sociology, comparable approaches are, in my view, Rational Choice and functionalist theories (Haller 2003); (3) models or stylized images of social reality; these can be considered as expedients of true explanations. I would add to these a fourth type, namely institutional approaches, which also consider aspects of economic power, political constitutions, politics and so on.

or inflation), aspects of economic growth (in this regard, the Kuznets thesis is relevant which will be discussed later) and demographic structures and trends are considered; however, these aspects are hardly able to explain the huge international differences in income inequality (see Bohnet 1999: 126ff.).

There are some economists who have developed models concentrating not on individuals but on structural aspects and mechanisms. Quite interesting (and very similar to interest and conflict theories of education in sociology proposed by Weber 1964 and Collins 1971) is the *job-competition model* of Thurow (1975). It assumes that there exists competition for good jobs and employers select those applicants who promise to be the most productive. In this perspective, educational upgrading of the whole labour force may just have the consequence that the same jobs today are filled by better educated individuals than in former times; as a consequence of educational expansion, higher education becomes necessary in order to get the same jobs today as in earlier periods. From this point of view, a policy of expansion of the educational system must not lead to a more equal income distribution (Klanberg 1981: 21). The focus of human capital theory on individual investment decisions about an educational career, furthermore, is inappropriate in all those countries (particularly in Europe) where individual costs of education are covered fully or to a large point by the state.

Economic 'explanations' often have a third characteristic which can surprise a sociologist who considers empirical research as an essential part of scientific work and progress. Galor and Zeira (1993: 50), for instance, conclude their article about 'Income Distribution and Macroeconomics' as follows: 'This study demonstrates that in the case of market imperfections the distribution of wealth significantly affects the aggregate economic activity ...' They arrived at this conclusion without looking at any data but just by starting from a basic production function model in an extremely escapist world (a one-good world with only two technologies and two forms of labour, skilled and unskilled, no population growth, perfectly competitive and mobile capital, labour and goods markets, fully rational expectations of all economic actors). Then they go on to introduce some additional assumptions and modifications and deduce several consequences. At the end, the conclusions are arrived at just on the basis of mathematical reformulations and deductions. A related fact, critically noted by an economist some time ago (Rivlin 1981: 273), is that there exist amazing data holes and economists themselves are quite uninterested in this fact. He wrote: 'To rise above problems of the provision of data is an in-built characteristic of structure of values and careers of economists'. According to the philosopher of science, Mario Bunge (1998: 147), it is taken for granted in the 'hard', factual sciences that the problem investigated must have some relation to the empirical world, and that theories, models and hypotheses must be testable empirically: 'Not so in mainstream economics. Here one may tog with ideas that have little if anything to do with the real world'. And he quotes the economist T.C. Koopmans who complained that 'nobody seems to keep track of confirmations and refutations of economic theories and that most mathematical economists seem to be allergic to data' (Bunge 1998: 148). Such an approach to 'explanation' seems somewhat wondrous on the basis of an epistemological perspective which assumes that concepts and theories have to be confronted systematically with empirical data and have to be supplemented by better theories if they are disproved (Popper 1968). An astute German critic has called this style of thinking 'Neo-' or 'Model Platonism' (Albert 1967); since it always presupposes an artificial world, its theorems might be untestable in reality. A further problematic aspect of these theories is that they are considering only relationships at the aggregate level and tend to make very simplifying assumptions about individual motives and behaviour (Haller 2003: 373–4). In this way it is hardly possible that concepts and theories induce researchers to look at and to detect new empirical phenomena not recognized within the framework of established theories.

Given this situation it is not surprising that economists themselves deliver critical judgements about the contributions of their discipline to this issue. Concerning neo-classical economic theories, such as that of Walras, Harold Lydall (1979: 283–4) wrote: '... the weakness of the theory is that in its exact – and highly detached – form it yields no predictions of any practical significance, while in its aggregative – and in exact – form it loses its logical coherence [...] the neoclassical assumption of perfect competition [...] is inconsistent with so many of the important facts of social life that the theory must be rejected for that reason'. It is also conspicuous – and in this regard a clear parallel exists with the situation in sociology – that the theme of income inequality has suffered a loss of interest in economics since the 1980s (Galor and Zeira 1993: 35). There exist only a few recent monographs on this topic (an exception is Atkinson and Bourguignon 2000b); in university textbooks on macro-economics one looks in vain for a chapter on the theory of distribution. Rather, this is the case in textbooks on finance (see, for example, Bohnet 1999, Ch. 6). It is certainly not by accident that Amartya Sen, one of the few, internationally prominent economists who investigates systematically income inequality, comes from India, a country where inequality and poverty are conspicuous at every turn (see Sen 2007, 2009, 2010). Not least because of this situation, even some economists, such as the Canadian David Green (2007), consider also the contribution of sociology to the explanation of economic inequality as essential (for a similar view, see Myrdal 1980: 26). Green argues that no scientific discipline can claim to hold exclusive expertise in any scientific field; only by the participation of researchers from different academic fields does it become possible to cut across disciplinary parochialisms and to develop new perspectives (see also Granovetter 1981). In the same vein, Armin Bohnet (1999: 125) argues that a mono-causal explanation of income inequality is impossible. The Swiss economist Henner Kleinewefers (2008: 276–8) mentions proper sociological themes when he argues that individual preferences are determined in a decisive way by the economic and social embedding of individuals; utility functions, in his view, are not independent but determined by location of individuals in different societies and cultures, social classes and strata. Significant gaps of neo-classical economic explanations based on the theorem of marginal utility were also noted early by the German economist Erich Preiser (1970); he mentioned the neglect of the fact that the development of wages is determined also by the power of unions and state interventions, as well as by legal and constitutional conditions usually taken for granted, such as the existence of private property. Thus, in spite of the foregoing critical review of mainstream economics, we can say that there have been and still are useful economic concepts and theorems which sociology should consider (for a review of economic concepts and theories which were influential in sociology, see Baron and Hannan 1994).

Let us now have a short look at sociological contributions to the explanation of income inequality. Economic inequality in general and income inequality in particular is in fact also a topic of sociology. It is treated in textbooks in a more descriptive manner in connection with issues of social inequality, social class and stratification in general (see, for instance, Giddens 1999: 274–5). More extensive discussions are contained in books on stratification and mobility. In one of the most widely used books of this sort, Harold Kerbo (2012: 21–39) describes extensively the patterns and trends of income and wealth distribution in the USA and compares them with other Western countries. Special sociological studies on income inequality usually are of two kinds. Some of them start from a specific general theory. An example is the well-known work of Erik O. Wright (1985). His theoretical background is Marxist theory, to which he adds elements of Weberian theory; on this basis he develops a schema of class locations in modern societies (with the new idea of 'contradictory class locations') and tries to show that this schema is able to contribute significantly to the explanation of income differentials between the incumbents of these positions. Another sociological approach is more inductive-empiricist and tries to find out by multivariate analyses which sociological variables contribute most to the explanation of income differentials. A well-known study of this sort is that by Christopher Jencks et al. (1977); using large US surveys, they estimate carefully the effects of social background characteristics (fathers and mothers education and occupation), gender and individual ability on income; they include also race and find a modest effect of this variable.[7] All of these works and studies give valuable insights into the problem of income attainment and inequality. Several aspects, however, are missing: they do not have an explicit theory of income inequality; they are restricted to advanced, Western societies; and they do not cover systematically the issue of ethnic differentiation and inequality which partly is a consequence of their concentration on Western societies.

However, a few major sociological works have investigated social and economic inequality from a comparative perspective. They are disappointing, however, if one looks at them from the viewpoint of the large international differences in income distributions within countries mentioned above. In his impressive work *Power and Privilege*, Gerhard Lenski (1973 [1966]) has investigated the development of stratification systems through human history, from the most simple and primitive societies to the most advanced, present-day societies. He finds an inversion of a long-term trend toward more inequality at the time when industrial societies emerge. However, differences between the present-day developed societies and other societies around the world are not picked out as a theme, probably under the tacit assumption that the differences will

---

7   For a study comparing the explanatory power of the Marxist and non-Marxist class theory see Robinson and Kelley, 1979.

assimilate. Lenski's key variables explaining differences in privileges and prestige are technical change and power. He assumes, following partly Marx, that the level of technological development of a society largely determines structures of distribution. In modern societies, technology became so complex that the dominant elites are not able any more to understand and control all activities of their subordinates. Therefore, they must divide some of their privileges with their vice-regents and substitutes so that overall inequality becomes smaller. A related theory of changes in income distribution has been developed by the economist Simon S. Kuznets (1955). He argues that the level of income inequality over time presents an inverted U-curve: it increases at the beginning of the process of industrialization because incomes in the industrial sector and in towns increase faster than those in the agricultural sector; later on, when industrial forms of production comprise the whole economy, including agriculture, they equal out.

What can be said about the role of industrialization and technical progress as a variable explaining income distribution? It is doubtless of central importance; however, it does not offer a clue for a sociological interpretation because it must be considered mainly as a limiting factor but not as an independent causal variable. So, it is not surprising that empirical findings concerning Kuznets' theory are controversial. Both Morrisson (2000) and Frazer (2006) found partial confirmations of the thesis. Frazer (2006), however, points to several cases which are not in accord with it: the UK and the USA as already highly developed countries experienced a strong increase of inequality between 1961 and 2003. Korea, Taiwan and Japan had large increases in GDP together with a rather low level of income inequality; inequality did only lightly increase in parallel; Sub-Saharan countries show persistent low levels of development and very high levels of income inequality. The limited explanatory power of Kuznet's theorem becomes also evident if we look at Table 1.1: among countries with extreme high income inequality, we find the very poor and little developed countries of Sub-Saharan Africa, but also industrializing nations like Brazil and South Africa. The same can be seen among advanced countries where quite equal countries co-exist with others which have a rather unequal income distribution. Bowles (2002: 235) notes that some small countries with open economies – in particular the Scandinavian countries, but also some Indian federal states like Kerala and West Bengal – have been able to create a relatively equal distribution of income through a consistent, forceful education and health policy, land reform and so on (see also Sen 2007; Bornschier 2008). Also the second factor in Lenski's theory, power, does not accomplish much for an explanation. Power is a much too general, amorphous concept as noted already by Weber (1964/1: 38). More concrete and useful, however, is Lenski's hint toward the relevance of democracy; I will come back to this idea later.

Of interest in our context is also the broad study of Hamilton and Hirszowicz (1987) about *Class and Inequality in Pre-Industrial, Capitalist and Communist Societies*. These authors start from the thesis that patterns of inequality are in the first instance determined by power differentials. They limit themselves, however, to a discussion of differences within advanced societies, in particular between Capitalist and State Socialist countries. However, these were relatively unimportant in a worldwide comparison; in addition, this distinction has become historically obsolete. State Socialist societies have in fact been able to reduce some inequalities, new ones, however, have come into existence (see Szelényi 1998 for a comprehensive study). The general conclusion drawn by Hamilton and Hirszowicz, however, is very relevant in this context:

> Contrary to the expectations of many nineteenth and early twentieth century sociologists, differences determined by gender, nationality, ethnicity and race have not been wiped out by the progress of industrial civilization or the advancement of socialist regimes and some of them act as powerful indicators of social change [...] Studies in class and stratification do not, therefore, constitute straightforward guidelines for forecasting future developments in any of the present societies. (Hamilton and Hirszowicz 1987: 276f.)

Thus, the results of this review of the relevant literature in economics and sociology are lean. As far as sociologists are concerned, it is possible, however, that they just did not investigate the problem of the large international differences in income, but their theories would be able to explain them. Yet, a review of the literature in this regard is also disappointing. On the one side, an old observation made by an eminent German student of inequality, Ralf Dahrendorf (1974a: 348), may still be true, namely, that there exists a considerable hiatus between class and stratification theories on the one side and empirical research on the other side. It seems, moreover, that theoretical sociological paradigms on inequality are taking turns not in correspondence with changes in social reality but because in each epoch new political and social currents gain prominence which then influence also the sociologists. In the 1950s and 1960s, functionalist theories of stratification were *en vogue*, which consider inequality as a basic and necessary characteristic of any society in order to motivate talented and able people for high achievements. In the 1970s and 1980s, neo-Marxist and neo-Weberian theories of stratification came to the fore; they see inequality as the result of conflicts of interests and power. Later on, also in connection with the breakdown of State Socialism in East Europe, these theories were displaced by theories of individualization and pluralistic differentiation, of post-industrialism and the rise of the knowledge society; in these theories, class-related interests and differentials of power and privileges do not appear. It is also evident that systems of interpretation of inequality, power and privilege which are dominant in specific countries have a large impact on the thinking of sociologists and economists. Functionalist theory gained prominence in the United States, class and conflict theories were (and still are) most strong in France and England and theories of the end of class societies, of individualism and pluralism were advanced mainly in Germany (Ossowski 1972; Hess 2001; Haller 2006; for the USA see also Verba and Orren 1985).

We can draw two general conclusions from this overview on the handling and explanation of international differences in national patterns of income inequality in social sciences like economics and sociology. First, the huge differences which exist in this regard have by far not received the attention they should merit; second, neither economics nor sociology have offered theories and hypotheses which seem to be able to explain them. A striking explanatory gap is obvious here. The thesis of this book is that we can close this gap to a considerable degree if the role of ethnic stratification is taken into consideration.

Summary and Outlook

Economic inequality is a fundamental problem of the world today. In the advanced North (which includes also developed countries in the Southern hemisphere, such as Australia), people live in abundance, compared with any earlier period in their history. In many countries of the Southern hemisphere, incomes and standards of living are far below; at least a billion people have to live on less than 1$ per day. These differences have led theorists of globalization to argue that the social sciences should concentrate on international patterns of inequality instead of continuing to look at national patterns of inequality within nation-states. In this chapter and in this book I argue that such a reorientation would be misleading. One the one side, it has been shown in this chapter that within-country income differences are not less, but probably even more pronounced than those between countries at the global level. The differences in economic inequality between countries which are the most unequal in terms of economic inequality – such as Brazil or the Republic of South Africa – and others which are most equal – such as the Scandinavian and some Central and East European countries – are extremely large. On the other side, there are also theoretical and political considerations which suggest that a focus on national patterns of income distribution remains as essential as ever. Also today, it is on this level where the social and political processes of the production and distribution of wealth, the creation of privilege and discrimination and the allocation of people to affluent and poor status groups are going on. A bulk of research has shown that countries which have a more equal distribution of income fare much better in many social, economic and political regards; those afflicted by pervasive inequalities have to suffer from massive problems, including corruption and violence.

How did economics and sociology, the two disciplines mainly concerned with patterns of distribution and issues of socio-economic inequality, handle this problem? A short review of the relevant literature provided only disappointing evidence: international differences in national patterns of economic inequality did not really capture their attention; neither of these disciplines has tried to develop a more or less coherent explanation for them. In fact, it seems hardly possible to explain them either in terms of standard economic theories of income distribution, as outcomes of different individual endowments with human capital or of market forces, nor in sociological terms, as results of the size, interests and behaviours of social classes. Thus, besides of the surprising neglect of a massive, present-day problem here also a striking theoretical gap seems to exist.

In the next chapters, I will argue that we can fill this gap to a large extent if we consider the role of ethnic differentiation and discrimination. Indications for the relevance of this dimension have been found already in this chapter: By and large, economic inequality is highest in countries which are extremely diversified in ethnic terms, while in others which are very homogenous in this regard – such as Japan – it is surprisingly low in spite of a rather weak redistributive welfare state. In the next chapter, I will show the relevance of ethnic-national differentiations and conflicts in the world today and give some explanations as to why they have escaped the attention of standard economics and sociology. In Chapter 3, it will be argued and shown that it is not ethnic differentiation as such but only its interaction with class structuration and exploitation and its earlier historical forms – such as slavery – which is highly relevant for economic inequality today. This argument will be tested in Chapter 4 empirically in a rigorous way and with the help of a new set of aggregate data on 139 countries around the world.

References

Adler, Alfred (1972 [1912]), *Über den nervösen Charakter*, Frankfurt: Fischer Taschenbuch Verlag

Aghion, Philippe, Eve Caroli and Cecilia García-Penalose (1999), 'Inequality and Economic Growth: The Perspective of the New Growth Theories', *Journal of Economic Literature* 37: 1615–60

Albert, Hans (1967), *Marktsoziologie und Entscheidungslogik. Ökonomische Probleme in soziologischer Perspektive*, Neuwied/Berlin: Luchterhand

Ali, Ali Abdel Gadir (2010), 'Demography, Growth, Income Distribution and Poverty: A Survey of Interrelationships', in Olu Ajakaiye, Germano Mwabu, eds, *Reproductive Health, Economic Growth and Poverty Reduction in Africa. Frameworks of Analysis*, Nairobi: The University of Nairobi Press, pp. 191–215

Angeles, Luis (2007), 'Income inequality and colonialism', *European Economic Review* 51: 1155–76

Arndt, Helmut (1979), *Irrwege der Politischen Ökonomie*, München: Beck

Atkinson, Anthony B. and Andrea Brandolini (2001), 'Promise and pitfalls in the use of ‚secondary data sets‘: Income inequality in OECD countries as a case study', *Journal of Economic Literature* 39: 77–799

Atkinson, Anthony B. and François Bourguignon (2000a), 'Income distribution and economics', in Atkinson and Bourguignon, *Handbook of Income Distribution*, pp. 1–58

Atkinson, Anthony B. and François Bourguignon, eds (2000b), *Handbook of Income Distribution*, Amsterdam etc.: Elsevier

Bales, Kevin (2004), *Disposable People. New Slavery in the Global Economy*, Berkeley etc.: University of California Press

Baron, James N. and Michael T. Hannan (1994), 'The impact of economics on contemporary sociology', *Journal of Economic Literature* XXXII: 1111–46

Batstone, David (2008), *Sklavenhandel heute. Die dunkelste Seite der Globalisierung*, München: Redline Wirtschaft (English ed.: *Not for Sale*, New York, Harper Collins)

Bayer, Michael et al. eds (2008), *Transnationale Ungleichheitsforschung. Eine neue Herausforderung für die Soziologie*, Frankfurt/New York: Campus

Beck, Ulrich (2002), *Macht und Gegenmacht im globalen Zeitalter*, Frankfurt am Main: Suhrkamp

Berger, Johannes (2005), 'Nimmt die Einkommensungleichheit weltweit zu? Methodische Feinheiten der Ungleichheitsforschung', *Leviathan* 33: 464–81

Berger, Peter A. and Anja Weiß, eds (2008), *Transnationalisierung sozialer Ungleichheit*, Wiesbaden: VS Verlag

Berthold, Norbert and Alexander Brunner (2010), Wie ungleich ist die Welt? Universität Würzburg, Wirtschaftswissenschaftliche Beiträge des Lehrstuhls für Volkswirtschaftslehre, Nr. 111

Bögenhold, Dieter (2010), 'From heterodoxy to orthodoxy and vice versa: Economics and Social Sciences in the Division of Academic Work', *American Journal of Sociology and Economics* 69: 1566–90

Bohnet, Armin (1999), *Finanzwissenschaft: Grundlagen staatlicher Verteilungspolitik*, München/Wien: R. Oldenbourg

Bornschier, Volker (2008), 'Zur Entwicklung der sozialen Ungleichheiten im Weltsystem: Fakten, offene Fragen und erste Antworten', in Michael Bayer et al., eds, *Transnationale Ungleichheitsforschung*, pp. 97–134

Borooah, Vani K., Bjorn Gustafsson and Li Shi (2006), 'China and India: Income inequality and poverty north and south of the Himalayas', *Journal of Asian Economics* 17: 797–817

Botton, Alain de (2004), *StatusAngst*, Frankfurt am Main: Fischer

Bourguignon, François and Christian Morrisson (2002), 'Inequality among world citizens: 1820–1992', *The American Economic Review* 92: 727–44

Bowles, Samuel (2002), 'Globalization and Redistribution: Feasible Egalitarianism in a Competitive World', in Richard B. Freeman, ed., *Inequality Around the World*, London: Palgrave, pp. 234–67

Brand, Ulrich (2011), *Post-Neoliberalismus? Aktuelle Konflikte. Gegen-hegemoniale Strategien*, Hamburg: VSA Verlag

Brandolini, Andrea and Timothy Smeeding (2008), 'Inequality (International Evidence)', in *The New Palgrave Dictionary of Economics*, Vol. 4, London: Palgrave Macmillan, pp. 273–82

Bunge, Mario (1998), *Social Science under Debate: A Philosophical Perspective*, Toronto etc.: University of Toronto Press

Carlsson, Gösta (1968), 'Ökonomische Ungleichheit und Lebenschancen', in *Soziale Schichtung und soziale Mobilität. Kölner Zeitschrift für Soziologie und Sozialpsychologie*, Sonderheft 6, pp. 189–99

Castles, Francis G. (1993), *Families of Nations. Patterns of Public Policy in Western Democracies*, Dartmouth: Aldershot

Chomsky, Noam (1993), *Wirtschaft und Gewalt. Vom Kolonialismus zur neuen Weltordnung*, Lüneburg: zu Klampen

Coates, Rondey D., ed. (2004), *Race and Ethnicity. Across Time, Space and Discipline*, Leiden/Boston: Brill

Cohen, Robin and Paul Kennedy (2007), *Global Sociology*, New York: New York University Press

Collins, Randall (1971), 'Functional and Conflict Theories of Educational Stratification', *American Sociological Review* 36: 1002–19

Collins, Randall (1975), *Conflict Sociology. Toward an Explanatory Science*, New York etc.: Academic Press

Dahrendorf, Ralf (1974a), 'Die gegenwärtige Lage der Theorie der sozialen Schichtung', in R. Dahrendorf, *Pfade aus Utopia*, Utopia, München: Piper pp. 36–352

Dahrendorf, Ralf (1974b), 'Über den Ursprung der Ungleichheit unter den Menschen', in R. Dahrendorf, *Pfade aus Utopia*, pp. 352–79

Deaton, Angus and Jean Drèze (2002), 'Poverty and inequality in India. A re-examination', *Economic and Political Weekly*, 7 Sept., pp. 3729–48

Delhey, Jan and Ulrich Kohler (2011), 'Is happiness inequality immune to income inequality?' *Social Science Research* 40: 742–56

Devine, Fiona and Mary C. Waters, eds (2004), *Social Inequalities in Comparative Perspective*, Malden, MA etc.: Blackwell

Dollar, David (2007), 'Globalization, Poverty and Inequality since 1980', in D. Held and A. Kaya eds, *Global Inequality*, Cambridge: Polity Press, pp. 73–103

Eicher, Theo S. and Stephen J. Turnovsky, eds (2003), *Inequality and Growth. Theory and Policy Implications*, Cambridge, MA/London: MIT Press

Engerman, Stanley and Kenneth Sokoloff (2005), Colonialism, inequality, and long-run paths of development, Working Paper 11057, National Bureau of Economic Research, Cambridge, MA

Esping-Andersen, Gøsta (1990), *The Three Worlds of Welfare Capitalism*, Cambridge: Polity Press

Firebaugh, Glenn (2003), *The New Geography of Global Income Inequality*, Cambridge, MA/London: Harvard University Press

Frazer, Garth (2006), 'Inequality and development across and within countries', *World Development* 34: 1459–81

Frey, Bruno S. and Alois Stutzer (2002), *Happiness and Economics. How the Economy and Institutions Affect Well-being*, Princeton: Princeton University Press

Gakuru, Octavian N. (2002), 'Globalisation of Social Structure and Politico-economic Development', *African Journal of Sociology* V: 23–38

Galor, Oded and Joseph Zeira (1993), 'Income Distribution and Macroeconomics', *Review of Economic Studies* 60: 35–52

Giddens, Anthony (1999), *Soziologie*, Graz-Wien: Nausner & Nausner

Goesling, Brian (2001), 'Changing income inequalities within and between nations: New evidence', *American Sociological Review* 66: 745–61

Graham, Carol and Andrew Felton (2005), Does inequality matter for individual welfare? The Brookings Institution/The John Hopkins University, CSED Working Paper 38

Granovetter, Mark (1981), 'Toward a sociological theory of income differences', in Ivar Berg, ed., *Sociological Perspectives on Labour Markets*, New York etc.: Academic Press, pp. 11–47

Green, David A. (2007), 'Where have all the sociologists gone?' *American Behavioral Scientist* 50: 737–47

Greve, Jens (2010), 'Globale Ungleichheit: Weltgesellschaftliche Perspektiven', *Berliner Journal für Soziologie* 20: 65–87

Haller, Max (1987), 'Positional and sectoral differences in income', in W. Teckenberg, ed., *Comparative Studies of Social Structure. Recent Research on France, the United States and the Federal Republic*, Armonk, NY/London: Sharpe, pp. 172–90

Haller, Max (1990), 'The Challenge for Comparative Sociology in the Transformation of Europe', *International Sociology*, 5: 183–204

Haller, Max (2003), *Soziologische Theorie im systematisch-kritischen Vergleich*, Wiesbaden: VS Verlag

Haller, Max (2006), 'Theorien sozialer Ungleichheit im nationalen und europäischen Kontext. Eine wissenssoziologische Analyse', in Martin Heidenreich, ed., *Die Europäisierung sozialer Ungleichheit. Zur transnationalen Klassen- und Sozialstrukturanalyse*, Frankfurt/New York: Campus, pp. 187–229

Haller, Max (2014), 'Die Ökonomie – Natur- oder Sozialwissenschaft? Wissenschaftstheoretische und wissenssoziologische Überlegungen zu einer alten Kontroverse', in Dieter Bögenhold, ed., *Soziologie des Wirtschaftlichen. Alte und neue Fragen*, Wiesbaden: Springer, pp. 31–65

Haller, Max and Markus Hadler (2004), 'Happiness as an Expression of Freedom and Self-determination. A Comparative, Multilevel Analysis', in Wolfgang Glatzer, Susanne von Below and Matthias Stoffregen, eds, *Challenges for the Quality of Life in Contemporary Societies*, Dordrecht etc.: Kluwer, pp. 207–31

Haller, Max and Markus Hadler (2004/05), 'Ist der Nationalstaat überholt? Überlegungen und Fakten über die sinnvollste Einheit bzw. Analyseebene in der international vergleichenden Sozialforschung', *AIAS-Informationen* 23: 141–61

Haller, Max and Markus Hadler (2006), 'How Social Relations and Structures can Produce Life Satisfaction and Happiness. An International Comparative Analysis', *Social Indicators Research* 75: 161–216

Hamilton, Malcolm and Maria Hirszowicz (1987), *Class and Inequality in Pre-Industrial, Capitalist and Communist Societies*, Sussex: Wheatsheaf Books, New York: St Martin's Press

Harrison, Bennett and Barry Bluestone (1998), *The Great U-Turn: Corporate Re-Structuring and the Polarizing of America*, New York: Basic Books

Hess, Andreas (2001), *Concepts of Social Stratification. European and American Models*, Houndsmill, Basingstoke: Palgrave

Hewlett, Sylvia A. (1997), 'Inequality and its implications for economic growth', in Irving L. Horowitz, ed., *Equity, Income, and Policy. Comparative Studies in Three Worlds of Development*, New York/London: Praeger, pp. 29–48

Hoover, Greg A. (1989), 'Intranational inequality. A cross-national dataset', *Social Forces* 67: 1008–26

Jencks, Christopher (2002), 'Does inequality matter?' *Daedalus*, Winter 2002, pp. 49–65

Jencks, Christopher et al. (1977), *Who Gets Ahead? The Determinants of Economic Success in America*, New York: Basic Books

Kanazawa, Sathoshi and Mary C. Still (1999), 'Why Monogamy?' *Social Forces* 78: 25–50

Katz, Lawrence F. (1999), 'Changes in the wage structure and earnings inequality', in O. Ashenfelter and D. Card, eds, *Handbook of Labor Economics*, Amsterdam: Elsevier, pp. 1463–555

Kerbo, Harold R. (2006), *World Poverty. Global Inequality and the Modern World System*, Boston etc.: McGraw-Hill

Kerbo, Harold R. (2012), *Social Stratification and Inequality. Class Conflict in Historical, Comparative, and Global Perspective*, New York: McGraw-Hill

Klanberg, Frank (1981), 'Paradigmen in der Erklärung der Einkommensverteilung', in F. Klanberg & J. Krupp, eds, Einkommensverteilung, Königstein/Ts.: Athenäum, pp 13–30

Kleinewefers, Henner (2008), *Einführung in die Wohlfahrtsökonomie. Theorie – Anwendung – Kritik*, Stuttgart: W. Kohlhammer

Korpi, Walter and Joakim Palme (1989), 'The paradox of redistribution and strategies of equality: Welfare state institutions, inequality, and poverty in Western countries', *American Sociological Review* 63: 661

Korpi, Walter (1983), *The Democratic Class Struggle*, London: Routledge & Kegan Paul

Kreckel, Reinhard (1992), *Politische Soziologie der sozialen Ungleichheit*, Frankfurt/New York: Campus

Kreckel, Reinhard (2008), 'Soziologie der sozialen Ungleichheit im globalen Kontext', in Bayer et al., *Transnationale Ungleichheitsforschung*, pp. 23–69

Kuznets, Simon (1955), 'Economic Growth and Income Inequality', *American Economic Review*, 45: 1–28

Lam, David (1999), 'Generating Extreme Inequality: Schooling, Earnings, and Intergenerational Transmission of Human Capital in South Africa and Brazil', Research Report, PSC Population Studies Center, University of Michigan

Lenski, Gerhard (1973), Macht und Privileg, Frankfurt am Main: Suhrkamp (Power and Privilege 1966)

Lydall, Harold (1979), *A Theory of Income Distribution*, Oxford: Clarendon

Manow, Philip (2002), '"The Good, the Bad, and the Ugly". Esping-Andersens Wohlfahrtsstaatstypologie und die konfessionellen Grundlagen des westlichen Sozialstaats', *Kölner Zeitschrift für Soziologie und Sozialpsychologie* 54: 203–25

Menard, Scott (1986), 'A research note on international comparisons of inequality of income', *Social Forces* 64: 778–93

Milanovic, Branko (2002), 'True world income distribution, 1988 and 1993: First calculation based on household surveys alone', *The Economic Journal* 112: 51–92

Milanovic, Branko (2005), *Worlds Apart. Measuring International and Global Inequality*, Princeton/Oxford: Princeton University Press

Milanovic, Branko (2007), 'Globalization and inequality', in Held and Kaya, eds, *Global Inequality*, pp. 26–49

Morrison, Christian (2000), 'Historical perspectives on income distribution: The case of Europe', in Atkinson and Bourguignon, *Handbook of Income Distribution*, pp. 217–308

Müller, Walter and Steffen Schindler (2008), 'Entleert sich die Mitte wirklich? Einige Überlegungen zur Milanovic-These über die internationale Ungleichheit', in Michael Bayer et al., eds, *Transnationale Ungleichheitsforschung*, pp. 71–95

Myrdal, Gunnar (1980), *Ein asiatisches Drama. Eine Untersuchung über die Armut der Nationen*, Frankfurt am Main: Suhrkamp. (An Asian Drama 1944)

Neal, Derek and Sherwin Rosen (2000), 'Theories of the distribution of earnings', in Atkinson and Bourguignon, *Handbook of Income Distribution*, pp. 379–427

Nollmann, Gerd (2006), 'Erhöht Globalisierung die Ungleichheit der Einkommen? Determinanten von Einkommensverteilungen in 16 OECD-Ländern 1967–2000', *Kölner Zeitschrift für Soziologie und Sozialpsychologie* 58: 638–59

Olson, Sven (1986), 'Sweden', in Flora, *State, Economy, and Society in Western Europe: 1815–1975*, Frankfurt/New York: Campus, pp. 1–116

Ossowski, Stanislaw (1972), *Die Klassenstruktur im sozialen Bewußtsein*, Neuwied: Luchterhand (1st Polish ed. 1957)

Perkins, John (2004), *Confessions of an Economic Hit Man*, San Francisco: South End Press

Persson, Torsten and Guido Tabellini (1994), 'Is inequality harmful for growth?' *American Economic Review* 84: 600–621

Pickett, Kate and Richard Wilkinson (2009), *Gleichheit ist Glück. Warum gerechte Gesellschaften für alle besser sind*, Berlin: Haffmans & Tolkemitt

Pogge, Thomas W. (2007), 'Why Inequality Matters', in Held and Kaya, eds, *Global Inequality*, pp. 132–47

Popper, Karl R. (1968), *The Logic of Scientific Discovery*, New York: Harper & Row

Preiser, Erich (1970), Politische Ökonomie im 20. Jahrhundert, München: Beck

Pries, Ludger (2010), *Transnationalisierung. Theorie und Empirie grenzüberschreitender Vergesellschaftung*, Wiesbaden: VS Verlag

Raffalovich, Lawrence E. (1999), 'Growth and distribution. Evidence from a variable-parameter cross-national time-series analysis', *Social Forces* 78: 415–32

Reich, Robert (2008), *Superkapitalismus. Wie die Wirtschaft unsere Demokratie untergräbt*, Frankfurt/New York: Campus

Rivlin, Alica (1981), 'Einkommensverteilung – sind Ökonomen zu etwas nutze?' in Klanberg and Krupp, *Einkommensverteilung*, Königstein, Ts.: Athenäum, pp. 269–89

Robinson, Robert V. and Jonathan Kelley (1979), 'Class as conceived by Marx and Dahrendorf: Effects on income inequality and politics in the United States and Great Britain', *American Sociological Review* 44: 38–58

Rousseau, Jean-Jacques (1967 [1754]), 'Abhandlung über den Ursprung und die Grundlagen der Ungleichheit unter den Menschen', in Jean-Jacques Rousseau, *Preisschriften und Erziehungsplan*, Bad Heilbrunn: Verlag J. Klinkhardt, pp. 47–137

Sagan, Leonard A. (1987), *The Health of Nations. True Causes of Sickness and Well-being*, New York: Basic Books

Scheff, Thomas J. (1990), *Microsociology. Discourse, Emotion, and Social Structure*, Chicago etc.: University of Chicago Press

Schumpeter, Joseph (1953 [1927]), 'Die sozialen Klassen im ethnisch homogenen Milieu', in J. Schumpeter, *Aufsätze zur Soziologie*, Tübingen: Mohr, pp. 147–213

Schwinn, Thomas (2008), 'Nationale und globale Ungleichheit', *Berliner Journal für Soziologie* 18: 8–31

Sen, Amartya K. (2007), *Ökonomie für den Menschen*, München: Deutscher Taschenbuch Verlag (English ed. 1999)

Sen, Amartya K. (2009), *Ökonomische Ungleichheit*, Marburg: Metropolis (English ed. 1973)

Sen, Amartya K. (2010), *Die Idee der Gerechtigkeit*, München: Beck (Development as Freedom 2009)

Sennet, Richard and Jonathan Cobb (1972), *The Hidden Injuries of Class*, New York: Vintage Books

Smeeding, Timothy et al., eds (1990), *Poverty, Inequality and Income Distribution in Comparative Perspective. The Luxembourg Income Study (LIS)*, New York etc. Harvester Wheatsheaf

Solt, Frederick (2008), 'Economic inequality and democratic political engagement", *American Journal of Political Science* 523: 48–60

Solt, Frederick (2009), 'Standardizing World Income Inequality Database', *Social Science Quarterly* 90: 231–42

Stiglitz, Joseph E. (1969), 'Distribution of income and wealth among individuals', *Econometrica* 37: 382–97

Stiglitz, Joseph E. (2004), *Die Schatten der Globalisierung*, München: Goldmann

Streissler, Erich and Monika Streissler (1986), *Grundzüge der Volkswirtschaftslehre für Juristen*, Wien: Manz

Sutcliffe, Bob (2007), 'The Unequalled and Unequal Twentieth Century', in Held and Kaya, eds, *Global Inequality*, pp. 50–72

Szelényi, Szonja (1998), *Equality by Design. The Grand Experiment in Destratification in Socialist Hungary*, Stanford, CA: Stanford University Press

Therborn, Göran (1995), *European Modernity and Beyond, The Trajectory of European Societies 1945–2000*, London etc.: Sage

Therborn, Göran (2006b), 'Meaning, mechanisms, patterns, and forces: An introduction', in Therborn, *Inequalities of the World*, London/New York: Verso, pp. 1–60

Thurow Lester C. (1975), *Generating Inequality*, New York: Basic Books

Tocqueville, Alexis de (1976[1835]), Über die Demokratie in Amerika, München: Deutscher Taschenbuch Verlag (Democracy in America 1945)

Verba, Sidney and Gary R. Orren (1985), *Equality in America. The View from the Top*, Cambridge, MA/London: Harvard University Press

Wade, Robert H. (2007), 'Should We Worry about Income Inequality?' in Held and Kaya, eds, *Global Inequality*, pp. 104–31

Weber, Max (1964/I+II), *Wirtschaft und Gesellschaft*, 2 vols, Köln/Berlin: Kiepenheuer & Witsch

Weiss, Linda (1998), *The Myth of the Powerlessness of the State. Governing the Economy in a Global Era*, Cambridge: Polity Press

Weiss, Linda (2002), *How to Argue With an Economist. Reopening Political Debate in Australia*, Cambridge: Cambridge University Press

World Development Report (2006), *Equity and Development*, Washington/New York: The World Bank/
    Oxford University Press
Wright, Erik O. (1985), *Classes*, London: Verso
Ziegler, Jean (2011), *Wir lassen sie verhungern. Die Massenvernichtung der Dritten Welt*, München:
    Bertelsmann

Chapter 2

Ethnic Differentiation, Stratification and Conflicts in the World Today. Concepts, Theories and Basic Facts

In the first part of this chapter, the general thesis of this book about the effects of class and ethnic stratification on economic inequality will be formulated. Then, we consider what classical and recent authors have written about the relation between ethnicity and stratification. Finally, the concept of ethnicity is defined more exactly and it is shown that most nation-states of the present-day world are characterized by significant degrees of ethnic differentiation and ethnic conflict.

Class Formation, Social Stratification, and Ethnic Differentiation. The Basic Triad in the Reproduction of Social Inequality

Following Max Weber[1] I start from the assumption that there are two basic processes by which social inequality is produced and reproduced, formation of economic classes and social stratification.[2] Besides class formation and social stratification, the *Castor and Pollux* (Hechter 1978; Bendix and Lipset 1966) in the reproduction of inequality, I assume that there exists a third principle, that of ethnic stratification, which must be considered as an independent source for the emergence of social and economic inequality.

The basic thesis of this study is that class formation, social stratification and ethnic differentiation are the basic triad when it comes to explain the distribution of socio-economic resources and privileges; these three processes play a central role also in connection with social integration and conflicts in general (see Figure 2.1).

It is a matter of fact that economically based class cleavages more seldom have led to social and political conflicts than one would have expected. Conflicts, however, typically emerge when class structures coincide with race, religious, linguistic and other ethnic divisions (Shibutani and Kwan 1965: 13; Collins 1975: 84; A.W. Marx 1998: 277) Decisive for the emergence of cleavages and the course and outcome of many conflicts is how class

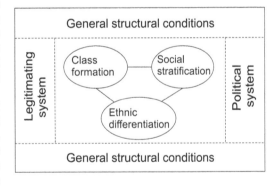

Figure 2.1 The basic triad in the production and reproduction of economic inequality and their macro-social embeddedness

---

1 Here, I refer mainly to the two relevant chapters in Weber's main work *Economy and Society* (Weber 1964/1: 223−7, 1964/II: 678−89). Classes and social stratification are issues, however, which are relevant and discussed also in most of his other works, including his research on the sociology of religion. On the Weberian class concept see also Giddens 1973; Parkin 1979; Haller 1983; Murphy 1988.

2 Weber himself in most instances does not write of 'social stratification' proper but of the formation of estates (*Ständebildung*) which he confronts to classes. Estates certainly are a specific historic form, connected with feudal society in the Middle and early Modern Ages. I follow the established interpretation, that we can use the more general term 'social stratification' in the same sense; this is all the more so, because Weber considers education and styles of life as the main characteristics of the formation of estates.

stratification[3] and ethnic stratification interact with each other. A sound theoretical conceptualization of this fact is missing in the relevant literature. We can develop such a conceptualization only by looking closely at characteristics of each of those three processes. Before going on to this problem, let us discuss shortly two related issues: the first is the thesis that there exists an additional basic dimension for the reproduction of inequality, namely gender; the second issue concerns an important corollary of class conflicts, namely the formation of (political) parties.

Starting with a seminal article by Kimberle Crenshaw (1991), feminist social scientists argue that also gender constitutes a basic form of social differentiation and inequality; they have developed the concept of intersectionality to denote the close interaction between class, ethnicity and gender. Crenshaw, for instance, showed that forms of violence like battering and rape affect women of all social classes, but particularly coloured women with childcare responsibilities and lack of job skills or immigrant women dependent on their husbands. She concludes, therefore, that the subordination and exploitation of women must be seen as 'a broad-scale system of domination that affects women as a class' (Crenshaw 1991: 124). In a similar vein, S. Walby argues that class, gender and ethnicity are social relationships which constitute clearly separate 'systems'. (Walby 2007: 460). I agree fully with the argument of these authors that it is necessary to carefully take account of gender inequalities and their interaction with class and ethnic differentiations. It is also correct that class, ethnic and gender inequalities do not simply add up; rather, in different classes, among different ethnic groups, quite varying forms of discrimination of women do exist (see, for instance, the collection of papers on this topic in Andersen and Hill Collins 1998 and the textbooks of Devine and Waters 2004; Chancer and Watkins 2006; L. Weber 2010; Healey 2010). In fact, ethnic and gender differentiation and stratification often interact very closely, and societies with extensive discrimination of women are often the same which exhibit large class and ethnic inequality; and, vice versa, societies with a high degree of female emancipation are also those with little ethnic and class discrimination.[4]

However, it is obvious that the resources, discriminations and privileges of women in different social classes and strata are diverging strongly; therefore, women as a whole are far from constituting anything like a 'class' or a 'system'. Women are – like men – connected with societal structures through their class positions and their roles in the system of social stratification; here, marriage, reproduction and the intergenerational transmission of social status tie men and women closely together (Haller 1981; see also below). Also ethnic membership embraces and interconnects men and women. Several authors have shown that the use of the concept of 'patriarchy' as a structure of equal theoretical status to capitalism is misleading, equating two very different forms of social relations, and collapsing explanation with description (Acker 1989; Pollert 1996; Kraemer et al. 2012). Rather, as one can look both at the separate effects of the two dimensions (see Cotter et al. 1999 as a good example), one can also look at the interaction between class and gender (Haller 1981, 1983) and gender and ethnicity. Pollert (1996: 8) has written, concerning the relation between class and gender: 'There is a subtle but crucial difference between dualist perspectives "positing analytically independent structures and then looking for the linkages between them" and the view "that social relations are constituted through processes in which the linkages are inbuilt" (Acker 1989: 239). This is because the first seeks abstract dynamics, and becomes caught up in the tangle of the non-equivalence of two types of social relations […], whereas the second seeks the answers in substantive historical process as the appropriate level of analysis of the mutual constitution of two conceptually different types of social relations'. A relevant example here is slavery, the most brutal form of ethnic exploitation; in all forms of historical (and actual) slavery, men and women were quite differently exposed to it (see Chapter 5, pp 142–15). Even within one ethnic-cultural group, women of higher and lower strata are confronted with very different life conditions. Particularly, in Arab-Islamic societies, but in principle everywhere around the world, women of the higher classes are

---

3   Here and in the following, I often use the term 'class stratification' in the relatively broad meaning of the German sociologist Theodor Geiger (1949, 1962); in this sense, it is used as a value-free, general concept including all the different forms of class formation and social stratification.

4   The UNDP Index of Gender Inequality shows that the Sub-Saharan countries have the highest scores on gender inequality, and the Scandinavian countries the lowest. However, there are also some partial exceptions. The USA and many Latin American countries exhibit comparatively more gender equality than socio-economic equality. See UNDP, Gender Inequality Index at https://data.undp.org

rather privileged, while those of the lower classes are deprived, and often also discriminated and exploited.[5] Myra M. Ferree and Elaine J. Hall (1996) have rightly pointed to a typical lop-sidedness in mainstream introductory sociology textbooks, published in English; rather than integrating the meso and macro-levels of social structure, problems of gender are usually discussed only at the micro-level, those of race at the group level and those of class at the macro-level. Out of these facts and considerations, my conclusion for this book is that when investigating class and ethnic inequalities, we must always also have an eye on related gender inequalities; I would not say, however, that gender establishes a stratification system of its own.

The second issue concerns the role of political parties. For Max Weber, (1964/II:688–89) parties were, besides the formation of classes and estates, a third principle of the distribution of power and privilege. In the sociological writings on social classes, this aspect has been largely neglected (see Haller 2008a: 400ff.). It is understandable given the fact that class stratification and party formation are quite different phenomena. In distinction to class formation, parties are processes of *Vergesellschaftung*, that is, consciously developed forms and strategies of association based on interests of the participants, not on their feelings of communality or togetherness (*Gemeinschaft*). They tend to arise in any form of human association, not only at the level of politics but also within groups and organizations of all sorts. If a conflict of interests arises within a human association, there exists a tendency that two groups form themselves who aim toward different solutions (Simmel 1923; Coser 1956). At the level of society and politics, political parties are the main organizations of group and class interests; they want to obtain their aims through access to political power and political offices, particularly seats in the legislature (Schumpeter 1946; Weber 1964/I: 211–7; Ware 1996). As a rule, there exist also two basic forms of parties: those who aim to preserve the existing order and the related structure of power and privilege and those who want to change it or to overthrow it. Political parties are of central importance in the interaction process between class formation, social stratification and ethnic differentiation. This is obvious in the ethnically, often very heterogeneous countries and societies of the South as will be shown in several case studies in Part II. But also during the emergence and formation of the political parties in Europe and America from the 18th to the 20th centuries, ethnic-national cleavages were highly relevant, such as the alliances between states and churches and religions, between towns and countryside, between centre and periphery (Lipset and Rokkan 1967).

Figure 2.1 assumes that class stratification and ethnic differentiation are embedded into three macro-social framework conditions. These are decisive for the way class stratification and ethnic differentiation develop and interact. The first of them are *general structural conditions*, such as geography, climate, population size and growth, level of technological development and the like. These aspects are not specific topics of this book, but they have to be considered as potential co-determinants of inequality. I will come back to some of them in several parts of this work. *Legitimating institutions* include all those institutions, organizations and movements which provide explanations and interpretations, justifications or critiques of existing patterns of inequality. Historically most important in this regard were religions and churches; since the early Modern Age, also secular ideologies legitimating or criticizing inequality (such as Communism and Socialism, or social Darwinism and racism) are highly relevant in this regard. The *political-economic system*, the third framework condition, includes not only the political party system pointed to before, but also the dominant national ideology, the structure of the constitution (centralistic or federalist) of a nation-state, the political-economic institutions relevant for processes of distribution, such as collective industrial interest groups, and the character and strength of the welfare state. I will come back to these aspects more generally in the following chapter, but – where they are particularly relevant – in more detail in the case studies in Part II of this book.

---

5   In a prosperous Arab household, a housemaid, who has to work very long and hard, earns about 140 Euros per month; to attend a higher education or find a well-off husband is nearly impossible; for daughters of such families it is possible to attend a university in Europe or America and often return earning a high income (reported by Judith Belfkih, 'Nur in Hammam sind alle gleich', *Wiener Zeitung*, 23.8.2012, p. 11).

How Social Science has Dealt with the Phenomenon of Ethnic Stratification

How did social science in general and sociology in particular come to terms with the problem of ethnic differentiation and stratification within the different societies of the world? To a large extent, one must speak here of neglect (see also Smith 1986; Yancey et al. 1976; Esman 2004; Fenton 2005). Only in recent times have some larger books on the topic been produced by sociologists (see, for example, Hill Collins and Solomos 2010). Much more work has been published on ethnic conflicts – not surprising in view of the fact these are an eminent problem in the present-day world (Gurr 1993; Gurr and Harff 1994; Eder et al. 2002; Lake and Rothchild 1998; Cordell and Wolff 2010, 2011; Premdas 2010). The complexity of ethnic differentiation and the high number and variety of ethnic groups has led some authors to deny the possibility of generalization in this field at all (see, for example, Esman 2004: 17) A similar statement has also been made in regard to ethnic conflict: 'Ethnic conflict is a phenomenon in international affairs that is almost as equally difficult to understand as it is to define' (Cordell and Wolf 2010: 1).

Also the interaction between classes, stratification and ethnic differentiation has rarely been investigated (see also Breen and Rottman 1995: 50; Williams 1994; Mann 2007: 15). In most sociological theories and studies on social classes, the issue of ethnic stratification is excluded altogether (see, for example, Dahrendorf 1959; Wright 1985). The general tendency is to look separately at these two phenomena.[6] This stance has clearly been expressed in the brilliant essay of the Austrian-American economist Joseph Schumpeter (1953 [1927]) entitled *The social classes in the ethnic homogeneous milieu*. In another well-known essay, written by the influential German economist and sociologist Werner Sombart (1906), *Why is there no socialism in the United States?*, race-related differences are explicitly (and erroneously) excluded as a relevant factor. There were some authors who took into consideration both class formation and ethnic differentiation. For them, however, it is the rule to see one of these two processes as dominant or primary, the other as dependent or secondary. Let us have a short look at some of these authors.

Classical Theories

Classes and their interests and actions are certainly dominant in the theories of Marx, Engels and Lenin. They saw the aspirations of small peoples within the multi-national empires of their times in the second half of the 19th century as a reactionary undertaking. In their view, only large states would be able to accomplish the *take-off* toward a dynamic capitalist development and thereby to create the preconditions for the coming Communist (world) revolution.[7] Multi-national empires, such the Austrian-Hungarian monarchy, were seen by them as outdated models of political communities. The subjugation and exploitation of slaves in the colonies was considered as an equivalent of exploitation of the proletariat in the capitalistic metropolises (Marx 1971/I: 281ff.; see also Balibar and Wallerstein 1990; for a critique Kolakowski 1977/1978: 406). Also at the level of individual actors, ethnicity was a peripheral phenomenon for Marx, 'a mask behind which actors conceal their class position both from each other and from themselves' (McAll 1990: 70) Later on, when the basic assumptions of Marxist theory were carried into effect in the Soviet Union, the Communists had to cope with their own ethnic and national problems. Therefore, the second leader of the USSR, Josef Stalin, who had learned about the explosive force of this issue during his stay in the Habsburg capital Vienna, developed a specific Socialist theory of nationalities. As second leader of the Soviet Union, he conceded the cultural autonomy of the many peoples of this huge empire and granted them a considerable degree in this regard. In political terms, however, the Soviet Communist Party kept all Republics and nationalities under firm control. It was expected that in the long run national peculiarities would disappear and merge into a common 'Soviet people'. This idea, however, was abandoned in practical Soviet policy in the 1930s and 1940s when some sub-nations and peoples different from Russians proper (like the Ukrainians) opposed the collectivization of agriculture; from now on, a hard policy of Russification was introduced. The same happened in China in 1949 when Mao Zedong occupied Tibet and carried through a brutal policy of subjugation of the Tibetan and other

---

6   This tendency is evident also in informative textbooks which cover both aspects such as that of Devine and Waters (2004) *Social Inequalities in Comparative Perspective*.

7   For the Habsburg monarchy, David F. Good (1984) and others have shown that this was not true.

minority peoples (Law 2010: 117). In Chapter 7, I will show that the misjudgement and suppression of the ethnic-national problem was one of the main reasons for the breakup of Soviet Communism and the USSR.

Also recent sociological works in the Marxist tradition insist on the thesis that ethnic domination in principle is a class phenomenon (Bonacich 1972, 1980; Wallerstein 1974, 1975; Wilson 1978; Pettigrew 1981; Olzack 1983; Ringer and Lawless 1989: 36; see also McAll 1990: 55, 69–82). Most notable in this regard is the work of the Afro-American sociologist Oliver C. Cox in his *Caste, Class and Race – A Study in Social Dynamics* (1959). In this comprehensive work, the author discusses extensively the Indian caste system (which he defines as a cultural phenomenon), the estates and classes in modern capitalist societies and the problem of race and race relations. Regarding the position of racial groups in different societies of the present-day world, he develops an interesting and useful typology (the stranger situation, the slavery situation, the ruling class situation and so on). Yet, Cox (1959: 322) also asserts that 'racial exploitation and race prejudice developed among Europeans with the rise of capitalism [...] and all racial antagonisms can be traced to the policies and attitudes of the leading capitalist people ...' Cox may well be right that race prejudice is a modern phenomenon and did not exist in antiquity. He overlooks (or underestimates), however, the political and cultural bases for race prejudices and restricts the phenomenon of ethnic conflicts (which comprise not only race conflicts but also language and religion conflicts) in an undue way.

In spite of these critical remarks, we can say that many of the arguments of the Marxist and Neo-Marxist authors are sound (see also Virdee 2010: 136 on Cox). It will be shown in many parts of this book that practically all ethnic differentiations and inequalities around the world contain a class-related aspect of domination and exploitation. Yet, the basic assumption of these authors that ethnic-national inequalities are phenomena only derived from class inequalities is untenable (see also Weber 1973; Rex 1980; Williams 1994: 64, Miles 1990). Even slavery, which could be considered as an extreme form of class exploitation, has a distinctive ethnic-racist component and is much older than capitalism (see Chapter 5). Marxists also underestimate the positive role of national self-determination for the development of a country and the willingness of workers to support national movements instead of their class-related organizations. When loyalties to a class and to an ethnic group or nation came into conflict with each other it was usually ethnic-national affiliation which was decisive (Vogler 1985; Haller 1992). This fact came to the fore most dramatically at the outbreak of the First World War when the Socialists in Germany, Austria and other countries voted to enter their nation into war. This decision ran not only against their own class interests, but also against the interests of their class comrades in the adverse countries. It betrayed the idea of brotherhood between the workers of all nations which was upheld by the second *Socialist International* which had united representations of workers from 20 states. As a consequence of the outbreak of war, the *Socialist International* collapsed. The national question has remained an unsolved problem for Marxists since that time (Kolakowski 1977/1978/II: 105ff.; James 1996: 47–82).

There exists a complementary theory assuming that ethnic and national differentiations are basic and that class-related economic and social inequalities are only consequences of them. A prominent representative of this theory was Ludwig Gumplowicz, a Polish-Austrian constitutional scholar and sociologist (1838–1909).[8] This author, also a proponent of conflict theory, as represented at his time by the American sociologist William G. Sumner, argued that at the beginning of human society there were only small, homogeneous groups which he called 'races' (Gumplowicz 1883, 1885, 1928).[9] Conflicts and fights between these groups, he argues, determine the course of history. A typical course is that strong, 'young' and aggressive ethnic groups from very meagre regions with harsh life conditions conquer the fertile territories and rich settlements of established nations and empires, subjugate them and establish new social and political institutions which ensure their continuous domination over the population of the conquered states (See also Nuscheler and Ziemer 1978: 23). Thus, domination of the mass of people by power elites and states ensuring this dominance over generations has emerged, according to Gumplowicz, out of the eternal race conflicts and fights.

---

8   It was no accident that Gumplowicz became interested in issues of ethnic and national conflict. He grew up in the Polish city of Krakov, at that time part of the Habsburg Empire, and he took part in the fights for the independence of Poland. After the suppression of that movement by Austria, he went to Vienna and entered into an academic career in administrative and constitutional law. In the last period of his career, when he was appointed as a professor in Graz, he gave lectures in sociology and wrote the first German book containing the word 'Soziologie' in the title (Gumplowicz 1885).

9   On Gumplowicz see also Timasheff 1955: 61ff.; Mozetic 1985; Ringer and Lawless 1989: 32ff.

It is obvious that also these approaches are one-sided. Gumplowicz's theory focusing on the interests of ethnic groups and related conflicts clearly is a one-factor theory, in formal terms similar to that of Marx. His theory of race fights and subordination of one race by another seems obviously true at superficial consideration. Asian tribes have conquered the fertile valleys and rich kingdoms of the Ganges and Indus in India; Germanic tribes have conquered the huge and all-powerful Roman Empire; the Ottoman Turks, originating from Central Asia, have established a vast empire ranging from Algiers in Northwest Africa to Baghdad in the Middle East; a few West European nation-states have subjected large parts of the non-European world. However, at closer inspection it is evident that neither the conquerors nor the conquered were homogeneous 'races' and in most cases the conquest and domination became possible only because parts of the conquered collaborated with the intruders. Moreover, it can never be proved that in the early phases of human society there existed only homogenous small groups or races. It is also a matter of fact that the ethnic groups invading and subjugating others, after some time intermingle with the local groups particularly if the latter are much larger in number.

Contemporary Authors

Let us look shortly also at some present-day sociological theories concerned with the explanation of ethnic stratification and see how they relate to the approach developed in this work. We might distinguish two kinds of theories in this regard: theories which have not much relevance or may even be irreconcilable with the approach developed in this book, and theories which are compatible with and relevant for this approach but which have focused on other aspects of ethnic stratification.

A distinct *socio-biological approach* has been developed by the American sociologist, born from Belgian parents in the Congo, Pierre van den Berghe (1978, 1981). Working in the tradition of ethology or behavioural biology, established by K. Lorenz, N. Tinbergen and others (see Haller 2003: 89–142), he looks for common characteristics of higher-level animals and humans and asks: Why are they social? Why do they cooperate? He finds one process common to both of them: kin selection to maximize 'inclusive fitness'. An animal can duplicate its genes directly through its own reproduction or indirectly through reproduction of relatives. Therefore, animals behave cooperatively to the extent that they can enhance their own fitness. This happens if they prefer kinsmen over non-kin people, that is, if they are nepotistic. The propensity to act altruistically is dependent on the cost/benefit ratio of an altruistic act; this is high if it is directed toward offspring and kinsmen. Thus, kin selection is a powerful 'cement of sociality' among all social animals. Among human beings, two additional processes come in: reciprocity (cooperation for mutual benefit) and coercion (use of force for one-sided benefit). In larger and more complex societies, the latter two processes become ever more important. Thus, as admitted by the author (van den Berghe 1978: 403), this theory is reductionist (based on very few, non-sociological principles), evolutionist (like all biology) and materialist. How can we evaluate this theory? First, it cannot be dismissed offhand. Several arguments of van den Berghe fit in quite well with the approach of this work. Ethnicity and race are seen as extensions of kinship and a clear differentiation is made between ethnic and class relations; the latter, according to van den Berghe, belong to the realm of reciprocal behaviour and are becoming more important in developed societies. In simple societies (which prevailed over many thousands of years in human prehistory), only kin-based, tribal forms of groups and societies existed. Van den Berghe takes care also not to equate ethnicity with race because only few groups and societies use morphological phenotypes to define themselves as specific groups. Interesting also is the idea that paternalism was an ideology legitimating coercion in small homogeneous societies, while in large multi-national (modern) societies, democratic and egalitarian ideologies have been developed.

However, the flaws in this theory are equally obvious (see also McAll 1990: 39–60; Haller 2003: 130–139) First, the narrow definition of ethnicity on the basis of blood relations (kinship) and the argument that cultural criteria (like language and religion) in the last instance are only indicators of kinship affinity are not acceptable. Cultural characteristics, particularly language and religion, can create feelings to belong to a common (ethnic) group also without a blood relation in the past. The great world religions include hundreds of millions of people and some of them (Christianity, Islam) are spread over several continents or the whole world. Without considering the specific content of different religions and worldly ideologies, but also of social and political institutions, which legitimate ethnic stratification, we cannot understand why and how the varying forms of ethnic relations, domination and discrimination have developed and continue to persist. Like other forms of reductionism, the idea that everything can be explained out of a few basic principles – such as utility, genetic fitness and the principle of natural selection – is too simple and does not consider the fact that everything is part of different systems (Bunge 1996: 128ff.). More generally, the problem with bio-sociological theories of this sort is that it might be impossible in principle to submit them to empirical testing: first, because they are focusing upon human evolution over tens, if not hundreds of thousands of years about which we have practically no empirical data; second, because any behaviour and structure can be interpreted in a way as to fit into the theoretical scheme.

A second general approach to the analysis of ethnic stratification has been developed in the framework of *Rational Choice theory* (Esser 1988, 1999, 2001b; Banton 1983; Hechter 1994). These authors start from the surprising fact that ethnicity – as a traditional, particularistic and 'primordial' basis of association – did not disappear with modernity, as predicted by functional theorists. Rather, modernization often seems even to trigger ethnic mobilization. The RC theory explanation is that in the course of migration and urbanization processes, many people find themselves in quite an anomic situation and, therefore, resort to others for support with similar characteristics in ethnic terms. Esser (1988: 245f.) supposes, however, that ethnic mobilization may only be a short-term reaction to actual problems of orientation, particularly if modernization remains unbalanced and partial; in the course of complete and full modernization which erases systematic and persistent deprivations, ethnic mobilization will in fact disappear. In the case of ethnic stratification, the tendency to form close new communities is particularly pronounced because objective and subjective criteria of deprivation and exclusion coincide. Ethnic stratification emerges if four conditions are present to a considerable degree: the existence of power differentials between the groups coming into contact; scarcity of resources and competition for these; and the enforcement of processes of social exclusion in favour of one's own group. Thus, ethnic movements are based on collective interests and the mobilization of collective groups in order to pursue these interests. In order to explain why a certain ethnic group comes into existence and begins to fight for its interests, six aspects are considered as relevant by these authors: the collective benefit in the case of success of the movement; the benefit of the individuals participating in the case of success; the probability of success; the private benefit independent of success; the private costs in the case of failure; and the private costs of participation and of non-participation.

This theory seems – as Rational Choice theory in general (see Haller 2003: 281–388) – quite plausible at first sight; at closer look, however, it turns out more as a conceptual scheme which denotes some relevant dimensions but not as a theory proper in the sense that it explains concrete events and processes (see also Eder et al. 2002: 67–80). The following four problems may be noted in this regard: (1) it is hard to imagine how the seemingly complex and exhaustive list of individual and collective utilities and costs connected with ethnic mobilization could be captured at all in empirical terms; actors will hardly have such a differentiated knowledge and they are not able to calculate (or are uninterested in calculating) in any precise way these costs and utilities; (2) other basic components of social action from the sociological point of view, such as values and emotions, do not enter the picture; sometimes this is done, but in a way which overstretches them. But we know that such factors are often of decisive importance in processes of ethnic group formation and conflict; (3) the focus is only on the situation of a group in the present time; in the case of ethnic collective consciousness and action, past history is of extreme significance (even if the past is relevant only in the form in which it is remembered); (4) the concept of 'modernization' is an all-embracing and vague term which is not very useful within explanations of concrete instances of ethnic group formation and of the huge international and intercultural variations in these processes; the concept of a partial or unbalanced modernization is no solution to this problem. If ethnic conflict has lost its relevance in advanced, 'modern' nations, this may have happened also because they encapsulate themselves against the import of ethnic problems though a restriction of immigration (Kreckel 1989).

Another point in the framework of RC theory has been made by M. Hechter (2004). He argued, along similar lines as Inglehart (1977) and Beck (1986), that post-Second World War prosperity has led to a shift from material values focused on class, to post-material ones focused on quality of life. In addition, the rise of the welfare state has reduced the incentive to join trade unions and has created new cultural divisions between those fully participating in its central institutions and those excluded; thus conflicts defined on the basis of culture have replaced class conflicts. It is certainly true that the consideration of the influence of the welfare state in changing class and ethnic identities and action is important. However, it is a way of throwing the baby out with the bathwater to argue that the dimension of class has been replaced by that of culture and ethnicity. Rather, we must focus on the interaction between the two.

A theory which is quite compatible with the approach developed in this book has been developed by sociologists Tamotsu Shibutani and Kian M. Kwan (1965) in a comprehensive book called *Ethnic Stratification. A Comparative Approach*. Working on the basis of symbolic interaction theory, these authors discuss in detail the micro- and macro-social processes whereby social strata and identification with ethnic groups develop; the relevance of the processes for the establishment of social distance between groups; the role of identity formation of ethnic strata; factors producing variations in ethnic stratification (in terms of complexity and magnitude of ethnic differences, of solidarity within strata, of extent of mobility and so on); the varying symbols of ethnic differentiation (cultural attributes and practices, status symbols, facial, skin and other body characteristics, language, religion, dress codes and so on); the character and role of ethnic stereotypes and prejudices and their relation to the status of a group. The discussion of all these concepts and processes is illustrated by an immense variety of empirical examples from all parts of the world in the course of recent history. We will use many of the ideas of these authors in this work. Nevertheless, there are some clear limitations in the work of Shibutani and Kwan in which the present work will try to be more precise. First, the definition of an ethnic group seems to be too narrow when it focuses only on the belief in a common ancestry and considers all other criteria as only secondary (Shibutani and Kwan 1965: 47, 56ff.). However, language and religion in many cases are at least equally important for the definition and self-understanding of ethnic groups, and are also persistent and stable, as other criteria such as status symbols, bodily gestures, dress codes and the like. As a rule, they are interconnected very closely. Second, although these authors discuss the relation between class, stratification and ethnic group formation extensively, they do so more in an impressionistic fashion, but do not try to develop concrete, testable hypotheses or develop a typology of ethnic stratification patterns, as shall be done in this work in the following chapters. Finally, their approach is primarily a micro-sociological one; it does not include a systematic discussion of institutions and structures at the macro-level, such as the forms of class and ethnic organizations, types of political systems, the content and influence of religious doctrines.

There were also some other authors who developed more specific concepts relating to the interaction between class and ethnic stratification which seem very useful for the present work in specific contexts. One of the most important among them is the work of Milton Gordon (1964, 1978) who carried out a pioneering study on patterns of ethnic stratification in American society and coined the term *ethclass*. He argues that each American belongs to one of the social classes of the overarching national (political) society, but at the same time also to an ethnic sub-group within a class; the main institutions and spheres of life related to the latter are religion, the family and recreation and leisure (Gordon 1978: 120). Gordon also distinguishes between the social structural and cultural aspect and argues that nationwide there exists in parallel a social structure and culture comprising the elements common to all Americans (particularly in the area of civic rights and politics), and a sub-structure and sub-culture connected with ethnic membership and affiliations. A somewhat related distinction has been made by German sociologist Hartmut Esser, who worked extensively on problems of migration, ethnic assimilation and integration. Esser (1999, 2001b) distinguishes between system integration and social integration concerning the situation of immigrants and minorities; the first aspect denotes the inclusion into the formal structure of a society (in economic and political terms, in labour markets and formal organizations), the latter the social relations between migrants and their ethnic compatriots as well as between them and other members of the society in the more informal social and cultural spheres. These distinctions may be useful also in this work when comparing the situation of ethnic minorities in different societies. Christopher McAll (1990: 124–37) in his insightful book, *Class, Ethnicity, and Social Inequality*, speaks of ethnicity's revenge when discussing the relation between long-distance labour migration and the re-emergence of ethnic discrimination and race prejudices in advanced societies. He points to one very important fact in this regard, namely the process of residential segregation: 'One factor that prevents that combination [i.e., of class and ethnic divisions and cleavages] from becoming an explosive one is that the greater the degree of material inequality, the more it can come to be hidden from view in select neighbourhoods, clubs, expensive hotels and private schools' (McAll 1990: 212).

A few authors have also picked out the issue of the whole societal structure in ethnically differentiated societies. The Canadian sociologist John Porter (1968) has devised the concept of a *vertical mosaic* to describe the ethnic stratification of his society. Porter's basic idea is that ethnic groups are not only differentiated in a horizontal way from each other, but occupy also different positions in the vertical stratification structure of Canadian society. This idea has been proposed forcefully also by Stephen Steinberg (1989) for the United

States. He criticizes the 'melting pot' thesis proposed by the Chicago sociologists in the early 20th century and argues that the position of the many different immigration groups in American society could not be understood by looking only at their cultural heritage. The relative success of Jewish and Asian immigrants and the failure of other groups (such as Afro-Americans or Puerto Ricans) were due to systematic processes of privilege usurpation and discrimination. This was particularly so in the case of Blacks after the abolishment of slavery. These observations seem well supported by the conclusion of Blau and Duncan in their pioneering study, *The American Occupational Structure*, in which they write that 'the American occupational structure is largely governed by universalistic criteria of performance and achievement, with the notable exception of the influence of race' (Blau and Duncan 1967: 241); they found that Blacks were the most discriminated racial group (see also Chapter 11, pp 288–92). The concepts and ideas of Porter and Steinberg seem quite useful and to the point; looking at the issue of ethnic stratification from a broader, comparative perspective, however, it is evident that they apply only to specific societies. (On the case of Canada, see also McAll 1990.) Relevant here is also the approach of Raymond Murphy (1988: 76). Writing in the neo-Weberian tradition, he argues that in a society, several different forms of social closure might exist, some of which can be considered as principal, while others may be seen as derivative or redundant. In addition, he distinguishes between different closure structures: A 'tandem' structure exists if one principal form of closure dominates all others, such as lineage in aristocratic society, or property in capitalist society; a 'paired structure' exists if two forms of closure dominate (such as private property and race in South Africa's Apartheid system); and a 'polar structure' if two principal forms of closure compete (such as private property and the Communist Party until 1989 on the world level). These seem to be plausible concepts, but so far its author has not implemented them in substantive research.

A Sociological Approach to Ethnicity and Ethnic Group Formation

Now, let us go on to the sociological concepts and theorems basic for this work. My theory of ethnicity and ethnic group formation shall be elaborated in two steps: first, ethnicity is defined and its three essential dimensions are discussed; then, the process of ethnic group formation is clarified.

The Definition of Ethnicity and its Three Components

Let us now discuss the concept of ethnicity. We can distinguish between a more specific and narrow and a more general, broader concept of ethnicity. An ethnic group in the more narrow bio-social sense defines an ethnic group as a group of people with common ancestry (blood) and with high levels of marriage within the group. In this sense also the contested concept of race is usually defined. It certainly includes also physical characteristics which are handed down from parents to children, such as skin colour, hairstyle and the like. However, this bio-social aspect is not sufficient to define an ethnic group. As noted already by Weber (1964/I: 303f.), what is at issue here is less (or not only) an objective biological ancestry and kinship, but also, or even mainly, more a belief in a common descent (see also Shibutani and Kwan 1965: 38ff.). We can denote an ethnic group in this regard with B. Anderson (1998) as an *imagined community*. However, the belief develops only if an ethnic group has some additional cultural characteristics in common. Thus, we need a broader definition. In such a wider sense, an ethnic group is defined as a group of people within a larger (state) society which is – in addition to its (factual or believed) common descent – also distinct from the majority or from other groups in important socio-cultural aspects and which understands itself as a community or 'we-group' (Ringer and Lawless 1989: 1ff.; Waters and Eschbach 1995). The two most relevant characteristics that come in here are language and religion. J.G. v. Herder and W. von Humboldt (1836) have first argued that language is the base for and result of the emergence and self-consciousness of ethnic groups and nations; for E. Durkheim (2001 [1912]) religion heightens and 'sanctifies' membership in the group. However, also the bio-social aspect has important cultural components. In Latin America, for instance, the indigenous Indian population is distinguished from that of Spanish and African origin also by styles of life; these are even more important than physical characteristics (see Chapter 9, pp 22–33).

It is very important, however, when speaking about ethnic-national affiliations – irrespective of the fact if bio-social or cultural characteristics are involved – to avoid two traps connected with the primordialist and constructivist theories of ethnicity (see also Yancey et al. 1976; Smith 1992; Yinger 1994; Lake and Rothchild 1998: 5; Momin 2009b). One is that of objectivism. Ethnicity is no criterion fixed once and for all. This is true both for the bio-social and the cultural aspects. It would be erroneous to assume that the bio-social characteristics of an ethnic group are fixed forever, while the socio-cultural characteristics are only acquired and changeable. In the course of life, it is possible to change one's language and religion. Also ethnic groups as a whole are often not clearly defined and circumscribed, fixed groups but rather the result of complex processes of boundary making, of classificatory struggles and negotiations between the several actors in the field (Wimmer 2008; Eder et al. 2002). But the same is true for ethnicity in the narrow, bio-social meaning. Even the belonging to a certain ethnic group or race, as indicated for instance by skin colour, is often not clearly defined and fixed. Who is considered as being 'Black' or 'White', to mention only the most obvious distinction in this regard, depends also on social conventions and even on bureaucratic-political definitions and codifications (for instance, at the occasion of censuses). It can even change in the individual life course (Coates 2004; Cohen and Kennedy 2007); a huge industry has developed which helps people with dark skin to develop a lighter skin. Changes in language use and religious affiliation are even easier both for the individual and for groups. Based on this fact, Caselli and Coleman (2006) have developed an economic theory of ethnic conflict; this theory assumes that ethnic group formation is based on the fact that in each society specific sub-groups try to form coalitions in order to wrest control of the societal assets (such as land or mineral resources); once a group has gained this control, it must enforce the exclusion of non-members. When a population is ethnically heterogeneous, coalitions can be formed along ethnic lines and ethnic identity is used as a marker for group membership. Skin colour is one of the most effective markers in this regard.[10]

At the same time, however, it must be asserted that all ethnic characteristics have an objective base which cannot be changed at will. In this regard we must admit that the biological aspects are important – against all 'culturalist' theories. Terry G. Jordan (1988: 69), for instance, states that the dominance of lighter-skinned peoples is one of the three basic human traits which help define 'Europe' as a unit; they are also referred to as *Caucasians* or *Caucasoids*, in distinction from the *Negroids* in the South and the *Mongoloids* in the East. 'Racism' in the sense that other peoples are also defined in biological terms, by blood ties and external physical characteristics, is a phenomenon known in all civilizations since Ancient Times (Law 2010: 1–10). Only if the concept of 'race' is used in this latter sense can we say that racial differences are something else than ethnic differences (Lee and Bean 2010: 85–6). To speak of 'races' from the neutral view sketched out before does not imply racism of any sort which assumes that there exist many bio-social physical, psychic and even moral differences between the races and that the races can be distinguished in a clear-cut way from each other. But also the cultural criteria language and religion are in a real sense very 'objective'. A language acquired in childhood is 'in born'. Even if one learns a new language or changes one's religions affiliation, the one which he or she has acquired in childhood will make a life-long imprint on his or her thinking (Haller 2009). It can also be the communality of language or religion which may contribute to a group regarding it in the course of generations as a quasi-natural base for the development of a strong feeling of being a community. This was and is most obvious in the case of 'people's religions' (as opposed to universal religions) which are closely connected to specific ethnic groups, tribes or peoples (Mensching 1968; Höllinger 1996; see also Mitchell 2006). Thus, also language and religion become significant hallmarks of ethnicity if they are seen as part of the identity of a person, group or a nation. I agree, therefore, with A. Smith's thesis (1986: 211) that 'neither the primordial-Parmemidan belief in the immutability and fixity, nor the Heraclitan commitment to eternal flux can do justice to the variety of ethnic phenomena and its persistence'.

Thus, in this book I presuppose a broader concept of ethnicity which includes all three aspects, the biosocial, the linguistic and the religious; all three have both ascriptive and self-selected constructed aspects. An indication that all these aspects are relevant is also proved by the fact that in American sociology till today the concept of 'races' is used, in spite of repeated critiques of it[11] (see also Horowitz 1985: 41ff.; Rex

---

10   This theory is certainly quite useful up to a certain point but it is evident that it lacks a historical-cultural anchorage. It is evidently too simple, for instance, to explain the fact that in the USA mainly the blacks but not the Irish, Italians and so on have been discriminated against only by reference to the fact of their skin colour. Such an exploration misses the most important fact that only the blacks have been brought to America and used there as slaves.

11   See the comprehensive study of Mathias Bös (2005) on the history of the concepts of race and ethnicity in American sociology.

1990). The reason is that both in history and in present time it was always the case that linguistic and religious differentiations can induce processes of forming communities and associations and can arouse social conflicts the same as ethnic origin or similarity in the bio-social sense do. Language is the foremost factor which comes into play when we ask how human communities emerge. Language is the most important characteristic or 'marker' of ethnic membership not only because it is the central medium of communication but also because it possesses high relevance for personal identity (Schöpflin 2000: 43; Haller 2009). Language associated with ethnic or national identity can even take on a sacred character (Anderson 1998). For this reason, nation-states are very reluctant to accord an official status to languages of minorities (Tichy 2001).

A factor of similar basic importance is *religion* whose influence on humans and their societies can hardly be over-estimated to the present day. Often, religious affiliation or membership in a church was more important for participation in unions and political parties than class situation (Vogler 1985; Strikverda 1991; Haller 1992; Joseph 2004; Oomen 2009). In many cases of purported 'races' – such as that of the Jews[12] – it cannot be doubted that a common religion is the connecting link of the ethnic-national community but not a common ancestry or 'race' (*Blutsverwandtschaft*) in the bio-social sense (I will come back to this issue in Chapter 12, p. 326). In South East Asia, religion was the main basis for state formation (Oomen 2009). Language and religion are acquired and implanted from early childhood onwards, so that later they are felt like having been inherited or innate. Often, they are also interconnected directly; religious identities can have their own linguistic markers and manifestations (Joseph 2004: 166) and certain languages are closely connected with certain religions not only in people's religions but also in universal religions (for example, Sanskrit with Hinduism, Latin with the Catholic Church and Arabic with Islam). Therefore, it is not surprising that ethnic origin and membership in the narrower (the bio-social) sense in many cases coincides with linguistic and religious communality. This fact can be observed most clearly in Sub-Saharan Africa; here, the larger countries usually include up to 100 or even more ethnic groups distinct from each other in all three aspects, that is, social origin, language and religious traditions (see Chapter 10). Language and religion per se, however, do not constitute an ethnic group particularly; if they do so; the cohesion of the group is strengthened. Religious and political leaders try to cultivate the identity of those whom they want to mobilize through their organizations; therefore, they are often deeply involved in politics (Stewart 2009; see also Höllinger 1996; Haller and Höllinger 2009). English, Spanish, French and other popular languages are spoken by people in many different nations and of different ethnic affiliations. But the same is true for the bio-social 'race' characteristics; neither the 'Whites' spread over all continents nor the 800 million 'Blacks' of Sub-Saharan Africa approximately constitute a race or an ethnic group. But we can probably say that all more or less clearly defined ethnic groups share a common language and religion. Moreover, even universal, widespread languages and religions can become the base for a rudimentary collective consciousness. For the Irish, for instance, English language possesses little relevance in this regard but Catholicism does so because the Irish share the first with their historical enemy England but are differentiated from it in the latter. In addition, many of the large world religions have split into sub-sections which often are quite hostile to each other. The most significant historical case was the Thirty Years' War (1618–38) in Central Europe which confronted Catholics and Protestants. Today, also in the Muslim world, confrontations between Shiites and Sunnites are frequent and often extremely severe.

Ethnic Group Formation

Ethnic groups are characterized by the fact that between their members exist closer and denser forms of communication and social interaction than between them and other groups. Membership in a clearly defined ethnic group is associated with strong feelings and loyalties in a similar vein as is the case in *kinship groups* (Horowitz 1985; Smith 1986: 21–46; van den Berghe 1978: 25ff.; Dittrich and Radtke 1990: 261; Ringer and Lawless 1989: 3; Hagendoorn 1993; Schwinn 2001: 390). It is no accident, therefore, that members of an ethnic

---

12　The common biological ancestry of the Jews is a myth (taken over and strengthened by National Socialism in Germany). It does not only contradict the religious-cultural 'spirit' of the Judaism, it can also not be proved from the historical point of view. Rather, it is a matter of fact that Judaism in Antiquity was an active missionary religion and many small Jewish Diasporas in Europe and Asia are native groups and peoples who were converted to the Jewish religion (see Shlomo Sand, 'Wie das jüdische Volk erfunden wurde', *Le Monde Diplomatique* (German edition, August 2008, p. 3. This topic is treated extensively in Sand (2010; see also Landmann 1981, Flapan 1988; Cohen and Susser 2000).

group often denote themselves as 'sisters', 'brothers' or 'cousins'; conflicts within ethnic groups often are denoted as 'family conflicts'; groups residing for a long time in a certain territory denote this as their 'native soil'; families and kinship groups are seen as the nucleus of larger ethnic communities; non-democratic regimes and leaders in Africa often are based mainly on their clan and tribe (see Chapter 10, pp 263–76). Tribes can be seen as extensions of families and kinship groups. The persistence of the clan and tribe is the highest good and value, it exceeds any individual interests (Mensching 1968: 44–6). The Arabic term *Asabiya*, coined by Ibn Chaldun (1332–1406), comes close to this meaning of an ethnic group. Originating from the clan consciousness and feeling of communality of the pre-Islamic nomadic tribes, it denotes the unconditional solidarity between members of all those groups who care for each other, defend each other and try to win dominance over other groups (Simon 1959: 48–62; Ibn Khaldun 1967). People well integrated into their ethnic group may be rather satisfied with their life – in spite of objective deprivation. This fact may explain why people in several Latin American countries are relatively happy compared to the objective socio-economic situation (Haller and Hadler 2006). The affinity between kinship and ethnic groups explains why demographic changes in the relative proportions of different ethnic groups and their statistical coverage are so contested and politically explosive issues (see Wasserstein 2003 and Chapter 12 (p. 315) for the case of Israel; Weber 1988 for India before First World War).

Ethnic groups comprise in principle – in contrast to social classes and strata – men and women of all social groups and categories. Within ethnic groups, there exist hierarchies and inequalities; some group members, particular women, may be discriminated and exploited. But the different ethnic groups are not necessarily – in principle – from each other by differentials of power and privilege. One could also say that ethnic groups differentiate society in horizontal terms (see Blau 1977 for this perspective). Since ethnic groups are inclusive societal groupings, they are also communities in terms of culture and identity; however, they have always also economic and political interests. Thus, a central aspect in the formation of any ethnic-national group is the question of its identity, its self-consciousness and its recognition by others. Ethnic conflicts are to a large degree conflicts about recognition.[13] We can speak of a really existent ethnic group only then if it recognizes itself as such a group, a fact which is most clearly indicated by its name (Smith 1986: 22f.). If an ethnic group possesses self-consciousness in this sense, it will also require recognition by other groups and by the society and the state as a whole. If this recognition is denied, extensive, prolonged and intense, social conflicts, violent fights and civil wars can be the consequence (see also Haller 1992; Rex 1995; Taylor 1997; Margalit 1999; Joas 1999: 205). Conflicts based on ethnic cleavages are often much more difficult to be solved than class conflicts because symbolic and moral issues of respect and recognition gain preponderance over economic and political interests (Williams 1994). We must be aware, however, that ethnic consciousness, identity and feelings are often aroused purposefully by ethnic leaders and elites for their own purposes. This aspect has been elaborated clearly in many studies on ethnic conflict (see references quoted above). I will come back to this issue in several of the case studies in Part II of this book.

There is one final, very important point which must be made in regard to ethnic groups. It is widely assumed (particularly in Marxist and modernization theories) that ethnic groups and movements are only traditional, 'tribal' forms of identification and association, determined to vanish in modern societies. However, considering their deep anchoring in the minds of individuals and collective units, this is a very misleading perspective. Rather we must consider ethnicity as a basic and positive form of belonging, association and collective action also in modern societies. The high correlation between ethnic differentiation and violent conflict, shown in the next section, is not a consequence of ethnicity as such, but only of the fact that ethnic groups 'are deprived of the opportunity to secure collective rights that could enable local governance institutions to take a more active role in democratizing state and development [...] The crux of the matter is that an enlightened ethnicity heralds a shift that would wrest power away from the monopoly of an exclusive political elite, and bring it closer to the people' (Salih 2001: 29–30).

It was already noted that ethnic and national identities and relations share similar characteristics. We speak of a nation-state or simply of a 'nation' if a political community, a state, is recognized as legitimate by its citizens, if they identify with this community and participate actively in its affairs (Weber 1964/I: 313–6; Francis 1965; Giddens 1987; Heckmann 1992; Guibernau 1996; Haller 1996a: 25). There were, and still today exist, states which

---

13   For the general relevance of this concept see Honneth 1992: 256ff.; Blumer 1958; Wimmer 1997; for a specific elaboration of the process of ethnic identity formation Eder et al. 2002; of ethnic nationalism Scheff 1990, 1994).

do not possess this legitimacy and anchoring among the citizens; the consequence is that they run the risk of falling apart in situations of serious crises. Compared with ethnic groups, the concept of nation implies the additional element of political autonomy and self-determination. There exist variable forms of transition from an ethnic group to a nation. Any ethnic group with some degree of self-consciousness will claim a certain degree of autonomy in political terms; the degree of this autonomy may vary. In some cases, such as that of the Catalans in Spain or the Hausa, Igbo and Yoruba in Nigeria, even ethnic sub-groups comprising millions of people do not aspire to become independent nation-states; thus, we speak of 'nations without a state' (Guibernau 1996: 100–114). We could speak of a transition from an ethnic to a national sub-group if an ethnic group demands political autonomy and self-government. If this, in the end, implies the quest for one's own state, that is, an independent nation-state, it depends on the circumstances. In general, one could say that a nation-state is stronger where the three aspects of ethnicity coincide more. The most spectacular and successful case in this regard is Israel; but the case of Israel also shows that a nation-state based mainly on ethnic criteria is not only a problematic special case in the present-day modern world but it also has significant implications for economic equality. In Chapter 12 I will investigate this highly interesting, and in a certain regard tragic, case in detail. The other case is ethnic heterogeneous societies which exist all over the world. It is not only in the South that the persistence of state unity is under threat; such cases exist also in the North (see, for example, Belgium, the United Kingdom or Canada). I will come back to these issues in Chapter 13.

Ethnic Differentiations in the State Societies of the Modern World

Let us now have a look at the countries around the world today: how many of them are homogeneous or heterogeneous in ethnic terms? First, we must indicate how ethnic differentiation was measured.[14]

An Index of Ethnic Heterogeneity

The measurement of the relevance and weight of ethnic differentiations within the present-day states of the world is no easy task; it is most difficult for the dimension of ethnic membership in the more narrow bio-social sense (common social descent), but for language and religion. As far as ethnic membership in the sense of ethnic origin and affinity is concerned. We started from a dataset compiled by the Finnish political scientist Tatu Vanhanen (1999). In addition, we used extensively a very informative handbook, *Ethnic Groups Worldwide*, elaborated by the cultural anthropologist David Levinson, former vice-president of the Human Relations Area Files at Yale University (Levinson 1998). In this book, a concise description of the ethnic composition of all countries around the world is given, including the history, composition and size of the different groups and the character (peaceful or conflictual) of the ethnic relations.[15] For the composition of the countries in terms of language and religion, standard encyclopaedias and handbooks have been be used.[16]

The index of Ethnic Heterogeneity (EH) developed out of these sources and used in this work captures the degree of ethnic differentiation of a state society in the three dimensions discussed before, those of common descent (that is, ethnicity in the narrow sense), language and religion.[17] The construction of the index proceeds

---

14   The empirical analysis in Chapter 4 was carried out together with Anja Eder and Erwin Stolz. They participated also in the development of this index.

15   Detailed information about ethnic groups in the bio-social sense is also presented in http://www.welt-auf-einen-blick.de/bevoelkerung/ethnische-gruppen.de

16   The main sources in this regard were the *Fischer Weltalmanach*, *The Statesman's Yearbook*, the yearbook *Aktuell 2001* (Harenberg 2000), *Wikipedia-the free encyclopedia* and others.

17   Comparable indices of 'Ethnic Fractionalization' (EF) have been developed by J.D. Fearon (2003) and Alesina et al. (2003). Both define EF as the probability that two individuals selected at random from a country will be from different ethnic groups. It is computed as the sum of the squares of the percentages of each group, subtracted from 1; thus, it varies between 0 and 1. Fearon developed also a measure for Cultural Diversity or Fractionalization which considers linguistic differences, taking into consideration also the similarity within 'language families'. Ethnic and cultural fractionalization correlated strongly with each other (0.79). Alesina et al. (2003) developed three separate measures for ethnic, linguistic and religious fractionalization. They found out that ethnic and language fractionalization correlated highly with each other (.70), but were only slightly correlated with religious fractionalization (0.14 and 0.27).

in two steps. First, the differentiation of a society in each of these three terms is determined; then, the degrees of differentiation in each dimension are summed up to a comprehensive index. The measurement of differentiation in each single dimension is as follows. First, we look if there exist ethnic sub-groups in a society according to this criterion. Then, we take the percentage of the largest sub-group and subtract this from 100; the resulting value is the index of differentiation in this dimension;[18] it varies theoretically from 0 to 99. The final step is to summarize the three partial indices into one comprehensive index. The indices reported in the original work of Vanhanen published in the 1990s seemed not to be plausible in some cases; in other cases in recent times significant changes have taken place. Therefore, the values for all countries were checked for plausibility and some changes were introduced using the Levinson (1998) handbook as well as printed and electronic encyclopaedias and yearbooks such as *Fischer Weltalmanach* and *The Statesman's Yearbook* and several specific Internet sources.[19] The index developed in this way varies between 2 and 240; its arithmetic mean is 89, its median 72, the standard deviation 64.

This index of Ethnic Heterogeneity does not capture the relative size of the different ethnic groups. To look at ethnic-heterogeneity from the viewpoint of ethnic fractionalization is also important (see also Alesina et al. 2003; Fearon 2003). Ethnic diversity may lead to conflicts more often if a few strong ethnic groups compete with each other than if many small ethnic groups exist in a country (for the relevance of this aspect in ethnic cleansing see Mann 2006:16); we have developed such an index and will describe and use it in the empirical analysis in Chapter 4.

I am aware that this definition of ethnic heterogeneity in many cases may capture rather statistical categories but not 'real' ethnic groups, that is, as groups who consider themselves as an ethnic group and are considered also by others as such a group. To catch such groups, special representative surveys would have to be carried out in all countries in order to grasp which and how many such groups are distinguished by the population (Fearon 2003: 198–9). It is evident that this would be an extremely large research venture. Nevertheless, we think also that the index developed here gives a good first approximation of the problems concerned. I will consider the aspect of the real perception and social significance of ethnic membership in several of the case studies in Part II of this book.

Table 2.1   The distribution of 158 countries by continents and by degree of ethnic-national heterogeneity in the late 1990s

Ethnic heterogeneity (EH)	Europe	North America, Australia, New Zealand	Latin America	Africa	Asia and Oceania	Total
	%	%	%	%	%	%
Very low (1–19)	22	0	4	4	10	10
Low (20–49)	42	0	46	8	19	25
Intermediate-lower (50–79)	17	25	25	10	33	21
Intermediate-higher (80–129)	17	50	8	11	26	17
High (130–199)	0	25	17	42	10	19
Very high (200–240)	0	0	0	25	2	8
Total	100	100	100	99	100	100
(No. of countries)	(40)	(4)	(24)	(48)	(42)	(158)

EH – Ethnic Heterogeneity Index (see text).

18   In the case of religion, the proportion of those reporting 'no religion' was first subtracted from 100. The assumption was that this group of people (quite large in the UK and several post-Communist states of Central East Europe) does not consider religion as a significant element of their life. Thus, in societies with a considerable number of these groups, religion will have less importance as a determinant of social and political processes.

19   Well-arranged overviews on the ethnic structure, religions and language in about 230 countries of the world are given at http://www.welt-auf-einen-blick.de/bevoelkerung/. (Additional end-headers: *ethnische-gruppen.php*; *religionen. php*; *sprachen.php*).

The basic facts about the ethnic differentiation within the 158 countries of the present-day world for which relevant data could be found are presented in Table 2.1 and Table 2.2. Six degrees of ethnic homogeneity and heterogeneity, respectively, are distinguished in Table 2.1. They show that only about 10 per cent of all included 158 countries can be considered as being more or less ethnically homogeneous (with an index of ethnic differentiation below 20); about one-third of all countries exhibit moderate levels of heterogeneity. On the other side, we can see that one-quarter of all countries show high levels of ethnic heterogeneity (EH indices 130 and more). Overall, we can say that nearly two-thirds of all countries (EH index 50 and more) around the world today are differentiated internally in a significant way in ethnic terms as defined before.[20] We can see in general that the different continents are strongly distinct from each other in terms of ethnic homogeneity and heterogeneity (for very similar findings see Alesina et al. 2003 and Fearon 2003). It is obvious that ethnic heterogeneity is lowest in Europe (about two-thirds of all European societies are not very heterogeneous), that it is somewhat higher in America and Asia and highest in Africa. A main reason for these differences is the history of nation-state formation and the duration of political independence: in Europe and in some parts of Asia, many states exist since the late Middle Ages (or even longer), in America most exist since the 18th and early 19th centuries, while in some parts of Asia and in Sub-Saharan Africa only since about 1960/1970.

Table 2.2   Ethnic heterogeneity in 152 countries of the world (around 1995–2005)

Ethnic heterogeneity (index)	Western Europe	Eastern Europe	America, Australia, New Zealand, Oceania	Africa	Asia
200–240			Papua New Guinea	Cameroon, Central African Rep., Chad, Côte D'Ivoire, Kenya, Mozambique, Nigeria, South Africa, Tanzania, Uganda, Zaire, Zambia, Zimbabwe	
130–199			Guatemala, Guyana, Fiji, Suriname, Trinidad & Tobago, USA	Angola, Benin, Burkina Faso, Congo Rep., Djibouti, Eritrea, Ethiopia, Gabon, Ghana, Guinea, Guinea-Bissau, Liberia, Malawi, Mali, Mauritius, Namibia, Sierra Leone, Togo	Indonesia
80–129	Belgium, Switzerland	Belarus, Bosnia-Herzegovina, Estonia, Latvia, Macedonia	Australia, Bolivia, Canada, Peru	Botswana, Gambia, Madagascar, Niger, Senegal	Afghanistan, India, Iran, Israel Kuwait, Kyrgyzstan, Malaysia, Nepal, Pakistan, Tajikistan

20   According to A.R. Momin (2006: 523) even more societies, namely 160 (86 per cent) of all member states of the United Nations, must be considered as being ethnically heterogeneous. According to Ted Gurr's comprehensive and detailed work, *Minorities at Risk* (1993: 11), in 1990 not less than three-quarters of the 127 large states of the world included ethnic minorities; the total number of members of these minorities is estimated by Gurr as 915 million people (see also Morris-Hale 1996: 7; Nash 1989).

Table 2.2   *Concluded*

Ethnic heterogeneity (Index)	Western Europe	Eastern Europe	America, Australia, New Zealand, Oceania	Africa	Asia
50–79	Germany, Luxembourg, Spain	Georgia, Lithuania, Moldova, Russian Fed., Ukraine, Turkey	Brazil, Cuba, Dominican Rep., Ecuador, Haiti, Nicaragua, New Zealand	Burundi, Lesotho, Morocco, Rwanda, Swaziland	Bahrein, China, Hong Kong, Iraq, Korea, Lebanon, Myanmar (Burma), Oman, Philippines, Sri Lanka, Thailand, Turkmenistan, Uzbekistan
20–49	Austria, Finland, France, Netherlands, Sweden, United Kingdom	Albania, Bulgaria, Croatia, Czech Republic, Hungary, Romania, Slovakia, Slovenia	Argentina, Colombia, Costa Rica, El Salvador, Honduras, Jamaica, Mexico, Panama, Paraguay, Uruguay, Venezuela	Algeria, Egypt, Equatorial Guinea, Mauritania	Arab Emirates, Azerbaijan, Cambodia, Cyprus, Mongolia, Syria, Taiwan, United Uzbekistan, Vietnam
1–19	Denmark, Greece, Ireland, Italy, Malta, Norway, Portugal	Poland	Chile	Libya, Tunisia	Armenia, Bangla Desh, Japan, Jordan, Yemen
No. of countries	18	20	30	48	36

Table 2.2 shows the position of all single countries in the different categories of ethnic homogeneity/ heterogeneity. Here we see that the group of rather homogeneous societies includes seven European countries (Portugal, Italy, Greece, Poland and two Scandinavian states), Chile, two North African countries (Libya, Tunisia) and five Asian countries, including Japan. On the upper fields of extremely high heterogeneity (EH Index 200 and more) there are 13 African states and only one country outside of Africa (Papua New Guinea). Again, it is evident that rather high degrees of ethnic homogeneity are typical for most European states, while most Sub-Saharan African countries are characterized by very high degrees of heterogeneity. America, North Africa and Asia are more similar to the European pattern. These extreme differences correspond by and large to the distribution of the countries in terms of economic inequality (see Figure 2.2). Thus, they provide a first confirmation of the central thesis of this book, saying that economic inequality will be greater the higher ethnic heterogeneity is. One clear exception to this pattern is Latin America with its extreme level of inequality; in Chapter 9, I will provide a convincing reason for this deviation which is also related to ethnic stratification, namely the history of slavery.

Three General Theses on the Actual Relevance of Ethnicity

From the background of these data and findings, we can formulate three general theses about the relevance and consequences of ethnic heterogeneity in the world today.

(1) Ethnic differentiation is highly important and its relevance within the present-day state societies of the world can hardly be over-estimated.
The fact that the majority of the present-day state societies around the world are quite heterogeneous in ethnic terms can easily be explained with two arguments. (1) The formation of the modern states in many cases occurred 'from above', by conquest or annexation of territories or smaller states in the neighbourhood (Giddens 1987; Mann 1994). In their course, often territories with 'alien' ethnic populations were affiliated to a state. (2) The forming of a homogeneous nation-state is a process which can be accomplished only during generations

and centuries; many of the states of the present-day world still are very young. Even in some small, seemingly homogeneous ethnic nation-states homogeneity has evolved or been created only in the course of time.

Let us have a look at the example of Austria which shows in a nutshell how ethnic homogeneity can be created over the centuries. Austria today is a small, eight million people country and in ethnic terms quite homogeneous (with a German-speaking, mostly Roman Catholic population); it was established after the breakdown of the multi-national Austro-Hungarian Empire in 1919. However, the ethnic origins of this population are quite manifold: Celtic and other native groups in pre-historic times; in antiquity, the Romans occupied the territory and connected it with their Empire; in the Middle Ages, Bavarians (a German tribe) and Slav people immigrated from North, East and South; in the 19th century and both after the First and the Second World Wars, Czechs, Hungarians, Slovaks and other East Europeans, but also Germans, were attracted to the capital Vienna and the main industrial areas of the Habsburg Monarchy; since the 1960s, again strong immigration waves came from former Yugoslavia and, recently, from Turkey and Germany. Also in terms of language and religion, homogeneity has been achieved in the last two centuries. Although the translation of the Bible into German by the religious reformer Martin Luther in 1522 had established some basic elements of a common German written language, up to the time of Empress Maria Theresia (1740–80) there existed no generally recognized, clearly defined common German language (as it is *Hochdeutsch* today) but many quite different dialects. Only around 1900 was a common German notation established. Religious homogeneity was imposed by the Catholic emperors in Central Europe after the peace of Augsburg in 1555 establishing the famous principle *cuius regio, eius religio* (the prince who reigns determines also a religion of his subjects) in the 17th century. Several hundred thousand Protestants had either to convert to Catholicism or to leave the country.

An extremely high degree of ethnic heterogeneity is typical for most states in (Sub-Saharan) Africa. It is related by the fact that the number of *ethnies* (tribes) existing on this sub-continent is also very high; practically all of the new states created by the colonial powers included dozens, if not hundreds, of ethnic groups differentiated from each other in terms of language, religious practices and socio-economic lifestyles. In the larger Sub-Saharan African states – such as Ethiopia, Kenya, Sudan, Nigeria and Congo – some 80 to 150 relatively small ethnic groups possessing by their own specific languages, religious traditions and social customs live side by side. The present-day borders of these states have been delineated mainly on the basis of political-military considerations by the former colonial powers. Thus, the functioning of the new, large political communities could be ensured only by establishing an overarching technical and administrative infrastructure, which included also the introduction of a common language (in most cases that of the colonial power). The independence movements and autochthonous governments which came to power in the 1960s and 1970s did not contest the existing state structures but subdued all movements aiming at regional independence. Rather, still today it is one of the principles of the *African Union* (formerly *Organization for African Unity*) not to challenge these state borders. This insistence on state unity is closely related to issues of ethnic class power and economic inequality which is so high in Sub-Saharan Africa. In Chapter 10 I will develop the thesis that in many Sub-Saharan African states, 'ethno-political classes' emerged whose main basis was the state apparatus that is, positions in political and public offices and the revenues resulting from their control. Thus, the preservation of the existing states became one of their overarching goals.

L. Popoviciu and M. Mac an Ghaill (2004) have argued rightly that the analysis of the relationship between race/ethnicity and class is currently 'of strategic political importance' in view of globalization and new liberal policies which seem to determine national immigration and welfare policies; they see also phenomena like a new Euro-racism and nationalism, Islamophobia, the arrival of new immigrants, refugees and asylum seekers in the context of class-related processes of social exclusion. I will come back to these issues in Chapter 13.

(2) The rise of ethnic-national movements aiming at the establishment of independent nation-states has not come to an end at the beginning of the 21st century.
Even in Europe, only two decades ago quite a number of new, small- and medium-sized nation-states emerged in the sequel of the breakdown of State Socialism. The break-up of the multi-national Soviet Union and Yugoslavia were the most spectacular among them. The USSR came apart into 15, Yugoslavia into seven new independent states. But also most of these succession states are not homogeneous in ethnic terms (for the Balkan countries see Geiss 1992). Some of the successor states of Yugoslavia (Kosovo, Bosnia-Herzegovina) still have not developed into a new 'nation', that is, established stable and well-functioning political

institutions; they are yet riven internally by ethnic conflicts. It is highly probable that processes of the creation of new states out of secession of provinces or through the division of larger states will continue in the 21st century, not only in Asia and Africa, but also in West Europe and North America. We must only think here of multi-national states like Spain, Belgium or Canada. In provinces of the latter two countries, political parties are active which aim toward a secession of their province and the creation of their own state. In Belgium, the decades-long ethnic-national conflict has made the country nearly ungovernable. We can observe, in addition, regional movements within several well-established old nation-states (such as the UK and Italy) and in many of the larger Sub-Saharan African countries which also have one or a few ethnic kernels and aim toward political autonomy (Hechter 1975). In one of those states such a secession has in fact happened recently; on 9 July 2011, South Sudan gained political independence as a new state after one of the longest civil wars recent African history. (See Chapter 10) Thus, it is very important to consider the conditions under which secession can be considered as a viable solution for the conflicts and inequalities within ethnically differentiated states; this will be done in Chapter 13 (pp. 342–45).

On the other side, on all continents there exist now also macro-regional integration processes which in many cases will lead toward the emergence of new and large multi-national units (Haller 2012). This process was most successful in Europe where the European Union has taken over many functions of the constituent 28 nation-states. All these new macro-regional units will have to grapple with the problem of ethnic and (supra-) national identity. This is obvious in regard to the development of a new European consciousness concerning issues of distribution and social justice (Delhey and Kohler 2006; Haller and Ressler 2006; Haller 2008b). As long as this has not been achieved, the functioning of the economic and monetary union and currency, the Euro, will remain on shaky foundations as the deep economic and monetary crisis in the Southern EU member states since 2011 shows. This will be so particularly because – as a concomitant of such macro-regional integration processes – ethnic-national sub-groups, regions and small member states will develop new sensibilities and worries to be dominated by the large members. This applies not only to economic matters (concerning taxes and redistributive politics), but also to ethnic-cultural aspects, for instance language.[21]

(3) Ethnic differentiation within a country is connected closely with ethno-social and ethno-political conflicts. Their consequence is that social integration is more feeble, political stability more fragile and economic development laggard.

The thesis that ethnic-national conflicts will be more frequent in ethnically heterogeneous societies seems to be logical. In homogeneous societies such conflicts cannot exist. It is not obvious, however, that conflicts in ethnic heterogeneous societies must exist in any case or even become very strong. We have seen that the majority of all state societies of the world are ethnically heterogeneous; yet, in many of them there are no serious ethnic conflicts. A paradigmatic example in the global North is the multi-national state of Switzerland with its four official languages and historical two religious groups (to which today a considerable minority of Muslims is added); a paradigmatic example in the South is Mauritius in the Indian Ocean; this small island-state of only about one million people is a multi-ethnic society, maybe the only real 'plural society' on the globe, with four major ethnic groups, 14 languages and three religions; they all live peacefully together. An opposite case is Sub-Saharan Africa as a whole and Nigeria, the most populous country in Africa in particular, which since its independence in 1960 has been shaken by bloody internal wars, military regimes and recurrent violent uprisings. Yet, the main reason for this tragic history was not its internal ethnic differentiation which in fact maybe the most manifold of any nation-state around the world. Rather, it was the suppression by force of most ethnic groups by military rulers as well as by autocratic civilian leaders (Akinwumi et al. 2007; Olaniyi 2007; Levinson 1998: 255). I will come back to these cases later (see Chapter 12). Ethnic-national conflicts can emerge, on the other side, also in cases where one might not expect them. So, it is often the case that quite small ethnic minorities in larger nation-states are well organized and can act militantly; an example being the Basks in Spain. However, in general the connection between ethnic heterogeneity and ethnic conflicts is rather strong, if investigated at the aggregate, macro-level.

---

21   An interesting example in this regard was the fear of many Austrians that as a consequence of its accession to the EU, several hundred words used only in Austria would have to be replaced by the corresponding terms used in Germany. Some literature scientists argue that 'Austrian German' is a language of its own. (Muhr & Schrott 1997).

Table 2.3   The relation between ethnic heterogeneity and ethnic conflicts in 149 nation-states

Ethnic heterogeneity		Ethnic conflict[*]						
		Very low	Low	Intermediate	High	Very high	Total	(n)
Very low (1–19)	%	64	36	0	0	0	100	(14)
Low (20–49)	%	21	58	13	3	5	100	(38)
Intermediate lower (50–79)	%	3	43	25	11	18	100	(28)
Intermediate higher (80–129)	%	7	15	19	48	11	100	(27)
High (130–199)	%	0	7	45	34	14	100	(29)
Very high (200–240)	%	0	15	31	39	15	100	(13)
Total	%	13	32	23	21	11	100	(149)

Note: [*]See text for the definitions and measurements.

For analysing this correlation, an index of ethnic conflicts was used also been developed by Tatu Vanhanen (1999); it was corrected by using the information in Levinson (1998) and Cordell and Wolff (2011). Table 2.2 shows the association between these two variables. We can see two facts. First: ethnic conflicts are a phenomenon and problem afflicting the majority of the present-day countries of the world. Only 13 per cent of the 149 countries included in the table have no or only rather weak ethnic conflicts; a relatively low level of conflict exists in 45 per cent of the countries. On the other side, 11 per cent of all countries are affected by a very high level of conflict. In 42 per cent of the countries, the level of ethnic conflicts is considerable, associated with all the problems mentioned before. Thus, it is unavoidable to see a phenomenon of utmost importance both for present-day social science and politics. As far as the relationship between ethnic heterogeneity and ethnic conflict is concerned, we must note an extremely strong association. In 64 per cent of the relatively homogeneous countries, there exists a rather low level of ethnic conflict. However, about half of the highly heterogeneous countries are afflicted by very high levels of ethnic conflict. The correlation coefficient between the two variables is as high as .49 (Pearson) and .60 (Spearman).

Ethnic conflict is 'one of the prevailing challenges to international security in our time. Left unchecked or managed poorly, it threatens the very fabric of the societies in which it occurs ...' (Cordell and Wolff 2011: 1). Ethnically based violent fights and civil wars are a central problem of many countries in the South, particularly in Sub-Saharan Africa (Shibutani and Kwan 1965: 10; Horowitz 1985; Gurr 1993; Williams 1994; Shultz 1995; Morris-Hale 1996; Easterly and Levine 1997; Esman 2004; Momin 2009a; Oomen 2009). Also one of the most violent, protracted and intricate conflicts in the present-day world, that in Israel-Palestine, has its roots in ethnic and national problems (see Chapter 13, pp. 313–18). Violent conflicts are a main reason for widespread starvation, poverty and under-development in the many poor countries of the South. Societies ridden by ethnic conflicts are characterized by lower levels of trust between people and less solidarity and social capital (Delhey and Newton 2005; Hooghe et al. 2006; Putnam 2007; DiPrete et al. 2008) Strong and persistent ethnic-national conflicts impair a society in many regards and can – in the extreme case – lead to decennial-long civil wars and to the breakdown of states altogether (Schöpflin 2000: 44–5). Recurring famines in the Third World, affecting millions of people, are often less a consequence of natural events (such as droughts) than of the collapse of order and security as a consequence of protracted conflicts and violent power takeovers (Sen 2009). Ethnic-national conflicts have probably been the main reason for the backdrop of Sub-Saharan Africa in terms of development in comparison to all other countries of the South (Easterly and Levine 1997; Bloom et al. 2010; Estes 2010). In his impressive work on ethnic cleansing, Michael Mann (2007) has shown that these extreme forms of atrocity and cruelty cannot be seen as outbreaks of ancient barbarism, but are intrinsic characteristics of modern civilization. They emerge from ideal visions of democratic nations and organic models of states in which *ethnos* and *demos* should coincide.

But also in developed and rich societies, ethnic diversity can have negative effects on social integration. B. Lancee and J. Dronkers (2008) found, following D. Putnam's (2000, 2007) well-known work, that ethnic diversity of a neighbourhood in the Netherlands tends to 'hunker down' the residents, to reduce their solidarity and social capital: interpersonal trust is lower, community cooperation is weaker, friends are fewer. From a

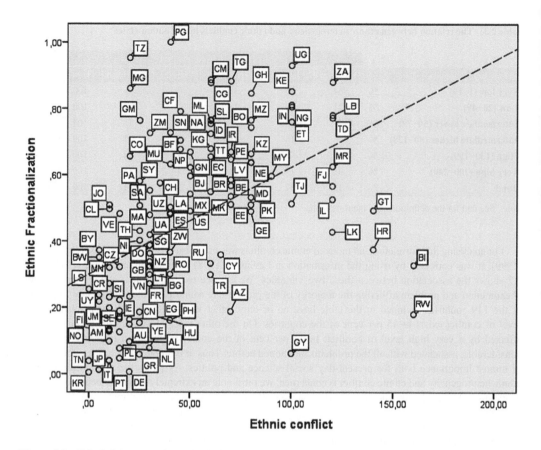

Figure 2.2   Ethnic heterogeneity and ethnic conflicts in 123 nation-states around the world in the 1990s
Data sources: See text.

cross-national perspective, Delhey and Newton (2005) report that ethnic homogeneity of a country has a direct negative impact on the level of interpersonal trust.

On the other side, we can say that a dynamic development and a high degree of social integration can be attained much more easily if a state is homogeneous in ethnic terms. In his recent, broad overview on the world situation, based on a comprehensive Weighted Index of Social Progress (WISP), Richard Estes (2010: 391) finds that countries with the highest values – which he calls the world's 'social leaders' – are predominantly small, culturally homogeneous countries. On top of the 162 countries included in his study are Sweden, Denmark, Norway, Germany (the only larger country), Iceland, Austria and Finland with a WISP between 90 and 98. At the bottom, we find the ethnically conflict-ridden countries Angola, Somalia, Chad, Liberia and Afghanistan (with a negative WISP between -4 and -14).[22]

Additional insight into the relations between ethnic heterogeneity and ethnic conflicts can be gained by looking at the scatter diagram of their relationship. Figure 2.2 again shows the very high association that exists between these two phenomena. It is indicated by the fact that most countries are positioned along a straight regression line, going from countries with low levels in both dimensions (lower left part) up to countries with high levels (upper right part). The figure also shows some particular exceptions or outliers from this general pattern.

---

22   The WISP includes 10 sub-indices (each with 1 to 7 variables) on education, health status, women's status, military expenditures, economic, demographic, environment, social chaos, cultural diversity and welfare effort measures.

In the left upper triangle of the figure, above the regression line, we see countries with a considerable or even a high level of ethnic heterogeneity, but a moderate level of ethnic conflict.[23] They include Mauritius (MU), India (IN), Guyana (GY), Chad (TD), and Suriname (SR). The most extreme, but 'positive' position concerning few ethnic conflicts is occupied by Suriname, a small South American country, located between Brazil and Venezuela. This is all the more remarkable because this country is internally highly differentiated in ethnic terms, with a population partitioned strongly in bio-social (racial) ethnic, religious and linguistic terms. The same is true for one of the largest nation-states of the world, India. In the right, lower triangle of Figure 2.2, we see countries with the opposed constellation that is a relatively high level of conflict in spite of only a moderate level of ethnic differentiation. Here we find Bosnia-Herzegovina (BA), Croatia (HR), Israel (IL), Burundi (BI) and Rwanda (RW). The first two countries are successor states to former Yugoslavia which came into being only recently through a cruel war. From the viewpoint of ethnic-national conflicts, Israel today is one of the most problem-ridden countries all over the world; it has both an unsolved internal ethnic-national problem, and distrustful relations with many of its neighbour states just because of the first problem. The two Central African countries Burundi and Rwanda are characterized by deep-going, protracted internal ethnic conflicts; in the case of Rwanda, these conflicts led to one of the cruellest genocides known in human history. I will come back to most of these cases in Part II of this book.

A comment may also be made concerning those countries which are positioned directly on the regression line where the strength of ethnic heterogeneity and ethnic conflict 'correspond' to each other. First, let us look on the lower left part of Figure 2.2, concerning the countries with low ethnic heterogeneity and a low level of ethnic conflict.[24] Here, we find countries on nearly all continents. In Europe, the mini states of Malta, Iceland and Luxembourg fall onto this position, but also Ireland, Portugal, Poland and Belarus; in Africa, this group includes Botswana, Lesotho and Swaziland; in East Asia, Japan and Korea; in Latin America, Chile, Costa Rica, Jamaica and Uruguay. On the upper end of the regression line, we find Sudan (SD), a country which is known for having been involved in one of the most violent internal ethnic-national conflicts and wars causing millions of deaths and refugees. That ethnic cleansing was involved in this conflict is documented by the fact that against its president, Omar al-Bashir, a warrant of arrest has been issued in 2008 because of genocide, crimes of war and crimes against humanity by the *International Criminal Court* (ICC). Sudan is also the only country in Africa where a part (South Sudan) has been split off as an autonomous new state recently, in 2011.

We can draw one general conclusion from these findings: although the correlation between ethnic heterogeneity and ethnic conflict is very strong, it is by far not deterministic. Some countries are able to manage heterogeneity without strong conflicts, while in others the relations between ethnic groups degenerate into brutal violence. This fact again shows the significance of the central topic raised here, that is, the elaboration of the conditions which can either lead to peaceful coexistence and cooperation between ethnic groups, or to protracted conflicts and violence. It is the thesis of this book that we can understand these ethnic-national conflicts only if their close connection with processes of class formation and social stratification is taken into account and their effects on patterns of economic inequality are elaborated. In the next chapter, I will develop a framework for investigating these connections.

Summary and Outlook

This chapter started with an outline of the fundamental theorem of this book, stating that economic inequality is produced by a triad of three processes: class formation, social stratification and ethnic differentiation. The first two are conceived in a Weberian tradition: class formation relates to processes of economic production and distribution, to interest group formation in the economic and political sphere, to power differentials and collective relations between the classes; social stratification relates to processes of status group formation, the development of lifestyles and prestige strata and their reproduction through patterns of marriage and intergenerational status transfer. From the sociological perspective, these two processes are essential when

---

23   The meaning of the abbreviations is given in Table 4A, p. 121).
24   Due to the high number of countries on this line, the acronyms for all the single countries cannot be seen in Figure 2.2.

it comes to explain the distribution of power and privilege, discrimination and deprivation. It was argued, however, that economic inequality is particularly affected by an interaction effect between these two processes and ethnic differentiation.

The next section gave a short review of the relevant literature on the relations between class formation and ethnic differentiation. Here, two tendencies were shown. The first is a constant neglect of this topic, often based on the argument that these issues are too complex to be accessible for sociological explanation. The second is to consider only one of the two processes, either class stratification or ethnic differentiation, as the most basic process. In the Marxist tradition, ethnic-national differentiations are recognized, but seen as secondary compared with class-related distributions of power and privilege. Also sociological rational choice theory argues that ethnic identities and conflicts are only relevant in an intermediate stage of history, when modernization develops too fast or creates imbalances and insecurities. The opposite position is taken in a theoretical tradition established by the Austrian sociologist L. Gumplowicz; here, ethnic differentiations and conflicts are seen as basic and the distribution of power and privilege as their outcome. Also the socio-biological theory of ethnic differentiation sees this as an 'eternal' phenomenon (common to higher animals and humans) whereby the members of an ethnic group cooperate because they improve group 'fitness' in this way. All these approaches have some merits, but ultimately were discarded for neglecting some or most of these facts/issues: that class organization often turned out as much weaker than ethnic-national consciousness and action; that there is no indication for ethnic-national consciousness to disappear in the foreseeable future; that ethnic differentiation is not always associated with inequality and conflicts; that both the degree of class and ethnic organization vary strongly historically and internationally; that political systems and secular and religious ideologies have a significant impact on the structure of class and ethnic relations.

A viable theory about the role of class and ethnicity in conflicts over power and privilege has first of all to start from a clear definition of ethnicity. Here, it was assumed that three core elements constitute an ethnic group: factual and/or believed common social descent (ethnicity or 'race' in the more narrow bio-social sense), a common language and a common religion. These three elements tend to cluster strongly together in most cases. This is so not the least because common descent includes also cultural aspects, and language and religion both have also an ascriptive quasi-natural component. In the self-consciousness of different ethnic groups, the relative weighting of the three components may vary, but as a rule ethnic identity is stronger the more they coincide. Members of ethnic groups tend to form communities based on feelings of belonging together; the recognition of their identity and interests by others is of crucial importance; if this is not given, much more violent and protracted conflicts may result than in the case of class conflicts.

The chapter concluded with the presentation of basic data and three general theses about the relevance of ethnic differentiations and conflicts in the world today. Using an index of Ethnic Heterogeneity first developed by T. Vanhanen, it was shown, first, that ethnic differentiation is a characteristic typical for the majority of state societies around the world today; between one-quarter and one-third of all world states exhibit a rather high degree of heterogeneity. Second, it was shown that heterogeneity is highest in Sub-Saharan Africa, and lowest in Europe. This indicates that ethnic heterogeneity must also be associated in a significant way to economic inequality since Sub-Saharan Africa is one of the two most unequal, and Europe the most equal macro-region around the world. A third significant fact is that ethnic conflicts are a pervasive characteristic of the present-day world; in at least one-third of all states, they are very intense. They may significantly contribute to persistent economic inequality and poverty and thus also impede socio-economic development. All these facts show that ethnic differentiation and its relation to processes of class formation and reproduction of economic inequality constitutes an extremely important topic for present-day social science.

In the following chapter, I will elaborate specific hypotheses on the way how the processes of class formation, social stratification and ethnic differentiation interact and how they lead to higher or lower degrees of economic inequality. In Chapter 4, I will submit these hypotheses to a rigorous empirical test, using a new aggregate dataset developed for this purpose. However, the relations pertaining to this process are rather complex, involving also structural and institutional conditions, like level of development, the size of a country, and its political constitution and welfare state. The effects of these factors are introduced in part into the regression analysis, but they cannot be really grasped by a quantitative linear analysis. Therefore, I will develop in Part II a typology of different forms of ethnic stratification and resulting patterns of inequality. This typology then constitutes the basis for case studies of the most relevant and interesting forms of ethnic stratification in different countries and macro-regions around the world elaborated in Chapters 5 to 12.

References

Acker, Joan (1989), 'The problem with partriarchy', *Sociology* 23: 235–40

Akinwumi, Olayemi et al., eds (2007), *Historical Perspectives on Nigeria's Post-Colonial Conflicts*, Lagos, Nigeria: Historical Society of Nigeria

Alesina Alberto et al. (2003), 'Fractionalization', *Journal of Economic Growth* 8: 155–94

Andersen, Margaret L. and Patricia Hill Collins (1998), *Race, Class, and Gender. An Anthology*, Belmont, CA: Wadsworth Publ.

Anderson, Benedict (1998), *Die Erfindung der Nation*, Berlin: Ullstein (*Imagined Communities*, 1983)

Balibar, Etienne and Immanuel Wallerstein (1990), *Rasse, Klasse, Nation. Ambivalente Identitäten*, Hamburg: Argument Verlag

Banton, Michael (1983), *Racial and Ethnic Competition*, Gower House, Aldershot (UK): Gregg Revivals

Beck, Ulrich (1986), *Risikogesellschaft. Auf dem Weg in eine andere Moderne*, Frankfurt am Main: Suhrkamp

Bendix, Reinhard and Seymour Martin Lipset, eds (1966), *Class, Status, and Power. Social Stratification in Comparative Perspective*, New York/London: The Free Press/Collier-Macmillan Ltd

Blau, Peter M. and Otis Dudley Duncan (1967), *The American Occupational Structure*, New York/London/ Sydney: J. Wiley

Blau, Peter M. (1977), *Inequality and Heterogeneity. A Primitive Theory of Social Structure*, New York/ London: Free Press/Collier Macmillan

Bloom, David E. et al. (2010), 'Realising the Demographic Dividend: Is Africa Any Different?' in Olu Ajakaiye and Germano Mwabu, eds, *Reproductive Health, Economic Growth and Poverty Reduction in Africa*, Nairobi: The University of Nairobi Press, pp. 235–49

Blumer, Herbert (1958), 'Race Prejudice as a Sense of Group Position', *The Pacific Sociological Review*, 1: 3–7 (reprinted in Cross, *The Sociological of Race and Ethnicity II*)

Bonacich, Edna (1972), 'A Theory of Ethnic Antagonism: The Split Labor Market', *American Sociological Review* 37: 547–59

Bonacich, Edna (1980), 'Class Approaches to Ethnicity and Race', *The Insurgent Sociologist* 10: 9–23 (reprinted in M. Cross, ed., *The sociology of Race and Ethnicity I*, Cheltenham: Elgar 2000)

Bös, Mathias (2005), *Rasse und Ethnizität. Zur Problemgeschichte zweier Begriffe in der amerikanischen Soziologie*, Wiesbaden: VS Verlag

Breen, Richard and David B. Rottman (1995), *Class Stratification. A Comparative Perspective*, New York etc.: Harvester Wheatsheaf

Bunge, Mario (1996), *Finding Philosophy in Social Science*, New Haven/London: Yale University Press

Caselli, Francesco and Wilbur J. Coleman (2006), On the theory of ethnic conflict, National Bureau of Economic Research, Cambridge/MA, Working Paper 12125

Chancer, Lynn S. and Beverly X. Watkins (2006), *Gender, Race, and Class*, Malden/MA etc.: Blackwell

Coates, Rondey D., ed. (2004), *Race and Ethnicity. Across Time, Space and Discipline*, Leiden/Boston: Brill

Cohen, Robin and Paul Kennedy (2007), *Global Sociology*, New York: New York University Press

Collins, Randall (1975), *Conflict Sociology. Toward an Explanatory Science*, New York etc.: Academic Press

Cordell, Karl and Stefan Wolff (2010), *Ethnic Conflict. Causes – Consequences – Responses*, Cambridge: Polity Press

Cordell, Karl and Stefan Wolff, eds. (2011), *The Routledge Handbook of Ethnic Conflict*, London/New York: Routledge

Coser, Lewis (1956), *The Functions of Social Conflicts*, New York/London: The Free Press/Collier Macmillan

Cotter, David A., Joan M. Hermsen and Reeve Vanneman (1999), 'Systems of gender, race, and class inequality: Multilevel analysis', *Social Forces* 78: 433–60

Cox, Oliver C. (1959 [1948]), *Caste, Class and Race*, New York/London: Monthly Review Press

Crenshaw, Kimberle (1991), 'Mapping the margins: Intersectionality, identity politics, and violence against women of color', *Stanford Law Review* 43: 1241–99

Dahrendorf, Ralf (1959), *Class and Class Conflict in Industrial Society*, London: Routledge & Kegan Paul

Delhey, Jan and Kenneth Newton (2005), 'Predicting cross-national levels of social trust: Global pattern or Nordic exceptionalism?' *European Sociological Review* 21: 311–27

Delhey, Jan and Ulrich Kohler (2006), 'From nationally bounded to pan-European inequalities? On the importance of foreign countries as reference groups', *European Sociological Review* 22: 125–40

Devine, Fiona and Mary C. Waters, eds. (2004), *Social Inequalities in Comparative Perspective*, Malden, MA etc.: Blackwell

DiPrete, Thomas et al. (2008), Segregation in social networks based on acquaintanceship and trust, WZB Discussion Paper SP I 2008–05, Berlin: Wissenschaftszentrum Berlin für Sozialforschung

Dittrich, Eckhard J. and Frank-Olaf Radtke, eds. (1990), *Ethnizität. Wissenschaft und Minderheiten*, Opladen: Westdeutscher Verlag

Durkheim, Emile (2001 [1912]), *The Elementary Forms of Religious Life*, Oxford/New York: Oxford University Press

Easterly, William and Ross Levine (1997), 'Africa's Growth Tragedy: Policies and Ethnic Divisions', *The Quarterly Journal of Economics* 112: 1203–50

Eder, Klaus et al. (2002), *Collective Identities in Action. A Sociological Approach to Ethnicity*, Aldershot, UK: Ashgate

Esman, Milton J. (2004), *An Introduction to Ethnic Conflict*, Cambridge: Polity

Esser, Hartmut (1988), 'Ethnische Differenzierung und moderne Gesellschaft', *Zeitschrift für Soziologie* 17: 235–48

Esser, Hartmut (1999), 'Inklusion, Integration und ethnische Schichtung', *Journal für Konflikt und Gewaltforschung* 1: 5–34

Esser, Hartmut (2001b), Integration und ethnische Schichtung (Gutachten), Arbeitspapier Nr. 40, Mannheimer Zentrum für Europäische Sozialforschung

Estes, Richard J. (2010), 'The World Social Situation: Development Challenges at the Outset of a New Century', *Social Indicators Research* 98: 363–402

Fearon, James D. (2003), 'Ethnic and cultural diversity by country', *Journal of Economic Growth* 8: 195–222

Fenton, Steve (2005), *Ethnicity*, Cambridge: Polity Press

Ferree, Myra M. and Elaine J. Hall (1996), 'Rethinking stratification from a Feminist perspective: Gender, race, and class in mainstream textbooks', *American Sociological Review* 61: 929–50

Francis, Emerich K. (1965), *Ethnos und Demos. Soziologische Beiträge zur Volkstheorie*, Berlin: Duncker & Humblot

Geiger, Theodor (1949), *Die Klassengesellschaft im Schmelztiegel*, Köln/Hagen: G. Kiepenheuer

Geiger, Theodor (1962), 'Theorie der sozialen Schichtung', in T. Geiger, *Arbeiten zur Soziologie*, Neuwied/Berlin: H. Luchterhand, pp. 188–205

Geiss, Imanuel (1992), 'Das alte, neue Pulverfass Europas. Explosives Gemenge von Völkern, Religionen und Kulturen', in *Das Parlament* Nr. 10–11, 28.2./6.3.1992

Giddens, Anthony (1973), *The Class Structure of the Advanced Societies*, London: Hutchinson

Giddens, Anthony (1987), *A Contemporary Critique of Historical Materialism*, vol. 2: *The Nation-State and Violence*, Cambridge: Polity Press

Good, David F. (1984), *The Economic Rise of the Habsburg Empire, 1750–1914*, Berkeley/Los Angeles: University of California Press

Gordon, Milton M. (1964), *Assimilation in American Life. The Role of Race, Religion and National Origins*, New York: Oxford University Press

Gordon, Milton M. (1978), *Human Nature, Class, and Ethnicity*, Oxford etc.: Oxford University Press

Guibernau, Montserrat (1996), *The Nation-State and Nationalism in the Twentieth Century*, Cambridge: Polity Press

Gumplowicz, Ludwig (1883), *Der Rassenkampf. Soziologische Untersuchungen*, Innsbruck: Wagner

Gumplowicz, Ludwig (1885), *Grundriß der Sociologie*, Wien: Manz

Gumplowicz, Ludwig (1928), *Soziologische Essays. Soziologie und Politik*, Innsbruck: Wagner

Gurr, Ted R. and Barbara Harff (1994), *Ethnic Conflict in World Politics*, Boulder etc.: Westview Press

Gurr, Ted Robert (1993), *Minorities at Risk: A Global View of Ethnopolitical Conflicts*, Washington, DC: United States Institute of Peace Press

Hagendoorn, Louk (1993), 'Ethnic Categorization and Outgroup Exclusion: Cultural Values and Social Stereotypes in the Construction of Ethnic Hierarchies', *Ethnic and Racial Studies*, 16: 26–51 (also in Cross, The Sociology of Race and Ethnicity II)

Haller, Max (1981), 'Marriage, Women and Social Stratification. A Theoretical Critique', *American Journal of Sociology* 86: 766–95

Haller, Max (1983), *Theorie der Klassenbildung und sozialen Schichtung*, Frankfurt/New York: Campus

Haller, Max (1992), 'Class and nation as competing bases for collective identity and action', *International Journal of Group Tensions* 22: 229–64

Haller, Max (1996a), *Identität und Nationalstolz der Österreicher*, Wien/Köln/Weimar: Böhlau

Haller, Max (2003), *Soziologische Theorie im systematisch-kritischen Vergleich*, Wiesbaden: VS Verlag

Haller, Max (2008a), *Die österreichische Gesellschaft. Sozialstruktur und sozialer Wandel*, Frankfurt/New York: Campus

Haller, Max (2008b), *European Integration as an Elite Process. The Failure of a Dream?* New York/London: Routledge

Haller, Max (2009), 'Language and identity in the age of globalization', in Mohamed Cherkaoui & Peter Hamilton, eds, *Raymond Boudon – a Life in Sociology*, Vol. I, Oxford: The Bardwell Press, pp. 183–96

Haller, Max and Markus Hadler (2006), 'How Social Relations and Structures can Produce Life Satisfaction and Happiness. An International Comparative Analysis', *Social Indicators Research* 75: 161–216

Haller, Max and Regina Ressler (2006), 'National and European Identity. A study of their meanings and interrelationships', *Revue Francaise de Sociologie* 47: 817–50

Haller, Max and Franz Höllinger (2009), 'Decline or persistence of religion? Trends in religiosity among Christian societies around the world', in Max Haller, Roger Jowell, Tom Smith, eds, *The International Social Survey Programme 1984–2009. Charting the Globe*, London/New York: Routledge, p. 281

Harenberg (2000), *Aktuell 2001*, Dortmund: Harenberg Lexikon Verlag

Healey, Joseph F. (2010), *Race, Ethnicity, Gender, and Class*, Los Angeles etc.: Sage

Hechter, Michael (1978), 'Group formation and the cultural division of labor', *American Journal of Sociology* 84: 293–318

Hechter, Michael (1994), '„Toward a Theory of Ethnic Change', in David Grusky, ed., *Social Stratification*, Boulder, CO: Westview Press, pp. 487–500

Hechter, Michael (2004), 'From class to culture', *American Journal of Sociology* 110: 400–425

Heckmann, Friedrich (1992), *Ethnische Minderheiten, Volk und Nation. Soziologie inter-ethnischer Beziehungen*, Stuttgart: F. Enke

Hill Collins, Patricia and John Solomos, eds (2010), *The Sage Handbook of Race and Ethnic Studies*, Los Angeles etc.: Sage

Höllinger, Franz (1996), *Volksreligion und Herrschaftskirche. Die Wurzeln religiösen Verhaltens in westlichen Gesellschaften*, Opladen: Leske + Budrich

Honneth, Axel (1992), *Kampf um Anerkennung. Zur moralischen Grammatik sozialer Konflikte*, Frankfurt am Main: Suhrkamp

Hooghe, Marc et al. (2006), 'Ethnic diversity, trust and ethnocentrism in Europe', Paper presented at the 102th Annual Meeting of the American Political Science Association, Philadelphia

Horowitz, Donald J. (1985), *Ethnic Groups in Conflict*, Berkeley etc.: University of California Press

Humboldt, Wilhelm von (1836), *Über die Verschiedenheit des menschlichen Sprachbaues und ihren Einfluß auf die geistige Entwickelung des Menschengeschlechts*, Berlin: Königliche Akademie der Wissenschaften/F. Dümmler

Inglehart, Ronald (1977), *The Silent Revolution. Changing Values and Political Styles among Western Publics*, Princeton etc.: Princeton University Press

James, Paul (1996), *Nation Formation. Towards a Theory of Abstract Community*, London etc.: Sage

Joas, Hans (1999), *Die Entstehung der Werte*, Frankfurt am Main: Suhrkamp

Jordan, Terry G. (1988), *The European Culture Area. A Systematic Geography*, New York: Harper & Row

Joseph, John E. (2004), *Language and Identity. National, Ethnic, Religious*, Houndmills: Palgrave Macmillan

Kolakowski, Leszek (1977/1978), *Die Hauptströmungen des Marxismus*, vol. s I/II, München/Zürich: Piper

Kraemer, Klaus, Philipp Korom and Sebastian Nessel (2012), 'Kapitalismus und Gender. Eine Auseinandersetzung mit der kapitalismuskritischen Intersektionalitätsforschung', *Berliner Journal für Soziologie* 22: 29–52

Kreckel, Reinhard (1989), 'Ethnische Differenzierung und ‚moderne' Gesellschaft', *Zeitschrift für Soziologie* 18: 162–7

Lake, David A. and Donald Rothchild, eds (1998), *The International Spread of Ethnic Conflict. Fear, Diffusion, and Escalation*, Princeton, NJ: Princeton University Press

Lancee, Bram and Jaap Dronkers (2008), Ethnic diversity in neighbourhoods and individual trust of immigrants and natives, International Conference on Theoretical Perspectives on Social Cohesion and Social Capital, Brussels, 15 May 2008

Law, Ian (2010), *Racism and Ethnicity. Gobal Debates, Dilemmas, Directions*, Harlow etc.: Pearson

Lee, Jennifer and Frank D. Bean (2010), *The Diversity Paradox. Immigration and the Color Line in Twenty-First Century America*, New York: Russel Sage Foundation

Levinson, David (1998), *Ethnic Groups Worldwide. A Ready Reference Handbook*, Phoenix, Arizona: Oryx Press

Lipset, Seymour M. and Stein Rokkan (1967), *Party Systems and Voter Alignments: Cross-National Perspectives*, New York: The Free Press

Mann, Michael (1994), *Geschichte der Macht*, Frankfurt/New York: Campus (The Sources of Social Power 1987)

Mann, Michael (2007), *Die dunkle Seite der Demokratie. Eine Theorie der ethnischen Säuberung*, Hamburg: Hamburger edition (*The Dark Side of Democracy*, New York 2005)

Margalit, Avishai (1999), *Politik der Würde. Über Achtung und Verachtung*, Frankfurt am Main: Fischer Taschenbuch Verlag

Marx, Anthony W. (1998), *Making Race and Nation. A Comparison of South Africa, The United States, and Brazil*, Cambridge: Cambridge University Press

Marx, Karl (1971 [1867]), *Das Kapital. Kritik der politischen Ökonomie*, 1. Bd., Berlin: Dietz Verlag

McAll, Christopher (1990), *Class, Ethnicity, and Social Inequality*, Montreal etc.: McGill-Queen's University Press

Mensching, Gustav (1968), *Soziologie der Religion*, Bonn: L. Röhrscheid Verlag

Miles, Robert (1990), 'Die marxistische Theorie und das Konzept der "Rasse"', in: Dittrich/Radtke, *Ethnizität*, pp. 155–77

Mitchell, Claire (2006), 'The religious content of ethnic identities', *Sociology* 40: 1135–52

Momin, A.R. (2006), 'India as a model for multiethnic Europe', *AEJ* 4: 523–37

Momin, A.R.(2009b), 'Introduction', in Momin, ed., *Diversity, Ethnicity and Identity in South Asia*, pp. 1–49

Momin, A.R., ed. (2009a), *Diversity, Ethnicity and Identity in South Asia*, Jaipur etc.: Rawat Publications

Morris-Hale, Walter (1996), *Conflict and Harmony in Multi-Ethnic-Societies. An International Perspective*, New York etc.: Peter Lang

Mozetic, Gerald (1985), 'Ludwig Gumplowicz: Das Programm einer naturalistischen Soziologie', in Kurt Freisitzer et al., eds, *Tradition und Herausforderung. 400 Jahre Universität Graz*, Graz: Akademische Druck- und Verlagsanstalt, pp. 189–210

Muhr, Rudolf and Richard Schrott, eds (1997), *Österreichisches Deutsch und andere nationale Varietäten plurizentrischer Sprachen in Europa*, Wien: Hölder-Pichler-Tempsky

Murphy, Raymond (1988), *Social Closure. The Theory of Monopolization and Exclusion*, Oxford: Clarendon Press

Nash, Manning (1989), *The Cauldron of Ethnicity in the Modern World*, Chicago/London: The University of Chicago Press

Nuscheler, Franz and Klaus Ziemer (1978), Politische Organisation und Repräsentation in Afrika, vol. II of the Handbook, *Die Wahl der Parlamente und anderer Staatsorgane*, eds Dolf Sternberger et al., Berlin/New York: Walter de Gruyter

Olaniyi, Rasheed (2007), 'Ethnic conflicts and the rise of militarised identities in Nigeria', in Akinwumi, *Historical Perspectives on Nigeria's Post-Colonial Conflicts*, pp. 56–69

Olzack, Susan (1983), 'Contemporary ethnic mobilization', *Annual Review of Sociology* 9: 355–74

Oomen, T,K. (2009), 'Plural society and pluralism in South Asia: A conceptual refinement and an empirical explication', in Momin, ed., *Diversity, Ethnicity and Identity in South Asia*, pp. 85–111

Parkin, Frank (1979), *Marxism and Class Theory: A Bourgeois Critique*, London: Tavistock

Pettigrew, Thomas F. (1981), 'Race and Class in the 1980s: An Interactive View', *Daedalus* 110: 233–55 (also reprinted in *The Sociology of Race and Ethnicity III*)

Pollert, Anna (1996), 'Gender and class revisited: Or, the poverty of "patriarchy"', *Sociology* 30: 639–59

Popoviciu, Liviu and Mairtin Mac an Ghaill (2004), 'Racism, Ethnicities, and British Nation-Making', in: F. Devine and M.C. Waters, eds, *Social Inequalities in Comparative Perspective*, pp. 89–115

Porter, John (1968), *The Vertical Mosaic. An Analysis of Social Class and Power in Canada*, Toronto: University of Toronto Press

Premdas, Ralph (2010), 'Ethnic conflict', in Hill Collins and Solomos, eds, *The Sage Handbook of Race and Ethnic Studies*, pp. 306–31

Putnam, Robert D. (2000), *Bowling Alone. The Collapse and Revival of American Community*, New York: Simon & Schuster

Putnam, Robert D. (2007), 'E Pluribus Unum: Diversity and community in the Twenty-first Century', *Scandinavian Political Studies* 30: 137–74

Rex, John (1980), 'The Theory of Race Relations – A Weberian Approach', *Sociological Theories: Race and Colonialism*, Paris: UNESCO, pp. 117–42 (reprinted in Cross, *The Sociology of Race and Ethnicity I*)

Rex, John (1990), "Rasse" und "Ethnizität" als sozialwissenschaftliche Konzepte', in Dittrich/Radtke, *Ethnizität*, pp. 141–53

Rex, John (1995), 'Ethnic Identity and the Nation State: The Political Sociology of Multi-Cultural Societies', *Social Identities* 1: 21–34 (reprinted in Cross, *The Sociology of Race and Ethnicity III*)

Ringer, Benjamin B. and Elinor R. Lawless (1989), *Race, Ethnicity and Society*, New York/London: Routledge

Salih, M.A. Mohamed (2001), *African Democracies and African Politics*, London/Sterling, Virginia: Pluto Press

Scheff, Thomas J. (1990), *Microsociology. Discourse, Emotion, and Social Structure*, Chicago etc.: University of Chicago Press

Scheff, Thomas J. (1994), 'Emotions and Identity: A Theory of Ethnic Nationalism', in Craig Calhoun, ed., *Social Theory and the Politics of Identity*, Oxford: Blackwell, pp. 277–303

Schöpflin, George (2000), *Nations Identity Power. The New Politics of Europe*, London: Hurst & Company

Schumpeter, Joseph (1946), *Kapitalismus, Sozialismus und Demokratie*, Bern: Verlag A. Francke

Schumpeter, Joseph (1953 [1927]), 'Die sozialen Klassen im ethnisch homogenen Milieu', in J. Schumpeter, *Aufsätze zur Soziologie*, Tübingen: Mohr, pp. 147–213

Schwinn, Thomas (2001), *Differenzierung ohne Gesellschaft. Umstellung eines soziologischen Konzepts*, Weilerswist: Velbrück

Sen, Amartya K. (2009), *Ökonomische Ungleichheit*, Marburg: Metropolis (English ed. 1973)

Shibutani, Tamotsu and Kian M. Kwan (1965), *Ethnic Stratification. A Comparative Approach*, New York: Macmillan/London: Collier-Macmillan

Shultz, Richard H. Jr (1995), 'State Disintegration and Ethnic Conflict: A Framework for Analysis', *Annals of the American Academy of Political and Social Science (AAPSS)*, 541: 75–88 (reprinted in Cross ed., *The Sociology of Race and Ethnicity* II)

Simmel, Georg (1923), 'Der Streit', in G. Simmel, *Soziologie. Untersuchungen über die Formen der Vergesellschaftung*, München/Leipzig: Duncker & Humblot, pp. 186–255

Simon, Heinrich (1959), *Ibn Khaldūns Wissenschaft von der menschlichen Kultur*, Leipzig: Harrassowitz

Smith, Anthony D. (1986), *The Ethnic Origins of Nations*, Oxford etc.: Blackwell

Smith, Anthony D. (1992), 'Chosen Peoples: Why ethnic groups survive', *Ethnic and Racial Studies* 15: 436–56

Sombart, Werner (1906), *Warum gibt es in den Vereinigten Staaten keinen Sozialismus?* Tübingen: Mohr

Steinberg, Stephen (1989), *The Ethnic Myth. Race, Ethnicity, and Class in America*, Boston: Beacon Press

Stewart, Frances (2009), Religion versus ethnicity as a source of mobilization: Are there differences? Centre for Research on Inequality, Security and Ethnicity (CRISE), University of Oxford, Working Paper No.70

Strikverda, Carl (1991), 'Three cities, three socialisms. Class relationships in Belgian working-class communities', in McNall et al., *Bringing Class Back in*, pp. 85–201

Taylor, Charles (1997), *Multikulturalismus und die Politik der Anerkennung*, Frankfurt: Fischer-Taschenbuch-Verlag

Tichy, Heinz (2001), 'Die Bedeutung der "Europäischen Charta der Regional- und Minderheitensprachen" für die ethnischen Grundrechte in Europa, insbesondere in Österreich', in: Chantal Adobati, ed., *Wenn Ränder Mitte werden*, Wien: WUV, pp. 162–70

Timasheff, Nicolas S. (1955), *Sociological Theory. Its Nature and Growth*, New York: Random House

Van den Berghe, Pierre L. (1978), 'Race and Ethnicity: A Sociological Perspective', *Ethnic and Racial Studies* 1: 401–11 (reprinted in Cross, ed. *The Sociology of Race and Ethnicity*, vol. I, 2000)

Van den Berghe, Pierre L. (1981), *The Ethnic Phenomenon*, New York etc.: Praeger

Vanhanen, Tatu (1999), 'Domestic ethnic conflict and ethnic nepotism: A comparative analysis', *Journal of Peace Research* 36: 55–73

Virdee, Satnam (2010), 'Racism, class and the dialectics of social transformation', in: Hill Collins & Solomos, *The Sage Handbook of Race and Ethnic Studies*, pp. 135–65

Vogler, Carolyn (1985), *The Nation-State. The Neglected Dimension of Class*, Aldershot/Hunts: Gower

Walby, Sylvia (2007), 'Complexity theory, systems theory, and multiple intersecting social inequalities', *Philosophy of the Social Sciences* 37: 449–70

Wallerstein, Immanuel (1974), *The Modern World-System I. Capitalist Agriculture and the Origins of the European World-Economy in the Sixteenth Century*, New York etc.: Academic Press

Wallerstein, Immanuel (1975), 'Class-formation in the capitalist world-economy', *Politics and Society* 5: 367–75

Ware, Alan (1996), *Political Parties and Party Systems*, Oxford: Oxford University Press

Wasserstein, Bernard (2003), *Israel und Palästina. Warum kämpfen sie und wie können sie aufhören?* München: Beck

Waters, Mary C. and Karl Eschbach (1995), 'Immigration and Ethnic and Racial Inequality in the United States', *Annual Review of Sociology*, 21: 419–46 (reprinted in Cross, *The Sociology of Race and Ethnicity I*)

Weber, Lynn (2010), *Understanding Race, Class, Gender, and Sexuality. A conceptual Framework*, New York/Oxford: Oxford University Press

Weber, Max (1964/I+II), *Wirtschaft und Gesellschaft*, 2 vols, Köln/Berlin: Kiepenheuer & Witsch

Weber, Max (1973), *Soziologie. Weltgeschichtliche Analysen*. Politik, Stuttgart: A. Kröner

Weber, Max (1986), *Gesammelte Aufsätze zur Religionssoziologie II. Die Wirtschaftsethik der Weltreligionen. Hinduismus und Buddhismus*, Tübingen: J.C.B. Moh

Williams, Robin M. Jr (1994), 'The Sociology of Ethnic Conflicts: Comparative International Perspectives', *Annual Review of Sociology* 20: 49–79 (reprinted in: Cross, *The Sociology of Race and Ethnicity II*)

Wilson, William J. (1978), *The Declining Significance of Race. Blacks and the Changing American Institutions*, Chicago/London: The University of Chicago Press

Wimmer, Andreas (1997), 'Explaining Xenophobia and Racism: A Critical Review of Current Research Approaches', *Ethnic and Racial Studies* 20: 17–41 (reprinted in Cross, *The Sociology of Race and Ethnicity II*)

Wimmer, Andreas (2008), 'The making and unmaking of ethnic boundaries: A multilevel process theory', *American Journal of Sociology* 113: 970–1022

Wright, Erik O. (1985), *Classes*, London: Verso

Yancey, William L., Eugene P. Ericksen and Richard N. Juliani (1976), 'Emergent Ethnicity: A Review and Reformulation', *American Sociological Review* 41: 391–402

Yinger, Milton (1994), *Ethnicity: Source of Strength? Source of Conflict?* New York: SUNY Press

Chapter 3
Ethnic Stratification and Economic Inequality.
Theory and Hypotheses

The analysis in the foregoing chapter has shown that ethnic differentiation and heterogeneity is a pervasive characteristic of the majority of present-day societies around the world. There is overwhelming evidence that ethnically heterogeneous societies are much more conflict-ridden than ethnically homogeneous societies. It is also evident, having in mind the basic facts about income inequality on the different continents presented in Chapter 1, that most of the ethnic heterogeneous societies are characterized by pervasive economic inequality. Thus, the issue of ethnic stratification seems to be highly relevant both from the scientific and from the political point of view. An international comparative analysis of societies in terms of ethnic stratification, however, must come to grips with the extreme variety and complexity of the patterns of ethnic differentiation which exists around the world today. It should be more than mere description; it should also detect and designate systematic patterns and regular processes, 'causal laws', from which testable hypotheses about the effects of ethnic stratification on economic inequality can be deducted. It was already suggested that such a claim cannot be fulfilled by either those approaches which concentrate on particular societal-historical cases (also denoted as *ideographic approaches*), or by those which try to find universal, ahistorical societal laws (the *nomothetic approaches*).[1] I start from the assumption that we have to combine the former, more qualitative approach with the latter, more quantitative one which attempts to detect general patterns behind singular cases. First, in the following section of this chapter, we will have a short look on these two approaches. Then we go on to develop specific hypotheses about the relations between class stratification and ethnic differentiation and their impact on economic inequality. In the final two sections, the relevance of political factors and of societal ideologies of equality and justice for the development of economic inequality shall be discussed. In all these sections, a few concrete testable hypotheses shall be elaborated.

Two Complementary Epistemological Approaches

There exists an old controversy in the sciences about the epistemological status of laws in the different sciences. Proponents of the nomothetic view argue that the social sciences should follow the model of the natural sciences, that is, develop general concepts and universally valid theories, deduce hypotheses from them and submit them to empirical testing. The tremendous success of the natural sciences and their application in technology, engineering and medicine proves the strength of this approach. In these sciences, out of successive and cumulative empirical research, impressive general causal theories were developed, but many of them later replaced by new and more powerful ones (Hempel 1965; Popper 1968). Some have argued that the situation in the social sciences is fundamentally different: their object, human beings, are not behaving like atoms, plants or animals, but have the capacity to reflect about their action and have a certain margin of freedom to decide how to act; in this, they can also follow ethical and moral principles; the societal context can alter the conditions fundamentally so that also human action will change; different societies and cultures are unique so that they cannot be compared directly. Exponents of this view argue, therefore, that the principal method in the social sciences must be that of understanding (*Verstehen*) the meaning and aims which are connected with human action. This method does not lead to general laws of behaviour but to 'rich' descriptions of the history and present structure of particular societies and cultures (see for example Geertz 1973: 3ff). Also the methodological emphasis differs between the proponents of these two approaches: those

---

1   The linguistic origins of these two concepts are Greek terms: *idios* (distinct, specific) and *graphein* (describe) in the first case, *nomos* (law) and *thesis* (constructing) in the second case.

of the nomothetic approach mainly use quantitative data, develop models of causal relations between variables and use multivariate statistical methods to test these relations. The proponents of the second approach use qualitative methods like in-depth interviews and anthropological, sociological and historical case studies in order to describe specific actions, situations and socio-cultural contexts as fully as possible. Theoretical statements, in their view, can only be developed out of such deep-going, comparative analyses of cases (see the concept of 'grounded theory' by Glaser and Strauss 1979). There is certainly some truth in all of the assertions connected with these two approaches. Today, however, we can see the strengths and weaknesses of both and combine them in a consistent and fruitful way (see also Acham 1995: 231ff.).

The strengths of the first, the causal-nomological approach, are evident. Here, we aim at the development of general theories and laws of human behaviour, which can be applied universally, in all historical epochs and in every human culture. Relations between two phenomena occurring regularly are interpreted as constituting 'causal laws'. Two developments in the philosophy of science made it possible to accept the aim of the discovery of such laws also in social science without denying the fundamental difference between the natural, physical and biological, and the human, social and cultural world (see also Haller 2014). First, 'causal laws' should be understood in a purely nominal sense, that is, as statements about our understanding of social reality, not about reality itself (Cuin 2006). The idea of *circular causation* (Bunge 1996: 35) is particularly suited for the human world where a certain state resulting out of a process can exert a feedback on the actor. We can also distinguish between *immediate* (*direct*) *occasions* (*Anlässe*) and *longer-term* (*indirect*) *causes* (Lorenz 1997: 189ff.). Examples of the first, in the present context, are land reforms or political revolutions, examples of the latter the long-term effects of slavery or of religious ideologies of equality and inequality. Finally, we should also distinguish between explanations at the micro- and macro-level. 'Causal laws' may exist both on the level of individual action and on the structural, aggregate level. 'Laws' at the aggregate level, however, must be based also on hypotheses and theories explaining individual behaviour (Coleman 1990; Maurer and Schmid 2010: 52–3; Albert 2011). This applies also to the general, macro-sociological hypotheses proposed in this book, namely, that economic inequality increases with ethnic heterogeneity. In the following chapter, the validity of this law is shown with multivariate statistical methods at the aggregate level; in the case studies in Part II, the concrete social and political mechanisms are elaborated to show how this association emerges and is reproduced in societies with different types of ethnic stratification.

In this regard, it is important to have in mind the idea of *probabilistic causation*, introduced by the Belgian astronomer and sociologist Adolphe Quetelet (1796–1874). It does not assume that certain causes by necessity produce certain effects, but that the causes are only increasing the probability of their occurrence (Goldthorpe 2000: 137).[2] Seen in this way, 'laws' relating to the human, social world can be interpreted as frame conditions which the actors can take into account in their decisions and actions. They will often, but not always act according to them. To give two examples related to subject theme of this book: it is well known that the cohesion of a group increases if a group feels threatened by another group, an 'enemy'. This law is used consciously by political leaders all the time when they invent such enemies in order to get support for their actions and demands, for instance for the sacrifices connected with a war. Political opponents and less xenophobic leaders, however, may also reveal the intent of these strategies and reduce the effects of the aforementioned law. The other example concerns the central thesis of this book, namely, that ethnic heterogeneity of a society increases economic inequality. This is no 'eternal law' but there are societies in which it ceases to be valid. Given the fact that many countries are highly heterogeneous today, these cases and the conditions under which such 'exceptions' do exist, are certainly of particular scientific (and political) interest.

The strength of the second, the qualitative approach, lies in the fact that it enables the researcher to cope with the immense variety and 'richness' of each human society and culture on earth, including those who look backward or even 'primitive' from the outside. Its weakness, however, is that by focusing upon only one or a few specific cultures and by collecting huge arrays of data, it often gets lost in pure description. A solution to this tension between uniqueness and generality is offered by the approach of Max Weber, called 'sociology

---

2   This idea of probability was also central for the thinking of Max Weber on whose approach I rely strongly in this work. He defines a sociological law as a probability, confirmed by observation, that a social action will occur in a certain way, following out of typical motives and meanings (Weber 1964/I: 13).

as a science of social reality'. (*Soziologie als Wirklichkeitswissenschaft*).[3] This approach accepts the necessity to look closely at singular cases, but it offers also a way to proceed to more general interpretations and conclusions. Three general assumptions are central for this approach when applied to the theme of this book.

First, any sociological explanation must be twofold, containing understanding of the meaning of human action and causal-statistical explanation at the same time. It is unique for the social sciences and even an advantage compared to the natural sciences that he or she can also ask individuals (or inquire our own mind) why they have acted in a specific way. However, since individual interpretations of action are often distorted, we have to use also statistical data about a larger number of people in order to prove if our hypotheses concerning subjective motivations or external reasons for an action are true. In this regard, a systematic relationship must be established between the behaviour and actions of individuals and the societal context. On the other side, we must take into consideration that men and women in different societies, socio-cultural contexts and sub-groups not only have different interests and act differently but also feel and think differently, have differing perceptions of reality. Black workers in societies with a Black minority might feel discriminated because of their colour; however, it could also be that the main source of their discrimination is not their race or ethnic group membership but their class status. What is true can only be proved by investigating the issue from a comparative, macro-sociological perspective, with an adequately large sample and taking into account objective and subjective data both on class status and ethnic membership.

Second, it is essential to develop specific types of interaction between class formation, social stratification and ethnic differentiation. Different societies are characterized by forms of class stratification and ethnic differentiation. Therefore, also specific patterns and types of their interaction can be found only in specific historical periods and in specific regional and cultural contexts. Even practices and institutions which have existed in most human societies and are denoted with a common term, in reality have meant quite different things. A pertinent example is slavery which has existed in practically every historical human society. However, the concrete meaning of slavery for those affected has varied enormously: in some African societies, slaves could become members of a family or clan; in America, slaves were imported from another continent, deprived of all signs of human dignity and exploited in a brutal way; the concepts of intrusive and extrusive slavery have been coined in order to come to grips with this fundamental difference (see Chapter 5) In methodological-empirical terms, the elaboration of such types requires to search for a 'third' way between quantitative, statistical methods and case-oriented, qualitative methods. The selection, presentation and comparison of the 'cases' itself must be a central issue in this procedure. An empirical-methodological approach of this sort has been developed with the method of *Qualitative Comparative Analysis* (Ragin 1989; Blatter et al. 2007); it shall also be applied in the following chapter.

Third, we must seriously and systematically include also the ideas and values which stand behind the actions of people in different contexts and societies. Only their consideration enables us to develop plausible and illuminating typologies and to make substantial deductions concerning political and social praxis. This is so because new ideas and far-reaching social reforms are accepted by the elites and citizens of a country only then if they are related in a meaningful way to their traditional and accustomed forms of thinking and living. From this point of view, we have to consider all societal influential systems of thinking which tried to explain and to justify or to criticize existing patterns of inequality, privilege and discrimination.

By taking into consideration all these three prerequisites, this approach can be designated as 'science of social reality', that is, as a science which starts from the concrete forms of thinking and acting, from the specific interests, aims and values of the actors and reflects and discusses these: (a) in the framework of general ideas and values; and (b) in connection with social structure and the related economic, political and social interests.

The application of this approach to the analysis of ethnic stratification must proceed in two steps. On the one side it is necessary to develop general concepts, theories and hypotheses and test them through quantitative methods. On the other side, it is also important to elaborate specific (individual and collective) strategies of thinking and acting concerning ethnic differentiation and stratification. On the basis of these strategies, we can then develop a meaningful and 'rich' sociological typology of systems of ethnic stratification. In this

---

3   For general outlines of this approach, see Weber 1973b; Lepsius 1988: 31–43; Albrow 1990: 78–94; Haller 2003: 489–621; Schluchter 2006; Albert 2009.

Chapter, the first aspect shall be elaborated. In the next Chapter, I will develop a typology of systems of ethnic stratification; the detailed analysis of them will be the topic of the second part of this book (Chapters 6 to 12).

Class Formation, Social Stratification and their Interaction with Ethnic Differentiation

In the foregoing chapter it was argued that class formation, social stratification and ethnic differentiation are the basic triad in the production and reproduction of socio-economic inequality. I have also elaborated on some central aspects of the process of ethnic differentiation. The same is necessary now in regard to class formation and social stratification before we can go on to develop hypotheses about the interaction between these three processes and their effects on economic inequality. The presentation of the concepts of class and stratification will be done here only in a summary way; there is no pretence to elaborate a new theory of class formation and social stratification.[4]

Class Formation and Class Structures

Classes are understood here, following Marx and Weber, as economic quasi-groups, distinguished by their sources of income and by their situation on the different markets (the labour, commodity and financial market). Such sources include ownership of property and of capitalist means of production (capital) and, among the non-propertied classes, the disposal over labour power and occupational qualifications. A division of modern society into the following five classes probably meets widespread support (see Weber 1964/I: 223–5; Giddens 1973; Lepsius 1988; Haller 1983; Goldthorpe et al. 1987): capitalists or *bourgeoisie* (the owners of means of production); the self-employed or *petty bourgeoisie* (internally differentiated into farmers and self-employed outside farming) – their characteristic is that they dispose of means of production (of widely varying size and worth) but employ no or only a restricted number of workers or employees; managers as a 'contradictory class location' between capitalists and workers/employees (Wright 1978) with stronger loyalties to the capitalists than to their fellow employees; the 'new middle classes' of white-collar and service workers with occupational qualifications; the working class in a more narrow sense, including skilled and unskilled manual workers and service workers with little qualifications and workplace autonomy. Classes per se do not form real groups capable of collective action; it is more adequate, therefore, to speak of class situations (*Klassenlagen*, as Weber called them) or class locations (Wright 1978). The common economic interests of the members of classes can, but must not necessarily, lead toward class consciousness and common action in the form of unions, collective bargaining and action (for example, strikes). This is all the more so because class interests are complex and certain groups can have different class positions in different types of markets (I will come back to this issue below; see also Wiley 1970). From this point of view, also the perspective of subjective consciousness of class membership is of central importance – a fact which has often been neglected in neo-Marxist class research (Nollmann and Strasser 2007). In the following, I will argue that exactly this subjective aspect is influenced decisively by the ethnic composition of a society.

One aspect of class structure which is particularly important when investigating ethnic stratification is the distinction between rural and urban classes. Rural class structure is peculiar because the main class base is land ownership which is much less mobile than ownership in the means of production. Social historians and historical sociologists have argued that the system of rural class relations was decisive for industrial and political development in the modern age. Barrington Moore (1993) showed that the strength of the landed upper classes vis-à-vis the small farmers and peasants determined the outcome of the social and political revolutions of the 18th and 19th centuries: in Western Europe, a strong non-farm bourgeoisie was decisive for the later introduction of democracy; in Germany and Japan, landed upper classes remained dominant, and initiated revolutions from above; in Russia and China, agrarian-based revolts led to Communist systems.

---

4   However, in an earlier work (Haller 1981, 1983) I have elaborated on the distinction between those two processes – a distinction which is only seldom recognized in the literature. A concise summary of my theses on this issue has been given by Reinhard Spree (2011).

Similarly, Jeffrey Page (1975) has argued in his *Agrarian Revolution* that political relations and conflicts at the countryside from 1948 till 1970 were strongly affected by types of rural ownership and class structures.[5]

Another important aspect is the distribution of land. This factor has certainly influenced massively the level of economic inequality in earlier centuries when the majority of the population was still working in agriculture. The Dutch social historian Ewald Frankema has shown in a recent series of work that the historical, colonial patterns of land distribution in Latin America are decisive determinants of income inequality today (Frankema 2008, 2009 a, b, 2010). One reason for the negative effects of inequality of the agrarian social structure on economic growth may be that landless rural families cannot afford to finance educational investments for their children. Because of the importance of the distribution of the arable land for socio-economic inequality and poverty, land reform has been a continuing aim of governments, but also a main contested issue in politics in many countries around the world from the 18th century till today.[6] In many cases, these reforms have led to significant improvements of the rural population; in those cases, where they had little or no effect, the reasons were that only a small percentage of the landless population benefited, and those who did often lacked the necessary qualifications, infrastructures and support services.[7] Land reform and rural development is a continuing and central issue particularly for the present-day poor countries in South Asia and Sub-Saharan Africa. In many of these countries, agriculture accounts for at least 40 per cent of the GDP and 80 per cent of employment; overall about 70 per cent of the world's poor live in rural areas and mostly depend on agriculture for their livelihoods. Rising rural-urban disparities and extreme rural poverty are major sources of social and political tensions in these countries and regions (World Bank 2007). This applies particularly to landlessness which affects a considerable proportion of the rural population, particularly in Asia (in India around 50 per cent, and in Indonesia and the Philippines around 80 per cent of all rural households are landless or near-landless), and is a major cause of poverty and starvation in the South (Sina 1984:17). I will come back to this topic in Chapter 13.

Class Relations, the Nation-state and Socio-economic Development

The relations between the classes, particularly those between capitalists and workers, can be characterized as *antagonistic cooperation*; they are based both on common and on conflicting interests. These interests exist both at the level of single enterprises and of societies as a whole. At the level of the individual enterprises, entrepreneurs and capitalists want to increase their profits and to ensure the growth and survival of the enterprise also in times of macro-economic hardship; workers are interested in secure jobs, appropriate wages and acceptable working conditions. At the level of society, we can also denote common interests of the propertied and non-propertied classes, although they are not so clear-cut. Capitalists will have the interest to secure macro-economic and political conditions beneficial for the realization of their interests; these might include easy access to means of production (land, productive assets, capital), little state intervention, low taxes on profits and so forth. Workers are interested in a strong and solvent welfare state, in full employment, laws protecting their rights and so forth. In order to promote their interests, both capitalists and workers establish associations (unions, employer associations, political parties) and try to influence politics through them.

In pursuing their interests, both capitalists and workers are relying strongly on their own nation-state. In this regard, the work of Carolyn Vogler, *The Nation State: The Neglected Dimension of Class* (1985), is very important. She argues, in accordance with Michael Mann (1980) and John Goldthorpe (1983), that trade unions have always been 'class national' rather than simply 'class actors'. The unions everywhere emerged within existing national units and their actors were always oriented toward nation-states – contrary to the basic assumption of Marx that they should and in some time also would become international actors. Since the 1970s, when the process of globalization set in, it would have become counterproductive for unions to

---

5   Anderson distinguishes four ideal types of rural systems; they are derived from a cross-classification of two classes (cultivators vs non-cultivators) and ownership, or not, of land. The types are: commercial haciendas (a landowning class paying the cultivators by giving them usufruct right to parts of the land; sharecropping or migratory labour estates; smallholding systems with many independent producers; and the plantation with paid labour.

6   For an overview see 'Land reform', http://en.wikipedia.org/wiki/Land_reform.

7   For such a fate of land reform in the case of India see Mohanty (2001), for that of Brazil under President Cardoso Ondetti (2007).

weaken the operations of capital at the international level. Thus, globalization strengthened the position of employers vis-à-vis workers as well as that of the nation-state as a unit in the world market – a trend which is fully in line with my argument put forth in Chapter 1 that the nation-state did not lose its importance. Vogler's investigation of the behaviour of the British unions from the 1930s till the 1970s showed that they 'now have more in common with their employers within the nation than with workers abroad. On both national and international policy, nations and struggles between them have thus come to take priority over, and mediate class relations within the nation' (Vogler 1985: 140). Such a view perfectly explains the paradoxical fact that the distribution of wealth is very unequal in Sweden – a country which otherwise is very proud of its strong welfare state and economic equality (see Chapter 6). In all these regards, however, we have to recognize significant differentiations within classes, related to disparities and interest conflicts between economic sectors,[8] different sorts of capital (industrial, trade and finance capital) and, among the dependent workers, by educational and occupational qualifications and the position in organizational hierarchies. Thus, both employers and workers in one sector are interested in preserving a particularly privileged situation of this sector. This fact is related directly to ethnic differentiation. For employers, an internal ethnic division within the working class might be welcome because it enables them to force wages of certain groups down. Workers can be divided in this regard; those in privileged sectors might accept or even welcome such cleavages.

One important, also often overlooked, common interest of classes is economic growth and socio-economic development; by creating new jobs, entrepreneurs-capitalists contribute significantly toward this aim. This aspect has been enthusiastically formulated by Marx and Engels when they wrote that the bourgeoisie has played a revolutionary role in history by destroying all feudal, patriarchal relations and by creating immense new forces of production (see Fetcher 1973: 383ff.). For the economist J. Schumpeter (1946), entrepreneurs are almost defined by the fact that they destroy old structures of production by inventing and offering new and better products and services. However, workers and employees in the old, declining sectors will be affected negatively by technological progress and shifts of the occupational structure. The availability of a large pool of cheap labour power will also delay efforts to increase the productivity of labour. We will see in Chapters 9 and 11, that the existence of slavery in the US-South and in Latin America had exactly this consequence. Fights against dominant classes are breaking off particularly in situations when people become overwhelmed by the feeling that these are living only as 'parasites' at the costs of all others but not contributing productively to development which is taking place in other parts of the world[9] (Davies 1962; Moore 1978; Seibel 1980). From this point of view, classes can be seen as the dynamic element in the triad of class formation, social stratification and ethnic differentiation.

Also in this regard, historical and present-day patterns of land ownership and rural class structures are very important. A strong thesis in this regard has been proposed by the American historian Robert Brenner in his article 'Agrarian class structure and economic development in pre-industrial Europe': he argued that '... most crudely stated it is the structure of class relations, of class power, which will determine the manner and degree to which particular demographic and commercial changes will affect long-term trends in the distribution of income and economic growth – and not vice versa' (Brenner 1987a [1976]: 11). The essence of this 'Brenner thesis' is that industrial capitalism emerged first in England because the landlords were able to gain control of an overwhelming proportion of the cultivable land and agricultural production was taken over by them; thus, they became agricultural capitalists (see also Aston and Philpin 1987; Bernhard n.d.).

Social Stratification and the Societal Status Structure

The origin of the process of social stratification and the formation of social strata (*Ständebildung*, in Weber's historical sociology; see Weber 1988/II: 41–2) is the tendency of social groups to establish borderlines and distinctions between them and other groups in terms of social honour and prestige. To think and to act in

---

8   Marxist authors used also the term of 'class fractions' in this regard and stressed particularly the interest differences between industrial and financial capital (see Hilferding 1986; Poulantzas 1974).

9   A recent confirmation of this thesis can be seen in the revolutionary development in the Arabic world, in North Africa and in Near East in the year 2011. In most of these countries, the same leaders had been in power for decades and economic development did not catch up with that in other parts of the Third World.

terms of higher and lower, of social hierarchies is a characteristic of people in all human societies (Svalastoga 1959; Ossowski 1972; Schwartz 1981). Most class theories since Marx have overlooked this fundamental process with the consequence that they expected too much from mere changes in (economic) class structures and overlooked their negative side-effects. Social strata emerge mainly through intergenerational status reproduction and the development of specific lifestyles. This is ensured by the transmission of social status over the generations and the complementary process of homogamy, the tendency to select a partner and to marry within one's own social stratum (Haller 1983: 106–21). The establishment and maintenance of social distance enables the members of the middle and higher social strata to avoid continuous challenges of their status position and related social identity (Banton 1960; van den Berghe 1960; Schmitt 1972).

Social stratification produces a status hierarchy in which as a rule three different strata are distinguished from each other: an upper, middle and lower stratum. The differences between and transitions from one to the next stratum are not sharp or clear-cut, however, particularly in the middle level. We can also use, with Max Weber and post-war British sociology (Marshall 1950; Giddens 1973; Parkin 1979; Goldthorpe et al. 1987; Goldthorpe and Marshall 1992; Breen and Rottman 1995), the term 'social classes' here. Members of the different strata try to limit their private interactions and relations to members of the same stratum; if relations to others are inevitable, they are restricted to the necessary and tend to be of a neutral-instrumental character (Archibald 1976). Often, however, status-related forms of social interaction are also forms of discrimination of the lower by the higher strata, implying elements of disrespect and contempt (Sennett and Cobb 1972). Members of the middle and higher strata, on their side, develop feelings of status anxiety (Botton 2004). Particularly members of the upper strata will hold on to the privileges of their situation, while members of the lower classes often will experience them as deprivation or discrimination (Sennett and Cobb 1972). Social stratification can be seen as a conservative principle tending to preserve an existing distribution of power and privileges. It can also be seen as a principle legitimizing inequalities; it reduces the envy which can develop among the less privileged and would undermine societal stability (Schoeck 1966).

In modern societies, in both processes of class formation and social stratification the educational system plays a decisive role. By its own vertical structure, it reinforces societal stratification (Bourdieu and Passeron 1971; Collins 1971; Haller 1986; Boudon 1974; Müller and Kogan 2011). From the comparative point of view and in connection with ethnic stratification, three aspects of education are important. The first is the structure or shape of the whole system; here we can distinguish between inclusive or comprehensive systems and segregative systems (Haller 1989:113ff.; Müller and Karle 1993). In the first, children and young people up to 15 or even 18 years attend the same type of school; in the second, pupils are differentiated at an early age (10–11 years) into different tracks, whereby only one of them leads to higher education. The second aspect is related to proportion of pupils and students who attend the schools of different types and levels. In some societies, the educational system is rather elitist: the mass of young people attends only lower levels of schooling, and only a minority the higher ones; in others, large cohorts of young people attend school up to higher tertiary levels. The third important distinction is that between public and private schooling; comprehensive school systems are typically public, financed by the state while private education typically is expensive and accessible only for well-to-do families. The tendency toward school systems which are segregative, elitist and divided into public and private sub-systems is particularly pronounced in ethnically heterogeneous societies. It is the rule that children of the privileged ethnic groups (mostly the Whites) attend the much better private schools while the rural and poor social classes must be content to send their children to the often rather poor public school system. In some countries (for example the UK), private and public systems exist at all levels in most countries: the higher school system is private, but in some, the relation is reversed; in Brazil and may Sub-Saharan African countries, the private elementary school system is much better than the public one. In this way, the school system contributes strongly to the reproduction of high inequality. I will come back to this issue in the final chapter.

Between classes defined in the more narrow economic sense and social strata or 'social classes' in the wider sense there exist close relations; from this point of view, we can also speak (and will do so in what follows) of 'class stratification'. Figure 3.1 presents the basic model of the effects of processes related to class structure, social stratification and ethnic differentiation on income inequality. Here, the connections between class formation, social stratification and ethnic differentiation are indicated by a non-direct line because it is assumed that they are reciprocal, working in both directions. Economic interests, resources and privileges

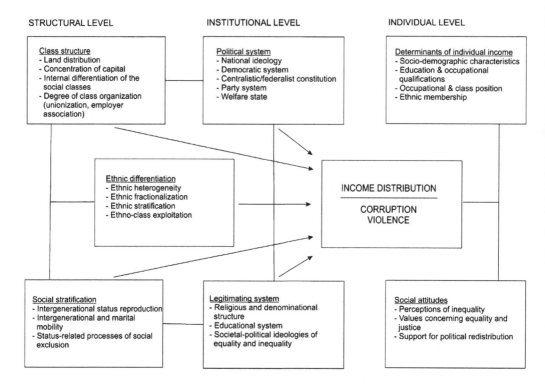

Figure 3.1   Central dimensions of class structures, social stratification and ethnic differentiation, of the political and legitimating system and their effects on income distribution (basic model)

connected with a class situation will never be pursued only as such, but always also because they tend to be connected with elements of social prestige and recognition that goes with social stratification. Economically rising and strong classes will try to become also recognized members of the higher social strata and circles. The concept of 'elites' might capture better this tendency than the concept of a 'dominant class'. In contrast to classes, elites are seen as closed, integrated groups or networks integrated also by a common distinct lifestyle, and they can act more or less directly in their own interests (Mills 1959; Etzioni-Halevy 1993). Joseph Schumpeter (1946) has argued that the replacement of owners by managers at the top of the great enterprises will lead to an exhaustion of entrepreneurial spirit because managers do not invest their income for an improvement in family status (for instance, by buying great houses and exhibiting a luxurious lifestyle) and thus will wear off the incentive to bequeath a large fortune to their offspring. This thesis evidently has been clearly disproved by history. Independent, hardworking individual entrepreneurs and managers who are able to amass big fortunes have not disappeared; they often also possess an exclusive education and exhibit elements of an elaborated upper class lifestyle; the same is true for managers of large enterprises (Coenen-Huther 2004; Bourdieu 2006; Hartmann 2007). As noted already by Weber (1964/II: 688), class formation comes to the fore in periods of rapid technological-economic change while a relative stability of economic life, and an absence of conflicts over distribution favours the formation of estates and social strata (see also Seibel 1980; Kreckel 1989). Aspects of the social situation and economic position outside the workplace and labour markets are also important for rank-and-file-workers. Dennis Smith (1990: 385) wrote, summarizing his study about workers in Birmingham in the early 1980s, that the job located them not only within the factory system and its battles and games (as elaborated in the work of M. Burawoy 1979), but 'also provided a ticket of entry to another sphere. This was the realm of the emancipated householder'. As such, a worker could participate in the material fruits of capitalism and control his own life with the ownership of a house as a significant symbol. Labour strikes and social revolts often emerge when economic discrimination and exploitation are connected with a lack of recognition of the personal worth of workers as individuals and as a class (Fraser and Honneth 2003). This happens particularly if the bulk of the workers is different from the higher classes also in ethnic terms, as in the case of many Latin American countries.

Sociological class theory has been used successfully to explain the distribution of income, but also a wide variety of inequalities in other domains, such as in social attitudes (perceptions of social structures, beliefs about social justice, political attitudes), educational and occupational aspirations, life chances in terms of health and life expectancy and happiness and so forth (Geissler 1994; Hradil 2001; Picket and Wilkinson 2009). I will do this also in some of the case studies in Part II, although I would not pretend that class theory and class analysis alone can explain socio-economic inequality. In this regard, one should be open to other approaches and explanations.[10] Since the 1960s, however, many authors, particularly in Germany, have proposed thesis of the end or 'death of classes' as a consequence of rising income and living standards, the extension of the welfare states, and the emergence of new life style differentiations and of identity politics (Beck 1986; Pakulski and Waters 1996; Berger 1996; Hradil 2001). However, recent research has shown that class stratification still is an important basic determinant of many aspects of private, public and political life also in advanced societies (see, for example, Goldthorpe and Marshall 1992; McNall et al. 1991; Müller 1999; Bouffartigue 2004; Bourdieu 2006). This is all the more so because in recent times in many Western countries income inequality is rising again. We will come back to this issue in Chapter 13. For the poor countries of the global South in which the majority of the world population is living, neither high standards of living, nor extended welfare state support and services are available.

The Interaction Between Class Stratification and Ethnic Differentiation

The concepts and theses discussed so far can be considered as received sociological knowledge. The new question which has to be posed and answered here concerns the relations between the process of class formation and social stratification on the one side, and ethnic differentiation on the other side which was denoted as the basic triad for the emergence and reproduction of socio-economic inequality (see Figure 2.1, Chapter 23). Several questions must be asked in this regard: What is the general nature of interaction between this triad? Is it the case that one of the three basic processes is dominant in a society? How does the concrete process of interaction between class formation, social stratification and ethnic differentiation look like? Are ethnic differentiations relevant at all levels of the social hierarchy and in all social classes, or do they affect only specific classes and strata? Of particular interest here are the possessing and upper classes on the one side, and the working and lower classes on the other side. Before going on to discuss these questions and developing concrete hypotheses, let us discuss shortly the general nature of the interaction between class formation, social stratification and ethnic differentiation.

It is rather obvious that class formation and social stratification will be closely related to processes of ethnic differentiation in ethnically heterogeneous societies. Processes of class formation are concerned about the acquisition and accumulation of economic, social and cultural resources and privileges, social and political influence and power. If specific social classes are homogeneous in ethnic terms, it will be facilitated for them to develop a consciousness of their common interests, to organize themselves collectively and to act in a concerted way (see also Giddens 1973: 111ff.). This may be the fact both for the privileged and dominant classes and for the deprived and lower classes. (Breen and Rottman 1995: 147ff.). Conversely, we might expect that ethnic differentiation will be a handicap for the development of class consciousness and action. This will be particularly so in the lower classes. They are much larger in numbers than the upper classes so that the probability of internal heterogeneity is higher and the development of a common consciousness will be more difficult. They depend much more than the upper classes on a 'dialogic' form of interest articulation and representation (Offe and Wiesenthal 1980). Conversely, the core of the *bourgeoisie* or upper classes might consist only of a few hundred or thousand big capitalists, allied professionals (for example lawyers) and top politicians. For them, it is much easier to interact regularly on a direct, personal basis. This will be even more so in small nation-states. In this way, they are able to preserve their interests in ways largely unrecognized by

_____

10   One particularly important other strand of thinking and research is organization and management theory (Westhues 1980).

the public. This situation helps to understand the surprising fact that the distribution of property in a rather equal country like Sweden is extremely unequal (see Chapter 6).

Likewise, it is evident that social stratification and ethnic differentiation will interact closely (see also Van den Berghe 1970, 1981). It is a definitional characteristic of both social strata and ethnic groups that they reproduce themselves through intergenerational transmission of group or status membership and homogamous marriage patterns. Ethnic differentiations have a strong impact on social stratification through processes of dissociation (*Distanzierung*) (Shibutani and Kwan 1965: 42). Strategies establishing social distance between the higher and lower are central also for the process of stratification (Haller 1983: 103–5). The relations between ethnic groups per se are not structured in a hierarchical way. However, there exists a communicative and social distance between ethnic groups, based on differences in languages, religious world-views and lifestyles. This communicative and social distance reduces the feeling of togetherness (*Zusammengehörigkeit*) and the readiness for reciprocal solidarity. Bruce Russett (1979: 73) has expressed this well: 'For most, our sense of moral responsibility for others recedes as their physical and social distance from us recedes. Our immediate families get highest priority, our fellow-nationals may occupy some sort of middle ground, and more distant inhabitants of the globe, about whom we know little, are farthest from our sense of responsibility. [...] Whatever the reason for a diminished sense of responsibility, these global inequalities are far greater than what we would tolerate within our own families, and greater than what we tolerate within the United States'. This communicative and social distance between members of the same social strata or ethnic groups within one society can even be larger than that between people from different societies. Language plays also a significant role in ethnic stratification. The language and associated family names can be a significant aspect of an existing hierarchy of power and status between ethnic national sub-groups. Therefore, some upwardly mobile Indians in Peru change their family names in order to blur the ethnic descent (Gugenberger 2001). In Francophone Africa, the use of French – mastered only by a small upper class elite – also served as a means to control the majority of the population (Bochmann 2001).

From these considerations it follows that emotions play an important role in the reproduction and transformation of stratification. Relevant here is *envy* which is a fundamental human emotion, largely neglected in the social sciences. The Austrian-German sociologist Helmut Schoeck (1966) has shown in an illuminating book that envy is connected closely with the problematic of social stratification. Envy is primarily a negative-destructive feeling and attitude which aims toward a constraint of the welfare and well-being of the envied person or group. It is directed toward people in similar social situations, but also toward other groups with which one comes in contact frequently. Now, if (vertical) social stratification and (horizontal) ethnic differentiation coincide, the difference and distance between the respective groups and strata will be pronounced particularly. The result can be that conflicts break out between ethnic groups who consider themselves as competitors. In Sub-Saharan Africa, for instance, many recent violent ethnic conflicts involved attacks of poor people against immigrant workers or refugees from other countries. Another emotion relevant in regard to social stratification is *status anxiety*. Alain de Botton (2004) has shown that this emotion is all the time present in our thinking and feeling and may also influence the behaviour of social groups which fear that economic crises or immigration might threaten their status. In regard to ethnic-national conflicts, the fear of becoming overrun in demographic terms is ubiquitous. We must assume, in general, that the relative position of a person, social group or class has significant impacts on their feeling status and emotions; these, in turn, have repercussions on their thinking and acting (Stryker 1980; Gerhards 1988, Kemper and Collins 1990; Scheff 1990). If class position, social status and a distinct ethnic membership coincide, the self-consciousness of a group may be enhanced strongly and may lead to social unrest and conflict in times of deep-going societal crises and changes. It could also be the case, however, that the members of a deprived class or group do not question their situation because they do not compare themselves with other groups in other groups in similar economic circumstances, but of a different ethnic membership. In principle, however, all human emotions play an important role in stratification and ethnic relations. This includes also the most basic emotions of love and hate. To speak of the love of one's country is not only a metaphoric use; many patriots and millions of soldiers were ready to sacrifice their life for their fatherland. The incredible atrocities committed in the several cases of mass genocide in recent history cannot be understood without taking into consideration the emotions of hostility and hate.

Class Stratification and Ethnic Differentiation as Determinants of Income Inequality

Let us now proceed to a discussion of the second question, namely, that of the effects of class stratification and ethnic differentiation on socio-economic inequality. In the following, I first present the basic model; then hypotheses are developed about class formation in ethnically homogeneous societies; and finally I analyse the effects of ethnic heterogeneity on income inequality.

The Basic Model

The basic model including the main variables and the relations between them is given in Figure 3.1. A first distinction concerns that of three different levels of analysis (from left to right in Figure 3.1): the social-structural level includes the dimensions, patterns and processes of class and ethnic stratification; the institutional level (centre) includes the political system and systems of legitimation; the third level concerns the issue of economic inequality, both at the structural level (the distinction of income) and at the individual level (the income of individuals in specific social strata and ethnic groups). In this regard, the model is somewhat inconsistent insofar as the distribution of income – a structural variable – is positioned at the right side; also the arrows – denoting causal patterns – may not be justified since in the following chapter we are carrying out only statistical analyses at the aggregate level. The idea, however, is that class stratification and ethnic differentiation are processes which have different effects on the processes determining the income distribution. In Part II of this book these processes will be elaborated on for specific types of countries and cases. On the left side of the chart, the relations between class formation, stratification and ethnic differentiation are displayed. They are connected with the political and legitimating systems in the middle of the graph. All these lines are not directed with arrows because I assume that there exist reciprocal relations. Income inequality, the central variable to be explained, is seen as being influenced by ethnic class structures and by the political and ideological systems. In addition, at the right side of Figure 3.1, two further aspects, concerning the determinants of individual income in different societies, are listed, along with their perceptions and evaluations of inequality. These two aspects, however, will be investigated empirically only in an exemplary manner, because the relevant data are available to me only for a restricted number of countries.

Class Formation in Ethnically Homogeneous Societies

The first question is that of the relations between class stratification and ethnic differentiation and the effect on income inequality. As it was noted already in Chapter 1, the issue of the relation between class and ethnicity has not been picked out as a theme in sociological class theories and research except by a few authors (for example, Murphy 1988). Neo-Marxist class theorists (Stephens 1979; Wright 1985; Hagelstange 1988), for instance, asked how it can be explained that in capitalist societies no majority emerges favouring a fundamental redistribution since more than 50 per cent of the population would profit from such a redistribution. Such a question is quite a keen simplification. As noted before, it is nearly impossible – particularly in the broad middle strata of a society – to define clearly privileged and deprived social classes and groups (Wiley 1967). An industrial worker, labouring hard for a modest pay in a job with low security, is clearly deprived in terms of his employment relation. However, he might have built (partly with his own hands) a house in the countryside. From this perspective, he might strongly oppose any taxation of house ownership – a measure which is oriented certainly toward the privileged who as a rule do have such ownership. In countries where the higher educational system is paid out of public funds, the upper classes – among which most children attend universities – might be strongly in favour of preserving such a system which was implemented first of all to enabling higher education for all gifted young people. We will see that this is a typical situation in countries with high inequality, such as Brazil.

Not only the neo-Marxists, however, but most class theorists do not ask at all if a society actually can be denoted as a 'class society' defined as one in which at least a rudimentary class consciousness and class-related organization (unions, left political parties) exist. I assume, following Theodor Geiger (1949) and Stanislaw Ossowski (1972: 175), that a society can be considered more or less as a 'class society', in the full sense, that its 'class character' can have a rather rich or only a restricted meaning. Classes in the 'objective' sense alone (workers, capitalists, small entrepreneurs and so on) certainly do exist in every society; but as long as these objective structures are not relevant for social processes, they are not relevant for social theory as well. The main question is, therefore, under which circumstances class societies in this sense come into existence (Dahrendorf 1959: 246). A fully developed class society would be one in which class-based differentiations and interests are highly relevant for many social and political processes. This must not imply that class conflict is strong or disruptive in such societies.[11] Rather, the relations between the classes have become 'institutionalized' which means that both employers and workers have developed strong organizations which guarantee that their interests are taken into consideration in negotiations about wages, work and labour market conditions and related political issues (Dahrendorf 1959; Lepsius 1988:142–50). The working classes are able to pursue their interests without ever-recurring strong or violent strikes and conflicts. Such a form of 'class compromise' has been established particularly in North and Central Europe; here the interests of all large classes are respected and incorporated.

In this regard, the relation between the classes and the state was also central. The emerging labour class organizations (unions, Socialist parties) emerged only within clearly defined national boundaries; the new 'national societies' were at the same time also new 'class societies': Carolyn Vogler (1985: 159) wrote in this regard: 'Classes became part of the state, while states themselves increasingly organized and regulated class relations within their boundaries. This resulted first in a blurring of the division between economics and politics at the national level [Goldthorpe 1983], secondly in a reinforcement of 'class' as the central structuring principle within the nation [Goldthorpe 1983] and thirdly in a very considerable reinforcement of the nation state itself'. Seen in world-historical and comparative perspective, it is more the exception than the rule that class societies in this sense have developed at all; it was mostly the case in Europe, but in very few societies outside of Europe. In this regard, the following hypothesis is proposed:

Hypothesis 1: *Class societies in the full sense have emerged only in ethnically homogeneous societies. Inequality of income distribution will be moderate in such societies because everybody is seen as a full member of society, the representatives of the main classes are able to pursue their interests in an effective way and the whole political process goes on in a non-violent way based on a fundamental consensus.*
Ethnic homogeneity, however, is not a sufficient reason for the emergence of a class society; it is only a necessary one. Japan is an interesting and important case of an ethnically homogeneous society with a weak class character of its society. Instead of it, an extremely fine-graded stratification hierarchy has developed in Japanese society (see Chapter 6). Thus, in order to explain the emergence of class societies, we have to consider additional factors. We will come back to them below.

Income Inequality, Privilege and Deprivation in Ethnically Stratified Societies

The next general thesis is quite straightforward after the considerations presented in this chapter: it is assumed that economic inequality will be significantly higher in ethnically heterogeneous societies than in ethnically homogeneous societies. This thesis must be specified additionally in four regards, however (see Figure 3.1): in regard to the kind of ethnic differentiation (ethnic fractionalization and polarization); in regard to the relation between ethnic differentiation and class stratification; in regard to the shape of the system of ethnic stratification, that is, the differentiation of the lower and the upper classes in terms of discrimination and privilege; and in regard to the existence or not of a history of ethnic exploitation.

The first aspect concerns *ethnic fractionalization* and *ethnic polarization*. The relevance and effects of the ethnic differentiation of a country on income inequality will vary dependent on the number and size of ethnic groups. This issue has been discussed extensively by economists who investigated the effects of ethnic heterogeneity on the quality of public service (for example corruption) and politics, and on economic growth (see, for instance, Easterly and Levine 1997; Fearon 2003; Alesina et al. 2003). Ethnic fractionalization is related to the number of discernible ethnic groups; the more groups exist, the higher fractionalization is; ethnic polarization is related to the relative strength of the different ethnic groups: it is greatest if there are

---

11   This contradicts also to the statement of Esser (2001:32) that class conflicts are the most important example of a lack of system integration.

only two ethnic groups competing with each other for economic and political power and resources. If in a country there exist many small ethnic groups it is difficult for any one of them to attain political power over the whole society. An example is Tanzania – one of the few countries in Sub-Saharan Africa which was able to avoid bloody and costly internal ethnic conflicts and wars. Tanzania is a large country with about 120 different ethnic groups, distinguished from each other in most regards (social descent, language, religion); the largest among them, the Sukuma, comprises only 12 per cent of the population; historically, it has also never been united as a singly, strong political community. This ethnic fragmentation was certainly an important pre-condition for its successful and peaceful political development since it gained independence in 1961 under the leadership of the charismatic Julius Nyerere (Müller Kmet 2012; see also Chapter 10, p. 260). Using large samples, most of the aforementioned economic studies found that ethnic fractionalization is related negatively to growth and the quality of democracy. The explanation given for the latter effect by Alesina et al. (2003) is that in more fragmented societies one group imposes restrictions on political liberty as a means to control other groups; in more homogeneous societies it is easier to rule democratically because conflicts in general are less intense. Concerning the effects of the different dimensions of ethnicity, some of these studies have reported that the effect of religious differentiation is smaller than that of racial or language differentiation (Alesina et al. 2003; Caselli and Coleman 2006). They explain this by the fact that religion is less visible in everyday life and can be changed more easily. I would add, however, that religion becomes highly relevant when it coincides with other dimensions.

The second question relates to the interaction between ethnic differentiation and class stratification. Here the general hypothesis is obvious:

Hypothesis 2: *In ethnically differentiated societies income inequality will be higher if ethnic differentiation and/or fractionalization coincide with class stratification.*
This central hypothesis can be tested in the following chapter only in an indirect way, by showing that ethnically differentiated societies are more unequal than homogeneous societies. It will be tested directly, however, Chapters 8 to 12 of Part II of this book where we can use individual-level data and show how ethnicity and class status interact and how this interaction impacts on levels of income in the different 'ethno-classes'.

The third question relates to the interaction between class stratification and ethnic differentiation at different levels of the social hierarchy. Here, we must distinguish between the situation in the upper and the lower classes (for arguments of the importance of this distinct from the economic point of view see Atkinson 2008: 15). Extensive privileges of the first must not necessarily imply a corresponding strong deprivation of the latter. A case which clearly proves this thesis is that of Sweden. I have already noted that this is one of the most equal countries worldwide in terms of income distribution but one of the most unequal in terms of ownership and asset concentration (see Chapter 6).

Let us first consider the relative privilege and internal differentiation within the upper classes. The privileged and dominant classes in a society are no monolithic block. This has been recognized clearly by class theorists. Marxist theorists argue that the capitalist class includes a series of 'class fractions' with considerable differences of interests; they unite themselves, however, in a common 'block of power' to pursue their overall common interests (Poulantzas 1974: 229ff.). The most important fractions within the capitalist class, the *bourgeoisie*, are the owners of large estates and the owners of capital (subdivided on their part into industrial, trade and finance capitalists). The Austrian Marxist Rudolf Hilferding (1986 [1919]) has shown in a path-breaking work that in advanced economies the finance capital gets more and more influence at the expense of industrial, productive capital. Many economists consider this fact as the main reason for the repeated deep world economic crises in recent times (Reinhart and Rogoff 2009; Krugman 2012). C.W. Mills (1959) saw the highest political leaders, the major corporate owners and high-ranking military officials as the core groups of the new 'power elite' in the United States; their power is backed by close relations between the members of these groups also in social and cultural terms. Since the declaration of independence in 1776, the White Anglo-Saxon Protestants (WASPs) constitute their socio-cultural kernel (Baltzell 1958; Mills 1959; Domhoff 1967). A similar situation exists in the United Kingdom and in France where an extremely selective and exclusive system of higher education ensures the social and cultural homogeneity of the elites till the present time (Boudon 1974; Marwick 1980; Ellis 1994). Particularly in Europe, two other groups must be added: the 'political class' (Mosca 1950 [1896]) and the public bureaucracy which gains ever more power in modern societies (Weber 1988); this is true also at the level of the European Union (Bach 1999; Shore 2000; Haller 2008b: 152–98). A similar point has been made by Robert Brenner (1987b: 254–9) from the historical point of view. He argues that the success of the English lords as extractors of surplus from their peasants was, in the Late Middle Ages, 'their superior self-organization; among the Norman aristocracy as a whole a high level of social solidarity existed. This stood in sharp contact to the disorganization of the French aristocracy.

However, if the upper class is divided internally, this will also have consequences and often very serious ones for the survival of a state and its political system. Mayer (2002) has shown using a dynamic model that the break-down of the State Socialist system of the Soviet Union was caused by a fundamental conflict between the political and the bureaucratic-administrative elites. Violent and bellicose ethnic conflicts in most cases are not related to the general ethnic diversity of a nation, but typically occur in those cases where the power centre is divided in ethnic terms (Wimmer et al. 2004). Emmerich K. Francis (1965: 163ff.), a pioneer in German research on ethnic differentiation, has pointed out that members of ethnic minorities often play an important role as leaders of militant *pressure groups*. On the other side, we can assume that if the economic and political elites are rather homogeneous they will not only be able to appropriate for themselves a high proportion of national income but will also be motivated to push the national interests concerning international competiveness and economic growth. It seems that exactly this has happened in East Asia, first in the four 'Asian Tigers' (Hong Kong, Singapore, South Korea, Taiwan) and more recently in Indonesia, Malaysia and Thailand. These states are all quite heterogeneous in ethnic terms but at the same time were able to accomplish a spectacular economic growth. This was possible due to a consistent macro-economic and educational policy pursued by responsible national elites (Page 1994; Ziltener and Müller 2007; Kerbo 2012: 501–13; Ziltener 2013). Quite the opposite of such behaviour was shown by many Sub-Saharan African elites and leaders.

An additional aspect in this regard concerns the relations of the upper classes and elites to the same classes in other nations. Dependence theory, inspired by Marxist ideas, has argued that the present-day unequal relations between the countries of the Third and the First World constitute a continuation of the unequal relations during the period of colonialism. The former direct exploitation has been supplanted by indirect methods, through unequal trade relations and the transfer of profits from the Third World to the home countries of the transnational corporations (see, for example, Amin 1976; Bornschier and Chase-Dunn 1985; Wallerstein 1975; Tausch and Prager 1993). This situation was particularly evident in the case of Latin America, one of the most unequal macro-regions of the world. There, industrial-capitalist development has been led from the beginning nearly exclusively by foreign born (Portuguese and Spanish) elites; the close intertwining of the economies of Latin America with those of Europe (and, later, the USA) was created by them and corresponded largely to their own class interests (Cardoso and Faletto 1979; Baronow 2000; see also Chapter 9). This was a clear contrast to the situation in East Asia (particularly Japan and China) where industrial development was sustained mainly by the local elites for which national interests were of central importance as pointed out before. It is certainly related to this fact that Japan was the only country of the non-Western world which was able to industrialize very early and to become an intense competitor for Western capitalism; in the same vein, most East Asian nations were able to achieve an impressive industrial take-off in the last decades. Thus, the internal ethnic structure and role of the elites plays a central role for the development of a country as a whole. We might suppose that the upper classes and elites will be less ready to consider their common interests and those of their state and society as a whole the more fragmented they are internally in ethnic terms. As a consequence, their power will be much more fragile and the danger exists of the breakout of intense and violent internal conflicts between their different factions to the point of civil wars and the breakdown of the state as a whole. We will see that such a situation has occurred over and over again in the young states of Sub-Saharan Africa (see Chapter 10).

At the aggregate level of the nations of the world, it will not be possible to test all the foregoing hypotheses empirically, both due to the lack of data and the qualitative character of many of these hypotheses. In order to get at testable hypotheses, we can distinguish between two types of upper classes in ethnically heterogeneous societies. The one is characteristic for the Latin American 'coloured class structure' in which the lower classes are predominantly Black or native Indian while the upper classes are rather homogeneous Whites. In this case, we can speak of a consolidated dominant upper class. In the other case, represented mostly by Sub-Saharan African societies, the upper class is recruited predominantly from one of the several large ethnic sub-groups in a society which, on their side, are not clearly distinct from each other in terms of privilege and status. Here, the dominant elites find themselves often in a precarious situation since they can be disempowered by other groups.

For the lower social classes and strata, we can postulate a complementary relation. If they are significantly differentiated internally, this enhances the competition for jobs and other resources and handicaps collective organization through unions and political parties (Bonacich 1972, 1980). Even if representatives of the working classes want to supersede ethnic fractionalization they often are unable to do so. Rather, they will pass over from strategies of usurpation to strategies of exclusion in the distributional fights (Parkin 1979). In the first, they try to unite the workers as a whole and to fight against employers. In the second, they fight only for specific groups of workers, at the expense of other workers who are excluded from certain sectors and jobs, or who have to pay higher prices for the products of the privileged economic sectors. For employers, an internal differentiation of the working class is advantageous and they will even actively further it if this is possible (in Chapter 9 it will be shown how this has happened in Latin America). These considerations permit also a very plausible interpretation of the fact that the working classes have played a key role in the first stages of democratization (in the late 19th, early 20th centuries) but much less so in recent times (Collier 1999). It is quite evident that after the Second World War, large numbers of foreign workers were recruited for industry in Western Europe and the working classes became more heterogeneous in ethnic terms; in the global South, this fact is even more obvious.

In this regard, an important process affecting both the global North and South is international migration. As a consequence of migration from poorer to richer countries it can be expected that ethnic heterogeneity in the latter will increase. It is usually the case that immigrants have to be content with the lowest occupational jobs (Hoffmann-Nowotny 1973; Castles and Kosack 1973; Esser 1980, 2001b; Han 2006). As a consequence, work conditions in these sectors will deteriorate and wages will be reduced so that general income inequality in a society will rise. This has actually happened in many Western countries (Atkinson 2008). A *race relation cycle* (Shibutani and Kwan 1965: 117 ff.) can emerge in this regard: new immigrants have to face competition with natives, but may be successful and rise in status; later on, new waves of immigrants arrive and they begin to occupy anew the lowest positions. This process explains why xenophobia is more widespread among the lower than among the higher strata, and why in poor countries of the Third World often violent fights are breaking out not between natives and immigrants, but between earlier and more recent immigrants (I will come back to the issue, the new patterns of international migration and ethnic stratification in Chapter 13, pp. 362–70). Based on these considerations, we can assume that the more heterogeneous the lower classes and strata are in ethnic terms, the less conscious they will be about their common class situation and the less they will be able to organize themselves collectively and to pursue their common interests. As a consequence, they will be more deprived in economic terms. Out of these considerations, the following testable hypothesis can be deducted:

Hypothesis 3: *In ethnically heterogeneous societies, people in the higher classes will receive a larger, and those in lower classes will receive a smaller amount of the total income than in ethnically homogeneous societies.*

A central question in the relations between class stratification and ethnic differentiation concerns the question how the different ethnic groups came into contact and how their relations developed later on. Two main forms may be distinguished here: the first is a violent encounter in which one group was able to subjugate, dominate and exploit the other; the second is a form where the different groups came into contact and are living together in a more or less peaceful way, connected to each other by economic relations and cooperation in the division of labour. However, in a society characterized by a close intertwining of class divisions and ethnic differentiation, the privileges and deprivations are often hidden by a strong separation of social interaction outside the sphere of work. R. McAll (1990: 213) wrote in this regard: 'One factor that prevents that combination [of class and ethnicity] from becoming an explosive one is that the greater the degree of material inequality, the more it can come to be hidden from view in select neighbourhoods, clubs, expensive hotels, and private schools'. What McAll explains here about the strategies and effects of social segregation of the upper classes can also be said about the involuntary segregation of the members of lower classes and deprived ethnic groups: children who have grown up in slums, for instance, may learn to perceive it as 'natural' that places of living are so extremely differentiated and unequal in many of the huge metropolizes of the present-day world. There were three main forms in which the relations between ethnic groups have been characterized by violent suppression and exploitation: slavery, which was very important in Sub-Saharan Africa, in the Arab-Islamic world and America from the 16th till the late 19th centuries; Apartheid, a system of legal separation and inequality between races, existent in the US-South and South Africa from the late 19th till the late 20th century; and the rise to power of ethnic groups in many of the new Sub-Saharan states after they had gained political independence in the aftermath of the Second World War. From the viewpoint of historical sociology, we can assume that these systems of exploitation have repercussions till the present day.

The historically most important and socially most pervasive of these three forms was slavery. I will come back to this form of ethnic-class exploitation from a general point of view in the following chapter. There, we will also see that the abolition of slavery did not lead to an abrupt change. Rather, both the objective discrimination of the freed slaves and their offspring continued, as well as racial stereotypes and prejudices which were transmitted to the Blacks in general. Therefore, the following hypothesis is proposed here:

Hypothesis 4: *A history of ethnic exploitation in the form of slavery of a country will be connected with a significantly higher economic inequality today, and in particular with a smaller proportion of income going to the lower income groups.*

Ethnic class structures are challenged in a fundamental way if far-reaching social and political transformations together with pervasive ideological reorientations are taking place in a society (Shibutani and Kwan 1965: 372ff.). Looking at world history in the last centuries, two events and trends, respectively, have been most consequential in this regard: first, the decline of the great imperial-colonial nations, connected with massive losses of power on the world scale; second, the implementation of a fundamentally new ideological world-view concerning the relations between nations and ethnic groups. Examples were the successful liberation fights of the former colonies in America in the 18th and 19th centuries, and in Africa and Asia after the Second World War. The pre-condition for the success of the liberation fights, however, was the long-term power decline and the military defeats of former imperial powers (such as Great Britain, France and Spain), the abolition of slavery and the condemnation of racism in the 19th and 20th centuries. In this regard, the United Nations Declaration of Human Rights in 1948 constituted a landmark.

The first governments in the new nations of the Third World often had a Socialist and Marxist orientation and they put through far-reaching economic and social reforms. Examples include Mexico in 1911, Russia in 1917, China in 1949, Egypt in 1949, Ethiopia in 1975 and Iran in 1979. However, the outcome of these revolutions and reforms was ambiguous in many cases; I will come back to them in Part II of this book. In other cases, ethnic inequality increased massively. In South Africa, the brutal exploitation of the Black majority by the White minority was replaced from 1911 onward by the Apartheid system which, at the surface, seemed to correspond to Western standards of human rights; in fact, however, a new system of exploitation was established. An early study on the issue of inequality between the ethnic groups in nine societies in the Third World found that it did not decrease, but even increased (Grove 1979). The experiences from suppression and exploitation and from the following violent fights for power of the leaders of liberation movements cannot be shaken off over night and will determine also their own thinking and actions after the rise to power (Waldmann 1977; Mann 2007). So, we find that one of the earliest liberated 'Black' nations in the New World, Haiti, today is also one of the most unequal societies (see Table 1.1, p. 56, and p. 103). Thus, we must conclude that the abolishment of ethnically based exploitation and the rise to power of hitherto suppressed ethnic groups did induce changes in incumbents of the higher positions but has not always led to a more equal distribution of power and privilege. Often it was connected only with a change in the composition of the dominant and privileged classes. I will come back to this fact in several of the case studies investigated in Part II of this book.

With the forgoing considerations, I have delineated the general contours of the relations between class stratification, social stratification and ethnic differentiation and their effects on economic inequality (in the three boxes on the left side in Figure 3.1). Now we can go on to look at the two main institutional and ideational context conditions which shape the emergence of patterns of ethnic stratification, namely the political system and the system of legitimation, that is, the values and norms related to class and ethnic relations.

The Modification of Ethnic Class Structures by the Distribution of Power in Different Political Systems

The distribution of political power in a society is determined by the constitution of a state and by the behaviour of the political and bureaucratic elites. The state is the main guarantor of the existing distribution of power and privileges, but also for its transformation in the interest of the less privileged and exploited groups and classes. In long-term historical perspective, the first aspect – the state as the guarantor of existing structures of privilege – was dominant. However, at the latest since the political and socio-economic revolutions in England, France and America from the 17th century onwards, also the latter aspect – the state as an agent of transformation – comes to the fore. Thus, the 'political sociology of social inequality' (Kreckel 1992) must be a central element of any theory of economic and social inequality. Before going on to elaborate the relations between the character of political systems and economic inequality, let us have a short look on this general issue.

The State and the Class Structure

The state has always played a central role in sociological class theory. We can distinguish three variants here. For Marx and Lenin, the state was an actor which mainly pursues the interests of capitalist classes. The bourgeois state is a product of antagonist class relations, 'an instrument for the exploitation of the suppressed class', as Lenin (1951 [1918] wrote in his programmatic article 'State and revolution'. Neo-Marxist authors admit that the state has 'relative autonomy' in relation to the economic sphere and the capitalist class. Nevertheless, they also consider the modern state as a political and ideological repressive instrument which has to be overcome by a Socialist order (see for example Poulantzas 1974). An opposite view is represented by the pluralistic theory of democracy (Dahl 1971). This theory assumes that in modern democracies all group and class interests have similar chances to organize themselves and to gain influence on politics. Many present-day, critical political sociologists disavowed both these positions. The Orthodox Marxist position has lost its credibility because of two facts. First, it has been falsified historically in a double way. On the one side it became evident that the Communist leaders in State Socialist societies themselves became a new power elite, governing and acting in many regards more in their own interests than in those of the population. Incredible facts about the cruelty of Communist leaders (first of all J. Stalin) came to the fore after the breakdown of the system in East Europe and Russia (Djilas 1957; Voslenskij 1980; Courtois 1998; I will come back to this issue in Chapter 7). Second, it clearly turned out that a system of central economic planning is in a hopelessly inferior position when it comes to develop science and technology, and to foster economic growth and increasing standards of life for the population as a whole. In this work, I pursue a third way of thinking about the relation between social classes, the state and the distinction of political power and socio-economic privilege. This position assumes that there are strong economic and class interests influencing political processes but we must not assume from the outset that some of them dominate the others. This assumption is based on the fact that democracy is a powerful instrument for establishing economic and social equality as political theorists since Alexis de Tocqueville (1945 [1835]) have argued (see also Kelsen 1965; Lenski 1973; Putnam 1976; Etzioni-Halevy 1993). However, they also insist that even in Western democracies, differential access to political power and a close association between economic and political power persists (Offe 1972; Miliband 1983). C.W. Mills (1959) has coined the term 'power elite' to describe this relationship in the case of the United States.

We can make significant progress in the analysis of the question of societal and political distribution of power and privilege if we include the issue of the ethnic-national homogeneity or heterogeneity of a state and society. Four aspects are relevant in this regard: the relation between state and ethnic groups; the democratic character of the state; the political constitution concerning centralization or federalization; and the character and comprehensiveness of welfare institutions.

Ethno-national States

Two issues are important in regard to the relation between state and ethnicity and the ethnically defined character of a state. Of utmost importance in this regard is the fact if ethnic membership is a characteristic relevant for social and political rights. If this is the case it has far-reaching implications for economy, state and society. The paradigmatic example of such a connection was the system of Apartheid in South Africa (1911–1994). To a somewhat alleviated degree, such a system existed in certain terms also in the US-South. In the first case, one could in fact speak of an 'ethnic class state' since race membership constituted a fixed, legally defined category which was closely related with the situation of privilege or discrimination of the four races defined by the South African Constitution (Whites, Blacks, Coloured and Asians). By separating these groups into different labour markets, settlement areas and educational systems and by establishing related inequalities in political rights (only the minority of the Whites had full political rights), race segregation in fact became ethno-class segregation (Duve 1965; Adam and Moodley 1977; Adam 2013; Cornevin 1980) (I will come back to this system in Chapter 11). Another example is the fatal development of the relations between Hutus and Tutsis in Rwanda in the 1980s and 1990s which led to one of the most brutal genocides in human history. It was caused by the fact that membership in one of these groups became closely related with political power during the colonial area and the first decades of the new nation (Mamdani 2001; Rwamapfa 1999; Mann 2007).

The other aspect concerns the degree to which a nation-state can be considered as having a certain ethnic character. A nation can be defined as a state which is well anchored in the minds of its citizens, including a strong identification of the citizens with the state, and its full acceptance by political elites (Weber 1964/I: 674ff; Deutsch 1966: 144; Haller 1996a, b; Schöpflin 2000: 35–65). Here, we can tie in again with Anthony Smith's (1986) thesis about the ethnic origin of nations discussed already in Chapter 2. There is some truth in this thesis insofar as even in ethnically heterogeneous societies a certain *ethnie* usually is able to imprint its character to a considerable degree on the nation as a whole. This character may not be formulated explicitly and officially, but it is operating effectively at the level of everyday behaviour and underpins official self-presentations of a nation (Billig 1995). A paradigmatic example is the United States. The character of this nation has been formed to a large degree by the Anglo-Saxon protestant heritage, in spite of immigrants from all over the world from the earliest days (Lipset 1979). Another well-known example is Germany whose constitution granted citizenship on the basis of blood and descent, in contrast to countries such as France, Switzerland and the USA where citizenship is granted to those who are residing a certain period of time on their territory.[12] The difference between France and Germany may not be as sharp as pointed out in Rogers Brubaker's first work on the topic, *Citizenship and Nationhood in France and Germany* (1992). However, it does exist and, as a consequence, it is easier for immigrants to become citizens in the latter group of countries than in Germany and others with a similar constitution. A recent example for a state which defines itself in ethnic terms is Israel; its state symbols and basic laws present Jewishness and Zionism as inherent characteristics of the state. It is evident that the sizable minority of nearly 20 per cent Arabs (Palestinians) living in Israel cannot feel to be represented fully by such a characterization. This issue is so controversial that still today the Israelian Government and Parliament have been unable to adopt a formal constitution which they resolved to do immediately after the declaration of independence in 1948. The reason was that some orthodox-religious Jews have an over-proportional influence on Israeli politics and oppose the idea of a constitution which could be regarded as nominally 'higher' in authority than religious texts. In this regard, Israel is comparable to fundamentalist Muslim states like Iran, Saudi Arabia or Pakistan who define their states as 'Islamic Republics' (see 5, pp. 153–54, for a more extensive discussion).

In this regard, we should finally mention an observation made by I. Wallerstein (1975: 374), namely, that all successful social revolutions of the 20th century (in Russia, China, Cuba and so on) were also national revolutions. This thesis seems to be valid also for earlier revolutions, such as the American War of Independence against Great Britain. Even in the falling apart of the Soviet Union in 1989/90 efforts at gaining more autonomy and even independence of the many provinces and territories distinct from Russia in ethnic-national terms played a significant role as will be shown in Chapter 7 (see also Lewada 1992: 154ff.). A similar mechanism is still relevant in some multi-ethnic Western nations, such as Belgium, Spain and Canada;

---

12   In recent practice, the difference between these countries became much less significant (see Chapter 13).

here, the people of provinces distinct from the majority (or what they believe is the more powerful group) feel that they are more and more deprived; thus, they enforce claims to full political independence. Out of these considerations, the following hypothesis is proposed:

Hypothesis 5: *The ethnic-national character of a state has significant consequences for power distribution and economic inequality: (a) if ethnic membership is associated legally with civic and political rights, economic inequality explodes; (b) if a nation-state defines itself officially in ethnic terms, minorities will be discriminated against and the integration of immigrants will become more difficult and they will also be discriminated economically.*
The dimensions pointed out in this hypothesis are difficult to measure in a quantitative way and for many states around the world because the necessary data do not exist. I will test this hypothesis, therefore, only through the case studies in Part II of this book.

Democracy, Ethnicity and Equality

The second characteristic highly important in the relation between the ethnic-national class structure of a society and the resulting degree of economic inequality is the democratic character and the quality of the social, economic and political institutions of a state. The basic principle of democracy is to establish equality between all citizens concerning access to political offices and power and to provide them with some influence on the substantive direction of politics. The selection of the holders of political offices by free elections in which every citizen has one and only one vote shall guarantee that also the less privileged classes and strata can bring their interests to bear in politics (Graubard 1973; Rubinson and Quinlan 1977). Democracy, however, is also important because it is closely related with 'good government' (Kerbo 2006: 35ff.), that is, the quality of societal and political institutions. A high level of institutional quality is indicated by the rule of law, efficient and responsible public administrations, stability of governments, the absence of clientelism, corruption, waste and misuse of public resources and a low risk of abrupt nationalization of foreign enterprises (Bloom et al. 2010; see also Rodrick and Subramanian 2003). A very important aspect of democratic systems in regard to income inequality is the possibility to establish independent interest organizations, particularly unions and political parties. They are the main forces working for more equality within a nation-state.

Thus, democracy is a decisive political-institutional mechanism leading toward greater equality. This fact was evident for classical social and political theorists such as Montesquieu and Alexis de Tocqueville; the latter used the concepts of democracy and equality nearly as convertible. More recent empirical research on the relations between democratic government and equality, however, has not found unequivocal support for a close connection (see Hughes 1997 for a summary). But one particular specific characteristic of modern, democratic societies, the existence of independent unions, has in fact been shown to be associated significantly with a more equal distribution of income (Freeman and Oostendorp 2002). Most of the aforementioned studies, however, compare only present-day societies with each other and cannot make valid conclusions about changes and trends. Seen from a world-historical perspective, the answer also to the question of the relation between democracy and economic inequality is unequivocal and positive. I have already quoted Lenski (1973) who notes that during the transition from agrarian to industrial societies a significant passage occurred from a long-term trend towards rising inequality towards one of increasing equality. The granting of political rights to the people in the course of the modern political revolutions certainly has played a significant role therein. Following Tocqueville (1945), we can assume that there exists a reciprocal relation in this regard: democracy leads to more equality but increasing equality also supports the establishment of democratic institutions. This idea has been proposed already by Aristotle who argued that a broad middle class is the most important pre-condition for a stable political system. In an empirical study including 50 countries, Rubinson and Quinlan (1977) found empirical support for this thesis, D. Lane (1996) has argued convincingly that the success of the Soviet Union in terms of the advancement of education for its population has in the end contributed to its downfall because a new, more critical social stratum came into existence.

In all these regards, the degree of ethnic differentiation within a state plays a significant role. Since ethnic differentiation can be closely related to patterns of social inequality and since ethnic minorities are often deprived, we can assume that a democratic constitution will reduce inequality also in ethnic heterogeneous nations. In addition, it is a matter of fact that in democracies violent ethnic conflicts are less frequent than in non-democratic states (Powell 1982; Gurr 1993; Stavenhagen 1996; Schlenker-Fischer 2009: 198–3). We can also understand the puzzle that some countries have managed to be rather egalitarian without being democratic: a high level of ethnic homogeneity may be the key to explain this fact in many cases. Out of these considerations, the following hypothesis is proposed:

Hypothesis 6: *Democratic countries will exhibit a lower level of economic inequality than non-democratic ones. In addition, ethnic heterogeneity will not be associated with higher economic inequality in democratic societies with well-established institutions and responsible, good functioning and stable political governments and bureaucracies.*

Federalism and Equality in Ethnically Heterogeneous Societies

The third important political factor in the relation between ethnic heterogeneity and economic inequality is the centralistic or federalist character of the political system. Federalism represents a horizontal division of power between the central state authorities and regional-territorial sub-units.[13] In a federal system, local or provincial governments can decide autonomously about important political issues; typical instances are regional development and planning, educational and social policy. Since many ethnic-national sub-groups are concentrated on certain territories, federalism is de facto an instrument for the autonomy of ethnic sub-groups. Thus, it will back their specific claims in the political process at the national level. We can expect, therefore, that economic and social inequality will be lower in ethnically differentiated nation-states which have a federal constitution than in those which have a centralized constitution (see also Singh 1979; Kößler and Schiel 1995).

An important related aspect is that a federalist structure contributes to fan out political tensions and conflicts onto more levels and actors and thus to mitigate their societal and political blasting force. Large nation-states which are internally highly differentiated in ethnic terms and which have a non-democratic and centralistic political system will show high levels of disruptive economic and political conflicts. Paradigmatic examples were the multi-national states of Yugoslavia and the Soviet Union which on paper had exemplary federalist constitutions. Because of the overall domination of the Communist party, however, they were de facto highly centralized political systems. The falling apart of Yugoslavia, however, has been caused by an additional fact which concerns the relationship between ethnic differentiation and the character of a federalist system. For Yugoslavia, the ethnic-national divisions correspond largely with the six autonomous Republics. This was a fundamental difference to the federal system of Switzerland where the 24 cantons (*Kantone*) do not correspond to linguistic or religious borders (except in the case of the Kanton Ticino); there are many cantons which are mainly German-speaking, and several in which French predominates. The difference between the two systems can well be captured by the 'primitive theory of social structure' developed by Peter M. Blau (1977). He distinguishes between two types of social structure: in a structurally consolidated society, several parameters of social structure coincide, in a multi-form heterogeneous society, they do not coincide. Evidently, social and political conflicts become attenuated in a multi-form heterogeneous structure because every person belongs to different groups whose membership does not overlap. Out of these considerations, the following hypotheses are proposed:

Hypothesis 7: *Economic inequality will be lower in ethnically differentiated state societies if they have genuine and effective federal political constitutions. This will be so particularly in multi-ethnic societies in which the political sub-units do not coincide with ethnic divisions.*

The Welfare State and Equality

The fourth important aspect of a political constitution and system affecting the distribution of income is the character and comprehensiveness of its welfare state. The aim of the welfare state is to provide political force

---

13   For an overview, see the article 'Federalism' in *Stanford Encyclopaedia of Philosophy*; available at http://plato. stanford.edu/entries/federalism.

to the idea of 'social equality' – one of the three fundamental forms of citizens' rights according to Marshall (1950; see also Stephens 1979; Korpi 1983; Alber 1987, 2001; Boix 2003; Kuhnle 2004). Two dimensions are relevant in this regard: the character of the welfare state and the extension of its transfers and services. The first dimension concerns the question if welfare state provisions are seen more as subsidiary, as a kind of charity, supplementing individual efforts only in cases of specific proven need, or if they are seen as basic rights to which every citizen is entitled in specific life circumstances, such as in the case of unemployment, sickness and disability, or in old age. One paradigmatic type (represented by the USA) is called a liberal or marginal welfare state, the second type (represented mainly by Scandinavian states) is called an universalistic or social-democratic welfare state (Esping-Andersen 1990). It is obvious that a universal welfare state will provide more services and transfer payments to its citizens than the first. Thus, it can be expected that in a strong welfare state equality is higher than in liberal welfare states.

Also in this regard, ethnic differentiation will be important. It can be expected that an extended welfare state can be developed only in ethnically homogeneous nation-states because it presupposes a strong feeling of togetherness and solidarity in the whole population; this must also include the support for a significant redistribution from the rich to the poor and a high level of taxation for the financing of the state expenditures. The development of such welfare states will be furthered significantly by strong unions based on a working class which is homogeneous in ethnic terms. I will show in Chapter 6 that all these conditions were given in Sweden in the first half of the 20th century. The counterpart of ethnically heterogeneous societies might be a liberal or marginal welfare state, focusing upon proven neediness because the deprived situation of the ethnically different lower classes and strata often will be explained by their irresponsible behaviour. Thus the following hypothesis is proposed:

Hypothesis 8: *Ethnically homogeneous societies will more frequently have a comprehensive welfare state than ethnically differentiated societies. In both cases, however, inequality will be lower if a state has a comprehensive welfare state.*

An extended welfare state is no necessary condition for an ethnic-homogeneous state to have a high degree of equality. In the case of Japan, the coherent political elites developed other means of redistribution which also assured a relatively high equality (see Chapter 6).

Cultural Values and Societal Ideologies Legitimating Ethnic Stratification and Inequality

In this section, I will first discuss briefly the relevance of ideas and values which legitimize inequality. Then, I will give an overview on the main secular ideologies of inequality and discuss the stance of the great world religions in regards to equality and inequality.

Ideologies and Inequality

The distribution of economic resources and social privileges is shaped not only by economic market processes and bold power but must also be legitimized in ideological terms (Weber 1964/I: 157–60; Ossowski 1972; Moore 1978). An ideology or philosophy of life (*Weltanschauung*) is a relatively comprehensive system of interpretation of social reality which includes scientific, cognitive-descriptive and non-scientific evaluative elements (Mannheim 1970; Boudon 1988; Borlandi et al. 2005: 338–41). Ideological systems and specific values (relating to patterns of behaviour in concrete spheres of life) have the function to provide orientation and guidance for individuals as well as legitimacy for social groups, organizations and societal institutions. It is a basic assumption of sociology – distinguishing it clearly from mainstream economic thinking – that ideas and values are fundamental for any human action and institution. Starting from such a Weberian approach, we must reject two influential interpretations. One is the Marxist view that ideas and values are nothing else than reflections of the interests and power of dominant classes and groups. The other is the assumption of functionalist sociology that values will always be the decisive cause for action. Values are in fact of fundamental importance in any form of human behaviour and social process but it cannot be assumed from the outset they will be determinative in every instance. Rather, as Weber wrote in a famous passage, concrete social action is guided in most cases by economic and other interests, but ideas determine in the long term which interests are selected (see also Lepsius 1988).

Ideas related to equality and inequality get social and political relevance when they become a part of the 'social consciousness' of a society (Ossowski 1972: 15); this consciousness includes the beliefs common to all members of certain societies and social milieus, which are strengthened by reciprocal persuasion. Such ideas have an objective existence and exert real social pressure upon the individual members of a collective unit (Durkheim 1982, 1993; Popper 1973). Dann (1975) and Majer (1995) have shown this for the history of the idea of equality through the centuries: only a tiny fraction of the peoples of ancient Greece and Rome were considered as free and equal citizens; the majority, the slaves, were deprived of any rights. Throughout millennia also most of the slaves accepted their fate as God-given and unchangeable. The exploitation and discrimination in the form of slavery was related closely to ethnicity: most slaves were members of non-Roman peoples, captured in wars. In the Middle Ages, brutal exploitation through slavery was substituted in most parts of Europe by serfdom which granted at least some basic rights to the exploited; in modern times, also this form has been abolished. Other forms of equality, such as that between men and women, have been achieved only in the last 100 years. Montesquieu (2002 [1748]) and Alexis de Tocqueville (1945 [1835]) have shown that the value of equality is basic for understanding the breakthrough and development of modern, democratic societies (see also Boudon 2000). Through public opinion, ideas related to equality retroact also upon the governing elites and reinforce the influence of citizens on political decisions and actions – and subsequently – on the shape of inequality in a society (Yinger 1994; Burstein 1998). Further, charismatic political leaders, inspiring confidence among the deprived and exploited, can contribute significantly to a peaceful overcoming also of systems of ethnic and national domination and exploitation; Mahatma Gandhi and Nelson Mandela were such personalities in recent times.

In this section, I will discuss briefly some of the main peculiar and religious ideas legitimating equality and inequality which have appeared in history and which are still relevant today. This aspect, however, cannot be included in the multivariate statistical analysis of the following chapter because in the highly mobile and secularized present-day world there are very few countries which can be characterized unambiguously in terms of a dominant ideology. In most countries – particularly in the larger ones – different secular-political ideologies of equality and inequality compete with each other (Haller et al. 1995); and people belong to several different religious denominations. A detailed discussion of some of these ideologies and values relevant in specific countries shall be carried out in the case studies in Part II of this volume. There are, however, a few, basic systems of ideas which later were further developed into more or less comprehensive theories of social equality and inequality. They can, similar to the theories of inequality, be classified according their emphasis on either class stratification or ethnic differentiation (see Table 3.1). I will discuss here shortly two of them: first, some secular ideas and systems legitimating equality and inequality and, second, the position of a few world religions in this regard. Special consideration is given to their stances concerning ethnic inequalities.

Table 3.1   Classification of ideologies of equality and inequality according to their view of the relation between class stratification and ethnic differentiation

Class stratification and class relations	Ethnic differentiation: strong, conflictive	Ethnic differentiation: weak, irrelevant
Strong, antagonistic and conflictive relations	Racism Social Darwinism Islam (Muslim – non-Muslim world)	Marxism, Leninism Conservative elite theories
'Organic' stratification, cooperative relations	Hinduism State Protestantism (Orthodox Christianity Church and state members – others)	Reform Socialism Catholic social doctrine Functionalist theory of stratification Buddhism, Confucianism Islam (relations within the Muslim world)

Secular Ideologies of Equality and Inequality

Since antiquity, there exist influential secular ideologies of equality and inequality. Of central importance for the modern world was the philosophical movement of *Enlightenment*, originating in the Italian *Renaissance* and in French and German philosophy in the 17th century. Enlightenment meant, in the words of Kant, that humans should escape from their self-inflicted immaturity and use their minds independently from the guidance of authorities. This attitude implied that equality and inequality were not seen any more as determined by God or by nature, but as created by humans themselves; therefore, one could challenge all forms of inequality and call into question their functions for different social groups. In this regard, Jean-Jacques Rousseau played a central role. In his essay 'About the origin of inequality among men' (Rousseau 1967 [1754]) he distinguished between inequality caused by nature and by society and argued that the first had always been much smaller than the last. Social inequality began when the first man fenced a piece of land and declared: this is mine. Cohabitation of men in large societies, increasing division of labour and amelioration of conventions led to feelings of privilege and deprivation, to vanity and contempt, to shame and envy, to conflicts of interest and to the overreaching of others. The blasting power of these Rousseauan ideas for structures of societal power and inequality turned out fully in the revolutions of the late 18th century. (Groethuysen 1989). These include the French Revolution with its slogan 'Freedom, Equality, Fraternity', and the American fights for independence with the aim to dispose of any estate privileges and to establish the first large democracy. The central ideas of these authors were incorporated as explicit principles of the constitutions of all states in the Universal Declaration of Human Rights of the United Nations in 1948. It is remarkable, however, that the Enlightenment in general did not call into question the institution of slavery, that is, subjugation of peoples in Africa, Asia and Latin America by Europe and America.

Another highly influential strand of secular ideas of equality were the Socialist and Communist theories of the 19th and early 20th centuries. They can be considered as children of the ideas of enlightenment claiming that civic and political equality had to be complemented by full economic and social equality between all men and women. These ideas inspired the fights of the labour movement in the late 19th century and the Communist Revolution in Russia in 1917. The aim of the first also included the quest for democracy and for the establishment of the welfare state; the latter should establish 'real' social equality by abolishing private property. Also many of the liberation movements in the Third World after the Second World War were inspired by Socialist ideas. As was shown already in Chapter 2, Marxism considered ethnic and national differentiations and inequalities only as secondary compared with class-based inequalities. The position of Marxists toward ethnic minorities within their own societies remained always ambiguous. In Chapter 7, I will show that the Soviet Union and Yugoslavia broke down not the least because of the neglect of the issue of ethnic-national differences and disparities. It will also be shown, however, that the idea of equality still is quite relevant for the people in former State Socialist societies (Lewada 1992: 62 ff.).

A secular ideological current, highly relevant when speaking about ethnic inequality, is *racism*. Its basic idea is that there exist natural, biological differences between the fundamental human races and that one can distinguish higher and inferior races. The founder of systematic modern race theory was the French J.A. Gobineau with his four-volume work *Essay on the Inequality of the Human Races* (1853–55). Gobineau argued that there exists a primordial German race, a *Herrenrasse* (master's race) which is superior to the yellow and Black race. In the 18th and 19th centuries, this concept of race was widespread among biologists, anthropologists, historians and philosophers. It was an ideology well suitable for the legitimation of colonialism and the enslavement of Black people. Another political consequence of race theory were the eugenic measures taken in Germany, Switzerland, Great Britain and the USA in the first part of the 20th century in order to keep 'clean' their own race. Adolf Hitler and his National Socialism has directly tied in with this doctrine and provided it with the most aggressive and inhumane moment; he did so by connecting race theory with the Social Darwinist argument that it is the duty of the German super race to provide more living space (*Lebensraum*) for itself in Eastern Europe and to blight the Jews, the incarnation of everything which is evil. In the latter regard he also built on the ideas of the English author J.S. Chamberlain (1855–1927). His anti-Semitism had grown not the least during a ten-year stay in Vienna, the capital of the multi-national Habsburg Empire, which at the turn of the century was a laboratory of ethnic-national tensions and conflicts (Kann

1993: 395–406; Fest 2004: 314 ff.). Today, racism is formally declared as illegal around the world; in practical life, however, it persists in many subtle forms (Wimmer 1997; Goldberg 2009; Law 2010; Virdee 2010).

A related ideology relevant for inequality is *nationalism* which says that a nation-state should also be characterized by the social and cultural community of its citizens. This concept has already discussed in Chapter 2. For primordial theorists of nationalism (for example Smith 1986), any nation has an ethnic core while constructivists (for example Anderson 1998) see the nation as created by political leaders through deliberate efforts to impose a common culture throughout society. Nationalism plays an ambiguous role as far as equality between ethnic-national sub-groups in a society is concerned. On the one side, it tries to assimilate all groups to the dominant culture; typical for this strategy was France since the Revolution (Lemberg 1964; Schieder 1964). On the other side, it is an instrument which can be used also by ethnic-national minorities within a state to attain political autonomy or even independence, and, thus, to foster better socio-economic development for them. In this regard, nationalism has also contributed to the break-down of the State Socialist systems in Europe around 1989/90. This was the main reason why many leaders of Third World countries after the Second World War based their politics on an ideological fusion of nationalism and Socialism. Nationalism exerts still enormous influence in many parts of the world today. By creating international barriers to mobility, and by encapsulating the rich countries of the North from the poor countries of the South through an invisible 'Iron Curtain', it supports a massive new form of social exclusion (Noiriel 1991; Schöpflin 2000; Wimmer 2002; Haller in print; see also Chapter 2, p. 74). Nation-states which define themselves in primordial terms, that is, the common ancestry of their citizens, may be more inclined to such processes of closure.[14]

How the World Religions Grappled with Inequality

Important strands of ideologies related to equality and inequality were also developed by the teachings of the religious communities and churches, particularly the 'universal' or world religions. They are characterized by the fact – in contrast to people's religions – that the single individual, not the community is the subject of religion. Thereby it became possible that they dispread over vast regions, including people and states with very different ethnic structures and cultural traditions (Mensching 1968: 103ff; Weber 1988a). As far as the stance of these religions toward equality and inequality is concerned, an ever-recurring ambivalence characterizes them. On the one side, many churches were and still are closely allied with the dominant classes; on the other side, they often were also quite astute critics of extreme forms of social injustice and exploitation, poverty and misery. Three such world religions developed consequential positions concerning equality and inequality, Christianity, Hinduism and Islam.

When looking at Christianity, we must discern quite different positions in history. Early Christianity was the religion of a hunted minority of poor people. It was not allied to any kind of social movement and did not aim at changing the worthy sphere (Weber 1986; Troeltsch 1994). Nevertheless, with its emphasis on the fundamental equality of the worth of all people, irrespective of gender, ethnic and national belonging, Christianity has paved the way for the modern idea of equality. Its position, however, changed fundamentally when it was declared the state religion toward the end of the Roman Empire (Mensching 1968: 111; Troeltsch 1994). From them on, and particularly in the Middle Ages, Roman Catholicism became the official societal doctrine for justifying the legal inequality between the estates and the political systems of the monarchies; natural and divine law were used as legitimating ideas. An apex of this inequality-legitimizing character of Catholicism was reached in 1452 when Pope Nicholas V authorized the king of Portugal in a *bulla* to conquer the territories of the 'disbelievers' outside Europe (mainly in Africa) and to subjugate and enslave their peoples. Thus, the idea of the propagation of the Christian faith all over the world also helped to legitimate colonialism and slavery – an institution which caused incredible suffering for millions of people in Africa, America and other parts of the non-European world (Rein 1953). Later on, however, the position of the Catholic Church changed again and it became one of the fighters against the excesses of slave trade from the 17th through the 19th centuries.

In the 19th century Catholic Church began to develop its own social doctrine, as a reaction to the negative consequences of industrialization, but also to the revolutionary doctrines of Socialism and Communism. In

---

14   For the case of Germany see Brubaker 1992; similar processes are at work also in other countries (see Billig 1995).

the encyclical *Rerum Novarum* of Pope Leo XIII (1891) a social doctrine was developed which declared that private property had to be respected and that society should be ordered according to the principles of individuality and personality, solidarity and subsidiarity (Klose 1979; Troeltsch 1994). The principle of personality says that the individual must be the ultimate target of all social and political efforts; he or she, however, is also seen as a social being. The intermediation of both aspects is achieved by the concept of the common welfare (*Gemeinwohl*); the principle of solidarity requires social justice, but no equalization; the principle of subsidiarity commits the individual to care for him- or herself as far as he or she can; societal-political institutions should help only in cases if this is impossible. The overall aim was seen in the 'ent-proletarization' of the proletarians and the establishment of a society ordered by occupational corporations in which the different interest groups of a society would balance out peacefully. Thus, the ideal society aspired to by Catholicism is also a society characterized by significant inequalities of status, of different occupational groupings ordered in a hierarchical way. This view of society has also been taken over later by state Protestantism in Germany and Scandinavia; it induced Martin Luther to condemn the fights of the peasants against serfdom (Troeltsch 1994).

In general, however, the principle of equality has been accepted particularly among the Protestant Christian churches. Here, it was associated closely with an individualist ideology of competition and achievement which considers certain forms of economic inequality not only as justified, but even as necessary. Important was the fact that Luther's reformation did not turn away from the church type of religion but on the contrary strengthened it by establishing national or 'state churches' (Troeltsch 1994). This close association between state and church later on furthered the development of welfare states. It is inherent in the Protestant ethic, especially its Puritan variant, which emphasizes individuals' autonomy, work and diligence, to differentiate between 'deserving' and 'undeserving' poor (Rodgers 1981). Therefore, in this regard, the strict Protestant churches, Calvinism and Puritanism, provided a strong (indirect) legitimation of ethnic discrimination through their emphasis on the principle of the 'elected people of god'. An example were the Boers or Afrikaaners in South Africa descending from French Huguenots and Dutch Calvinists. They legitimated their dominance over the Blacks, later codified in the Apartheid system, not the least by the consciousness to be a people elected by God; this helped them to dissociate themselves not only from the Blacks, but also from the English who opposed racially based separation and exploitation (see also Chapter 11). The most recent example for a people which considers itself as 'chosen by God' are the Jews. Their state was established through massive immigration and a war against the local Arab population in 1948. This war and the whole existence of the state is based on the idea that Palestine is the land promised to the Jews by God (see Chapter 12).

A short remark is in place here also concerning the Orthodox Churches, the third large variant of Christianity, prevalent in East and Southeast Europe. Although these churches have been split off quite early from Catholicism, they share many characteristics with the latter, such as a strong differentiation between the clergy and laypersons, a hierarchically structured church organization and all basic dogmas which have been pronounced before the schism in the year 1054 (Eliade 1983: 62–8). Two significant differences compared to Catholicism are relevant for the attitudes of the Orthodox churches toward equality and inequality. First, there exist relatively independent, 'national' churches, connected closely with the state and culture in which they prevail. Particularly in Russia, the state and church early in history established a 'pact' in order to protect both of them against the ever-threatening invasions of Mongolians and Tatars from the East. As a consequence, the church had to accept the basic Russian institutions: Despotism, bondage, suppression of independent thinking (Noetzel 1970: 11–13). Thus, Orthodox Christianity tends to foster nationalism and to legitimize the existing social hierarchy, distribution of power and inequalities; in this regard, it is comparable to medieval Christianity and present-day Islam. The second characteristic of the Orthodox Church is its focus on elaborated, mystical rites, and its lack of an elaborated religious dogma and doctrines concerning worldly matters (Eliade 1983: 643ff.). Connected with this characteristic is the deep anchorage of the Orthodox Church among the poor and exploited peasants where it helped to establish a kind of 'village communism'. From this perspective, Orthodox Christianity may also have provided a legitimation for revolutionary movements. Overall, however, equality in Orthodox thinking relates only to the members of one's own church (Papp 2006: 205f.) which in practice overlaps with the nation-state.

A religion which also does not challenge inequalities but interprets them as part of a harmonic social and world order is *Hinduism*. In a strict sense, one cannot speak of a religion in the case of Hinduism since it has neither an explicit statement of beliefs nor a clearly defined ecclesiastic institution and church authority. One can call Hinduism an 'ethnic religion' because it exists today only in India (partly also in Bali); as a traditional faith, it is also declining in demographic terms and the secular state has encroached into some of its religions practices (Sharma 1997: 299, 366ff.). Hinduism, however, had a tremendous influence on societal and political development in India, particularly through the caste ideology. This ideology is founded in the interpretation of life and death as a continuous cycle and in the idea of reincarnation after death as a being of lower or higher status, corresponding to one's conduct during life (Eliade 1979; Weber 1988: 1–133; Mensching 1968, 1989; 112–56). The caste system, although not existing any more in institutional-legal terms, still has a significant impact on Indian society and its patterns of class stratification. It says that all people are strictly separated since birth according to their rights and duties and that every man and woman must stick to his position and the related duties throughout his or her life (see Chapter 8 for an extensive discussion). The positive side of the caste system is that all people are integrated into society and its status structure. This applies even for the Untouchables (Dalit) at the lowest end of societal hierarchy; they can be considered as being integrated relatively well and this is certainly the reason why the underprivileged resort less to violence as one could expect given their massive discrimination. Also the teachings of Buddhism which historically was quite influential in India have contributed significant to this situation. Relevant in this regard are the basic Buddhist ideas about the emptiness of the self, the favouring of contemplation and compassion instead of activism, of austereness instead of greed and its view of the world and the universe as an endless stream or whole which also includes suffering (Mensching 1968; Weber 1986, 1988, 1991; Sharma 1997).

Islam is a Third World religion whose impact in many countries of the world was and still is immense, also in regard to the issues of equality and inequality. I have already pointed to the fact that Islamic states were strongly involved in slave capturing and store holding. Today, two general characteristics of Islam are relevant in this regard. First, it is the most mundane or profane among all large world religions. It came into being as an alliance between religion and political power; the new religion was propagated with the help of arms, and the community established by Mohammed in the early 7th century on the Arab Peninsula was a true theocracy, that is, a coherent political and religious community. The integration of Islamic societies is supported by the law of *Sharia* which covers not only religious behaviour, but all spheres of life. Thus, contrary to Christianity and Buddhism, Islam is also a social order. A consequence of it is that, until today, the Western idea of democracy is not accepted fully among most Muslim states (Mensching 1968: 109; Boisard 1982; Mensching 1989; Antes 1982; Enayat 1982; Eliade 1983; Ende and Steinbach 1984; Huntington 1996). Second, Islam created a universal community between all members of the faith, transcending barriers of race, nation and culture. This sense of community and equality, however, soon broke down because Islamic equality relates only to the community of believers and their religious practices but does not include non-Muslims who became very numerous in the course of the expansion of the new Muslim regimes. This stance also legitimated the widespread enslavement of Africans by Muslim states in North Africa, the Near East and South Asia; according to recent estimates, the number of slaves made by Muslims over the centuries was much higher than of those made by Europeans.[15] Still today, foreign workers in Islamic states have few rights and are often subject to exploitation, even if the majority of them are Muslims; they are recruited from Pakistan, Indonesia and other poor Muslim countries. As far as the economic order and the ideas of justice, freedom and equality are concerned, present-day Islam has no elaborate theory. Although extreme forms of wealth concentration and exploitation are condemned, Islam limits itself to prescribing charity to well-off people (Boisard 1982: 58ff.). The Islamic order is said to be opposed to capitalism and germane to Socialism (they both share collectivist thinking), but little is said about actual social and economic problems in connection with inequality and poverty. Both the idea of economic and social inequality and that of a public sphere, important in its own right, are not recognized, although in some countries Islamic political movements have contributed to the alleviation of poverty and social problems (Antes 1982: 73; Enayat 1982: 139; Reissner 1984; Halm 2000; Ruthven 2000). Thus, we can conclude that Islam in theory is opposed to pervasive privilege and inequalities, however in practice it legitimizes them. This is particularly so in regard

---

15   It is estimated that since 1500 about 12 million Africans were enslaved by Europeans, but about 17 million by the Arabs and Muslims (see Flaig 2009; N'Diaye 2010).

to the exceptional position of the dominant elites and the discrimination and exploitation of foreign workers; in Chapter 6, I will denote some of those societies as 'ethnocracies'.

Summary and Outlook

Ethnic stratification is an extremely complex and variegated phenomenon if one looks at the present-day world as a whole. Considering the findings concerning ethnic heterogeneity on the different continents of the world presented in the previous chapter, it is obvious that this heterogeneity must be closely correlated with social and economic inequality. In this chapter, I have argued that we can come to grips with this complexity and the effects of ethnic heterogeneity on inequality only by applying two approaches in parallel: first, a causal-quantitative approach which tries to specify general dimensions and variables and to develop causal models to explain variations in economic inequality in the different countries around the world; second, by using a qualitative-typological approach and the historical-sociological perspective which makes it possible to reduce the variety of systems of ethnic stratification to a few, paradigmatic 'ideal' types. Nine general hypotheses have been developed about the relations between class formation, social stratification and ethnic differentiation (the basic trias in the process of the reproduction of inequality) which serve as bases for both types of analyses. They relate to the general question of the emergence of class societies (a question seldom asked in research on this topic); to the relevance of the ethnic homogeneity of the upper and the lower classes; to the interaction between ethnic differentiation and class stratification; to the relevance of the ethnic homogeneity of the upper and the lower classes for their relative privilege and deprivation; to the effects of a history of ethno-class exploitation (slavery); and, finally, to the role of two context factors, of political institutions (a federal constitution and a welfare state) and of religious and secular ideologies of social and economic equality and inequality. In the next chapter, we will carry out an empirical test of most of the hypotheses developed in this chapter. This shall be done in two forms: first, by a multivariate, quantitative causal analysis which investigates the effects of the single dimensions on economic inequality; second, by a qualitative approach which looks at the effects of different combinations of relevant variables in producing the outcome of an equal or an unequal society. Further tests of the hypotheses developed in this chapter shall be carried out in the second part of the book where we can use individual-level data in several country case studies; here, we can investigate in particular the interaction effects of ethnic membership and class status on income chances.

References

Acham, Karl (1995), *Geschichte und Sozialtheorie. Zur Komplementarität kulturwissenschaftlicher Erkenntnisorientierungen*, Freiburg/München: K. Alber

Adam, Heribert and Kogila Moodley (1977), *Südafrika ohne Apartheid?* Frankfurt/Main: Suhrkamp

Adam, Heribert (2013), 'Siedlungskolonialismus: Ökonomische und ideologische Motive in der Konfliktlösung in Apartheid-Südafrika und Palästina', in Daniela Klimke and Aldo Legnaro, eds, *Politische Ökonomie und Sicherheit*, Weinheim/Basel: Beltz, pp. 62–73

Alber, Jens (1987), *Vom Armenhaus zum Wohlfahrtsstaat. Analysen zur Entwicklung der Sozialversicherung in Westeuropa*, Frankfurt/New York: Campus

Alber, Jens (2001), 'Hat sich der Wohlfahrtsstaat als soziale Ordnung bewährt?' in Karl Ulrich Mayer et al. eds, *Die beste aller Welten? Marktliberalismus versus Wohlfahrtstaat*, Frankfurt/Main: Campus, pp. 59–111

Albert, Gert (2009), 'Weber-Paradigma', in Georg Kneer and Markus Schroer, eds, *Handbuch Soziologische Theorien*, Wiesbaden: VS Verlag für Sozialwissenschaften, pp. 517–54

Albert, Gert (2011), 'Makrosoziologie für Individualisten. Zur Kritik und Verteidigung kollektivistischer Erkenntnisziele', *Österreichische Zeitschrift für Soziologie*, 36: 65–89

Albrow, Martin (1990), *Max Weber's Construction of Social Theory*, Houndsmill, Basingstoke/London: Macmillan

Alesina Alberto et al. (2003), 'Fractionalization', *Journal of Economic Growth*, 8: 155–94

Amin, Samir (1976), *Unequal Development: An Essay on the Social Formations of Peripheral Capitalism*, New York: Monthly Review Press

Anderson, Benedict (1998), *Die Erfindung der Nation*, Berlin: Ullstein (Imagined Communities, 1983)

Antes, Peter (1982), *Ethik und Politik im Islam*, Stuttgart etc.: Kohlhammer

Archibald, Peter W. (1976), 'Face-to-Face: The Alienating Effects of Class, Status and Power Division', *American Sociological Review*, 41: 819–37

Aston, T.H. and C.H.E. Philpin, eds (1987), *The Brenner Debate. Agrarian Class Structure and Economic Development in Pre-Industrial Europe*, Cambridge etc.: Cambridge University Press

Atkinson, Anthony B. (2008), *The Changing Distribution of Earnings in OECD Countries*, New York etc.: Oxford University Press

Bach, Maurizio (1999), *Die Bürokratisierung Europas. Verwaltungseliten, Experten und politische Legitimation in Europa*, Frankfurt/New York: Campus

Baltzell, E. Digby (1958), *Philadelphia Gentlemen. The Making of a National Upper Class*, New York/London: Free Press

Banton, Michael (1960), 'Social distance: A new appreciation', *The Sociological Review*, 8: 169–83

Baronov, David (2000), *The Abolition of Slavery in Brazil. The 'Liberation' of Africans Through the Emancipation of Capital*, Westport, CN/London: Greenwood Press

Beck, Ulrich (1986), *Risikogesellschaft. Auf dem Weg in eine andere Moderne*, Frankfurt am Main: Suhrkamp

Berger, Peter A. (1996), *Individualisierung. Statusunsicherheit und Erfahrungsvielfalt*, Opladen: Westdeutscher Verlag

Bernhard, Michael (n.d.), The Moore thesis: What's left after 1989? Working paper, University of Florida

Billig, Michael (1995), *Banal Nationalism*, London/Thousand Oaks: Sage

Blatter, Joachim K., Frank Janning and Claudius Wagemann (2007), *Qualitative Politikanalyse. Eine Einführung in Forschungsansätze und Methoden*, Wiesbaden: VS Verlag für Sozialwissenschaften

Blau, Peter M. (1977), *Inequality and Heterogeneity. A Primitive Theory of Social Structure*, New York/London: Free Press/Collier Macmillan

Bloom, David E. et al. (2010), 'Realising the Demographic Dividend: Is Africa Any Different?' in Olu Ajakaiye and Germano Mwabu, eds, *Reproductive Health, Economic Growth and Poverty Reduction in Africa*, Nairobi: The University of Nairobi Press, pp. 235–49

Bochmann, Klaus (2001), 'La littérature franco-africaine en quête de sa/ses langue/s. Considérations sociolinguistiques', in Chantal Adobati, ed., *Wenn Ränder Mitte werden*, Vienna: Facultas, pp. 200–212

Boisard, Marcel A. (1982), *Der Humanismus des Islam*, Kaltbrunn: Hecht (first French ed. 1979)

Boix, Carles (2003), *Democracy and Redistribution*, Cambridge: Cambridge University Press

Bonacich, Edna (1972), 'A Theory of Ethnic Antagonism: The Split Labor Market', *American Sociological Review*, 37: 547–59

Bonacich, Edna (1980), 'Class Approaches to Ethnicity and Race', *The Insurgent Sociologist*, 10: 9–23 (reprinted in Malcolm Cross, *The Sociology of Race and Ethnicity* I, Cheltenham/Northampton/MA: E. Elgar)

Borlandi, Massimo et al. eds (2005), *Dictionnaire de la pensée sociologique*, Paris: Quadrige

Bornschier, Volker and Christopher Chase-Dunn (1985), *Transnational Corporations and Underdevelopment*, New York, NY: Praeger

Botton, Alain de (2004), *StatusAngst*, Frankfurt am Main: Fischer

Boudon, Raymond (1974), *Education, Opportunity, and Social Inequality. Changing Prospects in Western Society*, New York: Wiley

Boudon, Raymond (1988), *Ideologie. Geschichte und Kritik eines Begriffs*, Reinbek: Rowohlt (*L'idéologie. L'origine des idées recus*, Paris 1986)

Boudon, Raymond (2000), *Il Senso dei Valori*, Bologna: il Mulino

Bouffartigue, Paul (2004), *Le Retour Des Classes Sociales. Inégalités, Dominations, Conflits*, Paris: La Dispute

Bourdieu, Pierre and Jean-Claude Passeron (1971), *Die Illusion der Chancengleichheit*, Stuttgart: E. Klett

Bourdieu, Pierre (2006), *Die feinen Unterschiede: Kritik der gesellschaftlichen Urteilskraft*, Frankfurt am Main: Suhrkamp

Breen, Richard and David B. Rottman (1995), *Class Stratification. A Comparative Perspective*, New York etc.: Harvester Wheatsheaf

Brenner, Robert (1987a), 'Agrarian Class Structure and Economic Development in Pre-Industrial Europe', in T.H. Aston and C.H.E. Philpin, eds, *The Brenner Debate. Agrarian Class Structure and Economic Development in Pre-Industrial Europe*, Cambridge etc.: Cambridge University Press, pp. 10–63

Brenner, Robert (1987b), 'The Agrarian Roots of European Capitalism', in Aston and Philpin, *The Brenner Debate*, pp. 213–329

Brubaker, Rogers (1992), *Citizenship and Nationhood in France and Germany*, Cambridge, MA etc.: Harvard University Press

Bunge, Mario (1996), *Finding Philosophy in Social Science*, New Haven/London: Yale University Press

Burawoy, Michael (1979), *Manufacturing Consent: Changes in the Labor Process under Monopoly Capitalism*, Chicago: University of Chicago Press

Burstein, Paul (1998), 'Bringing the Public Back In: Should Sociologists Consider the Impact of Public Opinion on Public Policy?' *Social Forces*, 77: 27–62

Cardoso, Fernando H. and E. Faletto (1979), *Dependency and Development in Latin América*, Berkeley, CA: University of California Press

Caselli, Francesco and Wilbur J. Coleman (2006), On the theory of ethnic conflict, National Bureau of Economic Research, Cambridge, MA, Working Paper 12125

Castles, Stephen and Godula Kosack (1973), *Immigrant Workers and the Class Structure in Western Europe*, London: Oxford University Press

Coenen-Huther, Jacques (2004), *Sociologie des élites*, Paris: Armand Colin

Coleman, James W. (1990), *Foundations of Social Theory*, Cambridge, MA/London: Belknap Press

Collins, Randall (1971), 'Functional and Conflict Theories of Educational Stratification', *American Sociological Review*, 36: 1002–19

Cornevin, Marianne (1980), *Apartheid: Power and Historical Falsification*, Paris: UNESCO

Courtois, Stéphane et al. (1998), *Das Schwarzbuch des Kommunismus. Unterdrückung, Verbrechen und Terror*, München: Piper

Cuin, Charles-Henry (2006), 'La démarche nomologique en sociologie (y a-ti-il des lois sociologiques?)' *Swiss Journal of Sociology*, 32: 91–118

Dahl, Robert (1971), *Polyarchy. Participation and Opposition*, New Haven, CT: Yale University Press

Dahrendorf, Ralf (1959), *Class and Class Conflict in Industrial Society*, London: Routledge & Kegan Paul

Dann, Otto (1975), 'Gleichheit', in Otto Brunner et al. eds, *Geschichtliche Grundbegriffe*, Vol. 1, Stuttgart: Klett, pp. 997–1046

Davies, James (1962), 'Toward a theory of revolution', *American Sociological Review*, 27: 5–19

Deutsch, Karl W. (1966*), Nationalism and Social Communication. An Inquiry into the Foundations of Nationality*, Cambridge, MA/London: The MIT Press

Djilas, Milovan (1957), *The New Class. An Analysis of the Communist System*, New York: Praeger

Domhoff, G. William (1967), *Who Rules America?* Englewood Cliffs, NJ: Prentice

Durkheim, Emile (1982 [1895]), *The Rules of Sociological Method*, Canada: Simon & Schuster

Durkheim, Emile (1993 [1893]), *The Division of Labour in Society*, New York: Free Press

Duve, Freimut (1965), *Kap ohne Hoffnung oder die Politik der Apartheid*, Reinbek: Rowohlt

Easterly, William and Ross Levine (1997), 'Africa's Growth Tragedy: Policies and Ethnic Divisions', *The Quarterly Journal of Economics*, 112: 1203–50

Eliade, Mircea (1979), *Geschichte der religiösen Ideen* (vol. II). *Von Gautama Buddha bis zu den Anfängen des Christentums*, Freiburg etc.: Herder (French 1978)

Eliade, Mircea (1983), *Geschichte der religiösen Ideen* (vol. III/1). *Von Mohammed bis zum Beginn der Neuzeit*, Freiburg etc.: Herder (French 1983)

Ellis, Walter (1994), *The Oxbridge Conspiracy. How the Ancient Universities Have Kept their Stranglehold on the Establishment*, London: Michael Joseph

Enayat, Hamid (1982), *Modern Islamic Political Thought*, London/Basingstoke: Macmillan

Ende, Werner and Udo Steinbach, eds (1984), *Der Islam in der Gegenwart*, München: C.H. Beck

Esping-Andersen, Gøsta (1990), *The Three Worlds of Welfare Capitalism*, Cambridge: Polity Press

Esser, Hartmut (1980), *Aspekte der Wanderungssoziologie*, Darmstadt/Neuwied: Luchterhand

Esser, Hartmut (2001), *Integration und ethnische Schichtung (Gutachten), Arbeitspapier Nr. 40*, Mannheimer Zentrum für Europäische Sozialforschung

Etzioni-Halevy, Eva (1993), *The Elite Connection. Problems and Potential of Western Democracy*, Cambridge: Polity Press

Fearon, James D. (2003), 'Ethnic and cultural diversity by country', *Journal of Economic Growth*, 8: 195–222

Fest, Joachim (2004), *Hitler. Eine Biographie*, Berlin: Ullstein

Fetscher, Iring, ed. (1973), *Der Marxismus. Seine Geschichte in Dokumenten*, München: R. Pipe

Flaig, Egon (2009), *Weltgeschichte der Sklaverei*, München: C.H. Beck

Francis, Emerich K. (1965), *Ethnos und Demos. Soziologische Beiträge zur Volkstheorie*, Berlin: Duncker & Humblot

Frankema, Ewout (2008), *Wage inequality in Twentieth Century Latin America: A comparative perspective*, Groningen Growth and Development Centre, University of Groningen

Frankema, Ewout (2009a), *Has Latin America Always Been Unequal? A Comparative Study of Asset and Income Inequality in the Long Twentieth Century*, Boston/Leiden: Brill

Frankema, Ewout (2009b) 'The Colonial Origins of Inequality: Exploring the Causes and Consequences of Land Distribution', in Klasen, S. and Nowak Lehman F., *Poverty, Inequality and Policy in Latin America*, Cambridge MA: MIT Press, pp. 19–45

Frankema, Ewout (2010) 'The Colonial Roots of Land Distribution: Geography, Factor Endowments or Institutions?' *Economic History Review*, 63: 418–51

Fraser, Nancy and Axel Honneth (2003), *Umverteilung oder Anerkennung? Eine politisch-philosophische Kontroverse*, Frankfurt: Suhrkamp

Freeman, Richard B. and Remco H. Oostendorp (2002), 'Wages Around the World: Pay across Occupations and Countries', in Richard Freeman, eds *Inequality Around the World*, New York: Palgrave pp. 5–37

Geertz, Clifford (1973), 'Thick Description: Toward an Interpretive Theory of Culture', in C. Geertz, *In The Interpretation of Cultures: Selected Essays*, New York: Basic Books, pp. 3–32

Geiger, Theodor (1949), *Die Klassengesellschaft im Schmelztiegel*, Köln/Hagen: G. Kiepenheuer

Geissler, Rainer, ed. (1994), *Soziale Schichtung und Lebenschancen in Deutschland*, Stuttgart: Enke Verlag

Gerhards, Jürgen (1988), *Soziologie der Emotionen: Fragestellungen, Systematik und Perspektiven*, Weinheim etc.: Juventa Verlag

Giddens, Anthony (1973), *The Class Structure of the Advanced Societies*, London: Hutchinson

Glaser, Barney G. and Anselm L. Strauss (1979), *The Discovery of Grounded Theory: Strategies for Qualitative Research*, Chicago: Aldine

Goldberg, David T. (2009), *The Threat of Race. Reflections on Racial Neoliberalism*, Malden, MA: Wiley-Blackwell

Goldthorpe, John H. and Gordon Marshall (1992), 'The promising future of class analysis: A response to recent critiques', *Sociology*, 26: 381–400

Goldthorpe, John H. (1983), The end of convergence. Corporatist and dualist tendencies in modern western societies, Paper presented at the SSRC Seminar on Labour Markets, Manchester

Goldthorpe, John H. (2000), *On Sociology. Numbers, Narratives, and the Integration of Research and Theory*, Oxford: Oxford University Press

Goldthorpe, John H., C. Llweellyn and C. Payne (1987), *Social Mobility and Class Structure In Modern Britain*, Oxford: Clarendon Press

Graubard, Stephen R. (1973), 'Democracy', in Philip L. Wiener, ed., *Dictionary of the History of Ideas*, vol.1, New York: Charles Scribner's Sons, pp. 652–67

Groethuysen, Bernhard (1989), *Philosophie der Französischen Revolution*, Frankfurt/New York: Campus

Grove, D. John (1979), 'A Partial Test of the Ethnic Equalization Hypothesis: A Cross-national Study', in D. John Grove, *Global Inequality: Political and Socioeconomic Perspectives*, Boulder, CO: Westview Press, pp. 135–62

Gugenberger, Eva (2001), 'Von Quispe zu Vargas. Identitätskonflikt am Beispiel peruanischer Familiennamen', in Adobati et al., *Wenn Ränder Mitte werden*, pp. 389–401

Gurr, Ted Robert (1993), *Minorities at Risk: A Global View of Ethnopolitical Conflicts*, Washington, DC: United States Institute of Peace Press

Hagelstange, Thomas (1988), *Die Entwicklung von Klassenstrukturen in der E.G. und in Nordamerika*, Frankfurt/New York: Campus

Haller, Max (1981), 'Marriage, Women and Social Stratification. A Theoretical Critique', *American Journal of Sociology*, 86: 766–95

Haller, Max (1983), *Theorie der Klassenbildung und sozialen Schichtung*, Frankfurt/New York: Campus

Haller, Max (1986), 'Sozialstruktur und Schichtungshierarchie im Wohlfahrtsstaat. Zur Aktualität des vertikalen Paradigmas der Ungleichheitsforschung', *Zeitschrift für Soziologie*, 15: 167–87

Haller, Max (1989), *Klassenstrukturen und Mobilität in fortgeschrittenen Gesellschaften. Eine vergleichende Analyse der Bundesrepublik Deutschland, Österreichs, Frankreichs und der Vereinigten Staaten von Amerika*, Frankfurt/New York: Campus

Haller, Max (1996a), *Identität und Nationalstolz der Österreicher*, Wien/Köln/Weimar: Böhlau

Haller, Max (1996b), 'The dissolution and building of new nations as strategy and process between elites and people. Lessons from historical European and recent Yugoslav experience', *International Review of Sociology*, 6: 231–47

Haller, Max (2003), *Soziologische Theorie im systematisch-kritischen Vergleich*, Opladen: Leske & Budrich (2nd ed.)

Haller, Max (2008b), *European Integration as an Elite Process. The Failure of a Dream?* New York/London: Routledge

Haller, Max (2014), 'Die Ökonomie – Natur- oder Sozialwissenschaft? Wissenschaftstheoretische und wissenssoziologische Überlegungen zu einer alten Kontroverse", in Dieter Bögenhold, ed., *Soziologie des Wirtschaftlichen. Alte und neue Fragen*, Wiesbaden: Springer, pp. 31–65

Haller, Max, Bogdan Mach and Heinrich Zwicky (1995), 'Egalitarismus und Antiegalitarismus zwischen gesellschaftlichen Interessen und kulturellen Leitbildern. Ergebnisse eines internationalen Vergleichs', in Hans-Peter Müller and Bernd Wegener, eds, *Soziale Ungleichheit und soziale Gerechtigkeit*, Opladen: Leske + Budrich, pp. 221–64

Halm, Heinz (2000), *Der Islam. Geschichte und Gegenwart*, München: C.H. Beck

Han, Petrus (2006), *Theorien zur internationalen Migration. Ausgewählte interdisziplinäre Migrationstheorien und deren zentralen Aussagen*, Stuttgart: Lucius & Lucius

Hartmann, Michael (2007), *Eliten und Macht in Europa*, Frankfurt/New York: Campus

Hempel, Carl G. (1965), *Aspects of scientific explanation, and other essays in the philosophy of science*, New York: Free Press

Hilferding, Rudolf (1986 [1919]), *Das Finanzkapital*, Frankfurt: Europäische Verlagsanstalt

Hoffmann-Nowotny, Hans-Joachim (1973), *Soziologie des Fremdarbeiterproblems*, Stuttgart: Enke

Hradil, Stefan (2001), *Soziale Ungleichheit in Deutschland*, Wiesbaden: VS Verlag

Hughes, Marion R. (1997), 'Sample selection bias in analyses of the political democracy and income inequality relationship', *Social Forces*, 75: 1101–16

Huntington, Samuel P. (1996), *The Clash of Civilizations and the Remaking of World Order*, New York: Simon & Schuster

Kann, Robert A. (1993), *Geschichte des Habsburgerreiches 1526–1918*, Wien/Köln/Weimar: Böhlau (Engl. ed. 1980)

Kelsen, Hans (1965), *Sozialismus und Staat. Eine Untersuchung der politischen Theorie des Marxismus*, Wien: Verlag der Wiener Volksbuchhandlung

Kemper, Theodore D. and Randall Collins (1990), 'Dimensions of microinteraction', *American Journal of Sociology*, 96: 32–68

Kerbo, Harold R. (2006), *World Poverty. Global Inequality and the Modern World System*, Boston etc.: McGraw-Hill

Kerbo, Harold R. (2012), *Social Stratification and Inequality. Class Conflict in Historical, Comparative, and Global Perspective*, New York: McGraw Hill

Klose, Alfred (1979), *Die katholische Soziallehre. Ihr Anspruch, ihre Aktualität*, Graz etc.: Styria

Korpi, Walter (1983), *The Democratic Class Struggle*, London: Routledge & Kegan Paul

Kößler, Reinhart and Tilman Schiel (1995), *Nationalstaat und Ethnizität*, Frankfurt: IKO-Verlag für interkulturelle Kommunikation

Kreckel, Reinhard (1989), 'Ethnische Differenzierung und ,moderne' Gesellschaft', *Zeitschrift für Soziologie*, 18: 162–7

Kreckel, Reinhard (1992), *Politische Soziologie der sozialen Ungleichheit*, Frankfurt/New York: Campus

Krugman, Paul (2012), *Vergesst die Krise! Warum wir jetzt Geld ausgeben müssen*, Frankfurt: Campus

Kuhnle, Stein (2004), *The developmental welfare state in Scandinavia: Lessons for the developing world*, Geneva: United Nations Research Institute for Social Development

Lane, David S. (1996), *The Rise and Fall of State Socialism: Industrial Society and the Socialist State*, Cambridge: Polity Press

Law, Ian (2010), *Racism and Ethnicity. Gobal Debates, Dilemmas, Directions*, Harlow etc.: Pearson

Lemberg, Eugen (1964), *Nationalismus*, 2 vols, Reinbek: Rowohlt

Lenin, W.I. (1951 [1918]), *Staat und Revolution*, Berlin: Dietz

Lenski, Gerhard (1973 [1966]), *Macht und Privileg*, Frankfurt am Main: Suhrkamp

Lepsius, Rainer M. (1988), *Interessen, Ideen und Institutionen*, Opladen: Westdeutscher Verlag

Lewada, Juri (1992), *Die Sowjetmenschen 1989–1991. Soziogramm eines Zerfalls*, Berlin: Argon

Lipset, Seymour Martin (1979), *The First New Nation. The United States in Historical and Comparative Perspective*, New York: Norton

Lorenz, Chris (1997), *Konstruktion der Vergangenheit. Eine Einführung in die Geschichtstheorie*, Köln etc.: Böhlau

Majer, Diemut (1995), *Der lange Weg zu Freiheit und Gleichheit*, Wien: WUV-Universitätsverlag

Mamdani, Mahmood (2001), *When Victims Become Killers. Colonialism, Nativism, and the Genocide in Rwanda*, Princeton, NJ: Princeton University Press

Mann, Michael (2007), *Die dunkle Seite der Demokratie. Eine Theorie der ethnischen Säuberung*, Hamburg: Hamburger edition (The Dark Side of Democracy, New York 2005)

Mannheim, Karl (1970), *Wissenssoziologie*, Neuwied/Berlin: Luchterhand

Marshall, Thomas H. (1950), *Citizenship and Social Class and other Essays*, Cambridge: Cambridge University Press

Marwick, Arthur (1980), *Class. Image and Reality in Britain, France, and the USA since 1930*, New York: Oxford University Press

Maurer, Andrea and Michael Schmid, eds (2010), *Erklärende Soziologie*, Wiesbaden: VS Verlag

McAll, Christopher (1990), *Class, Ethnicity, and Social Inequality*, Montreal etc.: McGill-Queen's University Press

McNall, Scott G. et al. eds (1991), *Bringing Class Back In. Contemporary and Historical Perspectives*, Boulder etc.: Westview Press

Mensching, Gustav (1968), *Soziologie der Religion*, Bonn: L. Röhrscheid Verlag

Mensching, Gustav (1989), *Die Weltreligionen*, Wiesbaden: VMA-Verlag

Miliband, Ralph (1983), *Class Power and State Power*, London: Verso

Mills, C. Wright (1959), *The Power Elite*, London: Oxford University Press

Mohanty, B. B. (2001), 'Land distribution among Scheduled Castes and Tribes', *Economic and Political Weekly*, 36: 3857–68

Montesquieu, Baron de (2002 [1748]), *The Spirit of Laws*, Berlin: Prometheus Books

Moore, Barrington (1978), *Injustice. The Social Bases of Obedience and Revolt*, White Plains, NY: M.E. Sharpe

Moore, Barrington, Jr (1993), *Social origins of dictatorship and democracy: Lord and peasant in the making of the modern world*, Boston: Beacon Press

Mosca, Gaetano (1950 [1896]), *Die herrschende Klasse*, Bern: Francke

Müller, Walter and Irene Kogan (2011), 'Education', in Stefan Immerfall and Göran Therborn, eds, *Handbook of European Societies*, Heidelberg: Springer, pp. 217–89

Müller, Walter and Wolfgang Karle (1993), 'Social Selection in Educational Systems in Europe', *European Sociological Review*, 9: 1–22

Müller, Walter ed. (1999*)*, *Soziale Ungleichheit. Neue Befunde zu Strukturen, Bewußtsein und Politik*, Opladen: Leske + Budrich

Müller Kmet, Bernadette. 2012. 'A Success Story of Creating National Identity in Tanzania: The Vision of Julius Kambarage Nyerere'. In: Crossing Borders, Shifting Boundaries. National and Transitional Identities in Europe and Beyond, Festschrift for Max Haller, Franz Höllinger and Markus Hadler, eds. Frankfurt/New York: Campus, pp. 125–148.

Murphy, Raymond (1988), *Social Closure. The Theory of Monopolization and Exclusion*, Oxford: Clarendon Press

N'Diaye, Tidiane (2010), *Der verschleierte Völkermord. Die Geschichte des muslimischen Sklavenhandels in Afrika*, Reinbek: Rowohlt (French ed. Paris 2008)

Noetzel, Karl (1970), *Die Grundlagen des geistigen Russlands*, Hildesheim/New York: G. Olms Verlag

Noiriel, Gérard (1991), *La tyrannie du national: Le droit d'asile en Europe, 1793–1993*, Paris: Calmann-Lévy

Nollmann, Gerd and Hermann Strasser (2007), 'The twofold class concept: Traditional limitations and new perspectives of class research', *Canadian Journal of Sociology*, 32: 371–98

Offe, Claus and Helmut Wiesenthal (1980), 'Two logics of collective action. Theoretical notes on social class and organizational form', *Political Power and Social Theory*, 1: 67–115

Offe, Claus (1972), *Strukturprobleme des kapitalistischen Staates. Aufsätze zur politischen Soziologie*, Frankfurt: Suhrkamp

Ondetti, Gabriel (2007), 'An ambivalent legacy. Cardoso and land reform', *Latin American Perspectives*, 34: 9–25

Ossowski, Stanislaw (1972), *Die Klassenstruktur im sozialen Bewußtsein*, Neuwied: Luchterhand (1st Polish ed. 1957)

Page, Jeffrey (1975), *Agrarian Revolution. Social Movements and Export Agriculture in the Underdeveloped World*, New York: Free Press

Page, John (1994), 'The East Asian Miracle: Four lessons for development policy', *NBER Macroeconomics Annual*, 9: 219–82

Pakulski, Jan and Malcom Waters (1996), *The Death of Class*, London et al.: Sage

Papp, Tibor (2006), *Die Grundprinzipien der christlichen Soziallehre in der westlichen und östlichen Theologie*, Dissertation an der Theologischen Fakultät, Universität Graz

Parkin, Frank (1979), *Marxism and Class Theory: A Bourgeois Critique*, London: Tavistock

Pickett, Kate and Richard Wilkinson (2009), *Gleichheit ist Glück. Warum gerechte Gesellschaften für alle besser sind*, Berlin: Haffmans & Tolkemitt

Popper, Karl R. (1968), *The Logic of Scientific Discovery*, New York: Harper & Row

Popper, Karl. R. (1973), *Objektive Erkenntnis. Ein evolutionärer Entwurf*, Hamburg: Hoffmann und Campe

Poulantzas, Nicos (1974), *Politische Macht und gesellschaftliche Klassen*, Frankfurt: Athenäum Fischer Taschenbuch Verlag

Powell, G. Bingham, Jr (1982), *Contemporary Democracies: Participation, Stability and Violence*, Cambridge: Harward University Press

Putnam, Robert D. (1976), *The Comparative Study of Political Elites*, Englewood Cliffs, NJ: Prentice-Hall

Ragin, Charles (1989), *The Comparative Method. Moving beyond Qualitative and Quantitative Strategies*, Berkeley, CA etc.: University of California Press

Rein, Adolf (1953), *Über die Bedeutung der überseeischen Ausdehnung für das europäische Staatensystem*, Darmstadt: Wissenschaftliche Buchgesellschaft

Reinhart, Carmen M. and Kenneth S. Rogoff (2009), *This Time is Different: Eight Centuries of Financial Folly*, Princeton, NJ: Princeton University Press

Reissner, Johannes (1984), 'Die innerislamische Diskussion zur modernen Wirtschafts- und Sozialordnung', in Werner Ende and Udo Steinbach, eds, *Der Islam in der Gegenwart*, München: C.H.Beck, pp. 155–69

Rodgers, James D. (1981), 'Zur Erklärung der Einkommensumverteilung', in Frank Klanberg and Hans-Jürgen Krupp, eds, *Einkommensverteilung*, Königstein/Ts: Athenäum, pp. 225–57

Rodrik, Dani and Arvind Subramanian (2003), 'The Primacy of Institutions. And what this does and does not mean', *Finance & Development*, 40: 31–4

Rousseau, Jean-Jacques (1967 [1754]), 'Abhandlung über den Ursprung und die Grundlagen der Ungleichheit unter den Menschen', in Jean-Jacques Rousseau, *Preisschriften und Erziehungsplan*, Bad Heilbrunn: Verlag J. Klinkhardt, pp. 47–137

Rubinson, Richard and Dan Quinlan (1977), 'Democracy and Social Inequality: A Reanalysis', *American Sociological Review*, 42: 611–23

Russett, Bruce (1979), 'Estimating the Marginal Utility of Global Income Transfers', in D. John Grove, ed., *Global Inequality, Political and Socioeconomic Perspectives,* Boulder, Col.: Westview Press, pp. 59–76

Ruthven, Malise (2000), *Islam: A Very Short Introduction*, Oxford: Oxford University Press

Rwamapfa, Jean Baptiste (1999), *Das Scheitern der Nationalstaatsbildung und der ethnischen Integration im zentralafrikanischen Raum*, Diploma Thesis, Department of Sociology, University Graz

Scheff, Thomas J. (1990), *Microsociology. Discourse, Emotion, and Social Structure*, Chicago etc.: University of Chicago Press

Schieder, Theodor (1964), *Der Nationalstaat in Europa als historisches Phänomen*, Opladen: Westdeutscher Verlag

Schlenker-Fischer, Andrea (2009), *Demokratische Gemeinschaft trotz ethnischer Differenz. Theorien, Institutionen und soziale Dynamiken*, Wiesbaden: VS Verlag

Schluchter, Wolfgang (2006), *Grundlegungen der Soziologie. Eine Theoriegeschichte in systematischer Absicht*, Vol. I, Tübingen: Mohr Siebeck

Schmitt, Madeline H. (1972), 'Near and Far: A Re-Formulation of the Social Distance Concept', *Sociology & Social Research*, 57: 85–97

Schoeck, Helmut (1966), *Der Neid und die Gesellschaft*, Freiburg/Basel/Wien: Herder

Schöpflin, George (2000), *Nations Identity Power. The New Politics of Europe*, London: Hurst & Company

Schumpeter, Joseph (1946), *Kapitalismus, Sozialismus und Demokratie*, Bern: Verlag A. Francke

Schwartz, Barry (1981), *Vertical Classification. A Study in Structuralism and the Sociology of Knowledge*, Chicago/London: University of Chicago Press

Seibel, Hans D. (1980), *Struktur und Entwicklung der Gesellschaft*, Stuttgart et al.: Kohlhammer

Sennet, Richard and Jonathan Cobb (1972), *The Hidden Injuries of Class*, New York: Vintage Books

Sharma, Arvind, ed. (1997), *Innenansichten der großen Religionen*, Frankfurt: Fischer Taschenbuch Verlag (Amer. ed. San Francisco 1993)

Shibutani, Tamotsu and Kian M. Kwan (1965), *Ethnic Stratification. A Comparative Approach*, New York: Macmillan/London: Collier-Macmillan

Shore, Cris (2000), *Building Europe. The Cultural Politics of European Integration*, London/New York: Routledge

Sina, Radha (1984), *Landlessness – A Growing Problem*, Rome: FAO (Food and Agricultural Organization of the United Nations)

Singh, Baldave (1979), 'Measuring Cross-national Ethnic and Racial Inequality: Alternative Perspectives', in Grove, ed., *Global Inequality*, pp. 163–79

Smith, Anthony D. (1986), *The Ethnic Origins of Nations*, Oxford etc.: Blackwell

Smith, Dennis (1990), 'Organization and class: Burawoy in Birmingham', in Stewart R. Clegg, ed., *Organization Theory and Class Analysis*, Berlin/New York: Walter de Gruyter, pp. 367–87

Spree, Reinhard (2011), 'Ein Konzept zur Analyse sozialer Ungleichheit', *Texte zur Sozial- und Wirtschaftsgeschichte* (available online: http://rspree.wordpress.com/2011/05/15/ein-konzept-zur-analyse-sozialer-ungleichheit/)

Stavenhagen, Rodolpho (1996), *Ethnic Conflicts and the Nation-State*, New York: St Martin's Press

Stephens, John D. (1979), *The Transition from Capitalism to Socialism*, London/Basingstoke: Macmillan

Stryker, Sheldon (1980), *Symbolic interactionism. A social structural version*, Menlo Park, CA: Benjamin Cummings

Svalastoga, Kaare (1959), *Prestige, Class and Mobility*, Copenhagen: Glydendal

Tausch Arno & Fred Prager (1993), *Towards a Socio-Liberal Theory of World Development*, Basingstoke/New York: Macmillan/St Martin's Press

Tocqueville, Alexis de (1945 [1835]), *Democracy in America*, New York: Vintage Books (here quoted after the German ed. 1976)

Troeltsch, Ernst (1994 [1912]), *Die Soziallehren der christlichen Kirchen und Gruppen*, 2 vols, Stuttgart: Mohr

Van den Berghe, Pierre L. (1960), 'Distance Mechanisms of Stratification', *Sociology and Social Research*, 44: 155–64

Van den Berghe, Pierre L. (1970), 'Race, class, and ethnicity in South Africa', in Arthur Tuden and Leonard Ploticov, eds, *Social Stratification in Africa*, New York/London: Free Press/Collier-Macmillan, pp. 345–71

Van den Berghe, Pierre L. (1981), *The Ethnic Phenomenon*, New York etc.: Praeger

Virdee, Satnam (2010), 'Racism, class and the dialectics of social transformation', in Patricia Hill Collins and John Solomos, eds, *The Sage Handbook of Race and Ethnic Studies*, Los Angeles, etc.: Sage, pp. 135–65

Vogler, Carolyn (1985), *The Nation-State. The Neglected Dimension of Class*, Aldershot/Hamps.: Gower

Voslensky, Michail (1980), *Nomenklatura*, Wien/Innsbruck: F. Molden

Waldmann, Peter (1977), *Strategien politischer Gewalt*, Stuttgart etc.: Kohlhammer

Wallerstein, Immanuel (1975); 'Class-formation in the capitalist world-economy', *Politics and Society*, 5: 367–75

Weber, Max (1964/I+II), *Wirtschaft und Gesellschaft*, 2 vols, Köln/Berlin: Kiepenheuer & Witsch

Weber, Max (1973a [1896]), 'Die sozialen Gründe des Untergangs der antiken Kultur', in M. Weber, *Soziologie*, pp. 1–26

Weber, Max (1973b), *Soziologie. Weltgeschichtliche Analysen. Politik*, Stuttgart: A. Kröner

Weber, Max (1986), *Gesammelte Aufsätze zur Religionssoziologie I*, Tübingen: J.C.B. Moh

Weber, Max (1988), *Gesammelte Aufsätze zur Religionssoziologie II. (Hinduismus und Buddhismus)*, Tübingen: J.C.B. Mohr

Weber, Max (1991 [1915–20]), *Die Wirtschaftsethik der Weltreligionen. Konfuzianismus und Taoismus*, Tübingen: Mohr

Westhues, Kenneth (1980), 'Class and organization as paradigms in social science', in Amita Etzioni and Edward W. Lehman, eds, *Organizations*, New York etc.: Holt, Reinhart and Winston, pp. 74–84

Wiley, Norbert F. (1970), 'The ethnic mobility trap and stratification theory', in Peter I. Rose, ed., *The Study of Society*, New York/Toronto: J. Wiley, pp. 397–408

Wimmer, Andreas (1997), 'Explaining Xenophobia and Racism: A Critical Review of Current Research Approaches', *Ethnic and Racial Studies*, 20: 17–41 (reprinted in Cross, *The Sociology of Race and Ethnicity II*)

Wimmer, Andreas (2002), *Nationalist Exclusion and Ethnic Conflict: Shadows of Modernity*, Cambridge/New York: Cambridge University Press

Wimmer, Andreas et al. eds (2004), *Facing Ethnic Conflicts: Toward a New Realism*, Lanham, MD: Rowman & Littlefield

World Bank (2007), *World Development Report 2008: Agriculture for Development*, Washington, DC: The World Bank

Wright, Erik O. (1978), *Class, Crisis, and the State*, London: New Left Books

Wright, Erik O. (1985), *Classes*, London: Verso

Yinger, Milton (1994), *Ethnicity: Source of Strength? Source of Conflict?* Albany, NY: State University of New York Press

Ziltener, Patrick and Hans-Peter Müller (2007), 'The weight of the past. Traditional agriculture, socio-political differentiation and modern development in Africa and Asia: A cross-national analysis', *International Journal of Comparative Sociology*, 48: 371–415

Ziltener, Patrick (2013), *Regionale Integration in Ostasien. Eine Untersuchung der historischen und gegenwärtigen Interaktionsweisen einer Weltregion*, Wiesbaden: Springer

Chapter 4

Income Inequality as a Result of Ethnic Heterogeneity and Ethno-class Exploitation. Macro-level Quantitative and Qualitative Analyses

Max Haller, Anja Eder and Erwin Stolz

The main thesis of this book is that present-day ethnic heterogeneity and a history of ethno-class exploitation, that is, slavery in a society leads to higher economic inequality. In this chapter, this thesis shall be submitted to empirical tests in two forms. The first is a multivariate statistical analysis, investigating the effect of ethnic heterogeneity as a causal factor determining income inequality. For this aim, a new aggregate quantitative dataset has been constructed, containing about 150 countries with about two dozen variables;[1] robust multivariate regression is the method of analysis applied. Three indicators for economic inequality – our main dependent variable – are used: The Gini index of economic inequality, and the relative deprivation and privilege of the lowest 40 per cent and the highest 10 per cent of income receivers. For the main independent dimension, ethnic heterogeneity, four sub-indices have been constructed and used. The first three were an index of ethnic heterogeneity, of ethnic fractionalization and of ethnic conflict. For all of them, we could rely on prior studies and indices; in some cases, they were updated using recent data collections. The new idea developed in this work – that historical patterns of ethnic domination and subjugation, that is, of slavery, are still decisive for economic inequality today – made it necessary to develop a completely new fourth index, 'historical ethno-class exploitation'.

In order to make sure that ethnic heterogeneity and ethnic domination and subjugation are in fact decisive factors for economic inequality today, additional independent variables have been controlled for. One set of them refers to socio-economic characteristics of the countries compared; most of them have been postulated also by economists as being relevant for income distribution. They include population size and growth, level of socio-economic development and land distribution. The other set of independent variables refers to indicators of the political system, including the age of a state, its democratic character and constitution (centralistic or federal) and the level of welfare spending.

The results of the analysis clearly show that ethnic heterogeneity and in particular historical ethno-class exploitation have significant effects on income inequality today. They also show, however, that linear regression models are only one way to investigate these effects. The applicability and explanatory power of this variable-based methodological approach is restricted by several facts: some of the independent variables are highly correlated among themselves, so that we cannot disentangle their specific single explanatory effects; several relations are not linear and effects may be relevant only in sub-groups of countries. We need, therefore, also another method to explain income inequality, a method which in particular takes into consideration the fact there exist significant interaction effects between the several factors. Such a method, qualitative comparative analysis (QCA) or Fuzzy Set Analysis (FSA), has been developed by Charles Ragin and others in recent times. The method allows to examine and to test hypotheses about the effects of different combinations of independent and intervening variables on a certain outcome variable. Thus, it is possible to make multiple comparisons of configurations. It seems that this method is very well suited to the problems analysed in this book. We have about 150 cases which shall be reduced to about a dozen or so different constellations of ethnic structures which all exert specific effects on income distribution. This method, thus, also constitutes a bridge between the variable-centred, quantitative analysis in this chapter and the case-based qualitative studies in Part II of the book.

---

1   Due to missing errors in some variables, this number reduces to 123 in some analyses.

Two clarifications have to be made right at the beginning of the quantitative-statistical analysis in the first part of this chapter. First, when speaking about causal effects, we do not think of deterministic, but only of probabilistic causality, as outlined in Chapter 3.[2] Thus, we postulate that ethnic heterogeneity will increase income inequality in most, but not in all cases. Second, the design of this analysis is restricted insofar as we investigate only a cross-section of countries but no time series. Changes in ethnic composition which have taken place in recent times and related changes in income distribution will not be investigated in a systematic manner. The use of cross-section data is a characteristic of much comparative social and political research on the aggregate level. There are many methodological critiques addressed to this method which are sound in several regards. However, we think – as many other researchers do – that it can well be used as a first approximation for the test of hypotheses; this is particularly true for cases such as ours, where we can see some very clear effects. We know, in addition, that changes in income inequality over time are much less conspicuous than the differences between countries (Li et al. 1998). In addition, we can balance out this restriction insofar as we will also look at data on changes in income distribution for specific countries or groups of countries over a considerable number of years or decades in the second part of this book. For these countries, we shall investigate if changes in income distribution in recent times have been associated with corresponding changes in ethnic differentiation.

General Question and Hypotheses

The general hypotheses proposed in this book, as outlined in Chapters 2 and 3, are the following: (1) societies which are heterogeneous in ethnic terms exhibit a higher level of income inequality than societies which are ethnically homogeneous; (2) societies in which the relations between ethnic groups have come about in more or less peaceful ways are more equal in economic terms today than those where one ethnic group subjugated and dominated others in earlier times. An extreme and globally widespread form of such exploitation was slavery. Thus, our hypothesis is that former 'slave holding societies' are much more unequal today than societies which did not know this form of exploitation. The empirical findings will show that this hypothesis contributes significantly to the explanation of the exceptionally high levels of economic inequality in Latin America and Sub-Saharan Africa. This latter fact has been noted also by economists. Some of them considered it an unexplained fact (De Gregorio and Lee 2002) while others explained it as general effects of colonialism (Acemoglu et al. 2001; Angeles 2005).

Our hypotheses have been specified in several regards. One aspect concerned the relation between ethnic differentiation and class stratification. It was argued that inequality will be highest if these two processes coincide, that is, if a consolidated ethnic stratification has emerged in a country. This hypothesis cannot be tested directly in this chapter because we do not have the relevant individual-level data for most of the countries compared. An empirical test of this hypothesis will be carried out, however, in Part II of this book when we focus on specific types of societies.

The aforementioned general hypotheses have been specified, secondly, in regard to several intervening variables, relating to the social structure and the political system of the different countries. In regard to the first, the effects of the demographic structure (population size and growth), the level of socio-economic development and inequality of land distribution are considered. We expect that income inequality will be higher in countries with a large and strongly growing population, in less developed societies and in societies with an unequal land distribution. In regard to the political system, four aspects have been considered: the age of a state, its democratic tradition, a federal or centralistic constitution and the level of welfare spending. The following theses have been proposed: inequality will be lower in state societies which have a democratic and a federal constitution and strong welfare states. In addition, we assume that older states which had a longer time to establish elements of a common culture among their citizens will exhibit a lower degree of inequality. In general, however, it is expected that the effects of these social-structural and political variables will not eliminate the effects of ethnic heterogeneity, discrimination and exploitation. Rather they might interact with these factors and either increase or decrease overall economic inequality. Such interaction effects will be investigated in the second part of the empirical analysis.

---

2   This shall be different in the second kind of analysis, the QCA or Fuzzy Set Analysis.

Let us now look in detail at our principal independent and intervening variables and their proposed effects on economic inequality.

The Main Independent Factors: Ethnic Differentiation and Stratification

From the methodological point of view, there exists a difficult situation in regard to the measurement of the central independent variable, the kind and degree of ethnic stratification within heterogeneous societies. This is a very complex issue which could only be grasped by detailed analyses of original data from each country, by looking at the ethnic composition of the different social strata. In addition, also the subjective aspect of ethnic differentiation would have to be considered, that is, the degree to which statistically defined ethnic groups are aware of their ethnicity and feel that ethnic group membership is significant for their own consciousness. To do such an analysis for a large number of countries is impossible here, firstly, because the data are not available for most of them and, secondly, because it would outrun the possibilities of this study by far (see also Alesina et al. 2003, 2005, 2012; Fearon 2003; Laitin and Posner 2001; Driessen 2008; Patsiurko et al. 2011). We can only take some first steps in such an analysis for a few countries, representing paradigmatic types of ethnic stratification systems (in Part II of this book).

However, there are several aspects of ethnic differentiation which we can grasp for a large number of countries with quantitative indicators. We have defined and measured ethnic differentiation in four different dimensions. The first is the number and size of distinguishable ethnic categories and groups existing in a country, that is overall *ethnic heterogeneity*. Ethnic groups in this sense are defined in one or all of the three dimensions in terms of bio-social ethnicity ('race'), and in terms of linguistic and religious commonality. A detailed description of the construction of this variable will be given in the next section. Overall, we expect that income inequality will be higher in ethnically differentiated societies.

The second dimension of ethnic differentiation used in the following analysis is the degree of *ethnic fractionalization*. Ethnic heterogeneity of a country may come in very different and complex forms, depending on the number and size and the socio-cultural and political power of the different groups. In some societies, one group (which in numerical terms can be a majority but in social and political terms a minority, as in South Africa during Apartheid) dominates one or all others; in others there exist a few large ethnic groups, some of which may be dominant (as in the cases of Ethiopia, Kenya and Nigeria); and yet in other societies, there may exist many small and medium-sized ethnic groups, none of which dominates the others (as in the case of Tanzania or in multi-ethnic nations like India). This dimension of ethnic fractionalization has been considered also in prior studies on which we will rely in our own analysis (Alesina et al. 2003; Fearon 2003; Driessen 2008; Patsiurko et al. 2011). The effects of ethnic fractionalization on economic inequality are ambiguous, however. In general, we could expect that the degree of economic and political conflicts and inequality will be higher in societies differentiated into a few large groups and lower in those with many small groups, none of which dominates the others (such a case is Tanzania). However, there exist many other constellations. Overall, however, the two dimensions of ethnic heterogeneity and ethnic fractionalization correlate strongly with each other. We expect, therefore, that also ethnic fractionalization will lead toward higher economic inequality.

A third aspect of ethnic differentiation is the level of *ethnic conflict*. In Chapter 2 (p. 40–43) it was shown that a very strong relation exists between ethnic differentiation and ethnic conflict. The level of conflict, on its side, is certainly highly important for the issue of economic inequality both as a consequence and as a cause. A low level of ethnic conflict may indicate that inequality between ethnic groups is moderate in a country; but it can also indicate that deprived groups may not be aware of their situation and accept the existing system. A high level of conflict, on the other side, can be a consequence of high inequality, but it can also contribute to the reduction of inequality if deprived groups are able to fight for their rights. Thus, the effects of ethnic conflict on income inequality are not clear-cut.

A fourth approach to grasp the effects of ethnic heterogeneity is to look at the origins of present-day ethnic heterogeneity. Hypothesis 4 (p. 66) has specified that ethnic heterogeneity will have the most pervasive effect on income inequality if it was established through the form of subjugation, domination and exploitation of one ethnic group by another. The most extreme form of such domination was *slavery*. Slavery was a form of ethno-class exploitation which was relevant historically nearly all over the world. In the next chapter, we will discuss in detail the different forms of slavery and their effects on the people – both slave-owners and slaves. We will also summarize historical literature which has shown that the transition from the slave status to that of free people was not connected with an immediate improvement of the social situation of the freed men and women. Out of these considerations, we suggest that economic inequality is higher in those societies which have practised slavery in former times; the more extensive this form of ethno-class exploitation was, the higher economic inequality today will be. In order to test this hypothesis, we have developed a new index of historical ethno-class exploitation. Its elements shall be described in the next section.

As far as ethno-class exploitation, that is, a history of slavery, is concerned, two additional hypotheses are developed here, one relating to the level of physical violence, the other to corruption.

Physical violence was a central element of slavery throughout the ages. Men and women became enslaved mainly through wars, or were kidnapped violently in other times on the homeland territories of their peoples and tribes. One additional element had to be present, however, in order to be able to enslave people through kidnapping and wars. This was the weakness of local communities to resist against foreign invaders and slave riders. This weakness included four aspects: first, their small size and political powerlessness. In West and East Africa where a few, strong kingdoms existed, they could well resist the invasion of foreigners for slave riding. (In the Middle Ages, however, some of them had sold slaves to Arabs and Europeans; see Engerman et al. 2001: 214f.) Second, weakness was caused by internal disunity and conflicts between the different tribes and peoples within a larger empire. This was one of the main factors which enabled Hernán Cortés to capture the Aztec empire of Moteczuma II with a group of only 500 soldiers against an army of tens of thousands of indigenous soldiers in 1519/1520 (Castillo 1982; Schmitt 2008). Third, the technological inferiority of the indigenous communities, particularly in their armament; and, finally, the effect of surprise because unknown, different-looking foreigners came to a country; this effect again was much more pronounced in America than in Africa. When Christopher Columbus arrived at *Hispaniola* (the present-day states of Haiti and the Dominican Republic) in 1492, the indigenous population, living on a moderate level of civilization, considered him and his companions as supernatural beings, 'White Gods', since all of their characteristics, their ships, weapons and instruments were totally new and shocking for them (Bitterli 1993).

The accuracy of these remarks can be proved in every slave society. Physical force and violence had to be used in order to keep the slaves obedient and working. This was particularly so in the slave societies of the New World, in the Americas. Here, violence was a pervasive feature: the master or his substitute could physically punish the slave; this occurred usually in public, with other slaves and free people attending the punishment (Schmitt 2008: 33–34; Grant 2010: 74ff.). The punishment often was very cruel, in disproportionate relation to the misbehaviour and offences of the slaves and it was carried out at will by the masters and their agents. In his *Voyage of a Naturalist round the World* (1831–36), Charles Darwin described the horrific treatment of the slaves in America by their male and female masters (see Pfaff-Giesberg 1955: 72ff.). Slaves, on their side, could often only react in a violent way to this maltreatment; homicides of violent masters occurred frequently, as did deadly fights between escaped slaves and guards. Thus in societies brutalized by violence and slavery, most people became brutalized, including the slaves themselves (Ross 1983; Bley et al. 1991: 152). Due to the disruption of communal relations between slaves (by separating slaves from similar tribes), the isolated settlement of the slave plantations and the paternalistic form of slave treatment in America, it was extremely difficult for the slaves to develop a group consciousness and to fight collectively against their exploitation; nevertheless, this happened frequently (Santos 1985; Engerman et al. 2001: 38; see also Marx 1971: 318). The only open means available for them was to resort to rebellions and violence. This included violence against themselves: many slaves committed suicide, particularly before they were constrained to enter into the slave ships and to leave Africa forever (Grant 2010: 61). Physical violence, crime and inequality are also correlated with each other (Blau & Blau 1982; Kelly 2000). Also people see a connection between inequality, violence and crime, as Morgan and Kelley (2010) have shown for Latin America. Thus, the following hypothesis is put forward: former slavery and the very unequal societies of today are characterized by a higher level of physical violence and crime than societies in which slavery was never pervasive.

There exists also a significant effect of slavery on the upper classes, the masters. Slave societies were characterized by an authoritarian social structure where a 'Big Man' was able to act to a large degree without respecting existing laws. Such men still can be found in Brazil and in other Latin American societies as well as in many Sub-Saharan African countries. In Brazil, for instance, today they are influential political personalities with an extended network of supporters, endorsed by a wealthy family background and a vast and complex system of enterprises, including ownership of media which is very useful for carrying out election campaigns. Their designation as *honoravais bandidos* (Dória 2009) seems quite adequate: what violent crime exists among the lower classes, corruption may exist among the upper ones. In contrast to small criminals, the latter are held in high esteem by the population of their home regions which profit in several ways from their actions. In Sub-Saharan Africa, such Big Men were responsible for extremely long and violent civil wars as well as for a dramatic economic decline of their countries (see Chapter 10, pp. 272–6). Clientelism and corruption in general are characterized by an inherently contradictory situation in which 'asymmetrical power and/or for inequality is combined with solidarity [...]' (Roniger 1994: 4; see also Miller 2007). However, we could expect that also inequality as such is connected with corruption. Corruption may help to preserve or even widen existing inequalities in income and wealth, on the one had; on the other hand, a high degree of inequality may promote corruption because the middle class is smaller in such societies and it is particularly this class which is interested in protecting its interests through organized groups and associations (Husted 1999: 342). Clientelism and corruption are general problems of both less and more developed industrial societies. Enormous damages and losses are caused by white collar criminality in its different forms (financial manipulations and fraud, bribery, tax evasion, violation of safety codes by firm owners, and so on). The societal losses from these forms are much higher than those from street criminality by murderers, thieves and robbers which are more typical for immigrants and lower classes (Coleman 1987: 7ff.). According to Coleman, the problem of white collar criminality is rooted generally in the modern, Capitalist culture of competition, and in particular in class conflict, that is, the struggle for power and profit of the dominant elite (Coleman 1987). The 'desire to prove oneself by "winning" in the competitive struggles' may be particularly acute in societies where civic ethics and democratic political processes are not yet strongly anchored. Clientelism and corruption are endemic in many developing countries, particularly in Africa (Wraith and Simpkins 1963) and they emerged as main problems also in the transition from State Socialist to Capitalist societies in East Europe and elsewhere (Stefes 2006).

The following hypothesis is proposed in this regard: in former slave societies, a much higher level of corruption exists than in societies without a history of slavery. In the former societies, inequality and corruption support each other.

Social-structural Country Characteristics Influencing Economic Inequality

Here, three main variables will be included as independent variables in the following quantitative analyses: population size and growth, the level of socio-economic development and inequality in land distribution. Concerning these variables, the following hypotheses are proposed:

Population size: we expect that in a very populous country income inequality will be higher than in one with a small population. This hypothesis can be deduced from classical sociological and economic thinking. Emile Durkheim (1993: 262), for instance, proposed that the division of labour in a society varies in direct ratio with its volume and density: as societies grow in size, their internal division of labour increases and leads to more complex social differentiations and distinctions. The resulting higher inequality, however, is no problem as long as it is based on individual endowments and merit and corroborated by a moral regulation of the economy. Also in economics it is a basic tenet that increasing size of a population leads to increasing differentiation of occupational and other functions; this, in turn, will lead to an increasing differentiation of incomes (see, for example Smith 1933 [1776]). Economist Leopold Kohr (1983) has argued that in small countries inequality will be lower because the distance between the upper and lower classes and the centre and periphery of the country is smaller; this, in turn, will be connected with a lower tolerance of extreme inequalities. The heterogeneous preferences of the population of large countries make it more difficult to deliver services and formulate policy in an optimal way; smaller countries can respond more easily to citizens' wishes (Alesina and Spolaore 2003). Thus, inequality will be lower in smaller countries. The same thesis can be deduced from organizational theories of income distribution which argue that differences in wages and salaries will be larger the more distinct hierarchical levels an organization has (Blümle 1975). In Chapter 3 (see p. 91) we have hinted at the fact that most of the world leaders in measuring quality of life are small countries; this fact is certainly related also to their moderate level of inequality.

Population growth: strong population growth will increase economic inequality, particularly in countries at lower levels of development. A growing population means that the existing or even expanding resources must be distributed between more and more people, while in a more or less stable population economic growth leads to rising incomes per head (Atkinson and Bourguignon 2000a). In a country with a strongly growing population there will be a heavy shortage of jobs particularly for the young cohorts entering work life; this then might increase income differences between persons in the formal and informal sectors of the economy and, thus, overall societal inequality. This thesis contributes to the explanation of the stagnation or even shortfall of many Sub-Saharan countries in terms of standards of living of the population over the last decades which took place in spite of growing economies. It is also consistent with the recent substantive reduction of poverty in China where fertility has effectively been controlled and restricted by government. It can be expected that excessive growth will mainly affect the incomes of the lower social strata. In countries with a highly unequal income distribution (such as Brazil and South Africa), educated persons have lower birth-rates than the less educated; this fertility differential increases the proportion of unskilled workers, if we assume that a higher proportion of children of persons with low education become unskilled workers (Kremer and Chen 2002). The consequence is that competition increases in the labour markets accessible to unskilled persons.

Level of education of the population: this is a central variable both from the sociological and economic perspective. The sociological theory of modernization sees the spread of education as a central factor contributing to and furthering modernization (Flora 1975; Lerner 1969; Zapf 1969; Lepsius 1988) Higher education is connected with a more rational approach to life, including family planning and a consequent decrease of fertility and better use of health facilities (Lutz et al. 2004; Lutz and Samir 2011); it also furthers participation in civic and political life. Therefore, we can expect that in societies in which large fractions of people who have a low education or are even illiterate, inequality will be higher. Education is a central variable also for economists; they see human capital as a main factor inducing both economic growth and an equalization of income distribution (Blümle 1975; Atkinson and Bourguignon 2000a; Wail et al. 2011). Low levels of schooling of significant segments of the population will correlate positively with poverty and, thus, also increase inequality. This thesis is also proved by the fact that the same groups of countries which exhibit a low or high economic inequality show also corresponding inequalities in education: the Gini index of educational inequality is .16 in Europe, around .30 in Latin America and East Asia and around .50 in Africa (Wail et al. 2011). However, economic growth might reduce the connection between schooling and income (Streissler and Streissler 1986: 292ff.). This is highly relevant because educational inequality is declining in most countries of the world with the educational advantage of Western Europe decreasing and the share of Asian countries increasing (Morrison and Murtin 2010; Crespo-Cuaresma et al. 2012). However, recent economic studies find only a weak or ambiguous connection between educational and economic inequality (de Gregorio and Lee 2002; Checchi 2000; Földvari and van Leeuwen 2011). In addition, it seems that in poorly developed economies, a slight increase in educational inequality is necessary to haul them out of poverty (Sauer and Zagler 2012). In spite of these ambiguous findings, however, we will include education as a control variable in our regression analyses.

Level of socio-economic development: the relevance of this dimension follows on from the famous Kuznets theory of the development of income distribution over the process of industrialization, discussed briefly in Chapter 1 (see p. 14). This theory says that the development of economic inequality follows an inverted U-curve: at the beginning of the industrialization process, inequality increases because incomes in the modern industrial sector and in the towns increase faster than those in traditional economic sectors and the countryside; later on, when industrialization captures the whole country and economy, inequality levels out. The Kuznets theory has been submitted to many empirical tests; some could confirm it, but many others not. Therefore, we will also investigate (and control for) the level of socio-economic development.

Inequality of land distribution: this is the last social-structural dimension which is very important for economic inequality. The relevance of agrarian property relations and class structures for the transition from feudal to Capitalist societies is incontestable since the works of Brenner (1987a, b), Moore (1993) and social historians like Bloch, Cipolla and Brunner. They have shown that the far-reaching social transformations and revolutions in the early Modern Age have been moulded to a significant degree by the existing patterns of land ownership and class structures (landlords, smallholders, farm workers). The differential access to land is still highly relevant today in the less developed societies around the world in which the agricultural population comprises over 50 per cent. In a country with a small landowner elite and a broad mass of smallholding farmers and poor farm workers (who often are employed only parts of the year) income inequality must certainly be higher than in one where most farms are middle-sized and run by families. Based on this fact, we can approximately use the proportion of family farms as an indicator of the equality of land distribution. Inequality in land distribution has also indirect effects on the distribution of non-land assets, wealth and income inequality and it may impede economic growth and democratization (Deininger and Olinto 1998; Helpman 2004; Ziblatt 2008; Ansell and Samuels 2010). Several authors found a positive correlation between historical inequality in land distribution and present economic inequality (Deiniger and Squire 1998; Li et al. 1998). Ewout Frankema (2009a, b, 2010) has shown in a series of recent publications that high inequality in land distribution was the central element producing the pervasive inequality in Latin American societies as shown in Chapter 1. He argues that the Iberian colonial administration redistributed land from indigenous peasants to the Spanish nobles and the new Creole elites in Latin America. The early colonists' efforts to conquest and settle the land were rewarded with this Crown land; Spanish and Indian estates were under separate political, juridical and administrative spheres. In Spanish Latin America, the institution of *economienda* provided the large estates (*latifundia*) and the silver mines with cheap indigenous labour; in Brazil and the Caribbean, slaves were imported from Africa to produce the tropical cash crops sugar, cocoa and coffee. The Catholic Church contributed significantly to the emergence and continuity of pervasive inequality in land distribution in two ways: first, because it was one of the largest landowners, and second because it provided an ideological underpinning for the unequal distribution of economic privilege and political power. If the landowning and other economic power elites largely overlap, they may develop policies which suppress democracy and social development in order to maintain existing inequalities (Bourguignon and Verdier 2000; Olson 2000; Acemoglu and Robinson 2012). This situation in Latin America was a marked contrast to that in North America where Indian land was occupied and developed in relatively small plots by immigrant White farm families.

In the analysis in this chapter, we will investigate the whole sample of countries and compare the effects of land distribution on income inequality. Indices for inequality in land distribution have been compiled by several authors (see, for example Deininger and Olinto 1999; Carter 2000; Frankema 2009a). They are usually based on data collected through the FAO World Census of Agriculture, initiated in 1924, and carried out every decade since the 1950s. The data presented in Frankema 2009 show that land inequality is more concentrated than economic inequality, but varies considerably between countries and continents: in some countries, the Gini coefficient for inequality in land distribution is relatively modest, around .40 to .50 (for example, Denmark, Finland, Canada, Ethiopia); in Europe, it is usually between .50 and .60; in the USA around .70, and in most Latin American countries around .80. The similarity of the rural class structures between the Iberian Peninsula and Latin America is reflected in the fact that also in Spain and Portugal land inequality is very high (.70 to .80). A methodological problem here is that data on land distribution are not available for many of the countries of our aggregated dataset. We will use, therefore, an approximate measurement, the proportion of family farms in a country (Vanhanen n.d.) which is available for all 123 countries.

Characteristics of the Political System as Determinants of Income Inequality

A second group of intervening variables, relevant for income inequality, was related to the political system and process. This aspect was discussed extensively in Chapter 3. Let us recapitulate the main hypotheses here:

1. Income inequality will be higher in states which have an 'ethnic character', that is, which connect the attainment of citizenship or the access to political rights and welfare state services on ethnic membership;
2. Income inequality will be lower in societies with a democratic tradition;
3. Income inequality will be lower in societies which have a federal constitution, that is, grant considerable autonomy to regional sub-units;
4. The more comprehensive the welfare state of a society, the lower economic inequality;
5. Income inequality will be lower in societies which have a Communist economic-political system today or had it in the past.

Datasets and Variables

As indicated in the introduction, a new aggregate dataset has been created for the quantitative analysis to be carried out in this chapter. First, data on income distribution were collected and compiled for as many countries as possible for the time period 2000–05; this could be done for 137 countries. The respective figures have been presented in Chapter 1 (see Table 1.1). For all these countries, additional data on the variables introduced in the foregoing section have been assembled, using existing compilations of international data. Here, in several dimensions no data could be found for some countries. Some of the regression analyses, therefore, are carried out only on the basis of fewer countries (123 in total). Let us have a short look at the source and definition of the variables. We can group them into three types: (1) the main dependent variables; (2) the main independent variables; and (3) the independent control variables.

The Main Dependent Variables: Income Inequality

Income inequality. One main data source for the central, dependent variable of this study was the World Development Report 2006, edited by the World Bank (2005).[3] These data are based on several sources: primary data collected by the World Bank; statistical publications of World Bank member countries; and studies by other research institutes and international organizations (such as the IMF and the OECD). Because the reliability of data from the different sources varies, the World Bank staff reviewed the figures in order to ensure that the most reliable data were presented (see also Deininger and Squire 1996).

The second source was the UNU-WIDER Database (WIID): this is quite a comprehensive dataset, containing time series data on income distribution for many countries. It has been checked thoroughly by Frederick Solt (2009) in order to ensure reliability and comparability over countries. Most of the time series in this dataset (called SWIID) begin in the 1980s; for some countries (for example Germany, Italy, Netherlands, Sweden, United States) they start already in the 1930s and 1940s, and for a few (Japan, United Kingdom), even in the late 19th century. In order to increase the reliability of the data presented in Table 1.1, we have computed the mean values for the years 2000–05 and added an additional figure in parenthesis if the deviation was pronounced.

The variables used in the regression analysis are described in Table 4.1. They include three indicators of income inequality, four variables related to ethnic differentiation and eight additional independent variables potentially relevant as factors explaining income inequality. The three indicators for income distribution have been taken over from the World Development Report 2006:

- The Gini-coefficient of net income inequality as reported in the SWIID dataset (Solt 2009); this gives a general indication of the amount of income inequality.
- Per cent of income going to the lowest 40 per cent of the population; the values vary between 7 per cent and less in the cases of Bolivia, Botswana, Lesotho and Sierra Leone, and up to around 24 per cent in the Czech Republic, Finland and Japan.
- Per cent of income going to the highest 10 per cent of the population. These values vary between 21 per cent and less in the Czech Republic, several Scandinavian states, Bosnia and Azerbaijan, and 47 to 64 per cent in Bolivia, Botswana, Namibia and Haiti.
- Violence: Fajnzylber et al. (2002) found in a survey of 39 countries during 1965–95 that rates of violent crime and inequality were positively correlated (for contrary evidence see Neumayer 2005). Violence is measured here by international homicides per 100,000 populations.[4]
- Corruption: high inequality increases corruption in two ways: the wealthy have more motivation and opportunities to engage in corruption when the poor are weak; and inequality undermines social norms and beliefs about justice and fairness (Gupta et al. 1998; Jong-Sung and Khagram 2005). Corruption was measured by the 'Corruption perception index' (2002).[5]

3   World Bank 2005, World Development Report 2006, pp. 289–90; see also other information at the World Bank website (See http://www.worldbank.org/).
4   UNODC Homicide Statistics 2012; http://data.un.org/Data.aspx?=UNODC&f=tablecode%311#UNODC
5   Source: Transparency International, Corruption Perception Index 2007 (see http://www.transparency.org/).

Table 4.1 Descriptive statistics for the main variables in the regression analysis

Variable	Definition (year of data collection)	Lowest observed value	Highest observed value	Mean value	Standard deviation
Gini index	Income distribution (Ø 2000–05)	21.7	73.2	38.6	8.9
Lowest 40%	Income share of the lowest 40% of the income recipients (%, ca [1996] 2000–03)	3.1	28.0	17.0	4.9
Highest 10%	Income share of the highest 10% of the income recipients (%, ca [1996] 2000–2003)	18.0	64.5	31.6	8.1
Ethnic heterogeneity	Ethnic heterogeneity (ca 2000–05)	2	240	88.1	64.1
Ethnic fractionalization	Ethnic fractionalization (ca 1995)	0	1	0.5	0.3
Ethnic conflict	Ethnic conflict (ca 1990–96)	0	160	48.9	37.6
Ethno class exploitation	Historical ethno-class exploitation	0	11	5.3	2.6
Population size	Population, millions (log. value 2003–07)	0.8	1307.5	49.1	159.,1
Population growth	Average annual growth (%, 2000–04)	-0.7	3.9	1.3	1.1
GDP/capita	Gross Domestic Product/capita in US-$	620	65.635	9.532	14.170
Democracy	Strength of democratic tradition (1960–2010)	0	1	0.3	0.4
Communism	Former or present communist system	0	1	0.3	0.5
Social spending	Public social expenditure in % of GDP (2000)	0.30	22.2	6.7	6.2
Land inequality	Family farms in % (2000)	1	98	48.5	24.,1
Federalism	Federal constitution (existence of federal elections)	0	1	0.6	0.5

Sources: See text; number of countries: 123.

The Main Independent Variables: Ethnic Differentiation

The main independent variable is ethnic differentiation. It was very important, therefore, to capture this dimension as comprehensively and reliably as possible. We tried to approach this problem by capturing the dimension of ethnicity in four different aspects and dimensions, respectively.

Ethnicity has been defined in Chapter 3 (see pp. 31–3) as consisting of three sub-dimensions, including the more narrow, bio-social aspect of ethnic origin and affinity ('race'), and the two cultural aspects of language and religion. For the measurement of ethnic membership in the bio-social sense we started from a dataset compiled by the Finnish political scientist Tatu Vanhanen (1999). The indices reported in the original work of Vanhanen published in the 1990s seemed not to be plausible in some cases; in other cases in recent times significant changes have taken place. Using additional sources, the Vanhanen data were updated. For this aim, the very informative handbook *Ethnic Groups Worldwide* by the cultural anthropologist David Levinson (1998) was consulted. In this book, a concise description of the ethnic composition of all countries around the world is given, including the history, the composition and size of the different ethnic groups, and the character (peaceful or conflictual) of ethnic relations in each country.[6] In addition, standard encyclopaedias

---

6 Detailed information about ethnic groups in the bio-social sense is also presented at http://www.welt-auf-einen-blick.de/bevoelkerung/ethnische-gruppen.de

and handbooks were used, particularly concerning the composition of the countries in terms of language and religion.[7]

The index of Ethnic Heterogeneity (EH) developed out of these sources captures the degree of ethnic differentiation of a state society in the three dimensions discussed before, those of common descent (that is, ethnicity in the narrow sense), language and religion. The construction of the index proceeds in two steps. First, the differentiation of a society in each of these three terms is determined; then, the degrees of differentiation in each dimension are summed up to a comprehensive index. The measurement of differentiation in each single dimension is as follows: first, we look if there exist ethnic sub-groups in a society according to this criterion. Then, we take the percentage of the largest sub-group and subtract this from 100; the resulting value is the index of differentiation in this dimension; it varies theoretically from 0 to 99. The final step is to summarize the three partial indices into one comprehensive index. The construction of the index Ethnic Heterogeneity (EH), thus, can be described formally as follows:

EH = EH(BS) + EH(L) + EH (R), whereby
EH (BS) = Ethnic Heterogeneity in bio-social terms;
EH (L) = Ethnic Heterogeneity in terms of language;
EH (R) = Ethnic Heterogeneity in terms of religion and
EH (BS)/EH(L)/EH (R) = 100 – largest Ethnic Group in BS/L/R terms.

The index developed in this way varies between 2 and 240; its arithmetic mean is 89, its standard deviation 64 (see Table 4.1).

We are aware that this definition of ethnic heterogeneity in many cases may grasp rather statistical categories but not 'real' ethnic groups, that is, groups who consider themselves as an ethnic community and are considered as such also by others. To capture such groups, special representative surveys would have to be carried out in all countries in order to gather how many such groups are distinguished by the population (Fearon 2003: 198–9). Such a database does not exist. However, in Part II when we look at specific countries and their ethnic composition we will be able to go into a more comprehensive understanding of the different ethnic groups and their social-structural characteristics.

An additional aspect here is the relative size of the different ethnic groups, the degree of *ethnic fractionalization* (see also Alesina et al. 2003, Fearon 2003). Ethnic diversity may lead to conflicts more often if a few strong ethnic groups compete with each other or if one or a few large ethnic groups dominate many others; if many small ethnic groups co-exist within a country the probability of conflict will be lower (Mann 2007:16). In the following analysis, the index of ethnic fractionalization developed by Fearon (2003) has been used.[8] This index is calculated on the basis of the probability that two individuals selected at random from a country will be from different ethnic groups. It gets the value 0, if a country is fully homogeneous; if there are two groups with the proportions 0.95 and 0.05, it is 0.10; with two groups 0.50 and 0.50 each it is 0.50; with three groups, each 0.33, it is 0.67; with four groups and each 0.25 per cent it is 0.75. The lowest observed values in this index (around 0.01 and less) can be observed in European countries such as Albania, Finland and Germany, and in Japan; the highest value (1.00) could be found in Papua New Guinea; most of the highest values (0.80 and more) are observed in Sub-Saharan countries, with Congo on top (0.93).[9]

It was argued before that present-day forms of ethnic differentiation, conflicts and patterns of privilege and deprivation in many world regions have their roots in the subjugation of indigenous people in the form of slavery. Thus, it was a central task to include this dimension also in the quantitative analysis. Slavery has been most important in modern times in Sub-Saharan Africa and Latin America – exactly the macro-regions with

---

7   The main sources in this regard were the *Fischer Weltalmanach, The Statesman's Yearbook*, the yearbook *Aktuell 2001* (Harenberg 2000), *Wikipedia-the free encyclopaedia* and others.

8   We have also developed our own index of ethnic fractionalization, but then preferred the one developed by Fearon (2003). The two indices correlated highly with each other.

9   Alesina et al. (2003) developed three separate measures for ethnic, linguistic and religious fractionalization. They found out that ethnic and language fractionalization were highly correlated to each other (.70), but were only slightly correlated with religious fractionalization (0.14 and 0.27).

the highest levels of economic inequality today. After experimenting with three dummy variables for these regions,[10] critical readers of the draft manuscript[11] reminded us of two facts: first, the relevance of slavery may have been variable within these regions; and, second, slavery was a form of exploitation existing nearly throughout the world for millennia. This made it necessary, therefore, to develop an index which could be computed for all countries in our dataset. Thus, for the measurement of the historical importance of slavery and similar forms of exploitation (EE), a new index called historical ethno-class exploitation was developed. This index was constructed as the sum of the following three sub-indices:

a. The existence and duration of slavery or comparable forms of exploitation (such as serfdom or peonage) in a country and the time of its formal abolition by law. Four categories were distinguished:
   0: No slavery or abolition of it before 1800;
   1: Abolition of slavery between 1800 and 1849;
   2: Abolition between 1850 and 1899;
   3: Abolition between 1900 and 1949;
   4: Abolition 1950 and later.
b. The proportion of the enslaved people among the whole population around 1850: 0 (0 per cent); 1 (1–15 per cent); 2 (16–30 per cent); 3 (31–45 per cent); 4 (46–60 per cent); 5 (61 per cent and more)
c. The degree of exploitation through slavery:
   0: No exploitation;
   1: Serfdom, peonage and similar forms of *enforced labour*. In these relations, exploitation was restricted in two regards: a) not the whole labour power of a person had to be provided to the landlord; he had to work only a part of the year for him; b) only certain members of a family or village had to contribute labour power.
   2: *Apartheid*, a comprehensive legal, political and socio-economic discrimination and exploitation, as it existed in extensive form in South Africa and, to a weaker degree, in the US-South and, maybe still exists in present-day Israel;
   3: *Extrusive slavery*; here, slaves were made within the own society or, when imported from other societies, were integrated into the destination society.
   4: *Intrusive slavery*, the most exploitative and cruel form of exploitation.[12] Here, slaves were imported from other countries or continents and used mainly as labour power. Due to their complete uprooting from their native lands and societies, the slaves had little power to escape or to organize and protest against their exploitation.

These data were collected from a wide variety of sources, including handbook and encyclopaedia articles, historical, anthropological and sociological and other works, and Internet sources on slavery and serfdom in whole continents and single countries.[13] Since many of the present-day countries around the world did not exist in the 19th century or in earlier times, two general principles were applied when assigning values to these countries: (a) they received the value of the larger state or empire of which they were a part (for example many African states); (b) they received values similar to other countries in the region (for example Middle East Arab-Muslim countries, Central-Asian Republics). Our experience has shown that data for index a) were not difficult to come by; for b) and c) it was more difficult although we believe that our categorizations are relatively reliable.

---

10   They were defined as 'African slavery', 'American slavery' and 'Apartheid'; all Sub-Saharan African countries (except the Republic of South Africa) were coded as 1 in the first variable, all Latin American countries as 1 in the second dimension.

11   We are grateful here, in particular, to Prof. Walter Müller, Mannheim.

12   For the distinction between extrusive and intrusive slavery see Flaig 2009.

13   A detailed list of the more than 100 sources used is available on request from the authors. We are grateful to Gerd Kaup who did most of this compilation work.

The resulting total index, historical ethno-class exploitation (EE), could vary theoretically between 0 and 14, but the highest value was only 11. Many European countries have the value 0; at the top are African and Latin American countries (Lesotho, Namibia and South Africa have the value 11, Jamaica and Swaziland 10, Brazil and other Latin American and African countries 9); overall, a very plausible rank order does emerge.

The Independent Control Variables: Social Structure and Politics

These are variables which according to some theories are relevant for the distribution of income, but are not directly connected with the central theoretical dimension of this book, ethnic heterogeneity and exploitation. They belong to two groups: social structural and socio-economic variables and variables relating to the political history and system of a state society.

The first group – social-structural and socio-economic indicators – includes five variables. If not indicated otherwise, these were taken from the World Development Indicators 2006 (World Bank 2005, Table 1). They include:

- *Population size of a country*: in order to cancel out the distorting effect of the extreme left-hand slope of this variable (many small and middle-sized, few very large countries) the square root of the values has been used.
- *Population growth*: average values of annual growth in per cent for the period 2000–04. The lowest values (about -1, that is, a shrinking population) have East European, post-Communist countries like Georgia, Bulgaria and Ukraine; the highest can be found in Sub-Saharan Africa (Angola and Niger 3.0, Congo 2.8).
- *Socio-economic level of development*, as measured by the Gross National Product (GNP) per capita in US-$ (in PPP-Purchasing Power Parity). This is lowest in Sub-Saharan Africa (around 600 to 700 US-$ in Burundi, Congo, Malawi), and highest in the developed Western countries (USA 39720, Norway 38550, Switzerland 35370, Austria, Belgium, Denmark and others around 32000).
- *Mean years of schooling of the population*: here, we used the UN-Education Index which constitutes one of the three components of the Human Development Index (HDI). It is based on mean years of schooling (of adults) and expected years of schooling (of children).[14] We computed and used the mean values 2005–07.
- *Inequality of land distribution*: our first source in this regard were the data compiled by Frankema. Since many countries were missing in his data, we used the index on the proportion of family farms, compiled by Vanhanen as part of his 'Index of Power Resources'.[15]

An additional variable which could be considered as an important determinant of income inequality is the educational structure of a population. Inequality will be much higher if a considerable part of the population is illiterate, for instance. The first analyses of our aggregate dataset have shown, however, that this variable was correlated strongly with the variable of social spending. We dropped the variable of Education, therefore, from the further analysis. We should keep in mind, however, its relevance for income distribution.

Four additional, independent variables are related to our hypotheses about the effects of the political system. We tried to capture this in four regards: the age of a state to its constitution (federalist or centralistic political system) and democratic character and its character as a welfare state.

- *Democracy Index*: in the data of the *Polity IV Project* (Marshall and Jaggers 2010), a country's democratic tradition was measured by the number of years between 1960 and 2010 in which it was democratic or autocratic. The available data consists of a 10-point-scale; the value 10 means that a country in this time span has always been a democracy. We dichotomized this variable into countries with values 1–6 (non-democratic) and those 7–10 (democratic).

14   The data are available at http://hdrstats.undp.org/en/indicators/1037056.html.
15   See http://www.fsd.uta.fi/en/data/catalogue/FSD2420/meF2420e.html

- *Federalism*: this variable was adopted from the *Polity IV Project* (Marshall and Jaggers 2010). The variable 'federal constitution' is based on the existence or not of elections at the level of sub-state (local or regional) administrative-political units. Its categories are:
    0: No elections at sub-state level;
    1: Executive is appointed by central government, legislative body is elected;
    2: Both executive and legislative body in sub-state units are elected.
- *Social spending/strength of the welfare state*: this variable was measured by the percentage of public social security expenditure (excluding health) as a percentage of GDP. The data, referring to 2000 (in some cases more recent years), were taken from the *World Social Security Report* 2010/11, International Labour Organisation, Geneva 2010. It varies from 0.30 (Zimbabwe) up to 22.2 (Sweden).
- *Communism*: the existence of a period in which the country had a State Socialist or Communist regime. The data were taken from Govindaraj and Rannan-Eliya (1994).
- *Age of a state:* In a first analysis, we investigated also the effect of the age of a state. A sixfold classification was used. Period of state foundation: (1) 1980–2000; (2) 1946–79; (3) 1915–45; (4) 1850–1914; (5) 1800–1849; (6) before 1800.

In a first regression analysis of income inequality it had a significant effect (older states are more equal). However, since the effect on income inequality is only indirect, we dropped the variable from the final analysis.

The presentation of the empirical findings in the next section proceeds in two steps: first, the results of the analysis of the newly created aggregate dataset of about 140 countries are presented. The main method applied here is the regression analysis. Since this method, focusing upon statistical relations between variables, is unable to grasp certain interaction effects and peculiarities of specific groups of countries, we supplement it by a qualitative comparative analysis (correctly, a Fuzzy Set Analysis) in the second part of this chapter.

Empirical results I: Quantitative Multivariate Analysis

Here, we look first at the correlations between all independent variables and – by using descriptive scattergrams and tables – describe the main patterns of relations. Then, the results of the multivariate regression analysis are presented, looking at income inequality (in the three dimensions introduced before) as the dependent variable.

Patterns of Relations Between the Independent Variables

A look at the bivariate correlations between the independent variables enables us to get a first understanding of the structural patterns into which the countries can be grouped. It helps us also to make sure that there are not severe problems of multicollinearity and that the estimates of the effects of the independent variables are not biased too much. The results in Table 4.2 show that there exist many significant correlations. This will complicate the regression analysis and make it difficult if not impossible to measure the net effect of some specific single variables. Let us look at the results.

First, the several indicators for ethnic heterogeneity are correlated with each other: a very strong correlation exists between ethnic heterogeneity and ethnic fractionalization. Thus, ethnic heterogeneity and ethnic fractionalization are measuring a rather similar dimension; this must be considered in the regression analysis where they cannot be entered simultaneously; we will enter only one of them into the analysis, therefore. Also the correlation between these two variables and ethnic conflict is rather high; this corresponds to the findings presented in Chapter 2 (see Table 2.2 and Figure 2.2, pp. 37–8, 42). Next, it is an important finding that ethnic heterogeneity and fractionalization are related much less strongly to ethno-class exploitation (historical slavery). This fact confirms that these are two different dimensions and suggests that ethnic heterogeneity also in historical times has not always been connected to ethnic exploitation.

A relatively high and positive correlation then exists between ethnic heterogeneity and fractionalization, respectively, and population growth; this is easy to understand since the most heterogeneous societies are located in strongly growing Sub-Saharan Africa. Finally, both variables related to ethnic differentiation are correlated significantly, but in a negative way, with GDP per capita, educational structure and social spending.

Table 4.2 Pearson-correlations between the variables used in the regression analysis (n=123)

	GINI	ILOW	IHIGH	EH	EF	EE	EC	PS	GDP	LD	DT	COM	FC	SS
Gini-index (Gini)	-													
Income lowest 40% (ILOW)	-.80**	-												
Income highest 10% (IHIGH)	.83**	-.94**	-											
Ethnic heterogeneity (EH)	.40**	-.33**	.33**	-										
Ethnic fractionalization (EF)	.39**	-.41**	.42**	.77**	-									
Ethno-class exploitation (EE)	.56**	-.44**	.47**	.34**	.41**	-								
Ethnic conflict (EC)	.20*	-.09	.08	.44**	.47**	.29**	-							
Population size (PS)	-.03	.11	-.10	-.01	.02	.03	-.02	-						
GDP per capita (GDP)	-.43**	.26**	-.30**	-.48**	-.52**	-.63**	-.36**	-.02	-					
Land distribution (LD)	-.29*	.18	-.20*	-.07	-.16	-.39**	-.10	.06	.25**	-				
Democratic tradition (DT)	-.27**	.18	-.23**	-.24**	-.31**	-.53**	-.23**	.04	.66**	.34**	-			
Communism (COM)	-.33**	.43**	-.40**	-.15	-.18	.01	-.09	-.09	-.11	.39**	-.28**	-		
Federal constitution (FC)	-.28**	.24*	-.22*	-.02	-.09	-.25**	.03	.01	.24**	.07	.25**	.05	-	
Social spending (SS)	-.60**	.46**	-.49**	-.52**	-.54**	-.65**	-.31**	-.10	.73**	.18*	.53**	.21*	.29**	-

Significance: ** p<0.01; * p<0.05.

This finding is fully in line with the pattern just mentioned: the typical multi-ethnic societies are concentrated in the South, particularly in Sub-Saharan Africa, and here we find also the poorer countries with a weaker democratic and welfare state tradition.

As far as ethno-class exploitation is concerned, some very interesting results come out: this variable shows a rather high correlation with several other variables, including GDP per capita, educational structure, democratic tradition and social spending (see Table 4.2). The high negative correlation between ethno-class exploitation and GDP per capita indicates that a history of slavery not only has led to extreme economic inequality persistent over the centuries, but has also retarded socio-economic development. This problematic connection was well known to critical observers in the United States at the times when slavery still existed there (see Chapter 5, p. 145). Also Figure 4.1 shows the negative connection between the two dimensions. However, also the outliers from the general patterns emerging in Figure 4.1 are interesting.

Fourteen countries exhibit a disproportional higher level of development compared to their history of ethno-class exploitation, but they can easily be subsumed under three groups: four African states, four Arab-Islamic states in the Near East and six American states.

The four African states with a disproportionately high level of development are the Republic of South Africa (ZA), Lesotho (LS), Namibia (NA) and Swaziland (SZ). It is quite evident why this is so: South African development was led by the White Minorities in numerical terms (Boers of Dutch origin and Britons) for centuries; they implemented modern agriculture and industry. Most of all, they exploited the rich mineral

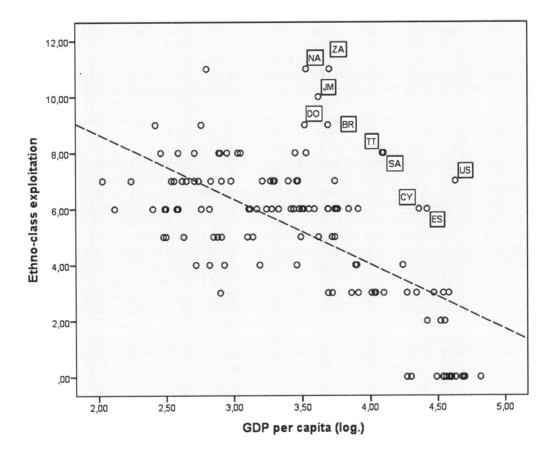

Figure 4.1 **The relation between ethno-class exploitation and level of socio-economic development today (GDP p.c.)**
Notes: Correlation coefficients: r= -.62[xx] (Pearson); r=-.45[xx] (Spearman).

resources of the country in a highly efficient manner, also by making use of slave work and – later – by the exploitation of Black labour power through the system of Apartheid. The case of Namibia is similar to South Africa insofar as a small White minority (in this case of German origin) developed the country's core economy (leaving most native Black people outside this sector, after having defeated a revolt of the Herero tribe in 1904 in a brutal way). After the First World War, Namibia became de facto a part of the Republic of South Africa which imported their Apartheid system but also contributed to the further economic development of the country. The two small states of Lesotho and Swaziland, territorial enclaves within the Republic of South Africa, are also very closely integrated into this country. With South Africa and Namibia, they are members of the South African Customs Union (SACU) and they form a common currency area with the *Rand*. Both countries are also characterized – as many other Sub-Saharan African countries are – by a dual economy with a small but highly productive Capitalist and market-orientated sector and a large poor sector of subsistence agriculture.

The second group of countries with a disproportionately high level of GDP per head, given their history of slavery, are the oil-rich Arab-Islamic Golf states Saudi Arabia (SA), Kuwait (RW), Oman (OM) and Qatar (QT). It is quite easy to understand why these states fall into one group; their extraordinary national incomes from crude oil catapulted them within an extremely short period of time (maybe half a century) from poor tribal communities into the group of the richest countries on earth.

The third group comprises six American states: the USA, in North America, four small Caribbean island states and Brazil. The case of the USA is again very easy to understand. This country, which in the early 20th century surpassed England in terms of Capitalist industrial production and became the world's leading economic power, had abolished slavery only a few decades ago, in 1865. For nearly a century, an extreme institutional inconsistency had characterized this (*The First New Nation*, Lipset 1979). On the one side it was very modern in terms of its democratic political system, but at the same time it was a nation of slave-holders in the South. In Chapter 11, we will show that the former predominance of slavery in the southern US states is closely related to higher income inequality in these states today.

The four Caribbean states with a relatively high level of development given their history of ethnic exploitation are Cuba (CU), the Dominican Republic (DO), Jamaica (JM) and Trinidad and Tobago (TT). The three latter countries are all small and poor island states in the Caribbean with different histories and socio-economic structures but also some commonalities. For all of them, the propinquity to the United States might have been a factor supporting development, for instance, by the establishment and management of large agricultural plants (for example, bananas in the Dominican Republic) through American corporations, and by tourism from North America and Europe into a region which includes some of the world's most beautiful landscapes and beaches. Trinidad and Tobago, situated near the coast of Venezuela, is an oil-rich country and was able to develop a petrochemical industry. The country has a large Indian ethnic group (about 25 per cent of the population); this group often includes many successful entrepreneurs. The relatively high GDP of Cuba is also no surprise. Already before the revolution led by Fidel Castro in 1959, this island was one of the richest in Latin America. The economic situation worsened since then significantly as a consequence of State Socialism and the embargo of the USA. Since 1989, an additional problem was caused by the breakdown of the Communist regimes in Eastern Europe which were the main trading partners of Cuba. But Cuba's social welfare institutions were strongly further developed under its peculiar State Socialist system. Already before 1959, the education and health systems of Cuba were among the best in Latin America and it also had a good infrastructure: 65 per cent of the populations are White, 25 per cent mulattos and mestizos, and 10 per cent are Black.

The South American case in this group of countries with a relatively high GDP per capita, given its history of slavery, is Brazil. In the last decades, Brazil has been able to become one the strongest rising countries of the global South; it is now among the 10 largest single national economies in the world. There are several reasons for this accomplishment: Brazil's immense territory (with 8.5 square kilometres) and a population of nearly 200 million provide a huge domestic market; it has rich natural resources; and Brazil's political system and welfare state institutions (education and health care systems) are comparatively well developed. I will come back to Brazil which is a highly interesting and unique case in terms of its ethnic stratification in Chapter 9.[16]

---

16   There are two further cases with a relatively high GDP/head, given their history of ethnic exploitation: Hong Kong, which is a very prosperous town-state in East Asia with a rather centralistic-authoritarian regime which, however,

Two countries, Haiti (HT) and Liberia (LR), are very strong deviations in the other direction, that is, ethno-class exploitation was rather weak in the last few centuries, but the level of socio-economic development is very low today. Their situation proves very clearly one of the central theses of this work, namely, that the experience of slavery makes a long-lasting imprint on all the persons involved in such a system, including the slaves and their descendants. Both these states had been established by former slaves and ruled by their descendants. Haiti is the poorest island state in the Caribbean; it has ten million inhabitants are composed of 60 per cent to 80 per cent Black, 10–20 per cent mulattos and only a few per cent White; 80 per cent of the population are Catholics. African slaves had been imported to this island by the Spaniards (who called it *Santo Domingo*) since the 16th century to work on their sugar and coffee plantations; one of the most cruel forms of slave labour exploitation was practised here. Later on, one part of the island became the French colony *Saint-Domingue* (the Spanish part later became the Dominican Republic). In 1804, a bloody slave revolt broke out which led to the murdering and expulsion of the French colonists; the slave rebels modelled their own upsurge on the French Revolution. This worldwide-only nation born from a slave revolt was able to preserve its autonomy and independence since then in spite of interventions by France, of embargos by the United States (they feared an export of the slave rebellion to their own country and recognized Haiti only in 1867) and of high reparation payments to France throughout most of the 19th century as compensation for the former land owners. The new government enacted far-reaching reforms: the large plantations were divided up into small parcels of land which were apportioned to the rural population. The consequence, however, was a sharp decrease of productivity and output. In political terms, the new Black power elites on the island were not democrats but soon acted as authoritarian leaders. As a consequence, the history of the new Republic was characterized by recurring terrible phases of public and state violence and continuous political instability.

A fairly similar story occurred in the West African state of Liberia which was colonized by freed Blacks from the United States who emigrated there and established an independent state in 1847 on this territory on the coast of West Africa. The founders of this state, the *Americo-Liberians*, as they were called, brought with them the American political culture including the idea of racial supremacy. Through their *True Whig Party* they fully monopolized political power and leadership in the country for 133 years even if they constituted only 5 per cent of the population. In 1980, the military coup of Samuel Doe dethroned the Americo-Liberian group; decades of brutal civil war was followed by the state-terrorist government of Charles Taylor from 1997 till 2003. Thus, both Haiti and Liberia had extremely tragic histories in the two centuries following their foundation and the hopes and expectations of millions inside and outside of these revolutionary nations connected with slave liberation, freedom and access to power were heavily disappointed.

Let us come back to the correlations between the independent variables. A very important finding here is that the variable ethno-class exploitation correlates strongly and negatively with most political system variables, particularly Democratic tradition and Social spending. The same applies to the variable Educational structure which on its side is closely correlated with social spending (see Table 4.2 above). These negative correlations mean that in countries with a strong tradition of ethno-class exploitation, the development of democracy and the welfare state were much weaker than in those without such a tradition. This finding is fully consistent with the theoretical concepts developed in this book: ethno-class exploitation, that is slavery, is a system in which one group of men are not recognized as a human beings; democracy and the welfare state, on the other side, are based on the opposite assumption, namely, that all members of a society are fundamentally equal and have the same political and social rights, including the claim to a decent standard of living.

The next variable which is strongly related to several others is the level of socio-economic development, GDP per capita. It correlates particularly with Democratic Tradition and Social Spending. In substantive terms, this is quite easy to understand; in fact, the positive correlation between democracy and economic development may be the strongest single empirical generalization in comparative politics (Boix 2003: 1–2). A positive socio-economic development resulting in prosperity and wealth enables a state to develop a welfare system and it also facilitates and strengthens democratic political processes. But a democratic system and a comprehensive welfare state on their side also further economic development by fostering interpersonal trust,

---

does everything to foster economic growth; and Estonia, which has one of the most dynamic economies among the post-Communist East European countries.

peaceful industrial relations and political stability. This high inter-correlation poses a substantial problem for the regression analysis, presented in the following section. In order to tackle this problem, let us look closer to their association.

Figure 4.2 shows a strong association between GDP per capita and the level of Social Spending: with an increasing level of GDP, usually also the level of Social Spending increases. The poorest countries around the world (with a GDP per capita below 1.000 US-$) spend less than 5 per cent of their budget for social purposes, while among most of the richest countries it is over 20 per cent. Thus, the absolute level of welfare spending will be extremely low exactly in those countries in which it would be most urgent in objective terms. There are, however, several exceptions to this pattern which can be subsumed under four groups.

The countries in the lower right triangle of Figure 4.2 are those in which social security spending is higher than to be expected according their socio-economic level of development. Two groups of countries are located here. The first group in the lowest left-hand side corner of the figure include four of the poorest countries in Sub-Saharan Africa (thus, also the poorest in the world), namely Burundi (BI), Congo (CG), Ethiopia (ET) and Liberia (LR). Several explanations are obvious for the specific position of the first two countries. One is the fact that they have extreme deficits in infrastructure (particularly in roads, public transport and energy supply); another is that they have been involved until recent times in bloody internal civil wars and violent conflicts with their neighbour states. (In Chapter 10, the negative effects of these conflicts in Sub-Saharan Africa will be discussed in detail.) In fact, military expenditure is rather high in all these three states, around

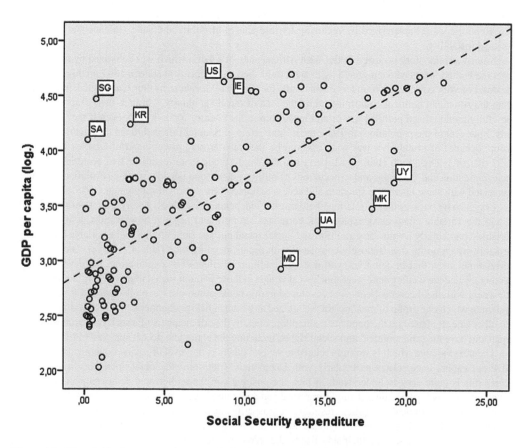

Figure 4.2   The relation between socio-economic development and level of social spending
Notes: Correlation coefficients r=,69 (Pearson); r=.71 (Spearman); statistical significance: p≤.01

3 per cent in Congo and Ethiopia, and nearly 6 per cent in Burundi.[17] Given the extremely low level of the state revenues[18] it is evident that the spending for social purposes is far away from the real needs of their populations (of which a majority lives in poverty) – even if it is higher than expected on the level of their GDP.

Also in the other group, Social Spending is higher than expected given their level of socio-economic development. Here, we find five post-Communist East European countries, Macedonia (MK), Moldova (MD), the Ukraine (UA) and Serbia (RS). The relatively high level of welfare spending in these states certainly is a heritage of their State Socialist past.

Finally, there are two groups of countries – located in the upper left corner of Figure 4.2 – which have a very high GDP per capita but spend comparatively little for social purposes. On the right side, we find some highly advanced nations which are well known for relying more on private insurance systems and obligations than public welfare; they include Switzerland (CH), the USA, Japan (JP) and – to a lower degree – Canada (CA), Luxembourg (LU) and Ireland (I.E.). The group on the upper left corner is that with an extremely low level of welfare spending, given their high GNP. This group includes two very rich Arabic Gulf states – Saudi Arabia (SA) and Kuwait (KW) – and three of the East Asian 'Tiger states': Hong Kong (HK), Singapore (SG) and Korea (KR) which since 1945 experienced stunning economic growth. The wealth of these states originated from very different sources. In the Gulf states, it was the extremely high income from crude oil. Here, the figures for the low state social spending are misleading: they in fact spend huge sums of money on their native citizens, providing them with free education, medical services and even free housing, and the proportion of them who are employed by the state is extremely high in comparative terms (see Chapter 5, pp. 151–3). All these benefits, however, are going only to the native Arabic population; the millions of foreign workers do not get any social subsidies in spite of the fact that most of them are also Muslims. In fact, not only a few of them are constrained to work and live under modern forms of slavery. Thus, in these states ethnic stratification is probably most sharply pronounced in the present-day world. In the case of the East Asian 'Tiger states', the source of present-day wealth was very different: it included a neo-liberal policy of openness for exchange and trade with the outside world, as well as definite state policies to support the development of a strong home industry competitive at the world level. At the same time, the educational and social services were well developed, even if they are financed to a considerable degree on a private basis.

The differences in social spending between all these groups of countries are clearly reflected in their highly differing degrees of economic inequality (see Table 1.1): it is rather low in the post-Communist East European countries, but very high in the liberalistic East Asian states: Hong Kong is the most unequal Asian country and Singapore follows just behind.

Determinants of Income Inequality at the Macro Level

Table 4.3 reports the findings of the multivariate linear regression analysis for the independent variable overall income inequality (Gini index) as indicated before. We applied robust regression instead of standard methods of regression (for example, ordinary least squares) because this method is highly stable also in the presence of strong single outliers from a general pattern (a problem particularly relevant in our data) and it also reduces problems of heteroscedasticity (Anderson 2008). Three variables included in our hypotheses were omitted from this analysis because of statistical problems. The first was ethnic heterogeneity which is correlated strongly with ethnic fractionalization (see Table 4.2). If they were both included here it resulted in too high VIF-values.[19] Several analyses in which Ethnic heterogeneity and ethnic fractionalization were entered alternatively as independent variables showed that the last variable was better able to capture our central dimension. Thus, we used only ethnic fractionalization as the predictor variable in the regression analysis.

---

17   See http://de.wikipedia.org/wiki/Liste_der_Streitkr%C3%A4fte_der_Welt; the data are based on the *World Defense Almanac 2006*, Bonn (Mönch Publ.) and *CIA World Factbook*. In the Scandinavian countries with the highest level of social spending, but also in Germany, the largest and economically most powerful EU member state, the defence budget is only 1.3 per cent of GNP.

18   The 90-million inhabitant country Ethiopia had a budget of around 4 billion US-$ in 2012 which is very low even compared with 18 billion US-$ of Kenya which had about 40 million people.

19   The value of VIF (Variance Inflation Factor) should not exceed .4 or so.

The second variable which caused the same problem was population growth. A separate analysis showed that it is strongly correlated with social spending and, to a smaller degree, with GDP per capita. These correlations are easy to explain: population growth is generally higher in the global South, and extremely high in Sub-Saharan Africa, the poorest macro-region in the world. The inclusion of the variable population growth in the regression analysis resulted in statistically inacceptable values of the Variance Inflation Factor (VIF); therefore, it was omitted from the analysis. We have to keep in mind, however, that population growth is one of the important determinants or concomitants of economic inequality and it is easy to understand why. If a rural family living off subsistence agriculture has to feed five or six children (as it is typically the case in Sub-Saharan Africa), the income per capita will be very low. Exactly for this reason, in Sub-Saharan Africa as a whole, the considerable economic growth in the last two decades has not been able to reduce widespread poverty – on the contrary it was even increasing.

The main findings in regard to the effects of the variables indicating the ethnic structure of the countries can be summarized as follows.

Table 4.3   **Robust regression analysis of overall income inequality (Gini Solt 2009; Beta-coefficients)**

	Independent variables	Basic model	Extended models			
		I	**IIa**	**IIb**	**IIIc**	**IIId**
Ethnic structure	Ethnic fractionalization	0.25**	0.24***	.24***	0.13*	0.06
	Ethnic conflict	-0.02	-0.02	-0.02	-0.04	-0.02
	Ethnoclass exploitation	0.41***	0.23**	.23**	.32***	0.15*
Other social structural variables	Population size		-0.03	-0.03	-	-
	GDP p.c.(log.)		-0.11	-0.11	-	-
	GDP p.c. (log. square)		-0.22***	-.21**	-	-
	Land distribution			0.02	0.27***	.27***
Political system variables	Democratic tradition				-0.05	0'01
	Federal constitution				-.13*	-.10*
	Communism				-0.39***	-0.31***
	Social spending					-.32***
Constant		-0.04	0.18*	0.18	-0.02	-0.04
Residual std. error		0.80 (df=119)	0.75 (df=116)	0.75 (df=115)	0.66 (df=115)	0.57 (df=114)

Statistical significance: *p<0.1; ** p<0.05; *** p<0.01; No of countries: 123.

In the basic model Ia, only the three variables related to the ethnic structure are included. Here, ethnic fractionalization and historical ethno-class exploitation are statistically significant; particularly the index of historical ethno-class exploitation has a strong effect. Thus, our central hypothesis is clearly confirmed at this level. Not significant, however, is the variable 'ethnic conflict'. This is not difficult to understand: the level of ethnic conflict depends not only on the degree of inequality between the ethnic groups, but also on their ethnic consciousness and organization; in addition, a high level of conflict may indicate that all (or at least some) ethnic groups are well organized and fighting for their rights which, as a consequence, can lead to a reduction of inequality. Thus, the level of ethnic conflict often can be higher in countries with lower objective inequalities between them as in those with high ethnic inequalities. The same relation has been observed in the occurrence of revolutions which typically do not break out in very poor and unequal societies but in societies with significant processes of growth and redistribution (Davies 1962; Tanter and Midlarsky 1967).

What happens if we include the social-structural control variables population size, level of socio-economic development and inequality of land distribution (Models IIa and IIb)? First, we can see that the variable population size is not significant. Thus, small countries are not necessarily more equal in economic terms than large ones, as our hypothesis has stated. This variable was omitted, therefore, in the extended models. The issue is more complex in the case of socio-economic development (GDP per capita). Our first analyses showed no overall significant effect, which indicated there exists no linear effect here. Therefore, we created a new variable, distinguishing four groups of countries (very low, relatively low, relatively high and very high levels of development). Such a categorization corresponds better to the Kuznets theory which proposes, in the course of economic development, an inverted U-curve, that is, first an increase and later a decrease of economic inequality (see Chapter 14). With this differentiation, one significant effect materialized: the most developed countries have a lower income inequality than the poorest countries. The significance of this effect is limited, however, because we know that a high GDP/capita is closely correlated with high social spending. In addition, since the relationship between GDP/capita and income inequality is not linear, we tested an additional interaction effect which turned out to be significant. Figure 4.3 shows that there seems in fact to exist a weak curvilinear relationship (as proposed by Kuznets) between GDP/per capita and income inequality: inequality is highest among countries with an intermediate level of development and clearly lower

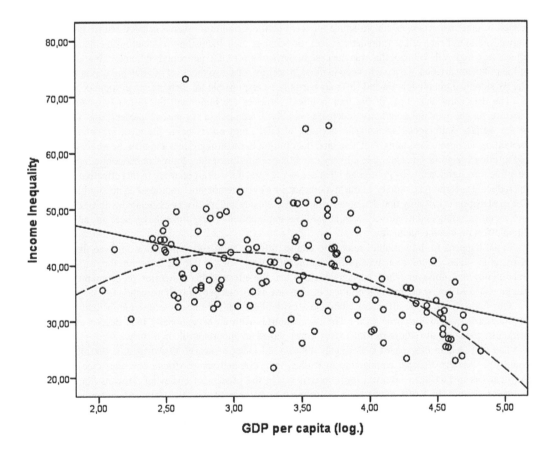

Figure 4.3 **The relation between level of socio-economic development and income inequality**
Notes: Correlation coefficients r=.69[xx] (Pearson); r=.71[xx] (Spearman).

in the most highly developed countries. We can also see that the introduction of GDP per capita results in a decrease of the explanatory power of ethno-class exploitation. This is quite easy to understand since heavy forms of slavery were practised mainly on continents which are rather poor today (Africa, Latin America).

An important question is the effect of land distribution. In model IIa, it is not significant, but it becomes significant and quite strong in models IIIa and IIIb. Thus, we must conclude that land distribution is a significant predictor of income inequality: the more unequal the land distribution, the more unequal also is income distribution. Thus, the findings of Frankema and Deininger and Olinto are clearly confirmed. From the perspective of the basic theorem of this work, it is important, however, that the variables ethnic heterogeneity and ethno-class exploitation retain their significant predictive value also in the extended model IIIa which includes land distribution. The connection between inequality of land distribution and income distribution is quite obvious in the case Latin America: when conquering and capturing this sub-continent, the Portuguese and Spanish invaders distributed the land among themselves similarly to how it was distributed at the Iberian Peninsula in Europe, that is, in a very unequal way. Huge estates were given to the invaders (often coming from noble families in Europe) and little or nothing was left to the native Indian population or the Black people introduced by force into the country. It is also symptomatic that Portugal and Spain today are among the most unequal countries in Western Europe (see Table 1.1). However, the exploitation of this land was possible only through the importation of slave labour or through enforced labour of natives. Thus, both unequal land distribution, slavery and bondage all were essential elements of the colonial mode of production and exploitation on this continent.

Finally, models IIIa and IIIb in Table 4.3 include also the political variables. In these models, all variables related to other aspects of social structure – except land distribution – were excluded, either because they showed no significant effect (population size), or because their inclusion produced problematic statistical effects (too high VIF-values); this was the case in particular for GDP per capita. When looking at the effects of the political variables we have to keep in mind, therefore, that also the level of GDP per capita (which was clearly significant in models IIa and IIb) may partially be responsible for their effects to some degree.

The data show that three of the four political variables are important: the residual standard error (a measure for the explained variance) decreases clearly. Communism (in past or present) and the strength of the welfare state (social spending as per cent of GDP) turn out as being the most important variables explaining economic inequality. But also land distribution has a strong effect and also the effect of a federal constitution is significant. These are all very important results since they show that economic inequality can be influenced significantly by politics and that democracy and the welfare state are in fact effective institutions for reducing inequality. Contrary to our hypothesis, however, democratic tradition has no significant effect. The explanation is certainly that democratic tradition is closely and positively associated with GDP per capita and social spending and negatively with ethno-class exploitation. Thus, it may have more an indirect than a direct effect on income inequality.

What happens to the variables related to ethnic differentiation and exploitation in these final models? Here, ethno-class exploitation retains its significant effect. This is not the case for the variable ethnic fractionalization, however. Thus, we can conclude that the effect of this dimension on economic inequality can be balanced out by the relevant political institutions, particularly by a welfare state.

Our findings about the effects of ethno-class exploitation on present-day economic inequality can well be illustrated by two European cases. The two countries with an exceptionally high degree of economic inequality today are also those in which slavery has played an important role in history.

The first case in this regard is Portugal. With a Gini-index of nearly 39, Portugal is the most unequal country in Western Europe, comparable to Russia, the USA and some African countries (see Table 1.1). Portugal has in fact been involved more intensively in the process of enslaving Africans than any other European country and this might have contributed to its present-day high level of inequality. Such an interpretation contradicts a widespread view of Portugal in regard to the development of slavery and the treatment of slaves. It is frequently mentioned – as a positive aspect – that the Portuguese did not separate themselves, as the British did, strictly from the slaves which mostly were Black and coloured populations. Particularly in Brazil, their main huge colony, there was a high level of miscegenation between the White and Black population, leading to a high proportion of mulattos. A continuous process of mixing of the races has been going on in fact in Brazil and is still going on today. While in 1940, there were 21 per cent *pardos* in the population, this proportion increased continuously; in the 2000 Brazil census 45 per cent were classified as *pardos*, that is of brown or coloured skin (Schmitt 2008: 77). Gilberto Freyre in his famous study of life on a slave plantation argued that Portuguese lifestyle and culture was in many ways akin to African culture; this enabled them to develop a unique and new kind of tropical society and culture in Brazil (Freyre 1964: 27ff.). Portugal, according to Freyre's interpretation, was a cosmopolitan and adaptable society, situated between Africa and Europe (more related to the former than to the latter), it always tended toward extremes, and – due to their high sexual appetites – Portuguese men impregnated women in all parts of the world where they arrived. In this way they adopted themselves to tropical life conditions and were able to create a strong and compliant population of mulattos. What is missing in this somewhat romantic and euphemistic view is the role of force and violence connected with slavery also in the Portuguese case. The first slave market in Europe was established in the Portuguese seaport Lagos in 1444, quite a time before the discovery of America. In the first half of the 16th century, at least 10 per cent of the population of Lisbon, around 9,000 persons, were slaves.[20] Portugal was the last European country which forbade the slave trade in 1836 (Grant 2010: 124; Schmitt 2008: 14). In their African colonies (Angola, Mozambique, Cape Verde, Guinea-Buissau), the Portuguese were quite racist and resourceful in the exploitation of Africans, applying forced labour, and detaining thousands in rehabilitation centres as punishment for strikes (Okuth 2006: 143–4). It is no accident that in some former Portuguese colonies the most long-lasting and cruel liberation wars were taking place.

The other case is Turkey. This country is even more distant from all other East and South East European countries in terms of its extremely high level of economic inequality; in fact, it corresponds to the very unequal Sub-Saharan, Latin American and Asian countries. This fact can also clearly be traced back to the historical past of Turkey. In the Arabic-Islamic world and in the Ottoman Empire, the precursor of present-day Turkey, slavery played a pivotal role: they were used as concubines, domestic servants and harem guards, as workers and craftsmen and as soldiers (*Janissaries*); even many high officials and military leaders who were bought slaves but raised free (Lewis 1992; Toledano 1993; Flaig 2009: 83–123; N'Diaye 2010). The latter certainly had a privileged position, but only as long as they were useful and absolutely loyal to their masters. Overall, however, it seems to be a myth that Islamic and Ottoman slavery was relatively mild, even benign, compared with American slavery (Toledano 1993: 52). The slaves were brought in from the Northeastern Slavic peoples (the Crimean Tatars sold 2.5 million slaves to the Ottoman Empire between 1450 and 1700; Flaig 2009: 88), from East Africa through the Red Sea and the Nile Valley and from Central Africa through the Sahara. In one Ottoman army operating in Hungary in 1777, there were about 64,000 Africans among a total of 350,000 soldiers (N'Diaye 2010: 157). After the Turks seized control of the Balkans in the 14th century, they continued with the import of slaves for half a millennium. In Istanbul, the proportion of enslaved among the population was about one fifth, in other parts of the country less.[21]

Arabic-Islamic and Ottoman slavery was characterized by one very peculiar feature, hardly present in such an extended form in any other slave society: the male slaves were castrated in order that they could not become dangerous as sexual competitors and could not establish their own family and kinship, but remained absolutely loyal to their masters. The castration of boys, an extremely painful and life-threatening process (only 10–20 per cent of the boys survived the operation), was done by middle men (mostly Coptic priests) during the transport of the slaves from Africa to the Mediterranean. Most of the slaves, however, were females, working as domestic slaves and concubines. Most wealthy men in Constantinople had several Black concubines but the number of their children remained low, either because the concubines were not allowed to give birth to them or because the babies were killed by their mothers after birth because they could only become slaves. In modern Turkey, which defines itself as a homogeneous nation-state and has ventured large-scale processes of ethnic cleansing and suppression (expulsion of Greeks, genocide among Armenians, suppression of Curds), some descendants of African slaves are still there but hardly conscious of their ancestry.[22] Thus, we can see here again the close connection between ethnicity and kinship, elaborated in Chapter 2 (see pp. 33–5). This treatment and use of

---

20   Wikipedia: 'Slavery'; according to other sources even one-fifth of Lisbon's inhabitants were slaves at this time.

21   'Slavery', in Encyclopaedia Britannica's Guide to Black History: see http://www.britannica.com/blackhistory/article-24157

22   See, for instance, Piotr Zalewski, 'Turkish descendants of African slaves begin to discover their identity', *The National*, 1 September 2012.

slaves in the Islamic and Ottoman world – which in fact can be described as ethnic cleansing (N'Diaye 2010) – is the polar opposite to that of the Portuguese in Brazil, which was characterized by miscegenation and the emergence of a new 'race' from the White and Black populations.

Also the history of the abolition of slavery in the Ottoman Empire is characteristic. Trade and possession of slaves was limited and formally forbidden only in the middle of the 19th century after European (particularly English) pressure but continued clandestine. It is indicative that in the reform movement Tanzimat (1839–76), which led to a new constitution restricting the absolute powers of the Sultan, slavery was not questioned. The same was true for the reformers called Young Ottomans (Toledano 1993: 46–8). This was an issue where these modern-minded social and political critics did not see a necessity to adopt modern Western values. So, it is not surprising that trade and use of slaves came under penalty only towards the end of the 19th century.

We may conclude and summarize the findings of the multivariate analysis of the determinants of income inequality as follows. It is obvious that ethnic differentiation and ethno-class exploitation are significant determinants of income inequality; the second variable retains its effect in the regression analysis even after a series of other relevant variables have been controlled for. The effect of ethnic heterogeneity and fractionalization is certainly also important but in a more indirect way, by leading to more ethnic conflicts and inhibiting the development of a strong welfare state and probably also by delaying economic development. Thus our hypotheses 1 and 2 have clearly been confirmed.

Now, let us also look at the additional important aspect of income inequality, the relative privilege of the highest income groups and the situation or deprivation of the lower income groups. As outlined in Chapter 1 (p. 4). the Gini coefficient gives only a mean value for the whole population but is not able to capture these groups well. In regard to the relative privilege of the well-to-do, the coefficients should be similar to those in the foregoing analysis; in the case of the lower income groups, they should have a different sign. That is, if overall economic inequality is high in a country, we expect that the higher social strata are more privileged and the lower less deprived. If overall inequality is low, we expect that the share of the lower income groups is higher.

The same regression analyses have been carried out with the two dependent variables – the income shares of the upper 10 per cent income and lowest 40 per cent income receivers, respectively – as with the Gini coefficient. In general, the results were quite similar, showing that in the first models, both ethnic differentiation/fractionalization and ethno-class exploitation were significant, but the demographic variable (population size) was not significant. Thus, for reasons of space we present here only the final models, in which the ethnicity variables and those related to the political system are included. Table 4.4 shows the regression analyses with both dependent variables (proportion of persons who are among the highest 10 per cent income receivers and those who are the 40 per cent lowest income receivers). The following four findings are most remarkable: (1) ethnic fractionalization has a significant impact on both proportions: in ethnically differentiated and fractionalized societies, the poorer get less and the richer get more income than in ethnically homogeneous societies; (2) ethno-class exploitation has an effect on the share of the lower income groups, reducing it significantly. This effect is easy to understand since slavery has long-lasting impacts both on society and on the individuals, as shown in Chapter 5 (pp. 145–7); (3) strong effects can be seen from inequality of land distribution and Communism, which parallels the findings on overall inequality; (4) a surprising difference is that public social spending has no significant effect on the income shares of the upper and the lower classes. This finding seems to confirm analyses of the effects of the welfare state which have shown that its main effect is not a vertical, but a horizontal redistribution, that is, from the employed to the non-employed people (children, old aged people) but not from the rich to the poor (Flora and Heidenheimer 1981; Flora 1986; Zijderveld 1986; Thakur 2003; Brooks and Manza 2006). This finding sheds also additional light on the first finding, the fact that ethnic fractionalization has significant impacts both on the higher and the lower classes. One could say that the welfare state is mainly able to redistribute in the middle of the class and social structure but not at the upper and lower margins. It corresponds to some surprising findings in Chapter 6 where it will be shown that Swedish society which is very equal in terms of income distribution is quite unequal in terms of wealth distribution. In general, we can conclude that ethnic differentiation, fractionalization and a history of ethno-class exploitation all turned out as important predictors of the relative income privilege and discrimination of groups located at the upper and lower ends of the class and social status structure.

Table 4.4   Robust regression analysis of the relative incomes of the lowest 40 per cent and the highest 10 per cent income receivers (BETA coefficients)

	Lowest 10 per cent	Highest 40 per cent
Ethnic fractionalization	-.19*	.23***
Ethnic conflict	.07	-.07
Ethno-class exploitation	-.19*	.12
Inequality of land distribution	-.27***	.21***
Democratic tradition	.03	-.07
Federal elections	.10	-.15**
Communism	.48***	-.40***
Social spending	.05	-.08
Constant	.004	-.06
Residual standard error	0,76 (df=103)	0,61 (df=103)

Statistical significance: *p<0,1; ** p<0,05; *** p<0,01; n = 112.

Corruption and Violence as Consequences of Ethnic Heterogeneity, Exploitation and Economic Inequality

We can now go on to the results concerning the findings of the effects of ethnic heterogeneity and economic inequality on violence and corruption. Also in these regressions, we have included some additional, potentially relevant social structural and political control variables.

Table 4.5 presents the analysis of the determinants of corruption.[23] The demographic variable population size shows no effect. This is the case, however, for the variable of GNP per capita; it has a highly significant, strong effect: the higher GNP, the smaller corruption. This effect, however, is strongly confounded with other

Table 4.5   Regression analysis of corruption (Corruption Perception Index 2002; Beta-coefficients)

	Independent variables	Basic model	Extended models	
		I	IIa	IIb
Inequality	Gini-coefficient	.01	'04	.04
Ethnic structure	Ethnic fractionalization	-.12	.06	-.00
	Ethnic conflict	-.10	-.04	-.08
	Ethno-class exploitation	-.64***	-.33***	-.25**
Other social structural variables	Population size		-.05	-
	GDP per capita		'.67***	-
Political system variables	Democracy			.27***
	Democracy square			.15*
	Federalism			.03
	Communism			-.04
	Land inequality			.11*
	Social spending			.29***
Explained variance (adjusted R²)		.52	.76	.73
Std. error		1.51	1.07	1.13

Statistical significance: *p<0.1; **p<0.05; ***p<0.01; n = 122.

---

23   The values for corruption have been taken from Tansparency International, a global civil society organization, based in Berlin, Germany. See http://archive.transparency.org/policy_research/surveys_indices/cpi/2002

variables (resulting in too high VIF-values). Thus we omitted this variable in models IIa and IIb. The findings can be summarized as follows:

- Economic inequality (the Gini coefficient) has no significant effect on corruption.
- Among the variables relating to the ethnic structure, ethno-class exploitation is statistically significant: the more widespread and/or stronger slavery was in the past, the higher the level of corruption today.
- A significant effect comes also from land inequality: the higher land inequality, the higher corruption.
- Most of the political system variables turn out as important: here, we can see a very strong effect of the variable Democratic tradition, but also a significant effect of the variable social spending: Democratic countries and countries with a strong welfare state have less corruption. A federal constitution has no effect.

What about violence and its dependence on the history of slavery and present-day ethnic differentiation and economic inequality? Violence was measured by the variable 'murderers per 100.000 persons in a country'.[24] Here, we can again see two significant effects (see Table 4.6). First, income inequality is highly relevant: the level of violence is much higher in unequal societies. Second, also historical ethno-class exploitation is important: in countries with extended slavery in history, there is more violence today. Surprisingly, the political variables have no significant effect. If we look at the distribution of violence in the different countries and macro-regions of the world today, the results presented so far are obvious. Violence is quite high in many Sub-Saharan African countries and in the Republic of South Africa, and it is extremely high in many

Table 4.6   Regression analysis of violence (murders per 1000 inhabitants; Beta-coefficients)

	Independent variables	Basic model	Extended models	
		I	IIa	IIb
Economic inequality	Gini-coefficient	.37***	.36***	.26*
Ethnic structure	Ethnic fractionalization	.09	.08	.10
	Ethnic conflict	-.01	-.02	-.01
	Ethno-class exploitation	.22**	.21*	.25**
Other social structural variables	Population size		-.09	-
	GDP per capita		-.05	-
Political system variables	Democracy			.21
	Democracy square			.04
	Federalism			-.03
	Communism			.00
	Land inequality			-.09
	Social spending			-.16
Explained variance (adjusted R²)		.30	.30	.29
Std. error		10.05	10.06	10.06

Statistical significance: *p<0.1; ** p<0.05; *** p<0.01; n = 123.

---

24   The data for murderers were taken from UN data, the UNODC Homicide Statistics (see http://data.un.org); they were compiled by the UN Office on Drug and Crime's International Homicide Statistics Database.

Latin American countries. This corresponds fully to the historical and empirical evidence mentioned in the earlier chapters of this work: it was mainly slavery in the Americas which was connected with a high level of physical violence. In Latin America, also in public opinion a positive correlation exists between violence, crime and inequality (Morgan and Kelly 2010).

We may summarize the findings of this additional analysis as follows: ethno-class exploitation has, as suggested, a significant effect on corruption and on violence; both these problematic social phenomena are much more frequent in societies characterized by slavery in former times. Economic inequality leads also to increased violence, while a lack of democracy and a weak or non-existent welfare state increase corruption.

Empirical results II: Qualitative Comparative Analysis

Another way to investigate the effect of historic ethnic exploitation and ethnic differentiation and fractionalization on income inequality on a global scale is Fuzzy Set Analysis (FSA) (Ragin 2000, 2008; Ragin and Sonnett 2005; Blatter et al. 2007). This method enables us to grasp at least approximately also the interaction effects between ethnic differentiation, class and economic structures and characteristics of the political system. The guiding question here is, in particular, how the characteristics of the variables discussed above combine in concrete countries and whether it is possible to minimize these combinations to a few dominant patterns. In the regression analysis, the net effect of each variable is of central interest, while qualitative comparative analysis (QCA) in general and Fuzzy Set Analysis (FSA) in particular explicitly seek to unravel the interplay of characteristic groupings of variables, that is, causal conditions. Thereby, the effects of different independent variables are not investigated in isolation to each other but interactive patterns of effects are investigated and thereby several different routes of dominant combinations of conditions to a specific outcome (causal equifinality) are assessed. This seems appropriate, considering the complexity and heterogeneity of the global scale of our analysis. This configurational approach to causal analysis was already proposed by Max Weber who wrote that 'a concrete result cannot be viewed as the product of a struggle of certain causes favouring it and others opposing it. The situation must, instead, be seen as follows: The totality of *all* the conditions back to which the causal chain from the 'effect' leads to 'act jointly' in a certain way and in no other for the concrete effect to be realized' (quoted in Ragin and Sonnett 2005: 5–6).

FSA provides both a descriptive overview of characteristics of combinations of conditions in the form of a truth table and a formal, logical reduction of empirical combinations of causal conditions.[25] After calibrating the variables and applying the Quine-algorithm, set-theoretic relationships, indicating necessary and sufficient conditions for a specific outcome, can be obtained.[26] A condition X is sufficient for an outcome Y if, whenever the condition is given, the outcome is present as well. There can be multiple paths to Y (X => Y but also Z => Y) and these causal paths are usually not conceptualized as single conditions (X or Z) but as configurations of several factors, causing the outcome (only) by their interaction (X*Z => Y). The concept of fuzzy sets allows opening this deterministic framework of causation in order to incorporate higher degrees of indeterminacy. Consistency values indicate the *degree to which the empirical evidence is consistent with the set theoretic relation.* This is the case if these values are high, if the Fuzzy Set values of X are less or equal to the outcome values and if there are none or only few inconsistent cases (Ragin and Sonnet 2005: 5–6).[27] After a condition is established as sufficient (consistency value > 0.80), the empirical relevance of a causal path,

---

25   The basic idea of the Quine algorithm performing the logical reduction can be outlined as follows: in each step of the formal analysis, two configurations leading to the same outcome (in our case high levels of income inequality) are compared. If they differ only in the characteristic of one condition, but still lead to the same outcome, this condition is considered causally non-important for the outcome in question and is excluded in the further iterative process of logical minimization. This process continues until no further logical reduction is possible. For a recent introduction to the application of Crisp and Fuzzy Set QCA see Rihoux and Ragin 2009.

26   The following software has been used for the computations: fs/QCA (v.2.5) by Ragin, Drass and Davey (2006) and the 'QCA' package (v.1.0–4) by Thiem and Dusa (2012).

27   In formal terms, this can be expressed in this way:

$$\text{Consistency } (X_i \le Y_i) = \sum \frac{\min(X_i, Y_i)}{\sum(X_i)} \quad \text{Coverage } (X_i \le Y_i) = \sum \frac{\min(X_i, Y_i)}{\sum(Y_i)}$$

that is, the number of cases covered by this combination of causal conditions, is indicated by its coverage value.[28] Figure 4.4 illustrates three different sub-set relations between outcome (UE = unequal country), condition (EC = historic ethnic exploitation) and consistency and coverage. Historic ethnic exploitation is a (perfectly consistent) sufficient condition, if all countries with a history of ethnic exploitation are a sub-set of the set of unequal countries (1a). The condition covers a substantial number of cases within the set of unequal countries, therefore it is an empirically important condition. There are, however, also unequal countries without this attribute, that is, there exist different causal pathways (causal equifinality). Subset 1b shows partial overlapping, that is, outcome and condition do not constitute a perfect sub-set but there are also some equal (more exactly: non-unequal) countries with a history of ethnic exploitation. Finally, a condition might constitute a perfect sub-set of an outcome but is empirically of little relevance if it covers only few cases (1c).

Variables, Fuzzy Sets and Hypotheses

The following variables will be included based on their theoretical relevance and their significance as shown in the regression analysis: ethnic exploitation, ethnic fractionalization, Communism, social spending level and land inequality. We use the direct method of calibration outlined by Ragin (2008) for continuous variables;[29] while history of Communism is entered as *crisp set* (that is, it can have only the values 0 or 1). In FSA, metric and pseudo-metric variables are calibrated into directed fuzzy sets. Thus, the variable democracy is transformed into the fuzzy set *democratic country*, where countries have varying memberships between one (full membership) and zero (full non-membership) based on set thresholds. The calibration of continuous variables is sensitive to the determination of the thresholds set by the researcher. Ideally, one would base the cut-off point (the point of maximum ambiguity: 0.5) and the level of fully-in and fully-out cases on theoretical and in-depth case knowledge. However, when dealing in an exploratory way with more than 120 countries as cases in a diverse and global setting, this procedure is not always applicable. Therefore, we combined information of the empirical distribution of cases (10th/50th/90thquantile) and case-knowledge for calibration.[30]

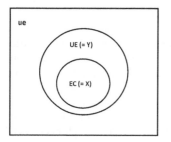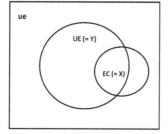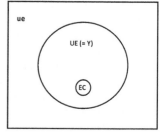

Figure 4.4   Subset relations

28   See Ragin 2009, page 118.

29   Thereby producing s-shaped fuzzy numbers by means of logistic transformation. For details see the 'QCA'-package for R by Thiem & Dusa (2012).

30   Calibration of both *ethnic fractionalization* and *land inequality* relies on the 10th/50th/90th quartile. The calibration of income inequality into *high income inquality country* (full membership/cross-over point/full non-membership: Gini 50/36.50/27.7) and *low income inequality country* (full membership/cross-over point/full non-membership: Gini 27.7/36.5/50) closely resembles the empirical distribution of the sample but is changed minimally in order to have the case of the United States of America above the cut-off point. The fuzzy sets *country with ethnic-exploitative history* (2/5.5/8) and *established welfare state* (social spending in per cent of GDP: 5/10/15) were calibrated after detailed inspection of the clustering of countries.

Our theoretical expectations formulated in the foregoing regression analysis as a series of single correlative statements (the higher ethnic heterogeneity, the higher income inequality and so on) have to be transformed into combinatorial set-theoretic causal relationships and formulated in terms of causal necessity and sufficiency. We have to distinguish here at the outset between unequal and equal countries. The following considerations belong to the sub-set of unequal countries. We expect neither high fractionalization nor historic ethnic exploitation or land inequality to be necessary or sufficient conditions on their own, but to act as *INUS* conditions (Goertz 2003). INUS is an abbreviation for an 'Insufficient (on their own) but Necessary Part of an Unnecessary but Sufficient Condition for a particular outcome'. It means that we expect that both ethnic fractionalization and ethnic exploitation are parts of different combinations of conditions leading towards high levels of economic inequality within a country. If countries experienced Historic ethnic exploitation (EE) and present day ethnic fractionalization (EF) or land inequality (LD), we assume that these countries show high levels of income inequality (EC). However, there are two important facts which theoretically could reduce the impact of ethnic exploitation and fractionalization on income inequality: the equalizing historic effect of decades of Communism (CO) and the existence of a welfare state (SS), that is, political redistribution. Framed in another way, this implies that high levels of income-inequality exist today if a country has a past of ethnic exploitation and present ethnic fractionalization and land inequality, but which has neither a Communist tradition nor a redistributive welfare state. The configuration of these conditions is deemed as a sufficient factor for high levels of inequality. If there is, on the other hand, a Communist past and/ or a present redistributive welfare state in such a country, we would expect lower levels of income inequality and in general less clear-cut results (that is, non-consistent solutions).

Our theoretical expectations for the outcome 'unequal countries' can be formalized as follows:[31]

$$EE*EF*LD*co*ss$$
$$EE*EF*LD*co*ss \qquad \rightarrow UE$$
$$EE*ef*LD*co*ss$$

According to the fuzzy-logic we do not expect the portrayed causal pathways to be the only solution towards high levels of income inequality, but we expect to cover a substantial proportion of the total cases with these pathways.

Results

Table 4.7 shows the truth table rows of configurations of conditions with at least three empirical instances, resulting in a total of 113 countries.[32] Countries appear here as instances of configurations of dichotomous variables but actually vary within this qualitative difference. Austria, for instance, appears as empirical instance of the vector combination 0, 0, 0 1, 0 (in row two) – that is, not having a history of ethnic exploitation, being neither ethnically fractionalized nor a highly land-unequal country, without a Communist past but with an established welfare state. But actually, it displays the following fuzzy values: 0.10, 0.05, 0.98, 0.99 (and 0 in Communist history). Rows with countries consistently showing the outcome of interest, that is, high economic inequality, indicated by the inclusion score ($> = .85$, shaded columns), are highlighted.

---

31 Following Rihoux and de Meur (2009: 34–5) the notations of Boolean algebra read as follows: upper case letters represent a value above the threshold of 0.5. Thus [EF] reads as ethnic fractionalized countries. Lowercase letters display values below the threshold of 0.5, that is, [ef] thus reads as non-ethnic fractionalized countries. The logical 'AND' is represented by the [*] symbol and the logical 'OR' is represented by the [+] symbol. EC*EF*dt + EC*EF*ws + EC*EF*dt*ws → UE then reads as: ethnic exploitation and ethnic fractionalization and absent democratic tradition or ethnic exploitation and ethnic fractionalization and absent welfare state or ethnic exploitation and ethnic fractionalization and absent democratic tradition and absent welfare state are sufficient for high levels of income-inequality. Expectations for the case of the outcome of 'equal countries' mirror the expectations for unequal countries.

32 The case number threshold per configuration set by the researcher corresponds to the overall case number and the number of conditions. Since our sample includes 125 countries, we decided to set a minimum case number threshold of three, in order to avoid empirically non-important configurations entering the formal analysis. This is necessary as all configurations of either positive or negative outcomes enter the formal analysis at equal weight as a valid configuration leading to one outcome type, irrespective of their case numbers.

Table 4.7 Truth table: unequal countries

	EE	EF	LD	SS	COM	OUT	N	INCL	Cases
1	0	0	0	0	0	0	6	0.83	BD, BW, I.E., KR, SG, LK
2	0	0	0	1	0	0	13	0.34	AU, AT, DK, FR, DE, GR, IT, JP, NL, NZ, NO, SE, GB
3	0	0	0	1	1	0	4	0.33	HR, FI, PL, SI
4	0	0	1	0	0	1	4	0.95	DZ, AR, CR, SV
5	0	0	1	1	1	0	3	0.43	CZ, HU, LT
6	0	1	0	0	0	1	5	0.91	GM, IN, ID, NP, PG
7	0	1	0	1	0	0	3	0.62	BE, CA, CH
8	0	1	1	0	0	1	4	0.97	CL, MU, PK, SN
9	0	1	1	1	1	1	3	0.66	EE, LV, MD
10	1	0	0	0	0	1	8	0.87	BI, EG, MA, RW, TW, TH, TN, TR
11	1	0	1	0	0	1	6	0.96	DO, GY, JM, PH, VE, ZW
12	1	0	1	0	1	0	8	0.68	AL, AM, AZ, CN, MN, NI,RU, UZ
13	1	0	1	1	1	0	4	0.52	BY, BG, RO, UA
14	1	1	0	0	0	1	16	0.93	BF, CM, TD, FJ, GH, JO, MG, ML, MR, NE, NG, SL, SY, TG, UG, US
15	1	1	0	0	1	0	3	0.82	BJ, CG, ET
16	1	1	1	0	0	1	20	0.96	BO, BR, CF., CO, EC, GT, GN, IR, KE, LB, MY, MX, NA, PA, PE, SA, ZA, TZ, TT, ZM
17	1	1	1	0	1	0	3	0.76	KG, MZ, TJ

Truth table rows with >= 3 empirical cases. EE: ethnic exploitative countries, EF: ethnically fractionalized countries, COM: Communist history, SS: welfare state countries, LD: countries with high levels of unequal land distribution, OUT: outcome, INCL: inclusion score; n = 110. For country abbreviations see Table 4.A, p. 121.

The truth table visualizes dominant combinations of conditions of unequal countries, thereby allowing a deeper insight into the patterns of how the different causal conditions outlined combine in different parts of the globe to lead toward high inequality. Here, first we see that although there are a number of pathways, only two combinations include a larger number of cases, that is, are empirically most important. Sixteen countries from Sub-Saharan Africa (row 14) follow the pattern of a history of ethnic-exploitation, present-day ethnic fractionalization and missing welfare and democratic structures. These countries, however, do not feature strong land inequality nor did they experience a history of Communist regime. In row 16, 20 geographically more heterogeneous countries (although including 10 Latin American cases) fully follow our expectations as they were ethnically exploitative and are ethnically fractionalized countries with an unequal land distribution, and lack a strong welfare state and a Communist past. Taken together, these 36 countries follow our expectations on the impact of historic ethnic exploitation and present-day ethnic fractionalization outlined in the hypotheses above. Other unequal countries following different trajectories show that these conditions can interact in multiple ways. Costa Rica, Argentina, El Salvador and Algeria (row 4), for example, did not experience historic ethnic exploitation, nor are they today ethnically fractionalized, but they show unequal land distributions and lack an established welfare state. Again others have had a history without ethnic fractionalization or land inequality (like Egypt, Morocco, Tunisia, Turkey, Rwanda, Thailand and Taiwan in row 10) or combine ethnic exploitation with land inequality without fractionalization like the Latin American islands appearing in row 11. While ethnic exploitation, fractionalization and land inequality vary over the country groupings, all combinations of unequal countries share two characteristics: none of them have had a Communist past nor do they maintain strong, redistributive welfare states. If we would focus only on the two logical combinations of conditions with the largest empirical coverage, we would conclude that historic ethnic exploitation and present ethnic fractionalization together with lacking a welfare state and a non-Communist past are sufficient for high levels of income inequality. High land inequality differs between these two configurations, that is, between Latin America where it is often present and Sub-Saharan Africa where it is often lacking. Thus, it can be regarded as non-essential for an unequal income distribution. If we include the other 30 unequal countries dispersed over a number of configurations of conditions, we cannot so easily infer a conclusion by visual inspection but must rely on an algorithm to derive dominant patterns.

Table 4.8 shows the intermediate solution[33] (overall consistency = 0.81) including three sufficient conditions of comparable empirical relevance, each a configuration of three conditions, covering in sum more than 70 per cent of the total number of unequal countries. All conditions are consistent (> 0.85) and overlap substantially as indicated by the large differences between raw (r-cov) and unique (u-cov) coverage in terms of both characteristics, that is, they all share the absence of a welfare state and have not been Communist. Forty-six cases are multiple covered, that is, they can be represented by more than one configuration.

The combination of a lack of an established welfare state or a Communist history is a necessary condition for unequal income distributions. Historic ethnic exploitation, present-day ethnic fractionalization and land inequality are characteristics shared by many unequal countries but not by all at the same time. These conditions can be seen as functional equivalents, representing – together with the lack of a welfare state and a Communist history – different pathways to unequal income distributions in different parts of the globe. If we compare the derived solution: EE*ss*com + EF*ss*com + LD*ss*com ➔ UE to our theoretical expectations outlined above, we can draw two conclusions. First, we see that we underestimated the empirical diversity on a global scale, causing our variables of interest ethnic exploitation and ethnic fractionalization to play a context-sensitive role across the globe only in unequal countries, that is, they are not present in all cases. Second, our specific expectations describe correctly the existing dominant empirical patterns in Latin America and Sub-Saharan Africa (see rows 11, 14 and 16 in Table 4.7).

Table 4.8 A fuzzy set analysis: complex solution unequal countries

Suff. configuration	R-COV	U-COV	CONS	Cases
EE*ss*com	0.59	0.05	0.85	BI, E.G., MA, RW, TW, TH, TN, TR, DO, GY, JM, PH, VE, ZW, BF, CM, TD, FJ, GH, JO, MG, ML, MR, NE, NG, SL, SY, TG, UG, US, BO, BR, CF., CO, EC, GT, GN, IR, KE, LB, MY, MX, NA, PA, PE, SA, ZA, TZ, TT, ZM
EF*ss*com	0.55	0.05	0.93	GM, IN, ID, NP, PG, BF, CM, TD, FJ, GH, JO, MG, ML, MR, NE, NG, SL, SY, TG, UG, US, BO, BR, CF., CO, EC, GT, GN, IR, KE, LB, MY, MX, NA, PA, PE, SA, ZA, TZ, TT, ZM
LD*ss*com	0.51	0.05	0.94	DZ, AR, CR, SV, DO, GY, JM, PH, VE, ZW, BO, BR, CF., CO, EC, GT, GN, IR, KE, LB, MY, MX, NA, PA, PE, SA, ZA, TZ, TT, ZM
Solution coverage	0.72			
Solution consistency	0.81			

EE: ethnic exploitative countries, EF: ethnically fractionalized countries, COM: Communist history, SS: welfare state countries, LD: countries with high levels of unequal land distribution, R-COV: raw coverage, U-Cov: unique coverage, CONS: consistency. For country abbreviations see Table 4.A, p. 121.

---

33 The used directional expectations to derive 'easy counterfactuals' follow our theoretical outlining. In case of the outcome 'unequal countries', the complex and the intermediate solutions are coincident.

In a second step, we analyse the opposite outcome: countries with low income inequality or, in other words, equal countries.[34] Our expectation is that absence of historic ethnic exploitation, little ethnic fractionalization or equal land distribution combined with present public welfare structures or historic Communism would be a sufficient condition for low income inequality.

Table 4.9 shows again the truth table of all those configurations of conditions, which display at least three empirical cases.[35] We see that all these configurations share one characteristic: they maintain redistributive welfare states. The largest group of 13 European countries (including Australia and New Zealand) follows our expectations outlined above as they were not subject to historic ethnic exploitation, are not ethnically fractionalized and have no high land inequality, but traditionally afford strong welfare states in a global comparison. Croatia, Poland, Finland and Slovenia (row 3) are distinct from this group only insofar as they have experienced decades of Communist rule. The Czech Republic, Hungary and Lithuania (row 5) diverge from the other Eastern European group insofar as they additionally have an unequal land distribution. The last set of Eastern European countries, comprising Belarus, Bulgaria, Romania and Ukraine (row 13), enlarges this configuration by also having experienced large-scale historic ethnic exploitation. All three configurations mentioned so far, however, share the absence of historic ethnic exploitation and present-day ethnic fractionalization. Belgium, Canada and Switzerland (row 7) are distinctive as they are ethnically fragmented.

Table 4.9   Truth table: equal countries

	EE	EF	LD	SS	COM	OUT	N	INCL	Cases
1	0	0	0	0	0	0	6	0.68	BD, BW, I.E., KR, SG, LK
2	0	0	0	1	0	1	13	0.94	AU, AT, DK, FR, DE, GR, IT, JP, NL, NZ, NO, SE, GB
3	0	0	0	1	1	1	4	0.96	HR, FI, PL, SI
4	0	0	1	0	0	0	4	0.54	DZ, AR, CR, SV
5	0	0	1	1	1	1	3	0.92	CZ, HU, LT
6	0	1	0	0	0	0	5	0.59	GM, IN, ID, NP, PG
7	0	1	0	1	0	1	3	0.95	BE, CA, CH
8	0	1	1	0	0	0	4	0.52	CL, MU, PK, SN
9	0	1	1	1	1	0	3	0.84	EE, LV, MD
10	1	0	0	0	0	0	8	0.58	BI, EG, MA, RW, TW, TH, TN, TR
11	1	0	1	0	0	0	6	0.47	DO, GY, JM, PH, VE, ZW
12	1	0	1	0	1	0	8	0.78	AL, AM, AZ, CN, MN, NI, RU, UZ
13	1	0	1	1	1	1	4	0.91	BY, BG, RO, UA
14	1	1	0	0	0	0	16	0.45	BF, CM, TD, FJ, GH, JO, MG, ML, MR, NE, NG, SL, SY, TG, UG, US
15	1	1	0	0	1	0	3	0.81	BJ, CG, ET
16	1	1	1	0	0	0	20	0.38	BO, BR, CF., CO, EC, GT, GN, IR, KE, LB, MY, MX, NA, PA, PE, SA, ZA, TZ, TT, ZM
17	1	1	1	1	0	1	0	0.81	KG, MZ, TJ

Truth table rows with >= 3 empirical cases. EE: ethnic exploitative countries, EF: ethnically fractionalized countries, COM: Communist history, SS: welfare state countries, LD: countries with high levels of unequal land distribution, SS: welfare social spending; OUT: outcome, INCL: inclusion score; n = 110.

---

34   'Not unequal countries' would be more precise. But since the empirical calibration of 'unequal countries' and 'equal countries' is symmetric, the verbal difference is not meaningful.

35   In order to avoid both inconsistent solutions or too complex solutions, we kept the consistency level of 0.85 and did not relax the consistency threshold to a lower level in order to include a number of ex-Communist countries like Estonia, Latvia, Azerbaijan or Uzbekistan (see rows 9 and 12), although some of these countries exhibit low levels of income inequality.

Table 4.10   Fuzzy set analysis: complex solution equal countries

Sufficient configurations	R-COV	U-COV	CONS	Cases
ee*ld*SS	0.40	0.31	0.94	AU, AT, DK, FR, DE, GR, IT; JP, NL, NZ, NO, SE, GB, HR, FI, PL, SI, BE, CA; CH
ef*SS*COM	0.21	0.12	0.91	HR, FIR, PL, SI, CZ, HU, LT, BY, BG, RO, UA
Solution coverage	0.52			
Solution consistency	0.88			

EC: ethnic exploitative countries, EF: ethnically fractionalized countries, COM: Communist history, SS: welfare state countries, LI: countries with high levels of unequal land distribution, R-COV: raw coverage, U-Cov: unique coverage, CONS: consistency.

The Fuzzy Set Analysis reduces these five configurations to two substantially overlapping, sufficient pathways of INUS conditions, covering 52 per cent of all equal countries or 27 cases. Both pathways share strong welfare state structures.[36] The first sufficient condition (ee*ld*SS) covers two-thirds of the selected equal countries and is highly consistent. The role of ethnic fractionalization of a country is not strongly associated with income distribution when there are welfare state structures and no unequal land distribution as can be seen in the cases of Switzerland, Belgium or Canada. The second pathway (ef*SS-H*COM) comprises exclusively Eastern European countries, being traditionally ethnically more diverse but also sharing a Communist past with present social welfare structures. This again implies that ethnic diversity does not necessarily imply inequality if hedged and balanced by high social spending (SS) in the form of democratic tax- or insurance-based welfare states and/or a heritage from decades of Communist rule.

Interim Conclusions

In the quantitative multivariate analysis we found that ethno-class exploitation and unequal land distribution are connected with higher income inequality today, while Communism and a welfare state reduced inequality. We could not test, however, how these two sets of factors interact. The findings of the qualitative comparative analysis, the FSA, supplement the results of the regression analysis. Factors of the political system in the form of welfare state structures and/or Communist rule make the difference whether historic ethnic exploitation and present ethnic fractionalization (and land inequality) lead to equal or unequal income distributions. In contrast to the regression analysis, the Fuzzy Set Analysis allows us to focus on the interplay of conditions and to allocate specific countries to specific configurations, thereby connecting the quantitative birds view with the case studies presented in the later chapters of this book. What can be learned from this analysis in addition to the previous regression analysis is that ethnic exploitation and ethnic fractionalization (and land inequality) are important causal conditions for present-day income inequality within countries in some but not in all regions of the world. The Fuzzy Set Analysis allows uncovering different pathways, each fully valid for a number of specific countries and it accounts for the vast differences in income inequality between most European countries on the one hand and Latin American and Sub-Saharan African countries on the other hand. In Europe, ethnic exploitation has never been significant, while most countries today have strong welfare states and a significant sub-set of countries have experienced Communism. In all these regards, historical and actual experiences and structures are almost mirror-inverted in Latin America and Sub-Saharan Africa.

---

36   This however does not imply that having an established welfare state is a necessary condition for equal income distributions as the analysis of sufficiency presented here is restricted to a smaller number of countries in highly consistent configurations. A separate analysis of necessity including all countries concludes that having an established welfare state does not meet the criterion (consistency score > 0.90) of necessity.

The North African and Asian countries fall into a wide range of differing constellations, connected also with highly varying patterns of economic inequality.

Summary and Outlook

In this chapter, the main thesis of this book – that ethnic heterogeneity and historical ethno-class exploitation will lead to higher economic inequality today – has been submitted to an empirical test in two forms. First, a multivariate analysis of the effects of ethnic heterogeneity and a history of ethno-class exploitation (slavery and other forms of forced labour) on economic inequality has been carried out at the aggregate level, using a new dataset for about 130 countries around the world. For this dataset, a new variable on historical ethno-class exploitation was developed. As dependent variables we used three indicators of economic inequality: overall inequality (as measured by the Gini coefficient), and the proportions of national income going to the larger, poorer section of the population (the lowest 40 per cent in terms of income) and to the smaller, richer population section (the highest 10 per cent). In addition, two additional sets of independent variables were introduced which can be considered as potential determinants of income inequality from the economic and sociological points of view. The first set included demographic factors (population size and growth), the level of socio-economic development of a country and land inequality; the second set was related to the political system of a country, including its age, its democratic tradition, its federal structure, a historical period of Communism and the level of welfare spending.

Our hypotheses concerning the effects of ethnic heterogeneity and historical ethno-class exploitation were clearly confirmed by the analysis. These variables are strong predictors of present-day economic inequality, and – as far as ethno-class exploitation is concerned – also after the introduction of all the additional independent variables mentioned before. The strong effect of land distribution on economic inequality is a clear hint to the fact that colonialism implied a closely connected bundle of institutions, structures and processes within which ethnic class exploitation played a central role. Also the findings on the effects of the control variables were highly interesting and relevant: particularly several of the political system variables have strong effects on overall economic inequality and equality. Inequality today is significantly lower if a state has a federal constitution, a Communist past (or present) and if its level of social spending is high.

Are ethnic heterogeneity and economic inequality significant predictors of political corruption and crime as postulated? Also in this regard, most of the findings confirmed our hypotheses: both corruption and violence are higher if a country has a history of ethno-class exploitation. Corruption, in addition, is also higher if there is no democratic tradition, if land is distributed unequally and if there is only a weak welfare state.

The Fuzzy Set Analysis presented in the last section confirmed and supplemented these findings. Focusing upon different combinations of independent factors, it showed also that ethnic fractionalization is an important concomitant of income inequality. While its effect did not remain statistically significant in the final regression model, it is obviously highly relevant in combination with other factors. Unequal land distribution on the other side seems to be crucial in some cases (for example, 'White' Latin America), but not so in other. The FSA also confirmed that particularly aspects of the political system (a Communist past, a strong welfare state) make a difference whether historical ethno-class exploitation and present-day ethnic fractionalization lead to economic inequality. This analysis sheds additional light on the vast difference between most European countries and those in Sub-Saharan Africa and Latin America.

In the following, second part of this book, these differences shall be elaborated more in detail by case studies of different patterns of ethnic stratification. Also in this regard, FSA has shown that the large number of countries can be combined into a limited set of types which include characteristic combinations of ethnic differentiation, political systems and patterns of economic inequality and equality. The most encouraging finding of this analysis – that ethnic stratification and the resulting economic inequality can be influenced significantly by politics – shall be taken up again in the final Chapter 13.

Appendix

Table 4.A   International country codes

Albania	AL	Greece	GR	Panama	PA
Algeria	DZ	Guatemala	GT	Papua New Guinea	PG
Argentina	AR	Guinea	GN	Peru	PE
Armenia	AM	Guyana	GY	Philippines	PH
Australia	AU	Hungary	HU	Poland	PL
Austria	AT	India	IN	Portugal	PT
Azerbaijan	AZ	Indonesia	ID	Romania	RO
Bangladesh	BD	Iran	IR	Russian Federation	RU
Belarus	BY	Ireland	IE	Rwanda	RW
Belgium	BE	Israel	IL	Saudi Arabia	SA
Benin	BJ	Italy	IT	Senegal	SN
Bermuda	BM	Jamaica	JM	Sierra Leone	SL
Bolivia	BO	Japan	JP	Singapore	SG
Botswana	BW	Jordan	JO	Slovenia	SI
Brazil	BR	Kazakhstan	KZ	South Africa	ZA
Bulgaria	BG	Kenya	KE	Spain	ES
Burkina Faso	BF	Korea, South	KR	Sri Lanka	LK
Burundi	BI	Kyrgyzstan	KG	Sweden	SE
Cameroon	CM	Laos	LA	Switzerland	CH
Canada	CA	Latvia	LV	Syria	SY
Central African Republic	CF.	Lebanon	LB	Taiwan	TW
Chad	TD	Lesotho	LS	Tajikistan	TJ
Chile	CL	Lithuania	LT	Tanzania	TZ
China	CN	Macedonia	MK	Thailand	TH
Colombia	CO	Madagascar	MG	Togo	TG
Congo (Brazzaville)	CG	Malaysia	MY	Trinidad & Tobago	TT
Costa Rica	CR	Mali	ML	Tunisia	TN
Croatia	HR	Mauritania	MR	Turkey	TR
Cyprus	CY	Mauritius	MU	Uganda	UG
Czech Republic	CZ	Mexico	MX	Ukraine	UA
Denmark	DK	Moldova	MD	United Kingdom	GB
Dominican Republic	DO	Mongolia	MN	United States of America	US
Ecuador	EC	Morocco	MA	Uruguay	UY
Egypt	EG	Mozambique	MZ	Uzbekistan	UZ
El Salvador	SV	Namibia	NA	Venezuela	VE
Estonia	EE	Nepal	NP	Vietnam	VN
Ethiopia	ET	Netherlands	NL	Yemen	YE
Fiji	FJ	New Zealand	NZ	Zambia	ZM
Finland	FI	Nicaragua	NI	Zimbabwe	ZW
France	FR	Niger	NE		
Gambia	GM	Nigeria	NG		
Georgia	GE	Norway	NO		
Germany	DE	Pakistan	PK		
Ghana	GH	Palau	PW		

References

Acemoglu, Daron, Simon Johnson and James A. Robinson (2001), 'The Colonial Origins of Comparative Development: An Empirical Investigation', *American Economic Review* 91: 1369–401

Acemoglu, Daron and James A. Robinson (2012), *Why Nations Fail. The Origins of Power, Prosperity and Poverty*, New York: Random House Inc.

Alesina Alberto et al. (2003), 'Fractionalization', *Journal of Economic Growth* 8: 155–94

Alesina, Alberto and Eliana La Ferrara (2005), 'Ethnic Diversity and Economic Performance', *Journal of Economic Literature* 43: 762–800

Alesina, Alberto and Enrico Spolaore (2003), *The Size of Nations*, Cambridge, MA: MIT Press

Alesina, Alberto F, Stelios Michalopoulos and Elias Papaioannou (2012), 'Ethnic Inequality' NBER WP 18512, CEPR Discussion Paper 9225

Anderson, Robert (2008), *Modern Methods for Robust Regression*, Los Angeles: Sage Publications

Angeles, Luis (2005), Income inequality and colonialism, Paper, University of Lausanne

Ansell, Ben and David Samuels (2010), 'Inequality and democratization: A contractarian approach', *Comparative Political Studies* 43: 1543–74

Atkinson, Anthony B. and François Bourguignon (2000a), 'Income distribution and economics', in Atkinson and Bourguignon, *Handbook of Income Distribution*, pp. 1–58

Atkinson, Anthony B. and François Bourguignon, eds (2000b), *Handbook of Income Distribution*, Amsterdam etc.: Elsevier

Bitterli, Urs (1993), 'Die Ankunft der weißen Götter', in W. Arens and H.M. Braun, eds, *Die Indianer. Ein Lesebuch*, München

Blatter, Joachim K., Frank Janning and Claudius Wagemann (2007), *Qualitative Politikanalyse. Eine Einführung in Forschungsansätze und Methoden*, Wiesbaden: VS Verlag für Sozialwissenschaften

Blau, Peter and Judith Blau (1982), 'The cost of inequality: Metropolitan structure and violent crime', *American Sociological Review* 47: 45–62

Bley, Helmut et al., eds (1991), *Sklaverei in Afrika*, Pfaffenweiler: Centaurus

Blümle, Gerold (1975), *Theorie der Einkommensverteilung*, Berlin etc.: Springer

Boix, Carles (2003), *Democracy and Redistribution*, Cambridge: Cambridge University Press

Bourguignon, F. and T. Verdier (2000), 'Oligarchy, Democracy, Inequality and Growth', *Journal of Development Economics* 62: 285–313

Brenner, Robert (1987a), 'Agrarian Class Structure and Economic Development in Pre-Industrial Europe', in Aston and Philpin, *The Brenner Debate*, pp. 10–63

Brenner, Robert (1987b), "The Agrarian Roots of European Capitalism", in: T.H. Aston and C.H.E. Philpin, eds, *The Brenner Debate. Agrarian Class Structure and Economic Development in Pre-Industrial Europe*, Cambridge etc.: Cambridge University Press, pp. 213–329

Brooks, Clem and Jeff Manza (2006), 'Why do welfare states persist?' *The Journal of Politics* 68: 816–27

Carter, Michael R. (2000), Land ownership inequality and the income distribution consequences of economic growth, UNU World Institute for Development Economics Research (UNU WIDER), Working Paper 201

Castillo, Bernard D. del (1982 [1568]), *Geschichte der Eroberung von Mexiko*, Frankfurt: Insel

Checchi, Daniele (2000), Does educational achievement help to explain income inequality? UNU WIDER, Working Paper 208

Coleman, James W. (1987), 'Toward an Integrated Theory of White-Collar Crime', *American Journal of Sociology* 93: 406–39

Crespo Cuaresma, Jesús, Samir K.C. and Petra Sauer (2012), Gini coefficients of educational attainment, Wittgenstein Centre, Vienna University of Economics and Business

Davies, James (1962), 'Toward a theory of revolution', *American Sociological Review* 27: 5–19

De Gregorio, J. and J.W. Lee (2002), 'Education and Income Distribution: New Evidence from Cross-country Data'. *Review of Income and Wealth* 48: 395–416

Deininger, K. and P. Olinto (1999), 'Asset distribution, inequality, and growth', World Bank Policy Research, Working Paper No. 2375

Deininger, Klaus and Lyn Squire (1996), 'A new data set measuring income inequality', *World Bank Economic Review* 10: 565–91

Deininger. K. and L. Squire (1998), 'New ways of looking at old issues: inequality and growth', *Journal of Development Economics* 57: 259–87

Doria, Palmerio (2009), *Honoraveis Bandidos. Um retrato do Brasil na era Sarney*, Sao Paolo: Geracao Editorial

Driessen, Michael D. (2008), 'Ethno-linguistic fractionalization: Dataset review', *APSA* Comparative Politics Newsletter, Winter 2008

Durkheim, Emile (1993 [1893]), *The Division of Labour in Society*, New York: Free Press

Engerman, Stanley and Kenneth Sokoloff (2005), Colonialism, inequality, and long-run paths of development, Working Paper 11057, National Bureau of Economic Research, Cambridge, MA

Engerman, Stanley, Seymour Drescher and Robert Paquette, eds (2001), *Slavery*, Oxford: Oxford University Press

Fajnzylber, Pablo et al. (2002), 'Inequality and Violent Crime', *Journal of Law and Economics* XLV: 1–40

Fearon, James D. (2003), 'Ethnic and cultural diversity by country', *Journal of Economic Growth* 8: 195–222

Flaig, Egon (2009), *Weltgeschichte der Sklaverei*, München: C.H. Beck

Flora, Peter and Arnold J. Heidenheimer, eds (1981), *The Development of Welfare States in Europe and America*, New Brunswick/London: Transaction Publishers

Flora, Peter (1975), *Modernisierungsforschung. Zur empirischen Analyse der gesellschaftlichen Entwicklung*, Opladen: Westdeutscher Verlag

Flora, Peter et al., eds (1986), *State, Economy, and Society in Western Europe: 1815–1975. A Data Handbook in Two Volumes*, vol. 1, Frankfurt/Main: Campus

Flora, Peter, ed. (1986), *Growth to Limits. The Western European Welfare State in Comparative Perspective*, Vol. 1, Berlin/New York: W. de Gruyter

Földvári, P. and B. Van Leeuwen (2011), 'Should Less Inequality in Education Lead to a More Equal Income Distribution?' *Education Economics* 19: 537–54

Frankema, Ewout (2009a), *Has Latin America Always Been Unequal? A Comparative Study of Asset and Income Inequality in the Long Twentieth Century*, Boston/Leiden: Brill

Frankema, Ewout (2009b) 'The Colonial Origins of Inequality: Exploring the Causes and Consequences of Land Distribution', in Klasen, S. and Nowak Lehman F., *Poverty, Inequality and Policy in Latin America*, Cambridge, MA: MIT Press, pp. 19–45

Frankema, Ewout (2010) 'The Colonial Roots of Land Distribution: Geography, Factor Endowments or Institutions?' *Economic History Review* 63: 418–51

Freyre, Gilberto (1964), *The Masters and the Slaves. A Study in the Development of Brazilian Civilization*, New York, Knopf (here quoted after the German ed. Herrenhaus und Sklavenhütte, Köln/Berlin: Kiepenheuer & Witsch 1965; original ed. Rio de Janeiro 1933)

Goertz, Gary (2003), 'The substantive importance of necessary condition hypotheses', in Gary Goertz and Harvey Staff, ed., *Necessary Conditions: Theory, Methodology, and Applications*, Lanham: Rowman & Littlefield, pp. 65–94

Govindaraj R. and Rannan-Eliya R. (1994), Democracy, Communism and Health Status: A Cross-National Study, Department of Population and International Health, Harvard School of Public Health, Boston

Grant, R.G. (2010), *Geschichte der Sklaverei*, London: Dorling Kindersley (Slavery, London 2009)

Gupta, Sanjeev, Davoodi Hamed and Rosa Alonso-Teme (1998), 'Does corruption affect income inequality and poverty?' International Monetary Fund, WP/98/76

Harenberg (2000), *Aktuell 2001*, Dortmund: Harenberg Lexikon Verlag

Helpman, E. (2004), *The Mystery of Economic Growth*, Cambridge, MA, London: The Belknap Press

Husted, Brian (1999), 'Wealth, Culture, and Corruption', *Journal of International Business Studies* 30: 339–60

Jong-Sung, You and Sanjeev Khagram (2005), 'A Comparative Study of Inequality and Corruption', *American Sociological Review* 70: 136–57

Kelly, Morgan (2000), 'Inequality and Crime', *The Review of Economics and Statistics* 82:530–39

Kelly, Morgan and Nathan J. Kelly (2000), 'Explaining public attitudes toward fighting inequality in Latin America', *Poverty and Public Policy* 2:79–111

Kohr, Leopold (1983), *Die überentwickelten Nationen*, München: Goldmann

Kremer, Michael and Daniel L. Chen (2002), 'Income distribution dynamics with endogenous fertility', *Journal of Economic Growth* 7: 227–58

Laitin, David and Daniel Posner (2001), 'The Implications of Constructivism for Constructing Ethnic Fractionalization Indices', *APSA-CP: Newsletter of the Organized Section in Comparative Politics of the American Political Science Association* 12: 13–17

Lepsius, Rainer M. (1988), *Interessen, Ideen und Institutionen*, Opladen: Westdeutscher Verlag

Lerner, Daniel (1969), 'Die Modernisierung des Lebensstils', in Zapf, *Theorien des sozialen Wandels*, pp. 362–81

Levinson, David (1998), *Ethnic Groups Worldwide. A Ready Reference Handbook*, Phoenix, Arizona: Oryx Press

Lewis, Bernard (1992), *Race and Slavery in the Middle East. An Historical Enquiry*, Oxford: Oxford University Press

Li, Hongyi, Lyn Squire and Heng-fu Zou (1998), 'Explaining International and Intertemporal Variations in Income Inequality', *The Economic Journal* 108: 26–43

Lipset, Seymour Martin (1979), *The First New Nation. The United States in Historical and Comparative Perspective*, New York: Norton

Lutz, Wolfgang, K.C. Samir (2011), 'Global human capital: Integrating education and population', *Science* 333: 587–92

Lutz, Wolfgang, Warren C. Sanderson and Sergei Scherbov (2004), *The End of World Population Growth in the 21st Century*, London: Earthscan

Mann, Michael (2007), *Die dunkle Seite der Demokratie. Eine Theorie der ethnischen Säuberung*, Hamburg: Hamburger edition (*The Dark Side of Democracy*, New York 2005)

Marshall, Monty and Keith Jaggers (2010), Polity IV Project: Regime Characteristics and Transitions 1800–2010 (online)

Marx, Karl (1971 [1867]), *Das Kapital. Kritik der politischen Ökonomie*, 1. Bd., Berlin: Dietz Verlag

Miller, Debra (2007), *Political Corruption*, San Diego, CA: Lucent Books

Moore, Barrington, Jr (1993), *Social Origins of Dictatorship and Democracy: Lord and Peasant in the Making of the Modern World*, Boston: Beacon Press

Morrison, Christian and Fabrice Murtin (2010), The Kuznets Curve of Education: a global perspective on educational inequalities, London School of Economics, Centre for the Economy of Education

N'Diaye, Tidiane (2010), *Der verschleierte Völkermord. Die Geschichte des muslimischen Sklavenhandels in Afrika*, Reinbek: Rowohlt (French ed. Paris 2008)

Neumayer, Eric (2005), 'Inequality and violent crime: Evidence from data on robbery and violent theft', *Journal of Peace Research* 42: 101–12

Okuth, Amo (2006), *A History of Africa, vol. 2: African Nationalism and the De-Colonisation Process*, Nairobi etc.: African Educational Publishers

Olson, Mancur (2000), *Power and Prosperity. Outgrowing Communist and Capitalist Dictatorships*, New York: Basic Books

Patsiurko, Natalka et al. (2011), 'Measuring cultural diversity: Ethnic, linguistic and religious fractions in the OECD', *Ethnic and Racial Studies* 35: 195–217

Pfaff-Giesberg, Robert (1955), *Geschichte der Sklaverei*, Meisenheim: A. Hain

Ragin, Charles C. (2000), *Fuzzy-Set Social Science*, Chicago: University of Chicago Press

Ragin, Charles C. (2008), *Redisigning Social Inquiry. fuzzy sets and Beyond*, Chicago: University of Chicago Press

Ragin, Charles C. (2009), Qualitative comparative analysis Using fuzzy sets (fsQCA), in: Rihoux and Ragin, *Configurational Comparative Methods*, pp. 87–122

Ragin, Charles C. and John Sonnett (2005), 'Between complexity and parsimony; Limited diversity, counterfactual cases, and comparative analysis', in Sabine Krapp and Michael Minkenberg, eds, *Vergleichen in der Politikwissenschaft*, Wiesbaden: VS Verlag für Sozialwissenschaften, pp. 180–97

Ragin, Charles C., Kriss A. Drass and Sean Davey (2006), *Fuzzy-Set/qualitative comparative analysis 2.0*, Tucson: University of Arizona, Department of Sociology

Rihoux, Benoît and De Meur, Gisèle (2009) '*Crisp-Set qualitative comparative analysis (csQCA)*', in Rihoux and Ragin, *Configurational Comparative Methods*, pp. 33–68

Rihoux, Benoît and Charles C. Ragin, eds (2009), *Configurational Comparative Methods*, Los Angeles etc.: Sage

Roniger, Luis (1994), 'The comparative study of clientelism and the changing nature of civil society in the contemporary world', in Luis Roniger and Ayse Günes-Ayata, eds., *Democracy, Clientelism, and Civil Society*, Boulder, CO: Lynne Rienner, pp. 1–18

Ross, Robert (1983), *Cape of Torments. Slavery and Resistance in South Africa*, London: Routledge & Kegan Paul

Santos, Ana Maria Barros dos (1985), *Die Sklaverei in Brasilien und ihre sozialen und wirtschaftlichen Folgen. Dargestellt am Beispiel Pernambuco (1840–1889)*, München: W. Fink Verlag

Sauer, Petra and Martin Zagler (2012), '(In)equality in education and economic development', Wittgenstein Centre, Vienna University of Economics and Business

Schmitt, Jucelmo L. (2008), *Die Lage der schwarzen Bevölkerung vor und nach Abschaffung der Sklaverei in Brasilien*, Bonn etc.: Scientia Bonnensis

Smith, Adam (1933 [1776]), *Natur und Ursachen des Volkswohlstandes*, Leipzig: A. Kröner

Solt, Frederick (2009), 'Standardizing World Income Inequality Database', *Social Science Quarterly* 90: 231–42

Stefes, Christoph H. (2006), *Understanding Post-Soviet Transitions. Corruption, Collusion and Clientelism*, London: Palgrave

Streissler, Erich and Monika Streissler (1986), *Grundzüge der Volkswirtschaftslehre für Juristen*, Wien: Manz

Tanter, Raymond and Manus Midlarsky (1967), 'A theory of revolution', *Conflict Resolution* XI: 264–80

Thakur, Subhash et al., eds (2003), *Sweden's Welfare State: Can the Bumblebee Keep Flying?* Washington, DC.: International Monetary Fund

Thiem, Alrik and Adrian Dusa (2006), *qualitative comparative analysis with R. A User's Guide*, New York: Springer

Toledano, Ehud R. (1993), 'Ottoman concepts of slavery in the period of reform, 1830s–1880s', in Martin A. Klein, ed., *Breaking the Chains. Slavery, Bondage, and Emancipation in Modern Africa and Asia, Madison*, WI/London: The University of Wisconsin Press, pp. 37–63

Vanhanen, Tatu (1999), 'Domestic ethnic conflict and ethnic nepotism: A comparative analysis', *Journal of Peace Research* 36: 55–73

Vanhanen, Tatu (n.d.), Index of Power Resources, available at: http://www.fsd.uta.fi)

Wail, Benaabdelaali, Hanchance Said and Kamal Abdelhak (2011), A new data set of educational inequality in the world, 1950–2010, Morocco: National Authority of Evaluation of the Educational System/LEAD, University of Toulon-Var, France

World Bank (2005), *Equity and Development. World Development Report 2006*, Washington: The World Bank, New York: Oxford University Press

World Development Report (2006), *Equity and Development*, Washington/New York: The World Bank/ Oxford University Press

Wraith, Ronald and Edgar Simpkins (1963), *Corruption in Developing Countries*, London: G. Allen & Unwin

Zapf, Wolfgang, ed. (1969), *Theorien des sozialen Wandels*, Köln/Berlin: Kiepenheuer & Witsch

Ziblatt, Daniel (2008), 'Does Landholding Inequality Block Democratization? A Test of the ,Bread and Democracy Thesis and the Case of Prussia', *World Politics* 60: 610–641

Zijderveld, Anton C. (1986), 'The ethos of the welfare state', *International Sociology* 1: 443–57

PART II
Historical-comparative Analysis and Case Studies

The Prevention and the Emergence of Ethnic Differentiation and Stratification. A Sociological-historical Typology

In Part I of this book, the process of the interaction between the triad of class formation, social stratification and ethnic differentiation have been in the centre. I have developed hypotheses as to how they interact and what effects these interaction processes have on economic inequality. These hypotheses have been tested at the aggregate level of nation-states. These analyses shall now be supplemented by investigating the question of whether ethnic differentiation and ethnic stratification come into existence at all in concrete societies and what they look like today. Such an analysis is necessary for two reasons. First, social historians and historical sociologists argue rightly that important past events and processes, the way how they originated and the course they took, can make a long-lasting imprint on societies (Tocqueville 1945; Wehler 1973; Braudel 1992; Tilly 1998; Lorenz 1997). This has been shown empirically for the effect of historical slavery on present-day economic inequality in the previous chapter. Second, it is necessary to look at the ways that ethnic heterogeneity comes about in a society because the related processes are going on all the time also in the present-day world. In fact, the issues of immigration control, integration, assimilation and exclusion of old and new minorities are top political agendas today in many countries. On the basis of the considerations and the concepts developed in Part I, I will elaborate in this chapter specific types of societies in terms of ethnic homogeneity and heterogeneity, and – in the latter case – their patterns of ethnic stratification. The basic theorems of Part I that are relevant here include the designation of class formation, social stratification and ethnic differentiation as the basic triad in the emergence, reproduction and transformation of inequality, the role of the state and the relevance of ideologies of equality and inequality. In addition, the concept of 'social closure', developed by Weber (1964), is highly useful here. (On this concept see also Giddens 1973; Parkin 1979; Haller 1983; Murphy 1988; Wimmer 2002.) It enables us to see that class stratification and ethnic differentiation within nation-states are also significantly shaped by attempts to control immigration in order to preserve or control their internal ethnic composition. I will argue that the interaction between all these processes has led to a restricted number of types – maybe a dozen or so – of ethnic differentiation and stratification. This fact facilitates qualitative comparative analysis enormously because we must not look at 150 or more societies but can limit ourselves to an in-depth analysis of a few characteristic cases from each of the general types.

I start from the assumption that there are three fundamental mechanisms or strategies to 'manage' (Lake/ Rotchild 1996; Kmezic et al. 2008; Marko 2012) ethnic differentiation: (1) strategies to preserve or to restore ethnic homogeneity; (2) strategies to deal with and to control ethnic heterogeneity; and (3) strategies to establish ethnically based systems of domination and exploitation (see Table 5.1). In this chapter, these strategies are defined and characterized in shortened form. A more extended discussion and analysis of the most important is given in the following Chapters 6 to 12. Only slavery, the historically most important form of ethno-class exploitation which does not exist anymore openly today, will be described more extensively in this chapter.

Strategies to Preserve or to Restore Ethnic Homogeneity

In Chapter 2 it was shown that ethnically homogeneous societies show a higher level of socio-cultural integration and political stability than ethnically heterogeneous societies. Governments generally aim to raise the level of socio-economic integration because it makes it easier for them to govern (Shils 1982; Olzak 2006). Therefore, they will try to avoid the emergence of ethnic differentiation or – if it already exists and if the ethnic minorities cannot be assimilated easily – to hide them and make them 'invisible'. Strategies of this sort have been applied to the present time.

A landmark in these efforts was the principle *cuius region, eius religio* established in the *Peace of Westphalia* in 1648 after the devastating Thirty Years' War in Europe. This treaty laid the foundations for the modern state system in Europe. It was put into effect most successfully in Scandinavia. In Sweden, for instance, the Protestant Lutheran church was the state church between 1527 until 1999 with the king as its head; still in 2005, 77 per cent of the Swedes were members of this church, all other religious denominations had less than 2 per cent members.[1] It was certainly related to this fact that in Sweden such a high societal consensus could emerge concerning economic and social equality, but probably also with the fact that in terms of the distribution of property, Sweden is one of the most unequal countries of the world (as Table 6.4 shows and as I will further elaborate in Chapter 6). In Catholic empires, such as France and Austria, Protestants were constrained to re-convert to Catholicism or to leave the country which hundreds of thousands did. Also the forced creation of linguistic homogeneity played a central role in this process of the establishment of the homogeneous nation-states in Europe between the 17th and 19th centuries (Lemberg 1964; Schieder 1964; Kohn 1967; Schulze 1999). The administration of the emerging absolutist states and the establishment of large standing armies made it necessary to establish a single, standardized language for nation-wide communication (Deutsch 1966). Empires characterized by cultural-linguistic heterogeneity, such as the Austro-Hungarian monarchy, disappeared not the least because of language conflicts between its ethnic-national subgroups. In East and South East Europe, the breakup of several states and the emergence of new ones in recent times occurred mostly along linguistic borders. But also religious cleavages – between Catholics and Orthodox peoples and between Christian and Islamic peoples – continued to be important to the present time. In Africa, some of the worst violent and long-lasting civil wars occurred in the countries at the southern end of the Sahara in which Muslims and non-Muslims were united by the colonial powers into one state, such as in the Sudan, Chad, Niger, Mali, Nigeria and others. In West Europe and North America, language conflicts and, to a lesser degree, religious cleavages are still acute and threaten the survival of whole nation-states in their present form, such as Belgium and Canada.

Political efforts to preserve ethnic homogeneity are typically pursued by conservative governments and propelled by right-wing, nationalist parties. They propose three main arguments: first, the cultural argument of the necessity to safeguard the nation against foreign infiltration, particularly in the case if the immigrants have a different religion to the natives (such as Muslims in West and North Europe); second, by the economic argument that immigrants crowd out native workers from jobs because they are ready to work at very low wages; and third, by political arguments stating that immigrants increase crime and misuse the welfare system. Political movements and parties which pursue these arguments are often supported by groups of people who are quite heterogeneous in their class situation. Among them are members of old and new middle classes who are concerned about the preservation of their social status and workers who fear unfair competition from the immigrants. Entrepreneurs and members of higher social classes and strata often display ambivalent attitudes and behaviours. On the one side, they are liberal and open concerning immigration because it offers direct advantages for them (availability of a cheap labour force for enterprises and private households); on the other side, they are anxious to distance themselves socially quite clearly from the immigrants.

Within the general aim of preserving the ethnic homogeneity of a society, we can distinguish four specific strategies: total isolation of a society, separation of minorities, constrained assimilation and secession (see Table 5.1, p. 136 below).[2]

---

1   Fischer Weltalmanach 2008, Frankfurt: Fischer Taschenbuch Verlag, p. 411.

2   A relevant additional form is ethnic cleansing. This topic would deserve a separate analysis. I can refer here to the comprehensive recent work of Michael Mann (2005). His provocative thesis that *ethnic cleansing* is a process which emerged only in modern democracies is fully compatible with my central thesis about the persisting relevance of ethnicity in the present-day world. Related, somewhat less cruel but also often violent, were population relocations between states which were effected in order to make the participant states (more) homogeneous in ethnic terms. Such 'exchanges', which often involved massive terror and violent expulsions, involved millions of people. Examples include that between Greece and Turkey in the 1920s (1.6 million) or between India and Pakistan in 1947–48 (20 million). Also the involuntary return or expulsion of over 15 million Germans from Central East Europe to Germany after 1945 belongs to this category.

Encapsulation of Whole Societies

There were several cases in history, in which whole nation-states attempted successfully to preserve their ethnic-cultural homogeneity throughout long periods. This was achieved by encapsulating themselves totally against the outside world (or significant parts of it). Attempts in this direction are made today as well, as a consequence of worldwide interconnections through communication, economic exchanges and people's movements; however, they are no longer really enforceable (for example North Korea, Cuba).

The most spectacular instance of such an isolation was carried out by Japan at the beginning of the Modern Age when first contacts with Western powers took place and were felt as potential threats. From 1615 till the middle of the nineteenth century, Japan isolated itself more or less completely from the rest of the world in order to keep away any foreign influences (Hall 1968). With the Meiji revolution in 1868, a complete turn was taken and Japan began to import systematically Western innovations, from science and technology up to educational and legal systems. This did not result in simple *Westernization*, however, but led to a modernization of Japan in which the Western elements were adapted to Japan's own culture. A Western country which in more recent times pursued a considerate policy of preservation of ethnic homogeneity was Australia. The Immigration Restriction Act of 1911 initiated a strategy of preserving White Australia with the aim to restrict immigration to Whites (first even to British) immigrants. This policy, which lastly was in contradiction to the Universal Declaration of Human Rights as amended by the United Nations in 1948, was fully brought to an end only with the Racial Discrimination Act of 1975. I will show in Chapter 13 (pp. 365 and 368), these policies have after-effects in both countries until today. Japan is formally open for all immigrants; as a consequence of the severe conditions connected being awarded with a visa and the peculiarities of its culture and language, immigration rates are still very low. A tendency to closure and a certain type of racism is still present also in Australia, as an Australian Commission for Human Rights has noted in 2001; one can recognize it also in political statements and actions of several political parties and governments (for more details see Chapter 13).

Isolation and Confinement of Ethnic Minorities

Here, we can subsume all those strategies of social exclusion of minorities which aim at their concentration in certain territories or living quarters, to leave them in these places to their own resources and – first of all – to take care that the majority will not be disturbed by them. This strategy is applied particularly against minorities which in their social structure and culture preserve traditional elements and, therefore, are significantly distinct from the dominant modern way of life so that an integration and assimilation is difficult. There were and still are many examples of such strategies around the world.

A first important case in point are the natives in the New World. The way of life of the *Native Americans* and *Indios* in North and South America, and of the *Aborigines* and *Maori* in Australia and New Zealand represented a very traditional lifestyle which was incompatible with modern Western civilization. Their clash with Western culture and military and political power through wars and genocides (in some cases till the extirpation of whole tribes), diseases and famines reduced their numbers sharply. With the creation of 'reservations', they were accorded their own *Lebensraum* (living space), however under conditions which worsened the situation because many of them in earlier times were accustomed to live in large, thinly populated areas. In Latin America where the indigenous population outnumbered the European immigrants by far this was not possible and the invaders (mainly men) intermixed with them through miscegenation. Their offspring, the *Mestizos* (descendants of Indios and Whites), today constitute the majority of the population; in these countries (such as Mexico and Columbia) social exclusion is attenuated, but discrimination still is strong.

A comparable group are the *Sinti* and *Roma* in Europe. There is no country where they are a majority or a sizable minority, although they are between one and two million in some Central East European countries (Bulgaria and Romania) there are between one and two million; the whole number of the *Gypsies* (their former designation which now is considered as racist) is estimated as high as 12 million. Because many of them were not sedentary in former times (today this is true, however, for less than 10 per cent), a considerable volume of them (those living in Romania) were enslaved and because of their particular language and lifestyle they were perceived over centuries as a threatening minority in Central and West Europe and often were even persecuted.[3] Their situation has worsened after the breakdown of Communism in East Europe, also as a consequence of social exclusion by non-Roma and by neglect from national governments. Roma children get less education; the level of unemployment is very high and villages inhabited mostly by Roma have a bad infrastructure (see Liégeois 2007; Henn 2011; Pusca 2012; Mappes-Niedick 2012; Scholze 2013). Their deprivation was one of the factors contributing to the increase of inequality in those countries. The normative pressure and financial support by the European Union, whose members these states have been for a decade, has not been able to overcome the deprived situation of the *Gypsies* in a significant way[4] (Henn 2011). Due to worsening of the situation of the Roma in Central and East Europe, many of them migrated to Western countries like Germany and France. Here, there again they aroused xenophobic attitudes among sectors of the population and harsh political measures, including expulsion by political authorities. In 2010, for instance, the French President and Government initiated a programme of Roma repatriation; in 2009–10, about 10,000 Roma were deported.[5] A comparable, tiny minority are the *Buraki* in Japan; they live in barrack settlements amidst the skyscrapers of modern metropolises.

This strategy to exclude and hide a national minority is applied also in one other form of exclusion, namely, that of hard penal treatment of delinquent members of minorities. Here, the United States are leading worldwide: in 2009, there were about two and a half million people in US-American prisons (1 per cent of the whole population); altogether 7.2 million persons (3.1 per cent of the population) were under correctional supervision. This was an incarceration rate of 743 per 100,000 population – one of the highest in the world; in the UK, it is about 150, in Norway 71.[6] The extremely high number of prisoners is closely connected with discrimination against minorities; two thirds of US prisoners are non-White (mainly Black and Hispanic). Imprisonment of peculiar members of minorities can be observed also in Australia. Here several states introduced compulsory arrest for adults who repeatedly committed small property offenses or other minor offences.[7] Since such offences are more common among Aborigines, they are mostly affected by these measures; they are 20 times more often in jail than other Australians.

Enforced Assimilation

Nearly all European nation-states which were established and developed in the 18th and 19th century tried to homogenize their populations in ethnic terms – mainly in the interest of an enforcement of centralized state power. A considerable pressure toward cultural integration was exerted already in those countries which had a historically continuous central power and administration; this was the case in France, England and in the European colonies in North and South America (Lemberg 1964/I: 92ff.; Anderson 1998: 52ff.). An important aspect of these homogenization efforts was the linguistic assimilation through compulsory education in the (new) national tongue of the population often divided by regional and local languages and dialects (Gardt 2000). The most exemplary case in point was France; the *Langues d'oil* which were spoken in the political centre around the Ile-de-France were imposed on all parts of the nation since the mid-17th century. Further examples for such strategies can be found in the second and third waves of national independence movements in Central, South and East Europe. Italy, for instance, at the time of its unification in the late 19th century – which occurred under the motto of the existence of a cultural-linguistic community – was no homogeneous country at all. In several border areas in the North, the 'unification' included territories with linguistic minorities (French-speaking people in the Valle d'Aosta, Slovenes in Friuli and Istria); the population in South Italy and Sicily spoke particular Italian idioms, and many considered the new lords from North Italy as aliens (Procacci 1983).

---

3   The National Socialist aimed at exterminating them like the Jews.
4   In Germany, see also http://de.wikipedia.org/wiki/Roma-Politik_der_Europ%C3%A4ischen_Union
5   See http://en.wikipedia.org/wiki/French_Roma_expulsion. I will come back to the question of the Roma in Chapter 13, p. 362.
6   See http://en.wikipedia.org/wiki/Incarceration_in_the_United_States (16.9.2011).
7   Vgl. Gesellschaft für bedrohte Völker, 'Rassismus in Australien' von Julia Hett, 31.8.2001 (http://www.gfbv.de/inhaltsDok.php?id=420&stayInsideTree=1; 6.1.2011).

Coerced integration and cultural assimilation in this sense can enforce also economic inequality in a country. A new polarization emerges between the centre and these (typical peripheral) areas where most members of the minority are living. This happens not only in terms of the dynamics of economic development and standards of living, but also in terms of culture, particularly at the level of elites. That the discrimination has an ethnic base is hardly recognized since the minorities are attached in a superficial way to the dominant 'high culture'. A full mastering of this culture and associated lifestyles, however, is a precondition for top careers in large organizations and in the political centre: in this sense, the studies of Pierre Bourdieu (2006) about the relevance of 'fine distinctions' are good descriptions of the particularly centralized French state society (Haller 2006). The fact that all South European countries show higher levels of inequality than the Central and North European countries may also be connected with these processes.

Secession

Another possible 'solution' for ethnic conflicts is the separation of a minority and its territory from an existing nation-state and the establishment of a new state. This strategy presupposes certain conditions: the minority must live in a concentrated way on a certain territory; it must have a minimal size; it must have developed a cultural and political self-consciousness; and it must possess a certain amount of economic power.

In the process of secession, questions about the distribution of power are important as motives for the pursuit of political autonomy: an ethnic minority will be activated particularly in cases when it does not feel recognized, if established rights are taken away and if the ethnic sub-group develops the feeling of being treated unfairly by or to be exploited economically in the existing political system. These elements can be seen in all successful secession movements of the last decades; they explain also why often not the weaker but the stronger ethnic-national sub-groups and territories aim toward secession.[8] The decline of state power, often connected with a lost war, frequently is the last impulse for establishing the quest for political secession.[9]

It is surprising, given the extreme diversity and the geographic huge extension of many new states in Sub-Saharan Africa, that only a few attempts of secession have taken place and only two of them (Eritrea, South Sudan) were successful. In a chapter entitled 'The limited allure of secessionism: Sudan, Congo, Nigeria or Chad', Paul Nugent (2004: 82–100) sees the following reasons for this fact: the under-development of the peripheral regions (for example South Sudan), the political opposition and military intervention of the central state governments against the newly established states (against Katanga in the Congo, and Biafra in Nigeria); and the intervention of European countries and the United Nations in form of the preservation of unity.

On the other hand, it is also possible that very strong ethnic-national sub-groups do not ask for their own state if they feel they have enough autonomy within the existing state and that they are able to preserve their cultural uniqueness. A good example is the Spanish province of Catalonia which attained a strong regional autonomy; recently, after extended public discussions, its parliament has defined Catalonia as a nation of its own.

However, in many cases when ethnic-national sub-groups were able to attain secession and recognition as a new state similar problems of new internal ethnic minorities may emerge. Since the former minority now is the official majority of the new country, it is hardly unavoidable that new minorities emerge within the new state. This is the case, for instance, in many former Republics of the USSR which now are independent states. Ethnic Russians were active in many of these provinces and settled there since generations; today, they are relegated to being minorities, often lacking basic political rights. In the Baltic Republics Estonia and Latvia, nearly one-third of the population are Russians; after these states acquired political independence, their national tongues were declared to be official languages and the Russians had to apply for citizenship in

---

8   In the Habsburg monarchy, not the poor eastern and south-eastern provinces, but the most highly developed northern and western ones (the Czechs, Italians) aimed first toward more political autonomy and (later) to secession. The same was the case in Yugoslavia between the 1960s and 1990s: not the poor Macedonians, Kosovars or Bosnians in the South, but the (relatively) rich Slovenes and Croats in the North aimed at establishing their own states, after the Serb leader Milosevic began to undermine their independent and autonomous position within the multi-national state of Yugoslavia.

9   To take again the example of the Habsburg monarchy: the Czech began to press for political secession only during the First World War; before, their aim was only more political autonomy within the monarchy.

the new states; they could obtain this only after a test in the local language and in constitutional knowledge. Thus, the situation of the Russians has changed in those countries fundamentally from that of a privileged to a deprived minority. Similar problems exist for the new Serbian minority in some of the non-Serbian successor states of Yugoslavia. In the case of the achievement of political autonomy of a national minority within an existing nation-state similar problems may emerge. In Catalonia, for instance, the language of Catalan has been declared the official language of the province (in addition to Castilian, the Spanish national language) in spite of the fact that it is mother tongue of only one-third of the people; considerable pressure is exercised on immigrants from other parts of the country to learn the provincial language. Similar trends facts and problems can be observed in the Canadian province of Quebec.

Founding of a New Ethno-national State

An ethno-nation is a state where citizenship and other social and political rights are based on a significant part on ethnic membership, that is, the possession of one or more of the three basic elements of ethnicity – social descent from a member of one's own ethnie and sharing its language and religion. Ethnicity in all its three components played a central role in the rise of modern nations.[10] Language was one of the foremost criteria in this regard; it inspired the nationalist movements in Germany, Italy, Greece and other countries in the 19th century (see also Deutsch 1966; Gardt 2000; Joseph 2004). Religion played an important role in the national movements in South and East Europe, as well as in Ireland and Poland (see also Smith 1986; Kößler & Schiel 1995). In a few cases, such as the Jesuit Reductions in southern Latin America, or in the case of the Vatican, a religious community itself established a state. The bio-social criterion of social descent from a father or mother (*ius sanguinis*) who already was a member of the ethic group or the nation was typically associated with Germany (after the work of Brubakers 1992); however, it was also practiced in Sweden and many other European countries. The fact that its origin goes back to democracy in ancient Greece shows that this principle (like ethnicity in this sense itself) cannot be interpreted in a biological way. It excludes others or can make their attainment of citizenship difficult, thus discriminating immigrants, for instance. However, it has also some strength from the perspective of democratic principles: it makes political membership independent from the exercise of political power and constitutes a protection against denaturalization for the first generation of emigrants from a country (Bauböck 1994: 38–49). Ethno-nationalism played and still plays a significant role also in present-day Europe: it led to bloody wars in former Yugoslavia; it produces tense relations between several southeast European states (Greece, Macedonia, Bulgaria, Turkey); and it inspires secessionist movements in West Europe which in some cases – as in the Basque country – often have no real base among the majority of the ethnic populations concerned.[11]

In the context of this work, the question is central if and how ethnic nationalism which has led to the foundation of ethno-nations is related to patterns of economic inequality. Here, we can certainly say that an exclusive ethnic foundation of membership in a nation will lead to discrimination of members of other ethnies, who often are immigrants. However, in most advanced Western countries, today the former specific ethnic criteria of national affiliation have been attenuated; the *ius solis*, that is, having been born in or living for some time on the territory of a state, became more relevant. However, there exists one state in which not only the *ius sanguinis*, but also the two other criteria of ethnicity – language and religion – still are of utmost importance. This case is Israel. I will devote a single chapter to this case because it is highly instructive and confirms the central hypothesis of this book, namely that a socio-economic and political system based on processes of ethnic exclusion sooner or later will also produce increasing economic inequality. The case of Israel is very complex: its history and present structure includes elements of Apartheid, even of theocracy; however, it is also a well-established modern democracy. Since the establishment and maintenance of the state of Israel has included the massive use of military and other forms of violence, and today is connected with pervasive processes of segregation and exclusion, its ethnic stratification can also be seen as an Apartheid system.

---

10   General historical works on this topic include Lemberg 1964; Schieder 1964; Kohn 1967; sociological works Smith 1986; Guibernau 1996; James 1996; Wimmer 2002.

11   See Carsten Wieland, 'Ethno-Nationalismus im modernen Europa, dpa-Hintergrund', März 2001.

Strategies to Control Ethnic Heterogeneity

In many cases it is impossible to preserve or to restore ethnic homogeneity in a country today. There are two main reasons for this: first because of extended processes of migration which imply that ethnically different groups often immigrate to a country; second, because ethnic minorities which have settled on the territory of a state for generations cannot be assimilated to the dominant culture and/or are too large to be isolated from the rest of society (as in type Ib discussed above). The first case became even more important as concomitant with globalization, but also due to the fact that on different continents and in different macro-regions of the world, population and economy are developing very unevenly. As a consequence, today many European countries have experienced massive immigration processes and have become ethnically heterogeneous 'immigration societies'.[12] In this regard, a state can act in two ways which are closely intertwined: (a) it can try to exclude unwanted immigrants as far as possible; (b) it can control the forms and the extent of immigration and can integrate the immigrants into the native society in selective ways, corresponding to the existing forms of class stratification and the interests associated with it. This strategy can also be applied for the 'management' of an autochthonous, long existing internal ethnic minority within a nation-state. In this regard, there is also the possibility of providing it with territorial political autonomy; this can be done only if the minority settles in a relatively compact manner on a certain piece of territory. In this case, the ethnic-national sub-group can develop its own 'sub-nation', including people of all social classes and strata. A third, very specific form of the control of ethnic heterogeneity has been developed in the form of castes in India.

Exclusion of the Poor – the New Iron Curtain between the South and North

As a consequence of new technological possibilities for worldwide communication and information, and of cheap and efficient intercontinental means of transport, a considerable global migration pull has developed from the poor to the rich countries and regions of the world. This pull is felt most strongly at those borderlines where poor, crisis-ridden countries directly adjoin highly developed rich countries and regions. This is the case in the Mediterranean which divides Africa from Europe and along the 3,200 km-long border (mostly along the Rio Grande) which separates the United States from Mexico and Latin America. A new worldwide division between 'North' and 'South' has developed whose borderlines are clearly recognizable: it separates the wealthy continents, sub-continents and countries of the earth in Europe, North America and in the Far East and Pacific region (Japan, Australia, New Zealand) from the poor countries and regions of the Global South (Africa, Latin America, Asia; see Table 5.1).[13] The first group of countries is confronted with massive immigration processes and birth rates which have been declining strongly in the past and now are at a level clearly below the level of demographic self-reproduction. Without immigration, the population would shrink and massive problems of finding workers and employees for jobs would arise. This could happen not only for those jobs which are not sought after by the native population because of harsh work conditions and low wages, but also for the qualified, professional jobs (for example, nurses, doctors and so on). In the South, particularly in Africa, birth rates are still extremely high and an enormous demand for work exists among the young cohorts of people entering working age and which therefore cannot be satisfied anywhere near enough (Michler 1988: 303–320; Zoubir 1999; Schmid and Wagner 2004; Haller & Müller 2010). Within Europe, a similar migration pull exists from East to West, although birth rates in the east have fallen sharply after the transition from State Socialism to Capitalist market societies.

---

12 In spite of this fact, however, it is misleading to equate these European societies with the old immigration countries in North America, Australia and so on because in the latter the vast majority of the population or their ancestors have immigrated and have ousted or subjected the native populations.

13 Latin America has an exceptional position in this regard. Due to the close historical, cultural and economic relations of Brazil with Portugal and the other Latin American countries with Spain, many of their citizens do not need a visa to enter the Iberian Peninsula and, thus, the EU. Some of the citizens of Latin America even have the right to get Portuguese or Spanish citizenship if they want.

Table 5.1 A historical-sociological typology of strategies to preserve, restore or control ethnic heterogeneity

Type of strategy	Historical and actual cases
I. Strategies to preserve or to restore ethnic homogeneity	
a. Encapsulation of whole societies	Japan (1615–1850) Australia (1911–75)
b. Isolation and confinement of ethnic minorities	Native peoples in the USA, Australia, NZ; Romas in Europe
c. Enforced assimilation of minorities	West European nation states (ca 1600–1900)
d. Secession of minorities from multi-national states	Successor states of the Habsburg and Ottoman Empires (1918ff.) and of the multinational Communist states in East Europe (1989ff.)
e. Establishment of a new ethno-national state	Israel (1948)
II. Strategies to control ethnic heterogeneity	
a. Foreclosure of the poor – erection of a new Iron Curtain between South and North	European Union, USA, Australia, Japan vs. global South
b. Selective immigration policy	Western Europe, North America, Australia, NZ, Japan
III. Establishment of ethnically based systems of domination and exploitation	
a. Enslavement	Sub-Saharan Africa, Arab-Islamic World, Latin America, US-South (ca 1500–1900)
b. Apartheid	South Africa 1910–90, US-South 1875–1965
c. Usurpation of power by ethno-classes	New states of Sub-Saharan Africa (1960–)
d. Establishment of ethnocracies	Saudi-Arabia, Iran and other fundamentalist Islamic states

Thus, immigration is necessary for the rich countries but mass immigration also presents a threat for their integration and stability. Given this contradictory situation, a pressure emerges for governments to control immigration and to accept only necessary 'welcome' immigrants but to prevent undesired and illegal immigration. In the framework of this selective immigration policy, political considerations about public order, safety and finances play a significant role (Shibuthani and Kwan 1965: 324ff, Milborn 2006). As a consequence of illegal immigration, many real and invented problems emerge, such as an increase in crime, exploitation of welfare state provisions and cultural infiltration; in their turn, ethnic and racial prejudices and hostility toward foreigners grow. These are used by right-wing political parties for propagandistic aims, and their election successes exert pressure on the other parties and on governments to endorse and enact restrictive immigration policies. The measures which are taken in this regard are backed and supported by governments, political parties and population groups from nearly the whole political spectrum. The propertied and dominant classes (for example entrepreneurs), elites and governments will accept or even further immigration if it is in their interest; this, in fact, is often the case. Classes and social strata, whose labour market situation becomes more difficult as a consequence of immigration, will be against it. Therefore, employers' associations usually are in favour of immigration, arguing with increasing shortages of skilled labour. Unions, however, are much more critical in this regard because they recognize that immigrant workers increase competition for working places and contribute to a depression of wages (Penninx and Rosblad 2000; Heschl 2009). Thus, interest constellations and conflicts related to specific class interests emerge about immigration. Employers, but also well-to-do private families and households, often try to bypass legal prescriptions by employing foreigners through moonlighting or even by recruiting them actively and indirectly supporting their illegal entry with the help of people smugglers. In this way, they contribute to the streams of illegal migration in spite of its problematic consequences for the sending and receiving countries and of the immense personal and social costs for the migrants themselves.

In 1989, the world celebrated the breakdown of the Berlin Wall as a triumph of freedom. However, many similar forms of Iron Curtains persist in the world today. By far the largest and most consequential among them are those which separate Europe from Africa and Latin America from the USA, and the poor countries of the South in general from the highly developed countries in the North. This new wall – which can be compared well with historical precursors such as the Great Wall of China or the Roman Limes – erects a factual barrier for maybe 99 per cent of the people of the South – that is, for more than 85 per cent of the world population[14] – against travelling freely toward and entering countries of the North (see Figure 5.1). The reasons for the establishment of this wall and its working mechanisms are closely related to the main topic of this book. Through this mechanism, governments want to restrict the number of unwanted immigrants and to keep their societies as homogeneous (and manageable) as possible. These measures can also be seen as a form of discrimination of the weaker ethnic-national groups by the stronger ones on a world scale. Let us look first at the reasons for the establishment of this new wall, at the forms it has taken and, finally, at some surprising similarities between this wall and its historical precursors, the Great Wall of China and the Roman Limes.

A series of push and pull factors in the South and North has contributed to establishment of this wall. In the South, three factors are obvious: a very strong demographic growth;[15] insufficient economic growth, thus extreme shortage of adequate jobs for the young cohorts entering the labour force; an unstable political situation often connected with internal ethnic conflicts, civil wars and forced movements of millions of people. All of these factors are most pronounced in Sub-Saharan Africa. As a consequence of the pervasive differences in educational, occupational and income chances between the North and South, there exists pressure for emigration, particularly among young people.[16]

Figure 5.1 The New Iron Curtain between South and North

Note: Serrated lines: tightened border control by walls, fences, mines and military patrols
Source: Le Monde Diplomatique, Atlas der Globalisierung, Paris: Armand Colin 2006, p. 58

---

14   The World Development Report 2006 (p. 293) classifies the world into high-, middle- and low-income countries; in the first live only about 1 billion people, that is, 16 per cent of the world population in 2004.

15   In many Sub-Saharan countries, a woman has 5 to 6 children; in Europe, the corresponding number is 1.3 to 2.0.

16   I have investigated this issue in a survey in Ethiopia with sociological students from the University of Graz in autumn 2009 and during my teaching at St Augustine University of Tanzania (SAUT) in Mwanza. In the Ethiopian survey, 300 persons from all ages were included, in the survey at SAUT 500 students; see Haller and Müller 2010, 2012; see also Heinsohn *2008*.

At the side of the rich countries of the North, governments are pushed to take strict measures against mass immigration from the South in order to preserve public order and security. Right-wing movements and political parties, but also some media and influential tabloids, exert pressure upon governments by constructing vivid images of an uncontrollable threat of mass migration from the South toward the North. At the same time, however, smaller groups of people in the North benefit from immigration, even if (or even because) it occurs in clandestine and illegal form. One group includes employers in countries bordering the poor South which can employ the illegal immigrants at low wages since they have neither protection nor interest representation. This happens in agricultural plantations in Spain as well as in California or in industrial plants owned by US entrepreneurs and established in the border regions of North Mexico. Another group gaining from the new Iron Curtain are people smugglers, persons employed in the trafficking industry at the borderlines, corrupt officers at embassies and consulates and many others.

As a consequence, emigration from the South and immigration toward the North is extremely restricted and can take place only in one of the three forms: as illegal immigration, as secretly steered immigration and as a very thin stream of legal immigration. Straightforward illegal immigration is connected with incredible personal and social costs – including deadly perils, for instance, when crossing the Sahara desert without adequate equipment, crossing the Mediterranean or other seas in overcrowded, small boats or making week-long journeys locked into shipping and truck containers (Sassen 1996; Schmid and Wagner 2004; Engbersen 2004; Milborn 2006). The fact that these people are ready to incur such costs testifies how desperately they see their fate in the home country. I will argue in Chapter 13 that the North, in particular the European Union and the United States, with their restrictive measures contribute in considerable part to these processes. Many of these legal, administrative and police and military measures against illegal immigration are in clear contradiction of human rights.

How does the new Iron Curtain work? We can distinguish three methods. The first and most obvious one is the building of extremely strong controlled border fortifications at the places where the poor regions directly adjoin the rich. This is the case in the north of Morocco where two Spanish enclave cities – Ceuta and Melilla – are located as outposts of the European Union. The same has happened along the Rio Grande which divides the United States from Mexico. In both cases, high concrete walls and barbed wire fences have been built; along the walls, roads were constructed so that motorized patrols, supported by helicopters, can patrol the length wall in order to detect immediately and detain any person trying to move across the border. At regions where natural borders separate the North from the South – such as the Mediterranean Sea – intense patrols at sea and air control are employed to detect illegal boats and ships; often, boats which have run ashore are given no assistance. The EU border control agency FRONTEX is said to hinder continuation of the boats of refugees journeying in the open seas – thus depriving them of the basic human right to seek asylum. It is estimated that since 1992 some 10,000 *boatpeople* have died in the Mediterranean.

A second method is to incorporate the poor countries located at the border into the control efforts of the North. The European Union, for instance, has concluded treaties with all North African governments which obliged them to capture migrants from Sub-Saharan Africa toward the North and send them back to the South. That these treaties contradicted humanitarian and democratic principles was obvious: they were concluded at a time when in all of these countries near-dictators were in power. The fate of the detained migrants through the Sahara or arrested at the Atlantic and Mediterranean sea towns was terrible, being detained often under inhuman circumstances or simply left to their fate in the plain Sahara desert; migration between the North African countries was inhibited and migrants from the South were criminalized.[17]

The third method seems to be the most 'humane', corresponding to human right principles; it is also the most effective one. This is the use of *visas* to limit migration from the South to the North. A visa or travel card is a document which gives someone permission to travel into a specific country and stay there for a set period of time. There are many different sorts of visas, distinguished by the groups of people for which they are available (tourists, students, businessmen, people looking for work) and by the duration of stay which they allow. For citizens of most northern countries, the passport or even just a personal identity card is enough for travelling to most other parts of the world; sometimes an easily obtainable visa must be applied for when entering. People from most countries of the South, however, must apply

---

17   See GIGA-Focus 8/2008 (www.giga-hamburg.de/giga-focus).

for a visa if they want to travel to the North. The conditions for obtaining a visa in all rich countries are so restrictive that a normal citizen from the South is unable to fulfil them. An example is the 'Schengen visa' which provides the holder with the right to enter all those European countries which are a member of the Schengen Agreement. This Treaty, first established in 1985 between five states, determined (by and large) that the internal border controls were removed and that all member states cooperate to enforce the borders surrounding the whole area. Today, 28 European states, mostly members of the European Union (except UK) take part in this agreement, thus, the Schengen area constitutes a huge and rich region which is highly attractive for immigrants and asylum-seekers from all over the world. The requirements to obtain a Schengen visa usually are the following:[18] the application for the visa has to be made in person only at the consulate; he or she must provide documents saying that he or she is enrooted well in his/her home country; the document must include: proof of stable employment (in many poor countries, only 20–30 per cent of the population have such an employment at all); proof of a valid social insurance; bank statements of the last three months documenting all receipts and expenses; proof of a travel insurance, covering at least costs of Euro 30,000. The whole process of granting the visa takes four to five months. Similar requirements are valid for immigration to the north for citizens of about 150 states of the world, that is, around three-quarters of the member states of the United Nations. The consequence is the creation of 'a global hierarchy of mobility' (Bauman 1998).

It seems appropriate here to discuss shortly the issue of the new Iron Curtain between South and North also from the perspective of historical sociology; this provides some additional surprising and highly significant insights. Two things may be noted here. The first is the fact that the obligation to carry passports and obtain visas for travelling over borders was established only during the First World War; before, people could travel freely through Europe without documents. The reasons for the introduction of the obligation to carry passports and visas were to keep away spies and to impede the escape of men obligated to do military service (Noiriel 1991). Thus, the fact that visas were invented for security and military considerations is obvious. After the First World War, the obligation to identify oneself and the related restrictions were retained.

The second aspect concerns the existence of similar forms of border control in history and the lessons which we can draw from them for the functions of this present-day world-dividing borderline. There were two large, well-known border fortifications in history, the Great Wall of China and the Roman Limes.

The Great Wall of China, usually denoted as the largest building on earth, was built over 2,000 years (between 500 B.C. until 1644 A.D.) and in total it was about 8,800 kilometres long. It was interrupted by about 25,000 signal and watch towers; fires on top of the towers informed soldiers on other towers and nearby military stations about incoming enemies (Zewen et al. 1990). The pre-condition for the building of the Wall was the political unification of China; its principal task was the protection of the fertile, densely populated and rich Chinese lands and cities from the invasion of aggressive nomads from the North. However, in spite of the existence of the wall, a variety of exchanges (economic, social, and cultural) were going on between China and its neighbours in the North. Subsidiary measures were taken in order to protect the frontier; these included the creation of 'dependent states', the seeding of discord and conflict among the peoples outside the wall, and the undertaking of military campaigns into foreign territory. But rather soon after the completion, parts of the wall lost their functionality because the Chinese empire enlarged its borders beyond the wall.

The other famous historical wall was the Roman Limes. This was a wall extending from the present-day Benelux states and north-west Germany along the rivers Rhine and Danube down to southeast Europe until the Black Sea. A similar, shorter one was Hadrian's Wall in England, separating the part of Britain controlled by the Romans (*Britannia superior and inferior*) from the northern part of Britain. These walls were only the most visible fortifications which surrounded the whole, huge Roman Empire in North and East, but also in the South (and the Near East). Here, North Africa belonged to the empire and the fortifications separated this region from the regions south of the Sahara (see, for instance, Klee 2006; Schallmayer 2006). The building of the Roman Limes began when the expansion of the empire came to a halt around 100 A.D. The Limes was fortified in varying degrees: first, by a concrete wall interrupted by watch towers and castles; in addition, minor fortifications and roads were built along natural borders, such as the rivers Rhine and Danube; these served also as channels of traffic and communication. The working of this Limes provides additional

---

18   Here, the regulations at the Austrian embassy in Tehran are taken as an example.

interesting insights: (1) it was less a military than an economic frontier, controlling mainly everyday life and movements at the border area; at the Limes, Roman law, administration and culture ended, but not Roman power and influence: people living on the other side of it were also considered as being subordinate to Rome; castles and camps served as bases for campaigns into their territory; (2) the Limes was a one-sided frontier: for Romans, unlimited passage into foreign territory was possible, but travel into Roman territory was allowed to inhabitants of the foreign countries only on market days, within a limited geographic area and without weapons; (3) the Limes also had a symbolic function, showing the people on the other side the power of the Roman Empire.

It seems obvious that the present-day Iron Curtain between the South and the North exhibits many similarities with these historical Great Walls. One could even argue that the North or its main components – the United States and the European Union – constitute a new empire or new empires. This is quite obvious for the United States whose character as an empire – given its outstanding military power and influence all over the world – can hardly be denied in spite of the fact that they are not an imperialistic power such as Great Britain in earlier centuries (Perkins 2004; Münkler 2005). But also the European Union is becoming more and more an empire of a new kind which not only exerts an immense economic influence on its neighbour countries and in the world as a whole, but which is also on the way to establishing its own military power base (Haller 2008b: 292–301). For the Dutch, who rejected the EU constitution in a plebiscite in 2005 with a majority of 63 per cent, one of the main reasons was the process of a covert militarization of the EU (Giorgi et al. 2006: 192ff.). Most of the rich northern countries are bound together by military alliances; the military alliance NATO joins the USA and most European countries; a similar military alliance exists between the USA and Japan.

Three aspects are most significant in regard to the similarities between the historical Great Walls and the present-day Iron Curtain: (1) walls are built in order to encapsulate the large, well-integrated, stable and rich countries and regions in the global North against the poor territories and countries in the South which are less developed, crisis-ridden and perceived as threatening; (2) the borders established by the walls are asymmetric and constitute a gradation of power and influence: for members of the empire, the passing over the border is no problem, for the outsiders it is strictly controlled and limited; (3) the effective functioning of the borders is restricted, however. First, many of them become obsolete after a short time because the 'empires' are continuously enlarged and new external states are accepted as members (in former times: were subjugated). Second, no border is impenetrable; there exist hundreds of possibilities how such borders can be traversed, particularly given their huge territorial extensions.

Two general questions arise out of these facts: the first relates to the handling of the Iron Curtain by different countries and regions of the world and the exceptions which they allow to people from the South to enter the North. These exceptions – their specific 'immigration regimes' – are closely related to the internal ethnic and class structures of the receiving countries. The second aspect concerns the evaluation of this foreclosure of people from the poor South from the North in terms of Human Rights. In the final Chapter 13, I will argue that the practices employed in this process contradict some principles of Human Rights, and that the basic assumptions behind them – that without the Iron Curtain an immense migration stream would turn over from South to North – contradicts sociological knowledge about migration processes.

Selective Immigration and Rudimentary Immigration Policy

All countries of the North today employ a selective immigration policy to their needs. They need immigrants not only in the short term, as a labour force, but also in the long term. This is so because fertility levels in Europe are considerably below the self-reproduction rate; therefore, in the long term many social services could not be provided due to lack of personnel and the increasing costs of the welfare state could not be borne any longer. The kind of policy which is pursued by different states depends on three factors: first, on its own history and ethnic composition; second, on its geographic position; and third, on the need for labour power and the effects of immigration on the internal economy. The last aspect is often more of a subjective than of an objective nature, since the overall short- and long-term effects of immigration are very difficult to grasp. Three main forms of immigration policies may be distinguished.

The first is typical for the United States. The US immigration policy is quite liberal and open, particularly since the removal of the ethnic quotas for immigration in 1965. Partly as a consequence of it, 38 million people have immigrated to the USA between 1965 and 2007.[19] This open policy, unique in the world, has several reasons: first, the origin and history of the United States which came into existence as an 'immigration country'. Today sizable numbers of people originating from all countries of the world are living in the USA; the largest groups of foreign-born persons are Mexicans, Filipinos, Indians and Chinese. A second reason is that the American economy grew very strong in the second half of the 20th century. It is widely believed that immigration has contributed to this growth and, thus, was positive for the economy. A third reason was the insular position of the USA which makes it relatively easy to control immigration. Thus, definite quotas for immigration from different countries and continents could be established, making it possible to select carefully among immigrants. An exception was the borderline to Mexico from where the strongest illegal influx in recent times came in.

An opposite model exists in central Europe, particularly in the German-speaking countries Austria, Switzerland and Germany. Their immigration policy is relatively restrictive for three reasons: first, because they border directly with East European countries with much lower wage levels; free admission could lead to high and uncontrollable immigration. Second, because the national ideology (more so in Germany than in Austria and Switzerland) and the laws concerning admission of citizenship were based on the concept of ethnic membership, that is, descent from German ancestors (Brubaker 1992; Bauböck et al. 2009). In these countries, immigration of foreign workers, which began (and was promoted actively by governments) during the years of the *Wirtschaftswunder* (economic miracle) in the 1960s and early 1970s, was first conceived as only a temporary phenomenon; the *Gastarbeiter* (guest workers) needed in those periods should return to their home country when they were not needed any more. Quotas were defined for different economic sectors and occupations determining the number of foreign workers which could be employed; these quotas were calculated according to the needs of the labour market and the enterprises.[20] Thus, at this time a close connection existed between West European class structures and immigration (Castles and Kosack 1973). This *Gastarbeiter* model, however, did not work out for two reasons: first, because many of the guest workers did not go back, but were accommodated to remain and live permanently in the host countries; second, because of family reunification which is a recognized human right today; because of this, immigration continued also in the 1990s and 2000s. The same was true for the United States, where family reunification in recent times accounts for two-thirds of all legal immigrants.[21]

A mixed immigration policy and experience was characteristic of the United Kingdom, Belgium, the Netherlands and France. For many decades in the aftermath of the Second World War, these countries admitted rather freely people from their former colonies. Later on, however, they also began to restrict the number of immigrants. In recent years, the UK has been noted for a liberal policy of immigration for people from other EU member states, particularly from Poland. The extensive immigration, however, also resulted in labour market problems and it has been abandoned recently. A mixed strategy was also followed by the Scandinavian countries. They were rather restrictive for a long time (which was also quite easy for them, given their location far away from the poor countries of the South), but recently relaxed their immigration policies and are particularly ready to accept refugees and asylum seekers. In recent times, however, all countries of the North, including the USA, are enacting more restrictions on immigration and determining more pre-conditions for immigration, such as a certain level of education or occupational qualification, knowledge of the language of the country and of its history and constitution. This happened not the least because in many of these countries, also in Sweden, the precarious life conditions of the immigrants (often concentrated in new ghettos like the French *Banlieues*) led to violent public uprisings. It is evident that an immigration policy which aims at excluding less qualified workers and accepting only well-educated people in occupations with a scarcity of workers is nationalistic-egoistic; from the viewpoint of the countries of the South, it can be called, rightly, a form of plundering of qualified workers and experts.

---

19   http://en.wikipedia.org/wiki/Immigration_to_the_United_States

20   In an Austrian publication, summarizing many studies on *Gastarbeiter*, it was written in 1973: 'Modern traffic means allow a mobility which can lead to new forms of living. Thus, it can be anticipated also that in the long term a rotation of *Gastarbeiter* will take place or a new kind of community migration between countries of settlement and countries of working' (Gastarbeiter 1973: 12).

21   See Footnote 19 above.

Concomitant and as a consequence of these varying forms of immigration and immigration policies, the status of immigrants is quite distinct in the different countries. While in German-speaking Central Europe, most employed immigrants occupy jobs at the lower level of the social hierarchy, in the UK and the USA considerable numbers of immigrants are employed as highly qualified workers and employees. At the same time, however, the more restrictive conditions for immigrants to get work permission in the German-speaking countries have led to a better integration compared with more liberal and open countries like the Netherlands and Sweden (Kesler 2006; Koopmans et al. 2005; Koopmans 2010). I will come back to this issue and its political implications in more detail in Chapter 13.

What happens to immigrants once they have settled in a country? This is also a question closely related to the issue of ethnic stratification. Also in this regard three models may be distinguished; they correspond, by and large, to the three models of immigration policy now sketched.

The first one may be called the *laissez-faire* strategy; it is typical for the United States. Its essence is to do nothing with or for the immigrants but to leave them to their own fate. The example of language is characteristic in this regard: although English is the dominant language of the United States, it has no official legal status, and so it is also not prescribed to immigrants to learn English. However, many US institutions (particularly universities) require a certificate of good English knowledge. The American model turned out as quite efficient for two reasons: first, because of the flexibility and openness of the US labour market. This market is characterized by the principle of *hire and fire*, but it is also relatively easy to find jobs and periods of unemployment are much shorter than in Europe (Haller et al. 1985). The second reason is that the immigrants to the United States do not expect any state support, but rely on their own capacities or on those of an extended family and ethnic network. For many immigrants (and their children) less successful on the labour market, this model, however, implies the risk of remaining or becoming poor and a member of a new 'underclass'.

A second model, characteristic for many European countries, may be called the *limited support model*. It includes several forms of public and private assistance for immigrants, such as the provision of language courses. In important aspects, however – such as the labour and housing markets – they are left to themselves with the consequence that they have to be satisfied with the simple and low quality apartments usually located in poor town districts.

A third strategy, the *multicultural policy model*, characteristic for countries like Canada and the Netherlands, implies an active policy of support for immigrants. This strategy is based on the idea of a multicultural society which implies that the immigrants should be able to preserve their native language and culture. This is certainly the most humane model and there are also human rights arguments and research findings in favour of it. One of the latter is the fact that the learning of a new language is easier if an immigrant commands his native language well (see, for instance, Hufeisen and Neuner 2003). The negative side of the multicultural model, however, is that it takes away the pressure for the immigrants to accommodate themselves to the new society and culture, including the acquisition of the dominant language; in the end, this has the consequence that they are less well integrated into the labour market than in the other two models (Esser 2011, 2006; Koopmans 2005 et al., Koopmans 2010).

A process observable more or less clearly in all countries, however, is that the largest volume of the immigrants occupies the lowest levels of the occupational, class and social structure. The German-Swiss sociologist H.J. Hoffmann-Nowotny (1973) has coined the term *Unterschichtung* (under-stratification) for this process. It usually occurs in the following way: immigrants take over the lowest position in a society or low-status jobs which are created particularly for them; as a consequence, the natives can experience a collective upward mobility (see also Esser 1980, 1999). This process, however, can also have negative consequences in the long run: it reinforces existing social structures and inhibits innovations (at the workplace, for instance, unskilled workers are employed instead of developing and applying technological innovations); the native groups who have risen upward in the hierarchy are captured by status anxiety since their position was not obtained always by achievement; neo-feudal tendencies arise connecting social positions with ethnicity; finally, also among the lower strata of immigrants, resentment and strains emerge because their upward mobility is blocked.

Establishment of a Comprehensive Ethnic Hierarchy

A third strategy which comes to terms with a social structure highly differentiated in ethnic terms is the establishment of an overarching, encompassing social hierarchy in which the place of all ethnic groups is clearly defined. Such a system has to a define a clear criterion which constitutes the basis for hierarchy; it must devise a functioning division of labour and exchange between the different ethnic strata; and it must devise norms and rules, obligations and gratifications so that all members of a society accept their position be it privileged or deprived.

An ingenious type of such a system has been developed in India in the form of castes. Castes and sub-castes are defined in a threefold way; by their vicinity or distance from the highest stratum (the Brahmins); by the prestige of their specific occupational activities (which are ranked in terms of purity); and by their social descent, family networks and customs. In this way, every person and his or her family occupies a recognized place in the social hierarchy. This place is not contested because the whole social order has a religious foundation. Only by following strictly the duties of his caste, an individual can be reborn in his next life in a higher caste or even enter the Nirvana, thus finding his or her ultimate salvation through being absorbed into the eternal universe. In Chapter 8 I will sketch out the main principles of this unique system and its implications for equality and inequality, as well for socio-economic development.

Establishment of Ethnically Based Systems of Domination and Exploitation I: Slavery

Several forms of the encounter of different ethnic groups and subsequent relations between them involve brute power and domination, suppression and exploitation. One of these forms has existed as a recognized social institution only in historical times, the others persist until today or have been abolished only recently. Even in the former case, however, we can expect that their repercussions are perceptible until today. The first form was enslavement – a system of exploitation which is incompatible with human rights. Apartheid was a pretended 'adaption' of ethnic relations and exploitation to modern principles of freedom and equality. The other two forms of ethno-class domination include the establishment of ethno-class regimes, and the foundation of ethno-national theocracies; they still exist today.

One of the most important historical forms of domination of one ethnic-national group over another was slavery. On two sub-continents of the world – Sub-Saharan Africa and Latin America – it existed in a very brutal form for nearly half a millennium. In these regions, slavery has made deep imprints on the societies concerned. In the foregoing chapter, it was shown that a history of slavery is a significant factor leading toward higher economic inequality in a society today. Also for this reason, it is necessary to discuss this unique and extreme form of ethno-class exploitation separately and in some detail here. This shall be done in three steps: first, arguments are brought forward pointing to the actual relevance of this phenomenon; second, slavery is defined and its implications for the respective societies are sketched out; and third, the long-term effects of slavery are described.

The Actual Relevance of Slavery

The social-scientific study of slavery is necessary still today because of four reasons. First, because slavery was connected with unthinkable forms of exploitation, the suffering of dozens, if not hundreds of millions of people, the displacing, expulsion and extermination of whole tribes and peoples, the disruption of couples and families and the abuse and exploitation of men, women and children. 'My eyes have seen deeds which are so alien to human nature and my hands are trembling as I write them down ...' wrote the Spanish bishop and jurist Bartolomé de las Casas in 1542, one of the early fighters against slavery (quoted in Grant 2010: 27). It is well known that extended slavery existed since antiquity until far into the 20th century and on all continents of the earth (Dal Lago and Katsari 2008: 37; Patterson 2008: 33); it is also well-known that slavery meant quite different things in different societies. The most recent form, the capturing of 10 to 12 million slaves in Africa, their freight to North and South America and their exploitation on the plantations there (Meissner et al. 2008: 47) was one of the most cruel forms in history. Another one, much less known, but quantitatively an even more extended form, was the Arabic and Ottoman enslavement of up to 17 million people who were captured in Europe, Asia and – most of all – in Africa over nearly a millennium (Flaig 2009; N'Diaye 2010). In other epochs and world regions enslavement was not so massive and slaves were not treated in such an inhumane way. Nevertheless, it was extremely uncommon that slaves were satisfied with their fate, or wanted to remain in this state. Even when slaves collaborated closely and freely with their masters, such as in the 18th and 19th century in South Africa, they were well aware of the fundamental difference between the state of free labour and of slavery (Bley et al. 1991: 146). The extreme diversity of slavery as an institution in different epochs and cultures has attracted the interest of social anthropologists and historians (Cooper et al. 2000). However, most of them were only looking backwards with little attention to the long-term consequences of slavery.

The study of slavery today is relevant, second, because it is a topic frequently underestimated, neglected or even suppressed in science and public discussion (Sala-Molins 1992; Heers 1996); an early example is Werner Sombart's famous essay 'Why is there no socialism in the United States?' In this essay (1906), the author does not mention the existence of slavery as a factor hindering the development of a unified and strong labour movement in America (as Marx did), and he also erroneously argues that the support of abolition among the northern Republicans had nothing to do with class interests. The publication of the works of the aforementioned B. De las Casas was forbidden for a long time in Spain, denouncing them as *Leyenda negra*.[22] Still in the 20th century, a leading Spanish historian (R.M. Pidal) tried to show that las Casas was mentally ill. Particularly Muslim slavery has been neglected and contested; one author speaks of a 'veiled genocide' in this regard (N'Diaye 2010). Among leftist authors, slavery is only seen as a relic of an earlier form of production but not as an essential element of early Capitalism in many countries.

The study of slavery is highly relevant and interesting, thirdly, from the theoretical point of view. Any present-day social philosopher and social scientist cannot be other than bewildered by the fact that the greatest and most enlightened thinkers in human history accepted slavery as a 'natural fact'. This was true for Aristotle and Cicero, for the greatest doctor of the Catholic Church, Thomas Aquinas, as well as for the modern French philosophers of the enlightenment. But also path-breaking, revolutionary religious texts, such as the Bible and the Koran, considered the exploitation of human beings by other people through slavery as legitimate. In the Bible, rules about the keeping of slaves are given; it is assumed that a man can sell even his daughter as a slave. In translations of this and other passages, the term slave was avoided and that of servant was used; the Bible itself, however, clearly distinguishes between the status of servants and slaves. In the Koran, slavery is also considered as a 'natural' institution; Mohammed and his co-fighters captured and used slaves as workers and concubines. However, slaves are not considered as things in the Bible and the Koran, like in Roman law. Since they are also seen as human beings, they are entitled to fair treatment and must be cared for in situations of need. Overall, however, slavery is one of the most spectacular cases which makes clear that both religious teachings and science can contribute to the development and propagation of ideologies which clearly contradict our present-day sense of justice. In specific historical circumstances and given certain social structures, men in general and specific societal groups in particular do not perceive a situation as others do; they perceive it only in a distorted or partial way (Boudon 1988: 98). The abolition of slavery – in spite of massive interests behind it – is, on the other hand, an outstanding example of the fact that universal values, 'axiological truths' in the sense of M. Weber (Boudon 2000), become enforced irreversibly at some point in history. One of the most consequential among them was the idea of equality of all people on earth.

A final reason why slavery should be an important topic for social science is that it is still relevant today. Although condemned by politics and public opinion, it is practised in a hidden form in many parts of the world. In West Europe, human trafficking involves women from East Europe and the South who are kept as real prisoners in brothels (Kreutzer and Milborn 2008); in the United States, agricultural workers have been practical slaves; in the Middle East, millions of foreign workers from poor (Islamic and non-Islamic) countries are employed under inhumane conditions, and many women as concubines; in Saudi-Arabia and some Sub-Saharan Muslim countries, true slavery persists in secret (Malek 2007); in Central Africa, as well as in Latin America, South Asia and China, people have to work under nearly openly, slave-like conditions. It was estimated that in 2006, 28 million people had to live under slave-like conditions, including bonded labour

---

22 See http://de.wikipedia.org/wiki/Bartolom%C3%A9_de_Las_Casas (1.7.2011).

or debt bondage (18 million), forced labour (7.6 million) and as trafficked slaves (2.7 million).[23] US President Bush told the UN General Assembly in 2003 that each year 800,000 to 900,000 people are sold, bought and transferred by force over national borders. The term 'slave-like-conditions' itself may be euphemistic since most of these people – mainly women and children – are kept as real slaves (Batstone 2008: 11).

It is not possible or necessary to discuss all the historical and intercultural variations of slavery here. Rather, I will first sketch out the central elements of slavery and then go on to discuss how this institution influenced social inequality in societies as a whole and the thinking and acting of the upper and lower classes in particular.

The Definition of Slavery and its Impact on Society

Slavery may be defined as a system or institution in which human beings (the slaves) are treated and used by other people (their masters) as their property and forced to work or to perform any kind of service for them. They can be held against their will from birth to death; in many cases, they could be punished and even tortured at will by their masters. Slaves are deprived of their free will, thus bereaved of personal autonomy and dignity, the central element of human beings and the basis for self-consciousness and happiness (Sen 1999; Haller and Hadler 2004/05). Slaves have little or no control over their own life, cannot decide about their work, often have no right to marry and to establish a family, and if they are allowed to do so, they have little to no control over the fate of their children. In most cases, the slave status is passed on over the generations (Miers and Kopytoff 1977: 3–4; Bley et al. 1991: 3; Berlin 2003). In America, there was only one instance when a slave was considered as a human being: if he committed an offence then he could punished as a responsible person (Schmitt 2008: 24). Already, in the Roman Empire, a paradigmatic 'slave society' (Dal Lago and Katsari 2008: 5), wars were made also in order to enslave people (Weber 1973a: 6). For Claude Meillassoux (1975), an eminent scholar of slavery in Africa, two elements were essential for slavery: violence and the destruction of social identity by bereaving persons of their kinship (Miers and Kopytoff 1977; Ross 1983; Bley et al. 1991: 15; Pfaff-Giesberg 1955: 15–18). In fact, slaves were sold and bought on markets like cattle – an extremely degrading experience (Grant 2010: 92–93). In Marx's terms (1971: 182) one can say that the slave became a commodity. Such a system which creates two classes of people, one of them deprived of all the characteristics of a true human being, cannot have other than profound impacts on society in general, as well as on the masters and slaves in particular. We must note, however, that this definition of slavery applies only or mainly to this phenomenon as it has evolved since the early Modern Age, when Europeans began to invade and subjugate peoples on the other continents of the world. In former historical periods and in societies outside of European invasion, slavery was less depriving.

The consequences of slavery on society as a whole have been well recognized by political thinkers in the early Modern Age. Let us quote three outstanding theorists of democracy in Europe and America. Charles de Secondat Baron de Montesquieu (1689–1755) wrote the following:

> Slavery in its proper sense is the establishment of a right which makes one man so much the owner of another man that he is the absolute master of his life and of his goods. It is not good by nature; it is useful neither to the master nor to the slave: not to the slave, because he can do nothing from virtue; not to the master, because he contracts all sorts of bad habits from his slaves, because he imperceptibly grows accustomed to failing in all the moral virtues, because he grows proud, curt, harsh, angry, voluptuous, and cruel (quoted in Engerman et al. 2001, p. 20).

Thomas Jefferson (1743–1826), the third president of the United States, living in a country which still practised slavery at that time, wrote much in the same vein:

> There must doubtless be an unhappy influence on the manners of our people produced by the slavery among us. The whole commerce between master and slave is a perpetual exercise of the most boisterous passions, the

---

23   Figures estimated by Kara (2009), reported in http://eu.wikipedia.org/wiki/slavery; see also O'Callaghan (1963), Bales (2004), Grant (2010: 184).

most unremitting despotism on the one part, and degrading submissions on the other. Our children see this, and learn to imitate it […]. From his cradle to his grave he is learning to do what he sees others do (quoted in Engerman et al. 2001, p. 29).

An extensive and lucid discussion of slavery is given in Alexis de Tocqueville's pioneering work *Democracy in America* published in 1835 (Tocqueville 1976: 394–421). Slavery, he argues, is the most dangerous evil for the United States, it is a kind of nightmare. It has only disadvantages for the economy as a whole because it develops more slowly; for the employers, because slaves work less efficiently than free workers and in the end are also more expensive because the master has also to pay for their living costs; and, finally, because the owners of slaves and their families live like parasites, broken of the habit to work and are interested only in preserving their privileged status.

The Long-term Effects of Slavery

Many authors agree that slavery has made a long-term imprint on the societies which practised it (Pfaff-Giesberg 1955: 74; Illife 1997: 172ff.). For J.L. Schmitt (2008: 11), it is possible only with the background of slavery to understand present-day social phenomena in societies formerly characterized by such a system. Given the pervasive impact of slavery on all aspects of society, it is obvious that its effects cannot have disappeared fully after only somewhat more than a century or four to five generations. Alexis de Tocqueville who visited North America in the 1830s wrote:

> Liberated slaves […] are in a similar situation like the indigenous population; in the middle of a population which is highly superior to them in terms of wealth and education, they remain poorly educated and without rights; they are helpless in the face of the tyranny of laws and the intolerance of the habits (Tocqueville 1976: 407).

He saw as the main problem in the situation of liberated slaves in North America the fact that they were Black. As a consequence of this, race as a permanent characteristic has been connected in a disastrous way with the transient situation of slavery: 'The memory of slavery degrades the race and in the race the memory of slavery persists' (Tocqueville 1976: 396). In order to understand better the effects of slavery on present-day societies, I shall now discuss shortly how the transition from slavery to freedom took place, how the situation of the descendants of the former slaves later on developed and what imprint slavery has made on the *collective conscience* (Durkheim 1965: 105ff.) and on the *cultural memory* (Assmann 1992).

What was the fate of the former slaves and their descendants after the abolition of slavery? The liberation of slaves is usually seen as a definite break with the former state but this is not true: enfranchisement leads 'rather to a transformation of the dependence band, rather than to its complete elimination' (Pétré-Grenouillon 2008: 239). Contemporary political and social philosophers foresaw the problems that would arise as a consequence of liberation. I have already quoted Alexis de Tocqueville; he also proposed a form of state ownership of the large plantations on which the former slaves could be employed. The early political theorist Jean Bodin (1529–96) argued that a profound re-education of slaves would be necessary (Engerman 2008: 270f.). Three forms may be distinguished as far as the concrete transition is concerned: one was to transform slavery and slave labour into constraint labour; the second was to establish a formal (and later, an informal) segregation between the former slaves and the rest of society; and the third strategy was to leave slaves to their own devices.

The transformation of slave labour into forced labour was realized most effectively in *South Africa* (Bley et al. 1991: 147–159; Bilger 1976). From 1809 on, children and youth continued to be held in bondage by their masters in exploitative work contracts, denoted as 'apprenticeship'. Later on, Black people were liberated, but their freedom was restricted in that they could not leave their living places without authorisation and documents. The ideological foundation of this practice was the idea that work would 'civilize' the Blacks. At the time of the liberation of slaves in 1833/34, 38 per cent of the 104,000 people in the Cape Colony were slaves. The abolition of slavery induced the *Boers* to their trek toward the north, to establish their own Republic there and to continue with the exploitation of the Blacks, the former slaves. From 1910 on, when the South African Union was established, a unique system of segregation and exploitation, *Apartheid*, was established as part of the constitution; it lasted until the mid-1990s (see Chapter 11).

A somewhat lighter form of continued exclusion of the former slaves was practised in the South of the US. The fate of the former slaves after their liberation during the Civil War (1863–65) was recognized as one of the most important problems facing the nation. Plans for a wholesale repatriation of the slaves to Africa had to be abandoned, although a small proportion (1 per cent) of them went to Africa and established the Republic of Liberia (see also p. 103). In the first decade after liberation, the new rights of the Blacks were not taken seriously; in economic terms, many of them worked as share croppers on small pieces of land and fell into a kind of bondage to the owners of land (Temperley 1977: 123ff). Later on, an informal terror of radical, right-wing enemies of abolition emerged (represented, for instance, in the Ku-Klux-Klan; see Eyerman 2001: 33ff.). Its origin was widespread status insecurity in the South among Whites for two reasons: they saw that some Blacks were quite successful, and they feared that the freed slaves would organize insurgences and massacres against their former masters (Meuschel 1981: 177ff.). From 1876 on, the *Jim Crow Laws* were enacted officially in the South which prescribed a formal separation between Whites and Blacks in public institutions and spaces under the embellishing label 'separate but equal'; some of them were effective until 1964 (see Chapter 11).

A third way of transition from slavery to a post-slave society took place in Latin America. Here, a strict separation was impossible given the small numbers of Whites and the close relations between Whites and Blacks, including widespread miscegenation. To many critical observers, it was quite clear that the situation of the freed slaves would become one of the most serious problems after the full abolition of slavery in 1888. Two different positions were developed: one was the idea of a natural inferiority of Black and coloured people (Azevedo 1987). The other was the idea of a harmonious co-existence, even an active intermixing whose outcome (the *mestizos* and *mulattos*) would be a new kind of man. This idea was developed particularly in Brazil (Hofbauer 1995: 78ff.; Holanda 1969), but also in Mexico and in other Latin American countries. In official Brazilian ideology, this position asserted itself in the concept of 'racial democracy' (see Chapter 9). Real behaviour and consequences, however, were rather different: the former slaves were largely left to themselves; they were offered no compensation (for instance, they got no land) in contrast to their masters who were given compensation and who could retain most of their privileges and power (Engerman 2008: 279). For many planters, abolition was even welcomed because it freed them from the slaves whose labour they did not need any longer because of technical progress and economic decline; they were discharged of any responsibility for the freed slaves (Fernandes 2008: 29). The consequence was that most slaves lost their former security and means of survival and slid into misery (Fernandes 2008; Schmitt 2008: 49ff.). In the countryside many slaves were dismissed by their masters, and in the towns they concentrated in marginal districts. Everywhere, they were excluded from education, social and cultural life and became the object of racist prejudices and actions; in the growing industry, immigrant workers were preferred to them. In his comprehensive study on this topic in the Brazilian case, David Baronov (2000: 3) argues that three non-market factors were essential: the emergence of systematic racism, continued reliance upon new forms of coerced labour and monopoly of the productive forces (and the state) by the dominant White class. A vicious circle unfolded between the legacy from the slave huts and the permanent exclusion of Blacks and mulattos from new forms of work and subsistence in the industrial society; both Blacks and Whites developed a kind of 'mythology of misery, promiscuity and hopelessness' (Fernandes 2008; Schmitt 2008: 59). It was only during and after the First World War that a Black press and movement began to develop. In addition, the idea of a natural inferiority of Blacks was not abandoned by influential groups; its effects were decided efforts to recruit immigrants from Europe for the newly developing industries rather than to hire Black and coloured people.

One additional long-term consequence of the 'cultural trauma' of slavery was the acceptance of massive deprivation and glaring inequality. Research by historians and historical sociologists has shown that important events and experiences can make a long-lasting imprint on the memories of societies and social groups (Assmann 1992). These can be positive events, such as consequential victories over an enemy, but also traumatic negative experiences. Ron Eyerman (2001) has investigated systematically the effects of slavery on the collective memory among African-Americans. It is not only slavery as such which still today constitutes such a trauma, but also the rejection of descendants of slaves by American society; it was the lack of integration which transformed the American Negroes from an ethnic group into a 'race'. As a consequence, the Blacks retreated from public life, and, with the help of churches and a few intellectual leaders, developed the idea of a distinct African American identity. Even in recent times, 'the dramatization of slavery' constitutes an important element of Black social and political self-consciousness, such as in the speeches of *Malcolm X* (Eyerman 2001: 185). In a study on Jamaica, a small Caribbean island state in which 90 per cent of the people descend from African slaves, Adam Kuper (1977: 113) found that the primary importance of racial features was as 'a symbol of the status of the [enslaved] ancestors'. This is so in spite of the fact that Jamaica has been called a paradigmatic 'plural society' by renowned authors such as F. Barth and J.S. Furnivall, and that people of African ancestry now dominate the political and administrative structure. Skin colour has little impact on employment prospects but 'continues to be a factor in politics, in self-image, and in the assessment of status' (Kuper 1977: 147). The spectacular success of the US TV series *Roots* among the general public also indicates the extreme significance of slavery for collective memory in the United States.[24] Similar observations have been made for Brazil: 'Still today, Blacks in Brazil are stamped by a strong and not erasable trauma of slavery which disadvantages and establishes additional bounds for them and prestresses their starting conditions' (Schmitt 2008: 91). A traumatic memory of Apartheid also persists in South Africa (Gobodo-Madikizela 2006).

The Two Main World Regions of Slavery

In the two sub-continents of Sub-Saharan Africa and Latin America, slavery not only was an important social institution far into the 19th century, but was also exercised in a particularly exploitative form. In America, we can distinguish between three sub-types of slave regimes.

In North America, the first slaves were acquired in the British colony of Virginia (in the present-day US-South) in 1619.[25] Between 1680 and 1700, the practice of indentured servitude practised in the beginning was substituted by chattel slavery; in the 18th century, slavery was fully legalized and also racialized, creating a caste system where practically only Blacks were defined as slaves. By 1860, four million slaves lived in the USA. They worked mainly on large plantations producing high-value cash crops such as tobacco, cotton, sugar and coffee. The treatment of slaves varied widely, but mostly it was brutal and degrading, including harsh punishment, sexual abuse and no provision of education and health services. In difference to Latin America, in the US-South the idea of racial purity inspired the laws, sexual relations between Blacks and Whites were forbidden. Between 1790 and 1850, a forced migration of nearly one million Black slaves from north-west US states (Maryland, Virginia, and Carolina) to the west and south took place where new large cotton plantations were established. In the USA, slavery was a contested issue already from the 1770s onwards. It was soon outlawed in the states north of the Ohio; many organizations were established advocating the liberation of slaves. In the extremely bloody Civil War, 1861–65, the conflict about slavery was a main issue and it was solved after the victory of the northern states by its abolition in 1864/65. However, the freed slaves and their descendants had to endure nearly a further century before they really got full political and social equality, as we have seen in the preceding section. Exploitation of the former slaves was sustained in a system similar to later Apartheid in South Africa. In 1876/77, Black people in the southern states lost their citizenship rights through the *Jim Crow laws* and were separated from Whites in schools and public spaces (Grant 2010: 177).

A second model existed in most *Spanish colonies* in *Middle and South America*. Here, large indigenous populations of Indians lived. However, their exploitation was not as easy as that of imported African slaves for two reasons: it was easier for them to escape and they were not resistant enough for the extremely hard work. As a consequence of this exploitation and of imported diseases, millions of Indians died[26] (Galeano 2003; Grant 2010: 18–20). As an alternative to enslavement, a new kind of serfdom was established. The communal land of the Indian population was expropriated and the new owners established big *latifundios*. In several regions of South America this process could set in only after violent military campaigns against

---

24   A parallel can be seen in the traumatic memory of the Holocaust among the Germans; over and over again, highly successful films and books are produced on this topic in Germany.

25   See 'Slavery in the United States', http://en.wikipedia.org (28.9.2011).

26   It is estimated that the indigenous population in America was around 50 million in 1500, but decreased to 10 million as a consequence of European invasion (Wikipedia, 'Slavery').

the native populations. On the *latifundios*, three types of workers were used: the *colonos*, Indians who had to work three to six days on the owners' land in exchange for the private use of a small plot; they also had to provide unpaid services to the household of the master; *agregados* who provided temporary labour; and *hatahuahuas*, proletarianized, nomadic workers (Calderón 1977: 197–9). In the region investigated by this author in Southern Peru and Bolivia, 100 Indian communities were dispossessed of land; their revolts were defeated violently; in 1950, 8 per cent of the landowners held 95 per cent of the land. Thus, the inequality in the distribution of land is a central concomitant of the Latin American slave-holding societies. Ewaut Frankema (2008, 2010) has considered it rightly as a main factor explaining present-day extreme inequality in this region.

A third, very peculiar model of societal integration of the former slaves ('race democracy') was developed in Brazil. For this model, the term *racial democracy* was coined after the influential book of the sociologist Gilberto Freyre (1900–87) *Casa-grande e senzala*, first published in 1933 (Freyre 1964). According to this model, Brazilian race relations were fundamentally different from those in the USA or South Africa. Instead of strict segregation and open exploitation, Indians, Blacks and Whites lived peacefully side by side and often had close relations with each other, including miscegenation. This would lead, in the end, toward the emergence of a new 'meta-race'. The concept of 'racial democracy' was widely accepted by the public and policy makers in Brazil. Later on, however, it came into sharp criticism because it entirely concealed racial discrimination and oppression and was promoted mainly by the White elites in order to obscure racial discrimination and oppression (Skidmore 1974). Because of its unique character, I will analyse the Brazilian model in detail in Chapter 9. Since class and ethnic membership are intertwined very closely in Brazil, I denote this model as 'coloured class structure'.

All South American countries, the United States and Mexico in North America, practised slavery till the second half of 19th century. In all these countries the origins of slavery were similar. Between the 16th and 19th centuries, millions of slaves had been imported from Africa in order to use their labour power on the large sugar, coffee, cotton and tobacco plantations of their British, Dutch, French, Portuguese and Spanish owners. Probably at no other time in history human beings had been uprooted in such a degree in social and cultural terms and brutally exploited (Blassingame 1972; Santos 1985). The masters of the slaves, the owners of the big *haciendas* and *facendas*, were connected to the international world through intensive trade with Europe, but also through direct personal, social and political networks with their 'mother societies', particularly on the Iberian Peninsula. In this regard, they can be compared to the owners of the *latifundia* in imperial Rome (Weber 1973a: 5–7; see also Marx 1971: 754–5; FN. 211; Wallerstein 1974).

The other region of the world affected massively by slavery was Sub-Saharan Africa. In many parts of Africa, slavery existed already in the Middle Ages (Meissner et al. 2008: 23–6). In the Arabic-Islamic countries in North Africa, it was allowed for the Muslim invaders to enslave non-Muslims. Prisoners of war and slaves were used as soldiers, administrators, as workers on wheat and rice cropping farms, in gold and salt mines. The majority of slaves, however, were females, used as housemaids, servants and as concubines or additional wives. The situation of some groups of slaves was relatively good, including rights for recreation and provision with the means of subsistence (Pfaff-Giesberg 1955: 31–2). One may say, however, that in North Africa slavery was not an institution which influenced societies in a fundamental way. The situation was different in Sub-Saharan Africa. Particularly in the regions along the African west coast, slavery was an established institution in many of the well-established political communities and kingdoms. One reason why slavery was important in this part of Africa was underpopulation while land was in large supply and often owned by the community; thus labour power was a more important source of wealth and influence for the dominant classes than land (Illife 1997: 172).[27] However, slavery in traditional Sub-Saharan Africa was very

27   This thesis is challenged, however, by O. Patterson (2008: 37). He argues, based on a reanalysis of Murdock's ethnographic data file of 186 societies, that there existed a crucial difference in the enslavement of men and women; while the first could be used only as labour power, the latter could be used, in addition, as concubines, additional wives and producers of children; in polygynous societies women were in great demand; if such societies engaged also in frequent warfare, the probability of slavery increased strongly. It is remarkable that two exceptions from the general African pattern (a lot of land, but few people) were Ethiopia and Rwanda; here, land was fertile, scarce and densely populated; it is no accident, therefore, that slavery was much less widespread in these two countries (see Chapter 10).

different from that in Latin America. It was embedded into a complex set of rights in persons: such rights implied that one person or group could exercise certain powers on (over) others. (Miers and Kopytoff 1977: 7ff.). These included rights and obligations, as in the selection of marriage partners, in the relations between parents and children, husbands and wives and so on. These rights were a result of complex transactions and they could be transferred between groups. A typical example was that a husband acquired certain rights from his wife through her kinship in the payment of bride wealth. A central aspect of slave life was belonging to a group, which included both to be a member of it and a part of its wealth (Miers and Kopytoff 1977: 8). Slaves were acquired through capture in wars and raids, but often without compulsion: strangers sometimes placed themselves in positions of dependence when they were forced to leave their own tribe; compensation for heavy crimes was paid through people, usually children. People fell into slavery along with other aspects of exploitation and inequality (Freund 1998: 30ff.; Grant 2010: 44–52). However, it happened also because of personal debts or even from free decisions when people were not able to provide for their family and children. Also the uses of acquired persons were many and variable: they provided extra labour and wives, soldiers for warfare, trading agents and so on. Thus, slaves were integrated in various ways into their new society. This was a way for them to gain freedom, which in Africa did not mean individual autonomy and independence in the Western sense but being member of a kinship group, attached to a patron and, in this way, belonging to a group and being secure and protected (Miers and Kopytoff 1977: 17). Thus, the situation of the slaves in traditional Sub-Saharan Africa was clearly better than that of the slaves in the New World in the early Modern Age. Slaves often became quasi-members of the local community and of the family of their owners, they could become free and some of them rose to influential administrative and political positions. The latter was possible because many of them did not have families and children and thus they had no possibility to hand on their positions or wealth to offspring (Pfaff-Giesberg 1955: 31–2; Santos 1985: 21ff.).

However, the practices of enslavement and the structure of slavery in Sub-Saharan Africa changed fundamentally after the advent of the first Europeans, the Portuguese, around 1500. Only at the beginning, the Portuguese themselves made slave-ridings into the villages near the coast. Later on, indigenous African chiefs and kings took an essential part in the process of enslavement and in the slave trade. They captured and sold the slaves to the Arab and European traders; this participation, in addition, strengthened the practice of slavery in the African societies themselves (Meissner et al. 2008: 46–69; Illife 1997: 175ff.; Freund 1998: 45ff.). For Europeans, it was impossible to enter African mainland because of tropical diseases and of the hostility of the tribes and the military strength of some of the regimes governing there. Even the European forts along the African coast were not able to control the territory; this was done by local potentates, tradesmen and officers who all had slaves. Therefore, the Europeans were dependent on local chieftains, leaders and warlords, 'African compradors' (Freund 1998: 47), who captured the slaves. These local kings and dominant classes profited clearly from the slave trade. But they did not only capture and sell the slaves, they used them also themselves. Enslavement occurred as a consequence of wars between adjacent African states, through raids of aggressive tribe leaders into neighbouring provinces and states, through organized systematic kidnapping of persons in remote villages and as punishment for crimes considered as grave, such as adultery or witchcraft (Reader 1998: 383–95). A crucial fact in this increase of enslavement in Sub-Saharan Africa was the import of guns and other firearms which provided local chieftains with an irresistible power over their neighbours and subjects (Reader 1998: 406–9). Thus, slavery was reinforced as a consequence of the hunger of the European powers for slaves in all well-established states in Sub-Saharan Africa, from those bordering the Sahara and the Arab-Muslim world in the North, down through the West African gold- and slave coast where the Empires of Benin, Dahomey, Oyo and the federation of the Asante existed along the east African coast (here, the sultanate Zanzibar was the most important slave owner and trader until 1875), but also deep into Central Africa to the Kingdom of Congo (Illife 1997: 174).

A recent summary of the situation of slavery in sub-Saharan Africa from the 16th till the 19th century reads as follows: 'Even if different regions suffered in different degrees because of wide-spread violence, slavery was everywhere a well-established and accepted institution [...] Slavery produced slavery' (Meissner et al. 2008: 60f.). According to these authors, the proportion of slaves among the African population around 1800 was about 10 per cent and increased again in the 19th century, in some countries up to two-thirds. According to Lovejoy (quoted in Reader 1998: 397), 'the interaction between enslavement, the slave trade, and the long-established practice of domestic slavery in Africa stimulated the emergence of a system of slavery that was basic to the political economy of many parts of the continent'. The slave trade strengthened the existing 'predatory ruling classes and intensified internal slavery, violence and social 'oppression' without any corresponding development of productive forces ...' (Freund 1998: 47). In a comprehensive work on the subject (Manning 1990) it is estimated that the shipping of 10 to 12 million slaves from Africa to America between 1700 and 1850 actually involved the capture of some 21 million Africans; 7 million of them were taken into domestic slavery and another 12 million died within a year of capture (Reader 1998: 404).

II. 'Modern' Forms of Ethno-class Domination and Exploitation

Slavery was the most open and brutal form of ethno-class exploitation and racism. It is incompatible with universal human rights as they have been declared and propagated at the global level since the Second World War and it has been eliminated in its open form all over the world.[28] Yet in a few countries and world regions, new forms of ethno-class exploitation have been developed which seemingly were compatible with modern principals of freedom and equality. These two forms are Apartheid and ethno-national theocracies. It is no accident that they have been invented and developed particularly by countries which in former times had practised slavery.

Apartheid

A particular system of exploitative race relations was developed in South Africa after the abolition of slavery. The fundamental initial condition for the emergence of it (as any Apartheid system) was the invasion and takeover of lands in South Africa by Europeans. In the wake of the military capture of a region, the immigration of a substantial number of civilians of the same ethnicity is arranged by the prospective Apartheid elites. Large numbers of indigenous people are allowed to stay as an exploited work force (Löwstedt 2012: 12). South Africa was the only African region where Europeans themselves also kept slaves (Michler 1988: 222–31; Illife 1997: 166–71; Mamdani 1996: 62–72; Bley et al. 1991: 137–52; Löwstedt 2012). Because of their needs for manual labour, the Dutch and British settlers in South Africa imported slaves from other parts of Africa and even from South Asia, and they themselves made slave-rides into the country among the *Khoisan* and *Khoikhoi* peoples (derisively called *Hottentotten*). The situation of the slaves in South Africa was unique in two regards: since the Dutch farmers (later called *Afrikaners* or *Boers*) were themselves working on the fields, they had close contacts with their slaves. On the other hand, slaves were strongly suppressed, internally very heterogeneous and not allowed to marry or to establish families. According to Illife (1997: 168) the Cape Colony had one of the most rigorous and repressive slave-holding systems in human history. Toward the end of legal slavery, one began to think how to continue with the exploitation of the Black and coloured people. The solution was to invent a kind of constrained labour and – later – the system of Apartheid. It was constitutionally enacted from 1910 on and in force until 1990.

Three elements are characteristic of the system of Apartheid (See also Nugent 2004: 131–7; Illife 1997: 366–84; Löwstedt 2012): (1) a racist ideology which sees humanity as divided into more significant White and less significant coloured and Black races; the first are seen as having the historical task to introduce the latter to modern civilization; (2) a legal differentiation between the races which excluded Blacks (and in many regards also all other non-White races) from the most important social, economic and political rights; (3) in addition, a social and territorial segregation between Blacks and Whites; mixed marriages were forbidden, Blacks were only allowed to enter the living areas of the Whites as a commuting workforce, and separate public services were established for Blacks and Whites.

Apartheid produced a systematic downgrading of the Black majority population: they were deprived of political rights (in particular the right to vote), and had to live on separate territories; in this way the Blacks living in separate rural enclaves had to contrive the costs of the reconstruction of a cheap labour force (that is, their demographic reproduction) by themselves (Nugent 2004: 131); mixed marriages between Blacks and coloured people on the one side, and Whites on the other side were forbidden. The ultimate aim of Apartheid was to establish a society fully segregated along racial, cultural and political lines. Since Blacks, however, continued to work for the Whites (the males mainly in mining and industry, the females in households) this

---

28   In Mauritania, it is still not yet abolished formally.

was a perfect system, allowing the employment of Black labour under very unequal, exploitative terms (Adam 2013; Adam and Moodley 1977; Downing 2004). Black South Africans not only lived in a different world from the Whites; Apartheid had also the intention to rob the Blacks of their honour and deference and to downgrade them to second class people in their own land (Gobodo-Madikizela 2006: 19). Thus even if the Apartheid system was not slavery in the strict sense, it is fully justified to consider it as a form of ethno-class exploitation.

A comparable, but somewhat less harsh system existed in the South of the United States and in some regards still exists to some degree today in Israel. The Southern US states could not accept the abolishment of slavery in 1865. Soon a massive intimidation of and terror against Blacks set in (3,500 Blacks were murdered between 1866 and 1875). This pressure led to a revocation of many of their civil and political rights, including suffrage, and to laws prescribing segregation in public spaces. This system significantly weakened the position of Blacks; it was abolished only in the course of the civil rights movement in the 1950s and 1960s. Also the system of ethnic relations and domination in present-day Israel and Palestine exhibits elements of an Apartheid system. The Palestinian groups living within the state of Israel or under its military control (such as in the Gaza strip) are subject to harsh forms of social and political exclusion: while the Arab citizens of Israel enjoy most political rights, Palestinians living on the West Bank and in the Gaza strip are extremely restricted in their socio-economic rights and opportunities (Löwstedt 2012). We will come back to both these cases in Chapter 11.

Ethno-class Regimes

In this form of ethnic domination and exploitation, a whole ethnic group within a country attempts and often achieves to monopolize political power and, in the wake of it, to monopolize the revenues from the resources of the state.

Such a specific form of a close interaction between ethnic differentiation and class domination came into being at least temporarily in many large central African countries in the 1960s and 1970s (for example Kenya, Nigeria, Sudan and Democratic Republic of Congo). In these countries, up to 100 different ethnic groups or tribes were united within the confines of a single state. Living together and relations between the different tribes in the new political communities, however, turned out to be quite difficult. Soon after these countries acquired their political independence, intense and violent fights broke out in which the elites of the different tribes wanted to get control of power in the central state government. The reason was obvious: this access would open up privileged access to the vast economic resources, controlled by the state, such as revenues from the export of mineral and oil resources, foreign support and donations, incomes from briberies of foreign firms and the allocation of privileged employment and occupational positions in the public sector.

Three factors contributed to these disastrous, violent internal conflicts which curbed economic development. The first was the fact that the colonial powers had installed persons from specific tribes as their representatives in local government and civil and military administration. In this way, a *re-tribalization* took place which enforced traditional hierarchies between the tribes. Such new kinds of unequal relations were very dangerous because they had never existed before colonization (Gurr 1993: 252ff.; Ellis 1996: 33). A second factor was that the new African states were used by the two world powers, the United States and the Soviet Union, during the period of the Cold War (that is, about 1945 to 1985) as chess pieces on the parquet of their power games and conflicts. By delivering huge amounts of weapons to their respective 'allied' governments and liberation movements, both the West (including France, the UK und Portugal) and the Soviet Union and its allies (for example the German Democratic Republic, Czechoslovakia, Cuba, Yemen Democratic Republic) heated up the conflicts and contributed to the establishment of military dictatorships (for the case of Nigeria see Zoubir 1999). Finally, the new political constitutions with democracies based on the majority principle and centralized political power did not correspond to African political traditions. Political processes in Africa usually occurred at the level of villages and tribes and implied long processes of discussion and negotiation, ending usually with a consensual decision (Sigrist 1967). The establishment of one ethnic group often supported by a foreign power, as a dominant elite or class, contradicted the African sense of equality in many regards (Fortes and Pritchard 1961; Sigrist 1967: 257).

However, it would be a mistake to assume that traditional (Sub-Saharan) African societies were very equal. Irving L. Markovitz (1977) has shown that many of those societies have been characterized by considerable class differences and inequalities in the distribution of power for centuries. The emergence of corrupt political networks also had its forerunners in traditional forms of African stratification structures. These were not based primarily on the occupational division of labour (which was very limited anyway), but on family and kinship, that is, ethnic groups. The rise of a person into a high office implied that from now on he had to engage his kinsmen and his clan in his success, either by providing them with financial benefits or by awarding public offices and sinecures (Fallers 1966; Nuscheler and Ziemer 1978: 7ff.; Peil and Oyeneye 1998). Clientelism and corruption were 'normal affairs', leading to an excessive staffing of the public sector, a neglect of private entrepreneurial activities and a foreclosure from foreign competition.

The extremely difficult processes of nation formation in Africa led to an immense amount of violence with millions of deaths and refugees, and it contributed also to economic stagnation and decline and to widespread poverty. Most of the young, ethnically heterogeneous new states were not integrated in economic, social and cultural terms, had not developed a national consciousness and were confronted with the real danger of falling apart. This danger was closely related to the inequality in the distribution of power and privileges between the different ethnic groups and the related tense ethnic conflicts (Bélanger and Pinard 1991). In the unclear, often anomic situation in which many of the new states found themselves after having gained political independence, the dominant ethno-classes often mainly strived toward maintaining and securing their power against subordinated ethnic groups. In order to justify their actions, they represented themselves as the main advocates of national unity since their privileges were closely connected with the survival of the new state. Violent oppression of other ethnic-national groups, however, awakened opposition and often had the contrary effect, namely that these began to digress from the aim of national unity and to think about secession.[29] From this point of view, it is nearly a miracle that so far secession has been obtained in only one case and only in recent times (in 2011), namely in the case of South-Sudan.[30] It is also remarkable that the ethnic conflicts in many cases existed only at the level of elites but not among the populations (Janowitz 1970; Sternberger et al. 1978; Williams 1994: 70; Haller 1996b). The governance of a single 'unity-party' (*Einheitspartei*) at the national level, established in many cases by the elites of a singular ethnic group, was not supported by the citizens (Bratton et al. 2005). In fact, many of the 'liberation movements' recruited the soldiers for their armies by force among the population, often among children. According to a comprehensive report of the United Nations in 1996, about 300,000 children were participating as soldiers in armed conflicts (UNO 1996). Between 1990 and 2000 about two million children died in armed conflicts. About 50 armed groups, most of them in Sub-Saharan Africa, employed child soldiers.[31] Thus, it seems that the term 'class domination' is quite well suited for these new African political elites because we can see a clear monopolization of political power connected with an appropriation of economic privileges. Since power and privilege rest in the first instance on the control of governmental power, we could speak here also of 'political classes' in the sense of Mosca (1950) or of 'state classes' (Engelhard 1994: 247; see also Maghezi 1976; Freund 1998: 210). I will come back extensively to this type of ethno-class domination in Chapter 10.

Ethno-national Theocracies

The second variant of a type of society in which ethnic criteria and domination play a central role are ethno-national theocracies. A theocracy in the full sense is a political system where the political leader is also the highest religious authority. Today, a formal (although not structural-substantive, strict) separation between political and religious leadership is the usual pattern worldwide (Hirschl 2010: 1f.; Moaddel 2002). Typical for theocracies, like Saudi Arabia, is 'a triangular relation between God (the source of legitimacy and legislation), the king (the guardian of the sacred laws) a and the Saudi nation' (Al Rasheed 1996: 359). Principles of theocratic governance have gained enormous public support worldwide; they include not only fundamentalist Islamic states like Saudi Arabia or Iran, but also the rise of the Christian right in the USA, the spread of Pentecostalism and politically oriented Catholicism in the South and the resurgence of the Orthodox church in Russia (Hirschl 2010:1).

---

29 Similar processes unfolded in the case of Yugoslavia, see Haller 1996b.
30 It is equally suggestive that even in this case violent conflicts broke out soon after independence.
31 See also Honwana 2006; http://de.wikipedia.org/wiki/Kindersoldat

From the viewpoint of ethno-class domination and economic inequality, the theocracies in the Islamic world are of particular importance. A problem in the characterization of this type of regime is that there exists very little data about it – a fact which itself is no coincidence. Thus, I can only give a short and provisional sketch of the social structure of these societies here. Included in this group are mainly Arab Islamic societies with high revenues from crude oil. In these countries, economic inequality is presumably the most extreme around the world today, not the least because ethnic stratification and exploitation play a central role in their socio-economic system. In these countries, foreign workers have been 'imported' in large numbers; they not only have to execute unskilled work and basic personal and social services, but are also employed to carry out the largest part of all industrial and other 'productive' work. This explains the paradox that in Saudi Arabia, which is a rather a populous (23 million in 2005) and rich country, a high level of unemployment exists among the national youth side by side with a very high proportion of foreign workers (about 25 per cent, in small countries like Kuwait and Quatar 60 and 85 per cent respectively). In Saudi Arabia, the royal family (a clan with a supposed number of 15,000 to 20,000 persons) resides over incredibly high revenues. These often come in a hidden form, through middle-men and a complicated network of firms, and include commissions on state purchases (particularly weapons), monopolization of lucrative industrial sectors (particularly the building industry), foreign trade and tourism (Sharif 1993). Overall, Saudi economy and state has become a high complex, uncoordinated system of vertically divided fiefdoms, but also some insulated islands of efficiency (Hertog 2011). The central circles of power and privilege, however, are clearly defined. In one of the few studies on such a *rentier state*, Jacqueline S. Ismael (1993: 129) wrote: 'In the post-oil era in Kuwait, the ruling family effectively controls a tremendous surplus that has made its life style on of the most opulent in the world and far out of reach of the average Kuwaiti'. Five per cent of the Kuwaitis capture 30 per cent of total income. The control and appropriation of oil revenues and public expenditure 'become the focus of intra-class competition, in effect consolidating rather than fragmenting class cohesion behind the ruling family' (Ismael 1993: 95). Thus, these cases clearly supports the respective hypotheses developed in Chapter 3. A similar situation may exist in other gulf oil states (such as in Irak, Iran, Bahrein, and the Emirates). The extreme wealth of the upper class families in these states may also constitute a problem for the global financial system and security, since some of the huge sums of money involved often arrives through obscure channels and is spent for dubious purposes.

Four factors are essential for such a system. The first is a specific religious-ideological background. It was pointed out in Chapter 3 that in Islam no clear division exists between religion and state. Islam originated as the religion of the dominant class (*Herrenreligion*) of the nomadic Bedouins and was used from the beginning as a legitimation of military expansion and political domination (Schluchter 1987; Moaddel 2002). This religious background also explains the nearly irresistible strength of the Arabic-Islamic armies, which were not very large when they overran and ruled ancient Egypt and all the North African kingdoms in the West including large parts of the Iberian peninsula and the very old kingdoms of Persia and others in the East between 630 and 900 AD. In the new states, religious law became the basis for political order up until today. Therefore, also students of Islam denote these societies as theocracies (Hourani et al. 1993). It is significant in this regard that non-Muslims in historic Islamic societies were tolerated but had always the status of second class citizens. The contemporary presence of a majority of an underprivileged expatriate population, disenfranchised from politics, constitutes a massive problem for the legitimation of these systems. This is even more so because retaining power is the dominant aim of the regimes.[32]

The second factor is closely related to the first; it is the absence of effective institutions of democratic participation and opposition. Instead of it, a massive police and military apparatus exists. The whole system is legitimized – particularly in Saudi Arabia – by the idea of 'Gods State' (*Gottesstaat*), in which the Islamic law of Sharia is reigning and all the powers are in the hands of the king. The huge rents from oil, which constitute 80 per cent and more of all state earnings, clearly contribute to the persistence of this system (Hertog 2010).

A third factor is connected with the immense revenues from crude oil. These enable their dominant classes to cede their own citizens to a considerable degree. This occurs both through privileged, well-paid employment in the public sector and through the provision of extensive and gratuitous public services in the areas of education, health and living. In Kuwait, the state guarantees a public job to every citizen and, in fact, over 72 per cent work in the public sector (Ismail 1993: 106–21). Some authors denote these systems

---

32   For the case of Kuwait see Ismail 1993, p. 123.

appropriately as 'rentier states' (Moaddel 2002). The high level of unemployment among the youth, however, constitutes a volatile social-political blasting composition which can explode any time. The revolutions in Tunisia, Libya and Egypt in winter and spring 2011 may be seen as a foretaste.

The fourth aspect concerns the ethnic and class structure. A sharp internal differentiation in ethnic terms, which has emerged only in recent times as a consequence of the massive employment of foreign workers, is a constitutive element of these societies. The privileged situation of the native Arab population contrasts extremely with the underprivileged status of the foreign population whose designation as *guest workers* is quite euphemistic in some regards. Most of them have very few, some no rights at all concerning their working conditions, union organisation and political participation. As a consequence, they have no possibilities to defend their basic rights as workers and as persons, often having lived for years in the country of employment (Esim and Smith 2004).[33] It is not surprising, therefore, that from time to time there is news about foreign workers and housemaids who are kept in slave-like conditions. The incomes of the foreign workers differ widely from those of the natives. There exists also a striking stratification within the expatriate labour force. On the top are highly specialized, well-paid technicians and engineers, doctors and university teachers; at the bottom are those who can hardly find alternative sources of employment and income in their home countries. It was no accident, for instance, that Palestinians (all in all about 300,000 living in Kuwait) were the main victims of Kuwait's occupation by Saddam Hussein's Iraq in 1990 (Ismail 1993: 171).

The extreme degree of inequality in these theocracies is not only their own internal social and political problem. It is highly relevant for the world as a whole, given their importance as the main furnishers of crude oil to many countries around the world. Political revolts could destabilize these countries massively and lead to serious threats for global security and peace. Therefore, social science in the North should also investigate this issue systematically and advise politicians in their own countries of this problem; at present it is a topic hardly mentioned at the international level or at state visits.

Two other strategies of this sort involve actions by ethnic minorities themselves. One is secession from a larger nation; this way is feasible for a minority only if it is settled on a relatively compact territory, situated at the edge of a nation-state. The other strategy is to establish anew a homogeneous ethnic nation-state and to bring together the dispersed members of this ethnic group from all parts of the world. I will return to these strategies in Chapter 13.

Summary and Outlook

Two main questions were raised in this chapter: how does ethnic differentiation in a society emerge? When does it lead to ethnic stratification and economic inequality? It was assumed that there exists a close connection between these two processes which must be taken into consideration when looking at present-day forms of ethnic stratification and inequality. Three basic processes and strategies were distinguished in this regard: strategies to preserve ethnic homogeneity, strategies to control an emerging ethnic heterogeneity and strategies to establish ethnically based systems of domination and exploitation.

The aim to preserve ethnic homogeneity – a situation which makes governing much more easy – can be achieved in different ways. One is to encapsulate a whole society from the outside world. Such a strategy is not possible any more in the globalized world of today; yet, we must not go back far into history in order to find such strategies. Japan and Australia were examples for the successful application of such strategies. Two other strategies are practised still today in many countries. One is the isolation and socio-economic and legal confinement of unloved indigenous or emerging new minorities within a society. Another one is to assimilate them with more or less pressure to the majority. Third, an ever recurring strategy is emanating from relatively strong minorities themselves, namely their secession from an existing multi-ethnic state.

In the present-day world, migration is a continuous and forceful process. Thus, governments willingly and unwillingly have to accept (or even foster) immigration. The immigrants, however, often are ethnically distinct from the native population. Therefore, governments try to control the flows of immigration and the integration of immigrants as far as they can. Three forms of such a control have been distinguished: one is

---

33   See also Human Rights Watch Report 2010; UNHCR, 'The Persian Gulf: the Situation of Foreign Workers', *Migration News*, 3(3) 1996; Rashid Al Amin, 'Migrant Workers in the Gulf', *International Human Rights*, 5(4), 1988.

the practical foreclosure of certain categories of potential immigrants, typically unskilled people or people from countries and world regions where adversary life conditions are pressing many to emigrate. The highly developed, rich countries of the North have in fact established a new Iron Curtain between the poor countries of the South and themselves. It consists of two elements. One is the construction of a concrete wall at the borderline between the poor and the rich countries. It has been shown that the walls established in North Africa and on the US-Southern borders are very similar, not only in their shape, but also in their functions, to historical walls around large empires, such as the Roman Limes and the Great Wall of China. The other strategy to keep away unwanted immigrants from poor countries is the refinement of an instrument invented during the First World War in Europe, namely the prescription that any immigrant from such countries must apply for a visa. The rich countries of the North, stagnating or even declining in demographic terms, however, need immigrants. Therefore, they must also come to grips with the fact that immigration is unavoidable and, as a consequence of it, new forms of ethnic differentiation will emerge. In order to control these as far as possible, two strategies are employed: a selective migration policy which favours certain groups of immigrants over others; and a rudimentary integration policy which assists certain groups of immigrants to integrate themselves in the host societies.

In many cases, however, the encountering of different ethnic groups does not occur in ordered and peaceful ways. Two such cases have been identified in which the application of brute power and domination of one group over the other came to the force: the enslavement and open exploitation of certain ethnic groups and the establishment of exploitative relationships between a dominant and a subordinate ethnic group (the Apartheid system). Two other forms also involving violent conflicts and civil wars include the usurpation of power by ethno-classes (which occurred in many Sub-Saharan African countries), and the establishment of ethnocracies, that is, systems of political domination by a small elite legitimized by religious ideologies.

The main assumption behind the considerations in this chapter was that the implementation of each of these forms of ethnic differentiation and relations has effective consequences for patterns of socio-economic inequality; this applies also to strategies which are not practised openly any more today or on a large scale. This is true particularly for the system of brutal enslavement, which existed in Africa and America from the 16th till the late 19th centuries. From the viewpoint of historical sociology it is obvious, however, that such forms of oppression and exploitation must have long-term consequences for all groups involved. In fact, we have already shown in the foregoing chapter, that there exists no other factor which is able to explain the excessive economic inequality which can be seen today on the two sub-continents of Sub-Saharan Africa and Latin America.

In Chapters 6 to 12, I will analyse the connection between ethnic differentiation and stratification and economic inequality in more detail for some of the most interesting and relevant cases around the world, using both historical and qualitative sources and actual quantitative data.

References

Adam, Heribert and Kogila Moodley (1977), *Südafrika ohne Apartheid?* Frankfurt/Main: Suhrkamp

Adam, Heribert (2013), 'Siedlungskolonialismus: Ökonomische und ideologische Motive in der Konfliktlösung in Apartheid-Südafrika und Palästina', in Daniela Klimke and Aldo Legnaro, eds, *Politische Ökonomie und Sicherheit*, Weinheim/Basel: Beltz, pp. 62–73

Al Rasheed, Madawi (1996), 'God, the King and the nation: Political rhetoric in Saudi Arabia in the 1990s', *Middle East Journal* 50: 359–71

Anderson, Benedict (1998), *Die Erfindung der Nation*, Berlin: Ullstein (*Imagined Communities*, 1983)

Assmann, Jan (1992), *Das kulturelle Gedächtnis. Schrift, Erinnerung und politische Identität in frühen Hochkulturen*, München: Beck

Azevedo, Célia M.M. de (1987), *Onda Negro, Mede Branco*, Rio de Janeiro: Paz e Terra

Bales, Kevin (2004), *Disposable People. New Slavery in the Global Economy*, Berkeley etc.: University of California Press

Baronov, David (2000), *The Abolition of Slavery in Brazil. The 'Liberation' of Africans Through the Emancipation of Capital*, Westport, CN/London: Greenwood Press

Batstone, David (2008), *Sklavenhandel heute. Die dunkelste Seite der Globalisierung*, München: Redline Wirtschaft (*Not for Sale*, New York, Harper Collins)

Bauböck, Rainer (1994), *Transnational Citizenship. Membership and Rights in International Migration*, Aldershot, UK/Brookfield: E. Elgar

Bauböck, Rainer, Bernhard Perchinig and Wiebke Sievers (2009), *Citizenship Policies in the New Europe*, Amsterdam: Amsterdam University Press

Bauman, Zygmunt (1998), *Globalisation. The Human Consequences*, Oxford: Polity Press

Bélanger, Sarah and Maurice Pinard (1991), 'Ethnic movements and the competition model: Some missing links', *American Sociological Review* 56: 446–57.

Berlin, Ira (2003), *Generations of Captivity. A History of African-American Slaves*, Cambridge/London: Belknap Press

Bilger, Harold (1976), *Südafrika in Geschichte und Gegenwart*, Konstanz: Universitätsverlag

Blassingame, John W. (1972), *The Slave Community: Plantation Life in the Antebellum South*, New York: Oxford University Press

Bley, Helmut et al., eds (1991), *Sklaverei in Afrika*, Pfaffenweiler: Centaurus

Boudon, Raymond (1988), *Ideologie. Geschichte und Kritik eines Begriffs*, Reinbek: Rowohlt (*L'idéologie. L'origine des idées recus*, Paris 1986)

Boudon, Raymond (2000), *Il Senso dei Valori*, Bologna: il Mulino (*Le Sense de valeurs*, Paris 1999)

Bourdieu, Pierre (2006), *Die feinen Unterschiede: Kritik der gesellschaftlichen Urteilskraft*, Frankfurt am Main: Suhrkamp (*La Distinction*, Paris 1984)

Bratton, Michael, Robert Mattes and E. Gyimah-Boadi (2005), *Public Opinion, Democracy and Market Reform in Africa*, Cambridge: Cambridge University Press

Braudel, Fernand (1992), *Schriften zur Geschichte*, Stuttgart (French ed. Paris 1969)

Brubaker, Rogers (1992), *Citizenship and Nationhood in France and Germany*, Cambridge, MA: Harvard University Press

Calderón, Fernando G. (1977), 'The Quechiua and Aymará pepoples in the formation and development of Bolivian society', in UNESCO, *Race and Class in Post-Colonial Society*, pp. 185–219

Castles, Stephen and Godula Kosack (1973), *Immigrant Workers and the Class Structure in Western Europe*, London: Oxford University Press

Cooper, Frederick, Thomas C. Holt and Rebecca J. Scott (2000), *Beyond Slavery. Explorations of Race, Labor, and Citizenship in Postemancipation Societies*, Chapel Hill/London: The University of North Carolina Press

Dal Lago, Enrico and Constantina Katsari, eds (2008), *Slave Systems. Ancient and Modern*, Cambridge: Cambridge University Press

Deutsch, Karl W. (1966), *Nationalism and Social Communication. An Inquiry into the Foundations of Nationality*, Cambridge, MA/London: The MIT Press

Downing, David (2004), *Apartheid in South Africa*, London: Heinemann

Durkheim, Emile (1965), *Die Regeln der soziologischen Methode*, Neuwied/Berlin: Luchterhand (Les régles de la mèthode sociologique, Paris 1895)

Ellis, Stephen, ed. (1996), *Africa Now. People, Policies and Institutions*, London: Heinemann

Engbersen, Godfried (2004), 'The wall around the welfare state in Europe: International migration and social exclusion', *Indian Journal of Labour Politics* 46: 479–95

Engelhard, Philippe (1994), *L'Afrique – Miroir du Monde? Plaidoyer pour une nouvelle économie*, Paris: arléa

Engerman, Stanley (2008), 'Emancipation schemes: Different ways of ending slavery', in Dal Lago/Katsari, *Slave Systems*, pp. 265–82

Engerman, Stanley, Seymour Drescher and Robert Paquette, eds (2001), *Slavery*, Oxford: Oxford University Press

Esim, Simel and Monica Smith, eds (2004), *Gender and Migration in Arab States: The Case of Domestic Workers*, Beirut: ILO Regional Office for Arab States

Esser, Hartmut (1980), *Aspekte der Wanderungssoziologie*, Darmstadt/Neuwied: Luchterhand

Esser, Hartmut (1999), 'Inklusion, Integration und ethnische Schichtung', *Journal für Konflikt und Gewaltforschung* 1: 5–34

Esser, Hartmut (2011), *Integration und ethnische Schichtung* (Gutachten), Arbeitspapier Nr. 40, Mannheimer Zentrum für Europäische Sozialforschung

Esser, Hartmut (2006), *Sprache und Integration. Die sozialen Bedingungen und Folgen des Spracherwerbs von Migranten*, Frankfurt am Main/New York: Campus

Eyerman, Ron (2001), *Cultural Trauma. Slavery and the Formation of African American Identity*, Cambridge: Cambridge University Press

Fallers, Lloyd A. (1966), *Class, Status, and Power. Social Stratification in Comparative Perspective*, New York/London: The Free Press/Collier Macmillan

Fernandes Dias, Maria S. ed. (2007), *Legacies of Slavery. Comparative Perspectives*, Newcastle, United Kingdom: Cambridge Scholars Publishing

Fischer Weltalmanach (2008), Frankfurt: Fischer Taschenbuch Verlag

Flaig, Egon (2009), *Weltgeschichte der Sklaverei*, München: C.H. Beck

Fortes Meyer and Evans Pritchard, eds (1961), *African Poliitical Systems*, London etc.: Oxford University Press

Frankema, Ewout (2008), Wage inequality in Twentieth Century Latin America: A comparative perspective, Groningen Growth and Development Centre, University of Groningen

Frankema, Ewout (2010) The Colonial Roots of Land Distribution: Geography, Factor Endowments or Institutions? *Economic History Review* 63: 418–51

Freund, Bill (1998), *The Making of Contemporary Africa. The Development of African Society since 1800*, Boulder, CO: William Mark Freund

Freyre, Gilberto (1964), *The Masters and the Slaves. A Study in the Development of Brazilian Civilization*, New York, Knopf (here quoted after the German ed. Herrenhaus und Sklavenhütte, Köln/Berlin: Kiepenheuer & Witsch 1965; original ed. Rio de Janeiro 1936)

Galeano, Eduardo (2003 [1971]), *Die offenen Adern Lateinamerikas. Die Geschichte eines Kontinents von der Entdeckung bis zur Gegenwart*, Wuppertal: Peter Hammer

Gardt, Andreas (2000), *Nation und Sprache. Die Diskussion ihres Verhältnisses in Geschichte und Gegenwart*, Berlin etc.: de Gruyter

Gastarbeiter. Wirtschaftsfaktor und soziale Herausforderung (1973), Wien: Europaverlag/Österreichischer Wirtschaftsverlag

Giddens, Anthony (1973), *The Class Structure of the Advanced Societies*, London: Hutchinson

Giorgi, Liana, Ingmar von Hoemeyer and Wayne Parsons, eds (2006), *Democracy in the European Union. Towards the Emergence of a Public Sphere*, London/New York: Routledge

Gobodo-Madikizela, Pumla (2006), *Das Erbe der Apartheid. Trauma, Erinnerung, Versöhnung*, Opladen: Budrich (*A Human Being Died That Night*, Boston 2004)

Grant, R.G. (2010), *Geschichte der Sklaverei*, London: Dorling Kindersley (*Slavery*, London 2009)

Guibernau, Montserrat (1996), *The Nation-State and Nationalism in the Twentieth Century*, Cambridge: Polity Press

Gurr, Ted Robert (1993), *Minorities at Risk: A Global View of Ethnopolitical Conflicts*, Washington, DC: United States Institute of Peace Press

Hall, John W. (1968), *Das Japanische Kaiserreich, Fischer Weltgeschichte vol. 20*, Frankfurt: Fischer Taschenbuch Verlag

Haller, Max (1983), *Theorie der Klassenbildung und sozialen Schichtung*, Frankfurt/New York: Campus

Haller, Max (1996b), 'The dissolution and building of new nations as strategy and process between elites and people. Lessons from historical European and recent Yugoslav experience', *International Review of Sociology* 6: 231–47

Haller, Max (2006), 'Theorien sozialer Ungleichheit im nationalen und europäischen Kontext. Eine wissenssoziologische Analyse', in Martin Heidenreich, ed., *Die Europäisierung sozialer Ungleichheit. Zur transnationalen Klassen- und Sozialstrukturanalyse*, Frankfurt/New York: Campus, pp. 187–229

Haller, Max (2008b), *European Integration as an Elite Process. The Failure of a Dream?* New York/London: Routledge

Haller, Max et al. (1985), 'Patterns of career mobiity and structural positions in advanced capitalist societies: A comparison of men in Austria, France, and the United States', *American Sociological Review* 50: 579–603

Haller, Max and Markus Hadler (2004/05), 'Ist der Nationalstaat überholt? Überlegungen und Fakten über die sinnvollste Einheit bzw. Analyseebene in der international vergleichenden Sozialforschung', *AIAS-Informationen* 23: 141–61

Haller, Max and Bernadette Müller, eds (2010), Europa in Afrika. Afrika in Europa. Ergebnisse des Forschungspraktikums Global Sociology, Graz: Universität Graz, Department of Sociology

Heers Jacques (1996), *Esclaves et domestiques au Moyen Age dans le monde méditerranéen*, Paris: Hachette

Heinsohn, Gunnar (2008), *Söhne und Weltmacht. Terror im Aufstieg und Fall der Nationen*, München/Zürich: Piper

Henn, Jessica (2011), *Minderheitenschutz der Roma in der Europäischen Union*, Berlin: BWV Verlag

Hertog, Steffen (2010), 'The sociology of the Gulf rentier systems; Societies of intermediaries', *Comparative Studies in Society and History* 52: 282–318

Hertog, Steffen (2011), *Princes, Brokers and Bureaucrats: Oil and the State in Saudi Arabia*, Ithaca: Cornell University Press

Heschl, Franz (2009), 'Shortage of skilled workers: myths and realities', in Fassmann et al., *Migration and Mobility in Europe*, pp. 31–50

Hirschl, Ran (2010), *Constitutional Theocracy*, Cambridge, MA: Harvard University Press

Hofbauer, Andreas (1995), *Afro-Brasilien*, Wien: ProMedia

Hoffmann-Nowotny, Hans-Joachim (1973), *Soziologie des Fremdarbeiterproblems*, Stuttgart: Enke

Holanda, Sergio Buarque de (2009 [1936]), *Raizes do Brasil*, Sao Paolo: Companhia das Letras

Honwana, Alcinda (2006), *Child Soldiers in Africa*, Philadelphia: University of Pennsylvania Press

Hourani, Albert et al., eds (1993), *The Modern Middle East. A Reader*, Berkeley, CA: University of California Press

Hufeisen, Britta and Gerhard Neuner, eds (2003), *Mehrsprachigkeitskonzept – Tertiärsprachenlernen – Deutsch nach Englisch*, Strasbourg: Council of Europe Publishing

Illife, John (1997), *Geschichte Afrikas*, München: C.H. Beck

Ismael, Jacqueline S. (1993), *Kuwait. Dependency and Class in a Rentier State*, Gainesville, FL: University Press of Florida

James, Paul (1996), *Nation Formation. Towards a Theory of Abstract Community*, London etc.: Sage

Janowitz, Morris (1970), *Political Conflict. Essays in Political Sociology*, Chicago: Quadrangle Books

Joseph, John E. (2004), *Language and Identity. National, Ethnic, Religious*, Houndmills: Palgrave Macmillan

Kara, Siddhardt (2009), *Sex Trafficking: Inside the Business of Modern Slavery*, New York: Columbia University Press

Kesler, Christel (2006), 'Social policy and immigrant joblessness in Britain, Germany and Sweden', *Social Forces* 85: 743–70

Klee, Margot (2006), *Grenzen des Imperiums. Leben am römischen Limes*, Stuttgart: Theiss

Kohn, Hans (1967), *The Idea of Nationalism*, New York: Collier-Macmillan

Koopmans, Ruud (2010), 'Tradeoffs between Equality and Difference Immigrant Integration, Multiculturalism, and the Welfare State in Cross-national Perspective', *Journal of Ethnic and Migration Studies* 36: 1–26

Koopmans, Ruud et al. (2005), *Contested Citizenship. Immigration and Cultural Diversity in Europe*, Minneapolis: University of Minnesota Press

Kößler, Reinhart and Tilman Schiel (1995), *Nationalstaat und Ethnizität*, Frankfurt: IKO-Verlag für interkulturelle Kommunikation

Kreutzer, Mary and Corinna Milborn (2008), *Ware Frau. Auf den Spuren moderner Sklaverei von Afrika nach Europa*, Salzburg: Ecowin

Kuper, Adam (1977), 'Race, class and culture in Jamaica', in: UNESCO, *Race and Class in Post-colonial Society*, pp. 111–49

Lake, David A. and Donald Rothchild, eds (1998), *The International Spread of Ethnic Conflict. Fear, Diffusion, and Escalation*, Princeton, NJ: Princeton University Press

Lemberg, Eugen (1964), *Nationalismus*, 2 vols, Reinbek: Rowohlt

Liégeois, Jean-Pierre (2007), *Roma in Europe*, Strasbourg: Council of Europe

Lorenz, Chris (1997), *Konstruktion der Vergangenheit. Eine Einführung in die Geschichtstheorie*, Köln etc.: Böhlau

Löwstedt, Anthony (2012), Apartheid. Ancient, Past and Present, Habilitation thesis, University of Vienna

Manghezi, Alpheus (1976), *Class, Elite, and Community Development in Africa*, Uppsala: The Scandinavian Institute of African Studies

Malek Chebel (2007), *L'Esclavage en Terre d'Islam. Un tabu bien gardé*, Paris: Fayard

Mamdani, Mahmood (1996), *Citizen and Subject. Contemporary Africa and the Legacy of Late Colonialism*, Princeton, NJ: Princeton University Press

Mann, Michael (2007), *Die dunkle Seite der Demokratie. Eine Theorie der ethnischen Säuberung*, Hamburg: Hamburger edition (*The Dark Side of Democracy*, New York 2005)

Manning, Patrick (1990), *Slavery and American Life*, Cambridge: Cambridge University Press

Mappes-Niediek, Norbert (2012), *Arme Roma, böse Zigeuner: Was an den Vorurteilen über die Zuwanderer stimmt*, Berlin: Ch. Links Verlag

Marko, Josef (2012), 'Ethnopolitics. The challenge for human and minority rights protection', in Claudio Corradetti, ed., *Philosophical Dimensions of Human Rights. Some Contemporary Views*, Dordrecht, etc: Springer, pp. 265–91

Markovitz, Irving L. (1977), *Class and Power in Africa*, Englewood Cliffs, NJ: Prentice Hall

Marx, Karl (1971 [1867]), *Das Kapital. Kritik der politischen Ökonomie*, 1. Bd., Berlin: Dietz Verlag

Meillassoux, Claude, ed. (1975), *L'Esclavage en Afrique*, Paris: Maspero

Meissner, Jochen, Ulrich Mücke and Klaus Weber (2008), *Schwarzes Amerika. Eine Geschichte der Sklaverei*, München: C.H.Beck

Meuschel, Sigrid, (1981), *Die langwierige Durchsetzung der bürgerlichen Gesellschaft in den USA*, Frankfurt: EVA

Michler, Walter (1988), *Weißbuch Afrika*, Berlin/Bonn: J.H.W. Dietz

Miers, Suzanne and Igor Kopytoff, eds (1977), *Slavery in Africa. Historical and Anthropological Perspectives*, Madison: The University of Wisconsin Press

Milborn, Corinna (2006), *Gestürmte Festung Europa*, Wien etc.: Styria

Moaddel, Mansoor (2002), 'The study of Islamic culture and politics: An overview and assessment', *Annual Review of Sociology* 28: 359–86

Montesquieu, Baron de (2002 [1748]), *The Spirit of Laws*, Berlin: Prometheus Books

Mosca, Gaetano (1950 [1896]), *Die herrschende Klasse*, Bern: Francke

Müller, Bernadette and Max Haller (2012), 'The Situation of Students in Sub-Saharan Africa: A Case Study of St. Augustine University of Tanzania', in *International Studies in Sociology of Education*, 22: 169–89

Münkler, Herwig (2005), *Imperien – die Logik der Weltherrschaft – Vom alten Rom bis zu den Vereinigten Staaten*, Reinbek: Rowohlt

Murphy, Raymond (1988), *Social Closure. The Theory of Monopolization and Exclusion*, Oxford: Clarendon Press

N'Diaye, Tidiane (2010), *Der verschleierte Völkermord. Die Geschichte des muslimischen Sklavenhandels in Afrika*, Reinbek: Rowohlt (*Le genocide voile*, Paris 2008)

Noiriel, Gérard (1991), *La tyrannie du national: Le droit d'asile en Europe, 1793–1993*, Paris: Calmann-Lévy

Nugent, Paul (2004), *Africa Since Independence. A Comparative History*, Houndmills, Basingstoke/New York: Palgrave MacMillan

Nuscheler, Franz and Klaus Ziemer (1978), Politische Organisation und Repräsentation in Afrika, vol. II of the Handbook, *Die Wahl der Parlamente und anderer Staatsorgane*, eds Dolf Sternberger et al., Berlin/ New York: Walter de Gruyter

O'Callaghan, Sean (1963), *Sklavenhandel heute*, München: Rütten + Loening (*The Slave Trade*, London 1965)

Olzak, Susan (2006), *The Global Dynamics of Race and Ethnic Mobilization*, Stanford: Stanford University Press

Parkin, Frank (1979), *Marxism and Class Theory: A Bourgeois Critique*, London: Tavistock

Patterson, Orlando (2008), 'Slavery, gender, and work in the pre-modern world and early Greece: A cross-cultural analysis', in Dal Lago and Katsari, *Slave Systems*, p. 32–69

Peil, Margaret and Olatunji Oyeneye (1998), *Consensus, Conflict and Change. A Sociological Introduction to African Societies*, Nairobi etc.: East African Educational Publishers

Penninx, Rinus and J. Roosblad, eds (2000), *Trade Unions, Immigration, and Immigrants in Europe, 1960–1993. A Comparative Study of the Attitudes and Actions of Trade Unions in Seven West European Countries*, New York/Oxford: Berghahn Books

Perkins, John (2004), *Confessions of an Economic Hit Man*, San Francisco: South End Press

Pétré-Grenouilleau, Olivier (2008), 'Processes of exiting the slave systems: A typology', in Dal Lago and Katsari, *Slave Systems*, pp. 233–64

Pfaff-Giesberg, Robert (1955), *Geschichte der Sklaverei*, Meisenheim: A. Hain

Procacci, Giuliano (1983), *Geschichte Italiens und der Italiener*, München: C.H.Beck (*storia degli italiani*, Roma 1968)

Pusca, Anca (2012), *Roma in Europe. Migration, Education, Representation*, New York: International Debate Education Association

Reader, John (1998), *Africa. Biography of a Continent*, London: Penguin Books

Ross, Robert (1983), *Cape of Torments. Slavery and Resistance in South Africa*, London: Routledge & Kegan Paul

Sala-Molins, Louis (1992), *Les misères des Lumiéres. Spous la raison l'outrage*, Paris: Homnisphères

Santos, Ana Maria Barros dos (1985), *Die Sklaverei in Brasilien und ihre sozialen und wirtschaftlichen Folgen. Dargestellt am Beispiel Pernambuco (1840–1889)*, München: W. Fink Verlag

Sassen, Saskia (1996), *Migranten, Siedler, Flüchtlinge. Von der Massenauswanderung zur Festung Europa*, Frankfurt: Fischer Taschenbuch Verlag (*Guests and Aliens*, New York 1999)

Schallmayer, Egon (2006), *Der Limes. Geschichte einer Grenze*, München: Beck

Schieder, Theodor (1964), *Der Nationalstaat in Europa als historisches Phänomen*, Opladen: Westdeutscher Verlag

Schluchter, Wolfgang (1988), *Religion und Lebensführung*, Frankfurt: Suhrkamp

Schmid, Eefje and Jutta Wagner (2004), *Migration in und aus Afrika*, ed. Bundesministerium für wirtschaftliche Zusammenarbeit und Entwicklung, Bonn

Schmitt, Jucelmo L. (2008), *Die Lage der schwarzen Bevölkerung vor und nach Abschaffung der Sklaverei in Brasilien*, Bonn etc.: Scientia Bonnensis

Scholze, Markus (2013), Integration der Roma in der EU, Master thesis, Department of Sociology, University of Graz

Schulze, Hagen (1999), *Staat und Nation in der europäischen Geschichte*, München: C.H. Beck

Sen, Amartya (1999), *Development as Freedom*, New York: Knopf

Sharif, Issam A. (1993), *Saudi-Arabien. Unter dem Joch der Ölprinzen*, Wien: Sharif

Shibutani, Tamotsu and Kian M. Kwan (1965), *Ethnic Stratification. A Comparative Approach*, New York: Macmillan/London: Collier-Macmillan

Shils, Edward (1982), *The Constitution of Society*, Chicago/London: The University of Chicago Press

Sigrist, Christian (1967), *Regulierte Anarchie*, Olten/Freiburg: Walter Verlag

Skidmore, Thomas (1992), *Fact and Myth: Discovering a Racial Problem in Brazil*, Notre Dame, Ind.: Helen Kellogg Institute für International Studies

Smith, Anthony D. (1986), *The Ethnic Origins of Nations*, Oxford etc.: Blackwell

Sombart, Werner (1906), *Warum gibt es in den Vereinigten Staaten keinen Sozialismus?* Tübingen: Mohr

Sternberger Dolf et al., eds (1978), *Die Wahl der Parlamente*. Bd.II: *Afrika*, 2. Halbband, Berlin: Walter de Gruyter

Temperley, Howard, ed. (2000), *After Slavery. Emancipation and its Discontents*, London: Frank Cass

Tilly, Charles (1998), *Durable Inequalities*, Berkeley, CA: University of California Press

Tocqueville, Alexis de (1945 [1835]), *Democracy in America*, New York: Vintage Books (here quoted after the German ed. *Über die Demokratie in Amerika*, München: dtv 1976)

UNESCO (1977), *Race and Class in Post-Colonial Society: A Study of Ethnic Group Relations in the English-Speaking Caribbean, Bolivia, Chile and Mexico*, Paris: UNESCO

Wallerstein, Immanuel (1974), *The Modern World-System I. Capitalist Agriculture and the Origins of the European World-Economy in the Sixteenth Century*, New York etc.: Academic Press

Weber, Max (1964/I+II), *Wirtschaft und Gesellschaft*, 2 vols, Köln/Berlin: Kiepenheuer & Witsch

Weber, Max (1973a [1896]), 'Die sozialen Gründe des Untergangs der antiken Kultur', in M. Weber, *Soziologie*, Weltgeschichtliche Analysen, Stuttgart: A. Kröner, pp. 1–26

Wehler, Hans-Ulrich (1973), *Geschichte als historische Sozialwissenschaft*, Frankfurt/Main: Suhrkamp

Williams, Robin M. Jr (1994), 'The Sociology of Ethnic Conflicts: Comparative International Perspectives', *Annual Review of Sociology* 20: 49–79 (reprinted in: Malcolm Cross, ed., *The Sociology of Race and Ethnicity II*, 3 vols, Northampton, MA: E. Elgar, 2000)

Wimmer, Andreas (2002), *Nationalist Exclusion and Ethnic Conflict: Shadows of Modernity*, Cambridge, New York: Cambridge University Press

World Development Report (2006), *Equity and Development*, Washington/New York: The World Bank/ Oxford University Press

Zewen, Luo, Dai Wenbao and Dick Wilson (1990), *Die große Mauer. Geschichte, Kultur- und Sozialgeschichte Chinas*, Augsburg: Weltbild-Verlag (*The Great Wall* 1982)

Zoubir, Yahia, ed. (1999*), North Africa in Transition: State, Society, and Economic Transformation in the 1990s*, Gainesville etc.: University of Florida Press

Chapter 6

Two Roads Toward Egalitarianism in Ethnic Homogeneous Societies: Sweden and Japan

There are three countries and groups of countries, respectively, which stand out worldwide according to the lowest degree of inequality (see Table 1.1 pp. 5–6): the four Scandinavian countries (Denmark, Finland, Norway, Sweden); several smaller, East Central European countries (Czech Republic, Slovakia, Hungary and Bosnia-Herzegovina); two Central Asian Republics (Azerbaijan and Uzbekistan); and Japan. In the case of two groups of countries, politics has certainly contributed significantly to the remarkable degree of economic equality. The East Central European and Central Asian countries had experienced a process of radical nationalization of land and industries after World War I and II, respectively, and they were subject to four decades of State Socialism whose declared intention was to equalize the living conditions of the whole population. But also in the case of Scandinavia, the political system and political processes – in this case, the social-democratic welfare state – were decisive for attaining the present-day remarkably high level of socio-economic equality. Sweden and the other Scandinavian countries today are among the richest of the world and they have also very well-established and stable democracies; they are considered by many as paradigmatic examples for the thesis that Capitalism and democracy are quite compatible. However, it is astonishing that also modern Japan seems characterized by a rather modest degree of socio-economic equality. According to our data (Table 1.1, p. 6) Japan's Gini index lies only somewhere between 25 and 31. This remarkable equality is all the more surprising because this large country has just a rudimentary welfare state. The proportion of social expenditures in terms of GNI was only 4 per cent in 1950, when it was already 14.8 per cent in Germany; in 2001 it rose in Japan to 16.9 per cent, but in Germany to 27.4 per cent, in Sweden to 28.9 per cent; even in the USA it was clearly higher than in Japan (Schmidt 2001). In spite of a high public deficit,[1] the Japanese state itself does little direct redistribution. Thus, we must say that a strong welfare state is not the only way to attain a high level of socio-economic equality.

In this chapter, it will be shown that in both cases, in Sweden and Japan, the high level of ethnic homogeneity was an indispensable pre-condition and supporting structure for the achievement of this remarkable equality. In the case of the Scandinavian welfare states this fact has been very seldom recognized. The findings that shall be presented in this regard do not invalidate the effectiveness of the Scandinavian welfare state. They cast doubt, however, on the thesis that this Scandinavian state could be a model for many other countries, particularly for the poor and conflict-ridden young nation-states in the Third World. For them, in some regards Japan rather than Sweden may be an example.

An Egalitarian Class Society. The Case of Sweden

Sweden has been selected as the paradigmatic example for the Scandinavian welfare state mainly for two reasons: first, with about 9 million inhabitants and 540,000 square kilometres, it is the largest among the four Scandinavian countries; second, its welfare state is the most distinctive. It is well-known internationally as the 'Swedish model' (Steinmo 2003), characterized by a deliberate and consistent policy over about half a century, and due to many excellent Swedish and other social scientists who have analysed this welfare state and its effects.[2] Sweden rightly has been designated as the Scandinavian 'welfare leader' (Olson 1986: 7). During the last 100 years, Sweden has also moved up from one of the poorest countries in Europe to one of the richest in the world, providing very high standards of living and levels of social security to all its citizens (see Table 6.1, pp. 164–5). In the late 19th century, out of a five million population, one million emigrated to

---

1 See, for instance, F.A.Z. Net (14.1.2008): 'Japan's Finanzpolitik auf Abwegen'.

2 On the Swedish welfare state see Korpi 1983; Henningsen 1986; Esping-Andersen 1990 and Huntford 1973 (a critical view); on welfare states in general see Flora and Heidenheimer 1981; Wilensky 1975; Flora 1986.

Country	(1) Population (in millions) (2010)	(2) Annual population growth 2000–10	(3) GDP (PPP) per capita (Int. $) (2005–12)	(4) Population below national poverty rate (%) (2002–12)	(5) Human development index (2012) (World rank)
Sweden	8	0.6	43.180	9.1	0.91 (7)
Norway	4	0.8	65.640	7.5	0.95 (1)
UK	58	0.6	36.901	9.9	0.87 (26)
France	60	0.7	36.104	7.9	0.89 (20)
Germany	82	-0.1	40.109	8.8	0.92 (5)
Austria	8	0.5	44.208	8.1	0.89 (18)
Switzerland	7	0.6	53.367	9.5	0.91 (9)
Italy	56	0.6	33.111	13.0	0.88 (25)
Spain	40	1.3	32.682	15.4	0.88 (23)
Portugal	10	0.4	25.411	11.4	0.81 (43)
Poland	38	-0.1	22.162	11.0	0.82 (39)
Czech Republic	10	0.2	26.590	5.8	0.87 (28)
Hungary	10	-0.2	22.119	6.8	0.83 (37)
Russia	146	-0.3	23.501	11.1	0.78 (54)
Turkey	63	1.3	18.348	19.3	0.72 (90)
Australia	22	1.5	44.598	14.5	0.93 (2)
Canada	30	1.0	42.533	11.9	0.91 (11)
USA	282	0.9	49.965	17.4	0.93 (3)
Mexico	100	1.3	16.731	51.3 (20.4)	0.77 (61)
Brazil	174	1.1	11.909	21.4	0.73 (85)
Argentina	40	0.9	12.034	.	0.81 (45)
Nigeria	123	2.5	2.661	54.7	0.47 (153)
Kenya	31	2.6	1.761	45.6	0.51 (145)
Tanzania	34	2.8	1.601	33.4	0.47 (152)
Ethiopia	65	2.3	1.139	38.9	0.39 (173)
South Africa	44	1.3	11.440	23.0	0.62 (121)
Palestine	4.0	(2.0/3.4)	(2.300)	21.9	0.67 (110)
Israel	6	1.9	28.809	20.9	0.90 (16)
India	1.053	1.5	3.876	29.8	0.55 (136)
China	1.262	0.6	9.233	2.8	0.69 (101)
Japan	126	0.0	35.178	16.0	0.91 (10)

(6) Life expectancy at birth (2012)	(7) Mean years of schooling (2010)	(8) Corruption perception score (2010)	(9) Homicide rate per 100,000 persons (2004–12)
81.6	11.7	9.2	1.0
81.3	12.6	8.6	0.6
80.3	9.4	7.6	1.2
81.7	10.6	6.8	1.1
80.6	12.2	7.9	0.8
81.0	10.8	7.9	0.6
82.5	11.0	8.7	0.7
82.0	10.1	3.9	0.9
81.6	10.4	6.1	0.8
79.7	7.7	6.0	1.2
76.3	10.0	5.3	1.1
77.8	12.3	4.6	1.7
74.6	11.7	4.7	1.3
69.1	11.7	2.1	10.2
74.2	6.5	4.4	3.3
82.0	12.0	8.7	1.0
81.1	12.3	8.9	1.6
78.7	13.3	7.1	4.5
77.1	8.5	3.1	22.7
73.8	7.2	3.7	21.0
76.1	9.3	2.9	3.4
52.3	5.2	2.4	12.2
57.7	7.0	2.1	20.1
58.9	5.1	2.7	24.5
59.7	2.2	3.3	25.5
53.4	8.5	4.5	31.8
73.0	8.0	*	4.1
81.9	11.9	6.1	2.1
65.8	4.4	3.3	3.4
73.7	7.5	3.5	1.1
83.6	11.6	7.8	0.4

Table 6.1 Basic socio-economic and political indicators for 25 countries around the world

Sources: (1)–(3) *World Development Indicators* 2012, Washington: The World Bank. (4)–(7), (9) *Human Development* 2013, New York: United Nations Development Programme (UNDP) (4) For OECD countries: www.stats.oecd.org/Index.aspx?DatasetCode=CRSNEW (8) Transparency International, Corruption Perception Score 2012 (www.transparency.org); *Values missing

America (*The Statesman's Yearbook* 2010: 1182). A historian has called this economic ascent, which placed Sweden already in the 1950s into the top group of European countries (Therborn 1995: 138), as 'one of the most astonishing achievements of mankind' (Findeisen 2003: 276). We will see later, however, that such a paean of praise may be somewhat exaggerated; there are also other countries in Europe which achieved a comparable rise in quite different ways. In addition, some important and astonishing historical and structural characteristics of Swedish society have been rather neglected by most social scientists.

We can assume that many characteristics of society and politics in Sweden are similar to those in the other Scandinavian states, due to the fact that they have rather similar social structures and political systems. The latter, on their side, emerged out of processes of close political collaboration between the Nordic states,[3] and reciprocal adoption of political instruments and measures. This political integration and cooperation goes back to historical forerunners. For many centuries, parts of Scandinavia were united under one political regime; between the early 15th and the early 19th centuries, Denmark was a great power, commanding also the territories of present-day Sweden and Norway; through most of the 19th century, Sweden also included Norway and Finland. In social structural terms, the four Scandinavian countries are very similar to each other: all are very homogeneous in ethnic terms (92 per cent to 95 per cent of the populations are members of the core ethnic group), they all had relatively low proportions of resident foreigners until quite recently (5 per cent or less), each nation has its own language, and the large majority of the population (77–85 per cent) are members of the Protestant Lutheran State Church (the bulk of the rest is not a member of any church). Thus, we can assume that many aspects characterizing Swedish society are similar in the other three Scandinavian countries, although it is not presumed that this must be so in all regards.[4]

In the first section of this chapter, I will proceed in two steps, considering all of the main dimensions sketched out in Figure 3.1 (p. 58). They concern, first, class stratification and socio-economic equality in Sweden, and, second, the ethnic structure and historical ideology of national unity. In the second section I will compare Sweden directly with Japan; this comparison will help us to find an explanation for the paradox that Sweden shows a much higher inequality in the distribution of wealth than Japan. In the concluding section, we will discuss the question of what the nations around the world can learn from the emergence and present-day functioning of the rather equal Swedish and Japanese models of state and society.

The Welfare State and Socio-economic Equality

Social scientists in Sweden (see, for example, Esping-Andersen 1990; Korpi 1983, 2006; Persson 1990; Korpi and Palme 1989), but also in other countries (Schmidt 1982, 2001; Thakur et al. 2003; Koch 2003) argue that the relatively high degree of equality and the factual elimination of poverty in this country (see Table 6.1, pp. 164–5) is due mainly to a decade-long and consistent social-democratic policy of redistribution. In fact, the Social Democratic Workers Party (*Sveriges Socialdemokratiska Arbetareparti*), established in 1889, already in 1917 attained nearly 40 per cent of the votes; in 1932 it was able to establish a stable government (in a coalition with the Farmers Party). Since then, it was – with short interruptions in the 1970s and 1990s – the largest and most influential political party of the country till the end of the 20th century. In 2006, however, it lost again the majority and got only 30 per cent in the election of 2010. It was characteristic and very important for the origins of the Social Democratic Party in Sweden at the end of the 19th century and its further development that it

---

3   The Nordic Council was established in 1952 between the four larger Scandinavian countries (Norway, Finland, Sweden, Denmark) and the smaller countries Iceland, Faroe Islands and Greenland. It is an assembly of members of the national parliaments. Later on, it was supplemented by the National Council of Ministers which oversees about 40 different commissions, sub-groups and other institutions. In 1972, treaties concerning culture and transport were added. Altogether, the Nordic cooperation, although in formal terms a rather loose association, covers nearly all areas of politics. See, for instance, http://www.globaldefence.net/artikel-analysen/buendnisse/europa/80-nordische-zusammenarbeit.html; Findeisen, 2003, p. 263ff.

4   A somewhat peculiar case is Finland which for a long period from the Middle Ages till the early 19th century was a part of Sweden, and after the Napoleonic Wars became a part of Russia (although with considerable political and cultural autonomy); it became an autonomous, political independent state only after the First World War. Finland is different from the other Scandinavian countries also in linguistic terms, using a language very unique in Europe. Also in a check-up of Esping-Andersen's typology of welfare states, Finland turns out to be more similar to Germany and the Benelux countries than to the other Scandinavian countries (Obinger and Wagschal 1998: 125).

established close links with the labour union movement (membership in the union was automatically connected with membership in the Social Democratic Party) and that its political orientation was not radical, aiming at an overthrow of private prosperity and Capitalism, but reformist. In spite of repeated large industrial strikes, it established a constructive working relationship with the associations of the employers (Findeisen 2003: 203ff.). In all these regards, Sweden can be seen as a paradigmatic case of the 'democratization of class struggle' (Korpi 1983) and of the 'institutionalization of class conflict' (Dahrendorf 1959). The aim of the establishment of a comprehensive welfare state system was propagated as a political strategy, and as an alternative to revolution.

This has been in fact achieved to a high degree: the Swedish welfare state is very active and intervenes in considerable part in market processes in order to secure an acceptable level of inequality; a comprehensive system of social insurance and benefits covers a large array of social risks; a central characteristic of these benefits is their universalism: they are not conceived of as supporting only the needy, but as basic social rights of everybody who is entitled to certain benefits; levels of taxation and social insurance payments are high because vast financial resources are necessary to finance the extensive public expenditures; many social and political institutions contribute to an efficient cooperation between private and public institutions and are responsible for the provision of many social services; there exist also extensive public regulations and controls, particularly on the labour market in order to make sure that welfare state provisions are not misused; wages are established in the form of peaceful negotiations; a 'social partnership' regulates the relationships between the employers and the strong, centralized unions (more than 80 per cent of the workers and employees are members union members – one of the highest rates internationally). The guiding principles behind all these measures are the assurance of a basic income and decent living standard for every person, the maintenance of full employment and peaceful negotiations between the representatives of the different classes (Thakur et al. 2003: 1–2; see also Persson 1990; Esping-Andersen 1990). A specific characteristic of the Swedish welfare state is also a high level of public employment, particularly in the education and health system, together with a relatively equal distribution of labour time; this has contributed significantly to the high level of equalization of men and women in terms of employment and income (Bjorklund and Freeman 1994).

Overall, Sweden and the other Scandinavian nation-states are within the group of the most equal countries worldwide in terms of income distribution. This fact is also reflected in public perceptions: very low proportions of Swedes and Norwegians consider their society as stratified according an elite-mass or a pyramid model, but large proportions as a diamond or even as an upper-middle-class society (see Table 6.2). Their attitudes are quite different from those of people in most other societies. For instance, they less often think that income differences are too large, that government should (further) reduce these differences and that there are conflicts between the rich and the poor (Table 6.3).

This model has high societal support (Svallfors and Taylor-Gooby 1999) and its success is undisputed: the Swedish system of social welfare and its social institutions, such as the educational and health system, are among the best worldwide; trust in government is high, the level of corruption is low; there exists also a high rate of employment, particularly among women, although since about a decade a considerable problem of unemployment has emerged (about 6 to 8 per cent); even birth rates are higher in Sweden today than in many central and south European countries.

The educational system in Sweden has long since been quite comprehensive with all pupils attending the same type of secondary school. As a consequence, nearly three-quarters of the respective age group qualify for admission to tertiary, university education (Mau and Verwiebe 2010: 65; see also Therborn 1995: 157ff.). The educational chances of children from farm families are significantly better in Sweden than in most other European societies (Müller et al. 1997).

Ethnic Structure and Historical Ideology of the Swedish Nation-state

The central thesis which I would like to propose here is that the high level of ethnic-cultural homogeneity of the Swedish society has played a significant, although in the social science largely underestimated, role in all these achievements. As indicated in the Introduction, Sweden is highly homogeneous in ethnic terms. Only a few decades ago, 90 per cent of the population were ethnic Swedes; the largest among the several small minorities were the Finns, many of whom have lived in Sweden for generations; they are not fundamentally distinct from the Swedes since both countries were interconnected closely centuries ago. Swedish society is very homogeneous also in terms of language and religion; about three-quarters of the Swedes are members of the Protestant Lutheran church which was the state church till the year 2000. The Swedish population is well aware of the high degree of the ethnic homogeneity of their society. Table 6.3 shows that the proportion of those believing that 'race is important for getting ahead in life' is only 7 per cent in Sweden; after Japan, this is the lowest proportion among all 24 nations compared in this table.

The Protestant state church played a very active role in former centuries concerning poor relief. In the course of Reformation in Lutheran Nordic countries, 'the property of the church and the religious orders

Table 6.2   Patterns of social stratification as seen by the people in the different countries

| Country | (N) | Stratification model | | | |
		A	B	C	D E
Sweden	(1078)	7	23	30	38
Norway	(1397)	2	11	24	56
Austria	(967)	17	27	31	25
Germany (W)	(921)	17	34	25	24
France	(2762)	16	54	16	14
Switzerland	(1212)	7	25	25	43
Great Britain	(931)	15	42	19	24
Spain	(1189)	17	41	22	20
Portugal	(993)	41	36	12	11
Czech Republic	(1183)	31	35	19	16
Hungary	(1006)	57	32	6	5
Bulgaria	(952)	64	27	6	4
Poland	(1233)	37	33	14	16
Russia	(1549)	41	35	12	12
Turkey	(1527)	40	36	12	12
Australia	(1441)	6	30	22	43
USA	(1508)	17	39	15	29
Argentina	(1102)	46	36	9	9
Chile	(1492)	24	48	13	15
South Africa	(3215)	51	32	9	9
Israel	(1180)	19	56	15	10
Philippines	(1191)	32	40	11	17
Japan	(1203)	11	39	26	24
China	(2963)	22	51	12	14
Total	**(52054)***	**27**	**34**	**18**	**21**

*All 38 countries in ISSP-2009.
Questions: 'These five diagrams show different types of society. Please read the descriptions and look at the diagrams and decide which describes best [country]. Type A: A small elite at the top, very few people in the middle and the great mass of people at the bottom; Type B: A society like a pyramid with a small elite at the top, more people in the middle, and most at the bottom; Type C: A pyramid except that just a few people are at the bottom; Type D: A society with most people in the middle; Type E: Many people near the top, and only a few near the bottom'.
Source: International Social Survey Programme (ISSP) 2009 – Social Inequality.

wcre confiscated and the clergy was incorporated into to bureaucracy of the territorial state. Thus, a concept of public welfare provision was able to develop relatively early in the North, at least partially legitimized by the Protestant churches' (Flora et al. 1986: XVIII; Rokkan 2000: 202ff.). In fact, already in 1686 the relief and welfare duties of the church were regulated by a law; in 1763, a law established that the state was responsible for the area of social welfare; some private mining companies established enterprise sickness funds (Menningen 1971: 21). A law prohibiting the youth below the age of 18 to work in factories was passed in 1852, long before industrialization took off in Sweden. But not only social welfare, also equality and freedom have traditionally been highly estimated values in Swedish society. This is indicated, for instance, by the fact that the American Revolution aroused great interest among intellectuals in Sweden (Gerste 1994).

Table 6.3   Perceptions and attitudes related to inequality in 24 countries

Country	(N)	(1) Income differences too large*	(2) Government should reduce differences*	(3) Conflicts rich–poor**	(4) Race is important for success***
Sweden	(1078)	32	21	35	7
Norway	(1397)	12	9	17	15
Austria	(967)	46	30	34	18
Germany (W)	(921)	45	22	56	16
France	(2762)	69	51	44	10
Switzerland	(1212)	39	16	26	9
Great Britain	(931)	29	18	41	9
Spain	(1189)	32	26	52	10
Portugal	(993)	60	50	68	10
Czech Republic	(1183)	51	29	30	18
Hungary	(1006)	77	55	91	29
Bulgaria	(952)	58	46	40	18
Poland	(1233)	53	39	43	10
Russia	(1549)	62	55	79	8
Turkey	(1527)	50	45	77	16
Australia	(1441)	29	18	27	8
USA	(1508)	29	8	59	11
Argentina	(1102)	38	30	61	9
Chile	(1492)	38	20	58	12
South Africa	(3215)	45	28	58	50
Israel	(1180)	54	45	37	23
Philippines	(1191)	21	19	51	31
Japan	(1203)	43	25	35	5
China	(2963)	39	27	65	38
Total	**(52054)******	**46**	**32**	**46**	**16**

*Strongly agree; **Very strong + strong conflicts; ***Essential + very important; ****All 38 countries in ISSP 2009.
Questions: (1) Differences in income are too large; (2) It is the responsibility of the government to reduce the differences between people with high incomes and those with low incomes; (3) In all countries, there are conflicts between different social groups; in [country] how much conflict is between poor people and rich people? (4) How important do you think is a person's race for getting ahead in life?
Source: International Social Survey Programme (ISSP) 2009-Social Inequality.

Even if the Swedish population today is characterized by a rather low level of religious ecclesiastic activity, the religious heritage may be still relevant. So, one could argue that the modern welfare state has substituted the state church in some regards. In all rich European countries with extended welfare states, people stand in considerable distance to the churches; high levels of religiosity are typical for poor, very unequal societies, such as Brazil; but also in South and several East European countries, religiosity is higher (Haller and Höllinger 2009; for Brazil see Chapter 9). The 'ethos' of modern welfare states may not be more 'moralistic' (based on a liberal ethos like in the USA, or on a Protestant ethos), but 'immoralist': it emphasizes an orientation toward consumption of the material and immaterial provisions of the welfare state, such as a high standard of living, ever more improved schooling, health facilities and so on (Zijderveld 1986). This was exactly the pattern which was found in surveys on the attitudes toward the welfare state which are very positive: '... most Swedes clearly believe they get a lot for the high taxes they pay. Survey after survey has shown that while Swedes (like virtually all citizens in modern welfare states) agree that "taxes are too high" only a minority of citizens support tax cuts if they are forced to choose them in exchange for reductions in public spending' (Steinmo 2003: 41; see also Olson 1986; Svallfors and Taylor-Gooby 1999). Such an attitude corresponds to the findings of Wilensky (1975: 47ff.) that the development of welfare states is mainly dependent upon economic growth, even if ideological factors also play a certain role.

If one looks more closely at the political aims of the Swedish Social Democratic Party, it becomes evident that the aspect of the ethnic-national homogeneity of the country ever since has played a significant, although often unexpressed role. Already in the programme of Per Albin Hanson, the influential Social Democratic prime minister 1932–46, the concept of the 'People's Home Sweden' (*folkhemmet*) was very important. He imagined Sweden as a close community, based on a strong feeling of togetherness; in Swedish society, no extended privileges and deprivations should exist and all barriers between the rich and the poor should be broken down (Menningen 1971: 23; Henze 1999; Blyth 2002: 116). Today, the concept of *folkhemmet* is not used any more and is replaced by that of the welfare state. This is understandable because it had first been coined 1916 in the framework of the organic-authoritarian political theory of Rolf Kjellén and was used also by the Swedish state church and in the politics of the farmers (Götz 2001). This concept, however, played also a significant role in the programmes of Social Democrats. In this regard, the *eugenics* movement and practices in the first half of the 20th century must be mentioned. Its most inhumane and criminal form was realized by the National Socialists in Germany who aimed at extinguishing Jews and other ethnic minorities (such as the Roma) considered as worthless races or even 'subhuman beings' or parasites. But also in many other Western countries, such as Switzerland, England and the USA, 'soft' eugenic measures were introduced in order to improve the biological quality of the people (*Volkskörper*). The method applied was constrained sterilization of persons who were mentally sick or suffered from genetic diseases. In Sweden, this programme was carried through in a particularly intense way.[5] A first, strong supporter of eugenics was Hjalmar Branting (1860–1925), the co-founder of the Swedish Social Democratic Party and its first *Riiksdag* deputy. After Branting's initiative, a State Institute for Race Biology was established in 1921; in 1935, a first law concerning coerced sterilization was decreed, in 1941 a second one. These laws were supported by the Swedish state church and also by public intellectuals like the renowned economists Alva and Gunnar Myrdal. The law included even persons showing anti-social behaviour, like alcoholism, as targets of constrained sterilization. Also Swedish immigration policy was quite restrictive during the first half of the 20th century, even against refugees from Hitler's Third Reich (Westin 2006).

The historically high level of cultural homogeneity and integration of Swedish society was relevant for the labour movement and its political success also in another regard. In continental Europe, there exists an old, significant ideological and political split between the rural population and the emerging workers' movement: the first support typically conservative, Christian and bourgeois parties, the latter support Socialist parties, which often are anti-clerical. The development of specific farmers' parties was a unique pattern in Scandinavia; it was one aspect of the internal cleavages of the bourgeois camp.[6] The fact that the Social Democrats were able to get the support of the farmers' parties was one of the main reasons for their political dominance over the next centuries. Also the workers' movement was much more compact in Sweden where

---

5   See http://de.wikipedia.org/wiki/Eugenik; Spektorowski 2004.

6   Detlef Jahn (2002), Die politischen Systeme Skandinaviens, SkanPolSYs1.doc (available at http://www.phil.uni-greifswald.de/fileadmin/mediapool/ipk/publikationen/jahn/jahn_die_politische_systeme_skandinaviens.pdf).

the Social Democratic Party was able to get the support of the majority of workers. This situation was very different in countries like France and Italy, where a strong Communist party challenged the Socialist parties, and where even within unions different political fractions emerged, such as between Communist, social-democratic and Christian wings. The absence of such partitions made the Swedish labour movement much more powerful (Esping-Andersen 1998: 48; Rokkan 2000: 405ff.).

A Stratified Egalitarian Political Community. The Case of Japan

Let us now look also at the case of Japan, considering first its ethnic and national structure, then the structures of equality/inequality and the mechanisms whereby its surprising level of economic equality came about and is sustained today.

The Emergence of Japan's State and Society: a Worldwide Unique Pattern of Ethnic Homogeneity and National Unity

All observers remark that there is probably no other large state society around the world which shows such a high degree of ethnic-national homogeneity and integration as Japan (Doi 1982: 8; Minami 1986: 3ff.; Ishida 1989: 144).[7] This homogeneity is also reflected in public consciousness: only 5 per cent – the lowest proportion worldwide – of Japanese consider 'race' as a significant factor for getting ahead in life (see Table 6.1). There are three evident historical and structural reasons for this fact (Hall 1968: 16): the age of the Japanese state, its remote geographic position and its landscape and the resulting structure of agriculture.

The Japanese state, in its present borders, has been established according to Japanese official self-description since 660 B.C.; in 1940, its 2600th anniversary was celebrated. While this date may be fiction (Hall 1968: 30), it is nevertheless a matter of fact that Japan as a distinct and independent political community is very old. The first recorded Japanese state was in fact established already in the 7th century A.D., its first capital Nara built in 708–12. Thus, this state is in fact much older than most European nation states which themselves are relatively old in a world perspective (*The Statesman's Yearbook* 2010: 716ff.). Already in the Heian-period (1192–1333) a high-level language and literature was developed. It was already mentioned (see Chapter 5, p. 131) that Japan closed itself off from the rest of the world over nearly three centuries (1600–1869); during this period, Japanese people were also forbidden to leave the country (Varley 1984: 146ff.). But also in the period before, Japan was rather separated from the rest of East Asia. Thus, although the original settlers of the Japanese islands from 20,000 B.C. on were rather mixed in ethnic terms, the time span was long enough so that a rather unique society and culture could develop itself. A Chinese report from the 1st century A.D. is astonishing insofar as the characteristics of Japanese society at that time seem to have been rather similar to its shape today; it describes a well-ordered society with strict rank-order distinctions; the people closely followed the law; and several practices of ritual cleanliness were used (Hall 1968: 31). Already in this time, the difference to China – from where many cultural influences were received in Japan – was marked in terms of the physical appearance of the population, in linguistic and religious terms, and in the political system. The continuity of the monarchy and the royal family was a central symbol of national unity in Japan; it was based on the principle of kinship affinity (Hall 1968: 16). Over these many centuries, no fundamental or revolutionary changes in the social and political structure of Japanese society took place. However, far-reaching reforms and changes were taking place in several periods; one of the most important was the abolishment of the feudal class system during the Meiji Revolution in 1867 (Kosaka 1994: 2). But in spite of this change, Japan did preserve many of its inherited social structures and cultural traditions. This was facilitated by the fact that all these reforms, including the Meiji Revolution of 1867, were 'revolutions from above' (Varley 1984: 205).

A main structural reason for this unique, continuous development of society was the geographic location of Japan as a group of islands at the eastern periphery of East Asia (Hall 1968: 10ff.). This helped it to remain free from direct foreign intervention and enabled a quiet and continuous development, in spite of the ability to take over cultural elements from China, such as Buddhism and Confucianism. A concomitant of this remote

---

7   For an excellent overview on Japan's social structure see Kerbo 2012, pp. 445–61.

geographical location, Japanese language and ways of life could develop their peculiar, unique character, thus making it more difficult for outsiders to enter the country.

A third structural characteristic of Japan is the configuration of its landscape: only 16 per cent of the islands can be used for agriculture which means that population density was very high already in historical times. This density was a consequence of the fact that a very intensive form of farming could be pursued. Already small pieces of land were enough for assuring the subsistence of a family given the high supply of water throughout the year (in the winter by heavy snowfall in the mountains, in the summer by the monsoons). The cultivation of the main product, rice, however, required very close social cooperation in the villages; it made necessary intelligent water management (Teruoka 2008: 21) and continuous artificial soil irrigation which could be achieved only by cooperating. In the course of centuries, extended and elaborate systems of irrigation were developed which enabled an extended farming population living in villages with a high density of dwelling (Hall 1968:15). Since the early 17th century and up to the post-Second World War, these villages have also been constituted in political terms as 'in-groups': the settlers were forbidden to leave their village, and the villages as a whole had to pay taxes to regional governments (Dore 1978: 25ff.; Ishida 1989: 143; Teruoka 2008: 21).

These patterns of collaboration in work were matched by the characteristic Japanese family structure. In this structure, both the stem family (focusing on vertical generational relations between grandparents, parents and children, with a patrimonial structure in which the eldest son remained in the household of the parents and become the new head) and the conjugal family (focusing on horizontal relations between husband and wife and their respective kinship) have been very important. This family system has traditionally fulfilled many functions of social assistance and support. In recent times, the proportions of firstborn sons who live in the same household with their parents have declined; this was not the case, however, for support between parents and children – support from wives' parents even increased (Liping 2010).

Family and Village Community as Models for a Highly Integrated and Stratified Society at Large

An apposite analysis of the basic structure of Japanese society has been given by a former professor of political science at the University of Tokyo:

> The solidarity which was partly based on blood ties which had contributed to the creation of conformity in the rural communities was expanded onto the whole nation. The idea "One state – one nation" which considered the imperial family as the main family of the nation and, as a consequence, the relation between the *tenno* and his subjects as a form of family relation, played an important role in the consolidation of national identity (Ishida 1989:143).

The community, that is, the family household or system, includes all those who are connected to each other by kinship ties but also living together. A student of Japanese law wrote:

> The hamlet or *buraku*, not the larger village, was in most instances the real locus of community cohesion, solidarity, and control. Without formal administrative or corporate status, the hamlet nonetheless existed by common assent and practice as a territorial unit. The mutual economic dependence of the cluster of households that constituted the hamlet on cooperative effort in maintaining common irrigation and drainage works and to assure access to their scattered landholdings compelled community; and from community, buttressed by shared pastimes and rituals, came the psychological satisfaction of belonging (Haley 1991: 170).

In his pioneering study of a Japanese village in the 1950s and 1960s, Ronald P. Dore (1978: 196) summarized life in a village community in this way:

> Shinohata people are, indeed, members one unto another in a way that, while normal for Japan, is not very common on a world scale in rural communities of fifty-odd households. […] The joys of one are the joys of all: the sorrows of one the sorrows of all, is the traditional way of putting it. And the honour and shame of one is the honour and shame of all too.

Personal relations are very important in all spheres of daily life in Japan. Their cornerstone are close personal and hierarchical relations, first between parents (mainly mothers) and their children, later on between superiors and subordinates in organizations and between people of lower and higher status in society at large. The vertical relation 'becomes the driving force in the relations between group members. As a consequence of the back-breaking overweight of this vertical orientation even a group composed of members equal in rank tends to create differences between them. If this tendency is reinforced, a surprisingly finely graded and hardly penetrable system of rank steps emerges' (Nakane 1970: 43). If two people have the same occupation, the length of service (seniority) becomes the differentiating element. Once it is established, this rank order, based more on ascribed than achieved characteristics, is of utmost importance in the determination of the social rank order position of a person. For the Japanese psychiatrist Takeo Doi (1982) the principle of *amae* underlines these hierarchical relations between persons higher and lower in the status scale. They imply a relationship of dependence, love and respect, in which the subordinate feels appreciated and accepted by the superior: thus, a relation in which one can feel oneself free and well. This model of the well-integrated and finely stratified community is valid also for work organizations and society at large. The vertical stratification of Japanese society is also recognized by the people: the majority (65 per cent) see the stratification pattern of their society as a pyramid or as a pyramid with a small bottom (Types B + C; see Table 6.2).

Concomitant with the high degree of social integration of Japanese society is the extreme low level of violence. In terms of indicators such as homicides and numbers of imprisoned people, Japan occupies one of the last best places in the world (see Table 6.1). The paradox is that this low level of crime is associated with little state and police control; people accept ruling norms with the assumption that government works 'with empathy and benevolence'; they tend to avoid legalistic approaches in conflict situations, and confession, repentance and absolution of criminals is preferred to punishment (Haley 1991: 115ff.; Komiya 1999).

Further, the enterprise in which one works is understood as one to which all employees belong (Nakane 1970: 16–21; Dore 1973; Dirks and Silke-Susann 1998). Like the village community, the company also has two main objectives: 'its collective reputation, and face and internal harmony and cohesion' (Haley 1991: 176). The enterprise does not only pay a salary to its employees but cares for them in many other regards. The egalitarian structure of the enterprise is secured on the one hand by the possibility for all new entrants to acquire the relevant qualifications on the job; and on the other hand by a system of job rotation between the different departments (Koike and Inoki 1990). The consequence is a strong commitment to the firm by the employees. Thus, it is not an overall class interest which is the basis for their organization, but the idea of the enterprise as a community (*Betriebsgemeinschaft*) (Kosaka 1994: 14). This structure is reflected also in the unions which are mainly based on the enterprise. Within large enterprises, different unions exist even within sub-firms and departments; Toyota alone, for instance, has 241 such unions.[8] The unions are restricted to the core employees of large enterprises. After 1945, hundreds of unions were founded in Japan and union density was rather high[9]; later on, it decreased considerably, however. In 1995, only 23 per cent of all dependent workers were still organized in unions; this percentage corresponds fairly to the proportion of people employed in life-long contracts in large enterprises. Umbrella union organizations (like *Rengo* and *Zenryoko*) have not much influence. As members of the 'enterprise community', the unions are closely integrated to the decision processes of the firm; many union leaders later become members of the personnel department. In the large enterprises, the unions have a strong position because the hiring of new employees is based mainly on general education and criteria; it is only within the firm where they acquire occupational qualifications (which again are more of a general character than specific). Because promotion and salaries depend to a large degree on seniority, an individual employee has a lot to lose if he leaves the enterprise.

As far as wage negotiations and the resulting income distribution are concerned, it is very important that unions can be seen as the representatives of the collective knowledge of the firm and command a power which cannot be ignored by management. The enterprise is not seen as being in the possession of the owners but in possession of a coalition between firm owners and staff. The management acts as a broker between the two, and

---

8   A comprehensive overview on Japanese unions is given in 'Gewerkschaften in Japan – Einführung', Friedrich-Ebert-Stiftung 1998; see http://library.fes.de/fulltext/stabsabteilung/oo41.htm#LOCE9E1_(28.11.2011).

9   According to Nakane (1970: 33f.) after the Second World War, 48,000 firm-based unions were founded with nine million members.

managers are typically recruited from the rank-and-file members of the firm. Twice a year, the employees get extraordinary dividends which can make up 40 per cent of their annual income. In this way, the relations between employers and employees within enterprises are not seen as a source of potential conflict but as a relation of cooperation. One consequence of this is the fact that the salaries of the managers are much more circumscribed than those of managers in West Europe or North America where they often have risen to astronomic scales in the last decade. So, the relation between the income of an employee in the core staff and a manager may lie somewhere between 1:3 and 1:6, while in Europe and North America it can well be 1:10 to 1:20.[10] Also political parties are not ideologically founded, broad class organizations but can be characterized more as factions organized around influential personalities (Pye 1989: 50ff.). The three parties with most votes in the 2005 elections in Japan were the Liberal Democratic Party (LDP) with 38.2 per cent of the votes (considered as conservative, with many voters from rural areas); the Democratic Party (considered as centre-left) with 31 per cent; and the New Komeito – New Clean Government Party with 13.3 per cent of the votes; this party is connected with the Buddhist organization *Soka Gakkei*. The Social Democratic Party has existed since 1945 and participated briefly in some governments; in 1995, it got only 4.5 per cent of the votes. The Communist Party, established in the underground in 1922, was never influential; in 2005, it got 7.3 per cent of the votes (*The Statesman's Yearbook* 2009: 719). Thus, also in this regard, the difference in comparison with Sweden is very pronounced.

Finally, also Japanese society as a whole is well integrated mainly because of the existence of manifold forms of class-crossing, vertical relationships of loyalty. The whole social world is divided into *sempai* (people higher in the rank order), *kohai* (those lower) and *doryo* (people of the same rank). This fact is reflected in the forms of address used in daily intercourse with others or in the exchange of business cards if people from two different organizations meet. The strict rank order requires that the *kohai* never criticize the *sempai*; it is always the latter who dominate conversation. In this way, however, a free exchange of ideas is drowned (Nakane 1970: 43–62). This principle undermines that of stratification by occupational positions so central in Western societies. Instead of horizontal relations and associations, such as between workers, employees and so on, that is, members of the same classes and status groups, vertical group and department relations are priority ranked in Japan; they include, for instance, a full professor, assistant professors, assistants and students. Stable and close relations between the higher and lower status members form the core element of all groups; the higher status person – the *oyabun* – has the status of a father, the lower status person – the *kobun* – that of a son or a child (Nakane 1970: 65). No other society, maybe except China, has developed the act of organizing everybody into some form of vertical organization so highly as the Japanese (Dore 1978: 49). Nearly every Japanese citizen is embedded into *oyabun-kobun*-relations, which exist in work and professional organizations, in political parties and in all other organizations. They are responsible for the strength and stability of organizations, as well as for their efficiency (which is high if a high level of social and emotional integration exists), but also for the reluctance of the Japanese to participate in voluntary activities and organizations. Also, competition which can be quite strong emerges not between individuals but between groups and organizations and it leads to the establishment of rank orders of organizations (Nakane 1970: 125ff.). In general, one can say that Japan is a society in which competition and consensus have assumed a close connection.

The cultural integration and socio-economic development of Japanese society has been supported by religion. At first sight, Japan seems to be very heterogeneous in this regard. All great Asian religions had a profound impact on Japanese society. But Shintoism, for a long time the '"state religion', is not a religion or church in the Western sense; it has no dogmatic teachings, no formal church organization and no membership but is more a collection of rituals. Socially significant is in the first instance the visit to the public Shrines (temples) which occurs at many different occasions, because of gratitude, in order to prey for help and so on (see Dore 1978: 362ff; Trobe and Streb 1985: 11ff.). The four main 'commandments' of Shintoism are reverence for family and tradition, respect for and love of nature, physical cleanliness and the commemoration of important feasts.

---

10   In 2007, the 30 top managers of Toyota together got 15 million Euros (including bonuses), that is 50,000 Euros per person. In Germany, the top managers of the firms listed in the Dax stock index in 1987 got 14 times as much as an average employee, in 2007 they got 44 times as much; the leading earner, Josef Ackermann of the Deutsche Bank, got 13.6 million Euros, that is 74 times the average and nearly the same as all Toyota managers together. In the United States, the 20 best-paid managers got 145 million Dollars each; funds manager even more. See *Focus-Money*, 2/2008: 'Managergehälter – gerechte Lücke?', available at: http://www.focus.de/finanzen/news/tid-11062/managergehaelter-gerechte-luecke_aid_261329.html

Historically, the main function of Shintoism was to secure social integration and harmony and to legitimate the domination of the emperor. Robert Bellah (1985) accentuates – more than Max Weber – the influence of Buddhism on Japanese society, in particular its focus on diligence and frugality as a basis for a modern, rational economic attitude. Some other authors ascribe the economic success of Japan also to the specific Japanese version of Confucianism, which laid stress on loyalty, collectivism and nationalism (Schwentker 2005: 84ff.). A high ethic of duty has characterized Japanese state officers; often, there existed mobility between leading positions in the state and the private economy (Minami 1986: 20; McMillan 1989:19ff.).

Even if Japan is highly homogeneous in ethnic terms, the country also houses several minorities. They include (in 2005) about 1.3 million foreigners (mainly South Koreans, Chinese and a few Americans), and some small indigenous ethnic groups, but they are nearly invisible (Kosaka 1994: 40ff.). Among them, about 20,000 *Ainu* living in the northern islands of Hokkaido and the *Buraku* or *burakumin*, living in central Japan, are the most important.[11] The attitude of the Japanese toward these minorities is to try to neglect them; this applies especially to the *Buraku* who were (and maybe be still are) considered as unclean people, comparable to the outcasts in India. They live in rather closed, isolated communities, located often in densely populated quarters of large towns (Wagatsuma and De Vos 1989). The social and political strategy to cope with these ethnic minorities is to isolate and confine them, as outlined in the foregoing chapter. The result is that these minorities in fact are seen more adequately as social 'outcasts' (De Vos and Wagatsuma 1967; Norbeck 1970: 183ff.) – a position which has been internalized by their members themselves. They do not want to be integrated into the majority society – a spectacular case of the so-called 'ethnic mobility trap' (Wiley 1970; Esser 2011: 36). The separation between the settlements of *Buraku* and those of the Japanese is so sharp that children recognize their specific status only when entering the higher school system outside of the quarter, experiencing for the first time discrimination in daily interaction (Okano and Tsuchiya 1999: 110ff.). This creates a feeling of strong deprivation among children; if they want to leave their community forever it will be associated with high personal costs. Nakane (1970: 37) compares the situation of the *buraku* with that of the *Untouchables* in India; he argues that the latter do not experience such a strong mistrust and disesteem as the former; the Indians do not know the sharp distinction between 'they' and 'us' as the Japanese do, for whom the own group ('we') stands in sharp contrast to the whole other world. Thus, the Japanese often exhibit a rather cold attitude toward foreigners (Doi 1982: 45). Official discrimination of ethnic minorities has only ended in 1997 when the first ethnic minority (the *Ainu*) were recognized politically (*The Statesman Yearbook* 2009: 718).

It is evident that all the aforementioned characteristics of social relationships in Japanese villages and cities, organizations and political associations and in society as a whole have the effect that economic inequality will be much more limited than in advanced Western countries. The figures on inequality appear quite reliable and the general belief that Japan is a rather equal society cannot be considered a myth.[12] We cannot really grasp the central aspects of this system from a Eurocentric view of the welfare state, by just denoting the Japanese welfare state as a 'hybrid model', combining elements of several European welfare states (Esping-Andersen 1997). Rather, economy and society as a whole have evolved in a fundamental different way in Japan compared to the West (see also Leibfried 1994; Miyamoto 2003). Japanese politics, however, has implemented additional measures which strengthen this effect and offset the low level of welfare spending which is typical for Japan compared with other rich nations.

Political Aims and Measures which have Consolidated Economic Equality

Japan is a very important case from the viewpoint of this book because it shows that equalization can also be obtained in other ways than that of direct state social spending (see also Weiss 1998: 157–62). Three areas might be mentioned particularly here: the first is the educational policy, the second the land reform and agrarian policy and the third economic policy.

The educational level of contemporary Japanese people and school attainment among children and youth is one of the highest in the world (see Table 6.1) The six-year elementary school and the three-year middle school are compulsory; about 97 per cent of the graduates from the latter go on to high schools and most of them complete it. (The facts presented in this section are largely from the comprehensive study of Okano and Tsuchiya 1999) Thus, 'a high school diploma is a prerequisite for the attainment of even modest aspirations' (Okano and Tsuchiya 1999:

---

11   http://en.Wikipedia.org/wiki//Ethnic_issues_in_Japan
12   This is the conclusion of Tachibanaki (2009). His critical view might be estimated from an inside perspective.

56): 38 per cent of the high school graduates go on to tertiary, university education and to attain an academic degree. The systematic development of the educational system has been a principal aim of Japanese politics since the first 1869 reform act and the 1872 education law. These laws represented a radical break with the former class-based school system and charged the schools with the aim to strengthen the nation and its economy. Already in 1905, 87 per ent of children attended the four-year compulsory school (Ishida 1989: 146). In the first half of the 20th century, the school was burdened also with imperialist and militaristic ideas. However, in 1947, a further reform was enacted which created the present-day system: the 6:3:3 years of elementary, middle and high school, the aim of 'a high school for everybody who wants it' and the foundation of many new universities. Practically all elementary schools are state-run; they provide a very positive social climate for the pupils with relatively little direction and control from the teachers and no ability-based streaming and competition (Dore 1978: 176; Okano and Tsuchiya 1999: 58).Only a small proportion (5 per cent) of the middle schools are private. The most important juncture of differentiation is taking place at entry into a high school. These are differentiated into several types: (elite and non-elite) academic high schools, vocational high schools, schools for the handicapped and others. The first prepare mainly for entry into university. At the universities, three-quarters of the students attend private institutions. In 1990, two-thirds of the population had attained secondary or higher education (Ishikawa 1997). Thus, even if inequality of chances by social origin and – quite sharply – by gender persist, 'to a large degree post-war Japan has achieved the "provision" of equal opportunities in education; and many would agree that education is one area in which individuals face the least overt institutionalised discrimination, and where individual achievement largely determines reward' (Okano and Tsuchiya 1999: 53f.). The high level of education of the majority of the Japanese population is certainly one of the factors contributing to its low level of economic inequality. It certainly has also contributed significantly to its impressive economic performance as the first country of the 'Third World' which was able to rise to the technical-economic level of the most advanced Western societies. It may also have produced a high cultural level of Japanese society in general; this is indicated, for instance, by the fact that Japan has the highest newspaper density in the world; in 2007, 121 daily newspapers (including four major English-language newspapers) had an aggregate circulation of 68 million (*The Statesman's Yearbook* 2009: 724).

Two other areas where policy has contributed to preserve or even create anew a considerable level of economic equality in Japanese society is the agrarian and economic policy. Although the state does not intervene much in a direct way into social and economic processes, it nevertheless has a strong indirect control power. This fact is also due to high level of elite cohesion and its commitment to sustain national economic and political strength and development (Kerbo 2012: 458–61). The huge industrial-financial conglomerates (*zaibatsu*) cooperate closely with the state; therefore, the term '*Japan Inc*' is often used (Murakami 1987: 36f.; McMillan 1989). A concise sketch of the development of the socio-economic policies from the post-war area up to the 1970s has been given by Tsuneo Ishikawa (1997), formerly professor of economics at the University of Tokyo. As will be shown in the following section, in this period a marked decline in economic inequality occurred. According to Ishikawa, this can be ascribed to a strong, but controlled influx of workers from rural into urban areas; many new jobs were created both in the countryside and in the towns. At the country side, the agrarian reform of 1947 had made a lasting impact. This reform was carried out with genuine rigor (Ishikawa 1997). In a recent study on Japanese agriculture, the reform is characterized in this way: 'Indeed, by dissolving the landowner class in a way that was very advantageous to the tenant farmer and by establishing owner-farming, land reform did create a productive capability in agriculture unknown in pre-war Japan and contributed to the improvement in the social and economic status of the farmers' (Teruoka 2008: 30–31). The land of absentee landlords was confiscated and sold completely; only one hectare was allowed to be kept. The price of this land was low and also income differences between large and small farmers were low; the latter were supported to get additional part-time jobs and incomes.

Important government policies in the economic realm included the encouraging of mergers of major firms, but also measures supporting the continuous establishment of small firms by preferential tax grants and relaxation of regulations, and the creation of public financial agencies for their support. Also farmers were supported in the introduction of technological innovations. Most important, however, were the sealing from foreign competition of farmers' products and considerable price-support measures for their products, mainly rice (see also Weiss 1998: 158f.). Interestingly, the same way of indirect support was provided for the ethnic minority of the *burakumin*; since this group dominated the leather and shoe industry, this industry was particularly strongly protected against foreign competition (Kotabe and Wheiler 1996: 143; Nakamura 1981:

151ff.). An additional state policy was passed with an equalizing effect on strong employment-maintenance programs; they included financial support for (re-)training, housing subsidies to encourage workers to move to new jobs and employment programs for workers aged 45 and over (Weiss 1998: 160); also the unique Japanese institution of 'life-time' employment is strongly supported by the state.

In this way, a polarization of income conditions between rural and urban areas, between agriculture and other sectors and between the employed and non-employed could be avoided because the level of unemployment has been low by international standards (most of the time less than 5 per cent). This certainly has also been facilitated by the low level of immigration – itself a consequence of the linguistic and cultural uniqueness and homogeneity of Japan.

Wealth Distribution and Long-term Changes in Income Inequality: Two Surprising Differences between Sweden and Japan

The direct comparison between Sweden and Japan – a comparison which to my knowledge nobody has ever carried out so far – helps us to solve a remarkable puzzle and to explain two significant differences between the two countries. These differences are much less surprising if we take into consideration the basically different class structures of these two countries as they have been outlined in the preceding sections. The puzzle is the fact that Swedish society, which is among the most equal around the world in terms of the distribution of income among dependent workers, may be one of the most unequal in terms of the distribution of wealth; Japan is significantly more equal in this aspect than Sweden. The second difference between the two countries is the fact that inequality of income among the dependent labour force has significantly decreased in Sweden over the 20th century, but remained more or less constant in Japan.

Table 6.4 shows that Sweden has a very high inequality in wealth distribution. In fact, with its Gini coefficient of 89 it is not only the highest in Europe, but in the world as a whole (see also Table 6.5). This is an extremely high value, comparable to income distribution among the dependent work force in the most unequal countries in the world, such as Brazil and South Africa. What is the explanation of this astonishing fact which recently has been noted also by other authors (Müller et al. 2010) but only in passing by a few Swedish social scientists? (for example Olson 1986: 59). I think it can be explained in a rather straightforward manner if we reconsider the process how present-day equality in Sweden has been achieved.

Table 6.4   Wealth distribution in west European countries (Gini coefficients)

	UNU-WIDER[1] (ca. 2000)	SHARE[2] (2006/07)
Sweden	89.0	83
Denmark	80.8	-
Ireland	70.7	-
UK	69.7	-
Finland	68.0	-
Norway	63.3	-
Netherlands	64.9	67
Belgium	66.2	-
France	73.0	62
Germany	67.1	63
Switzerland	80.3	69
Austria	64.6	56
Italy	60.9	56
Spain	56.5	57
Portugal	66.7	-

Sources: [1]World Institute for Development Economics Research (UNU-WIDER); available at: http://wikipedia; [2]HARE-Project: Panel study of 33.281 persons aged 50 and over in 13 EU member states; reported in Mueller et al. (2010).

This was the process of the *institutionalization of class conflict* (Dahrendorf 1959) as pointed out in the foregoing section. A corollary of this process was the emergence of *corporatism* which 'integrates organized socioeconomic producer groups through a system of representation and cooperative mutual interaction at the leadership level and mobilization and social control at the mass level' (Rothstein 1987; see also Schmitter 1974; Korpi 1983; Schmidt 1982). It is characteristic that most Western states with corporatist structures also have an influential and reformist labour movement, organized in strong unions and strong Social Democratic Parties (besides Sweden, this is typical also for Austria, Norway and partly Denmark and Germany). In such systems, an agreement about distribution has been reached between the major classes and their political representatives, which are the entrepreneurs, employers and owners of different capital assets on one side, and the workers (and small farmers) on the other side. The agreement between these large class groupings enabled a considerable redistribution in favour of the working classes through the welfare state. In this regard, the findings in Chapter 4 concerning the significant and strong effect of social spending on economic equality have clearly been confirmed. The institutionalization of class conflict, however, did not constrict in a serious way the power and privileges of the Swedish capital owners and of the wealthy in general.

Table 6.5   Wealth distribution in 100 countries around the world (outside West Europe)

Gini index of wealth distribution	Countries (grouped by continents)
50–54	Japan (54.7)
55–59	China (55.), Macao, Korea
60–64	Albania, Belarus, Czech Republic, Slovakia, Slovenia Australia (62.2) Yemen
65–69	Bulgaria, Croatia, Estonia, Hungary, Moldova, Poland, Romania, Russia (69.9), Ukraine, Lativa, Lithuania, Macedonia Algeria, Burundi, Chad, Ethiopia, Ghana, Mauritania, Marocco, Mozambique, Senegal, Tanzania, Kongo Armenia, Azerbaijan, Bangla Desh, Egypt, Pakistan, Kazakhstan India (66.9), Singapore (68.9), Sri Lanka, Taiwan, Vietnam, Israel, Jordan Canada (68.8), New Zealand (65.1) Jamaica
70–74	Argentina, Costa Rica, El Salvador, Honduras, Mexico, Uruguay, Venezuela Botswana, Cameroon, Central African R., Congo D.R., Gambia, Malawi, Mali, Niger, Nigeria, Ruanda, Uganda Georgia, Turkey (71.7)
75–79	Nicaragua, Paraguay, Peru, Brazil (78.4), Chile, Colombia, Dominica, Ecuador, Guatemala, Haiti, Puerto Rico South Africa (76.3), Botswana, Central African R., Gabon, Lesotho, Mali, Swaziland, Zambia Indonesia, Lebanon
80–84	WORLD MEAN (80.4) USA (80.1) Namibia (84.7), Zimbabwe (84.5)

Source: Diverse sources; compiled in: http://en.wikipedia.org/wiki/List_of_countries_by_distribution_of_wealth

The high level of inequality in wealth distribution has been observed casually by a few Swedish social scientists, although there are as far as I know no systematic studies on it. Olson (1986: 59) noted that wealth distribution is much less equitable than income distribution in Sweden (a fact which exists everywhere), and notes also that between 1920 and 1975 the relative privilege of the rich had declined. According to S. Steinmo (2003), the Swedish taxation policy supported large export-oriented capital firms with explicit tax incentives even while Socialists were in power. He makes this rather surprising observation: 'Contrary to many people's expectations, it was never true that Sweden used taxes directly to "redistribute" income between social classes. Quite the contrary, to the extent that the tax system redistributed income it was from wage earners to capitalists'. (Steinmo 2003: 33) In fact, the huge public expenditures were financed 'virtually exclusively through taxation on income earners'; corporate profits were never a major source of revenue; they were always low and stable. (Ibidem, p. 35) A similar observation was made by Pfaller et al. (1991: 286) who wrote that Sweden 'has for a long time relied heavily on the taxation of households to finance its expensive welfare state while capital has been taxed rather modestly in international comparison. Thus, by its very design, Swedish welfare statism has entailed less redistribution from capital to labour and more 'solidarity' among wage earners …' These facts are remarkable also because Sweden has had for a long time – compared to other countries of similar size – a considerable number of worldwide active, large Capitalist enterprises (for example, Volvo, SKF, ASEA); about 15 rich and influential entrepreneurial families (the most famous among them are the Wallenbergs) control 70 per cent of all private enterprises (Menningen 1971: 17). Since the time of King Gustavus II Adolphus (1594–1632), Sweden was a great European power in which the upper classes were a highly privileged stratum (Findeisen 2003: 120). In fact, already in 1319, the constitutional foundations for its 'nobility democracy' were laid; in the early Modern Ages, several attempts of the kings to centralize the state and to disempower the nobility failed. There exists one further reason which explains the surprising high level of 'tolerance' of Swedish unions and Social Democrats concerning the inequality in the distribution of wealth. Here we can tie in with the general thesis that the labour unions in Sweden, as in all other Western societies, were not only 'class actors' but 'class national' actors, as pointed out in Chapter 3 (Mann 1980; Goldthorpe 1983; Vogler 1985). Thus, the interests and efforts of the large enterprises to remain competitive on the world market were strongly supported by the state and accepted by the unions and Social Democrats.

As I have outlined, Sweden was a very unequal society until the 20th century. In Japan, on the other side, inequalities have never been very extensive. Table 6.3 shows that also inequality of wealth distribution is quite high in Sweden – in fact one of the highest among about 100 countries around the world. Contrary to this, wealth distribution is – in relative terms – quite equal in Japan: in fact, Japan has the lowest inequality in wealth among 100 countries around the world! (see also Tachibanaki 2009: 14–15). Out of these surprising facts, a clear hypothesis follows concerning the change in income distribution over the last century in the two countries: in Sweden, we would expect that income inequality has declined significantly, but in Japan no such change should have occurred.

Fortunately, we have data on income distribution for Japan going back to 1890, and for Sweden, going back to the 1930s, that is, exactly the period when the Social Democrats took over government and began to build up the Swedish welfare state. Figure 6.1 presents the corresponding figures. We can observe exactly the

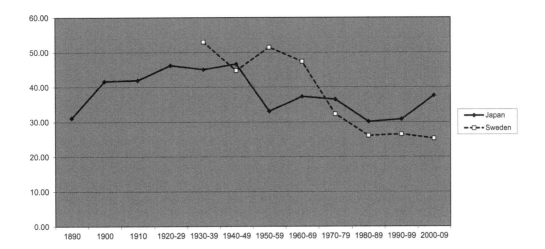

Figure 6.1   The development of income inequality in Japan (1890–2005) and Sweden (1930–2005)
Source: UNU-Wider.

tendency which follows from our hypothesis: in Sweden, income inequality declined massively from a value of over 50 in the 1930s to its present-day value of around 30 and less. A similar although somewhat weaker decrease of income inequality took place also in Denmark and Norway. In Japan, on the other side, no long-term linear trend can be observed. The figure available for 1890, a Gini coefficient of 31, is surprisingly low and corresponds largely to present-day figures. A change within this period has been taken place in Japan. It seems that there was an increase of income inequality from the late 19th century till the 1920s, and remained high till the 1940s; afterwards, however, it began to decline and reached the 1890 value again at the end of the 20th century.

This very different trajectory of economic inequality in Japan can also be explained quite well. The increase in income inequality was certainly a consequence of the general changes in Japanese society and politics going on in the late 19th and early 20th centuries. In this period, Japan became a strong power with imperialist ambitions and corresponding military actions, such as the war with China 1894/95 and with Russia 1904/05 (Varley 1984: 238ff.). The success of these wars contributed to the rise and establishment of a new 'dominating power bloc' constituted by old and new powerful interests and elites, such as old aristocrats, higher public employees, large landowners, leaders of the rising large industrial concerns (*zaibatsu*) and the military leaders (Hall 1968: 303). Also, the development of the unions did not keep pace with the concentration process in industry; as a consequence, the profits of *big business* rose faster than workers' wages. At the same time, agriculture slithered into a crisis and many independent farmers slumped into the status of tenant farmers on the lands of big landowners; in 1920, nearly half of all farm land was tenant land (Teruoka 2008). In the course of the 20th century, however, different events and changes were taking place. Political parties got influence; already in 1913, a factual two-party system was established. The First World War and the social changes in its wake led the basis for unrest and agitations after the war (in 1918, for instance, the so-called 'rice riots' broke out) and all political parties began to lay the focus more on the solution of civil problems. Unions and the Socialist and Communist party were not able, however, to gain significant influence before Second World War; in fact, they were suppressed most of the time (Dore 1978: 49; Varley 1984: 240). A massive change came with the Second World War and Japanese defeat. Given far-reaching devastations of many cities, widespread hunger and demoralization, the allied forces were able to implement a far-reaching program of reform which changed Japanese society in a fundamental way (Hall 1968: 343–8). A new constitution provided more influence to the people; the divestiture of the large enterprise conglomerates *zaibatsu* and a law against monopolization were enacted; the unions got more support and could increase their membership strongly; a land reform improved significantly the status of rent farmers and farm workers and increased the proportion of land handled by the owners of the land from 53 per cent to 87 per cent; and a reform of the educational system was carried out which included a decentralization of the school system, a massive increase of secondary education, and the establishment of many new universities.

Summary and Conclusions

In a comparative view, Sweden and Japan are two countries characterized by a very low level of economic inequality. In this chapter, it was argued that this fact was due in both cases not only to political factors but also to the fact of ethnic-national homogeneity. In the case of Japan, the relevance of this factor is obvious. This country was able to close itself off from the rest of the world over centuries; when it opened its borders it took in many inventions and achievements of the West but integrated them well into its own social structures and cultural system. Economic equality has been the consequence of the specific characteristics of Japanese society, that is, a very high level of socio-cultural integration through close family- and community-based social relations throughout society. The essence of these relations is that they are of a vertical nature, criss-crossing the class cleavages which were of central importance in Europe. But Sweden, too, has been a very homogeneous country since the Middle Ages. Economic inequality which was quite high until the 1930s levelled off since then due to the development of an extensive and efficient welfare state. It was argued, however, that Sweden's fast industrialization in the 20th century and the development of its unique, redistributive welfare state was possible only because of the high level of socio-cultural integration of the population and the close connection between state and Protestant church in former times. It was shown that the idea of societal homogeneity and national unity underlined also much of the Social Democratic ideology of an egalitarian welfare state in the first half of the 20th century.

Can other countries learn something from the experiences and achievements of these two cases which in many instances are very rather unique compared to other countries around the world? I think that this is in fact the case. We can learn four general lessons from them. The first is that there exists no contradiction between economic growth and achievement and equality. Sweden and Japan are not only among the most equal countries around the world, they have also been among the most successful in terms of socio-economic development, as pointed out already in the introduction.

A second conclusion is that ethnic homogeneity of a country is in fact a very important, although much underestimated fact. The aims of national minorities within existing states to attain political independence cannot be seen only as the outcome of striving toward power and prestige, but have also a foundation in the expectation that many social and political processes will work more smoothly in a small or medium-sized, homogeneous nation-state (see also Kohr 1983, 2002). Table 1.1 (pp. 5–6) shows that also four central European countries – Hungary, Bosnia-Herzegovina, Slovakia and the Czech Republic – exhibit a high level of economic equality. The fact that, with the exception of Hungary, all of them came into existence only at the time of the break-down of the State Socialist systems around 1990–94 and through a process of secession from larger, multi-national states is highly significant here. The leaders of the secession movements may well have had in mind also the fact that a smaller, more homogenous political community will exhibit less economic inequality. Thus, efforts toward secession must be taken seriously everywhere in the world. I will come back to this issue in Chapter 13.

A third lesson is that it is essential for the successful socio-economic development of a country that the elites develop the feeling that 'we are all in the same boat'. Only if this is the case, they are able to develop a coherent and consistent policy, and to retain it over long periods of time – a pre-condition for their success. The outstanding importance of this fact can be shown also in other cases around the world. The recent spectacular economic rise and success of many countries in East Asia was due in large degree to responsible elites focusing mainly on the development of their nations (Austin 2001: 80ff.; Kerbo 2012: 507). The same was true in the 'African miracle', the outstanding economic development of Botswana (Samatar 1999).

A final, fourth lesson to be learned from the Swedish and Japanese cases is that the role of the state is pivotal for development. The state must not play a very strong role – as it does in Sweden – but it must be powerful enough to ensure the smooth functioning of the basic social and political processes, to bring together under one umbrella the major classes and power groups of society and to ensure a coherent, continuous and efficient economic and social policy. From this point of view, it is not necessary that the state intervenes directly and massively into economic and social processes. In this regard, Japan may be a better model than Sweden particularly for the poorest countries in Sub-Saharan Africa because none of these countries has an old, well-established state, but all have very close-knit local communities and family and kinship systems like Japan (see Chapter 10). Political redistribution through a welfare state and social integration through community – like relationships – may be seen as functional equivalents in this regard. From such a perspective, political scientists Stephan Leibfried and Linda Weiss (1998: 162) aptly characterized Germany as a 'social state' (*Sozialstaat*), and Japan as a 'welfare society'.[13]

There are certainly also several shortcomings and challenges both for the Swedish welfare state and the Japanese model of a well-integrated 'community at large'. For the Swedish model, the following problems exist or may become more important: the high levels of taxation (although so far no upper limit of tolerable taxation is in sight); the emergence of the new 'welfare classes' (such as the public employees or the pensioners) which develop their own interests in a continuous further expansion of state expenditures (Olson 1986: 99); the integration of new immigrants. In this regard, an increasing pressure on national welfare states is emerging from globalization. The bureaucratization of the welfare state could incapacitate personal initiative and its focus on individuals could lead to problems such as boredom and loneliness, alcoholism and criminality (Huntford 1974; Haller et al. 2013).[14] In recent decades the Swedish economy has shown severe

---

13   See also the clear-sighted discussion in Miyamoto 2003.

14   Alcoholism among youth and binge drinking on weekends is most frequent in Scandinavia; see 'Binge drinking and Europe', Institut for Alcohol Studies, Cambridgeshire (UK), 9 April 2010. This fact is also a reason why Sweden has

symptoms of crisis. Its position in GDP per capita slipped down, growth rates and industrial investment and production have been weaker than in the OECD mean, unemployment rose to levels (8–9 per cent) unknown before. Linda Weiss (1998: 88ff.) argues that the reason for this was an increasingly strong role of the expanding public sector in wage setting which led to a rising reluctance of industry to invest and create new jobs. Thus, the redistributive capacity became stronger than the transformative complement, that is, pressure from world markets to invest in new technologies and products, the emphasis on consumption was stronger than that on innovation and industrial transformation. One further problem which is much in line with the central arguments of this work has been noted by Sven Steinmo (2003: 449): 'Potentially more troubling [than the aging of the population and the rising costs associated with it] is the possibility that the growing ethnic heterogeneity of this nation will one day undermine the traditional "nordic" Swede's willingness to pay taxes for social programmes that may increasingly go to racial and ethnic minorities'. Although so far in Scandinavia no excessive violence against foreigners has occurred in some other European countries, some indications for this problem are showing up as well. One may note here the rise of right-wing parties in Denmark and Norway already in the 1970s,[15] and the violent attacks of single right-wing persons on public institutions or civilians. The immigration policy of Sweden in the last decade was quite liberal, accepting high numbers of asylum seekers and refugees from the Third World. This has increased the proportion of foreign-born people to 12 per cent (Westin 2006).[16] However, this immigration has also caused problems since many immigrants could not be integrated well into Swedish society. A study has shown that immigration has had a negative effect on the incomes of the Swedish population in the 1990s (Ekberg 1999). The gaps in joblessness between immigrants and natives are larger in Sweden than in Britain and Germany, controlling for relevant personal characteristics (Kesler 2006). Another study found that activity rates of foreigners from former Yugoslavia are significantly lower in Sweden than in Austria (Kogan 2002). In a reanalysis of data from the annual Swedish Living Conditions Survey for the period 1993–2000, Mikael Herm (2005) found that in comparison with Swedish nationals, immigrants displayed lower employment participation rates, earned less and were more frequently poor, and participated much less in political discussions. Herm (2005: 135) concludes: 'It is clear, in Sweden as in other countries that efforts toward integration have failed […] It has become increasingly clear that social exclusion in Sweden, as elsewhere, is amalgamating with constructed ethnic boundaries in the backwash of changing institutional and policy frameworks, labour markets and identities. Exclusion is visible in all of Marshall's three areas of citizenship …' As a consequence of all these problems, Swedish immigration politics in most recent times became more restrictive.

A more general questioning of the redistributive mechanisms of the Swedish welfare state emerges from the new large, interdisciplinary project Gini-Growing Inequalities' Impacts, sponsored by the EU, and including 30 European countries over 30 years. István Tóth (2013) reports in a working paper that quite different trends in economic inequality in Europe can be observed in recent times. In some countries (for example, Austria, France, Belgium, Italy) it did not change, in others it increased significantly. Among them were some East European transitions countries and, to a lesser degree, the Nordic countries, particularly Sweden and Finland. He concludes that in the long run a shift between unequal regions could take place, involving in particular the Nordic countries: 'This group of countries has long been celebrated as the countries with the lowest levels of inequality in Europe. After decades of gradual but incessant increase of inequality they no longer belong to the lowest division of the inequality "league table"' (Tóth 2013: 2).

Also the Japanese model has shown clear crisis symptoms in recent times. First, there is a strong attenuation of economic growth. Japan was falling behind most other OECD countries in the last decade; expectations for the next years are also quite low. A second problem concerns demographic growth. Japan has already today one of the oldest populations in the world. If present-day fertility and mortality rates continue, the

---

long since had a definite policy combating alcoholism (see also Österberg and Karlsson, n.d.).

15   See Walter Bauer, Rechtsextremistische und rechtspopulistische Parteien in Europa, Österreichische Gesellschaft für Politikberatung und Politikentwicklung, 2011 (available at http://www.politikberatung.or.at/typo3/fileadmin/02_Studien/6_europa/Rechte_Parteien.pdf).

16   This is evidently not the highest rate in Europe, as Therborn (2006b: 17) writes; also his remark that Sweden maintained its egalitarian socio-economic orientation, has to be qualified in the light of the findings reported in the text.

population of Japan will shrink from 127 million today to 100 million in 2050 and 64 million in 2100.[17] The restrictive present-day immigration policy, based on the *ius solis* (and a somewhat vague criterion of 'correct behaviour') probably cannot be perpetuated in the future. The exit of young people from the countryside (Dore 1978: 109) has left many old people living alone in their villages and being visited only occasionally and briefly by their children and grandchildren living in the urban agglomerations. These trends and problems are closely related to a fundamental change of Japanese agriculture. As in Europe, the percentage of part-time farmers has increased massively between 1960 and 2005 from 32 per cent to 62 per cent; the percentage of farmers over 65 years old increased from 10 per cent to 60 per cent.[18] At the same time, gross agricultural output declined significantly, including rice production. Thus, the policy of supporting small farmers through a high price of rice (which requires also high tariffs on import) cannot be pursued further for long. However, given the fact that also the Japanese today consume more imported foods (wheat, meat and so on) and a shifting of agricultural production to larger farms could ensure enough rice production. Fourth, there may emerge an increasing split between the sector of the large enterprises with the model of life-long employment and the rest of the economy with small and medium-sized enterprises with worse job and income conditions (Ishikawa 1997). Fourth, women have experienced significantly less positive changes in academic higher education, in the labour market and in politics. While in Sweden in 2000, 42.7 per cent of parliament deputies were women, in Japan in 1998 there were none.[19] Fifth, the traditional policy of subsidizing the price of rice in order to preserve fair incomes for the farmers does not work anymore in the same manner. This is so on the one hand because the average consumption of rice has halved over the past 40 years. On the other side, there exist international pressures to reduce the high import tariffs. Figure 6.1 shows that income inequality in Japan has increased in recent times, this may be a consequence of all these trends, particularly of the emergence of a dual labour market (see also Tachibanaki 2009: 7). A final problem is the disturbing fact that subjective well-being, as measured with a question on overall life satisfaction, has declined between the 1980s and late 1990s – a period in which per capita GDP rose significantly (Kusago 2008). Thus, it seems that the Japanese perceive the aforementioned new social problems. In addition to all these trends, the declining capacity of families and enterprises to care for their members make an extension of the welfare state in Japan inevitable (see also Tachibanaki 2009: 35–42).

References

Austin, Ian P. (2001), *Pragmatism and Public Policy in East Asia: Origins, Adaptations and Developments*, Singapore: Fairmont International Private Ltd.

Bjorklund, Anders and Richard B. Freeman (1994), Generating Equality and Eliminating Poverty. The Swedish Way, Cambridge, MA: National Bureau of Economic Research (NEBR Working Paper 4945)

Blyth, Mark (2002), *Great Transformations. Economic Ideas and Institutional Change in the Twentieth Century*, Cambridge: Cambridge University Press

Dahrendorf, Ralf (1959), *Class and Class Conflict in Industrial Society*, London: Routledge & Kegan Paul

De Vos, George and Hiroshi Wagatsuma (1967), *Japan's Invisible Race: Caste in Culture and Personality*, Los Angeles: University of California Press

Dirks, Daniel and Otto Silke-Susann (1998), 'Das 'japanische Unternehmen', in Deutsches Institut für Japan Studien, ed., *Die Wirtschaft Japans*, Berlin, pp. 211–44

Doi, Takeo (1982), *Amae. Freiheit in Geborgenheit. Zur Struktur japanischer Psyche*, Frankfurt/Main: Suhrkamp

Dore, Ronald P. (1978), *Shinohata. A Portrait of a Japanese Village*, Berkeley/Los Angeles: University of California Press

---

17 See de.wikipedia.org/wiki/Demografie-Japans (30.11.2011).

18 See Kazuhito Yamashita, 'Ensuring Japan's food security through free trade not tariffs', EastAsiaForum, 10 March 2010.

19 Jahn 2002; see also footnote 6 above, p. 170.

Ekberg, Jan (1999), 'Immigration and the public sector: Income effects for the native population in Sweden', *Journal of Population Economy* 12: 411–30

Esping-Andersen, Gøsta (1990), *The Three Worlds of Welfare Capitalism*, Cambridge: Polity Press

Esping-Andersen, Gøsta (1997), 'Hybrid or unique? The Japanese welfare state between Europe and America', *Journal of European Social Policy* 7: 179–89

Esping-Andersen, Gøsta (1998), 'Die drei Welten des Wohlfahrtskapitalismus. Zur politischen Ökonomie des Wohlfahrtsstaates', in Stephan Lessenich and Ilona Ostner, eds, (1998) *Welten des Wohlfahrtskapitalismus. Der Sozialstaat in vergleichender Perspektive*, Frankfurt/New York: Campus, pp. 19–58

Esser, Hartmut (2011), *Integration und ethnische Schichtung (Gutachten)*, Arbeitspapier Nr. 40, Mannheimer Zentrum für Europäische Sozialforschung

Findeisen, Jörg-Peter (2003), *Schweden. Von den Anfängen bis zur Gegenwart*, Regensburg: Friedrich Pustet

Flora, Peter and Arnold J. Heidenheimer, eds (1981), *The Development of Welfare States in Europe and America*, New Brunswick/London: Transaction Publishers

Flora, Peter et al., eds (1986), *State, Economy, and Society in Western Europe: 1815–1975. A Data Handbook in Two Volumes*, vol. 1, Frankfurt/Main: Campus

Flora, Peter, ed. (1986), *Growth to Limits. The Western European Welfare State in Comparative Perspective*, Vol. 1, Berlin/New York: W. de Gruyter

Gerste, Ronald D. (1994), Schweden und die amerikanische Revolution, Dissertation, Universität Düsseldorf

Goldthorpe, John H. (1983), The end of convergence. Corporatist and dualist tendencies in modern western societies, Paper presented at the SSRC Seminar on Labour Markets, Manchester

Götz, Norbert (2001), *Ungleiche Geschwister. Die Konstruktion von nationalsozialistischer Volksgemeinschaft und schwedischem Volksheim*, Baden-Baden: Nomos

Haley, John O. (1991), *Authority without Power. Law and the Japanese Paradox*, New York/Oxford: Oxford University Press

Hall, John W. (1968), *Das Japanische Kaiserreich, Fischer Weltgeschichte*, vol. 20, Frankfurt: Fischer Taschenbuch Verlag

Haller, Max and Franz Höllinger (2009), 'Decline or persistence of religion? Trends in religiosity among Christian societies around the world', in Max Haller, Roger Jowell and Tom Smith, eds, *The International Social Survey Programme 1984–2009. Charting the Globe, 1984–2009. Charting the Globe*, London/New York: Routledge, pp. 281–301

Haller, Max, Markus Hadler and Gerd Kaup (2013), 'Leisure time in modern societies: A new source of boredom and stress?' *Social Indicates Research* 111: 403–34

Henningsen, Bernd (1986), *Der Wohlfahrtsstaat Schweden*, Baden-Baden: Nomos

Henze, Valeska (1999), Der schwedische Wohlfahrtsstaat. Zur Struktur und Funktion eines politischen Ordnungsmodells, Working Paper 19, European University Institute, Firenze

Herm, Mikael (2005), 'Integration into the social democratic welfare state', *Social Indicators Research* 70: 117–38

Huntford, Roland (1973), *Wohlfahrtsdiktatur. Das schwedische Modell*, Frankfurt etc.: Ullstein (*The New Totalitarians*, 1971)

Huntford, Roland (1974), *Wohlfahrtsdiktatur. Das schwedische Modell*, Frankfurt etc.: Ullstein

Ishida, Takeshi (1989), 'Die Integration von Konformität und Konkurrenz', in Ulrich Menzel, ed., (1989), *Im Schatten des Siegers. Japan, vol. 1: Kultur und Gesellschaft*, Frankfurt/Main: Suhrkamp, pp. 140–170

Ishikawa, Tsuneo (1997), 'Growth, human development and economic policies in Japan: 1955–1993' (Online)

Kerbo, Harold R. (2012), *Social Stratification and Inequality. Class Conflict in Historical, Comparative, and Global Perspective*, New York: McGraw Hill

Kesler, Christel (2006), 'Social policy and immigrant joblessness in Britain, Germany and Sweden', *Social Forces* 85: 743–70

Koch, Max (2003), *Arbeitsmärkte und Sozialstrukturen in Europa*, Wiesbaden: Westdeutscher Verlag

Kogan, Irena (2002), Labour market inclusion of immigrants in Austria and Sweden, Working Paper 44, Mannheimer Zentrum für Europäische Sozialforschung (MZES)

Kohr, Leopold (1983), *Die überentwickelten Nationen*, München: Goldmann

Kohr, Leopold (2002), *Das Ende der Großen. Zurück zum menschlichen Maß*, Salzburg/Wien: Müller

Koike, Kazuo and Takenori Iniki, eds (1990), *Skill Formation in Japan and Southeast Asia*, Tokio: University of Tokyo Press

Komiya, Nobuo (1999), 'A cultural study of the low crime rate in Japan', *British Journal of Criminology* 39: 369–90

Korpi, Walter and Joakim Palme (1989), 'The paradox of redistribution and strategies of equality: Welfare state institutions, inequality, and poverty in Western countries', *American Sociological Review* 63: 661

Korpi, Walter (1983), *The Democratic Class Struggle*, London: Routledge & Kegan Paul

Korpi, Walter (2006), 'Power Resources and Employer-Centered Approaches in Explanations of Welfare States and Varieties of Capitalism: Protagonists, Consenters, and Antagonists', *World Politics* 58: 167–206

Kosaka, Kenji, ed. (1994), *Social Stratification in Contemporary Japan*, London/New York: Routledge

Kotabe, Masaaki and Kent W. Wheiler (1996), *Anticompetitive Practices I Japan. Their Impact on Foreign Firms*, Westport, CT/London: Praeger

Kusago, Takayoshi (2008), 'Japan's development: What economic growth, human development and subjective well-being measures tell us about?' *Thammasat Economic Journal* 26: 28–116

Leibfried, Stephan (1994), '"Sozialstaat' oder 'Wohlfahrtsgesellschaft"? Thesen zu einem japanisch-deutschen Sozialpolitikvergleich', *Soziale Welt* 45: 389–410

Liping, S.H.I. (2010), 'Continuities and changes in parent-child relationships and kinship in postwar Japan', *GEMC Journal* 2: 48–67

Mann, Michael (1980), *Political Power and Social Theory*, vol. 1, Greenwich, CN: JAI Press

Mau, Steffen and Roland Verwiebe (2010), *European Societies. Mapping Structure and Change*, Bristol: The Policy Press

McMillan, Charles J. (1989), *The Japanese Industrial System*, Berlin/New York: Walter de Gruyter

Menningen, Walter, ed. (1971), *Ungleichheit im Wohlfahrtsstaat. Der Alva-Myrdal-Report der schwedischen Sozialdemokraten*, Reinbek: Rowohlt

Minami, Ryoshin (1986), *The Economic Development of Japan. A Quantitative Study*, Houndsmill, Basingstoke/London: Macmillan

Miyamoto, Taro (2003), 'Dynamics of the Japanese welfare state in comparative perspective. Between "Three Worlds" and the Developmental State', *The Japanese Journal of Social Security Policy* 2: 12–24

Müller, Nora, Sandra Buchholz and Hans-Peter Blossfeld (2010), *Wealth Inequality in Europe and the Delusive Egalitarism of Scandinavian Countries*, University of Bamberg, Department of Sociology

Müller, Walter, Susanne Steinmann and Reinhart Schneider (1997), 'Bildung in Europa', in Stefan Hradil and Stefan Immerfall, eds, *Die westeuropäischen Gesellschaften im Vergleich*, Opladen: Leske + Budrich, pp. 177–246

Murakami, Yasusuke (1987), 'The Japanese Model of Political Economy', in Kozo Yamamura and Yasukichi Yasuba, eds, *The Political Economy of Japan*, Vol. 1, Stanford, CA: Stanford University Press, pp. 33–90

Nakamura, Takafusa (1981), *The Postwar Japanese Economy. Its Development and Structure*, Tokyo: University of Tokyo Press

Nakane, Chie (1970), *Die Struktur der japanischen Gesellschaft*, Frankfurt: Suhrkamp

Norbeck, Edward (1970), 'Continuities in Japanese Social Stratification', in Leonard Plotnicov and Arthur Tuden, eds, Essays in Comparative Social Stratification, Pittsburgh, PA: University of Pittsburgh Press, pp. 173–201

Obinger, Herbert and Uwe Wagschal (1998), 'Drei Welten des Wohlfahrtsstaates? Das Stratifizierungskonzept in der clusteranalytischen Überprüfung', in Stephan Lessenich and Ilona Ostner, *Welten des Wohlfahrtskapitalismus*, Frankfurt/New York: Campus, pp. 109–36

Okano, Kaori and Motnori Tsuchiya (1999), *Education in Contemporary Japan. Inequality and Diversity*, Cambridge: Cambridge University Press

Olson, Sven (1986), 'Sweden', in Flora et al., *State, Economy, and Society in Western Europe: 1815–1975*, pp. 1–116

Österberg, Esa and Thomas Karlsson, eds (n.d.), 'Alcohol Policies in EU Member States and Norway. A Collection of Country Reports', pp. 17–42 (Online: http://ideas.repec.org/p/hdr/hdocpa/hdocpa-1997-01.html)

Persson, Inga, ed. (1990), *Generating Equality in the Welfare State. The Swedish Experience*, Oslo: Norwegian University Press

Pfaller, Alfred, Ian Gough and Göran Therborn, eds (1991), *Can the Welfare State Compete? A Comparative Study of Five Advanced Capitalist Countries*, Houndmills/UK: Macmillan

Pye, Lucian W. (1989), 'Das japanische Rätsel: Die Verbindung von Wettbewerb und Konsens', in Menzel, *Im Schatten des Siegers: Japan*, pp. 41–75

Rokkan, Stein (2000), *Staat, Nation und Demokratie in Europa. Die Theorie Stein Rokkans*, ed. by Peter Flora, Frankfurt: Suhrkamp

Rothstein, Bo (1987), 'Corporatism and reformism: The social democratic institutionalization of class conflict', *Acta Sociologica* 30: 295–311

Samatar, Abdi I. (1999), *An African Miracle. State and Class Leadership and Colonial Legacy in Botswana Development*, Portsmouth, NH: Heinemann

Schmidt, Manfred (1982), *Wohlfahrtsstaatliche Politik unter bürgerlichen und sozialdemokratischen Regierungen*, Opladen: Leske & Budrich

Schmidt, Manfred, ed. (2001), *Wohlfahrtsstaatliche Politik: Institutionen, politischer Prozeß und Leistungsprofil*, Opladen: Leske & Budrich

Schmitter, Philippe (1974), 'Still the century of corporatism', *Review of Politics* 36: 85–131

Schwentker, Wolfgang (2005), 'The spirit of modernity. Max Weber's Protestant Ethic and Japanese Social Sciences', *Journal of Classical Sociology* 5: 73–92

Spektorowski, A. (2004), 'The Eugenic Temptation in Socialism: Sweden, Germany, and the Soviet Union', *Comparative Studies in Society and History* 46: 84–106

Steinmo, Sven (2003), 'Bucking the trend? The welfare state and the global economy: The Swedish case up close', *New Political Economy* 8: 31–48

Svallfors, Stefan and Peter Taylor-Gooby, eds (1999), *The End of the Welfare State? Responses to State Retrenchment*, London: Routledge

Tachibanaki, Toshiaki (2009), *Confronting Income Inequality in Japan: A Comparative Analysis of Causes, Consequences, and Reform*, Cambridge, MA/London: MIT Press

Teruoka, Shuzo, ed. (2008), *Agriculture in the Modernization of Japan 1850–2000*, New Delhi: Manohar

Thakur, Subhash et al., eds (2003), *Sweden's Welfare State: Can the Bumblebee Keep Flying?* Washington, DC.: International Monetary Fund

The Statesman's Yearbook ed. by Barry Turner, Houndsmills, UK/New York: Palgrave Macmillan (Annual Publication)

Therborn, Göran (1995), *European Modernity and Beyond, The Trajectory of European Societies 1945–2000*, London etc.: Sage

Therborn, Göran (2006b), 'Meaning, mechanisms, patterns, and forces: An introduction', in G. Therborn, *Inequalities of the World*, London, New York: Verso, pp. 1–60

Tóth, István György (2013), Time series and cross country variation of income inequalities in Europe on the medium run: are inequality structures converging in the past three decades? GINI Policy Paper 3

Trobe, Mitsue de la and Inga Streb (1985), *Alltag in Japan*, Düsseldorf/Wien: Econ

Varley, H. Paul (1984), *Japanese Culture*, Honolulu: University of Hawaii Press

Vogler, Carolyn (1985), *The Nation-State. The Neglected Dimension of Class*, Aldershot/Hants: Gower

Wagatsuma, Hiroshi and George A. De Vos (1989), 'Die Tradition der Ausgestoßenen im modernen Japan. Ein Problem der gesellschaftlichen Identität', in Menzel, *Im Schatten des Siegers: Japan*, pp. 208–42

Weiss, Linda (1998), *The Myth of the Powerlessness of the State. Governing the Economy in a Global Era*, Cambridge: Polity Press

Westin, Charles (2006), 'Sweden: Restrictive immigration policy and multiculturalism', *Migration Information Source*. Migration Policy Institute, Washington

Wilensky, Harold (1975), *The Welfare State and Equality*, Berkeley: University of California Press

Wiley, Norbert F. (1970), 'The ethnic mobility trap and stratification theory', in Peter I. Rose, ed., *The Study of Society*, New York/Toronto: J. Wiley, pp. 397–408

Zijderveld, Anton C. (1986), 'The ethos of the welfare state', *International Sociology* 1: 443–57

Chapter 7
Ethnic-national Cleavages and the Rise and Fate of Communist Systems

Introduction

Going westward from Japan, it is a logical route to look at China, but not only in geographic terms. China shares many characteristics with Japan as one of the oldest states on earth and as a society which is also quite homogeneous in ethnic-national terms. It was already noted in the preceding chapter that Japan had close relations with China throughout its history: it owes considerable parts of its cultural traditions to the Chinese heritage; the fact that both states entered into wars repeatedly between 1839 and 1945 is also an indication of their close relation (Simmel 1923). However, with China we encounter a state-socialist system whose declared intent was to establish a fundamental, revolutionary change in order to erase pervasive inequalities and to establish 'real' economic and social equality among all members of society. The same goal was pursued also in a few other macro-regions and states around the world, particularly in Russia in 1917, in Central East Europe after the Second World War and in Cuba in the 1950s.

In this chapter we shall look at all these systems under the general framework developed in this book. To consider the state-socialist systems here seems appropriate also in view of the fact that nationalism and Socialism/Communism are seen as the two main contending and most influential political ideologies shaping the history of the world in the 19th and 20th centuries (see, for instance, Rejai 1995; Beyme 2002; Baradat 2012). In Chapter 2 I outlined that in Marxist theory nationalism was seen not as an original and creative force but only as class conflict in disguise; in order to prevent workers from pursuing their class interests, they were spurred to nationalist emotions by the bourgeoisie and their intellectuals. Therefore, the aims of State Socialist regimes in ethnic nationally mixed societies was to develop a new supranational (Soviet, Yugoslav and so on) identity and to further the attachment of people to the new, overarching Socialist society.

As far as the pre-conditions and reasons for the outbreak of the Communist revolution in East Europe are concerned, three general interpretations are well-established: (1) they emerged in rather backward countries and regions of the world where large groups of the population – particularly farmers – were living under miserable conditions; therefore, they welcomed and supported the revolutionary program and leaders; (2) the regimes and political systems established by the Communists instituted a high degree of economic and social equality, although a new split emerged between the mass of the population – rather equal within but living under modest socio-economic circumstances – and a new and small but all powerful elite or *Nomenklatura*; (3) most of these systems have collapsed because of political discontent and unrest of the population at large, following economic inefficiency and stagnation.

In this chapter, I would like to show that these theses, while not incorrect, are clearly incomplete. I will argue that ethnic-national identities, divisions and conflicts have played a decisive role both during the rise and fall of the Socialist and Communist revolutions and in the political systems which afterwards were established. I propose the following four theses: (1) the outbreak and success of these revolutions was due in a decisive manner to aggression from outside and to rule and suppression from foreign powers, thus to national suppression; later on, it often involved the subjugation of indigenous ethnic-national subgroups; (2) the take-over of power by the Communist elites was possible only in (a) centralized political systems and multi-national imperial states where it occurred typically after violent internal fights and civil wars for power and (b) in other nations it occurred only in the sequel of a war and under the pressure of a foreign Communist power; (3) the state-socialist regimes did in fact establish more 'substantive' socio-economic equality among the broad mass of the population, but at the same time the victorious Communist cadres established a new 'dominant elite'. However, the ways in which this happened were quite distinct in different state-socialist societies and they were closely related to the ethnic-national dimension: (a) in multi-national societies, that is, in societies characterized by strong and self-conscious sub-nations, each living on a relatively compact territory (such as in Russia and Yugoslavia), the revolution had to concede a federalist constitution; this constitution, however, remained on paper only because real power was exercised by the central Communist Party. As a consequence, there was also no effective regional redistribution and economic inequality remained relatively high; (b) in small and ethnically homogeneous societies (as most Central East European countries were), economic inequality did not change very much as a consequence of the revolution; they have ever since been characterized by considerable equality; (4) even the huge Communist state of China was able to create and preserve a considerable degree of economic equality, due to a relatively high degree of ethnic homogeneity and a strict centralistic policy. In recent times, however, the liberalization of the economy and its integration into the global market, as well as the preferential treatment of the eastern provinces has led to a massive increase of inequality; (5) finally, also the eventual fall of state-socialist systems (such as in Central East Europe, the USSR and Yugoslavia) was caused by ethnic-national suppression and connected closely to the striving for national independence and the emergence of new political and economic inequalities between the different ethnic-national groups and their regions.

Theories of State Socialism and the Role of Ethnic-national Cleavages and Conflicts

Let us first discuss shortly the main theories of state-socialism and the role of the ethnic-national factor in these theories. We may distinguish four groups of theories in this regard. Two of them are opposite to each other – the one fully legitimizing, the other criticizing State Socialism – and the third and fourth posit some similarities, but also differences between State Socialism and Capitalism. All of these theories contain some truth although none of them is able to explain the downfall of the Communist System in East Europe. One reason for it is that all of them neglect the role of ethnic-national cleavages and conflicts which in my view have been decisive in many regards.

The first theory of State Socialism is *Orthodox Marxist theory*, as developed by Marx, Engels and Lenin and later used as an ideological weapon by the dominant elites in the State Socialist societies. It proposes that Communism is a system which enables the proletariat to take over power by the working classes at the work place, in society and politics, and realizing in this way far-reaching equality in all regards, between manual and non-manual workers, men and women, town and country and so forth. Communist revolution also establishes 'real democracy', that is, possibilities for broad participation of the people in political decision-making processes at all levels and in all spheres of society. As pointed out in Chapter 2 (see pp. 26–7), for Marx and Lenin ethnicity and nationalism were only time-dependent phenomena, determined in the last instance by class interests. In the course of time, a new Socialist personality and society would emerge under Communism; ethnic-national thinking and acting would fade away in this new society. The founders of Communism in the Soviet Union, Lenin and Stalin, did not deny some positive aspects of nationalism and they argued that nations have the right to self-determination (see the texts in Fetscher 1973: 571–97). However, in practice it was the political leaders who decided about the official recognition of an ethnic minority as a 'national' sub-group; and these were considered more as pure culturally based entities, not to be granted political autonomy. Lenin himself was 'a staunch believer in state unitarism; the promise to the nations in the Russian empire which did not want to remain in the state after the revolution should be granted the right to secede was only a sop' (Kolsto 2001: 2002).

We need not go into a detailed critique of this theory here. Historical facts have clearly shown that the high aspirations and expectations have not been met: State Socialism has not been able to develop the productive forces more dynamically than Capitalism, it has rather fallen more and more behind the Western, Capitalist countries; some inequalities have been erased, but others have persisted and new ones emerged; the political and bureaucratic apparatuses have not disappeared altogether but have been expanded strongly by taking over more and more tasks thus becoming very powerful; none of the multi-national Communist societies has been able to erase ethnic-national affiliations and to produce internationally minded 'socialist personalities' and societies. The dogmatic version of orthodox Marxist-Leninist theory is not endorsed any more today. However, there are some authors who claim that 'real' State Socialism was not an adequate implementation of the principles of Socialism and Communism; hence we cannot disprove this theory altogether because of the fall of State Socialism (Therborn 1995: 341). It is certainly true that there is no one-to-one correspondence between classical Marxist-Leninist theory and real State Socialism: I think nevertheless that this is a misleading position. There was no real gulf between Marx and Stalin; Lenin with his totalitarian, black-and-white view of Capitalist and Socialist ideology and praxis provided the bridge between them (Goldfarb 1989: 210–215). Central characteristics of 'real' State Socialism (as it was called in the German Democratic Republic) are indeed following directly from Marxist theory. We can mention here the abolition of private ownership in the means of production and of free markets in the area of distribution which were a main reason for the falling behind of State Socialism against Capitalism in economic terms; and the contempt for representative, parliamentary democracy which was a main reason for the degeneration of the political system into authoritarian patterns. For two reasons, however, it is important to look at this official Marxist theory still today: first, because it was the dominant ideology of State Socialism; second, because some of its central tenets have also been incorporated into the public consciousness in the former State Socialist societies.

At the opposite pole of the spectrum, there is the theory of *totalitarianism*, proposed by authors such as C.J. Friedrich, Z.K Brzezinski, S. Huntington and H. Arendt (see Lane 1976: 44ff.). It posits that State Socialism, on the one side, was a system where the Communist Party exerted absolute control over all spheres of society and life using, if necessary, police terror and concentration camps; an ideology explaining and legitimizing anything in the interests of the dominant party; on the other side, this system presupposed masses which had no influence at all, and even accepted total control which provided them with security and satisfaction of basic needs. Recent research on the history of State Socialism, supported by the implementation of a critical attitude toward history in many former Communist societies, has brought to light incredible facts and misdeeds of State Socialism, particularly by the extremely powerful leaders Stalin and Mao Tse-tung. An estimated number of 20 million dead persons were victims of Stalins purges: in the 1920s they included competing Communist leaders; in the 1930s *kulaks*, that are farmers who opposed the nationalization of agricultural properties; in 1936–38 leaders in all spheres of politics and economic life, in 1948–53 Jews (Heinsohn 1998; Courtois 1998). Mao's repeated 'revolutions' – such as the land reform after 1949, the 'Great Leap Forward' and the 'Culture Revolution' – have led to an estimated number of 45 to 70 million death people (see also Halliday and Chang 2007). The totalitarian position, however, is also open to criticisms: the control of state and party has never been total, and it has been relaxed in recent decades (Lane 1996, 2011). The basic view of this approach concerning human nature is one-sided and pessimistic, assuming that political elites strive only for power, and citizens are hardly ever ready and able to oppose and dethrone a totalitarian regime. A very strong counter-argument, in my view, is that this theory cannot explain the collapse of State Socialism and also the fact that this fall in the largest Socialist state, the USSR, occurred without bloodshed (Beyme 1994).

In the 'middle' between these two extremes we find the *theory of convergence*. This theory has been proposed in the west as well as within State Socialist societies. D. Bell (1973) and others have argued that the development of industrial society undergoes a similar logic in all countries; it is correlated with an increasing division of labour, rising importance of education and knowledge, science and technology, expansion of markets and the like. These processes are universal tendencies spreading out worldwide and they must be emulated everywhere in order for a society to remain competitive. A variant of this theory has been proposed also by state-socialist reformers, such as by economists in Czechoslovakia (for example, Ota Sik) and maybe even by Gorbachev when he tried to reform the Soviet system from inside. Their idea might have been that State Socialism can be transformed to a system comparable to the Nordic welfare states, with an extended social welfare state and elements of democracy in the Western sense. Also this theory has some merits. Particularly in the less developed East European countries – such as Russia, but also Bulgaria or Romania – State Socialism has in fact achieved a strong developmental jump by rising massively the educational level of the population and establishing industry; in a certain regard, one can even argue that Communism has been digging its own grave because the better educated, urbanized population also became more critical toward the system (Lane 1996, 2011). Empirical research on class structures provides some support to this theory. For Walter Connor (1979: 204ff.), the transition in East Europe produced just another variant of an industrial society. Based on the data of the International Project on Class Structure and Class Consciousness, carried out in 1991, the last year of the Soviet Union, M. Kivinen (1994: 129ff.) found no significant difference in the size of the new middle classes in Russia and Western countries; the most notable was the absence of an entrepreneurial class; some further differences concerned a larger bureaucratic-administrative stratum and a higher proportion of women in professional occupations in Russia. Szonja Szelényi (1998: 52), in her accurate study on State Socialist Hungary, writes that the changes have led to 'a hybrid of classic postindustrial upgrading and low-wage proletarianisation'. An American journalist, Hendrick Smith (1979), wrote a book full of rich materials on the way the Russians lived in the 1970s. He found that a new privileged class, composed of leading party members and cadres, had emerged; it could not be grasped by official statistics, but could be clearly recognized through its distinct style of life, based on a vast network of separate shops, hospitals, recreational facilities and clubs. While the proportion of this privileged stratum among the population was small, its privileges were highly problematic given the depressed consumption standards for the general population (Connor 1979: 248ff.). Heike Solga (1995: 210) investigated the changes in the German Democratic Republic 1945 to 1989 and found an increasing self-recruitment of the privileged classes there as well, leading toward a 'social class society' (see also Haller/Mach 1984). Thus, while the theory of convergence has rightly noted some trends in which State Socialist societies became more similar to Western societies, it has basically failed. In 1989/90, the idea of convergence was fully abandoned in favour of an overthrow of Communism and a transition (or return) to Capitalist and democratic societies of Western style.

The fourth group of theories posits the emergence of a *new class character of State Socialism* and – maybe – even Capitalism. Authors like J. Burnham (1972 [1941]) and J. Schumpeter (1946) have argued that in any advanced society the managers will form the new dominant class because they control the most important, centralized economic assets and processes. They have argued that this will happen not only in State Socialist societies, but even in Western, Capitalist societies so that these will become Socialist themselves in the future (from this point of view, their theory can be seen as a variant of convergence theory). Two Hungarian authors, G. Konrad and I. Szelenyi (1978), have proposed that *intellectuals* will form the new dominant class in State Socialist societies; in support of their argument, they assemble an impressive picture of the Revolution in Russia and other East European countries which shows that the *intelligentsia* in those countries in fact played a crucial role in destroying the old order and establishing the State Socialist system. Also these theories contain important insights. However, the establishment of State Socialism has implied the emergence and action of more classes than just these two; in fact a new dominant 'political class' has emerged. In this, I am following authors like Djilas (1959), Sik (1976) and Bahro (1977) who already in the 1960s and 1970s have pointed out, based on their own experiences under State Socialism, that a new dominant, political class had come into existence comprising the leading political, bureaucratic and ideological cadres. In my view, this new dominant class in State Socialism, with the *Nomenclatura* in the centre, showed all characteristics of a class in the Marxist and Weberian sense: their members controlled vast economic resources; they had their own political interests; they were closely interconnected and enjoyed wide privileges. They were also on the way to develop their own styles of life and to reproduce themselves through patterns of intra-class marriage and intergenerational inheritance.

The thesis proposed here is that the rise, the form and the eventual decline of State Socialism can only be explained if it considers the emergence of the new class structure – an elite-mass model – in connection with the relevance of the ethnic-national component. As far as the victory and rise of Communism is concerned, these facts are more than obvious in the case of the first country where it was established, in Russia. The coup through which Lenin's small group of Bolsheviks came to power in 1917 was possible only as a consequence of the fact that Russia had lost the First World War and that a revolution carried out by soldiers and workers at the base, and supported by social democratic and other political parties, was already under way. But also in China, the revolution was a consequence of a series of national humiliations in the wake of foreign invasions and military defeats from the middle of the 19th till the middle of the 20th centuries.

An additional crucial element in these revolutions was the fact that both Russia and China were empires controlling a vast territory with large peripheral regions and many ethnic-national minorities. The revolutions were carried out by small, determined politically parties whose leaders were members of the core natural ethnie. This fact may explain the crucial difference between the modern history of Japan and China: while in Japan, new elites were coming into power in a non-violent way during the Meiji revolution, in China a bloody civil war for the control of central power was carried out between Chiang Kai-shek and Mao Tse-tung.

Military suppression of oppositional groups was also necessary in Russia. The continuous bloody purges both in the Soviet Union under Stalin and in China under Mao can only be understood fully if one takes into consideration the multi-ethnic and multi-national character of these empires. From this point of view, also the persistence of State Socialism in China and its fall in the Soviet Union, Yugoslavia and East Europe can be explained by taking into consideration the fact that the USSR and Yugoslavia were multi-national empires and states, respectively, while this was much less true for China where the Han was and still is the numerically preponderant and politically dominating and unchallenged ethnic group.

It is also evident that ethnic-national divisions and conflicts cannot be neglected in the fall of State Socialism in central and southern East Europe. Their crucial role in the case of Yugoslavia is more than obvious. The same was true, however, also in the Communist East Central European countries where the union with the USSR in the COMECON was seen by many as a kind of foreign domination. The unrest and uprisings in the GDR 1953, in Hungary 1956, in Czechoslovakia 1968 and in Poland in the 1970s were all motivated to a large degree by the wish for more independence from the USSR and for more autonomy concerning the design of socialism. But even in the USSR, interest conflicts between the centre and the governments of the large Republics were quite important for the dissolution of the system; they were closely intertwined with ethnic-national divisions. In this regard, also the theory of the new classes under State Socialism has to be supplemented by including the ethnic-national component producing a significant latent discord within the dominant class. Let us now have a closer look at three paradigmatic cases of State Socialism, China, the Soviet Union and Yugoslavia.

The Manipulation of Socio-economic Differentiation by the *Great Leviathan*. The Case of China

From the viewpoint of this study, China is a particularly interesting and important case. This is so not only because of the sheer size of this state which is the largest in the world in terms of population – about 1.3 billion people, nearly 20 per cent of world population – and the fourth in terms of surface area – 9.5 million square kilometres and because of its stunning economic growth since the 1980s. China is also – despite of its huge size – a rather homogeneous country in ethnic terms and it has over many centuries, if not millennia, a highly centralized government system.[1] Let us have a short look on the characteristics of China in this regard.

Historical China: a Highly Integrated, Centralized and Elitist Society

In spite of the existence of many ethnic minorities, China must be considered as a relatively homogeneous country. About 91 per cent of the Chinese people belong to the dominant ethnic group of the Han[2] and in most parts of the country the language of Standard Mandarin is spoken.[3] A decisive pre-condition for the emergence and persistence of the huge state of China was the fact that efficient internal connections in the northeastern central area made it possible that already in ancient times a common language and culture were developed (Deutsch 1966: 43). They were fostered mainly through the early invention of scripture (around 1250 B.C.) and of the letter press around 900 A.D., that is, much earlier than in Europe (Vogelsang 2013: 60, 296). The emergence of this community was supported and cemented by political integration and domination. In fact, the history of China is a continuous fight of central powers to unite (or reunite) and integrate this huge, heterogeneous territory (Vogelsang 2013). Large parts of China, particularly in the region around the *Yellow River*, became politically united already around 1500 B.C. Since more than two millennia (approximately from 200 B.C. on) a series of dynasties created the Chinese Empire which existed till 1911. No other political community on earth, including Japan, can look back at such an old and continuous form of political centralization and cultural integration.

---

1   For an overview see Hsieh 1986.

2   See http://en.wikipedia.org/wiki/Ethnic_minorities_in_China; Fischer, *Weltalmanach* 2008, p. 104.

3   See http://en.wikipedia.org/wiki/Languages_of_China. China was not always so mono-lingual. During the Qing-dynasty (1645–1795) China had four official languages (Vogelsang 2013: 416). Even today, there exist significant regional linguistic differences in the spoken Chinese (see Bodmer 1989: 231–56).

These two facts – cultural homogeneity and political centralization – reflect themselves clearly in present-day public perceptions of the form of the social structure: a very high proportion (51 per cent) of the Chinese considers the shape of their society as a pyramid (see Table 6.1, pp. 164–5). The persistence of the empire was furthered in a decisive way by the fact that the huge Chinese landmass is separated in the West from the rest of Asia by nearly impassable deserts and mountains, and in the East by the Pacific Ocean which could not be transcended in historical times (Fitzgerald 1956: 15). Ethnic minorities are living mainly in the remote, vast and thinly populated regions in the West and North; most of them were incorporated into the empire only in later times. However, due to geographical mobility into and out these regions, today many members of ethnic minorities are living all over China, and in the autonomous provinces of the minorities, millions of people from the dominant Han ethnicity are living. Overall, there exist 55 officially recognized ethnic minorities in China with their own languages; nine of them have more than five million members.[4] Although the total number of these minorities is over 100 million, they have little influence in the centre of China in spite of the fact that their suppression is continuously and rightly denounced at the international level (Hour and Stone 2009). The ever recurring unrest of the minorities – often as a reaction to oppressive acts by the central government – may lead to a relatively high level of consciousness of their problems also in China. This could explain the fact that a very large proportion (38 per cent compared to a mean of only 16 per cent in 38 countries) of the Chinese consider 'race' as an important factor for getting ahead in life (see Table 6.2, p. 168).

In religious terms, China is not homogeneous. There exist five officially recognized religious communities (Buddhism, Daoism, Islam, Catholicism and Protestantism) but they play only a minor role in public and private life. This is so because some of them can be considered more as traditional rituals and ethics (such as Buddhism and Confucianism) but are not organized in churches, and because Communism suppressed them as much as possible. However, the basic doctrines of Confucianism were highly important in the history of China till the present day.[5] They stressed general humanism and altruism, loyalty to the family and friends, filial piety and social harmony. The latter was particularly important in connection with the stress on etiquette, rites and morals, including education and polite behaviour. The 'gentleman ideal' saw the perfect men and women as ones who acted as a moral guide to the rest of society. This ideal was developed through the millennia, since China's political unification 200 B.C. It was essential for the development and power of the state bureaucracy, the force mainly responsible for the cohesion of society and state. As elaborated in Max Weber's (1991) path-breaking work on Confucianism, China was very different from eternally divided Europe insofar as it attained unification and integration under a centralized officialdom. Neither military power nor land ownership were crucial for attaining power, wealth and status in historical times, but the access to political offices in the service of the emperor, the fees and taxes from these offices. Thus, the goal of ambitious men in Confucianism was 'a cultured status position' (Bendix 1977: 141). This clearly implies an elitist view of society and politics. We can again look here to the view of the Chinese of their society as a perfect pyramid (see Table 6.2, p. 168). I would argue that this elitist view is still valid for the leading Communist cadres in China today. However, in difference to the old 'gentleman officers', they are also strongly orientated toward political action. In former times, the lack of such an orientation was responsible for the stagnation of the Chinese economy in difference to Europe where Capitalism began to develop after the Reformation.

Activist Elitism: Changes and Continuities through the Communist Revolution

In China in 1949 a Communist Party under the leadership of Mao Tse-tung took over political power which had as one of its central slogans the establishment of socio-economic equality in all spheres of life and society. Also the Chinese Communist revolution was not based on the industrial working class, but on soldiers and farmers. The undisputed leadership, however, remained in the hands of the Communist Party. In its organization and ideology one can see a continuity to the traditional highly educated Chinese bureaucracy

---

4   These are the Zhuang (16 million), the Manchus and the Huis (both about 10 million and Muslims), the Miao, Uygurs, Tujia, Yi's, Mongols and Tibetans. See also Hsieh (1986).

5   For a short overview see http://en.wikipedia.org/wiki/The_Religion_of_China:_Confucianism_and_Taoism (20.11.2011). See also Vogelsang 2013: 157–64, 321–5.

which understood itself as an elect and efficient body of mundane management; the reference to religious ideologies, gratifications and punishments in the afterlife was irrelevant. After the unification of the country, following a decade-long civil war, Mao Tse-Tung in his 'Great Leap Forward' from 1958 on tried to carry through a far-reaching, egalitarian reform, including the establishment of agricultural production cooperatives, small production units and people's communes in the countryside (Bian 2002: 98; Vogelsang 2013: 536–72). This reform was not only forced on the people, but carried through with broad participation of the millions of Communist functionaries in the small villages, of leading personalities and also the whole village populations.[6] Only the large land-owners, living off rents, were considered as 'class enemies'; they had been expropriated already in 1947. Before this time, less than 10 per cent of the population owned 70 per cent to 80 per cent of the land and exploited the rest of the agricultural population in a brutal way (Hinton 1972/II: 391). As far as the ethnic-national minorities were concerned, the several constitutions enacted in Communist China between 1954 and 1982 established the formal recognition and equality of the nationalities, the right to regional autonomy and use of the native language, but not – as in the Soviet Union – the right to national self-determination. In fact, several accomplishments for the nationalities were attempted: the establishment of autonomous regions with various kinds of indirect rule; the decree of formal equality and the abolition of insulting terms for minorities (such as 'beast' or 'clay'); the enforcing of subregional economic development and the recognition of minority languages; the establishment of a nation-wide system of transportation and communication, of educational and health systems (Hsieh 1986). Yet, in practice these rights were limited and the minorities, particularly those living in remote areas, remained backward in many regards.

The extremely encompassing Chinese revolution, steered by the Communist Party, can be understood only at the background of the high ethnic-cultural homogeneity of China. In this way, the Communist functionaries stressed their closeness to the common people – in agreement with the principles of Mao Tse-tung – and showed this also in their behaviour (Fitzgerald 1956: 150). For Mao Tse-tung the concept of 'people' played a central role; it included also parts of the bourgeoisie (Schram 1972). The principal aim of the Communist revolution was the collective improvement of the life of the nation as a whole (Fitzgerald 1956: 153ff.). This reform doubtless led to a revolutionary change in the social structure and mindsets of the rural population; in the first period, it was also successful insofar as China could provide itself with food. But from 1958 on, when new economic shortcomings and an increasing domination of the party apparatus emerged, Mao proposed the movement 'Let's Blossom Hundred Flowers' in which everybody was invited to formulate grievances.[7] In its wake, an ambitious economic and developmental programme, the *Great Leap Forward*, was initiated; it led to the establishment of the agricultural communes (People's Communes) and of thousands of small, rather primitive production plants at the countryside. However, this strategy turned out to be an immense failure and it ended in a huge famine which produced the estimated deaths of 30 million people (Courtois 1998). This fact proves A. Sen's (2009) thesis that most big famines are man-made. Later on, in the mid-1960s, Mao tried anew to induce a turnaround with his 'Culture Revolution'; but this again led to chaos.

After Mao's death in 1976, an opening of the economy toward a special form of 'social market economy' was introduced which continues to today. Within its frame, private economic activities are permitted to a considerable degree[8] (Vogelsang 2013: 580–617). At the eastern coastline, special economic zones were established in which Western enterprises could operate and foreign trade increased strongly. In agriculture, where still the majority (about 700 millions) of the population is living, a transfer of use rights of land was installed in which families could loan their soil to others for a fee. The main problem of economy and the population in the countryside is that acreages per family are too small to enable an adequate subsistence.[9] In

---

6   A very vivid report of this time and events has been given by the American journalist William Hinton (1972).

7   See http://de.wikipedia.org/wiki/Hundert-Blumen-Bewegung (19.11.2011).

8   According to Rajnash Tiwary (Chinesische Wirtschaft und Wirtschaftspolitik, Universität Hamburg 2004), the proportion of the private economic sector was already 63.7 per cent in 2001; this seems implausible, however; it can be assumed that also the new 'collective enterprises' are subsumed under the label 'private' (see http://www.global-innovation.net/team/tiwari/PDF/China-Globalisierung.pdf; 2011). According to Herr (2000: 6) the proportion of private enterprises among all industrial enterprises is only marginally over 30 per cent.

9   200 million households cultivate about 1.4 million square kilometres, that is, 0.6 hectares per household. See Peter A. Fischer, 'Chinas Kommunisten wollen erneut die Landwirtschaft modernisieren', *Neue Zürcher Zeitung*, 11.10.2008.

the 1980s, income in the countryside decreased, not least because of the low prices for agricultural products (a clear difference to Japanese agricultural policy); rural poverty was very widespread (Ping 1996).

The leadership of China today pursues a strategy of transition from State Socialism to a market society which is fundamentally different from that in East Europe and Russia (Brainerd 2010; Myant/Drahokoupil 2010; Herr 2000). Reforms are implemented in a piecemeal manner, beginning in only a few areas or regions and testing their effects.[10] Furthermore, China does not practice the neo-liberal policy of unrestrictive liberation of market forces which has led to strong disparities and new inequalities in Russia (Haller 2009: 205ff.). Rather, the state keeps control of the main sectors of the economy, such as foreign trade, finance system and credit lending. Thus, we can say that this is a very centralistic and elitist way of developing a country. This way has turned out to be highly successful from the macro-economic point of view. Since the beginning of the 1980s, the Chinese economy has been growing with breathtaking speed; the extremely high growth rates (around 10 per cent) are also due to the import of foreign technological know-how which often disregards ownership rights (Mayer 2006: 43). The number of poor people has been reduced significantly. According to World Bank, the percentage of people living in absolute poverty has been reduced from 80 per cent in 1981 to only 8 per cent in 2001 (see also Yao 2000; Mayer 2006: 50ff.). This high growth rate is also perceived by the population at large. It seems that the Chinese are ready to accept income inequality, given the general prospects of improvement in standards of living. Table 8.1 (p. 223) shows that 88 per cent of the Chinese – much more than in any other of the 11 nations included in the table – think that poor people have a chance to escape from poverty; 8 per cent believe that people can get rich only at the expense of others.

Changes in the Distribution of Income as a Consequence of the Deliberate Creation of Two Classes of Citizens

How did economic inequality develop in China during this transition? The general trend is rather clear: as in all other countries undergoing a transformation from a State Socialist to a liberal market society. During the revolutionary period 1950–1970 economic inequality declined strongly, but since then, it has again increased significantly (Figure 7.1). Table 1.1 (pp. 5–6) has shown that China, with a Gini coefficient of around 35 to 40, today shares the position with other large countries like the USA and Russia. But economic inequality in China is significantly higher than in India, not to speak of Japan. Looking at the development of economic inequality since the 1960s and 1970s, it turns out that it has increased strongly. According to some authors, the increase of inequality was the strongest in the world since this time (Mayer 2006: 59; see also Ohtake et al. 2013).[11] Thus, we must speak of an explosion of economic inequality which was specific for China and a few other countries. As argued in Chapter 1, we cannot speak of a general worldwide increase of inequality in the course of economic development. Figure 7.1 shows inequality increased (Gini) from 24 to 38 between the 1960s and the first decade of the 21st century. According to other data (Goldman 2008: 2) the Gini increase was even stronger, from 22 in 1978 to 49.6 in 2007.

These trends are also reflected in public consciousness. A rather high proportion of the Chinese think that income inequality is too high and two-thirds see conflicts between rich and poor people (see Table 6.2, p. 168). Why did economic inequality rise so strongly in China? In fact, we can see a U-curve, the opposite of the prediction of Kuznets: from the 1950s to the 1970s, inequality decreased strongly, but afterwards it increased (similar data are reported in Mayer 2006: 9).[12] What were the reasons for this increase?

---

10   Sebastian Heilmann, 'Chinas Wirtschaftspolitik. Autoritäre Staatstätigkeit in einem lernenden autoritären System', *Bundeszentrale für politische Bildung*, Bonn (available online: http://www.bpb.de/internationales/asien/china/44279/chinas-wirtschaftspolitik?p=all).

11   Friedrich Ebert Stiftung, 'Digitale Bibliothek: China: Soziale Konfliktpotentiale' (http://www.fes.de/fulltext/stabsabteilung/00409004.htm; 30.1.2009). According to Zhijia Zhou ('Soziale Ungleichheiten in China'), the Gini coefficient in 1980 was only 23 (see http://www.socio.ethz.ch/education/fs08/ksc/notes/nb07_Ungleichheit.pdf; 30.1.2009). See also Qingbin Wang/Guanming Shi (2009), *Economic growth and income inequality in the transition to market economy: China's experience and policy implications*.

12   However, there are extreme differences in the Gini values reported for China. In the UNU WIDER Database (V2.0c May 2008), for the decade 1990–99 the lowest value is 17.0, the highest 45.2. For the years 2000 to 2004, the lowest is 25.3 and the highest 46.9. The main reason for these differences is that gross and net incomes, personal and household incomes are mixed (in the Solt data on which I rely mainly, these differences are corrected). Yet, we must be aware of these measurement problems.

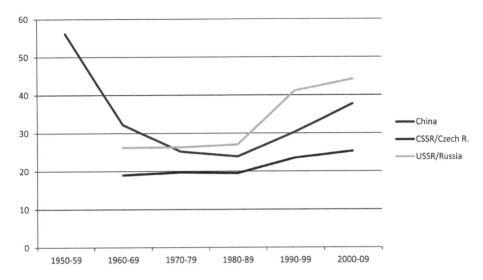

Figure 7.1   The development of economic inequality (Gini coefficients) in China, the USSR/Russia and Czechoslovakia/Czech Republic (ca 1950–2009)

I think we can mention two main aspects here. First, the economic reforms since 1978 did introduce only a partial market economy. The collective communes in the countryside and the work units in the urban economy have been divided in favour of more individual and family initiatives (Bian 2002). As a result, however, a new split emerged between rich and poor peasants, and rural state property and urban industrial assets were diverted into private hands of cadres (Wu 2002). This 'informal privatization' (Bian 2002) contributed to the emergence of a new, very rich bourgeois class. Although human capital became more important and opportunities to upward mobility increased, social networks (*guangxi*) remained (or became) a central factor for economic success (Bian 2002). I would propose the thesis in this regard, that both ethnic homogeneity of the dominant elites in the central and coastal regions of China as well as political centralism unchecked by democratic control mechanisms, have contributed significantly to this change. Although reliable data are lacking, it is quite sure that the new rich strata have been able to accumulate immense privileges.[13]

Also the second central factor contributing to the increase of income inequality was closely related to the ethnic-national structures of Chinese society. This factor was the high development of the different macro-regions of China. The vast rural areas in the West where also the ethnic minorities are settling (see also Hsieh 1986) have been systematically disadvantaged in comparison with the fertile, densely populated central and coastal areas (Mayer 2006). This was the consequence of a deliberate policy in two regards.

First, the eastern regions have been privileged by state politics in receiving more resources. The main factor in this policy was the establishment of *Special Economic Zones* (SEZs). These SEZs are open to foreign investment and trade, they are granted considerable legislative autonomy and foreign capital is attracted by tax incentives, joint ventures with Chinese firms and infrastructural support. Beginning in the 1980s with Shenzen, the island of Hainan and other coastal zones, many others with varying privileges have been added up to the 1990s. The zones have a dual role as 'windows' in developing the economy, advancing foreign trade and importing advanced technologies.[14] A correlated change was a massive power of urbanization which took

---

13   Just one press report about this fact: it was detected that the Chinese power elite and super-rich established – like their Western counterparts – bogus firms in well-known tax havens around the world. It was reported that 21,000 such firms from China and Hong Kong exist today (January 2014); since 2000, the sum of four billion Dollars may have been transferred to them. See 'Chinas Machtelite hortet Vermögen in Steueroasen', *Die Presse* (Vienna), 22.1.2014.

14   See http://en.wikipedia.org/wiki/Special_Economic_Zones_of_the_People%27s_Republic_of_China: 12% of all global sales of luxury handbags, shoes, jewellery and perfumes are made in China (Goldman 2008: 3).

place in the last three decades. In 1949, only 10 per cent of the Chinese were living in cities, in 1978 it was still less than 20 per cent, but in 2010 about 50 per cent; 129 Chinese cities had over 1 million residents (Ren 2013: xiii). These changes were correlated with the rise of huge corporations and a new generation of billionaires in China, often connected with the booming real estate sector.

The second aspect of the establishment of a systematic division within China was that the huge poor, mainly agricultural western inland areas have been hampered in their development in two ways. One mechanism contributing to this was the limitation of migration out from the countryside into the towns. The instrument for this policy was the *Hukou* system, established in 1951–55, which prescribed to every person to register him- or herself in a certain place; in this regard, rural and urban areas were distinguished (Yao 2000; Bian 2002; Cai et al. 2002; Lu and Wang 2005). In the countryside, the village is the registration unit, in the urban areas the household. To be registered in the latter, either an academic degree or the release from military service is necessary. The educational system, social services and infrastructure institutions of all sorts are significantly better in the towns and cities. The far-reaching functions of the *Hukou* system have been described by two experts in the following way:

> In comparison with the residence recording systems bearing the same name in Taiwan or Japan, the Chinese system serves far more important functions, broadly dividing citizens into two classes for a variety of purposes essential to the function of the state and seriously affecting the livelihood of hundreds of millions of ordinary people. Under this system, some 800 million rural residents are treated as inferior second-class citizens deprived of the right to settle in cities and to most of the basic welfare and government-provided services enjoyed by urban residents […] As is well established, the *hukou* system is a cornerstone of China's infamous rural-urban 'apartheid'. Creating a system of cities with invisible walls. It is a major source of injustice and inequality, perhaps the most crucial foundation of China's social and spatial stratification, and arguably contributes to the country's most prevalent human rights violations (Chan and Buckingham 2008: 582f.).

Also other authors compare the Hukou system with the Apartheid system of South Africa.[15]

A positive consequence of the *Hukou* system was that in Chinese cities no slums were developing as in other megacities of the global South. However, since the Hukou system has been attenuated in the course of the liberalization program and migration is tolerated to some degree, there are millions of people in the towns who are exploited due to their lack of social and legal protection. In recent times, the media announced the complete abolishment of the *Hukou* system; in fact, however, this did not happen, except some administrative changes in the authorities responsible for registration, such as devolution to local governments (Chan and Buckingham 2008). Thus, also a new urban underclass is emerging, consisting of unemployed, laid-off and low-paid workers. They include 20 to 35 million registered urban workers and their family members and a large proportion of poor migrant workers, so that all in all as many as 200 million Chinese lived in poverty in the first half of 2000 (Ren 2013: 149; Yao 2000).

How the Striving Toward Equality was Overruled by Ethnic-national Domination in Multi-national State Socialist Societies: the Soviet Union and Yugoslavia

It is more than evident that ethnic-national heterogeneity, subdivisions and conflicts have played a decisive role in the fate of Communism in East Europe. In this chapter, I will show this first by looking at the Russian Revolution at the end of the First World War and at the distribution of power in the State Socialist system; then I will investigate the transition to State Socialist societies in Central East Europe after the Second World War, the changes in the socio-economic equality in this period, and, finally at the collapse of the Communist system in the Soviet Union and Yugoslavia.

---

15   See references in http://en.wikipedia.org/wiki/User:Cerejota/chinese-apartheid, and http://en.wikipedia.org/wiki/Human_rights_in_the_People%27s_Republic_of_China (19.11.2011).

The Russian Revolution 1917

I would like to propose four arguments here: the first points to the fact that Russia's transition to Communism in 1917 was no 'proletarian revolution'; the second point is that the farmers were used as a strategic power base in the first phase of the revolution, but later on were deprived of their independence – a stark contrast to the situation in Japan; the third argument relates to an important split within the Russian elites, the *Intelligentsia* versus the political dominating classes; the fourth argument points to an important continuity in the social structures from the Tsarist empire to the Soviet Union.

The Russian Revolution of 1917 is often characterized as having been attained by a small elite of decided members of the Bolshevik Party with Lenin on top. This argument is based on the fact that Russia was still largely an agrarian society around the time of the First World War and industry was only in children's shoes. However, the revolution of February 1917 in fact was led and supported mainly by industrial workers in Petrograd which at this time constituted a large group of about 400,000 workers out of a population of 2.1 million inhabitants (Moore 1982: 471ff.). The revolution itself was to a large degree a spontaneous process of mass organization, in which councils of workers and soldiers, but also social-democratic and Communist parties (*Menscheviks*) played a decisive role. It was only during the later course of the revolution that Lenin and his Bolsheviks came to play the dominant role. The success of the revolution was possible to a large degree because state power had been weakening strongly during the war and because the provision of food for the population was breaking down. Thus, while it may be true that this was not a 'proletarian revolution' in the sense foreseen by Marx, with the proletariat as the largest and most deprived class in the whole society – in a country of 147 million inhabitants there were only 1.5 million industrial workers (Goerke et al. 1973: 301) – nevertheless it is true that the 1917 revolution had an important class base.

Second, the role of the peasants and farmers was decisive for the success of the revolution as well as for the later fate of Soviet Communism. The Soviet army was composed mainly of men from the countryside; after it became clear that the continuation of war would be only in the interest of big landowners and nobles, the readiness to continue to fight declined significantly among the soldiers. Then a crucial decision of Lenin was to promise to the farmers that the landowners would be expropriated and land distributed to the farm families. The later fate of peasants and farmers under State Socialism is well known. While the expropriation of big landowners was carried through, the further economic, social and political fate of the peasants was quite different from that which they had hoped for. Beginning in 1918, the prices and distribution of farm products were subject to strict state control (leading toward their freezing) with the effect that farmers as a whole became an exploited class. This policy was relaxed after peasant rebellions, but from the mid-1920s on, when the New Economic Policy (granting more freedom of markets and small enterprises) ended, the pressure on farmers increased massively, especially in connection with the collectivization of farms. Under Stalin, cruel measures were taken particularly against larger farmers (the Kulaks) and farmers in non-Russian provinces, such as the Ukraine. This policy, however, may have been one of the greatest mistakes of Soviet policy. Agrarian productivity never rose in way comparable to Western societies and terrible famines were the consequence in the decades of enforced collectivization.

Third, the important role of the *Intelligentsia* is beyond doubt in the Russian Revolution. It was a peculiarity of many East European societies that a special grouping of intellectuals emerged who found no place in state administration or in the churches and who felt compassion for the suppressed and exploited groups of the population (Konrad and Szelenyi 1978). It was from these strata that the leaders of the Russian oppositional anarchist, Socialist and Communist groups and parties were recruited at the beginning of the 20th century up to the revolution of 1917. Hypothesis in Chapter 2 has argued that a split within the upper classes in ethnic terms might be of crucial importance for the political development of a country. Although the Russian *Intelligentsia* was not different from the rest of the upper classes in ethnic terms,[16] this split was nevertheless of decisive importance.

---

16   It was a matter of fact that Jewish intellectuals were overrepresented among the Bolshevik leaders; however, it was only a polemic slogan of the National Socialists in Germany that the Russian Revolution was a Jewish-Bolshevik conspiracy. Between 1936 and 1940, Stalin during his *Great Purge* largely eliminated all Jews from senior positions in all spheres.

Fourth, I think that we can also see a considerable continuity of the social structures and political institutions from the Tsarist empire to the Soviet system. Here, we have to remember that already Peter the Great (1682–1721), who tried to reduce Russia's economic backwardness and military weakness compared to West Europe, had initiated reforms which created an efficient bureaucratic-military state and solidified Russia's position as a large imperial East European and Asian empire. His reforms are 'comparable to Stalin's revolution from above by subjugating all citizens through collectivization, industrialization and enforced consumer abdication' (Goerke et al. 1973: 175). Two measures were crucial for this purpose: the transformation of the nobility from an independent, powerful estate to a service class fully loyal to and employed by the state, with merit as the decisive criterion for privileges instead of birth; and the implementation of the 'second serfdom' through peonage (Leibeigenschaft) on the peasants which defined them legally as an 'inventory' of the landowners, bounded them on their soil, and saw them mainly as a reservoir for taxes and soldiers. This peonage coined the character of the Russian people in a similar way as it did the continuous threat of invasions from the East (Noetzel 1970). A peculiarity of Russian peasant and farm life was the importance of the village community (*Mir*): taxes had to be paid by the village as a whole; the village councils (*s'chods*) and leaders decided how much each family had to contribute (depending on its specific situation). Therefore, a high level of communality developed in the villages (Hosking 2000: 228ff.). Deeply ingrained characteristics of farm and village life expressed a protest attitude against exploitation by the landowners. It included a sense of equality, solidarity and communality, but also – especially among the young – the feeling of being trapped in a modest and dull life.

Pseudo-federalism: the Centralization of Power in the Hands of the Communist Party

Access to political power and influence was very unequally distributed in state-socialist societies. Despite an elaborated system of councils and elected representatives, factual power remained in the hands of a few: at the very top of the political system there was a powerful, small group of leaders in the *Politburo* and in the larger political and administrative apparatus, the members of the *Nomenklatura*, all those who were listed personally in a directory of able and loyal members of the Communist Party, and occupants or candidates for important administrative and steering positions in economy, society and politics (Voslensky 1980; Stölting 1990). In the German Democratic Republic (ca. 18 mio population), the closest circle of powerful functionaries included about 30 persons, the inner circle about 500 to 600, the total *Nomenklatura* between 250,000 and 340,000 persons,[17] which would be about 0.2 per cent or so of the adult population. For the Soviet Union, Smith (1979: 48) estimated that only a few million people were members of the *Nomenklatura*. While also some prominent scientists, artists, sportsmen and others could enjoy privileges of many sorts, only the members of the political elite had real access to power. Such a concentration of power both reflects and facilitates state control over human and material resources. This, in turn, gives politics great control over economics, and produces a system of economic stratification shaped to political goals as well as economic realities. Here, the East-West divergence is substantial indeed (Connor 1979: 307). This exceptional position of the political power elite had also a clear ethnic-national component. The Communist Party of the Soviet Union had during the whole time of its existence a preponderant Russian-Slavic nucleus. In 1922, 72 per cent of all party members were Russians in the narrow sense, while the proportion of these among the whole population was only 53 per cent (Kolarz 1976: 16). Ukrainians, 20 per cent of the whole population, were represented with only 6 per cent. At the 13th Party Congress which included the leading party members, only 1 per cent of the delegates were from Turko-Tataric peoples who at this time comprised 11 per cent of the population.

In contrast to the tiny, highly influential group of the *Nomenklatura* (Voslensky 1980), 'power is scarce to the point of nonexistence for most socialist citizens, and extremely abundant for the few' (Connor 1979: 337). A central crux of this situation is, so the same author states, that the monopoly power of the Socialist regime restricts the ability of groups to defend themselves and to press their interests. While, on the one side, the state may check claims to disproportionate shares of society's rewards by specific groups, the problem is that the state (or party) alone decides what is proportionate. In this way, also groups like the security

---

17   http://de.wikipedia.org/wiki/Nomenklatura (29.3.2010).

policy and other surveillance specialists are elevated (Connor 1979: 338; see also Parkin 1979; Lane 1982). The dominant power groups have also defined and controlled access to leading positions, the upper 'service classes' in State Socialist societies (Solga 1995: 212). The Communist parties at large, however, were not a fully 'unrepresentative elitist group'; non-manual workers were overrepresented, but also manual workers were represented to some degree (Lane 1982: 118; Kivinen 1994: 120). Finally, on the bottom of the political power hierarchy there was a considerable stratum of people who were excluded or even imprisoned for political reasons. Soviet detention camps had an estimated number of six million political prisoners in Stalin's days (Lenski 1978: 371f.); today, the number is much smaller and the treatment less severe, but the group of political prisoners did not disappear altogether.

Thus, overall egalitarianism has been delivered in State Socialism on the basis of a lack of group and individual freedom. There exists one further area, besides politics in the more narrow sense, where differences in power and lack of freedom and autonomy played a significant role in State Socialist societies. This area concerns the position of national and ethnic subgroups and the related regional inequalities. In the case of the Soviet Union, the importance of this aspect cannot be overestimated. In 1979, only 52 per cent of the population of the Soviet Union were Russians; this huge 'empire' included no less than 21 different national sub-groups with at least one million people, the greatest among them being the Ukrainians with about 40 million people (Stölting 1990). The conquest, settlement and development of the huge territories of Siberia can in fact be considered as a colonial enterprise. Walter Kolarz (1976) has investigated the Soviet 'Nationality Policy' (particularly as it was carried through by Stalin) and he shows many similarities between British colonization around the world and Russian expansion to the Pacific Ocean. About 3 million Russians moved toward the East (many of them only half-freely), and 500 cities were newly established. The political self-determination of these and all other peripheral Republics was only on paper; they had very few things to decide by themselves, over 80 per cent of state revenues were distributed by the central government in Moscow. Attempts by regional leaders to get more influence were denounced as 'local chauvinism' and Russian was imposed everywhere as the official language. Also David Lane (1982: 83ff.) confronts the attempts of the Soviet Union to create 'a supra-national multiethnic socialist community' with the facts. He concludes from the outset that 'it would be surprising if there were equality of treatment of ethnic groups in the USSR' because the Bolsheviks inherited a system of severe inequality between nationalities. While the USSR made some efforts to reduce the inequalities between these groups and the regions where they lived, it was clear, nevertheless, that the northwestern Russian territories were privileged in many regards, such as in investments in strategic industrial sectors, in the development of cities with better infrastructures.

In some cases, there occurred an open suppression of ethnic-national minorities. The most extreme form of it happened in the Ukraine. During the years 1932–33, following a law that stipulated that all produced food was state property, in the Ukraine a big famine broke out which lead to the deaths of an estimated 2.5–7 million people.[18] As a result of the neglect of peripheral regions and other nationalities, these regions and the smaller national groups had to be content with worse educational opportunities, lower incomes and weaker political representation and cultural autonomy (for instance, because Russian language became dominant in all regions), often even in their own provinces. Thus, Lane concludes, there was a certain domination of the others by the white Slavic, especially Russian national groups (Stölting 1990). The same was true in *Yugoslavia*: while the constitution of this country, consisting of six autonomous Republics, was an ideal federalism, in reality the Serbs were dominant over the other five large ethnic-national groups in politics and administration. When the northern Catholic and and economically more advanced Republics Slovenia and Croatia planned to introduce democratic reforms, a conflict emerged between them and the central Communist Party. It led to a brutal war, first between Slovenia and Croatia against the Serbian-dominated Yugoslav National Army (JNA), later on within Bosnia-Herzegovina between the militias of the Serbian, Croatian and Muslim ethnic-national groups. One must indeed say that the attacks of the JNA Slovenia and Croatia were an act of aggression since

---

18   The famine was caused by a resistance of Ukrainian farmers to follow the strict new guidelines and by general economic problems of the USSR at this time. But it is also without doubt that Stalin used the Ukrainian famine to reprimand this province which had always shown some resistance to its incorporation into the Russian Empire and the Soviet system. So, among other measures, a strict cordon was established around the Ukraine in order to make sure that nobody could escape and no foodstuffs could be imported (see Dolot 1985).

the Yugoslav Republics had a constitutional right to secede from the federal state. From this point of view, the war in Yugoslavia can well be compared to the American Civil War and many civil wars in Sub-Saharan Africa; there, however, the central power was able to boar down the secession movements. I will come back to this important issue in Chapter 13.

Ethnic-national heterogeneity is an important factor even in Russia today; still, only about 80 per cent of its population are ethnic Russians and there are no less than 20 million Muslims living in Russia. We can assume that ethnic differentiation is also correlated with the higher level of economic inequality of Russia, as shown in Table 1.1. The issue of national and ethnic independence and freedom has also played a central role in the fall of State Socialism as I will show below.

The Transition to State Socialism and Failed Revolts in Central East Europe, 1953–80

It is out of question that the transitions to State Socialist systems in the smaller Central East European countries after the Second World War were only possible because they were induced from outside, by the Soviet Union. Certainly, there were some notable differences between the countries. In Hungary and Poland, a rather large class of landowners was living side by side with a poor and humble peasantry; in the Czech lands, industry was more developed and this country had also experienced a true democratic phase in the interwar time; in Yugoslavia, a relatively independent and original form of Socialism was established which included significant elements of participation also at the level of enterprises and communes. In the first free elections after the war, in none of these countries the Communists got absolute majorities of votes (only in Czechoslovakia, the proportion was rather high). The establishment of one-party rule was possible only by forbidding the bourgeois, liberal, Christian and other parties, and by including the social-democratic parties by force into an alliance with the Communist parties. This forced abandonment of democratic political life had the consequence that in the most advanced countries of the Communist bloc, those of Central East Europe, successively revolts against Communist and Soviet rule broke out.

Figure 7.2 shows a very interesting finding in this regard, namely the connection between the number of political riots and demonstrations between 1948 and 1967, and the level of economic development of the different European countries at this time. It comes out that in West Europe, political unrest and riots were more frequent the lower the economic level of development of a country (they were highly frequent in Portugal, Italy and Greece, but rare in Switzerland, the Netherlands, Denmark and Sweden). In East Europe it was exactly the reverse. The largest number of riots could be observed in the Czech and the German Democratic Republic, certainly the highest developed countries; then came Hungary and Poland; at the left, lower part of the figure, we find Romania and Bulgaria, Yugoslavia and – at the very lowest position – Albania. Also in these riots, class forces played a significant role.

Let us look briefly at the historical significant cases of such riots, the popular revolts in Central East Europe between 1945 and 1980. We will see that political freedom was a central issue in all those riots, but again that the working classes played a significant role.

The first of these riots emerged already in the first postwar decade, in 1953 in the capital of the *German Democratic Republic*, East Berlin. In the early 1950s, the economic situation was catastrophic in the GDR; because of high military expenditures, obligations to pay high war reparations, a focus of investment in heavy industry, and collectivization of agriculture, the provision of the population with basic consumer goods and food became worse and worse. People certainly felt this strongly since from their own front door they could witness the much better development and conditions in West Germany; many emigrated there. On 30 June 1953, the Central Committee of the Communist Party SED decreed that work norms had to be raised without a rise of wages. This was the occasion for a spontaneous strike and demonstration of workers in East Berlin; immediately, tens of thousands of citizens joined their demonstration march. Since the event was communicated by radio, very quickly in other GDR cities similar marches were organized, involving over a million people altogether. The participants occupied party and public buildings, and opened political prisons. In the West, the far-reaching importance of the riot was not recognized for some time. However, the GDR leaders soon asked the Soviets for help and they entered East Berlin with heavy tanks; 6,000 people were arrested, seven executed. We can say that there were three main motives of this insurrection: economic decline and misery, political suppression and national heteronomy. Due to heavy suppression, no riots emerged later

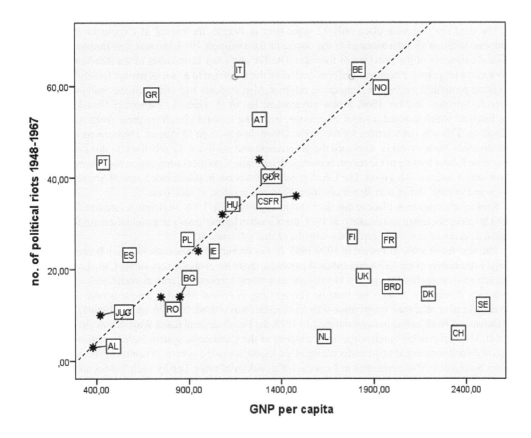

Figure 7.2   The relation between level of economic development and the frequency of political riots in West and East Europe in postwar time (1948–67)

Note: Pearson Correlation Coefficients for West Europe: r=-40; East Europe: r=.92. For abbreviations of countries see Table 4.A, p. 121.

Sources: Haller 1990; data from Taylor/Jodice (1983).

on in the GDR. However, the dissatisfaction of the people within the system expressed itself in a continuous stream of emigration, particularly of young, skilled people, to West Germany. This stream could only be stopped in 1961 when the infamous Berlin Wall was built between east and west Berlin.

Only three years later, in Hungary a similar upheaval broke out. Already during the mid-1950s, groups of students had discussed critically the practices of the Stalinist government of Prime Minister Matyas Rakosi and written a pamphlet asking for reforms. On 23 October 1956, students organized a peaceful demonstration asking for democratic changes. The military, after initial aggressive actions, however, defected to the students and hundreds of thousands of people joined the demonstration on the streets of Budapest. In contrast to the GDR, a new government under the leadership of Imre Nagy was formed which soon introduced reforms, declared an exit from the Warsaw Pact and the neutrality of the country. Here, however, the Soviets decided on their own to intervene; a large army occupied Hungary and violent fights broke out in the streets of Budapest lasting for a week. After the defeat of the rebellious Hungarians, hundreds of people were executed, including Prime Minister Nagy, and tens of thousands imprisoned; about 300,000 Hungarians escaped from Hungary, most of them toward Austria. In this case, it is evident that political freedom and national independence were the decisive factors for the upheaval.

The third uprising took place only 12 years later in Prague, the capital of Czechoslovakia. Here, the economic situation also deteriorated in the course of the 1960s; in 1960, the new constitution restricted the political autonomy of the province of Slovakia. Ota Sik and other economists of the Academy of Sciences elaborated a program for economic reform, including the transition to a 'social market society'. Intellectuals published pamphlets asking for democratic reforms. Also students had criticized the Stalinist government under A. Novotny. In May 1968, a new government led by A. Dubcek, the former Slovak party leader, was installed which enacted a series of reforms, including cultural pluralism, press freedom and political federalism. This was not tolerated by the Soviet Union, however; on 21 August 1968, troops of the Warsaw Pact invaded Czechoslovakia, displaced the government and put down the rebellion. In this case, we can see three main factors leading to the revolt: economic deterioration, political suppression and disempowerment of a province or national sub-group. The Czech population was not hostile-minded against Socialism as such: a survey in 1968 had shown that 89 per cent were for a preservation of socialism.[19]

Smaller uprisings took place at this time also in Yugoslavia. In 1968, in Belgrade, student demonstrations asked for more Socialism and equality; in 1971, the 'Croatian Spring' involved nationalist mass demonstrations against a perceived economic exploitation by the central government.

The next revolt arose in Poland in 1979/1980. In this country, the economic situation became particularly dismal in the course of the 1970s and 1980s. A particular factor here was the very strong Catholic Church which both served as an anchor for national identity and as a moral supporter of critical intellectuals challenging the ideological dominance of the Communists. The uprising in Poland was also unique insofar as the workers played a decisive role; their cooperation with intellectuals was crucial. In 1976, an intellectual Committee for the Defense of Workers had been established. In 1978, the Polish cardinal Karol Woytila was elected Pope John Paul II; his charisma, his unrelenting, open criticism of the Communist system State Socialism and repeated visits to Poland contributed to the undermining of the legitimacy of the system. In summer 1980, an independent Union, *Solidarnosc*, was established in the sequel of an industrial strike. Led by Lech Walesa, and continuously supported and advised by critical intellectuals, *Solidarnosc* was able to grow into a mass movement which State Socialist societies never had seen before. At the height of its influence around 1980, it had 9.5 million members. Its aims became more and more political, aspiring toward a general change of the system away from State Socialism. This was not tolerated by the Communist Party, and its leader W. Jaruzelski declared a state of war over the country, forbidding *Solidarnosc* and returning to the old, authoritarian system. However, over the course of the 1980s, *Solidarnosc* and other movements for reform became again more and more influential; in 1989, it was recognized officially and its representatives became heads of the state (T. Mazowiecki and L. Walesa). It can be said that this Polish fight for freedom in the end was successful because it had far-reaching consequences for the fall of State Socialism also in the Soviet Union and all over East Europe in 1989/91.

Changes in the Distribution of Income and Social Stratification in Communist East Europe

How did the distribution of incomes change in Communist East Europe? Connor (1979: 215ff.) investigated income distribution in the mid-1960s and found that Central European countries like Hungary, the Czech Republic, Poland and Yugoslavia showed similar patterns to Austria and Germany, while the Soviet Union was clearly more unequal. This is in fact also shown by Figure 7.1: there we can see that income inequality did not change very much in Czechoslovakia and the Czech Republic, respectively, from the 1950s till the first decade of the 21st century. It was and still is one of the lowest among all countries compared in Table 1.1. The situation and changes were very different in the Soviet Union. Here, income was levelled soon after the revolution in the 1920s; it became more unequal under Stalin, but again more equal after the Second World War; this trend is also recognized by Lane (1982: 54ff.). In State Socialism, 'the working class is given pride of place', as the creator and builder of a new society (Lane 1982: 35). However, although male skilled industrial workers earned good incomes, the line between blue- and white-collar work was not blurred and the hierarchy between them did not alter except that most of the low-earning non-manual workers were women (Connor 1979: 259); clear differences between blue- and white-collar strata were preserved in family incomes (Lane 1982: 54ff.). As to the incomes of the upper strata, an important fact is that the size of their incomes was grossly underestimated

---

19   See http://wikipedia.org/wiki/Prager_Frühling (30.3.2010).

because there were a high number and variety of non-monetary, direct benefits; these were largely hidden from the general population (Smith 1979: 50ff.). Already Lenin had introduced special food ratios for specialist workers and academics; under Stalin this system of hidden privileges was brought to perfection.

A significant achievement by state-socialist societies has certainly been attained in the realm of *education*. Russia was a backward country before the Communist revolution; only 21 per cent of the population could somehow read and write; in the countryside, only 12 per cent of people went to school for more than three years (Haavio-Mannila and Kauppinen 1994: 176). Soon after 1917, the Soviet Union made strong efforts to increase the level of education of the population, as did also the East European countries after becoming part of the Soviet system. Radical egalitarian policies were introduced, such as abolishment of school fees, provision of scholarships for children from lower classes, building of student dormitories, introduction of quotas for children of workers at higher schools, establishment of adult education facilities and the like. These measures had significant effects in that children of workers increased their proportions in higher education significantly. However, after the successful establishment of comprehensive schools everywhere, educational expansion slowed down, and access to higher educational institutions become again more closed in favour of students from well-educated backgrounds (Szelényi 1998: 13ff.; Solga 1995: 210f.). With the maturation of industrial society, three tendencies decreased the equalizing potential of higher education (Lane 1982: 114): a replenishment of the higher occupational strata from within these strata; a slowing-down of upward mobility; and an increase of downward mobility from non-manual to manual work. A detailed comparison of educational changes in Austria and Poland 1945–70 (Haller and Mach 1984) found significant differences; but they were mainly related to the different educational systems (a much higher weight of on-the-job vocational training in Austria than in Poland) and a stronger connection between educational degrees and occupational positions in Poland. Education in general expanded in both countries, as well as the relevance of educational degrees compared to social descent.

The opening up of chances for *intergenerational mobility* was also one of the central aims of State Socialist policy. In the 1970s, Lane (1982: 104) noted that the Polish intelligentsia had been recruited to high degrees from working classes; however, a tendency toward increasing internal recruitment was already observable. Among the elite groupings, a systemic difference between Capitalist and Socialist societies existed, since in the former members of political dominant and other privileged classes cannot inherit their position directly to their offspring. Szelényi (1998: 120) argued that the ability of the members of the *Nomenclatura* to retain their elite standing has been over-estimated. However, for the GDR Heike Solga (1995: 210) found an increasing self-recruitment of the privileged social classes. According to Szonja Szelényi (1998: 70), there is 'nothing to suggest that socialism has fundamentally altered exchanges between class categories'. Her conclusion – that there is rather a trendless fluctuation in patterns of mobility, but no trend toward more openness – has also been confirmed in the many studies by Rudolf Andorka and colleagues who could rely on long-time statistical series of data collected by the Hungarian statistical office. They found that 'the contours of interclass mobility remained essentially unchanged despite much egalitarian rhetoric and policy in the immediate post-transition period and despite the relaxation of such policy later' (Szelényi 1998: 93; for similar conclusions on other countries see Connor 1979: 162). Haller, Kolosi and Robert (1989) carried out a systematic comparison of patterns of occupational change and mobility in Austria, Hungary and Czechoslovakia, whereby for the last country two sub-samples were analysed, that for the Czech lands and for Slovakia because the first was more advanced in industrial terms (and on a similar level as Austria), while the latter was similar to Hungary. In this way, four hypotheses could be tested: that of an effect of the political system (in this case, the main difference should have been between Austria and the other three cases); an effect of industrial development (main difference Austria and Czech lands versus Slovakia and Hungary); an effect of market liberalism (in this case, Hungary with its 'Goulash Communism' should have been similar to Austria, and both different from the Czech and Slovak samples); and a country effect, positing a peculiar pattern in all four cases. Findings showed that the country effect was the strongest of all; the system effect was also significant but weak and the liberalism and industrialism theses had to be rejected.

What about patterns of *prestige-based social stratification*? D. Lane (1982: 67f.) quotes studies on the prestige of occupations which were carried out by several US authors (Inkeles, Treiman and others). They showed that the ranking of occupations was rather similar all over the world thus confirming the aforementioned results about minor differences in occupational and class structures. Societal prestige is also related to and reproduced by patterns of homogamy in marriage; here, high levels of homogamous marriages prevailed also in the state-socialist countries (Lane 1982: 97ff.). The same was reported for the GDR (Solga 1995: 207) and for Yugoslavia (Lazic 1987; see also Tomić-Koludrović and Petrić 2012). Connor (1979) makes an interesting comparison between the Soviet Union, state-socialist Central East Europe, West Europe and the United States; he argues that both the Soviet Union and the United States were characterized less by deferential behaviour than Central East and West Europe. He found it remarkable that in the state-socialist Central East European countries, traditional like forms of politesse, deference and use of academic titles in everyday life were frequent; in some regards, 'the East presents an older Europe than the West' (Connor 1979: 329). Smith (1979: 340ff.) concludes on the basis of his personal observations in Soviet Russia that as a consequence of the determination of power and authority from above, a much more strict hierarchical class consciousness had developed than in Western societies; the resulting rank order was clearly defined, not only in the political realm, but also in other areas and occupations, such as in science. Rank order insignia, awards and decorations of all sorts played a significant role in the Soviet Union. Also in this regard, a significant difference between the Soviet Union and the Central European state-socialist societies might have existed. In Yugoslavia, for instance, there was a general impression of the dissolution class and status differences (Tomić-Koludrović and Petrić 2012).

The Collapse of State Socialism and the Development thereafter in Russia and Central East Europe

It is not possible to tell the story of the transition from Communism and State Socialism toward Capitalism and democracy in Russia in detail here. I have discussed four theories of State Socialism in the first section and it seems that the first three of them are unable to explain the fall of this system. For orthodox Marxist theory, such a fall seems unbelievable since the Soviet Union was declared as the first society were the workers had the power; for totalitarianism, it was also highly improbable since a totalitarian government is in full control of state and society and would never be ready to give up power; convergence theory has also failed since we must clearly say that the former state-socialist societies have become Capitalist and democratic countries in the Western sense (although some of them have yet to cover some distance toward such a system). It seems clear, however, that the fourth group of explanations, the theories of class and ethnic-national stratification and conflict have to say a lot about this fall.

Generally, we can mention five factors which played a decisive role in the collapse of Soviet Communism. In at least three of them, class-related, ethnic-national cleavages were important.

1. Economic decline, associated with increasing problems of the provision of the population with basic necessities (shelter, food, clothes and so on) and with consumer goods which had already become a matter of course in Western societies (television sets, electric and electronic household equipment, private cars and so on). This decline was felt most acutely by the mass of the population which had no access to privileged provision with housing, food and consumer goods. The neoliberal market reforms and politics of Margaret Thatcher and Ronald Reagan which were implemented during the 1970s and 1980s in England and the United States have certainly made a deep impression on economic and political leaders in Russia (Lane 1996, 2011).
2. Claims for cultural and political freedom, although these claims were expressed mainly by small groups of intellectuals. Some of these, however, may have been quite influential because they had gained prominence also in the West (Sacharow, Solshenitsyn). During the revolutionary demonstrations supporting the change in Moscow, when B. Yeltsin defeated the counter-revolution by Conservative Party leaders, it became evident that also citizens at large were in support of democratic changes. In 1989, people throughout the Soviet block and beyond were 'really enthusiastic about the changes the Gorbachev has initiated' (Goldfarb 1989: 197). Later on, with the worsening of the economic situation and the increasing corruption of the political class, support declined strongly.
3. A continuous loss of military power and national prestige vis-à-vis the main opponent on the global scene, the United States; some authors argued that the instalment of missiles with atomic warheads in West Germany in the 1980s was decisive in this regard.

4. Problems with the multi-national character of the Union, and increasing requests for more economic and political autonomy from the side of the Republics of the Union. A consequence of the three aforementioned factors clearly was a loss of legitimacy and power of the central political authorities. In the case of Yugoslavia, this was the decisive factor for the continuous worsening of the socio-economic and political situation in the 1980s and the breakdown of the system and the dissolution of the state in the early 1990s.
5. The fifth element was class-related. It concerned an internal split within the political-bureaucratic class, whereby the politicl elites, the power-oriented and long-serving party members took a different stance than the reformers who were recruited more frequently from scientific-technological cadres and managerial positions in industry (Lane and Ross 1999; Mayer 2002). A prominent example was Boris Yeltsin, the first president of the Russian Federation, who dissolved the Soviet Communist Party and the Soviet Union itself; in his earlier career, he was chief engineer and manager in agricultural administration. Also in this regard, divisions and conflicts of interest between the Russians, dominating the centre, and the leaders of other Republics and sub-nations may have played a significant role.

It is not the place here to discuss in detail the development of economies and societies in Russia and Central East Europe since the downfall of the Communist systems. A short remark is necessary, however, concerning the fact that economic inequality has developed very differently in these two regions. An obvious expectation in this regard would have been an increase of inequality since Capitalism is also associated with a much higher level of economic differentiations than a state-socialist system and Western democracy is fully compatible with rather high levels of inequality. However, a significant increase can be observed only in Russia and China but not in the Central East European countries outside the Former Soviet Union (FSU; see Figure 7.1). In most of these countries, inequality remained at a very low level; only in Hungary and Poland, a slight increase (from a Gini of about 24 to one of 28 and 30) took place. These differences in regard to the development of economic inequality are closely related to general differentiations in development. This was much less positive in Russia and the FSU countries than in Central East Europe (CEE). In Russia, real GDP per capita and the Human Development Index fell sharply between 1992 and 1996; they have reached the 1990 levels only in 2005. Unemployment doubled, and life expectancy for men fell from 65 to 57 years; today, it is about 62 years – 16 years less than in Western Europe (see also Silverman and Yanovitch 1997). Russia and the other FSV states are at the bottom, worldwide, in regard to life happiness (Haller and Hadler 2006). In contrast to this deterioration, the CEE countries had a much more positive development in many socio-economic aspects; they are now comparable to some South European countries. Their overall economic performance was comparable to East Asia, and much more positive than in Latin America.

   The following reasons can be given for these divergent developments in Central East Europe and the FSV states (Hildebrandt 2002; Fabrizio 2009; Myant and Drahokoupil 2010; Brainerd 2010): (1) in the CEE countries, more comprehensive and systematic institutional economic reforms were enacted including privatization, price and trade liberalization, and macro-economic stabilization programs; they have certainly been assisted in this regard significantly by the EU. In Russia, the transition from Communism to Capitalism has been characterized as a 'devolution' instead of a revolution (Silverman and Yanovitch 1997: 128–38). A consequence of the shock therapy pursued by Yeltsin and his advisers (Gaidar), a misinterpretation of social order occurred, and the state lost the ability to control the transition process, leading to the rise of a 'Gangocracy', of a new business stratum which is highly educated but in its behaviour it is 'at the edge of the criminal world' (see also Stefes 2006). What is most significant is that there exists a high continuity between the late Soviet Nomenclatura and the new political leaders and businessmen; (2) the more positive economic development in CEE made it also possible to maintain the basic social services, to prevent minimum wages from falling to a very low level, and to confine poverty; (3) more political pluralism and possibilities for civic and democratic participation have exerted pressure on the elites to consider issues of distribution and social justice also during and after the transition; (4) last but not least we must mention here also the effect of ethnic-national and regional differentiation and inequality. While most of the relatively small CEE countries are rather homogeneous in ethnic terms, this is not the case for Russia which still is the largest world country in geographic terms with 17 million square miles, subdivided into 21 Republics and 68 partly autonomous territorial units. About 18 per cent of the total population of Russia are not ethnic Russians, for 14 per cent Russian is not the main language, and about 7 per cent are Muslims. Regional inequalities are closely related to ethnicity and nationality. GDP per capita varies extremely between the Western and Eastern Russian Republics and Oblasts (it is about 40,000 in Moscow and St Petersburg, and only between 5,000 and 7,000 in the Altai Republic, Chechnya and Ingushetia, all inhabited by non-Russians). These inequalities have increased significantly since the transition.

How do subjective perceptions of inequality and class structures in the post-Communist countries look today? Has the existence of half a century of State Socialism made an impact on people's views about equality and inequality? In the International Social Survey Programme (ISSP) in 2009 (Inequality III), the respondents were asked if they considered income inequality in their country as being too high or not. Table 6.3 (p. 169) gives an unequivocal answer in this regard: 50 per cent and more of people in the post-Communist countries agree very strongly with the statement 'Income differences in my country are too large'. A similar high consent – much higher than in most of the other 24 countries – exists in regard to an obligation of the government to reduce income differences. Among Western societies, only the French and the Portuguese are also highly critical about income inequality. If we compare Germany and Austria with their neighbour countries Czech Republic, Hungary and Slovakia, a large difference comes out: objective inequality is somewhat higher in the former two countries, but fewer of their citizens consider it as too high compared to the latter. Table 8.1 (p. 223) shows that particular people in Russia are very pessimistic and critical: they see little chance to escape from poverty; the government does too little in their view; and a very low proportion believe that democracy is the best political system. In the ISSP-survey 2009, the respondents were also confronted with five graphic models of how a society could be structured and asked what their own society looked like. Two of these models are most of interest here: one presented a society with a large base and a narrow middle and upper stratum, the other as a diamond with a large middle class, and narrow lower and upper strata. We can say that the first is a typical elite-mass structure, the second a 'middle-class society'; the latter is considered since Aristotle as being the ideal social structure. Table 6.2 (p. 168) presents the findings on how the respondents in five post-Communist societies, compared with Western countries, perceived their society in terms of these structures. Again, large differences appear: in all advanced Western societies, only between 5 per cent and 17 per cent think that their society looks like an elite-mass structure (with the exception of Portugal), and between one-quarter and one-third think that it is predominantly a middle-class society (here, Portugal and France are exceptions). In the post-Communist countries, however, the first picture has been selected most frequently, by 31 per cent to 64 per cent of the respondents, and the second (the diamond model representing a middle class society), by only 4 per cent to 16 per cent.

The very critical view of the social structure and inequality in the post-Communist countries is confirmed by a further question which asked if the government should reduce income differences. This statement is supported strongly by about 20 per cent to 30 per cent in Western societies (in West Germany and in the USA only by about 10 per cent), but by 40 per cent to 60 % in the post-Communist countries.

Concluding Remarks

In this chapter, four very different societies and groups of societies were investigated: China, the Soviet Union and Russia, and the smaller Central East European former state-socialist societies. They shared the same fate insofar as they all had a long period of Communist rule in the 20th century. In China, it still exists, although in a considerably different form, as a hybrid system combining political centralism with a partly liberalized economy. The case of China looks paradoxical at first sight and seems to contradict the central thesis of this work: in spite of its considerable ethnic homogeneity, today it is a country characterized by a rather high level of economic inequality. It was only from the 1960s till the end of the 20th century that inequality was reduced; before that time inequality was rather high, and afterwards, it increased again. The explanation given for the high level of inequality in historical China was that this was a society characterized by a deep split between a very poor, mainly rural population and a small stratum of high officers working in service of the empire in the regional and national capital cities; this prescinded elite was well-educated and very distinct from the mass of the people in their style of life. The Communist system can be seen as a continuation of this system insofar as a small elite continues to dominate political life. However, some significant changes took place. First, the highest and most privileged strata of society today include more and more persons who became super-rich due to their entrepreneurial activities and huge private businesses. Also in the structure of the population at large, significant changes took place. By selective furthering of different regions and economic sectors of the country and by imposing strict limitations on free migration on the rural population through the *Hukou* system, the Communist regime contributed to a freezing of inherited inequalities under Deng Xiaoping's rule (1978–1992) elements of a market society were introduced which led to high levels of economic growth and a significant reduction of poverty. But the preferential treatment of the leading economic areas and centres in the East and near the East China Sea continues until today. This is certainly one of the factors which contributed toward the increase in economic inequality.

The situation was very different in Russia, in the smaller East European countries and in Yugoslavia. In Russia and the USSR, throughout history, from the taking over of power by the Bolsheviks till the breakdown of the system in the 1990s, issues of ethnic-national cleavages have been of decisive importance. National unity was preserved or attained only through the use of external and internal military violence. In the smaller, more developed nations in Central East Europe all the time signs of unrest against domination by the Soviet Union were evident. In Yugoslavia, the persisting ethnic-national conflict were closely connected with an accelerating economic decline (indicated, toward the end, by hyper-inflation); both of them led to increasing political and national unrest, and – in the end – to internal war and the collapse of state unity. Historical Russia has certainly been a rather unequal society; State Socialism had reduced inequality significantly, after the transition to a market society inequality again increased strongly. In the smaller, ethnic homogeneous countries of Central East Europe, economic inequality has always been modest and State Socialism may have made more of a difference in people's thinking about equality and inequality than in factual structures (except from the fundamental changes in ownership of land and enterprises). Thus, in all these cases, it is obvious that inequality has been shaped strongly by ethnic-national ideas and forces. In the end, they clearly turned out as stronger than the Marxist-Leninist idea of classless and egalitarian 'a-national' societies.

References

Bahro, Rudolf (1977), *Die Alternative. Zur Kritik des real existierenden Sozialismus*, Köln: Europäische Verlagsanstalt

Baradat, Leon P. (2012), *Political Ideologies. Their Origins and Impact*, Glenview, IL: Pearson Education

Bell, Daniel (1973), *The Coming of Post-Industrial Society. A Venture in Forecasting*, New York: Basic Books

Bendix, Reinhard (1977), *Max Weber. An Intellectual Portrait*, Stanford, CA: University of California Press

Beyme, Klaus von (1994), *Systemwechsel in Osteuropa*, Frankfurt: Suhrkamp

Beyme, Klaus von (2002), *Politische Theorien im Zeitalter der Ideologien: 1789–1945*, Wiesbaden: Westdeutscher Verlag

Bian, Yanjie (2002), 'Chinese social stratification and social mobility', *Annual Review of Sociology* 28: 91–116

Bodmer, Frederick (1989), *Die Sprachen der Welt*, Herrsching: M. Pawlak (English ed: *The Loom of Language*, New York 1944)

Brainerd, Elizabeth (2010), *Human development in Eastern Europe and the CIS since 1990*, United Nations Development Programme, Human Development Report No. 2010/16

Burnham, James (1972 [1941]), *The Managerial Revolution. What is happening in the world?* Westport, CT: Greenwood Press

Cai, Fang, Dewen Wang & Yang Du (2002), 'Regional disparity and economic growth in China. The impact of labor market distortions', *China Economic Review* 13: 197–212

Chan, Kam Wing and Will Buckingham (2008), 'Is China abolishing the Hukou system?' *The China Quarterly*, Sept. 2008, pp. 582–606

Connor, Walter (1979), *Socialism, Politics, and Equality. Hierarchy and Change in Eastern Europe and the USSR*, New York: Columbia University Press

Courtois, Stéphane et al. (1998), *Das Schwarzbuch des Kommunismus. Unterdrückung, Verbrechen und Terror*, München: Piper (*Le livre noir du communisme*, Paris 1997)

Deutsch, Karl W. (1966), *Nationalism and Social Communication. An Inquiry into the Foundations of Nationality*, Cambridge, MA/London: The MIT Press

Djilas, Milovan (1957), *The New Class. An Analysis of the Communist System*, New York: Praeger

Dolot, Miron (1985), *Execution by Hunger: The Hidden Holocaust*, New York: W.W. Norton

Fabrizio, Stefania et al. (2009), The second transition: Eastern Europe in perspective, Economic Papers 366, European Commission, Economic and Financial Affairs

Fetscher, Iring, ed. (1973), *Der Marxismus. Seine Geschichte in Dokumenten*, München: R. Piper

Fitzgerald, C.P. (1956), *Revolution in China*, Frankfurt: Europäische Verlagsanstalt

Goehrke, Carsten et al. (1973), Rußland, in: *Fischer Weltgeschichte*, Vol. 31, Frankfurt:Taschenbuch Verlag

Goldfarb, Jeffrey C. (1989), *Beyond Glasnost. The Post-Totalitarian Mind*, Chicago/London: The University of Chicago Press

Haavio-Mannila, Elina and Kaisa Kauppinen (1994), 'Changes in the status of women in Russia and Estonia', in Timo Diirainen, ed., *Change and Continuity in Eastern Europe*, Aldershot: Dartmouth, pp. 173–203

Haller, Max (1990), 'The challenge for comparative sociology in the transformation of Europe', *International Sociology* 5: 183–204

Haller, Max (2009), 'Language and identity in the age of globalization', in: Mohamed Cherkaoui and Peter Hamilton, eds, *Raymond Boudon – a Life in Sociology*, Vol. I, Oxford: The Bardwell Press, pp. 183–96

Haller, Max and Bogdan Mach (1984), 'Strukturwandel und Mobilität in einer kapitalistischen und sozialistischen Gesellschaft', in Manfred Nießen et al., eds, *International vergleichende Sozialforschung. Sozialstruktur und öffentliche Institutionen in Ost- und Westeuropa*, Campus Verlag, Frankfurt/New York; Campus, pp. 63–149

Haller, Max, Tamas Kolosi and Peter Robert (1989), 'Soziale Mobilität in Österreich, Ungarn und der Tschechoslowakei', *Journal für Sozialforschung* 30: 33–72

Haller, Max and Markus Hadler (2006), 'How Social Relations and Structures can Produce Life Satisfaction and Happiness. An International Comparative Analysis', *Social Indicators Research* 75: 161–216

Halliday, Jon and Jung Chang (2005), *Mao. Das Leben eines Mannes, das Schicksal eines Volkes*, München: K. Blessing Verlag

Heinsohn, Gunnar (1998), *Lexikon der Völkermorde*, Reinbek: Rowohlt

Herr, Hansjörg (2000), 'Der gradualistische Reformprozess in China im Vergleich zu anderen Transformationsländern', *Prokla* 30: 240–265

Hildebrandt, Antje (2002), Central and East Europe in Transition. Economic and Institutional Aspects, Dissertation, Humboldt University Berlin

Hinton, William (1972), *Fanshen. Dokumentation über die Revolution in einem chinesischen Dorf*, 2 vol.s, Frankfurt: Suhrkamp (*Fanshen*, Harmondsworth 1972)

Hosking, Geoffrey (2000), Russland. *Nation und Imperium 1552–1917*, Berlin: Siedler (*Russian People and Empire 1552–1917*, London 1997)

Hsieh, Jiann (1986), 'China's Nationalities Policy: Its development and problems', *Anthropos* 81: 1–20

Kivinen, Markku (1994), 'Class relations in Russia', in Timo Pirirainen, ed., *Change and Continuity in Eastern Europe*, Darthmouth: Aldershot, pp. 114–47

Kolarz, Walter (1976), *Die Nationalitätenpolitik der Sowjetunion*, Frankfurt: EVA

Kolsto, Pal (2001), 'Territorial autonomy as a minority rights regime in post-Communist societies', in Will Kymlicka and Magda Opalski, eds, *Can Liberal Pluralism be Exported? Western Political Theory and Ethnic Relations in Eastern Europe*, Oxford: Oxford University Press, pp. 200–219

Konrad, György and Ivan Szelenyi (1978), *Die Intelligenz auf dem Weg zur Klassenmacht*, Frankfurt: Suhrkamp (*The Intellectuals on the Road to Class Power*, 1979)

Lane, David and Cameron Ross (1999), *The Transition from Communism to Capitalism. Ruling Elites from Gorbachev to Yeltsin*, New York: St Martin's Press

Lane, David S. (1976), *The Socialist Industrial State. Towards a Political Sociology of State Socialism*, Boulder, CO: Westview Press

Lane, David S. (1982), *The End of Inequality? Class, Status and Power under State Socialism*, London: G. Allen & Unwin

Lane, David S. (1996), *The Rise and Fall of State Socialism: Industrial Society and the Socialist State*, Cambridge: Polity Press

Lane, David S. (2011), *Elites and Classes in the Transformation of State Socialism*, New Brunswick/London: Transaction Publishers

Lazic, Mladen (1987), *U susret zatvorenom društvu? Klasna reprodukcija u socijalizmu*, Zagreb: Naprijed

Lenski, Gerhard (1978), 'Marxist experiments in destratification. An appraisal', *Social Forces* 57: 364–383

Lu, M. and E. Wang (2005), 'Institution and inequality: The Hukou system in China', *Journal of Comparative Economics* 33: 133–57

Ludwig, Klemens (2009), *Vielvölkerstaat China. Die nationalen Minderheiten im Reich der Mitte*, München: Beck

Mayer, Philipp (2006), The dual economy of the PR China: Causes and extent, Diploma thesis, Karl Franzens-University Graz

Mayer, Tom (2002), 'The collapse of Soviet communism: A class dynamics interpretation', *Social Forces* 80: 759–811

Moore, Barrington (1982), *Ungerechtigkeit. Die sozialen Ursprünge von Unterordnung und Widerstand*, Frankfurt: Suhrkamp (*Injustice*, White Plains, 1978)

Myant, Martin and Jan Drahokoupil (2010), *Transition Economies: Political Economy in Russia, Eastern Europe and Central Asia*, Hoboken, NJ: Wiley

Ohtake, Fumio et al. (2013), Growing inequalities and their impacts in Japan, Gini Growing Inequalities Project, Impacts (https://www.google.at/?gws_vol=ssl#9=ohtake+gini+growing)

Parkin, Frank (1979), *Marxism and Class Theory: A Bourgeois Critique*, London: Tavistock

Rejai, Mostafa (1995), *Political Ideologies. A Comparative Approach*, Armonk, NY etc.: Sharpe

Schram, Stuart R. (1972), *Das politische Denken Mao Tse-Tungs. Das Mao-System*, München: Deutscher Taschenbuch Verlag

Schumpeter, Joseph (1946), *Kapitalismus, Sozialismus und Demokratie*, Bern: Verlag A. Francke

Sen, Amartya K. (2009), *Ökonomische Ungleichheit*, Marburg: Metropolis (English ed., Oxford 1973)

Sik, Ota (1976), *Das kommunistische Machtsystem*, Hamburg: Hoffmann & Campe

Silverman, Bertram and Murray Yanovitch (1997), *New Rich, New Poor, New Russia. Winners and Losers on the Russian Road to Capitalism*, Armonk, NY/London: Sharpe

Smith, Hendrick (1979), *Die Russen*, München/Zürich: Droemer Knaur (*The Russians*, London 1976)

Solga, Heike (1995), *Auf dem Weg in die klassenlose Gesellschaft?* Berlin: Akademie Verlag

Stefes, Christoph H. (2006), *Understanding Post-Soviet Transitions. Corruption, Collusion and Clientelism*, Houndmills: Palgrave-Macmillan

Stölting, Erhard (1990), *Eine Weltmacht zerbricht. Nationalitäten und Religionen in der UdSSR*, Frankfurt: Eichborn

Szelényi, Szonja (1998), *Equality by Design. The Grand Experiment in Destratification in Socialist Hungary*, Stanford, CA: Stanford University Press

Taylor, C. and D. A. Jodice, eds. (1983), *World Handbook of Political and Social Indicators*, Vol. 2, New Haven/London: Yale University Press

Therborn, Göran (1995), *European Modernity and Beyond, The Trajectory of European Societies 1945–2000*, London etc.: Sage

Tomić-Koludrović, Inga and Mirko Petrić (2012), The dissolution of class differences: The Socialist roots of the postsocialist anomia, Conference 'Bringing class back in: The dynamics of social change in (post) Yugoslavia', Centre of Southeast European Studies, University of Graz

Vogelsang, Kai (2013), *Geschichte Chinas*, Stuttgart: Reclam

Voslensky, Michail (1980), *Nomenklatura*, Wien/Innsbruck: F. Molden

Weber, Max (1991 [1915–20]), *Die Wirtschaftsethik der Weltreligionen. Konfuzianismus und Taoismus*, Tübingen: Mohr

Wu, Xiaogang (2002), 'Work units and income inequality: The effect of market transition in urban China', *Social Forces* 1069–99

Yao, Shujie (2000), 'Economic development and poverty reduction in China over 20 years of reform', *Economic Development and Cultural Change* 48: 447–74

Chapter 8
The Ethnic Hierarchy.
India's Caste System in Comparative Perspective

Introduction

From the viewpoint of the central problem of this work, India represents an extremely important and challenging case. First, with its 1.2 billion inhabitants (Census of 2011), it is one of the two most populous countries on earth; it is called, rightly, a sub-continent.[1] What is particularly relevant from the social-scientific and political perspective, is that in the early 2000s, at least about one-quarter of all Indians (about 300 million people) were poor by national standards, and 41 per cent by international standards (450 million), having less than 1.25 Dollars a day at their disposal.[2] With a mean life expectancy of 65.8 years, 4.4 mean years of schooling and an HDI of 0.55, India's position is somewhat better than that of Sub-Saharan Africa, but clearly below that of China, not to speak of the developing countries in East Asia and Latin America (see Table 6.1) Second, what is particularly relevant from the central question of this book, is that there is no other country in the world which is characterized by a similar high degree of ethnic heterogeneity. Twenty-one languages are recognized by the constitution; in addition, English and more than 100 different languages (not only dialects) are spoken, many of them written in a particular script. There exists a multitude of ethnic groups, including over 600 officially recognized 'scheduled tribes' with, collectively, 83 million members (Rath 2006: 16). Four important religions have developed in India (Jainism, Sikhism, Hinduism and Buddhism), but this nation includes also 145 million Muslims (about 13 per cent) and members of several other religious groups (for example, Christians). Third, in spite of its immense ethnic diversity and its huge problems of poverty, India was able to preserve a relatively stable and well-functioning democratic system since it gained political independence in 1947. Fourth, historically, Indian society was distinct from all other societies of the world due to its unique stratification system of the castes. With the implementation of the Constitution in 1950 this system and its customs and practices have been abolished legally, but it still exerts a significant influence on society and politics. I don't think that it makes sense to speak of a caste system in other parts of the world, although it is striking how similar the forms of social exclusion and discrimination were concerning the Black population in the US-South, the small ethnic minorities in Japan or some ethnic groups in the central African states of Burundi and Rwanda. Mainly because of its caste system India has sometimes been denoted as the most strongly stratified society on earth (Gupta 1991: 1). Fourth, in spite of its huge size (3.2 million square kilometres), its geographic and cultural diversity and its political partition into 25 states, distinguished from each other separately in many regards,[3] India's unity was never sincerely threatened by movements of secession.[4] Fifth and finally: in spite of its huge size and immense ethnic-cultural diversity, economic inequality in India is relatively modest. With a Gini coefficient of about 32–3, it is comparable to that of the relatively egalitarian West and East European societies (see Table 1.1).[5] The astonishing low level of

---

1 For overviews see http://de.wikipedia.org/wiki/India; Schmitt 1982; Farndon 2008.

2 World Development Report 2011, p. 346ff.

3 A main difference between the states is language, although many states are also multilingual. A somewhat more pervasive socio-cultural difference exists between the four southern states (Kerala, Karnataka, Andra Pradesh and Tamil Nadu), whose languages are Dravidian, not Indo-European as in the rest of the country.

4 One such attempt was made by a Dravidian movement in South India (Rothermund 1995: 396).

5 It is probable, however, that these figures underestimate economic inequality in India somewhat. This might be so for two reasons: first, because data collection is much more difficult and less reliable in such a huge and poor country; usually, the higher incomes are underestimated (Milanovic 2007: 38). Second, and particularly in rural areas, significant aspects of wealth and inequality (for instance, personal services, household production) are not covered in monetary terms

economic inequality contrasts particularly with the significantly higher level in China – a country which is much more homogeneous in ethnic terms which still has a Communist system – two facts which would one lead to expect a lower inequality.

The comparative analysis of this unique system is a very important task, as noted rightly by one of its outstanding scholars, Louis Dumont (1980 [1966]; see also Sharma 1999: 93; Verba et.al 1971). It is not only in order to understand Indian society, but it is also an important task of general and comparative sociology. By comparing it with other systems of social stratification, I will try to do exactly that in this chapter. I think that the denotation of the caste system as a variant of ethnic stratification provides a very concise description. As a matter of course, I can give only a very succinct outline of the Indian (caste) society in this chapter. This is no problem as far as traditional India is concerned; with the works of Weber (1988) and Dumont (1966) I can rely on two excellent studies (a few studies exist also about recent changes of the caste system). The intent of this chapter is threefold: first, to outline the central characteristics of the caste system and to compare it with other types of ethno-class stratification; second, to look at the factors which contribute to the surprisingly low level of economic inequality of India; and third, to discuss the relation between the caste system and socio-economic development. Here, a central question is if globalization and the recent industrial take-off of India will lead to a similar increase of inequality as it was shown for China in the preceding chapter.

The Caste System

The first task here is to elaborate the essential characteristics of the caste system. Then I will argue that it was mainly this system which is responsible for the surprising low level of economic inequality in India.

Defining Elements of the Caste System

It seems that we can grasp the essential characteristics of the caste system in four aspects: the existence of a comprehensive societal rank order and its religious-ritualistic foundation; the occupational specialization of the castes; the transmission of caste status through families; and the function of caste membership to provide security and protection.

Let us first bring to mind what castes are (or have been).[6] Traditionally, four castes (*varnas*) are distinguished: the *Brahmins* (the intellectual elite, scholars, teachers, priests, that is, the interpreters of the texts and conductor of religious ceremonies), the *Kshatriyas* (the political and military rulers, kings, princes, warriors, administrators), the *Vaishyas* (tradespeople, land owners and farmers, artisans) and the *Shudras* (workers, craftsmen, tenants, day labourers and service providers).[7] Only the first three are considered as *dvija*, thus allowed to participate in Vedic rituals. Outside of the caste system, there were the *Harijans* (denoted also as *Dalits* or *Untouchables*) who exercised works and activities which were considered as being unclean. They had to avoid, therefore, being within touching distance (or even in the sight) of the caste members, in particular the Brahmins. Also foreigners were in principle considered as casteless. The castes are usually described as social strata ordered in a vertical hierarchy; a person belonged to them from his or her birth on. In reality, however, the caste system is much more complex than this simple classification suggests. While there exists no single, generally recognized definition of castes, there exists unanimity concerning the five aforementioned characteristics of the system as a whole. Let us have a closer look at them.

(1) In formal terms, it was decisive that the caste society as a whole constituted a relatively clearly structured rank order; this has been stressed particularly by Louis Dumont (1980: 65ff.; see also Böck and Rao 1995: 111) The aforementioned, four-caste structure (the Varnas) alone, however, is completely unable

---

(Myrdal 1980: 109). However, this aspect could also lead to an overestimation of inequality as measured in market incomes by the Gini coefficient.

6   See, among many others, the works of Srinivas 1962; Dumont 1966; Bellwinkel 1980; Schmitt 1982; Davis 1983; Weber 1988 [1921]; Gupta 1991; Sharma 1999; Rath 2006; Schlensog 2006: 63–5.

7   See Cox 1959; Dumont 1980; Böck and Rao 1995; Weber 1996. See: http://en.wikipedia.org/wiki/Caste_system_in_India and http://en.wikipedia.org/wiki/Varna_%28Hinduism%29

to capture the reality. For social life, the many, differentiated sub-castes, designated as *Jatis*, were much more important; it is only these which can be seen as birth groups.[8] The hierarchical, vertical order of castes (which was based on the Brahmin classical texts) and the horizontally, functional ordered structure of the Jatis constitute two different principles (Sharma 1999: 3ff.). They combine the principles of hierarchy and of differentiation (Gupta 1991: 10,111ff.). The latter aspect is frequently overlooked. The constitution of the Jatis is based on the principle of endogamy and commensality, that is, the community of cohabitation and meals. It contains also an element of a racial division: the highest caste of the Brahmins usually is also characterized by a lighter, the lowest group of the Untouchables by a darker skin colour (Weber 1988a: 123–5; Beteille 1991). This bio-social difference, however, is only secondary; it is superimposed strongly by socially determined, more 'cultivated' forms of appearance and behaviour of the higher castes and by caste-specific, ritualized social practices, particularly at common meals and family celebrations. The number of sub-castes could vary significantly by regions, and there could be different bases for their differentiation. Most often it was occupation, but it could also be territory; sometimes a sub-caste coincided with the inhabitants of a whole village. Max Weber (1988a: 6) reports about the attempt in the Indian census of 1911 to capture the number and size of the different castes statistically; in this endeavour, between 2,000 and 3,000 castes were identified (see also Schlensong 2006: 64). This census was criticized sharply by many contemporaries, however. In the census of 1901, significant differences between North and South India were found concerning who is clean or unclean (Dumont 1980:79–80). The caste structure was clearly defined and known to all people only within a village or region; in different villages and regions, the same occupational groups who in another place occupied a certain position, could be placed in different castes. Therefore, the overall society caste structure was not so clear. From this point of view, one could designate the caste system as a segmented social structure (Beteille 1991: 156). Gupta (2003: 516) considers the caste structure as a closed system because each caste or sub-caste tried vigorously to keep up their specific characteristics and customs, distinct from other castes. Contrary to this system, in the West an open system of stratification exists because everybody agrees about the main principles of stratification (for example, education, occupational achievement and so on) which basically are accessible to everyone and, therefore, allow upward social mobility. The decisive difference is that in a stratification system the principle of hierarchy is important, but in a caste system it is not only more important but also supplemented by the principle of difference (Gupta 2003). From this point of view, the caste system differs also from the medieval European estate system (*Ständesystem*) where the estates included people of many different occupations and were open to individual ascent. This difference, however, has often been overstated; research has shown that also in India a considerable amount of social mobility both in collective and individual forms was possible (Srinivas 1962; Silverberg 1969).

(2) The caste order as a whole was justified in religious terms. This constitutes a significant difference to the legally and politically defined feudal estate system in Europe while, in other terms, the two principles showed some striking similarities. Strictly speaking the caste system was based in a religious-ritualistic way since Hinduism, his primary pillar, was no church religion in the Western sense but a general world-view and system of belief whose intent was to steer human behaviour (Weber 1988a: 6). The decisive religious element of the caste system was the deeply internalized distinction between the clean and the unclean (Dumont 1980: 46–54). Only the Brahmins were considered as fully clean while the *Dalits* were considered as being fully unclean. Therefore, the members of the lowest castes and the Untouchables could not serve the Brahmins and had to carry out all unclean jobs and activities, those which were connected with waste, excreta and the like; the members of the higher castes had to avoid contact with them in order not to infect themselves. The status of the highest castes was based, not the least, on the adherence to strict rituals and the avoidance of certain habits and practices, including the consumption of meat and alcohol (Dumont 1980: 130–151). From this point of view, there existed a high degree of consensus about the societal stratification order (Shibutani and Kwan 1965: 253ff.).

(3) The caste order is closely connected with the occupational division of labour. As mentioned before, certain castes and sub-castes were obliged to or forbidden to carry out certain occupational activities; these activities could be defined differently in different regions, however. An exception in a certain regard were the two highest castes and the Outcastes. The first had everywhere the privilege of carrying out the religious-

---

8   In the following, I continue to use the general term 'caste', having in mind, however, more the *Jatis*.

ritualistic and political-military functions, respectively; the latter were constrained to perform the unclean activities. A basic distinction was between the castes who owned land and those who did not; the first were the dominant castes (Dumont 1980: 106). The connection between the castes and occupations was, in one sense, much closer, in another, less close than in the medieval occupational guilds in Europe. The European guilds were mainly economically based, could be selected more or less freely by young people and tried to monopolize work and income chances for a whole occupation; the castes did not monopolize a whole occupation and a caste could also change and overtake another occupation if they were able to continue with the adherence to their ritual obligations (Weber 1988a: 37).[9] J.P. Mencher (1991: 93ff.) argues that also the aspect of domination played a significant role in the system of caste stratification: 'It is quite clear that it was the superior economic and political power of the upper castes that kept the lower ones suppressed'. This thesis is supported by the fact that in densely populated regions with intensive agricultural cultivation, the proportion of Untouchables was higher than in arid, less fertile regions.

(4) A person is assigned to a caste by birth; within the castes there exists exogamy. Social ascent is difficult (although not impossible) for a single person, but not so for a caste as a whole; such a process is called *sanskritization* (Srinivas 1966). Thus, social ascent is hardly a primary aim of a single person – a fundamental difference to Western thinking (Verba et al. 1971: 69). In this regard, a caste is also different from a tribe. Although many castes were concentrated in one or a few villages, none of them occupied only a definite tribal territory; many castes were spread over a large territory, some over the whole of India (Weber 1988a: 33). Familial inheritance of social status is closely correlated with the role of skin colour as a characteristic of caste. Even if this is not a primary criterion of allocation, as mentioned before, it has considerable importance still today. Two authors write in this regard:

> Even today in India, the lighter-skinned Indian of Aryan descent is somehow identified with higher caste background. And judging by the matrimonial columns in Indian newspapers, "fair-skinned" (an often repeated adjective used in ads to describe a prospective bride) is not only an indication of high caste background, but is also completely synonymous with beautiful. In fact, for the aesthetically narrow-minded Indian, "tall, fair and light-eyed" are still considered the essential characteristics of the ideal human body type (Wanjohi and Wanjohi 2005: 216).

In summary, we can say that a caste is a specific form of an ethnic group, a 'closed estate', (Weber 1988a: 99); I think one must call it more exactly a 'closed ethnic estate'. This view has been explicitly expressed by Weber (1964/II: 684): 'The "caste" is really the normal form in which ethnic communities who believe in blood kinship and who exclude outward are connubium and social intercourse, are living together'.

The Caste System and Equality: a Paradox

The central question now is: Was the caste system a source producing inequality or was it also a force restraining it? Can we explain the comparatively moderate level of economic inequality in India with reference to the caste system? Why have there never been consequential revolutionary upheavals in India? We could also ask, varying the famous question of Werner Sombart, quoted in Chapter 1 (p. 6): Why has there never been a radical Socialism in India? In fact, repeated efforts to organize a social movement of the *Dalits* have been without success until recent times in spite of their high number (about 160 millions).[10] Also the descendants of this deprived social group usually vote for the Congress party, a broad people's party with no strong class basis (Verba et al. 1971). I think in fact that the first and main factor explaining the paradox of

---

9   In this regard, Weber is grossly misinterpreted by Dumont (1980: 26) when he writes that Weber equated the castes with the estates.

10   See http://de.wikipedia.org/wiki/Dalit (21.11.2011). A conscious caste politics was initiated around 1980 when affirmative action for the *Dalit* was initiated by the state, reserving exclusive access to government jobs and public universities. As a reaction, members of higher castes protested massively; also political parties now appeal increasingly to specific groups, such as the *Dalits* or the Brahmin community.

relative economic equality in India is its caste system. In addition, we have to consider the impact of religion, the political system and the dominant societal ideology; their effects shall be discussed in the next section.

Looked at from the internal Indian perspective, the caste system certainly constitutes in the first instance a factor producing fragmentation and inequality leading to deep divisions and conflicts.[11] The economic privileges of the higher castes and the deprived of the lowest have been have been noted already by Weber (1988a: 114ff.). Some recent studies have investigated in particular the relative income position of the Scheduled Castes and Tribes (SC/ST). Borooah (2005) analysed data from 28,922 households in 16 Indian states and found out that at least one-third of the average income differences between Hindu and SC/ST households was due to discrimination of the latter. Zacharias and Vakulabharanam (2005) investigated wealth among rural households, using the All India Debt and Investment Surveys of 1991–92 and 2002–03. They found that the SC/ST groups owned significantly less than the members of the 'forward' Hindu castes. The variation between castes was only 13 per cent; however, while the Hindu castes had a low degree of overlap with the other, this was clearly so for the SC/ST groups. They conclude that a 'nouveau riche' group may be emerging within the Scheduled Castes and Tribes. Rawal and Swaminathan (2011) investigated differences in rural household incomes using data from eight villages in four states. They found very large differences with Gini coefficients of the regions ranging from 49 to 68. From the comparative perspective, however, we cannot overlook the powerful integrative force of castes. Here, we must compare the persistence of the huge nation-state India with other large multi-national states which disappeared from the world map in the last decades (such as the Soviet Union) or which were shaken by terribly violent internal wars, like Nigeria, Sudan, Congo and many other new Sub-Saharan African states. The editor of a relevant volume rightly states in this regard:

> The success of democracy in India defies many prevailing theories that stipulate preconditions for democracy: India is not an industrialized, developed economy; Indian businessmen and middle classes do not fully control the country's politics; India is anything but ethnically homogeneous; and India would probably rank low on a number of attributes of 'civic culture' (Kohli 2001: 1).

In Chapter 4 we found that a history of ethno-class exploitation in combination with unequal land distribution was a significant factor leading toward high economic inequality. The relations between the castes in India have never been of the sort which characterized brutal exploitation through slavery. The member of a low caste was of menial status; he or she was not the servant of a single other person, but of the higher castes altogether (Weber 1988a: 126). All castes, focusing upon certain occupations, had to rely on the products and services of other castes; thus, the castes were closely interrelated through the division of labour and economic exchange. This exchange certainly was strongly asymmetrical; the Brahmins at the top of the hierarchy enjoyed privileges unknown to any other priesthood on the world (Weber 1988a: 62). In some regards, the caste system could be compared to the Apartheid system which also involved economic cooperation, but with a separation in socio-cultural terms and political discrimination. However, the Apartheid system distinguished only between two classes of people, differentiated from each other in terms of race; and it came into being by force and military violence.

A similar comment is in place concerning the general relevance of the idea of equality in the caste system. Overall, the caste system is certainly a system of inequality, even of privilege, discrimination and exploitation (Mencher 1991: 93). This point is made explicitly in a very informative article about caste and politics of Myron Weiner:

> Perhaps no other major society in recent history has known inequality so gross, so long preserved, or so ideologically well entrenched. In the traditional civilizations of Islam and China, the ideal if not always the practice of equality had an honourable and often commanding place in the culture. But in India the notion that men should remain in the same occupation and station of life as their forefathers was enshrined in religious

---

11 In a letter of 15 December 2012, commenting on a first version of this chapter, Professor Rahman Momin (Mumbay) wrote to me: '… it will be inappropriate to describe social stratification (caste system) as the main principle of integration – as either a reality or a social ideal … even within the fold of Hindu society, which is characterized by a great deal of diversity and differentiation, the case system has been a mjor source of division and fragmentation, rather than integration' (see also Weiner 2001: 194).

precepts and social custom [...] the idea of social equality never became as widespread in Hinduism as it did in other great traditions. It was not simply that India has had gross inequalities in material standards, but more profoundly, social relations were marked by indignities: the kissing of one's feet by a beggar and supplicant for a jog, the outstretched hands of the groveling poor, the stooped backs of low-caste sweepers (Weiner 2001: 194–5).

All these observations are certainly true. Modifications are necessary, however, when looking at inequality in India from the comparative perspective. First, the impossibility of social ascent through the generations (which often was more semblance than reality, as noted before) relates only to equality of opportunities. Income distribution and inequality, the topic of this book, however, refers to equality of outcome. From this point of view it is not true that 'a half century after independence, India still remains one of the world's most inequalitarian societies' (Weiner 2001: 211). Second, the ideal of equality in China and Islam was largely restricted in terms of coverage, either to the educated classes (as in China) or to members of the Muslim community. In the Islamic world, people from other social classes and groups, nations or continents could be treated in even much more inhumane ways than the Untouchables in India. In addition, if the caste system had been a source of high inequality, this should have decreased since the introduction of the Constitution in 1948 which abolished it; however, there is no indication of such a decrease as was indicated in the introduction.

In general we can say that the caste system was an ingenious invention to legitimize inequality, but at the same time it did not allow excessive inequality. In this regard, caste membership had a strong integrative and protective force even for the Outcastes. First, it provided them with a recognized place in the whole social structure; second, the caste members supported each other in many ways. It is clear that the first aspect was more important for the higher castes, the latter for the lower castes and for the Untouchables. This difference corresponds to the fact that today for the higher castes the small family is the ideal, but for the lower ones it is the extended family (Bellwinkel 1980: 144–63).

Additional Factors Explaining the Moderate Level of Economic Inequality

I have already hinted at the surprising low level of economic inequality in India which, in overall terms, corresponds to that of West European countries like France and Belgium. There is also no indication of a significant change in the patterns of economic inequality in India in recent times. The SWIID dataset, going back to 1960, shows that the Gini throughout the five decades since then always was rather similar, fluctuating between 31 and 34; only in a few years (1968, 1975–77) it increased slightly to 36 (Solt 2009). Deaton and Dreze (2002) found an increase of regional disparities in economic terms, but not in other regards (school participation, life expectancy).

Also in terms of the privileges of the upper and the disadvantages of the lower classes, the impression of a relatively egalitarian socio-economic structure of India is confirmed. The highest 10 per cent income receivers earn 28 per cent of all income, which is a little bit more than in most West European states and Japan, but less than in China, Russia, and the USA (here, they get 30–33 per cent), not to speak of Brazil (46 per cent).[12] The lowest 40 per cent of income earners receives 21 per cent, which corresponded to that in France and Germany, but was significantly higher than that in China, Russia and the USA.

I think that three additional aspects can be mentioned which help to understand the paradox of the moderate level of inequality in India: its most influential religious systems (Hinduism and Buddhism); three elements of the political system (its democracy with a dose of Socialism and its federal constitution); and its general value system which can be denoted as 'multi-communitarianism'.

The Formative Religions of India: Hinduism and Buddhism

In Chapter 3 (p. 73) I have argued that in the long term religious ideologies of equality and inequality have a significant impact on objective patterns of inequality as well as on their perception and evaluation by the

---

12   These are the data which served as the basis for the aggregate level, multivariate analysis in Chapter 4; data sources are given there.

people. This thesis can probably nowhere be proved so clearly than in the case of India. In fact, the religion of Hinduism, and – to a weaker degree – also that of Buddhism had a relevance for the stratification system of India which cannot be overestimated. In fact, once could say that the Hinduism is unconceivable without the caste system and this system itself cannot be understood without looking at Hinduism. Three characteristics may be mentioned in this regard.

First, Hinduism cannot be considered as a religion in the Western sense, as a system of dogmatic beliefs and rituals with a church, a body of professional priests and clearly defined membership rules. Rather, Hinduism is a comprehensive system or philosophy of life (*Weltanschauung*) which allocates a person to his or her individual place in family, society and the Cosmos, providing the believing Hindu with a sense of life and an ethical-moral orientation here and beyond this life; it constitutes an ideal typical model for human behaviour in all spheres of life (Schlensog 2006: 17; 142ff.; Weber 1988a; Stietencron 1995).

Second, Hinduism is a specific Indian religion. One becomes a Hindu only by birth; it is hardly possible (and probably few would like to do so) to convert to Hinduism during one's life time. Hinduism was established in India by the Aryan Brahmins immigrating from the North in the last pre-Christian centuries; they contributed significantly to the religious and cultural integration of the vast subcontinent (Eliade 1979: 45). The essential element of Hinduism is not the religious doctrine or the aim of salvation, but the compliance to general social norms and, above all, to extended rituals (Weber 1988a). It was mainly through these rituals, prescribing different places for living, restricted intercourse between castes of different status, eating habits and so on, that the caste spectrum and its inequalities were kept alive and effective.[13]

The third aspect, the overarching importance of the caste community is most important for the system of ethnic stratification in India. One became a Hindu not as an individual person, but only as a member of a group, and in particular, as a member of a caste. It is possible, however, that whole groups collectively became members of the caste system. Through a process of 'hinduization' (Weber 1988a: 15ff.), immigrating tribes or groups migrating from one place to another could establish themselves as new castes by adopting a 'slave yoke' of ritual obligations. This process of integration into the hierarchical order of castes was in the interest of the kings and of the dominant classes (particularly the Brahmins) because in this way they could legitimate their domination and privileges. But also the subordinated new castes were interested because so they also could become, although at a low level, legitimized members of society. Since the order of the castes was eternal in principle, the duty of a person was to follow the obligations connected with his or her caste membership. The doctrine of reincarnation is highly relevant here: if a person did follow strictly the caste obligations, he or she had the chance to be reborn in a higher status; if not, he/she would be reborn in a lower status. In this way, caste obligations were strongly anchored in individual salvation expectations – more strongly than in any 'organic' societal ethic (Weber 1988a: 121ff.). To aspire toward personal social improvement or to develop fundamental innovations of any sort was hardly imaginable on the basis of this ethic. In this regard, the Hindu caste system had so strong an assimilative power that it captured also the Muslims and to some degree even the Christians.

Two additional important elements of Hinduism where also influenced by Buddhism. Further, Buddhism was no organized religious system; rather, it was a kind of a philosophical-ethical system which was founded by Siddharta Gautama in India around 500 B.C., but later on disappeared before being exported to East Asia (Schlensog 2006: 143ff.).

One of the elements shared by Hinduism and Buddhism was religious tolerance; this was practised already by the Brahmins when they disseminated Hinduism in India in prehistoric times. It is highly relevant that the dissemination of Hinduism did not occur mainly by force, supported by military expansion (Kulke/ Rothermund 1998: 123) – a clear difference to Islam, for instance. The Brahmins did not suppress the myriad of religious beliefs and practices which they came across on the huge sub-continent, but tolerated their survival. In fact, they integrated the multiplicity of popular, autochthonous rituals and deities into the Brahmin scheme of thinking (Eliade 1979: 45). Up to several thousand if not hundreds of thousands of Gods are adored in Hinduism (Schlensog 2006: 216–43). These Gods share several characteristics. They all possess power, exhibit unity in diversity, are unspecific in their characteristics and there exists an identity of Gods and people. However, the Gods are internally clearly stratified: on top are the highest Gods (Brahma, Visna,

---

13   For an overview on those rituals see Schmitt 1982: 301–12.

Siva), followed by high Gods, people's Gods, half-Gods, demons and ghosts. Thus, one could say that the heaven of the Gods is a mirror image of the diversity of human society in India with its manifold vertical and horizontal differentiations.

The other common element of Hinduism and Buddhism was a basic tenet of Indian philosophy and theology in general, namely the focus on human suffering and the striving toward its overcoming not in this life but in the other, eternal world. In this regard, the influence of Buddha was important who had declared: "'Everything is pain, everything is fading'. The rescue and redemption from pain became the primary aim of religious doctrine and ritual praxis (Eliade 1979: 46; Conze 1977: 13ff.). But this view did not lead to nihilism and pessimism. Rather, it was a positive value insofar as it reminded the wise and ascetic man that there is only one way toward happiness, namely, to withdraw from the world here and now, to disengage from material possessions and claims. The four 'Noble Wisdoms' of Buddha correspond to this view of life: everything is suffering, life is intrinsically connected with aging and death; the origin of suffering is avidity; salvation from suffering can only be found in the Nirvana; the only therapy is the 'middle way', the avoidance of striving either toward excessive material-sensual enjoyment or toward an exaggerated asceticism. This middle way consists in the virtues of having the right opinions, ways of thinking, speaking and acting (Eliade 1979: 87f.). Central in this regard was also the belief that humans have no unique, permanent self or individual personality independent from the rest of the universe. Belief in such a self was seen as the main source for all forms of suffering in Buddhism (Conze 1977: 16–18). Rather, there exists only an ever-changing process of 'dependent arising' which implies that humans will take on the life of another being which can be a higher (the highest: that of a deity) or a lower being (which could be even an animal), corresponding to the way of life one has led. Therefore, the Hinduist belief in reincarnation was crucial: only if one's way of life did correspond to the obligations of one's caste, reincarnation in a higher being was possible (Schlensog 2006: 277–86; Farndon 2008: 66).

Thus, we can conclude with Max Weber in his pioneering study about the significance of Hinduism for the caste and stratification system of India:

> Without the penetrating, everything dominating influences of the Brahmins this social system which does not find his own kind anywhere in the world would not have emerged in its closeness or at least would not have become dominant. It must have been finished as an ideal image long before it had conquered even the larger part of northern India. The specific ingenious connection of caste legitimacy with the Karman teaching, thus with the specific Brahmin theodicy is virtually a product of rational ethic thinking, not of any 'economic necessities'. And only the marriage of this thought product with the real social order through the promise of reincarnation provided this order with an irresistible power over the thinking and hoping of the people embedded into it, the firm schema according to which the social position of the single occupational groups and pariah peoples could be ordered (Weber (1988a [1921]: 131f.).

The Political System: Democracy, 'Socialist Centralism' and Federalism

The next set of characteristics which is relevant for the surprising low level of inequality concerns the political system of India. In Chapters 3 and 4, I have argued and shown that several aspects of political system are important factors leading toward more equality; they include democracy and federalism, a history of Communism and a strong welfare state. At least three of these factors have been highly relevant in India.

First, India is the largest democracy on earth, and the foremost example of a successful post-colonial democracy. Since 1947, India had more than five decades of periodic elections in which all political offices were contested, the long-dominating Congress party had been voted out of power, there existed free and lively media, freedom of association and assembly, and considerable scope to express dissent and protest. At the elections in April–May 2009, 369 political parties nominated 8,070 candidates; 714 million people were elective, 428 million people did vote; 4.7 million election aids and 2.1 million security personnel were active; the election itself occurred on five different days, but counting of votes on only one (!) day.[14]

---

14   Heinz Nissel, Indien hat gewählt, ISS Flash Analysis 5/2009, Landesverteidigungsakademie Wien.

These facts are highly remarkable, given the low incomes, weak industrialization, widespread poverty and illiteracy of the country and its immense cultural diversity (Kohli 2001: 1–4). From this perspective, India clearly contradicts Przeworski's thesis (2004) that democracies 'are extremely fragile when facing poverty', and 'when countries are poor there is little they can do'. It is also conspicuous if one compares India with its neighbour states Pakistan and Bangladesh with whom they formed a common political community under British rule. The contrast to Pakistan is outstanding: political instability and ethnic conflicts have been the leitmotif of Pakistan's history (Samad 2009: 208; see also Ahmed 1996; Momin 2009: 23). The reason for this was not only that Pakistan was established from the beginning as an Islamist state – a recipe for suppression of freedom and democracy (see also p. 76) – but it was also because behind the Islamic façade, in fact, a hegemony of the dominant ethnic group of the Punjab was established (Samad 2009) – this produced an explosive situation similar to that in many Sub-Saharan postcolonial societies (see Chapter 10, pp. 260–63). Similar attempts to establish hegemony also were made in India by some Hindus, both terroristic and in formal political ways, when they established the Bharatija Janata Party (BJP) in 1980. This party became quite strong (in 1998–2004 a member of it led government), but it did not win permanent political hegemony, not to speak of re-Hinduization of India. The significance of democracy can be well illustrated in regard to the problem of fertility control. The high population growth is a main problem of India (as it is for Africa). In India, however, no such strict measure as the one-child policy could be established as in Communist China. Only during the government of Indira Gandhi who declared a state of emergency in 1975 were compulsory measures implemented in the course of which – among other measures – 8.3 million people were sterilized (Schmitt 1982: 64). However, people were so strongly focused negatively against these measures that Gandhi was dropped in the elections of 1997. The continuing later, nonviolent efforts to reduce population growth remained ineffective. Today it becomes more and more evident, however, that the central planning of China in this regard may not be the better solution in the long term. China now has to confront the problem of a significant over-population of male births and in the not so distant future of the excess of an aging population.

Second, also the idea of equality was very important for India from the beginning. Already in the 1940s and even more so after the Second World War, Indian nationalists turned toward Socialism from which they expected a way out of the depressing socio-economic situation of the country (Sinha et. Al 1979: 24; Myrdal 1980: 145; Rothermund 1995: 488). The highly influential first Prime minister of India, Jawaharal Nehru (1947–64), considered himself a Socialist – as did many other members of the Assembly which drafted the Constitution (Austin 1966: 41–3). The policy of Nehru, however, was quite pragmatic. He and the other leaders avoided reliance on dogmatic economic-political recipes and on the use of coercion and force in the implementation of political measures, as they have been applied extensively in the Soviet Union and China. In 1951 the first Five-Year Plan was enacted, establishing a kind of 'planned economy' in China with a high proportion of public ownership or control of important industries and services (including banks and the huge railway system). Also a comprehensive land reform was tackled; at this time, about two-thirds of agricultural soil was in the hands of large land owners and the mass of farmers had either only small pieces of or hardly any land. The results of this land reform were modest, however (Schmitt 1982:101ff.). The centrally planned measures of programmes often served only the stronger farmers (Arora 1995). The Constitution, moreover, institutionalized affirmative action measures for the Scheduled Tribes and Castes, the descendants of the Untouchables and of the ethnic minorities (Galanter 1991; Deshpande 2005). The people belonging to the Scheduled Tribes and Castes constituted nearly one-third of the population of India. A similar percentage was reserved for them in the parliament, and the same quota was foreseen also in public higher education and state administration: 22.5 per cent of all government jobs and places in higher educational institutions are reserved for members of the Scheduled Castes and Tribes. Since 1991, also for the other Backward Castes a quota of 27 per cent was reserved, summing up a proportion of 49 per cent of reserved places (Weiner 2001: 201; Deshpande 2005). This measure caused huge public protest and widespread violent student agitations across many universities with public opinion supporting them. However, the achievements of the quota system were limited. The system is fulfilled only in the electoral sphere; here, it has led to a significant change in the caste composition of the elected politicians. In higher government jobs and university education, however, the proportion of people from the preferentially treated cases remains as low as 10 per cent or less. What did increase massively, however, was the proportion of workers and employees in the public sector; from 7 million in 1961 to 21 million in 2001 (Rothermund 1995: 497). In the light of a total workforce of 470 million, this was a very high number, given the fact that all in all in 2001 only 35 million Indians (an extremely low proportion of 7 per cent) altogether had a formal job where they paid taxes (Farndon 2008: 18). While the people employed in the public sphere certainly enjoyed considerable privileges, the mass of Indians, however, did not profit at all from this form of provision of employment. Industrial employment was even shrinking since enterprises were reluctant to hire personnel due to tight restrictions on firing. Economic stagnation and poverty are a particular problem in rural areas where the mass of Indians live, often with no ownership of land or other productive assets (Simha et. al. 1979). Also the economy as a whole went into a deep crisis until the 1980s, given the low productivity of many sectors (due also to import restrictions), and the increasing public debt. After the state went nearly bankrupt, in 1991 a political turn was taken from an interventionist to a regulatory state which provided more space for market forces (Rothermund 1995: 533ff.; Kulke/Rothermund 1988: 393ff.). This turn was certainly an important factor for the successive take-off of economic growth.

The third relevant aspect of the political system of India in relation to the issue of equality is its *federalism*. In stark contrast to China, historical India has never been a strongly centralized state. That independent India should be federalist was supported unambiguously by all those who fought for Indians' liberation from British colonialism before and after 1900. The Constitution of 1948 implemented a very special kind of 'centralized federalism' or 'cooperative federalism', as it was called in a comprehensive historical study: 'National unity and integrity were to be served by the Constitution's highly centralized federalism, characterised ... by central government distribution of much revenue, national development planning, continuation of the inherited civil services ... and a wide variety of state-centre coordinating mechanisms' (Austin 1966: x). There were never, as in the US Philadelphia Constitutional Convention in 1787, harsh disputes between federalists and centralists; all agreed that both centralist and federal principles were important. A reason for this consensus was also that India had to undergo a threefold revolution at this time: a democratic revolution, a national revolution (which demanded the unity of the sub-continent) and a social revolution (which demanded a strong central state). The actual extensive constitution of India lists the tasks of the federal government (in total 100 items) and of the states (in total 61); the latter have exclusive authority to legislate in important areas such as public order, administration of justice, local government, public health, agriculture, land rights and many forms of taxation. Thus, the states can carry out an independent policy in many regards (Austin 1966; Kohli 2001). In this way, political parties such as the Communists who have little influence at the federal level were able to gain much influence in the states of Kerala and West-Bengal; they have adopted a quite efficient egalitarian policy here. Particularly the 'Kerala model' became known worldwide as a successful strategy of human development in poor countries of the South, focusing not on economic growth but on social investments in education and health.[15]

Multi-communitarianism – the Dominant Ideology of Politics and Society

A third important aspect which supports the surprising high level of equality in India is the unanimity concerning the general value of equality. Stanislaw Ossowski (1972) has argued that the existing social structure of a country is clearly reflected in its 'public consciousness', which expresses itself both in official statements (constitutions, speeches, literary works) and behaviours as well as in the perceptions and attitudes of the population at large. We can assume that this consciousness has significant impacts on policy and objective social structures (Haller et al. 1995). For the Indian sociologist, A.R. Momin, the dominant societal model of India today is that of *multi-communitarianism*. Its basis is 'living together on the basis of the recognition of equality, cultural diversity, of respect for the feelings of others, and of the communal division of social, cultural and civil living spaces and societal engagement' (Momin 2006: 527; 2009a: 15–20). Although in such a characterization the distinction between an ideal type and social reality may be blurred somewhat, it certainly contains a lot of truth. Important elements of this model include comprehensive social networks and relations between the different sectors and segments of society; a deeply ingrained religiosity which, at the same time, recognizes the principles of secularism and tolerance; and a comprehensive, inclusive concept of national identity which also accepts diversity and disapproves of violence. An essential basis for the development of this model certainly were the

---

15   Also Sen has used Kerala as a model of a politic which can advance equality and social advancement despite low levels of development. For a discussion see Askhok R. Chandran, 'Amartya Sen: Sense or nonsense', *The New Indian Express* (Kerala), 25.9.2000.

religions of India (Hinduism and Buddhism), as outlined before, with their idea of the community between all living creatures and the ideals of wisdom and compassion. Compared with its immense internal differentiations and inequalities, the level of violence in India is in fact relatively circumscribed (see Table 6.1, pp. 164–5) although in the last decades individual assaults on *Dalits* have been frequent and also several collective 'ethno-political' rebellions have appeared (Schmitt 1982; Gurr 1993; Schlenker/Fischer 2009: 188f.). One reason why such rebellions do not happen more frequently may also be the relative weakness of the Indian central government and its federal constitution which makes it much more difficult to strike down rebellions by massive concentrated repression, as occurred with the Tiananmen Square protests in Beijing in spring 1989. Caste-based conflicts occur mainly at the level of states. Another relevant characteristic of India is the leaning toward non-violent solution of conflict and the striving toward consensual decisions. In fact, this striving has deep roots in India. Comparable to Sub-Saharan Africa, the Indian village *panchayats* traditionally reached decisions in this way (Dumont 1980: 170–172). Indians in general prefer an exhausting discussion of problems instead of moving to quick decisions. This habit was important also in the drafting of the Constitution in 1945–47 when the Constitutional Assembly sometimes took years (as in the problem of language) to arrive at a decision. G. Austin (1966: 313) wrote about this process: 'Consensus, and the decision making process in general, was made possible largely by the atmosphere of unity, of idealism, and of national purpose that pervaded the Assembly'.

In this regard, we must also recognize the importance of charismatic political personalities who played a decisive role in the birth of modern India as they did on other continents (for former Communist societies see Chapter 7; for Sub-Saharan Africa see Chapter 10). First of all, we have to mention here the founder of its state, Mahatma Gandhi (1869–1948) who is internationally the most renowned representative of the principle of non-violent conflict resolution. Such a unique personality could unfold only in India, although his education and his occupational and political activities in two foreign countries provided him with a comprehensive basis for his political activities in India. Growing up in a well-to-do family in India, with a liberal father and an educated religious mother, he went to London to study jurisprudence; later on he lived for 21 years in South Africa (eight of them in prison) and was engaged successfully with the improvement of the situation of the Indians there. After his return to India, he became the leader of the independence movement. In this he combined, as few others did, deeply rooted religious and ethical beliefs with political prudence, pragmatism and a strict rejection of violence (Schlensong 2006: 381ff.). The extremely high reputation in which he enjoyed among Indians (and, maybe throughout the world) was attested by the fact that nearly a million people attended his funeral on 31 January 1948, after his death at the hands of a Hindu terrorist (Fischer 1983: 9). One biographer writes about Gandhi: 'Nobody of those who survived him confronted powerful opponents in his own country and abroad with so much benevolence, sincerity, humility and nonviolence and has achieved so many victories with these weapons' (Fischer 1983: 10). In these regards, Gandhi can well be compared to Julius Nyerere, the founder of independent Tanganyika (see Chapter 10), and he also got the honorary title 'Mahatma' (literally the 'Soul of India'). Similar attitudes and political behaviour patterns were practised also by other influential political personalities during the period of India's way to independence and in the first years of the young Republic. One must mention here Vallabhbhai Patel, Ambekdar R. Bhimrao (originating from a *Dalit* family and converted to Buddhism; see also Farndon 2008: 74) and Jawaharal Nehru (1889–1964), the first Prime Minister. Austin (1966: 21) writes about these people: 'Their honour was unquestioned, their wisdom hardly less so. In their god-like status they may have been feared; certainly they were loved'. In this regard, there exists a sharp contrast to Sub-Saharan Africa: In India, the influence of these enlightened men continued also after the gaining of independence, while in most African states the first generation of idealistic national leaders was dethroned and replaced by ruthless and power-hungry political and military leaders.

What are the perceptions and attitudes of the general population in India concerning equality and inequality? One particular question here is how it was possible that the members of the lowest social classes and groups, the descendants of the Untouchables, did accept a system which discriminated them so clearly? Three aspects are relevant in this regard.

First, India never knew a rigorous system of domination, open suppression and exploitation as it existed in other parts of the world. As pointed out before, the distinction between the thousands of castes was to a large degree also one of horizontal differentiation and did not involve direct domination and exploitation. Second, the protective and supporting functions of caste and *jati* membership are important. Every caste and group, also the lowest, in many regards excludes social groups, and provides emotional affiliation and social assistance to their members when they are in need. This fact has existential importance, not only in regard to physical survival but also in regard to social existence in general because otherwise one would be excluded from society altogether. According to Cox (1959: 18), castes can be designated as 'fraternities' which all have their place in society. In this way, even the *Harijans* or Untouchables had a significantly better position as, for instance, slaves in the New World.[16] Third, also the general population in India is quite critical about inequality and supports measures leading toward more equality.

India is not a member of International Social Survey Programme (ISSP) in which detailed questions on these issues were asked and which I use in other chapters of this book. However, we can look at a few data from the World Values Surveys which did include also India. They show that the Indians are quite critical about the wealthy and the way a person can become rich (see Table 8.1) 42 per cent support the statement that people can get rich only at the expense of others – more than in any of the other 11 nations compared. The same applies to the support of redistribution: 48 per cent of the Indians agree with the statement that incomes should be made more equal – also more than in most other countries. In spite of the country's moderate level of development and high poverty, Indians are not particularly pessimistic; half of them believe that poor people have a chance to escape from poverty. Finally, these data also confirm that democracy is anchored well among Indians at large: 46 per cent consider democracy, in spite of its problems, as better than any other form of government; in several countries (for example, Russia, Mexico, Japan) this proportion is much lower.

It would also be erroneous to say that the lower castes and groups fully accepted their deprivation and discrimination. Formal, external acceptance of an inegalitarian system must not be connected with its inner approval (Shibutani and Kwan 1965: 294). Empirical evidence shows that the Untouchables have used many strategies to reinterpret their hard fate; in private life they often neglected formal norms and often they rebelled openly and violently (Sharma 1999: 47ff.). The official conception of the social hierarchy, not only propagated but also kept in existence by the superior power of the upper castes (Mencher 1991: 94), was accepted by the lower castes and tribes only to a limited degree (Gupta 1991: 12f.). In spite of their demographic weight (about one-quarter of the population), the Scheduled Castes and Tribes have not emerged as a politically powerful group. Mohanty (2001: 3858) writes about them:

> They continue to be ruled by the upper castes because of their submissiveness, tolerance and survival-mindedness. The ruling minorities, who find the existing social order beneficial, remain apathetic or lukewarm towards issues concerning the upliftment and empowerment of the people at the lower rungs as it tends to challenge their spectral dominance.

Mohanty here speaks also of a 'submission serfdom syndrome'. A consequence of this was that factual redistribution in India, propagated in the Constitution, public declarations and official policy, remained modest. The demands of rural *Dalit* workers for the observance of legal norms concerning minimal wages and decent work conditions and their protest actions against encroachments of large land owners are often responded to by violent actions, such as the burning of their huts. Given the high inequality of land distribution and the exploitation of landless workers one can indeed speak of *Klassenkampf* (class fight) there (Schmitt 1982: 101–5). In fact nearly all of these exploited groups were *Dalits* or *Adivasis*, and a small proportion of them were even submitted to forms of forced labour still in the 1990s.[17] Thus, one must also say that the caste ideology camouflages the extreme socio-economic inequalities (Mencher in Gupta 1991: 108). Today, the traditional caste system and, in particular, the related rituals, continue to be relevant particularly in the rural areas; in the towns and cities, its influence has been weakened and the underprivileged are more ready to fight against discrimination (Schmitt 1982: 301ff; M. Marriott in Gupta 1991: 49ff.; Sharma 1999: 59ff.). This might be a reason why violent ethnic conflicts are much more frequent in the towns than in the countryside (Schlenker-Fischer 2009: 239ff.).

---

16   E. Schmitt (1982:197ff.) argues that today the Indian *Dalit* workers in the countryside are more discriminated against than blacks in the United States. I think, however, that this applies only to the deprived blacks living in urban ghettos, but not to the majority of black Americans (see Chapter 11).

17   Schmitt (1982: 193) reports a study according to which in 10 states 2.3 million workers in such new forms of slavery were found. Their proportion among all rural workers was estimated at 5 to 10 per cent.

Table 8.1   **Perceptions and attitudes related to inequality and politics in 12 countries around the world (1995–2005) (% agree)**

	(V130) People can only get rich at the expense of others	(V173) Poor people have a chance to escape from poverty	(174) Government is doing too little for people in poverty	(V163) Democracy is better than any other form of government	(V116) Incomes should be made more equal
West Germany	22	17	66	49	53
Spain	27	31	69	40	33
Sweden	26	47	66	69	26
Russia	20	15	94	11	*
USA	15	71	40	49	18
Mexico	25	41	73	22	30
Brazil	14	29	65	50	37
South Africa	26	49	62	40	37
Nigeria	32	26	83	59	*
India	42	53	57	46	48
China	8	88	41	*	35
Japan	14	80	60	19	15

Source: World Value Surveys 1995–97 (V130–V163), World Value Surveys 2005 (V116).
*Question not asked.

Summary and Outlook

With its caste system, India has developed a worldwide unique model of stratification. In terms of the theoretical approach developed in Chapter 3, it can be characterized as a system where the principle of social stratification entered into a very close relationship with that of ethnic differentiation, together producing the unique, hierarchical caste system. Thus, stratification and ethnic group formation were clearly predominant. The differentiation between the castes and *jatis* includes elements of occupational specialization and economic class formation, but these were subordinated to the first two processes. The interaction between these three processes gave rise to an extremely differentiated and hierarchical social structure. The ideological background of this complex system of vertical and horizontal diversity is a remarkable level of tolerance of diversity, and a high degree of social integration and support within the sub-groups thus formed. These principles have been incorporated into the constitution and politics of India; they are backed by the religious tradition of Hinduism and of Buddhism, emphasizing the virtues of wisdom and frugality, non-violence and meditation and they are also supported by the population at large.

In conclusion, let us discuss shortly the following questions: How did this system come into being? What is the relevance of the caste system today? What was the effect Indian *Weltanschauung* (world-view) and its caste system on socio-economic development? And, in particular: How were this system and the politics of 'democratic Socialism' related to old and new inequalities and the aim of erasing widespread poverty?

How did the unique Indian caste system come into being? I have argued in this chapter that it had deep roots, originating several thousand years ago from Indian civilization which was influenced significantly by the religious traditions of Hinduism and Buddhism. But also one additional event of recent Indian history has to be mentioned here. This is the fact that also India had experienced a phase of traumatic events shortly before, during and after its declaration of independence. A deep conflict emerged between Hindus and Muslims when India and Pakistan were established as two separate nations in 1947. In the ensuing riots against Muslims in India, and against Hindus in Pakistan, several hundred thousand people lost their lives and nearly 20 million had to effectively 'swap' countries from one to the other. These were deeply tragic and embarrassing traumatic events, years of communal genocide and enforced mass migration (Austin 1966: 23f.). Maybe also because of these experiences the leaders of the new nation India tried to avoid similar events later at all costs; it was not impossible that they would arise anew given the fact many Muslims remained in India. (Today their number is over a 100 million.) This positive twist of events could be seen as sign of hope for Sub-Saharan Africa where the bloody civil wars from the 1970s till today may have convinced many leaders to try to avoid their recurrence.

What is the relevance of the Indian caste system today? In legal constitutional terms, the caste system was abolished completely in 1948, and many official declarations and decisions since then confirmed the intent to eliminate its aftermaths.[18] The profound structural transformations of Indian society in the last century (Dumont 1980: 217–38) and particularly in recent decades certainly changed the caste structure significantly. Work in large and modern, often multi-national enterprises, migration toward and settlement in the growing megacities and more individualistic patterns of consumption have reduced the relevance of caste. Personal identity in present-day India is multifaceted, probably stronger than anywhere else in the world: a Brahmin from Benares may understand himself as an Indian when he watches at a hockey match with India against Pakistan; as a Benarsi when travels to Delhi; as a Brahmin when he is asked about his descent; as the head of a family if the division of family property is at stake. However, the caste structure and the related attitudes and patterns of behaviour have retained their power to a considerable degree. This is most obvious in marriage and family life. In marriage advertisements ethnic criteria are dominant when describing the characteristics of a desired partner: religion is in first place, caste membership second, followed by regional provenience, language and occupation (Schlensog 2006: 64–5). Traditionally, often quite strict rules of marital endogamy and exogamy are still valid. In a national survey in 1997, 72 per cent said they would not allow their son or daughter to marry someone from another caste.[19] Wedding remains the most festive ritual in the life of an Indian. The family is still structured along quite patrilineal and patriarchal lines; the position of women is subordinated to that of fathers and sons; for the marriage of a young woman to another family, often a high bride price has to be paid; the main duty of women in the family is to bear children and to care for their husbands; it is difficult for many women to survive without being integrated into a family (Schlensog 2006: 411–4). The horrific cases of mass rape of women in India, reported in recent times, also document that the subordinated position of women is one of the main social problems of Indian society today.[20] In a sociological study, Maria Mies (1980) found that for many women these traditional conceptions have not lost their relevance, in spite of new ideas and achievements in the spheres of education and work.

A comprehensive study about the caste and status system in about 400 households in the large industrial city of Kanpur, carried out in the early 1970s by the German social anthropologist Maren Bellwinkel (1948–2011), is very informative in this regard. Her findings can be summarized as follows. The personnel of the new industrial enterprises which were established in the city after the Second World War included people from all castes, although Brahmins mostly worked in white-collar office jobs and as foremen, and the *Dalits* as blue collar workers. There was no strict separation at the workplace; this happened only at meal times when commensality was avoided. Also the formation of larger unions was inhibited by caste distinctions to the advantage of entrepreneurs and employers (Weber 1988a: 113; Rothermund 1995: 549ff.). Membership in the many unions (there were about 350 in Kanpur) did not create a common class consciousness. Geographical mobility from the countryside to the town did not correspond to a socially upward mobility; members of the higher castes relocated only to the town when a white-collar job was prospective. Those working in the city continued to keep alive the relations with the village; for the *Dalits*, unskilled work as a rickshaw driver, for instance, was often only temporarily taken over as a substitute when no industrial job was attainable. The higher castes preferred the ideal of a small family, the lower that of the extended family; education and a good occupation were highly valued also for women, particularly in the higher castes. The overall status system consisted of two strata, an upper one, composed of white-collar workers, state employees (in terms of castes

---

18 A recent example was that the Indian Supreme Court holds that inter-caste marriages are in the 'national interest' as a unifying force. See *The Indian Express*, 20 April 2011.

19 Reported by *India Today International*, 18 August 1997; quoted in Weiner 2001, p. 195, footnote 2.

20 These cases may have recognized by the world press, however, mainly because of their sensational character. Sen argued in an interview that the relative rates of rape are significantly higher in the UK, Sweden and the USA than in India. Reprinted in 'Amartya Sen Interview: India must fulfill Tapore's vision, not Gandhi's', *The Spectator*, 20 August 2013.

the three higher ones), and a lower one, composed of former *Dalits* and blue collar workers; overall status resulted from a combination of caste position and (achieved) occupational status; alone in the town district investigated by Bellwinkel, 26 castes were distinguishable. Residential segregation, particularly the separation of *Dalits* into specific streets, was loosened; relations between the lower and upper classes were reciprocal insofar as the former seek support of the later in times of elections, while the latter used representatives of the first when it came to act against the outside world; in this way they accepted that their true interests were often betrayed. Thus, caste membership and relations have changed fundamentally, but they retained high significance. The same conclusion was drawn in a study about the role of castes in political life by Myron Weiner. He wrote that caste as an ideology may be almost moribund, but as a lived-in social reality it is very much alive: 'Caste is not disappearing, nor is "casteism" – the political use of caste – for what is emerging in India is a social and political system which institutionalizes and transforms but does not abolish caste' (Weiner 2001: 195–6). Caste, Weiner concludes, 'has been a far more potent form of social identity and action in India than class, notwithstanding the history of kisan (agricultural and farming) movements and trade unions. India now has a plethora of caste-based educational institutions, caste associations, and caste-based political parties' (Weiner 2001: 210). A political science professor at the Indian Institute of Public Administration New Delhi states: 'Many of the state policies have not only sustained but also furthered gender, caste and class based inequalities by worsening the status of those at the weaker end of the relationship' (Arora 1995: 959).

What is the relation between the Indian caste system, socio-economic development and socio-economic inequality? The first issue was discussed in detail already by Max Weber in 1920–21 (Weber 1988a: 109–21). He argued that the traditionalistic and anti-rational caste system as a whole clearly impeded modernization; craftsmen and merchants persisted in their traditions and had the habit of working only until they had enough money to become self-employed or to stop working – in spite of the fact that the Indian craftsmen (more than the Muslim) are hard-working; as a consequence it was difficult to recruit workers for industry. One could add here a social 'declassation' of the farmer in India took place; because he killed creatures with his plough and bred cattle, he was ritually unclean (Weber 1988a). As additional reasons for the slow development of Indian economy, Weber mentions the negative impacts of British colonialism which did not allow the emergence of an independent industry and economy in India but relegated it to a furnisher of raw materials and semi-finished products (see also Wendt 1978). India in fact was lagging behind China for decades in the dynamics of economic growth,[21] although it was able – contrary to China – to avoid big famines since 1945. However, since the 1990s growth has been accelerated also in India and has reached very high values: 8 per cent and more in recent years. In sectors such as electronics, pharmaceuticals and exclusive health services, India today offers services for a worldwide rich clientele (Farndon 2008; Momin 2009a: 26–7). However, the boom of these high-tech sectors (including IT) was more capital than labour intensive and did not translate into jobs for the masses. Huge problems inhibiting economic development persist, such as deficient infrastructure in traffic, transport and energy provision, an inefficient public administration and high corruption.

A particular relevant area here is education. Education and knowledge were traditionally held in high esteem in India, particularly among the higher castes. Weiner (2001: 214) argues that also the new leaders from lower castes got what *they* wanted but they did not care a lot about the poor masses. It was mainly higher education on which India's educational policy was focusing in the first decades. In this regard, both the caste system in which learning was a prerogative of the Brahmins and the ideas of Gandhi were influential. In contrast to the great Indian writer Rabindranath Thakur (Tagore) (1861–1941), Gandhi was sceptical of formal education. The consequence is that there exists a clear status bias in this regard. Also the success of non-Brahmins in high political offices and public administration did not lead to a satisfying improvement of the educational situation of the deprived social groups. In terms of general basic education, India is lagging behind China; about one-fourth of the adult population are illiterate.[22] India's expenditure on education is lower than that of many developing countries and a disproportionate amount of the budget is going to higher education and grants for private schools; pubic primary schools, however, are given inadequate resources. Also in this regard, the situation in Sub-Saharan Africa is quite similar (see Chapter 10) Affirmative action

---

21 The relatively low rate – about 3 per cent between 1950 and 1990 – was called 'Hindu rate of growth' (Farndon 2008: 15).

22 World Development Report 2011, pp. 344ff (Tables 1–3).

– reservations of places in the education system and public administration – was preferred as a low-cost political strategy because it permitted government to pay little attention to the primary and secondary school system. For Dreze and Sen (2013) the relative neglect of education is a main reason for the lagging behind of India's economic growth, after that of China and the successful East Asian countries. One could add here that increasing the education of the masses would be the most effective means for reducing population growth. In Chapter 13, I will also argue that a focus on the general improvement of the public school system is a better strategy than affirmative actions in the form of quotas.

What can other nations of the global South learn from the Indian experience? First, I think that India in fact can be considered as a model for many other multi-ethnic and multi-national states around the world, even for Europe (Momin 2006). The US Secretary of State Condoleezza Rice was right when she called India 'a great multi-ethnic democracy' (quoted in Farndon 2008: 1). The case of India confirms that it is possible to avoid glaring inequality, even in a huge and ethnically highly diverse nation. Among the positive side of India's achievements we can mention particularly four aspects: (1) the attainment of political continuity and stability as a democratic nation which never practised open suppression of minorities; (2) in recent times, the attainment of a very high level of economic growth; and – as a fundamental difference to China – the avoidance of terrible, homemade mass famines; (3) the more or less peaceful co-existence of many ethnic and national sub-groups and the respect of their traditions, customs and practices, including the languages; (4) last, but not least, the retention of a moderate level of economic inequality.

The idea that the autonomy of 'every race and community in India' should be preserved was widespread already in the early 20th century among Indian politicians as Sarkar writes:

> A discourse of 'unity in diversity' became standard in mature Indian nationalism, particularly in the context of deepening Hindu-Muslim conflicts. This was often vague, platitudinous, and open to diverse interpretations, yet it did involve a recognition of plurality or religions, languages, and cultures that logically favoured federalism rather than any totally centralized polity (Sarkar 2001: 31).

Thus India is an outstanding example, proving that peaceful social integration and a moderate level of inequality is possible also in a society highly differentiated in ethnic terms. Today, India is facing extremely large and serious problems as well; they include a high population growth rate and widespread poverty; the highest incidence of child labour in the world, with half of the children dropping out of school by the fifth grade (Weiner 2001: 211). Nevertheless, both the practice of tolerance, the ability to live peacefully together in spite of extreme diversity and the constitutionally engrained commitment to equality allow a positive outlook for India's future.

References

Ahmed, Feroz (1996), 'Pakistan: Ethnic fragmentation or national integration?' *The Pakistan Development Review* 35: 631–45

Arora, Dolly (1995), 'Addressing welfare in Third World contexts. Indian case', *Economic and Political Weekly*, 29 April 1995, pp. 955–62

Austin, Granville (1966), *The Indian Constitution. Cornerstone of a Nation*, Oxford: Oxford University Press

Bellwinkel, Maren (1980), *Die Kasten-Klassenproblematik im städtisch-industriellen Bereich. Historisch empirische Fallstudie über die Industriestadt Kanpur in Uttar Pradesh, Indien*, Wiesbaden: F. Steiner

Beteille, André (1991), 'Caste in a South Indian Village', in Gupta, *Social Stratification*, pp. 146–62

Böck, Monika and Aparna Rao (1995), 'Die Vielfalt der indischen Sprachen', in Rothermund, *Indien*, pp. 112–31

Borooah, Vani K. (2005), 'Caste, inequality and poverty in India', *Review of Development Studies* 9: 399–414

Conze, Edward (1977), *Der Buddhismus. Wesen und Entwicklung*, Stuttgart etc.: W. Kohlhammer (Buddhism, Oxford 1953)

Cox, Oliver C. (1959 [1948]), *Caste, Class and Race*, New York/London: Monthly Review Press

Davis, Marvin (1983), *Rank and Rivalry: The politics of inequality in rural West Bengal*, Cambridge: Cambridge University Press

Deshpande Ashwini (2005), Equity and Development, World Development Report 2006, Background Papers

Dreze, Jean and Amartya Sen (2013), *An Uncertain Glory: India and its Contradictions*, Penguin Books: Allen Lane

Dumont, Louis M. (1980), *Gesellschaft in Indien. Die Soziologie des Kastenwesens*, Wien: Europaverlag (Homo hierarchicus, Paris 1966)

Eliade, Mircea (1979), *Geschichte der religiösen Ideen (vol. II). Von Gautama Buddha bis zu den Anfängen des Christentums*, Freiburg etc.: Herder (*History of Religious Ideas*, 1978)

Farndon, John (2008), *India Booms*, London: Virgin Books

Galanter, Marc (1991), *Competing Equalities: Law and the Backward Classes in India*, Oxford: Oxford University Press

Gupta, Dipankar (2003), 'Social stratification, hierarchy, difference, and social mobility', in Veena Das, ed., *The Oxford India Companion.to Sociology and Social Anthropology*, Oxford: Oxford University Press, pp. 502–31

Gupta, Dipankar, ed. (1991), *Social Stratification*, Delhi: Oxford University Press

Gurr, Ted Robert (1993), *Minorities at Risk: A Global View of Ethnopolitical Conflicts*, Washington, DC: United States Institute of Peace Press

Haller, Max, Bogdan Mach and Heinrich Zwicky (1995), 'Egalitarismus und Antiegalitarismus zwischen gesellschaftlichen Interessen und kulturellen Leitbildern. Ergebnisse eines internationalen Vergleichs', in Hans-Peter Müller and Bernd Wegener, eds, *Soziale Ungleichheit und soziale Gerechtigkeit*, Opladen: Leske + Budrich, pp. 221–64

Kohli, Atul, ed. (2001), *The Success of India's Democracy*, Cambridge: Cambridge University Press

Kulke Hermann and Dietmar Rothermund (1998), *Geschichte Indiens. Von der Induskultur bis heute*, München: C.H. Beck

Mencher, Joan P. (1991), 'The caste system upside down', in Gupta, *Social Stratification*, pp. 93–109

Mies, Maria (1980), *Indian Women and Patriarchy. Conflicts and Dilemmas of Students and Working Women*, New Delhi: Concept

Milanovic, Branko (2007), 'Globalization and inequality', in D. Held and A. Kaya, eds, *Global Inequality: Patterns and Explanations*, Cambridge: Polity press, pp. 26–49

Mohanty, B.B. (2001), 'Land distribution among Scheduled Castes and Tribes', *Economic and Political Weekly* 36: 3857–68

Momin, A.R. (2006), 'India as a model for multiethnic Europe', *Asia-Europe Journal* 4: 523–37

Momin, A.R.(2009b), 'Introduction', in Momin, ed., *Diversity, Ethnicity and Identity in South Asia*, pp. 1–49

Momin, A.R., ed. (2009a), *Diversity, Ethnicity and Identity in South Asia*, Jaipur etc.: Rawat Publications

Myrdal, Gunnar (1980), *Ein asiatisches Drama. Eine Untersuchung über die Armut der Nationen*, Frankfurt am Main: Suhrkamp (*Asian Drama: An Enquiry into the Poverty of Nations*, 1968)

Ossowski, Stanislaw (1972), *Die Klassenstruktur im sozialen Bewußtsein*, Neuwied: Luchterhand (1st Polish ed. 1957)

Rath, Govinda C., ed., (2006), *Tribal Development in India. The Contemporary Debate*, New Delhi etc.: Sage

Rawal, Vikas and Madhura Swaminathan (2011), 'Income inequality and Caste in village India', *Review of Agrarian Studies* 1: 108–133

Rothermund, Dietmar, ed. (1995), *Indien. Kultur, Geschichte, Wirtschaft, Umwelt. Ein Handbuch*, München: C.H. Beck

Samad, Yunas (2009), 'Pakistan or Panjabistan: Crisis of National Identity', in Momin, ed., *Diversity, Ethnicity and Identity in South Asia*, pp. 208–30

Sarkar, Sumit (2001), 'Indian democracy: The historical inheritance', in Kohli, *The Success of India's Democracy*, pp. 23–46

Schlenker-Fischer, Andrea (2009), *Demokratische Gemeinschaft trotz ethnischer Differenz. Theorien, Institutionen und soziale Dynamiken*, Wiesbaden: VS Verlag

Schlensog, Stephan (2006), *Der Hinduismus. Glaube, Geschichte, Ethos*, München-Zürich: Piper

Schmitt, Eberhard, ed. (1982), *Indien. Politik, Ökonomie, Gesellschaft*, Berlin: EXpress Edition

Sharma, Ursula (1999), *Caste*, Birmingham/Philadelphia: Open University Press

Shibutani, Tamotsu and Kian M. Kwan (1965), *Ethnic Stratification. A Comparative Approach*, New York: Macmillan/London: Collier-Macmillan

Silverberg, James (1969), 'Social Mobility in the Caste System in India: An Interdisciplinary Symposium', *The American Journal of Sociology* 75: 443–4

Sinha, Rada, Peter Pearson, Gopal Kadekoki and Mary Gregory (1979), *Income Distribution, Growth and Basic Needs in India*, London: Croom Helm

Solt, Frederick (2009), 'Standardizing World Income Inequality Database', *Social Science Quarterly* 90: 231–42

Srinivas, M.N. (1962), *Caste in Modern India and other essays*, Bombay: Media Promoters & Publishers

Stietencron, Heinrich von (1995), 'Die Erscheinungsformen des Hinduismus', in D. Rothermund, *Indien. Kultur, Geschichte, Wirtschaft, Umwelt. Ein Handbuch*, München: C.H. Beck, pp. 143–66

Verba, Sidney, Ahmed Bashiruddin and Amil Bhah (1971), *Caste, Race and Politics. A Comparative Study of India and the United States*, Beverly Hills/London: Sage

Wanjohi, Gerald J. and G. Wakuraya Wanjohi, eds (2005), *Social and Religious Concerns of East Africa. A Wajibu Anthology*, Washington, DC: Paulines Publ.

Weber, Max (1964/I+II), *Wirtschaft und Gesellschaft*, 2 vols, Köln/Berlin: Kiepenheuer & Witsch

Weber, Max (1988a), *Gesammelte Aufsätze zur Religionssoziologie II* (Hinduismus und Buddhismus), Tübingen: J.C.B. Mohr

Weber, Max (1988b), *Gesammelte Aufsätze zur Religionssoziologie III* (Die Wirtschaftsethik der Weltreligionen), Tübingen: J.C.B.Mohr

Weiner, Myron (2001), 'The struggle for equality; caste in Indian politics', in Kohli, *The Success of India's Democracy*, pp. 193–225

Wendt, Ingeborg (1978), *Japanische Dynamik und indische Stagnation?* Darmstadt: Wissenschaftliche Buchgesellschaft

World Development Report (2011), Washington: The World Bank

Zacharias, Ajit and Vamsi Vakulabharanam (2009), Caste and wealth inequality in India, The Levy Economics Institute, Annandale-on-Hudson, New York, Working Paper 566

Chapter 9
Coloured Class Structures:
Brazil and Hispanic America

Latin America is the most unequal macro-region in the world. Table 1.1 (pp. 5–6) shows that practically all of its countries have a Gini coefficient of over 40, four among them (Colombia, Bolivia, Brazil and Haiti) larger than 50.[1] Even in Africa, where we also find about a dozen countries with comparable high levels of economic inequality, there are at least a dozen countries with Gini coefficient below 40. Latin America was called the 'lopsided continent' (Hoffman and Centeno 2003) in which the unequal distribution of inequality is specific insofar as the highest tenth is extremely privileged and detached from the rest. On this continent, one almost 'breathes in inequality' (Gillian 1976).

This extreme inequality has not been reduced in the period since the Second World War; while poverty and inequality decreased somewhat as a consequence of earlier economic growth, they increased again in periods of economic crises and recession (Ocampo 1998; Janvry and Sadoulet 1999; Singh et al. 2005; Campos et al. 2012). Figure 9.1 shows that between the 1950s and 2005, economic inequality increased significantly in Brazil and Chile; in Argentina and Venezuela, the general trend was also upward. Such a trend contradicts economic expectations according to which trade liberalization (which occurred in most Latin American countries since the mid-1980s) should lead to an increase of incomes of unskilled labour and, thus, to a reduction of income inequality (Angeles-Castro 2011). In Mexico, it has remained stable, but on a very

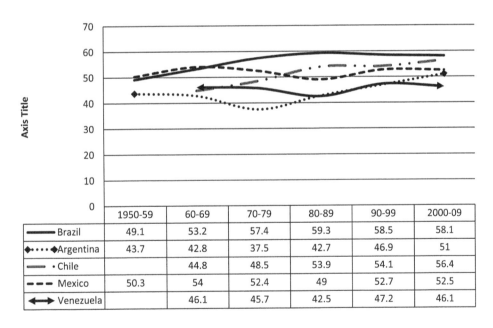

	1950-59	60-69	70-79	80-89	90-99	2000-09
Brazil	49.1	53.2	57.4	59.3	58.5	58.1
Argentina	43.7	42.8	37.5	42.7	46.9	51
Chile		44.8	48.5	53.9	54.1	56.4
Mexico	50.3	54	52.4	49	52.7	52.5
Venezuela		46.1	45.7	42.5	47.2	46.1

Figure 9.1 The development of economic inequality in five Latin American countries, 1950–59 to 2000–09 (Gini coefficients)
Source: UNU-WIDER dataset (Solt 2009).

---

1   Only Jamaica's Gini is marginally smaller (37.9).

high level. Even in such a case, however, significant structural changes may have been going on in particular sectors. One of the most conspicuous changes in this regard was a large increase of an urban 'underclass', composed of people in informal service sector employment (see below). Concomitants of this increase were an expansion of informal self-employment, a rise of violent crime and emigration abroad (Portes and Kelly 2003). Similar trends are shown in Ewout Frankema's analysis (2008) who investigated the changes in income distribution from the longer term perspective. He found that in the 1920s a levelling of incomes took place in Latin America, leading to a relatively moderate inequality, but afterwards inequality began to increase again.

It is out of question that the extreme structures of economic and social inequality in Latin America cannot be understood without considering the ethnic differentiation of its societies. To consider this dimension as a central aspect of social structure and inequality is not taken for granted. Important articles and books about Latin American class structures neglect it completely (examples include Skidmore and Smith 2001: 399–411; Portes and Hoffman 2003; Figueiredo Santos 2006a; Boris et al. 2008). As a consequence, they are unable to provide an explanation for the extremely high level of economic inequality and for the related fact why a vast mass of workers must procure a living through unregulated employment or direct subsistence activities (Portes and Hoffman 2003: 44). They are also surprised by the apparent contradiction between the extreme socio-economic polarization and the relatively weak political articulation of the most negatively affected social groups (Boris et al. 2008: 326).

There are, in fact, two specific issues which make the discussion and analysis of race or ethnic differences more complex in Latin America than elsewhere. The first is that ethnic differentiations on this sub-continent interact in a peculiar way with the societal class and status structure. I call the model of class stratification and its interaction with ethnic differentiation in Latin America 'coloured class structures'. Brazil presents the most paradigmatic example of such a type and I will discuss the situation in this largest Latin American country in more detail in this chapter. In the Spanish-speaking countries the situation looks somewhat different. This is particularly so in the Caribbean with Blacks and mulattos and in the southern Latin American countries of Argentina, Chile and Uruguay, with Whites of European origin predominating.[2] The second peculiarity is that the issue of race has been officially relativized or even neglected; in Hispanic America the idea of *mestizaye* was developed, with the emergence of a new race from inter-marriages; in Brazil, ethnic stratification was disclaimed altogether in the idea of the race 'democracy'. Both these views have a grounding in social and cultural reality, but they are also used to obscure rural and ethnic discrimination (see also Graham 1990; Mignolo 2005).

In this chapter, I will proceed as follows: in the first section, a short characterization of the variation of ethnic differentiation and class structures of the main sub-regions of Spanish Latin America shall be given, including some of the main factors and forces producing these patterns; the second section discusses two essential forces sustaining and legitimating inequality, political power structures and the role of religion; in the last section, the Brazilian model of 'coloured class structure' is investigated in more detail, showing the close interaction between ethnic differentiation and class structure and its perception by the people.

Patterns of Ethnic Stratification in Latin America

Latin America can aptly be divided into four sub-regions in terms of its ethnic composition (see Table 9.1): in the Caribbean, the majority of the population is Black or mulatto (descendants of Blacks and Whites); in the former Spanish colonial area, from Mexico across the headland of Central America and the west coast countries, Colombia and Ecuador down to Peru, the main ethnic groups are *mestizos* (descendants of Whites and Indians) or *Amerindos* (native American Indians); two large countries in the north (Colombia and Venezuela) have also sizeable proportions (about 20 per cent) of mulattos. Finally, the two states in the South – Argentina and Uruguay – are mostly White. Portuguese-speaking Brazil, the largest and most populous country on the sub-continent is ethnically mixed (in socio-biological terms), with a slight majority of Whites, a large proportion (38 per cent) of mulattos and a small group (6 per cent) of Blacks. These different ethnic compositions are closely related to the histories and patterns of colonization in the respective regions (see also Fagg 1963; Donghi 1991; Skidmore and Smith 2001; Andrews 2004). Let us have a short look at them.

---

2   For detailed information on the internal diversity of Latin America see also Beyhout 1965: 11–17; Dirmoser et al. 1994; Davis 1995; Skidmore and Smith 2001; Meissner et al. 2008: 205ff.

Table 9.1   The ethnic structure in the four different macro-regions of Latin America

Region/countries (population in millions)[*]	Ethnic composition[**]
I. Black and mulatto Latin America: the Caribbean	
Jamaica (2.7), Haiti (10)	90–95% Black
Cuba (11)	37% White, 51% Black, 11% mulatto
Dominica (9.7)	16% White, 11% Black, 73% mulatto
Trinidad & Tobago (1.3)	40% Indian Asian, 37% Black, 20% mulatto
II. Mestizo & Indian: North and Central America, North and North-East South America	
Mexico (118), Guatemala (15)	60–70 mestizo, 30–40% Amerindian
Honduras (8.5), El Salvador (6.6)	90% mestizo
Costa Rica (4.6), Nicaragua (6.2), Panama (3.6)	10–17% White, 70–90% mestizo (Panama: 15–20% Amerindian)
Colombia (47), Ecuador (15), Venezuela (29)	10–20% White, 50–70% mestizo, 10–15% mulatto (Col, Ven)/25% Amerindian (Ec)
Bolivia (10), Peru (30)	15% White, 30–40% mestizo, 40–50% Amerindian
Paraguay (6.8)	95% mestizo
Chile (16)	65% mestizo, 30% White
III. The coloured class structure	
Brazil (193)	54% White, 38% mulatto, 6% Blacks
IV. White Latin America	
Argentina (40)	88–97% White
Uruguay (3.2)	(Uruguay: 8% mestizo)

*Ca. 2010–13
**Sources*: see Chapter 4, pp. 95–6.

The Black and Mulatto Caribbean: from Exploitation to Revolutions with Ambivalent Results

The Caribbean is the only Latin American region with a dominance of Blacks and mulattos. This goes back to the fact that this was the first region colonized and exploited by the Spaniards, and – to a smaller extent – also by the French and Britons. For this aim, millions of Africans were imported from the 16th century on and used as labour slaves from the 16th till the 19th century.[3] The reason was that these islands with plentiful sunshine, abundant rainfall and no frosts were very well suited for the large-scale plantation of sugar – a crop which in Europe at this time was a luxury good in very scarce supply which could be sold at high prices. The work on the Caribbean (and later Brazilian) sugar plantations and mills, however, was extremely hard and needed a robust and docile labour force. There were too few indigenous people who could be constrained to do this work; many of them died because the conditions were unbearable for them and because of imported diseases (smallpox, measles, flu) for which they had no resistance. In addition, the Indians had also the possibility to escape from their exploiters into the bush although this was less possible on the small Caribbean islands than on the main lands of Latin America. Therefore, a massive and systematic import of slaves from Africa was initiated. It became one of the three essential links in a triangular business in which all European colonial powers were involved, including the Portuguese and Spanish Crown, British industrialists and financial entrepreneurs and solvent consumers (nobles and prosperous businessmen) throughout Europe. The ships transported slaves (mostly men) from Africa to Latin America, returned from there with raw materials (silver and other precious metals) and tropical agricultural products (sugar, cacao, coffee) to Europe and then sailed again back from Europe to Africa and Latin America with industrial products (for example textiles) and goods often of little use value but estimated highly by the natives (for example tinsel and alcohol; see Fausto 1994: 42).

---

3   For an overview see http://en.wikipedia.org/History_of_the_Caribbean; see also Chapter 5, pp. 142–9.

The work and life conditions of the slaves on the Caribbean (and in Brazil) may have been among the worst history had ever seen: Far away from their homelands, they were subject to an oppressive legal control, which denied them any civil (for example marriage) and political rights. Many of their masters treated them in the most inhumane and violent ways in order to make sure that they worked as hard as they could (Burkholder and Johnson 2010: 218ff.; Meissner et al. 2008: 99ff.). If they did not work hard or if they even tried to escape, they were subjected to the most severe punishments, including torturing till death. It is no wonder that over and over again slave revolts occurred, not the least because the slaves often outnumbered their White masters. Between 1700 and 1850, both in Cuba and Jamaica more than a dozen slave revolts broke out. They were all suppressed by force, but one was successful, namely that in Haiti in 1804. The tragic history of this first independent state of former Black slaves has been described in Chapter 4 (p. 103).

The recent socio-economic and political development in Caribbean countries like Jamaica and Dominica has been mixed (Skidmore and Smith 2001: 289–315). On the one side, economic reforms and an opening up to the outside have led to economic growth, but also an increasing public debt and even a financial collapse in 1996 in Haiti. Important revenues are coming from tourism, but also from remittances of the many émigrés to other countries in North and South America. Massive problems that remained unsolved are a high level of crime (in Haiti), an insufficient educational system and a high rate of poverty in the Dominican Republic. To cope with the latter, only ad hoc measures, such as direct food support (*Lomer es primero*), have been developed.

A short note might be in place here also about Cuba, which today is one of the few Socialist states remaining around the world because the history and consequences of this revolution are quite similar to other cases (see Chapter 7 on Cuba; Fagg 1963: 761–7; Skidmore and Smith 2001: 259–88; Ranis and Kosack 2004; Mesa-Lago 2009; Meissner et al. 2008: 208–13). The outcomes of the Cuban revolution must be considered as highly ambivalent. When Fidel Castro overthrew the authoritarian Batista government in 1959, Cuba was one of the best developed countries in Latin America. Violence and suppression were involved also in the Cuban revolution which saw thousands of deaths (among them, many due to executions); till today, nearly all forms of political dissent are suppressed by force. The coercive character of the regime manifests itself also in a continuous emigration which at times was suppressed by the government with legal, military and police measures. The socialization measures – a land reform in 1959 which expropriated all estates with more than 1,000 acres – and the abolition of private property contributed significantly to an increased overall economic equality. However, they also led toward a shrinking economy and widespread poverty. Certainly also the boycott by the United States contributed to the economic difficulties. The Soviet Union, and recently Venezuela, supported Cuba massively; it is questionable, however, if this support (which created strong dependency) was really beneficial in the long term. Additional achievements on the positive side of the Cuban revolution are significant improvements in terms of social programs and spending for the educational and health provision of the population at large; they have produced one of the best educated peoples in the region and a comprehensive provision of health services throughout the country. Overall, the aim of achieving more equality was certainly attained in the first decades of the revolution. According to Mesa-Lago (2009: 377), the Gini coefficient decreased from 55 in 1953 to 25 in 1989, but then rose again to 41 in 1999. The cost, however, was an 'overwhelmingly negative economic performance' (Mesa-Lago 2009: 380) and a suppression of civil liberties and political freedom. However, given the highly qualified workforce and the well-developed social system, Cuba has very positive opportunities for the future if it is able to pursue efficient, gradual reforms of the economic system and to maintain its commitment to human development (Ranis and Kosack 2004).

Hispanic Latin America: Toward New National Races?

The next and largest area which shows a relatively homogeneous ethnic composition are the countries which have a predominant *mestizo* population and large proportions of indigenous Indians; they include Mexico and the countries along the Pacific coast down to Chile, Bolivia and Paraguay. These were the main and most profitable colonies of Spain: Mexico because of its silver sources and fine woods, and later as a producer of sugar, cacao and coffee; the present-day Bolivia and Peru because of their silver deposits, mainly in Potosi. Here the Spaniards introduced the *encomienda* system in which large estates were given to the *conquistadores*, including the right to exploit the people living on the territory (see Fagg 1963; Wolf 1982; Donghi 1991; Fausto 1994). In these regions, the indigenous Indian population was much larger than in the Caribbean. It remained the basic population stock (Fagg 1963: 311) in spite of the fact that it had been decimated radically through epidemics, slave riding and ethnic cleansing – probably the greatest demographic and cultural catastrophe in human history.[4] Since the Indios were exploited massively after the conquest of these territories, in 1542 the *Leyes Nuevos* by Spain were enacted to restrict the worst forms of exploitation. The Indios were concentrated in their own communities (*repartimientos*) which collectively were responsible for providing labour to the owners of the land and to the state or to work in the silver mines. Thus, exploitation took the form of enforced labour[5] and peonage – somewhat less cruel than the slavery in the Caribbean and Brazil. This system also made it possible for the Indians to survive and grow again in demographic terms. However, the Indios were seen very negatively by the White population until the early 20th century; they were considered as being trapped in archaic traditions, as barbaric and non-rational people, even similar to animals (Fagg 1963: 312; Wünderlich 1999; Burkholder and Johnson 2010: 135–43).

Since intermarriage was frequent between the Indians and the Creoles (the descendants of the original Spanish invaders), in the course of time the *mestizos* became the largest population group. For instance, in Mexico in 1800, the population of about 6 million consisted of one million Whites, 3.5 million Indios and 1.5 million *mestizos*, that is, only about 25 per cent of the population were White. Today, about 90 per cent are *mestizos*. Therefore, it became impossible to define countries like Guatemala, Honduras and Nicaragua as Creole (that is, White) nations. In this process of intermixing of the 'races' also a new cultural and political identity developed. Today the term 'Mexicans' is used and preferred by the people of Mexico instead of the term *mestizos*. This term has some pejorative connotations, denoting the outcome of a mixing (*mestizaje*) of European and Amerindian (and to a weaker degree also African) social and cultural elements. In this sense, also the Constitution of 1917 devotes a special paragraph to the name and definition of 'Mexicans'.[6] Consequently and in contrast to the United States and Brazil, race or skin colour is not a category used in the census or any other official survey. Thus, *mestizaye* became an official ideology, positing that race differences are not relevant any more.

Several recent studies have shown, however, that the reality does not correspond fully to this ideal. Andrés Villarreal (2010) analysed the large Mexican Panel Study of 2006 in which interviewers were asked to code the respondents' skin colour. Two results are most important here: first, it turned out the interviewers were able to classify in a reliable way the skin colour of the respondents (as indicated by the fact that the classifications of the same individuals by different interviewers showed a high correspondence); and, second, the colour of the respondents was significantly correlated with educational attainment, occupational status and socio-economic poverty, controlling for other relevant characteristics (see also Telles 2004; Wade 1997). Villarreal as well as ethnographic research shows that 'White' is considered as superior and desirable, and 'Black' as inferior. Flores and Telles (2010) have recently supplemented the analysis of Villarreal, showing that skin colour exerts its effect mainly through education, while parents' occupation appeared as a stronger predictor of occupational status. Telles (2004: 107–38) has shown in his detailed analysis of ethnic discrimination that in terms of the different dimensions of social class and status (employment, occupation, income), the expansion of higher education has benefitted disproportionately the Whites. Thus, the difference to Brazil (and even to the USA) may not be as large as indicated by the distinct ideologies of race. Villarreal (2010: 672) concludes with a critical comment on this specific Mexican ideology of *mestizaye* that it 'impedes social mobilization to address disparities across individuals of different skin colour ... an ideology of non-racialism that is avowedly antiracist may actually deter the kind of mobilization that could bring about the social reforms necessary to realize racial equality'. While the recent rise of indigenous liberation movements (such as the Zapatistas in Chiapas in south-eastern Mexico) indicates such a mobilization, a similar one is hard to imagine for individuals with darker skin colour.

---

4   According to some estimates, there were 50 million people living in America at the time of the arrival of the Europeans; their number was reduced to a few millions within a short period of time.

5   In the *quatequil* system, the able-bodied males of a village had to work for two weeks and four times a year for state projects or Spanish employers (Fagg 1963: 311).

6   Ch. II: Mexicans are all those born in the territory of Mexico or outside it but from Mexican parents. See http://www.oas.org/juridico/mla/en/mex/en_mex-int-text-const.pdf. Similar strategies were pursued in Paraguay in the early 19th century (Riekenberg 2009: 58).

'White' Latin America – an Exception?

The third sub-group of Latin American countries are the 'White' countries in the South of the sub-continent, Argentina and Uruguay. In part, also Chile with its sizable proportion of Whites (about 30 per cent) belongs to this group. The ethnic composition of these countries resulted from the fact that these 'frontier' regions were inhabited only by few indigenous people and settled by Whites only later (Riekenberg 2009: 15). The majority of the present-day population in the mega-cities of Buenos Aires and Montevideo in the Rio de las Platas area are the descendants of immigrants between 1880 and 1930, mainly Italians and Spaniards (Riekenberg 2009: 106ff.). However, the low proportion of *mestizos* was also a consequence of their discrimination and an official policy of keeping the countries 'White' (comparable to the Australian policy; see Chapter 5, p. 131) by facilitating immigration from Europe. The same policy of 'Whitening the Black out' was pursued by Brazil between 1870 and 1940 (Telles 2004: 29–33; Andrews 2004: 119–24), but with less success given the higher proportion of Blacks imported as slaves in earlier times. Economic inequality in these 'White' Latin American countries is somewhat lower than in those where extended slavery and forced labour was used. The fact that in worldwide comparative terms it is also very high could be seen as disproving the central thesis of this book, that historical ethno-class exploitation (slavery) was one of the main forces producing the extreme inequality in Latin America. Several authors (for example Deininger and Squire 1998; Li et al. 1998; Frankema 2009a, b) have argued that unequal land distribution was the main historical factor decisive for later economic inequality. In Chapter 4 we found in fact a significant effect of this variable on income distribution.

However, there are two counter-arguments against the thesis that land distribution per se was the decisive factor for the extreme inequality. First, the colonizers and dominant classes in these 'White' Latin American countries made sure that their regions developed in a similar way as in the other parts of the sub-continent. Thus, even if they did not practice slavery on a large scale, they practiced a massive exploitation also of the labour force 'imported' from Europe and – in earlier periods – in part also from Asia. Second, during colonial times there were substantial numbers of slaves – Blacks and others – also in these regions. As early as in 1580, Portuguese businessmen carried out a slave trade through the port of Buenos Aires. Around 1800, nearly 30 per cent of the population in this city were slaves (Riekenberg 2009: 23, 38). In the early 19th century, Blacks made up nearly 30 per cent of the population in Argentina and Chile.[7] The historical influence of the Blacks is also documented by cultural elements in Argentina such as the *tango*, the *milonga* and the *zamba*, all words of Bantu origin (see also Geler 2005). In addition, there were and still are considerable numbers of Indios in these regions. This is contrary to the 'founding myth' of Chile as consisting of one homogeneous *mestizo* race which was claimed as early as in 1907 after the publication of census results. Skin colour or race is relevant for income still today also in Chile (Barandiarán 2012).

Interim Résumé

The main patterns of social, economic and political inequality throughout Hispanic America include three main elements: (1) a privileged economic elite which historically was based on the ownership of large estates and today controls the profitable export-oriented enterprises (maybe together with or on behalf of foreign capital owners); this economic elite is intertwined closely with the political class (including the military); (2) a very unequal land distribution which offers few opportunities for smaller independent farmers and – together with effective processes of mechanization of agricultural work – produces a growing rural surplus population whose alternative is only to migrate to the emerging mega-cities; (3) since the labour markets of these cities are unable to absorb the incoming people, a large new underclass develops whose life and income conditions are highly precarious. Most of the members of this class are constrained to seek an income in marginal service sectors as 'penny capitalists', as unregistered and unprotected street vendors and retailers of cheap (mainly imported) products (textiles, toys, electronic devices and so on). In Mexico, up to 60 per cent of the economically active population are employed in these forms of marginal self-employment (Sernau 1994: 85; Bayón 2008).[8] It is evident that many of these people are of indigenous origin.

---

7   http://en.wikipedia.org/wiki/Miscegenation

8   See also *Instituto Nacional de Estatistica Geografia*, Census y Conteos de Poblation y Vivienda; http://www.censo2010.org.mx/

The main lines of ethnic discrimination, however, may not be related to the gulf between the better developed central parts of the large cities and the slums (*favelas*) which have developed around them. Rather it is the indigenous population living in the more remote, rural regions and villages which is most disadvantaged. Here, the whole infrastructure is deficient and opportunities for jobs and for educational and social advancement are the worst (Sernau 1994: 114–8). An important factor which contributes to rural underdevelopment in Mexico – which to a large part is an indirect form of ethnic discrimination – is language. Although the use of Indian languages has declined somewhat in relative terms, still 7 per cent to 8 per cent of the population are speaking them; in remote regions (such as Yucatan), the proportion of their speakers rises to 50 per cent (Sernau 1994: 115). The consequence is not only economic deprivation, but a comprehensive social or 'class isolation'. Such isolation occurs

> ... when the characteristics of one sector of the economy render the workers less suitable or marketable in another sector ... this is compounded when those subcultural class traits [e.g., the ability to make frequent job changes, subordinate job demands to immediately family needs] are interwoven with long-standing ethnically based cultural attributes (e.g., fatalistic passivity).

Visible ethnic characteristics reinforce the cycle of stereotyping demonstrated by Gunnar Myrdal already in the 1940s (Myrdal 1980). Low-income Mexicans with predominantly Indian characteristics are likely 'to find the social isolation of their class ethnically reinforced and the resulting exclusion from more secure and remunerative sectors to be even more complete' (Sernau 1994: 116–7).

Origins and Structural Forces which Produced and which Sustain Glaring Inequality

The Political Pillars of Inequality

The extremely high level of economic inequality has been produced and safeguarded by the political systems in Latin America. In the colonial period, the Spanish system of *castas* was transposed to Hispanic America. Here, a clear caste hierarchy emerged, with the White Spaniards on top in command positions, their offspring, the Creoles, on the next level, followed by different groups of *mestizos* (people of mixed, often brown colour), and the Black population, the descendants of the African slaves, as well as the indigenous Indios, on the bottom (Donghi 1991: 50ff.; Nash 1995; Andrews 2004). Thus, one can also speak of the existence of 'societies of caste' in Latin America (Burkholder and Johnson 2010: 194). The Spaniards were keenly honour- and prestige-oriented. In their colonial societies, the principle of *limpieza de sangre* was important (Burkholder and Johnson 2010: 198). This concept had been developed in Spain in the course of the prosecution and expulsion of Muslims and Jews in the early Modern Age and was used to distinguish to 'old' Christians from the proselytes descended from Muslims or Jews (Riekenberg 2009: 20). The designation *negro* used in Hispanic America for the Blacks contained an aggressive overtone, although the Blacks themselves were also proud of their African cultural heritage (Gillian 1976; Hofbauer 1995).

Most countries of Latin America became politically independent Republics already in the first third of the 19th century. But the emerging regimes were unstable and corrupt, dominated by the oligarchic and wealthy White elite, including powerful regional land owners and military chiefs (*caudillos*; see Bakewell 1997; for Argentina Riekenberg 2009: 79–85). In this regard, the world systems theory of Immanuel Wallerstein (1974) and the related dependency theory (Frank 1978) are clearly valid analyses. They argue that since the onset of the Modern Age, a tripartition of the world economy evolved, with the core, dominant countries in Europe, the peripheral countries in the least developed South, and a group of semi-peripheral countries in-between. The first were focusing upon the new industrial productions and worldwide trade activities, requiring new technologies and skilled labour, while the peripheral countries had to provide raw materials, labour-intensive products and low-skilled work and productions. Imperialism was the political side of this global division of labour, leading to the conquest, domination and exploitation of the territories and peoples in the South by the European core nations (see also Meissner et al. 2008: 34–98). Also in the case of Latin America, it is evident that foreign economic and military interests played a decisive role in its development. Brazil became a Republic in 1889 and today it has a democratic and federal constitution. Political rights for the whole population, however, were granted quite late; still in the 1930s, only 5 per cent of the adults had voting rights. A military regime had dethroned the last emperor in 1889 – not the least for the reason that slavery was abolished the year before. One important reason for the resistance against abolition was that the Whites perceived the *negroes* as a danger. Therefore, also plans to relocate the Blacks to Africa were developed (de Azevedo 2004). A quasi-authoritarian populist system, the *Estado Nuevo*, was established under the leadership of President Getúlio Vargas in Brazil; he was brought to power in 1930 by the military and governed till 1945.[9] The military governed also during many periods of recent Brazilian history, at the last between 1964 and 1985; it is well known that this regime used brutal force against many oppositional groups. An authoritarian political system was also imposed in Argentina between 1946 and 1955 by the former military leader Juan D. Peron. He enacted an extensive program of nationalization and social reform which became known as *Peronism* (Riekenberg 2009: 145–60).

The power of the military regimes which were ruling between the 1930s and the 1980s in many Latin American countries was based on a corporatist alliance between government and state bureaucracy on the one side, and the land-owning feudal 'lords' and Capitalist entrepreneurs on the other side. It is quite evident that the high degree of ethnic homogeneity of this dominant class was a decisive factor for its power, thus confirming the general hypothesis proposed in Chapter 3 (pp. 64–6). The laws enacted by the military governments restricted civil and political liberties and the possibilities for leaders of oppositional groups to act as candidates for political offices. The predominant interest of the economic and political elites was not to develop their countries but to preserve their power and privileges. They have been called, appropriately, a 'rentier bourgeoisie' in Eduardo Galeano's critical history of Latin America (Galeano 2003: 334). Their main 'capital' were slaves who not only provided labour power but were also an indicator of an aristocratic status and style of life (Freyre 1964). Since the early 20th century, the United States displaced the United Kingdom as the most important and powerful foreign economy for Latin America; their oligopolistic and monopolistic corporations strengthened the external dependence of Latin American economy (Galeano 2003: 313ff.; Boris et al. 2008: 16ff.).

One can, with reference to Latin America as a whole, speak of an alliance between the internally dominating classes and the foreign bourgeoisie which invests in these countries in the interest of high returns on the placed capital (Bonacich 1980: 19; see also Wallenstein 1974). At the level of the Brazilian federal states, the system of *coronelismo* is dominating political life and undermining the strengths of federalism. Regional oligarchs, in most cases large land owners and other wealthy personalities, exert a nearly unrestrained power, based on a complex, obscure system of clientelism, corruption and violence (Speck 2010; Schönenberg 2010). In the last decades, this system has even been strengthened in some countries (Hoffman and Centeno 2003: 371): caused by the state's financial crisis and in connection with the worldwide spread of neoliberal principles of economic policy, governmental activities were restricted more and more. The resulting weakness of the state has increased the problems of the insufficient social protection (still in 1969, only 3 per cent of the Brazilians had a social insurance) and of the unequal treatment of different groups in terms of taxation (Portes and Ferguson 1977: 86).

The population in Latin America clearly perceives these facts. Table 9.2 shows that the proportion of those who have no confidence in government is significantly higher (mean value: 39 per cent) in the nine Latin American countries than in any country included in the table. The same is true for the trust in other people (83 per cent vs. 40 per cent to 70 per cent in most other countries). Also the proportion of people who have no political interests is higher than elsewhere (in many Latin American countries between 28 per cent and 33 per cent compared with only 10 per cent to 20 per cent in most other countries). Three-quarters of the Latin Americans believe that their country is run by big interests, one-third thinks that public officials are corrupt and two-thirds that the poor have no chance to get ahead in life. Only people in Nigeria, South Africa and Russia show similar high levels of pessimistic and critical views and political discontent.

---

9   In 1954, Vargas was elected again as president, but lost the support of the military; he shot himself death in the same year.

Table 9.2   Social and political attitudes in 29 countries around the world (1995–97; per cent agree)

	Little trust in other people*	No political interest	No con- fidence in government	Country is run by big interests	The poor have no chance	All public officials are corrupt
Argentina	82	33	41	88	74	37
Brazil	97	32	32	75	71	57
Chile	79	14	48	68	59	16
Peru	95	13	34	43	50	23
Mexico	72	27	35	71	59	41
Venezuela	86	44	64	84	59	44
Uruguay	78	26	34	77	76	13
Dominican Rep.	74	33	20	92	62	49
Colombia	89	28	44	79	56	29
(Mean value)	(83)	28)	(39)	75)	(63)	(34)
South Africa	84	10	22	44	51	16
Nigeria	81	41	30	86	74	57
USA	64	14	13	73	29	15
W-Germany	58	21	6	64	83	6
Spain	69	23	41	67	73	17
Sweden	40	11	12	59	52	5
Switzerland	63	12	19	61	–	8
Russia	76	3	18	93	85	41
Japan	57	15	7	23	20	–
India	62	12	29	71	47	27

*The variable numbers in the WVS are: v27, v117, v142, v166, v173, and v213.
Source: World Value Survey (WVS) 1995–97.

Religion as Ideology. The Ambiguous Role of the Catholic Church

A problem for Latin America was and still is the fact that no ideology of equality exists which is effective and well-anchored in society and which could challenge the unequal system of power and privileges. Catholicism, the dominant religion in Latin America, played an ambivalent role in this regard. On the one side, it had a positive influence in regard to the relations between the races, as indicated above, because it was less exclusive than Protestantism for parts of the population. In colonial times, it also performed most of the functions of the modern state in education and welfare (Fagg 1963: 230). However, in historic times also it represented a corporatist ideology which legitimized imperial expansion and exploitative colonial practices (including slavery) (Donghi 1991; Hofbauer 1995: 110–113). The Catholic Church was the largest land owner; the Jesuits, convents and many individual priests owned slaves (Burkholder and Johnson 2010: 153). Still today, the Catholic Church supports the political and economic status quo by and large. Thus, it contributes to the justification of the position and privileges of the powerful and requires the poor to remain quiet and fulfil their daily duties (Portes and Ferguson 1977; Gonzalez 2006; Höllinger 2007). In addition, the Catholic Church from the beginning was practising a magical cult of saints and organizing vast religious festivities which included many elements of the pagan cults of the Indians and Blacks (such as voodoo). At the same time, it attempted to keep at a distance the modernizing tendencies in European Catholicism. For common people, which de facto practices a religious eclecticism, the participation in church festivities, magic rituals and old and new religious movements generates a certain kind of consolation given the glaring inequalities and injustices (Hofbauer 1995: 127ff; Höllinger 2007: 239; Haller and Höllinger 2009). For poor people, however, the participation in formal religious ceremonies, like baptism, marriage or funerals, often is impossible because they cannot afford the high fees asked for them (Borsdorf 1999). Today, Brazilian society is very pluralistic in religious terms: while Catholics remain dominant, the proportion of its adherents is shrinking; Pentecostal churches have strongly increased, as have the numbers of people without formal church membership.

The proponents of the liberation theology in the 1960s, such as Gustavo Gutiérrez, Dom Helder Camara, and Leonardo Boff, tried to sensibilise the Church for social problems and processes of exploitation but could not reach the masses. After the conservative turn of Roman Catholicism after the Second Vatican Council they were themselves suppressed by the Church hierarchy. Recently at least, also the official Catholic Church has criticized excesses of political suppression and economic exploitation. An encouraging event in this regard was the election the arch-bishop of Buenos Aires, Jorge Mario Bergoglio, as the first pope of the Catholic Church from the Southern Hemisphere.[10] He had criticized excessive inequality and corruption in Latin America already in his former position. As newly elected pope, he attacked unbridled Capitalism and said that he would like to have 'a poor church, a church for the poor'. Such statements by a pope of the Catholic Church may not have direct political consequences. Nevertheless, they are important both because they remind politicians of their duties, and because they give some hope and strengthen self-consciousness among the exploited poor masses who suffer also from societal and political neglect and depreciation. In view of these facts, it is surprising that it seems to be a characteristic of the poor in Brazil that they try to make the best out of adverse life circumstances without becoming immersed in pessimism and despair as seems to be the case in many post-Communist East European countries. In fact, given the moderate level of economic development of their countries, people in Latin America show a surprising high level of happiness (Haller and Hadler 2006). A study on the youth population in a poor residential area in Salvador found that it was very important for them 'to emanate optimism, to demonstrate personal strength and capacity to act instead of quarrying with the past' (Kühn 2006: 137; see also Galeano 2003; Moritz Schwarcz 2003).

Brazil: the Coloured Class and Status Structure

Brazil is the fifth largest state on earth both in terms of geographic extension and population (about 190 million people in 2010), and by far the largest country in Latin America. Table 1.1 (p. 56) shows that Brazil is also one of the three Latin American countries with the highest degree of economic inequality (Gini 59); only half a dozen Sub-Saharan African countries are more unequal (see also Boekle 2010). Also its specific form of ethnic stratification makes Brazil a particularly important and challenging case for this book. In this section, I will first discuss some relevant aspects of the recent economic and social structural developments, including the concept of 'race democracy' and its validity today. Then, I will present statistical data and a reanalysis of the ISSP survey 1999 on inequality in order to prove the existence of a 'coloured class and status structure', that is, of a close interaction between class and ethnicity.

Development of Economy and Society in Recent Times

The European settlement of Brazil began with its discovery by the Portuguese Pedro Alvares Cabral in 1500. After a period of slow development, from the mid-16th century on, plantations for sugar, cocoa and tobacco were established in the northeast. The workers needed were found among Indians captured by mercenaries (*bandeirantes*) in the interior of the country, but soon slaves from Africa were imported because the Indios could not supply enough labour power as outlined before. Later on, the detection of gold in the interior of the country (the present-day province of Minas Gerais) led to a rush of new immigrants from Europe. In the 19th and 20th centuries, Brazilian economy, population and settlement patterns changed again fundamentally because the plantations in the ortheast lost their profitability and millions of Blacks moved to the southeast, attracted by the prosperous new industrial and commercial region around the growing mega-cities Sao Paolo and Rio de Janeiro. Also new waves of immigration from Southern Europe took place.

---

10   See http://en.wikipedia.org/wiki/Pope_Francis

The differences between Brazil and the other Latin American countries have historical roots in their different forms of colonialism. They are based – among other things – on the fact that Brazil was colonized by Portugal, but the rest of Latin America by Spain. The Portuguese conquistadors were more ready from the beginning to intermix with the native population and the slaves whom they had 'imported' from Africa and with the descendants of the slaves (Freyre 1964). This was due firstly to demographic reasons because the majority of the Portuguese settlers were men. In addition, however, already in Europe the Portuguese had more close relations with their African neighbours than Spaniards and were also the first involved in the slave trade, as pointed out in Chapter 5 (p. 148): the Spaniards had already waged a war against 'heretics' (the Moors and Jews) on their own territory and driven them from their country in the early Modern Age.

Brazilian economy has been based since the early days of colonization on two pillars: a system of large land holdings – *haciendas* – which produced precious products for export to Europe (sugar, cotton, tobacco and so on). They were based on the labour of imported African slaves. In addition, international concerns exploited mineral resources. The basis of this economy was a very unequal land distribution. Land on the new continent was not owned privately by the Indians living there; in fact, as in many other parts of the South, the concept of land ownership was unknown to the indigenous peoples. The Portuguese and Spanish invaders declared the land as belonging to their kings. The kings distributed the land to the *conquistadores* and immigrants. While the Spanish tried to avoid a concentration of land ownership, the Portuguese Crown enabled the emergence of huge *haciendas* (Fagg 1963: 181ff., 385ff.; Konetzke 1965: 42–58; Bakewell 1997). This was made possible by the fact that together with a few nobles, many poor people, unskilled workers, agricultural labourers and servants also emigrated to Brazil; the latter, however, were not able to establish their own farms. The apportionment of the land was influenced strongly by the social position and the personal networks of the nobles to the Crown. The large land owners concentrated on the cultivation of products for export, such as sugar and cotton. In order to provide for the scarce and much needed labour power, during three centuries (1548–1850) at least 2.5 million Africans were imported as slaves, particularly to the northeast region of Brazil. In Salvador de Bahia, for instance, 50 per cent of the 800,000 inhabitants in the early 18th century were Blacks of African origin (Gillian 1976). This fact has had far-reaching consequences for Brazilian society up to today (Skidmore and Smith 2001: 24).

In colonial times, non-White people were considered as 'uncivilized', nearly as non-human savages; this racism legitimized their brute exploitation (Silverio 2004). However, between many owners of *haciendas* and their slave servants a patrimonial relation existed which comprised elements of domination and provision at the same time; the first had to care also for the basic needs of the latter. These relations have been described in the brilliant, worldwide acclaimed best-seller of the sociologist Gilberto Freyre *Casa grande & senzala* (literally 'Big house and slave cottage'), first published in 1936 (Freyre 1964). The African slaves brought many elements of their culture and ways of life to Brazil and the Caribbean; they contributed significantly to the development of the new society and culture (Davis 1995; Schröter 1999).

After the prohibition of slavery, which occurred in Brazil only in 1888, slaves were partly replaced until the 1930s by workers hired in Southern Europe. The liberation of the slaves and the other members of the lowest classes (which included also coloured and White people), however, did not improve their lot very much, as was shown already in Chapter 4 (pp. 145–7). Many of the former slaves had to leave the countryside and the impoverished northeast region as they lost their work. Large *haciendas* were simply abandoned because the world prices of their products often broke down within a short time; in the sequel, whole villages and towns decayed (Meissner et al. 2008: 217–8). As a consequence of the migration of former slaves from the countryside to the towns, huge *favelas* emerged at the outskirts of the large cities. They were populated with a new sub-proletariat composed of people of all skin colours, who had to live on casual labour and precarious forms of trade and services.[11] This lowest social stratum, called *ralé*, is deprived in economic terms and also excluded in socio-cultural terms (de Souza 2006, 2009). Today, there are millions of landless

---

11   This can clearly be observed in megacities like Mexico City. During my participation in the annual ISSP conference in this town in May 2005, my wife and I were impressed but also saddened by the fact that in very long streets in the centre of the town on both sidewalks and in the middle of the streets retail dealers were offering their merchandises (which we would consider often as junk). A newspaper article reported that not less than half a million people were living off such kinds of trade and that the city administration was under hard pressure to find a way to regulate their activities legally.

people who are constrained to earn their livelihood as day labourers and migrant workers. Many of them are recruited on the peripheries of the megacities by *gatos* and brought to mines, plantations or rain forests thousands of kilometres away; there, they have often to give up their documents to the employer and work under miserable conditions and starvation wages, thus, as real 'modern slaves' (Bales 2004: 121–48; Meissner et al. 2008: 270).[12] The continuity of the situation of all these groups with the traditions of the slave system can hardly be overlooked. Also for the slave it was stated that he/she had 'been transformed into a commodity and deprived of his human dignity in the eyes of society' (Santos 1985: 152). But also large groups of urban workers and labourers are deprived in many regards. One main cause for this is the poor state of the Brazilian public education system which is not able to provide school leaving certificates for most people from lower strata and in peripheral rural regions (Perez et al. 2010). At the other side, there exist expanding, but quite heterogeneous middle classes. Altogether, this leads to 'the two fundamental and permanent characteristics of Latin American societal development: Determination from outside and high [internal] heterogeneity' (Boris et al. 2008: 209): particularly the urban working class in Brazil was and still is characterized by a very low degree of ethnic homogeneity. Its weak political participation is a direct consequence. This fact is of utmost importance since already in the 1970s, 70 per cent of the population were living in cities.

The Brazilian 'Race Democracy' and its Limits

As a consequence of the specific relations between masters and servants, in Brazil a peculiar system of race relations emerged. There was no open race discrimination and a considerable amount of intermarriage (miscegenation) took place although the Black and coloured women were subject to many forms of exploitation (Gillian 1976). These specific race relations were designated as 'race democracy' by the prominent Brazilian sociologist Gilberto Freyre (1964) in his book mentioned above. This concept became accepted and used frequently also in Brazilian politics because it provided the elites with a legitimation of the existing social structure. In fact, there are significant differences in the system of race relations in the USA and Latin America and Brazil (Marx 1998): aside of the lack of open race discrimination, in Latin America the concept of race is related less to skin colour as such, but to a broad ensemble of social characteristics, including social descent and place of residence, occupational position and activity, appearance and style of life. A *negro*[13] is in the first instance considered as a slum dweller (among them, there are in fact also coloured and White people). The inhabitants of Indian villages are called *Indios*; since they occupy the lowest position, the concept of Indio is also used to characterize the lowest stratum (Pitt-Rivers 1969). People with darker skin, however, are also described as being more emotional and sexually sensible, a light skin colour indicates higher status, but also frigidity. One reason for the absence of racial discrimination in terms of a prohibition of intermarriages in Latin America, in stark contrast to Anglo-Saxon North America, was the position of the Catholic Church in this regard. It can be traced back to passages in the Bible (New Testament) which only forbid marriages between Christians and non-Christians, but admits that 'persons of all nations, tribes, peoples, and tongues' will stand before God's throne after the Apocalypse.[14] This is a clear difference to the exclusivist position of many Protestant churches which relied to a larger extent on the Old Testament which stresses the uniqueness of the 'chosen people' and of Judaism; both these religious traditions have laid the ideological basis for systems of Apartheid (see Chapters 11 and 12). Particularly the Portuguese men were ready to mix with Black and Indian women as noted before. The frequency of ethnic intermarriages can clearly be seen in the significant increase of the mixed population (the browns) in the Brazilian population during the last century. In 1835, the proportion of Whites was 24 per cent, of Blacks 51 per cent and of brown-skinned people 18 per cent; till 2008, that of the Whites increased to 49 per cent (due to immigration and high birth rates), that of the Blacks decreased to only 6 per cent; but the proportion of the mixed group (those of brown skin) increased most strongly to 44 per cent (Skidmore 1992). Certainly, a part of this increase is artificial as mixed colour is less and less seen as a stigma.

---

12   See also 'Geht's der Wirtschaft gut …' Welthaus-Info (Graz), 2011, no. 9, p. 9.

13   This word for Blacks should not be confounded with the derogatory American word *Nigger*.

14   This and additional quotations are collected in Nil Desperandum, On interracial marriage: The moral status of miscegenation, see http://faithandheritage.com/2011/05/the-moral-status-of-miscegenation/

Recent sociological research has strongly criticized the concept of 'race democracy', the most extensive and systematic discussion is provided by Eduard Telles (2004: 47–77). Many studies have shown that skin colour still is a highly significant determinant of life chances in Brazil (Silverio 2004; Twine 1998; Villarreal 2010; Barandiarán 2012). In addition, it was argued that the concept of race democracy could be used even against Black and coloured people because it suppressed the feeling of discrimination among them (Marx 1998: 164). However, in a representative survey, Bailey (2002) could disprove the thesis that the Blacks had fully internalized the ideology of race democracy. The population in Brazil in fact holds structural reasons but not personal or socio-cultural factors as mainly responsible for the deprivation of the Blacks. Between 70 per cent and 90 per cent of people in Latin America (except Peru) think that their country is run by the interests of the capital, the rich; owners of large businesses (see Table 9.2); in other countries, this proportion is at most 60 per cent. Nevertheless, it is a matter of fact that the concept and the reality of 'race democracy' made it difficult for the deprived Black and coloured people in Brazil to organize themselves against a common enemy. Since the 1980s, significant changes have been going on. First, a Black movement is developing which speaks openly about racism and denounces its practices, and also Afro-Brazilian politicians are emerging (Andrews 2004: 197–201). Second, the concept of race democracy has become a thing of the past in Brazilian politics as well; there is now recognition of racism and the state has initiated surprising activities of affirmative action (Telles 2004: 75) – I will come back to them in the final Chapter 13.

In place of collective fights for more equality both in Brazilian politics and civilian life, individual mobility was propagated through 'Whitening' (*branqueamento*) (Gillian 1976; Telles 2004: 28–9). This is in fact possible in several forms: one is by marrying a person with a lighter skin colour, another one by taking over the outfit and behaviour of White people of higher status. The first way is more typical for females (who also describe themselves more often as White than males), the latter among males. In their case, 'Whitening' is often a consequence of occupational success and upward mobility. In both these ways, persons with relatively dark skin colour can classify themselves as 'Whites'. We can say, therefore, that 'colour is an ingredient not a determinant of class' (Pitt-Rivers 1969: 386; see also Moritz Schwarcz 2003). Comparing race relations in the USA and Brazil, Luisa Farah Schwartzman (2007: 9602) concluded that in the United States, racial boundaries among Blacks and Whites 'serve to keep class boundaries in place', while in Brazil, 'class boundaries serve to keep racial boundaries in place'. For Brazil, Schwartzman found in fact that 'money Whitens' and 'poverty darkens'; dark parents from higher classes have possibilities to assign their children to a 'Whiter' status, while the reverse is true for White parents in the lower classes. In fact, there exists an extremely finely differentiated continuum of skin colours: besides the three main types – White, brown-skinned and Black – many intermediate shades of colour are distinguished in daily life. In the Brazilian census of 1991, people used about 100 different words to describe their race (Hoffman and Centeno 2003: 378; Telles 2004: 78–106). Usually, a distinction is made between five groups: Whites (*brancos*; about 50 per cent of the population), Blacks (*pretos*, about 6 per cent), brown-skinned (*pardos*, about 43 per cent), Indians (*indigenos*, less than 1 per cent), and yellow-skinned (*amarelos*, people of Asiatic origin). If the partners in a couple have a different colour, they try to classify their children in the respective lighter category. Here we see clearly the close interaction between social stratification and ethnic group membership: because it is unequivocal that the dominant and privileged people are White, and the deprived and exploited are Black, everything positive is an associated with 'White', everything negative with 'Black'. To be White, however, does not automatically mean to belong to the higher classes (Moritz Schwarcz 2003: 39).

The Coloured Class Structure

Social structures in Latin America and Brazil can be seen as a particularly strong and problematic interaction between class stratification and ethnic differentiation ('problematic' from the perspective of its perdurability). The research results presented so far make clear that the discrimination by colour to a large degree is class discrimination. This is quite evident also if we look at patterns of land distribution. In 1985, three million small farmers (*campesinos*) owned only 2.7 per cent of the arable land, but an extremely small group of about 50 large land owners owned 43.7 per cent (Höllinger 2007: 83). Incomes of the Black population in Rio de Janeiro stand at only half the incomes of the White population (Marx 1998: 172). Even if the interaction between ethnic differentiation and class stratification is more than evident, it is overlooked in many relevant social scientific works as noted in the introduction to this chapter (p. 230). In reality, however, we can understand the extreme inequality between the classes as well as the weakness of unions and leftist political parties only by considering just this interaction between class and ethnicity: the extreme power of the dominant classes is based on their ethnic homogeneity, a religiously legitimized hierarchical-patriarchal societal ideology and latent, but nevertheless quite effective, race discrimination. Such a discrimination is forbidden officially and in the public sphere – corresponding to the ideology of 'race democracy' effective for a long time – but is nevertheless practised in private life. Surveys have shown that 90 per cent of Brazilians say they have no racial prejudices and had not experienced personal discrimination; when asked, however, if somebody in the personal social context has experienced them, they indicate this frequently (Moritz Schwarcz 2003: 5). Hoffman and Centeno (2003: 373) point to the political consequences of the deep split between the rich and the poor in Brazil: 'The concentration of power in the first (that is the rich) and the heterogeneity of the second has made it practically impossible to organize a coherent political program, resulting often in illusionary populist appeals that do nothing but reproduce the same class structures'. My designation of the ethnic and class stratification in Brazil as 'coloured class structure' indicates that class power and class and status-based social relations are the dominant base for patterns of privilege and deprivation, but that they are closely related to patterns of race[15] or ethnic differentiation. I argue, in fact, that cannot be understood rightly without taking into account this aspect. Let us look more closely at this interaction, first by summarizing some pertinent studies, second, by presenting results of the census of 2010 and a reanalysis of ISSP 1999 in Brazil.

Several sociologists have carried out comprehensive studies on social inequality and the educational, employment and occupational chances of coloured Brazilians today which strongly confirm my argument. Their results can be summarized in four points (see Twine 1998; Cireno Fernandes 2005; Figueiredo Santos 2006b; Costa Ribeiro 2007; Guerreiro Osório 2008; Bailey 2009): (1) ethnic membership determines life chances independently of other factors in a significant way; this effect does not decrease among younger cohorts; (2) an important factor is regional location. Life chances are much worse in the thinly settled north and northwest regions of Brazil, including the huge Amazon Basin where the proportion of Blacks and Indios comprises two-thirds of the population (in the south it is between one-third and one-quarter) (Kohlhepp 2010); (3) the discrimination of the Black population in terms of education and income is particularly strong at the higher levels of the educational and income structure; (4) but also at the lower levels, discrimination by skin colour exists. The Brazilian sociologist Jessé de Souza (2009) argues, based on his comprehensive in-depth qualitative study, that a 'structural underclass' (*ralé*) has been formed which is not only discriminated economically, but also in social and cultural terms.

These facts can be documented and analysed further with some recent data: Table 9.3 presents the distribution of the population by education and income, using data from the most recent Brazilian census (2010). Here we see that Whites have a clear edge over the Blacks and brown-skinned population (whose situation appears as rather similar): the proportion of illiterate White people is only half (7.1 per cent against 14–15 per cent) that of the coloured population, and the proportion of graduates from high schools is three times as much (about 13 per cent vs. 4 per cent). The same pattern emerges in relation to income: Whites have a significantly higher income. Quite interesting is also the position of the people of Asian origin (*amarelas*): just as in the United States (Lee and Bean 2010l; see also Chapter 11, pp. 290–93), they are in a good position comparable to Whites. The most disadvantaged group, however, are the Indigenous people in Brazil (although they constitute only 0.4 per cent of the population): one-quarter are illiterate, half have no income at all and one-third only a very low one. Thus the concept of 'race democracy' seems to apply least to this group.

Brazil was a member of ISSP in 1999 and a Brazilian research team collected the data for the ISSP module 'Inequality III'. It is possible, therefore, to investigate here directly the interaction between ethnic membership and class position, thus the central hypothesis of the formation of a 'coloured class structure'. The Brazilian ISSP survey covered 2,000 persons and distinguished between three racial groups: Whites, Blacks and mixed. Table 9.4 shows the findings of a regression analysis of personal and household income with socio-demographic variables and ethnic membership as predictors. It turns out that ethnic membership is a significant determinant of income even after controlling for gender, age, education and occupational position

---

15   In the Brazilian context, the concept of 'race' has no ideological underpinnings like the German word 'Rasse' (connected with the racist idea of immutable biological characteristics and a hierarchy of races). Also in US social sciences, the concept of race is used quite neutrally, but there it is usually associated with the dichotomy White–Black.

Table 9.3   Education and income of the four main ethnic groups in Brazil (2010)

	Ethnic (skin colour) groups					All
	White	Brown-skinned	Black	Yellow-skinned	Indigenous	
	(branca)	(parda)	(preta)	(amarela)	(indigena)	
(N in 1,000)	(77,788)	(68,779)	(12,974)	(1,824)	(616)	(161,920)
%	48.0	42.5	8.0	1.1	0.4	100
Education	%	%	%	%	%	%
Illiterate	7.1	14.2	14.9	9.9	26.2	10.9
No school/leaving certificate	42.7	57.2	57.0	42.9	71.3	50.2
Higher school graduates	12.7	4.0	3.9	14.3	2.5	8.3
Monthly income						
No income	33.5	41.2	35.1	36.7	52.9	30.7
Salario mínimo or less	22.2	32.1	34.9	25.5	30.0	24.5
Tenfold of *salário mínimo*	2.8	0.5	0.5	3.5	0.4	1.6
Mean income (Real)*	1019	495	539	995	344	777

*1 Brazil Real = 0,30 Euro/0,41 US-$ (23.8.2013). Thus mean income was 226,– Euro/309,– US-$.
Source: Population Census; data reported by *Instituto Brasileiro de Geografia* e *Estatística* (IBGE).

Table 9.4   Linear regression models of personal earnings and household incomes in Brazil by socio-demographic variables (1999)

	Personal earnings	Household income
Variables	Beta coefficients	Beta coefficients
Gender	-.24**	-.04
Age (centred)	.10**	.08*
Education (reference group: no formal education)		
Primary education	.17**	.22**
Secondary education	.25**	.25**
University degree (completed and not completed)	.37**	.27**
Occupation (reference group: operators, unskilled workers)		
Professionals, technicians, office workers	.12**	.11**
Service workers, skilled workers	.00	-.07*
Household size (number of persons)	-.00	.14**
Ethnic groups (reference group: Blacks)		
Whites	.12**	.15**
Mixed	-.01	-.01
Employment status (reference group: employed)		
Unemployed	X	-.22**
Housewife	X	-.16**
Other than employed	X	-.07*
Retired	X	-.13**
Observations	1,189	1,160
R² (adjusted)	'26	.29
S.D. of the estimate	1.81	2.07

Statistical significance: **p<0.01; *p<0.05
Source: ISSP-1999 – Inequality (Brazil).

Table 9.5   Linear regression models of personal earnings in Brazil: Interaction effects between ethnic membership and occupational group (1999)

Variables (dummies)/interaction effects	Personal earnings Beta coefficients	Personal earnings Beta coefficients
	A: Ethnicity and occupation (reference group: Black professionals, technicians, office workers)	B: Ethnicity and occupation (reference group: Black operators, unskilled workers)
Black professionals, technicians, office workers	X	.03
Black service workers, skilled workers	-.04	-.04
Black operators, unskilled workers	-.03	X
White professionals, technicians, office workers	.21**	.21**
White service workers, skilled workers	.05	.05
White operators, unskilled workers	.04	.04
Mixed professionals, technicians, office workers	.05	.05
Mixed service workers, skilled workers	-.03	-.03
Mixed operators, unskilled workers	-.10*	-.09*
Observations	1,237	1,237
R² (adjusted)	.06	.06
S.D. of the estimate	2.04	2.04

Statistical significance: **$p<0.01$; *$p<0.05$
Source: ISSP-1999 – Inequality (Brazil).

of the respondents (which all exert also significant effects). Table 9.5 directly tests the interaction effect between occupational group (as an indicator of class position) and ethnicity on income. It clearly turns out that there exists such an interaction effect: Whites in professional, technical and office jobs earn significantly more than Blacks in the same occupational categories. An additional finding is that mixed people appear as the most discriminated if they are employed as operators or unskilled workers, earning significantly less than Whites in the same low-level occupations. Thus, the central thesis of this chapter (and book) is clearly supported. The findings are remarkable also because it was only possible to use rather broad occupational categories, due to the restricted sample size of the survey. If we had used narrower occupational groups, the effects might have been even more pronounced.

A consequence of the strongly consolidated patterns of inequality and the difficulty to articulate them in political terms is a massive decline of civil society. In Latin America, crime and violence have grown in a dramatic way. In a rank order of 61 countries around the world, four Latin American countries (Colombia, Mexico, Jamaica and Venezuela) are among the six with the highest levels[16] (Paul 2010; Schönenberg 2010). The murder rate in Brazil is three times higher that of the USA and about 20 to 30 times higher than in Europe. Blacks are much more often a target of assaults by the police. The Whites think more frequently that delinquent Blacks should be punished severely (also by death penalty) (Mitchell and Wood 1998). The one-sided behaviour of the police can be explained on the grounds that it was a main duty in the times of slavery to control the Black slaves in the cities. Also the justice system often doesn't really work impartially: if a middle-class White Brazilian knocks over a Black person a court procedure is initiated but often turned down after a short time. Trust in the political system but also in fellow citizens is very low in Latin America – comparable to Nigeria and South Africa, also two countries with extremely high levels of inequality (see Table 9.2). The well-off Whites are constrained to live in strictly separated ghettos in order to provide for their security. It is quite probable that this high level of distrust also impedes economic growth in a significant way.[17]

---

16   See www.NationMaster.com. Brazil is not included in this list.

17   See Eric Uslaner, *Trust and Economic Growth in the Knowledge Society*, University of Maryland (see http://www.esri.go.jp/en/workshop/030325/030325date2-e.pdf).

Summary and Conclusions

Latin America is one of the two most unequal macro-regions around the world. This seems quite surprising at first sight, given the fact that all countries are quite homogeneous in linguistic and religious terms. A differentiation seems to exist, at first sight, only in the dimension of bio-social ethnicity, that is, race or skin colour. However, in this regard, both Hispanic Latin America and Portuguese Brazil have praised themselves for not being racist like the US Americans but for having developed a race democracy (Brazil) or new national races (Hispanic America) in which all major races – Blacks, Indios and Whites – not only live peacefully together but are even merging into a new race. This aspect of Latin American race relations is doubtless a positive one; however, it is only one side of the coin. The other side is a very strong interaction between class position and ethnic differentiation. Given the fact that through processes of 'Whitening', ethnic boundaries seem permeable, the whole system operates in a way so that economic inequalities and discriminations are less visible and less understood as reproduced by an unequal distribution of economic and political power. In the chapter, these mechanisms have been traced back to the history of one of the most brutal forms of slavery in the colonial age and to the corresponding development of political and religious institutions. Recent research as well as a reanalysis of ISSP data for Brazil has clearly proved that we can understand the pervasive economic inequality in this country only if we understand it as a 'coloured class structure'.

In concluding this chapter, two remarks may be in order: one concerns political prospects for a reduction of the glaring inequality in Latin America, the other relates to a methodological issue. There are certainly several trends in this region which can be evaluated as positive. One is that for the first time in the history of the independent Latin American states throughout the region – with the exception of Cuba – democracy reigns. A second fact is that in many countries leftist governments came to power which have enacted important social and political reforms. In Brazil such reforms have been carried out by President Luiz J. Lula da Silva in his two terms of office (2003–11). But already his forerunner, President Fernando Cardoso, an internationally renowned sociologist, had realized some important social reforms and he was able to reduce inflation significantly. In Mexico, the economic opening and liberalization reform programs enacted by Ernesto Zedillo (president, 1994–2000) and his predecessors since the mid-1980s have resulted in positive economic outcomes and they have also consolidated the democratic process (Jouannet 2004). In the Chapter 13 I will come back to the question if the reforms enacted by these governments were really sufficient to cope with the extreme degrees of inequality and deprivation in these countries. To achieve such a result was also particularly difficult given that the power of labour market institutions and unions which protect rank-and-file workers declined (Angeles-Castro 2011).

A third fact indicating an improvement of the political and social situation in Latin America is that in 2005 for the first time in history a president with an indigenous background, Evo Morales, was elected in Bolivia. One could consider this as a similar breakthrough of the election of Black US president Barack Obama. Not only the reform program but also the willingness to include other political groups and movements into the political process were important measures of President Morales. However, his government and those of all other Latin American countries continue to face gigantic problems. Among them are the extremely high proportion of poor people – about one-quarter of the population in several countries – and the high budget deficits.[18] Another problem, also of leftist governments in Latin America, is that their leaders often begin to act in quite an autocratic way once they have attained power. A case in point is Venezuela where social reforms enacted by its president Hugo Chavez (in power from 1999 till his death in 2013) were thwarted by restrictions in civil liberties and democratic rights. Similar problems emerged in the course of the earlier 'populist' governments of Juan Peron in Argentina, Getúlio Vargas in Brazil and Lázaro Cárdenas in Mexico. They had established new alliances between industrialists and the emerging working classes and, thereby, challenged the established land-owning classes. But their governments were severely hampered by internal conflicts, fuelled by autocratic styles of leadership (Galeano 2003; Skidmore and Smith 2001: 55, 399). Today, a main issue in Latin America is

---

18 See Mark Manderer, Brasilien: Zwölf Jahre liberaler Reformkurs vor dem Ende? See http://www.weltpolitik.net/print/1511.html

> ... the contradiction between an investment in recently achieved democratic reform, which tends to politically include and broaden popular participation, and the dynamics of an economy that historically has caused the highest rates of social and economic inequality, and which today tends to deeper exclusion massively and deny citizenship by the withdrawal of previously acquired rights (Leal Ivo 2005: 72).

Maybe the problem of most consequence for the persistence or even increase of inequality is the retreat of the state from many areas of policy in the connection with liberalization (Dirmoser et al. 1994).

What can we learn from the Latin American case in regard to the central question of this work, the interaction between class stratification and ethnic differentiation? It seems evident that an international comparison in this regard appears as very important and fruitful: it is only through such a comparison that the peculiar features of the Latin American case come fully to light. We can see much more clearly why this continent in its degree of socio-economic inequality, violence and corruption and many other problems is set worlds apart even from other poor world regions or countries such as India or China, not to speak of European countries like Portugal and Spain which are very close to Latin America in cultural terms. These differences and their long-term causes become clear only if one carries out systematic international studies from the perspective of historical and comparative sociology. All kinds of empirical evidence – qualitative in-depth research, standardized representative surveys, analysis of statistical Cenus data – are relevant and necessary. In this sense, two eminent scholars of Latin America have rightly concluded: 'We strongly urge an alliance of interests between the sociological community interested in stratification and that of Latin American scholars who would encourage the development of a regional research strategy, including a large-N multiyear household survey' (Hoffman and Centeno 2003: 381). The extreme level of inequality in Brazil and other Latin American countries can only be explained if one considers the interaction between class stratification and ethnic differentiation. The dominant class in Brazil is distinct from the others not the least in its skin colour, and the same applies to the lower classes. The fact that this ethnic stratification and class structure is seen as surmountable (and is in fact often superable) prevents a societal polarization along class lines. One consequence is that is extremely difficult for political movements and organizations to mobilize the deprived classes and strata. In Latin America, unrest and rebellion manifest themselves mainly in the forms of individual violence and societal anomie. Neither a class theory nor a theory of ethnic differentiation alone is able to explain this particular constellation.

References

Andrews, George Reid (2004), *Afro-Latin America, 1800–2000*, Oxford/New York: Oxford University Press

Angeles-Castro, Gerardo (2011), 'Economic liberalisation and income distribution', in Angeles-Castro, G. et al., eds, *Market Liberalism, Growth, and Economic Development in Latin America*, London/New York: Routledge, pp. 195–219

Bailey, Stanley R. (2002), 'The race construct and public opinion: Understanding Brazilian beliefs about racial inequality and their determinants', *American Journal of Sociology* 108: 406–39

Bailey, Stanley R. (2009), *Legacies of Race. Identities, Attitudes, and Politics in Brazil*, Stanford, CA: Stanford University Press

Bakewell, Peter (1997), *A History of Latin America*, Oxford/Malden, MA: Blackwell Publishers

Bales, Kevin (2004), *Disposable People. New Slavery in the Global Economy*, Berkeley, CA etc.: University of California Press

Barandiarán, Javiera (2012), 'Researching race in Chile', *Latin American Research Review* 47: 161–76

Bayón, Maria C. (2008), 'Konturen des informellen Sektors in Mexico und Argentinien', in Boris, *Sozialstrukturen in Lateinamerika*, pp. 147–170

Beyhout, Gustavo (1965), *Süd- und Mittelamerika. II. Von der Unabhängigkeit bis zur Krise der Gegenwart*, Frankfurt: Fischer

Boekle, Bettina (2010), 'Soziale Ungleichheit und Brasiliens Politikantwort in den Neunziger Jahren. Ein Rückblick', in Sergio Costa et al., eds, *Brasilien heute. Geographischer Raum – Politik – Wirtschaft – Kultur*, Frankfurt: Vervuert, pp. 429–39

Bonacich, Edna (1980), 'Class Approaches to Ethnicity and Rac', *The Insurgent Sociologist* 10: 9–23 (reprinted in Cross, The Sociology of Race and Ethnicity I)

Boris, Dieter et al., eds (2008), *Sozialstrukturen in Lateinamerika. Ein Überblick*, Wiesbaden: VS Verlag für Sozialwissenschaften

Borsdorf, Axel (1999), 'Lateinamerika zwischen Sakrament, Voodoo und Zungenrede', in Manfred Büttner and Frank Richter, eds, *Beziehungen zwischen Religion (Geisteshaltung) und wissenschaftlicher Umwelt (Theologie, Naturwissenschaft und Musikwissenschaft)*, Frankfurt: P. Lang, pp. 1–21

Burkholder, Mark A. and Lyman L. Johnson (2010), *Colonial Latin America*, New York/Oxford: Oxford University Press

Campos, Raymundo, Gerardo Esquivel and Nora Lustig (2012), The rise and fall of income inequality in Mexico, 1989–2010, United Nations University, UNU-WIDER, Working Paper 2012/10

Cireno Fernandes, Danielle (2005), 'Race, Socioeconomic development and the educational stratification process in Brazil', *Research in Social Stratification and Mobility* 22: 365–422

Costa Ribeiro, Carlos A. (2007), 'Class, race and social mobility in Brazil', *Dados* 49/4: 833–73

Costa, Sergio et al., eds (2010), *Brasilien heute. Geographischer Raum, Politik, Wirtschaft, Kultur*. Frankfurt a. M./Madrid: Vervuert

Davis, Darien J., ed. (1995), *Slavery and Beyond. The African Impact on Latin America and the Caribbean*, Wirmington, DC: Jaguar Books

De Azevedo, Celia M. Marinho (2004), *Onda Negra, Medo Branco, O Negro no Imaginário das Elites Séculao XIX*, Sao Paolo: ANNABLUME

De Souza, Jessé and Thomas Kühn eds (2006), *Das moderne Brasilien: Gesellschaft, Politik und Kultur in der Peripherie des Westens*, Wiesbaden: VS Verlag für Sozialwissenschaften

De Souza, Jessé (2009), *A Ralé Brasileira: quen è e como vive*, Rio de Janeiro: Record

Deininger. K. and L. Squire (1998), 'New ways of looking at old issues: inequality and growth', *Journal of Development Economics* 57: 259–87

Dirmoser, Dietmar et al., eds (1994), *Jenseits des Staates?* Bad Honnef: Horlemann

Donghi, Tulio Halperin (1991), *Geschichte Lateinamerikas von der Unabhängigkeit bis zur Gegenwart*, Frankfurt: Suhrkamp

Fagg, John E. (1963), *Latin America. A General History*, New York/London: Collier-Macmillan

Fausto, Boris (1994), *Historia de Brasil*, Sao Paolo: Fundação para o Desenvolvimento da Educação

Figueiredo Santos, José A. (2006a), 'Class effects on racial inequality in Brazil', *Dados* 2: 21–65

Figueiredo Santos, José A. (2006b), 'A socioeconomic Classification for Brazil', in *Revista Brasileira de Ciencias Sociais* 2: 27–45

Flores, René and Edward Telles (2010), 'Social stratification in Mexico: Disentangling color, ethnicity, and class', *American Sociological Review* 77: 486–94

Frank A.G. (1978), *Dependent Accumulation and Underdevelopment*, London: Macmillan

Frankema, Ewout (2008), Wage inequality in Twentieth Century Latin America: A comparative perspective, Groningen Growth and Development Centre, University of Groningen

Frankema, Ewout (2009a), *Has Latin America Always Been Unequal? A Comparative Study of Asset and Income Inequality in the Long Twentieth Century*, Boston/Leiden: Brill

Frankema, Ewout (2009b) 'The Colonial Origins of Inequality: Exploring the Causes and Consequences of Land Distribution', in Klasen, S. and Nowak Lehman F., *Poverty, Inequality and Policy in Latin America*, MIT Press: Cambridge MA, pp. 19–45

Freyre, Gilberto (1964), *The Masters and the Slaves. A Study in the Development of Brazilian Civilization*, New York, Knopf (here quoted after the German ed. Herrenhaus und Sklavenhütte, Köln/Berlin: Kiepenheuer and Witsch 1965; original ed. Rio de Janeiro 1936)

Galeano, Eduardo (2003 [1971]), *Die offenen Adern Lateinamerikas. Die Geschichte eines Kontinents von der Entdeckung bis zur Gegenwart*, Wuppertal: Peter Hammer

Geler, Lea (2005), 'Negros, pobres y argentinos. Identificaciones de raza, de clase y de nacionalidad en la comunidad afroprotena, 1870–1880', *Nuevo Mundo* (Online)

Gillian, Angela (1976), 'Clase, raza y etnicidad en Brasil y Mexico', *Nueva Antropologia* 5: 91–104

Gonzalez Eurico Antonio, Cursion dos Santos (2006), 'Die soziale Konstruktion des Sklaven: Die Religion Brasiliens', in: de J. Souza and T. Kühn, eds, *Das moderne Brasilien: Gesellschaft, Politik und Kultur in der Peripherie des Westens*, Wiesbaden: VS Verlag für Sozialwissenschaften, pp. 213–28

Graham, Richard, ed. (1990), *The Idea of Race in Latin America, 1870–1940*, Austin, Texas: University of Texas Press

Guerreiro Osorio, Rafael (2008), Is all Socioeconomic Inequality among Racial Groups in Brazil Caused by Racial Discrimination? Working Paper 43, International Poverty Centre, United Nations Development Programme, New York

Haller, Max and Markus Hadler (2006), 'How Social Relations and Structures can Produce Life Satisfaction and Happiness. An International Comparative Analysis', *Social Indicators Research* 75: 161–216

Haller, Max and Franz Höllinger (2009), 'Decline or persistence of religion? Trends in religiosity among Christian societies around the world', in Max Haller et al., *The International Social Survey Programme 1984–2009. Charting the Globe*, London/New York: Routledge, pp. 281–301

Hofbauer, Andreas (1995), *Afro-Brasilien*, Wien: ProMedia

Hoffman Kelley and Migua Centeno (2003), 'The lopsided continent: Inequality in Latin America', *Annual Review of Sociology* 29: 363–90

Höllinger, Franz (2007), *Religiöse Kultur in Brasilien. Zwischen traditionellem Volksglauben und modernen Erweckungsbewegungen*, Frankfurt/New York: Campus

Janvry, Alain de and Elisabeth Sadoulet (1999), *Growth, poverty and inequality in Latin America. A causal analysis, 1970–1942*, Inter-American Development Bank, Washington DC

Jouannet, Andres Valderrama (2004), Politische Parteien in Lateinamerika, Dissertation, Universität Heidelberg, Institut für Politische Wissenschaft

Kohlhepp, Gerd (2010), 'Regionale Disparitäten und Regionalplanung', in Sergio Costa et al., eds, *Brasilien heute*, pp. 93–109

Konetzke, Richard (1965), *Süd- und Mittelamerika I. Die Indianerkulturen Altamerikas und die spanisch-portugiesische Kolonialherrschaft*, Fischer Weltgeschichte, vol. 22, Frankfurt: Fischer Taschenbuch Verlag

Kühn, Thomas (2006), 'Alltägliche Lebensführung und soziale Ungleichheit – eine exploratorische Studie in Salvador (Bahia)', in de Souza and Kühn, *Das moderne Brasilien*, pp. 129–43

Lee, Jennifer and Frank D. Bean (2010), *The Diversity Paradox. Immigration and the Color Line in Twenty-First Century America*, New York: Russel Sage Foundation

Li, H., L. Squire and H. Zou (1998), 'Explaining International and Intertemporal Variations in Income Inequality', *The Economic Journal* 108: 26–43

Marx, Anthony W. (1998), *Making Race and Nation. A Comparison of South Africa, The United States, and Brazil*, Cambridge: Cambridge University Press

Meissner, Jochen, Ulrich Mücke and Klaus Weber (2008), *Schwarzes Amerika. Eine Geschichte der Sklaverei*, München: C.H. Beck

Mesa-Lago, Carmelo (2009), 'Economic and social balance of 50 years of Cuban revolution', in *Cuba in Transition*, Papers and Proceedings of the 19th Annual Meeting of the Association for the Study of the Cuban Economy, vol. 19, Washington, DC: ASCE, pp. 368–82

Mignolo, Walter D. (2005), *The Idea of Latin America*, Malden, MA/Oxford: Blackwell

Mitchell, Michael J. and Charles H. Wood (1998), 'Ironies of citizenship: Skin color, police brutality, and the challenge to democracy in Brazil', *Social Forces* 77: 1001–20

Moritz Schwarcz, Lilia (2003), Not Black, not White: just the opposite. Culture, race and national identity in Brazil, Working Paper CBS-47–03, Centre for Brazilian Studies, University of Oxford

Myrdal, Gunnar (1980 [1944]), *Ein asiatisches Drama. Eine Untersuchung über die Armut der Nationen*, Frankfurt am Main: Suhrkamp (*An Asian Drama* 1968)

Nash, Gary B. (1995), 'The hidden history of mestizo America', *The Journal of American History* 83: 941–64

Ocampo, José A. (1998), Income distribution, poverty and social expenditure in Latin America, Paper presented at the First Conference of the Americas, Washington, DC

Paul, Wolf (2010), 'Strafrecht und Rechtstaat in Brasilien. Ein kriminologisches Portrait', in Sergio Costa et al., eds, *Brasilien heute*, pp. 219–44

Perez, Aparecida et al. (2010), 'Brasilien – ein Land mit Zukunft(?). Bildungssystem und alternative Bildungspraktiken', in Sergio Costa et al., eds, *Brasilien heute*, pp. 623–36

Pitt-Rivers, Julian (1969), 'Race, color, and class in Central America and the Andes', in C.S. Heller, ed., *Structured Social Inequality. A Reader in Comparative Stratification*, London: MacMillan/Collier-Macmillan, pp. 380–396

Portes, Alejandro and D. Frances Ferguson (1977), 'Comparative ideologies of poverty and equity: Latin America and the United States', in I.L. Horowitz, ed., *Equity, Income, and Policy. Comparative Studies in Three Worlds of Development*, New York/London: Praeger, pp. 70–105

Portes, Alejandro and Hoffman Kelly (2003), 'Latin American Class Structures: Their composition and change during the neoliberal area', *Latin American Research Review* 38: 42–82

Ranis, Gustav and Stophen Kosack (2004), *Growth and Human Development in Cuba's Transition*, Institute for Cuban and Cuban-American Studies, University of Miami

Riekenberg, Michael (2009), *Kleine Geschichte Argentiniens*, München: C.H. Beck

Santos, Ana Maria Barros dos (1985), *Die Sklaverei in Brasilien und ihre sozialen und wirtschaftlichen Folgen. Dargestellt am Beispiel Pernambuco (1840–1889)*, München: W. Fink Verlag

Schönenberg, Regine (2010), 'Gewalt, Kriminalität und Drogenhandel', in Sergio Costa et. al., eds, *Brasilien heute*, pp. 265–81

Schröter, Bernd (1999), 'Die Stellung der Schwarzen im kolonialen Uruguay: Eingliederung und Konfrontation', in Heinz-Joachim Domnick et al., eds, *Interethnische Beziehungen in der Geschichte Lateinamerikas*, Frankfurt: Vervuert, pp. 79–114

Sernau, Scott (1994), *Economies of Exclusion. Underclass Poverty and Labor Market Change in Mexico*, Westport, CT/London: Praeger

Silverio, Valter R. (2004), 'Movimento Negro und die (Re)Interpretation des brasilianischen Dilemmas', *Stichproben. Wiener Zeitschrift für kritische Afrikastudien* 4: 21–41

Singh, Anoop et al. (2005), *Stabilization and Reform in Latin America. A Macroeconomic perspective on the experience since the early 1990s*, International Monetary Fund, Washington, DC

Skidmore, Thomas E. (1992), Fact and myth: Discovering a racial problem in Brazil, Kellog Institute for International Studies, Notre Dame/Indiana, Working Paper 173

Skidmore, Thomas E. and Peter H. Smith (2001), *Modern Latin America*, New York/Oxford: Oxford University Press

Solt, Frederick (2009), 'Standardizing World Income Inequality Database', *Social Science Quarterly* 90: 231–42

Speck, Bruno W. (2010), 'Korruption und Korruptionsbekämpfung', in Sergio Costa et al., eds, *Brasilien heute*, pp. 245–63

Telles, Edward E. (2004), *Race in Another America. The Significance of Skin Color in Brazil 2004*, Princeton/Oxford: Princeton University Press

Twine, France Winddance (1998), *Racism in a Racial Democracy. The Maintenance of White Supremacy in Brazil*, New Brunswick, NJ: Rutgers University Press

Villarreal, Andrés (2010), 'Stratification by skin color in contemporary Mexico', *American Sociological Review* 75: 652–78

Wade, Peter (1997), *Race and Ethnicity in Latin America*, London: Pluto Press

Wallerstein, Immanuel (1974), *The Modern World-System I. Capitalist Agriculture and the Origins of the European World-Economy in the Sixteenth Century*, New York etc.: Academic Press

Wolf, Eric R. (1982), *Europe and the People without History*, Berkeley, CA: University of California Press

Wünderlich, Volker (1999), 'Das Bild des 'Indianers' und das ethnische Dilemma des Nationalismus in Guatemala, 1920–1930', in Domnick Heinz-Joachim et al., eds, *Interethnische Beziehungen in der Geschichte Lateinamerikas*, Frankfurt: Vervuert, pp. 239–55

Chapter 10
Ethno-class Regimes.
The Origins and Forces Sustaining Glaring Economic Inequality in Sub-Saharan Africa

In this chapter, one of the most interesting but also disturbing macro-regions from the viewpoint of ethnic stratification and economic inequality shall be investigated. Africa contains many countries with extremely high, but also a few with rather low levels of, economic inequality. At the same time, most of its countries are characterized by an extreme degree of ethnic differentiation. It is obvious that these two characteristics are connected to each other (Easterly and Levine 1997). To investigate this issue in the case of Africa is highly important also from the view of Africa's development in the last decades. Sub-Saharan Africa is the poorest and least developed sub-continent on earth; between one-third and a half of the populations (except South Africa) live in poverty, and life expectancy is less than 60 years (see Table 6.1, pp. 164–5). Sub-Saharan Africa has also the fastest growing population around the world. This was one of the reasons why income per capital fell in the last decades, in contrast to all other macro-regions in the Global South – a second 'African tragedy' (Davidson 1992: 9; Collier and Gunning 1999; Easterly and Levine 1997; Hyden 2006: 16ff.; Kerbo 2006: 153–70; Njogu et al. 2009; Ali 2010; Bloom et al. 2010).[1] Thus, it is imperative to look for all possible reasons for these facts both from the viewpoint of universal values of equality and justice, as well as from the perspective of the developed world, particularly of Europe, which is seen as a destination country by millions of Africans who do not see a future on their own continent: 'the immensity of the problems of the 'forgotten continent' makes Africa globally relevant' (Adam and Moodley 1993: 11). In this chapter I will investigate the intersection between ethnic differentiation, class formation and economic inequality in Sub-Saharan Africa; it is argued that a specific form of ethno-classes has emerged here and still persists in several countries. The chapter is structured in five parts: first, an overview on the different patterns of ethnic differentiation and economic inequality within the whole continent is given; then the role of ethnic relations in three historical periods (the pre-colonial and colonial periods and that of transition to independence) is discussed; the third part analyses the historical origins and pre-conditions for the outbreak of the many terrible civil wars in Africa – the first and greatest 'African tragedy' in my opinion – and of their ethnic character; the fourth part analyses the patterns of present-day ethno-class domination and privilege;[2] in the final section, the attitudes of Africans are investigated, related to the issue of ethnic stratification and inequality.

Introduction and Overview

Africa in general and Sub-Saharan Africa (also called Black Africa) in particular constitute a natural laboratory for the central topic of this book, ethnic stratification and its effects upon socio-economic inequality, for at least four reasons. First, this continent encompasses worldwide the highest ethnic diversity as shown in Chapter 2 (see Table 2.2, pp. 37–8). Overall, several thousand ethnic groups ('tribes') exist in Africa, clearly

---

1   The deterioration of living standards in Sub-Saharan Africa shows itself even in body sizes of the population which decreased since 1965 in many countries; ethnic heterogeneous countries were characterized by the highest degree of inequality in this regard (Moradi 2005).

2   This chapter is somewhat longer than the others in part II. One reason for this is that the author has travelled through, teached and made some research in East Africa (Tanzania and Ethiopia) and could gain a personal insight into a few of its societies. But there are also several objective reasons why Sub-Saharan Africa deserves particular attention in this work as outlined in the text.

differentiated from each other in terms of (actual or believed) social origin, language and culture (Michler 1988: 56–8; Ungar 1989; Levinson 1998; Schicho 1999). They range from groups containing only a few thousand members up to groups with 20 or 30 million people, such as the Hausa, Yoruba and Igbo in Nigeria and adjacent countries, the Oromo in Ethiopia and Kenya and the Fula in Guinea and adjoining countries. Second, Sub-Saharan Africa is – together with Latin America – also a continent with extremely high levels of income inequality. Inequality in Namibia tops all other countries in the world; its neighbour states, including the Republic of South Africa, follow suit. No single African country belongs to the groups of relatively equal countries (Gini below 30) which include most European and also many Asian countries. For received theories of inequality, this fact appears as a 'paradox', since Africa, in difference to Latin America, 'has no large-scale land ownership, no ex-slave plantations, no preserved colonial race hierarchy' (Therborn 2006b: 19). Third, even in Sub-Saharan Africa economic inequality varies strongly. While Namibia and Lesotho are on top worldwide in terms of economic inequality, a few countries are much less unequal; they include Benin, Ethiopia, and Tanzania. Fourth, inequality is rather narrow in all Arab-Islamic North African countries (Gini coefficients between 34 and 40).[3] That ethnic differentiation plays a central role in this regard is also evident. While Sub-Saharan Africa exhibits an extreme degree of ethnic differentiation, the contrary is the case in North Africa. In fact, Libya and Tunisia are among the most homogeneous countries in the world, and ethnic heterogeneity is rather limited also in all other North African countries. This homogeneity is the result of a domination of Islam and the Arab language since over a millennium. Consequently (and confirming the central hypothesis of this work), economic inequality is much lower in North Africa.

In this chapter, the focus is on Sub-Saharan Africa. Although some of the main problems of this part of Africa have been relevant also for North Africa – such as violent colonialism and liberation wars, authoritarian regimes and suppression of internal minorities (Zoubir 1999) – Sub-Saharan Africa has quite a different history and culture. What is most important here, though, is that it is much more differentiated internally in ethnic terms than Arab-Islamic North Africa. What are the reasons for the extreme inequality in this region, and why have some countries been able to avoid it? In Chapter 4, we found strong empirical evidence for the thesis that the historical experience of slavery has been a decisive factor for the emergence of the present-day extreme income inequality. The high ethnic diversity of Sub-Saharan Africa and its experience with centuries of terrible slavery also support the general thesis of this book that ethnic heterogeneity increases economic inequality particularly if it is connected closely with class stratification and exploitation. In this chapter, I will investigate the historical evolution and the present-day patterns of interaction between ethnic differentiation and class stratification. Looking at history, the *long duree* in Braudel's terms, is very important also for Africa (Nugent 2004: 4).

We have to distinguish between three periods of African history: (1) the period before Africa came into contact with higher developed non-African civilizations; this period ranged up to the early Modern Age, but in some up to the late 19th century; (2) the period of the encountering of Africa with non-African civilizations and with colonialism; and, (3) the period since the 1960s and 1970s when most African states gained political independence. In this historical excursus I will show three facts: first, in none of these three periods, ethnicity and ethnic membership was a given fact, it was continually transformed in connection with people's movements, the dissolution of old and the establishment of new political communities and the fights for influence and power. The view of traditional Africa being uniformly composed of fixed and stable 'tribal societies' is certainly a simplification; nevertheless, it is a matter of fact that ethnic groups and divisions have been and still are highly important for an understanding of the persistence of glaring inequality in Sub-Saharan Africa. Contrary to established wisdom, however, I do not assume that ethnic affiliation and identities are only a 'tribal' relic, in conflict with modern society and democracy. Rather, it was exactly the neglect and forceful suppression of these identities which led to the tragedy of violence in the new states after the end of colonialism (Salih 2001). Second, in pre-colonial Africa many different forms of ethnic and political communities existed; some of them exhibited high levels of inequality, others considerable equality (Peil and Oyeneye 1998: 57). This diversity of traditional Africa will also help to understand present-day variations in regard to economic inequality. The thesis is that equality, internal peace and economic development in some

---

3   It should be noted, however, that the geographic and cultural divisions do not coincide fully. There are several Sub-Saharan countries which are part of the Arab-Islamic culture: Comoros, Djibouti, Mauritania, Somalia, and in part, also Sudan (see also Abusabib 2004).

countries were achieved exactly because the established traditional ethnic differentiations were respected and integrated positively into the political process. Third, a new perspective will be developed also concerning the colonial period. It is a widely shared belief that the basis for ethnic competition and conflict, strife and violence was laid during this period, because colonial powers often used and strengthened ethnic differentiations in order to gain control over their subjugated peoples. This is quite a simplification both when looking backward and forward in the history of Africa. It is argued that we have to make a clear distinction between the period of exploitative colonialism exerted in Sub-Saharan Africa when the interests of Europeans were mainly in getting access to slaves and a few mineral resources, and the later stage of colonialism, where the whole continent was divided up by the European powers. My thesis is that it was in the first period (which in many parts of Africa lasted till the mid-19th century) that Europe has most strongly devastated (Sub-Saharan) Africa (see also Ziltener 2013a). It is true that most ethnic conflicts did emerge only during the later period, that is, between about 1800 and 1960. This was the case, however, already simply because of the fact that many tribes and political communities which existed side by side before now became integrated into larger political communities. All the governments of the new independent states had to come to terms with this problem (Elaigwu and Mazrui 1981; Young 1994; Herbst 2000).

The central thesis of this chapter is in line with the general argument of this book: it says that we can understand patterns of income distribution and socio-economic inequality in present-day Africa only by looking at the intersection between interests, resources and conflicts related to class and status on the one side, and to ethnic membership on the other side. The peculiar feature of African societies is that no powerful bourgeoisie and proletariat, based on industrial enterprises, did develop but that the state became the main economic power base of the rising classes. Specific ethnic groups were able to usurp state power and to establish themselves as dominant ethno-classes in many countries. But the relations between ethnic differentiation and class stratification remain a central problem for many countries still today. Political leaders try to avoid broaching this issue of ethnic conflicts altogether; this should not be done in scientific research as often happens.[4]

A limitation of the analysis in this chapter is the lack of specific, pertinent data and research. I must rely, therefore, often on only indirect indicators for the existence of economic inequalities between ethnic groups. Some data could be taken from international surveys which were carried out also in Africa, such as the political science project *Afrobarometer*. For some basic data, also figures of African national statistical offices are available.

In concluding this introduction, let us have a short look at the differences in the patterns of ethnic differentiation and economic inequality within Sub-Saharan Africa. Table 10.1 distinguishes three patterns in this regard. The first group of countries was characterized by the Apartheid system which was a legally enforced, exploitative institutional structure; it was covered briefly already in Chapter 5 and will be analysed in Chapter 11. Such a system was implemented fully in the Republic of South Africa, but *de facto* came into force also in the neighbour countries of South Africa which were under its strong influence. All of these countries are characterized still today by extreme levels of economic inequality. The second group includes countries in which one or a few ethnic groups were clearly dominant over the others; in many of them, the consequence were prolonged and bloody civil wars, authoritarian political systems and a delayed socio-economic development in spite of high state revenues from the export of natural resources. An additional reason for the pervasive internal conflicts in these countries was the fact that in historic time slavery made a big impact and the main present-day divisions still reflect this split. This is obviously the case in the two largest Sub-Saharan African countries, Nigeria and Sudan, where the most protracted conflicts broke out between the Islamic northern and non-Islamic southern territories and groups. The Islamic Arabs were slave rioters and slave traders throughout almost a millennium; the Black Africans were their victims (N'Diaye 2010). The third group comprises African countries which exhibit a surprisingly low level of economic inequality. They include two Sub-Saharan countries – Tanzania and Rwanda – which are clearly an exception in this region.

---

4   An example is an interesting study on the elections 2006 in Uganda by Kiiza et al. (2008). Throughout the 302 pages of their book the authors avoid any reference to ethnicity – which was very important in Uganda and played a decisive role in the terrorist regimes of Milton Obote and Idi Amin. A similar tendency is evident in Crawford Young's work *The African Colonial State* (1994). He makes hardly tenable statements, for instance, that the Acholi and other ethnic groups in Uganda were 'novel ethnic identities' (on the Acholi: see Kasozi 1994).

Table 10.1　The main types of ethno-class stratification and domination and the resulting patterns of economic
inequality in Africa

Type of ethnic stratification Factors producing inequality	Factors attenuating inequality	Macro-regions/countries	Economic inequality (Gini)
I. Apartheid systems a. *'Classical' Apartheid system* Polarized, consolidated ethnic structure; ethno-class domination; rentier state	Economic growth, diversified economy	Republic of South Africa	Extreme (ca 60)
b. *Satellites of 'classical' Apartheid system* Doubly exploited lower ethno-classes; polarized, consolidated ethnic structure; rentier states	Economic growth	Botswana, Lesotho, Namibia, Swaziland	Extreme (60–75)
II. Ethno-class domination or hegemony a. *Ethno-class domination* Extensive historic slavery; consolidated ethnic structure, dominant ethnic group; centralized authoritarian systems; rentier states; extensive violence and civil wars		Sudan Chad	Probably very high (no data)
b. *Pervasive ethno-class hegemony* Consolidated, polarized ethnic structure; ethnically based civil wars; divisive regionalism; rentier states	(Sierra L.: plural ethnic structure; integrative political parties and leaders)	Nigeria Sierra Leone	Very high (40–60)
c. *Moderate ethno-class hegemony* Consolidated, polarized ethnic structure; ethnically based violence and civil wars; partly liberal-Capitalist systems; weak federalism		Kenya, Uganda	Very high (40–50)
III. Heterogeneous, but integrated and stable societies a. Moderate historical slavery	Segmentary-plural ethnic structure; reconciliatory national movements and leaders; impact of Socialism	Tanzania	Moderate (ca 35)
b. Moderate historical slavery; consolidated ethnic structure; at times pervasive ethnic violence (genocide)	Old traditions and cultural homogeneity; centralized political system	Rwanda (Burundi)	Moderate (30–40)
III. Ethnically homogeneous, authoritarian states Moderate historical slavery; liberal-Capitalist systems; centralized suppressive regimes	Ethnic and cultural homogeneity; Socialist regime periods/ influence	Morocco, Tunisia Algeria, Libya, Egypt	Moderate (35–40)

I will discuss the first case in detail in Chapter 13. Finally, the Arab-Islamic North Africa countries are the relatively egalitarian (see Table 1.1). The lower level of inequality in these regions is also easily explained by the general thesis of this book: they are very homogeneous in ethnic-national terms, particularly in terms of language (everywhere Arab is spoken, with some regional variations) and religion (here Islam predominates). This homogeneity and their old traditions of statehood were certainly a main factor for the early independence movements which started in Egypt in 1900 and became a model for all other African countries (Illife 1997: 308ff.).

Historical Origins and Pre-conditions for the Rise of Ethno-classes

In all three significant periods of recent African history, important foundations for the present-day ethno-class regimes and socio-economic inequality have been laid down. The three periods are: the time before Africa came into close contact with non-African civilizations; the colonial era beginning in the 16th century, and culminating the 19th and 20th centuries; and the era since most African states gained political independence in the 1960s and early 1970s up to the early 21st century.

Characteristics of the Traditional Social Organization of African Societies

I start from two basic assumptions concerning the first two periods which run counter to widespread descriptions of African history in textbooks and in the public: (1) it is misleading to denominate all the centuries between the first exploration of the West African coast by the Portuguese around 1500 and the attainment of political independence by most African states in the 1960s as the 'colonial period'. Throughout much of this period, there was no colonialism at all; in the first period, the relation between European and African powers was often one of cooperation, in positive and negative terms; (2) it is also too narrow to consider only the contact of Africans with European, Western civilization as having been of decisive importance for Africa. A similar, profound impact was the contact by Africa with Islamic civilizations and empires; even Asian (particularly Indian) influence was and still is important. The contact with Europeans was most influential in West and South Africa, that with the Arab, Islamic and Asian civilizations in East and Central Africa. The present-day *lingua franca* in East Africa, Swahili, has taken over quite a number of Arabic vocabularies (Reader 1998: 175–6). Sailing over the Red Sea and the Indian Ocean, the Arabs, Persians and Indians developed an intense trade (with ivory, slaves and cash-crops as main merchandises) between East Africa, the Near East and South Asia. The Sultanate Zanzibar was an important Arabic-Islamic economic and political centre in the 19th century, controlling the slave trade in the region (Albertini 1976: 349–50).

Strictly speaking, there was never a period when Africa was fully closed off from contact with peoples and powers outside of the continent. Throughout pre-history and antiquity, particularly North Africa was an integral part of a cultural and political macro-region whose centre was the Mediterranean. Egyptian high culture which was developed already in 2000 B.C. was influenced strongly by Greece and on its own terms had a profound impact on Jewish and Christian culture. Later on, the Roman Empire included all North African coastlands. In the second half of the 8th century, Egypt and the whole of North Africa were seized by Arab-Islamic troops within a short period; in the following centuries, the region was fully assimilated to Islam and the Arab language. In the early 16th century, Ottoman Turks conquered the countries of the Near East and Egypt and established – in parallel with the Europeans in West and South Africa – dependent states there. Also West Africa had contacts with Europe long before the advent of the European colonists (Albertini 1976: 380). The apex of European settler colonialism was reached only in 1884 when at the Berlin conference the whole territory of Africa was divided among the European powers, and these began to occupy and exploit their colonies systematically in economic terms. Thus, the period of this kind of colonialism was relatively short in most parts of Africa, maybe one century or less. This was offset by the fact, however, that the colonial powers had a wide experience from other parts of the world which they could apply immediately to Africa (Young 1994; Mamdani 1996: 9).

The characteristics of the traditional Sub-Saharan African social and political systems can be summarized in the following five points (see also Fallers 1966; Manghezi 1976; Freund 1998; Reader 1998; Herbst 2000; Illife 1997: 9ff; Mafeje 1998; Mwijage 2004):[5]

1. The economic system and the division of labour was rather simple; most production occurred in the household, there was no development of specialized crafts; dinnerware, tools and other basic commodities were produced part-time. The restricted level of technological development (Ziltener and Müller 2007) was also due to the limited degree of contact and the absence of technological competition between tribes and political communities. This fact was caused by the huge geographical size and the linguistic fractionalization of the continent. A central impediment was the lack of scripture and the reliance on oral tradition (Bozeman 1976; Illife 1997: 125; Reader 1998: 103–10). The low level of technology was most consequential in agriculture where the plough and the wheel were never introduced but the hoe remained the most important tool. Thus, agrarian productivity remained low. Given the abundance of natural food resources (domesticated crops, nutritive fruits like bananas, huntable wildlife) it was adequate to feed the people in normal times.[6]

2. All these facts can be understood against the background of the dispersion of the population over a huge, thinly populated territory which was not interconnected by navigable rivers or well-established streets (Illife 1997: 39–40; Reader 1998: 2). There was an abundance of land (Herbst 2000: 37–9; Robinson 2010: 84), given the low density of the population; around 1900, Africa had not much more than a hundred million inhabitants. Some peoples (for example in Rwanda) did not even have a sense of a territory in the political meaning (Mafeje 1998: 16). Therefore, not land but people were the scarcest resource of power and influence, income and wealth; the command over people included members of a family or household, clan or tribe, or of a larger political community. Women, children and slaves were those who carried out daily work both in the household and in the fields. Since child mortality was very high (particularly in periods of aridity), 'children were precious, and the drive to reproduce became a central feature of African culture and social order' (Reader 1998: 247; Illife 1997: 94–131). Therefore, it was highly profitable for a household head or a chief to have several wives and many children (see also Mamdani 1996: 91). The extremely high birth rate in Sub-Saharan Africa today (see Table 6.1, pp. 164–5) and the reluctance of many governments to carry out a deliberate policy of birth control are a consequence of this aspect (for Kenya see Ungar 1989: 183f.). Also slavery was widespread in pre-colonial Africa, although it was quite distinct from chattel slavery later practised by the Arabs and Europeans. African slavery was based on 'rights-in-persons' (Miers and Kopytoff 1977: 7–14) These rights took many forms: it included the rights of a man over his wife (and of tribes in all wives) as a consequence of the payment of bride wealth; the buying of orphans who otherwise would have died; the transformation of unredeemed hostages or pawns into servitude; and the kidnapping of people in wars and raids. While the transfer of these people from one group to another was often violent and painful, later on they were integrated into the new group or tribe.

3. This leads to the third characteristic of African societies, the central role of the family and household head in the fate of a clan or tribe. Given the abundance of land and the restricted means of chiefs and kings to control their subjects, it was possible and frequent that young men, dissatisfied with their subordinate position, left their tribe to affiliate themselves with another one or establish their own clan. Many tribes adopted the names of their founders as their names. In some regards, these founders and chiefs of clans and tribes can be seen as the forerunners of the 'Big Man' who still play a decisive role in the many African states today (see pp. 272–6, below). Generally, however, the head of a clan or tribe could not rule alone but had to share power with a council of elderly men and to consider also the wishes of his subjects (Mamdani 1996:43). According Evans-Pritchard (1969: 5), a chief was a sacred person without political authority. The role of the oldest members was so important that one

---

5   An informative map of African states between the 16th and 19th centuries is presented in Michler 1988: 79.
6   It might have been the case that the Africans knew the plough and the wheel but did not take it over for their own use. (Mafeje 1998: 87).

can speak of *gerontocracy* as the dominant form of political organization (Reader 1998: 259; see also Kasozi 1994: 18).

4. There existed two or three forms of social and political communities in Africa. One was relatively egalitarian, decentralized village communities with self-government (an example were the Igbos in Nigeria), a second one was larger political communities and kingdoms (like the Buganda in the Great Lakes District); a few of these (like Ethiopia) developed further into long-lasting empires (Mwijage 2004: 17–42). The former were internally quite diversified, 'multi-ethnic' societies (Mafeje 1998: 38) without a strong central authority and political organization; they have been characterized as an 'ordered anarchy' (Evans-Pritchard 1969: 6; Sigrist 1967). But also the stronger integrated kingdoms can hardly be compared with European or Asian states which were much more strictly organized, richer and vaster, and stronger in political and military terms. The huge and inhospitable territory was a fundamental problem for all state-builders in Africa (Herbst 2000: 11–31). A central form of establishing and holding together larger political communities in Africa was through the establishment of personal, client relationships between the king and the local chiefs. Mafeje (1998: 118–9) writes about the Great Lakes Region shortly before colonialism: 'In these societies, virtually every adult male was somebody's client and loyal clients were rewarded materially and politically ...'; with the passing of traditional society, patron-client relations gradually replaced kinship politics. Mafeje speaks here of *tributary relations*, tying in with Amin (1980).

5. This leads to the final aspect of social systems in Africa which is particularly of interest here, their degree of socio-economic inequality. Given the low level of technological development and the relatively small size of most communities, the overall level of inequality was restricted. The privileges of chiefs and kings were limited also by the possibility of their subjects to escape. In addition, there existed a strong consciousness of equality and a resistance against the power striving of single personalities (Sigrist 1967: 251–63). The degree of overlap between kinship and political roles, power and influence was by far less perfect than in ancient Europe, India or China. Solidaristic kinship groups included persons of widely varying degrees of power and wealth (Fallers 1966: 146). A significant aspect of inequality was that between men and women; only in a few societies did women have considerable rights (Sigrist 1967: 163–7). Male dominance was widely prevalent; women were mainly seen as bearers of children and providers of labour (Illife 1997: 156). In traditional and even in present-day rural Africa women do most of the work (Lamb 1984: 38–9). One important source of power for the leaders of clans and tribes was their capacity to organize other people (tenants, wives, slaves) to work for them; in this regard, their rhetoric skills and the capacity to persuade others to follow their proposals were crucial. Servile institutions (the readiness to trade rights-in-persons among Africans themselves) were widespread; their roots were the needs for wives and children, the wish to enlarge one's kin group, and to have clients, dependents and servants (Reader 1998: 289). Also poverty was widespread and many of the poorest 'gravitated inexorably towards enslavement' (Reader 1998: 290). The inexistence of property right does not imply that domination and exploitation were absent (Mafeje 1998: 113). In larger political communities and kingdoms, the use of brute physical violence as a means of domination was frequent. For male youth, it was a main instrument to gain power (Illife 1997: 130). This explains also why the guerrilla fighters in the wars for independence mostly were young volunteers (Illife 1997: 339). While disputes within clans were resolved peacefully, violence between clans was widespread and resulted often in deadly conflicts with hundreds of people killed. In kingdoms, such as that of Buganda, 'the kings massacred their subjects whenever it pleased them' (Kasozi 1994: 20). The Buganda people accepted the king's right to kill. In the period of enslavement, Buganda had become a 'military machine, a predatory society'. This latter characteristic was crucial for the enslavement of people throughout Sub-Saharan Africa in which African leaders participated significantly.

A short note is necessary here on the concept of tribe. A tribe is defined by five central characteristics (Evans-Pritchard 1969: 122): a distinct name; a common sentiment of affiliation and pride; a moral obligation to unite in war; and the settlement of internal disputes and feuds by negotiation. Within tribes, there existed clans as sub-divisions; a clan is defined as group of people connected to each other by factual or believed kinship (a common ancestry) or a common language and religion. It is certainly erroneous to consider tribes as fixed and stable entities and traditional Africa as consisting only of 'tribal societies' (Fried 1975; see also Mafeje 1998: 111ff.). However, tribe was a highly relevant social category in the past (Atkinson 2010: 12–17), as it remains it even today in Africa, as everybody who has lived there for some time will note (Lamb 1984: 9–16).[7] The words clan and tribe may be used interchangeably; since some 'tribes' today include a few million people, it is difficult to conceive these as kinship groups; in such cases, people refer to a 'clan' which is a smaller unit. The membership and characteristics of tribes can change significantly over generations. Tribes have often been mobile over large distances and/or were subjugated by others. In the course of such events, they could change their names, their social and political constitution, and in sequel, also their language (Atkinson 2010: 80). In recent times, the identity of the tribes and ethnic groups became attenuated and blurred by the massive migrations from rural areas into the large urban agglomerations (Mamdani 1996: 6).

The European Conquest of Africa and the Heritage of Colonialism

The contacts and relations between African and European states developed in two forms. One of them was reciprocal, the other one was conquest and domination. In some cases, political and military alliances were established in which European powers helped African states and regimes to persist in their conflicts with other states. The earliest was the Portuguese support for Ethiopia in its 1543 war against the Muslim Sultanate Adal; later on, several European countries assisted regimes in Sub-Saharan Africa with whom they had established advantageous trade relations. Another form of 'partnership' between Africans and Europeans occurred in the slave trade from Africa to the Americas. There was a relatively clear division of labour in this regard: African chiefs, kings and military leaders literally hunted and captured the slaves in the interior of the continent, and brought them to the bases of the Europeans at the West African coast to sell them there; then, European traders shipped the slaves to the Americans (Illife 1997: 172–98). Therefore, several African chiefs and kings were against the abolition of the slave trade (Mwijage 2004: 87). It is estimated that up to 12 million slaves were sold and protracted in this way. In Central and East Africa, the Sahara, the Nile valley and the East African coast were the main slave trade routes toward North Africa, the Near East and South Asia. Here, up to 17 million slaves were captured and sold over the course of a millennium (from the 10th till the 19th century) (Mwijage 2004: 57–64; N'Diaye 2010). The total number of people captured may have been 21 million (Reader 1998: 404; Miers and Kopytoff 1977; Lamb 1984: 134–70; Illife 1997: 69–77; Flaig 2009). The slave hunters in these regions were Islamic Sudanese and Arab groups from Central and North Africa and from the Near East. As a consequence of this division of labour, new, militaristic and highly aggressive states and regimes emerged in Sub-Saharan Africa, such as those of Asante, Dahomey, Ghana and Songhai.

This participation of African regimes was possible because slavery was a practice which had been used in Africa for a long time. According to some authors, between 30 and 60 per cent of the entire African population were slaves in historical times. In Ibadan (Nigeria), 104 families owned more than 50,000 slaves (Reader 1998: 284, 423). From this point of view, the shipping of slaves across the Atlantic could be seen as an extension of the internal African slave market (Reader 1998: 285). Also in traditional Africa, slaves were mostly acquired through violent raids into and wars with neighbouring tribes and states. However, the later capturing of slaves on a commercial basis on behalf of Europeans and Arabs left large areas of interior Africa depopulated and devastated (Reader 1998: 383). It led to a radical direct and indirect depopulation; the people left behind (old, disabled, children) were less productive than the captured; many families were broken with negative effects on wives and children; a general atmosphere of insecurity was created as violent inter-tribal and inter-village conflicts became normal; the development of African culture was hindered; existing, well-functioning political systems broke down, new aggressive states emerged; the local traditions in craft work (pottery, weaving, iron smelting and so on) were destroyed; general standards of living declined while some African traders, chief and societies became wealthy (Mwijage 2004: 75–8).

---

7   The author experienced this during his teaching at *St. Augustine University of Tanzania* (SAUT) in Mwanza at the Lake Victoria. It was common among the students to ask each other from which tribe they came. In classroom discussions about social problems, a usual comment was: 'In my tribe, we do as follows …'. The members of a tribe are called 'brothers' and 'sisters' – a practice which can be easily misinterpreted by a European in the first time.

Thus, the colonial period cannot be seen as an abrupt break in African history, but rather as a bridge between the pre-colonial times and post-colonial events and structures (Nugent 2004: 4). In this period, three new developments were significant in addition to the slave trade (see Cohen 1972; Michler 1988: 85–8; Meditz 1994; Young 1994: 278–1): (1) the creation of large new administrative units which later became states, each of which included some 100 or more different ethnic groups.[8] Since large administrative and political units were established, most of these new states became highly differentiated internally in ethnic terms. If the colonial powers made a failure in this regard it was that they considered their colonies mainly as administrative-economic units but not as future nation-states (Albertini 1976: 389; Welsh 2000). The aggregation of many different ethnic groups into the new, often very large and heterogeneous political-administrative units has often intensified ethnic conflicts. A particular tragic example was Nigeria where the British united the Muslim North and the non-Muslim South even against the ideas of the native leaders. Overall, however, 'colonialism rarely created ethnic conflict where none existed previously' (Hannum 1990: 456); (2) the arousing and strengthening of ethnic conflicts by applying the principle of *divide et impera*, used by the colonial powers to assure their domination. This principle implied that the members of certain ethnic groups and their chiefs were favoured over others by assigning them the power to participate in colonial government and administration; in this way, deep-rooted ethnic hatred and violence was sowed. Also the role of the traditional clan and tribe chiefs changed significantly; the chief as a 'full-blown village-based despot shorn of rule-based restraint' (Mamdani 1996: 43); a 'decentralized despotism' came into being only in the colonial period. It was supported by the British model of indirect rule which delegated local authority to the indigenous leaders; (3) there was a further problematic negative consequence of colonialism. Capitalism came to Africa with the imperative of acquisition and consumption but without the Protestant work ethic and frugality. Joseph Ki-Zerbo et al. (1981: 493f.) wrote in this regard: 'The white man himself in Africa set a dangerous example. The luxurious aristocratic life of White settlers as they played master to African servants was detrimental to the spirit of capitalism ...'

Not all aspects of colonialism were negative. The colonial powers eradicated some of the most inhumane traditional African practices, such as human sacrifices, they developed technological infrastructures, established educational systems, administrations and governmental institutions and introduced modern legal and institutional principles in their colonial territories (Illife 1997: 263–84). Many Christian missionaries had humanitarian ambitions and supported the abolition of slavery (Mwijage 2004: 95). Some of them also contributed in cultural terms by collecting comprehensive information about the language and culture of the African peoples and tribes.[9] They may have been a counter-force to the missions in general which established spiritual confusion and an inferiority complex among Africans (Lamb 1984: 140). Certainly, these modern, universal principles and innovations were first applied mainly for the advantage of the dominant Whites and a restricted, privileged number of their native subjects. But after the Second World War, when the independence movement began, the new African leaders had ideas and models which they could claim for themselves and apply in the new independent states.

The Dawn of the African Tragedy: Transition to Independence

Three stages may be distinguished in the more recent history of Africa: (1) the period immediately following independence, connected with far-reaching expectations both among the leaders and the populations; (2) the period approximately between 1970 and 1995 in which many dictatorial military regimes took over governments and violent internal fights and wars were unleashed; and (3) the recent period in which civilian governments resumed political power in many countries and formal multiparty democratic systems were introduced. Many countries managed it in this period to mitigate the former, fatal ethnic conflicts, although ethnic tensions persist beneath the surface.

---

8   The establishment of state borders corresponding to ethnic divisions, often implicitly considered as the better alternative to the arbitrary borders established by the colonial powers, would have been no solution in most cases. In any case, it would have created an extremely large number of very small states; with its 54 states, about half of which have only 10 million inhabitants or less, Africa is politically a very fragmented continent (Herbst 2000).

9   One representative was Father Crazzolara of the Catholic missionaries *Verona Fathers* who published extensive documentations of the languages of the Nuer, Acoola and Logbara in East Africa.

The time when most African states gained political independence in the 1960s and 1970s brought four additional developments, changing again significantly the structures of socio-economic inequality: (1) the first was that the state structures and state borders established by the colonial powers were taken over, unchallenged and preserved – with very few exceptions (secessions of Eritrea and South Sudan) till today (Herbst 2000). This can on the one side be considered as an achievement since it provided for political stability. On the other side, however, it was connected with the bloody suppression of fights for more local or regional autonomy or for even political independence of specific (often ethnic) sub-groups; (2) in politics, public administration, the armed forces and state and semi-state enterprises, tens of thousands of new jobs formerly held by representatives of the colonial powers, became accessible for Africans; (3) new sources of income opened up, such as revenues from taxes imposed on the population and the export of mineral resources, and from subsidies of foreign governmental and private donors. It is typical for the latter that they are not based on individual work efforts but can be considered as *rentier income*. States which rely to a large degree on such incomes can be denominated as *rentier states* (Yates 1996; see also pp. 154, 260); (4) deadly weapons were delivered into the hands of African state leaders and guerrilla fighters; their application led to much bloodier wars than those which in pre-colonial time African tribes and kingdoms had fought against each other (see also Mafeje 1998: 109; Reader 1998: 260, 408). Once political independence had been achieved, the nationalist movements 'all too often fractured into political groupings whose struggles for power and wealth polarized economic and social discontent along ethnic lines ...' (Reader 1998: 627). In addition, during the Cold War, Sub-Saharan Africa was used as a substitute battlefield of the Cold War between the Capitalist Western and State Socialist countries.[10]

Two aspects are crucial for the development of inequality in the transition from the colonies to independent states. First, in most countries the independence movements became political parties after the attainment of independence. Those who were able to gain control of the government soon established one-party systems (Ungar 1989; Young 1994; Herbst 2000; Dzimbiri et al. 2000). Western multiparty systems were considered as a luxury which Africa could not afford (Ki-Zerbo et al. 1981: 490). In most cases, the victorious movements had their main base in one or a few tribes and they soon established centralized, authoritarian systems, sawing the seed for the later brutal and protracted ethnic conflicts and civil wars. A second, important trend was a fundamental change in the typical political leader. Many of the first-generation leaders of the new states had been educated at European or American universities, and were enlightened fighters for independence (many of them wrote books) who – together with other intellectuals – foresaw a peaceful autonomous development of their nations. Examples include Kwame Nkrumah of Ghana, Leopold Senghor of Senegal, Julius Nyerere of Tanzania and Yomo Kenyatta of Kenya (see also Ki-Zerbo et al. 1981; Elaigwu and Mazrui 1981: 435–6; Davidson 1992: 33; Shils 2000; Müller 2012; Aminzade 2013). But even some of these leaders soon became autocratic. Most of them, however, were soon dethroned in coups by ruthless political and military leaders who used all their means to establish authoritarian systems and to suppress any opposition by brute force. This then led to an outburst of violence which was unique in global terms. Since this period was so devastating for Sub-Saharan Africa, let us have a short look at them. I will show that in the vast majority of these internal conflicts and civil wars ethnic division were of decisive importance.

Ethnic Violence Unbound: Civil Wars in Africa

Certainly the most disturbing aspect of the development of Africa since most states gained their independence in the 1960s and 1970s was the unbelievable amount of violence and atrocities which broke out and often lasted for decades. Collier and Hoeffler (2002) list 78 civil wars (defined as wars within a state involving at least 1,000 war-related deaths) around the world between 1962 and 1999 (see also Michler 1998: 271–301; Illife 1997: 345–54; Ali and Matthews 1999): 41 per cent of them occurred in Africa – far more than its share among the countries of the world. In the largest of these wars – such as in Nigeria, the Congo and Sudan – millions of people have died directly and indirectly as war victims and many more millions have

---

10   See F. Forsyth (1976) on the fatal intervention of Britain and other foreign powers in the Biafran civil war in Nigeria.

been displaced internally or became refugees in adjacent countries. Alone in four African countries (Angola, Mozambique, DRC and Sudan) around eight million people must be counted as direct and indirect war victims (Hoeffler 2008). The present-day extremely high level of civil violence (homicides) in Sub-Saharan Africa (see Table 6.1, pp. 164–5) is certainly an inheritance from this terrible period.

Civil wars also have significant impacts on socio-economic inequality. First, they delay development and often throw a country backwards in levels of wealth and welfare for decades (Hoeffler 2008). They have negative effects on education, through the destruction of school buildings, the loss of teachers and the drawing away of funds for military spending (Lai and Thyne 2011). State expenses for military are very high in many African countries. While they were less than 3 per cent of GDP in practically all European countries (except Russia), and also in most Asian countries, they were 3–4 per cent in 11 African countries, and 5 per cent and more in six further African countries (Angola, Burundi, Eritrea, Mauritania, Morocco and Namibia).[11] Second, civil wars directly contribute to an increase of inequality by impoverishing the lowest sections of the population and enriching the highest ones (Bircan et al. 2010). Millions of people find their houses and villages destroyed; the death of male family members means that many widows and orphans are left; starvation and war-related disabilities and diseases (such as HIV/Aids) spread. Middle- and upper-class people are not subjected as much to all these consequences because they are able to escape earlier and in safer ways from areas where violence breaks out. On the other side, unscrupulous warlords, political leaders and businessmen can enrich themselves by shuffling together big fortunes through the confiscation and rubbing of civilian property, the control of large areas with mineral resources, such as oil or diamonds and the production and trade of weapons (see also Sklar 1967; Ali and Matthers 1999; Anugwom 2006; Herbst 2000). Certainly, causality may also run in the other direction, that is, blatant inequalities may fuel conflicts. This has been so, for instance, in Uganda where the Northern Muslim tribes were deprived in economic and political terms but had considerable influence in the military (Kasozi 1994: 30–55).

The thesis that ethnic fractionalization has been the main factor for the emergence of the bloody civil wars in Africa has not been unchallenged. Some authors do not even mention this factor.[12] Paul Collier and Anke Hoeffler (2002) distinguish two theories about the role of ethnic fractionalization in civil wars. *Grievance theory* focuses on objective grounds for rebellion and war, such as ethnic discrimination, political repression or extreme inequality. According to this theory, people take up arms because of their misery and starvation, repression and exploitation. Collier and Hoeffler (2002) provide an alternative approach called *greed theory*; this economic theory sees a high degree of similarity between rebellion and crime. Its main thesis is that it is very costly to organize a rebellion and carry through a long civil war which makes necessary the support of a considerable army and the control of a large area. Rebel leaders are well aware of this and take these costs into account. This theory makes a lot of sense. However, I would not subscribe to the conclusion of Collier and Hoeffler (2002: 2) that those factors which determine 'the financial and military viability of a rebellion are far more important than objective grounds for grievance'. We need an additional approach which can be called the *mobilization theory* of civil war. In this theory, the focus is on the capacities to release unrest and uprisings among the population, to organize rebel groups and to carry through a prolonged civil war. Four factors are relevant in this regard. The first is ethnic fractionalization. As outlined in Chapters 2 and 3, ethnic group formation and consciousness can significantly inhibit, but also foster the development of collective consciousness and action. Second, the socio-cultural level of development of an ethnic group; the higher it is, the better it will be able to organize itself to defend its interests: significant in this regard is the fact if an ethnic group disposes of something like 'organic intellectuals' in terms of Gramsci's class theory (Gramsci 1975). In fact, often students and intellectuals were the driving forces behind rebellions, such as in Ethiopia (Balsvik 2005) or in the West Sahara. A third factor significant for the outbreak of civil wars was the rise of strong *Big Man* whose actions often were decisive. Finally, also ideologies related to ethnic and national autonomy and political power and domination played a significant role. Here, we have to look particularly at the role of religious communities and churches.

Ethnic differentiation and cleavages may affect the emergence of civil wars mainly in an indirect way. Randall J. Blimes (2006: 539) argues that ethnic diversity often serves as a natural fault line on which a

---

11   The data refer to 2005. See http://de.wikipedia.org/wiki/Liste_der_Streitkräfte-der-Welt
12   An example is Michler (1988: 271–302).

society, subjected to other variables that have a direct influence on the outbreak of civil war, can act as a solution to collective action problems that might otherwise prevent a cohesive rebellion from forming. These other factors include: a prior war history; a low per capita income; political instability; the youth of a state; if a state is an oil exporter; if it has a large population and a high proportion of mountainous surface (which makes it easier for rebel groups to operate); and the existence of a dominant ethnic group. It is obvious that this theory of several indirect effects of ethnic fractionalization is well in line with the general argument of this book about the intersection between class stratification and ethnicity proposed in Chapter 3. My thesis is that unscrupulous political and military leaders used their power – grounded in their ethnic clientele – to monopolize the means of violence and state revenues in order to consolidate their domination and to suppress any challenge to it. Their particular targets were movements which threatened the territorial integrity of the state. In this case, ethnicity certainly operated as a destructive force.

If we have a systematic look at the 17 larger civil wars in Africa between 1960 and 2005,[13] it becomes evident that ethnic divisions were in fact present in most of them. In eight cases, they were crucial (Algeria, Burundi, 1st and 2nd Congo Wars, Nigeria, Rwanda, Sudan, Uganda); in a further seven cases, they played a significant, although not the decisive role (Angola, Chad, Cote d'Ivoire, Liberia, Morocco, Sierra Leone, Somalia). This was the case, however, particularly in some of the cruellest conflicts, such as in the Congo, Nigeria, Rwanda, Uganda and Sudan (for Uganda see Atkinson 2010: 275ff.; Kasozi 1994).

In not less than five cases a religious cleavage was also involved, namely that between an Islamic north (or an Islamic fundamentalist movement) and non-Islamic parts of a country; this was the case in Algeria, Chad, Nigeria, Rwanda, Uganda, Sierra Leone and Sudan. Here, the thesis of Huntington (1996) seems to be true that a 'clash of civilisation' is taking place between the Islamic world and the Western world. In fact, in countries like Chad, Nigeria and Sudan, one can identify a kind of 'bloody borders' between Islamic and non-Islamic civilizations. However, these bloody fights and wars did not originate from the religions as such (as Huntington claims) but only from their instrumentalization for fights for political domination and exploitation. The Muslim Arabs are hated among many Africans in the border regions between Islamic and non-Islamic Africa due to the memory of slave riding. Also the close relation between the religious and secular-political sphere in Islam is relevant here, including the attempt of fundamentalist Islam to establish *Sharia* law in the civic and political sphere (for the case of Sudan see Mathok 2009, for Nigeria Reader 1998: 274).

A further factor which seems to be relevant in nearly all cases of bloody civil wars is the experience of former wars and terroristic regimes; the same is true for foreign military interventions (Blimes 2006). Here, we have again to bear in mind the period of slave riding during which many aggressive African regimes were established. Particularly shameful in this regard is the fact that Africa was used as a substitute battlefield by the United States and the Soviet Union during the Cold War. In this period, the USSR, West European countries and the USA supplied masses of deadly weapons to the contending parties, thus heating up violence and wars.

There is one more crucial factor which is not seen in the two theories sketched out before, but which is clearly decisive from the viewpoint of a sociological organization and mobilization theory of civil wars. This is the role of single political leaders. Here, we can rely on Max Weber's concept of the charismatic personality; it says that in certain periods specific kinds of individual personalities arise which propose new ideas and aims, and which are able to gain mass support for these (Weber 1947: 328, 258). It is my thesis that single political personalities have played an outstanding role in Africa in the second half of the 20th century.[14] Both positive and negative characteristics of these leaders may have been particularly important.

The typical autocratic leaders of the new independent African states were no gloomy warlords from the bush even if many of them had been successful guerilla fighters. It has already been noted that many were highly intelligent and knowledgeable men who had acquired their ken either through academic studies or through autodidactic self-learning. They often had a high degree of personal charm and excellent oratorical skills which enabled them to gain the approval of the masses and the trust and admiration of foreign heads of states. We see here clearly the elective affinities (*Wahlverwandtschaften*) between the traditional African

---

13   In the first version of this chapter, a detailed section was presented characterizing all these civil wars, particularly the role of ethnic divisions in them. Due to limits of space, this overview cannot be included here.

14   For a similar view see Lewis 1966; it is contested, however, by Markovitz (1977: 209).

leaders and chiefs and these modern warlords. Many of them, however, later developed extremely negative traits including the lack of any civic or political morale, an unscrupulous power striving, the tendency to enrich themselves, to engage in corruption and to act as true *cleptocrats* looting public income and revenues for personal purposes. Some of the worst personalities in this regard include Mobutu Sese Seko, autocratic president of the Democratic Republic of Congo (1971–97); Milton Obote (1925–2005) and Idi Amin (1925–2003) of Uganda; Muammar Ghadaffi (1942–2011) of Libya; Mengistu Haile Mariam of Ethiopia (1971–91) (see also Lamb 1984: 43–76). One of the most long-term reigning (1971–97), power-hungry and corrupt leaders, Mobutu of Zaire, was described as follows: 'Mobutu's position has also been strengthened by his ability ... to incite ethnic violence, thereby promoting instability, fostering anarchy, weakening the opposition, and undermining mass political mobilization against his regime' (Meditz 1994: l); his 'consummate political skill' to divide the opposition and to co-opt key opponents was a very important factor for his ability to retain power. It is certainly a positive sign that one of these brutal autocrats, Charles M.G. Taylor, president of Liberia 1997–2003, has been sentenced to 50 years in prison by the *International Court of Justice* in Den Haag because of 11 charges, including terror, murder and rape.

According to Weber, also the historical and social circumstances are decisive under which the chance increases that charismatic personalities in this sense emerge. Here, it is evident that the foundation of new, independent states all over Central Africa created a situation in which entrepreneurial personalities could unfold their political capacities. We may mention several crucial factors in this situation: the weakness of the new states which had no history and a low level of social integration and national identity; the lack of strong and independent public institutions; the weakness of collective civic and political actors, such as political parties, trade unions, confederations of employers and so on; the availability of high state incomes through sources such as mineral exports or development aid from foreign donors.

My conclusion about the most important factors leading to the many violent civil wars corresponds largely to that of Ali and Matthews. They also argue that the main reasons were neither the colonial heritage nor interventions from outside but internal forces, in particular the action of leaders and elites:

> Often ruling elites were made up of self-seeking cynics with no vision for the future of their countries. They perpetuated their power by maintaining the inherited structures and policies of the colonial state, by manipulating ethnic loyalties, and by trampling on the economic, cultural and political rights of marginalized communities. (Ali and Matthews 1999: 291).

Socio-economic Privilege and Deprivation Today

Three points shall be dealt with in this section: (1) the rise of the new dominant ethno-classes; (2) the use of the state as the main employer and the privileges of state employees; (3) ethnic biases in the educational policy and resulting educational inequalities.

The Uusurpation of State Power by Ethno-classes

The most widely used concept for the analysis of the development of political systems in the new African states is that of *neopatrimonialism*. It says that patron-client networks organized around a powerful individual are the main structure which determines political processes. The concept in fact captures an aspect which is present in nearly all African societies. Patron-client relationships have not only negative consequences, leading to corruption and similar processes, but are also a means to facilitate social integration, protection and support for weaker groups and communities (Theobald 1982; Bratton and Valle 1994). Neopatrimonialism is seen as a hybrid political regime consisting at the same time of a formally modern, rational-legal state apparatus and a patrimonial 'spoils network' in which central elites mobilize political support by using their position to distribute jobs and resources as personal favours.[15] Recently, this concept has been criticized for

---

15 A.H. Francisca, 'Neopatrimonalism in contemporary African politics', *e-International Relations*, 24 January 2010.

several reasons: the focus on selected countries, limited empirical evidence and the tendency to overgeneralize about Africa; the construction of a simplified model which provides a convenient policy-relevant message; the tendency to functionalist explanation at the expense of historical-causal analysis; the transformation at Weber's ideal type 'patrimonialism' into a diffuse empirically induced term (de Grassi 2008; Pitcher et al. 2009; see also Mamdani 1996: 3ff.).

In this work, I start from the thesis that political processes and conflicts about distribution in the African context can be understood better by a class-theoretical approach, including processes of ethnic stratification, and supplemented by the concept of the 'rentier state'. Several authors have anticipated such a class-theoretical interpretation. Manghezi (1976: 73–6) reports several authors who saw the new African societies as divided into an elite and the masses. They saw the elite as a small, homogeneous group with a similar social background: coming from a humble social background, and continuing to maintain links with their villages and kin, they were 'Westernized' by education, and 'reside in the national or regional capitals where they share the same salubrious residences afforded them by their high salaries' (for Nigeria see Ungar 1989: 131f.) In French-speaking Africa, René Dumont (1969: 81) discovered a new type of 'a bourgeoisie of the civil service' (see also Cohen 1972). In his comprehensive work, *The Making of Contemporary Africa*, Bill Freund (1998: 210f.) wrote that the new ruling classes are neither aristocrats nor planters, but 'are attached by an umbilical cord to the state bureaucracy'. In his well-documented book *Power and Class in Africa*, Irving L. Markovitz (1977) argues that a new class, the 'organizational bourgeoisie', was formed; the nationalist movements and their leaders in the new African states 'sought above all to consolidate and take a firm grip on power'. They relied mainly on indirect taxation and non-tax revenues (such as from export of minerals or foreign aid); in this way, it was easy for them to divert large amounts of revenue to themselves and their followers (Herbst 2000: 131). In the same vein, Basil Davidson (1992: 111f.) writes about Nigeria that tribal-based associations played a significant role in the fight for independence, but as soon as independence was gained, 'the new parties at once became instruments of national rivalry ... and the interests of the "elites" took primary over the combined interests of the "masses"' (see also Lloyd 1966; First 1970). But social scientists were not alone in noting the emergence of a new powerful and privileged class. Also some of the most respected first-generation independent African leaders, such as Kwame Nkrumah and Julius Nyerere, expressed critical views in this regard, as did several literary writers and others.

The new 'organizational bourgeoisie' (Markovitz 1977) formed itself in the first years after independence in all states. It was based primarily on the steady growth of the public sector and the expansion of government expenditures for his administrative personnel. In the mid-1960s between 50 per cent and 80 per cent was devoted to administrative salaries in some of the new independent states. Members of this new ruling organizational class (Markovitz 1977: 208; for the Congo see Meditz 1994: 151ff.) were 'top political leaders and bureaucrats, the traditional rulers and their descendants, and the leading members of the liberal professions and the rising business bourgeoisie' as well as top members of the military and police forces. In all these regards, we see astonishing similarities with characteristics of pre-colonial Africa; already there, 'the extraction of economic value took a political form' (Mafeje 1998: 39). Markovitz also quotes many studies showing that the new political and bureaucratic elites soon formed a new social class because they were distinct also in their lifestyles. In contrast to the simple huts and cottages of most people, they lived in massive buildings with glass windows, hardwood doors and air conditioners. Lobban (1985: 171) wrote that 'the wealthy Sudanese are bond to have the finest clothing for their wives, perhaps drive a Mercedes Benz, and life in the prestigious sections of the city [Khartoum]' (see also Kasozi 1994: 47). Middle-ranking civil servants received a smaller salary but had almost the same other privileges as their superiors. The houses of the well-to-do and ruling people in African cities (as in Latin America) are surrounded by high walls often reinforced with barbed wire. This fact clearly shows that here a highly privileged new class is detaching itself from the outside world of common people and feels endangered by them. Also the structure of imports of the new states sheds a significant light on the rise of this new class. In the former French colonies, much more was spent in importing alcoholic beverages, cosmetics and private cars than in importing fertilizers and agricultural equipment or machine tools (First 1970: 110; quoted in Markovitz 1977: 208; Ki-Zerbo et al. 1981: 493). The favouring of capital cities and urban centres by the new elites was supported by a preferential financing of food and imports through an implicit taxation of exports (Collier and Gunning 1999: 68). Thus, we can say that here a truly new 'ethno-class' has emerged in many African states and societies. It can be called a class in the sense of Marx (1974 [1848]) and of Weber (1964/I: 223–9; 1964/II: 678–89) who defined a class in terms of its own sources of income and by a specific style of life. Following Gaetano Mosca (1950 [1896]), we could also speak of ethno-political classes.

A corollary of the theory of the rise of these new dominant ethno-classes is the concept of the 'rentier state' which was introduced already in Chapter 5 (p. 154). A rentier economy or state is one in which the main income comes from foreign sources, such as oil exports, development aid and so on; economic policy is concerned mainly with spending the income; and the state controls the income and its use (Yates 1996: 15ff.). Such a situation leads to a devaluation of work and produces a 'rentier mentality': An expectation of a continuous stream of income; 'conspicuous consumption' in order to arouse envy among others; investment in large, prestigious prospects; a swelling of the third sector (Yates 1996: 11–40). This theory was developed first for oil-rich Arab countries like Persia and Kuwait (Ismael 1993), but is applicable also to African countries like Gabon (Yates 1996), Nigeria and Sudan.

An additional aspect of the new ethno-classes also mentioned by Markovitz was that 'they have to seek a social base' in a developing commercial and business class. In fact, the new state-based ethno-class continually tried to establish its influence and privilege by cooperating closely with the rising private business classes and by developing and accumulating their own private enterprises and income sources. However, the business class did not overtake the politically based ethno-class. Several facts show that the political ethno-classes were able to procure a continuous stream of income for themselves.

First, there were hundreds of cases in which it became known in public that European corporations had paid huge sums of bribery to African political leaders in order to get orders for their products (often weapons) and investments. Recently, the international tolerance for such practices has declined massively, however. Another form of cooperation between African politicians and Western corporations is the possibility offered by banks in countries to deposit Black money in a safe way. Most helpful in this regard were banks in Switzerland (Ziegler 1992), but also banks in other West European countries such as France (given the close relationships between France and Francophone Africa) and Great Britain (with its many off-shore banks). Second, political leaders and high officials cooperate closely with local entrepreneurs and businesspeople. This happens typically through tender contracts (coined as *tenderpreneurism*) mostly based on personal connections and relationships, as documented in the famous *Warioba Report* about corruption in Tanzania (Warioba 1996). The cooperation between political and business elites may be particularly close and intransparent in cases where a state gets huge incomes from the export of mineral resources, such as in Nigeria (Reader 1998: 664). Third, the political elites themselves have an interest and many possibilities to assemble additional incomes through private business ventures, both in order to get a high return on their money and to build a kind of insurance for the time when they eventually would not be in office any more. There are many examples of high-level African political leaders whose investments in private businesses became known in public after they had been dethroned. They include Rupiah Banda, the former president of Zambia; the Ethiopian emperor Haile Selassie; and Omar O. Bongo, the autocratic president of Gabon, one of the richest men in Africa (Yates 1996: 209).

Economist John M. Mbaku (2004: 48–54) has described very well the process how the new political leaders in Africa usurped state instruments for accumulating privileges. The earlier colonial 'decentralized despotism' was substituted by a 'centralized despotism' (Mamdani 1996: 25). In many of the new independent states all import and export businesses were nationalized and the government took over the majority of all companies, mines and industries and financial institutions (Kasozi 1994: 90). Its policy instruments included: '(1) the protection of domestic producers through import taxes (tariffs), exchange rationing/controls, and import quotas; (2) subsidies to foreign entrepreneurs/firms to encourage them to establish subsidiaries; and (3) the creation of so-called development banks' (Mbaku 2004: 51). In addition, a large number of para-state enterprises were created and many sectors including the financial one were targeted to fall under state control. The idea was that through these state activities and investments development could be accelerated. However, two factors made implementation of this well-meant policy impossible, even perverted it: first, a lack of institutional constraints on the politicians and civil servants and second, the absence of a strong and critical civil society (Mbaku 2004: 51f.). Thus, the effects of government-led development plans were 'rent-seeking, corruption and the promotion of perverse economic policies'. Another important factor was state politics which held prices for agricultural products low while those of industrial goods increased much more

(Illife 1997: 359). In this way, surpluses were extracted from the rural sectors and they were used to provide subsidies to urban dwellers, special payments to the armed forces, civil servants, labour leaders and other politically influential individuals and groups (Mbaku 2004: 53).

The State as Main Employer Outside Agriculture and the Privileges of State Employees

The fact that employment by the state's governments is of utmost importance can be shown clearly when we look at some recent Labour Force Surveys. Table 10.2 shows the distribution of the employed population in five countries according to different institutional contexts (central and local government, parastatal organizations, NGOs, private sectors, farming and household services).[16] Looking at the total working population, employment by the government in Ethiopia, Tanzania and Zambia is less than 5 per cent of total employment; in Botswana and Namibia, it is about 21 per cent. The bulk of the population in all countries work in self-employment in- and outside agriculture as well as in private households: also in Nigeria, Namibia and Ethiopia only about 8 per cent of the working -age population have a formal, paid employment contract (Ogwumike et al. 2006). The proportion occupied by government in the group of paid, employed persons, however, is similar and vey high in all countries (in Tanzania 37 per cent, in Ethiopia 40 per cent and in Zambia 53 per cent).

It is often said that state employees in Sub-Saharan Africa (SSA) earn much less than those in the private sectors. As a consequence, they are under constraint to polish up their income by other means, including bribery and corruption. In statements of this sort, two false arguments are contained: first, a misleading equalization of all employees in the public sector; second, the assumption that public sector employees as a whole are paid lower wages than people employed in other sectors.

Data for Uganda and Tanzania show that employees in the private sector, even those in NGOs, earn significantly less than those in government services, not to speak of those in agriculture (see Table 10.3). Only employees in parastate enterprises earn more, a fact well known also in other countries. A special survey among urban employed people in Ghana and Tanzania in 2004/05 (sample sizes about 1.000) showed similar results (Teal 2010). The privileged income situation of the public employees may also be a kind of *tabu* for researchers so that they do not report the respective data.[17]

The argument about the low incomes in the public sector also overlooks the massive inequalities within this sector. A reanalysis of the Nigerian General Household Survey 1999 found that income inequality is more pronounced in paid employment than in self-employment. This fact is completely different from the situation in Europe and America; here, the income dispersion within the self-employed is much higher than that among the paid employees. The African situation may be explained by the fact that most self-employment consists of simple agricultural, trade and service activities which provide only very low, subsistence incomes. Statistical figures are confirmed by case studies. They show that the income of people employed by the state is often improved significantly by additional revenues, such as those from independent businesses.

In this regard, we can also look at state budgets as mirrors of societal power constellations (Goldscheid and Schumpeter 1976) and the indirect benefits going to the dominant ethno-classes. Politicians and leaders of parastatal organizations also profit from government expenditures which usually are purported to support the poor or the population at large. In most African nations, the largest part of government investments and spending goes to the central, economically most prosperous parts of the country, often to the capital alone. This applies to infrastructural investments such as roads, transport facilities, energy, security and so on. This concentration of state funds on the centres is connected with the high level of administrative and judicial centralization of the African states and the concentration of power in the presidencies (see below). A good example is the subsidizing of the provision of electrical energy. The building and maintenance of power plants and overhead power lines requires a high level of technological expertise and accurateness which many

---

16   It was only for these five countries, that these tables were given in the respective Labour Force Surveys. In many SSA-countries, no such surveys have been carried out at all.

17   A case in point is the informative study of Ogwumike et al. (2006) which does not report data on the income of public employees, but in the policy recommendations includes 'the need to address the wage gap between private and public paid employees'.

Table 10.2 The distribution of the total and the employed population by institutional sectors in five Sub-Saharan African countries, 2000–2008

Sector	Botswana 2005 Total %	Botswana 2005 Paid employment %	Ethiopia 2004 Total %	Ethiopia 2004 Paid employment %	Namibia 2008 Total %	Namibia 2008 Paid employment %	Tanzania 2000 Total %	Tanzania 2000 Paid employment %	Zambia 2008 Total %	Zambia 2008 Paid employment %
Central and local government	20.7	34.6	2.6	33	20.9		2.0	30	4.5	45.2
Parastatals	2.6	5.9	0.6	7	8.9		0.5	7	0.8	7.7
NGO, Church, international organisations	0.6	1.0	4.3	6	4.8		x	x	0.7	3.5
Private sector	43.1	45.3	40.9[1]	36	51.0[3]		4.5	56	16.9	43.1
Private household	7.8	13.2	-	18	14.1		3.5	7	76.1[7]	-
Subsistence farming	24.0	-	50.3[2]	-	-		81.0[4]	-	-	-
Total	100	100	100	100	100		100	100	100	100
(N in 1.000)	(539)	(326)	(31400)	(2480)	(272)		(16911)	(1150)	(5221)	(522)

[1] Self employed; [2] Unpaid family workers; [3] Probably incl. farming; [4] Traditional farming; [5] Informal sector; [6] Incl. "private farming; [7] Probably incl. farming; [x] Incl. "private other"; [x] Category not included.

Sources: Botswana Labour Force Survey 2005/06 (ca. 9.000 respondents); Ethiopia Labour Force Survey 2004/05 (24.861 households); Namibia Labour Force Survey 2008 (N ca. 6000); Tanzania Integrated Labour Force Survey 2000/01 (only Tanzania mainland covered); Zambia Labour Force Survey 2008 (ca. 30.000 households. All surveys are available at the homepage of the respective Statistical Bureaus and Offices and also through the homepage of the International Labour Organisation; see http://www.ilo.org/dyn/lfsurvey/lfsurvey.home.

Table 10.3   Income and expenditures, respectively, by institutional sector of the employed population in Tanzania and Uganda (2005/06)

	Tanzania 2000/01				Uganda 2005/06		
	Mean monthly income[1]				Pop. share	Mean CPAE[2]	% poor
Sector	All	Men	Women	Sector			
Government	77.8	80.1	73.3	Government	4.7	76.700	7.2
Parastatal organiz.	129.5	131.3	121.8	Private empl.	11.9	50.200	24.0
NGO's and similar	37.6	51.5	33.6	Self-empl.	79.7	35.500	33.6
Private informal sect.	22.3	25.6	12.5	Inactive	1.3	72.800	19.2
Private agriculture	13.4	15.3	8.2				
Housework	11.8	18.2	10.8				

[1]In 1.000 Tanzanian Shillings (TSH); [2]Consumption per Adult Equivalent of each Decile in Uganda Shillings (UGX)
Sources: Tanzania Integrated Labour Force Survey 2000/01 (mainland Tanzania), available at http://www.nbs.go.tz/. Uganda National Household Survey 2005/06, available at http://www.ubos.org/onlinefiles/uploads/ubos/pdf%20 documents/UNHSReport20052006.pdf (15.1.2012).

countries are lacking. Therefore, power blackouts are a recurring problem not only in Africa but also in many other countries of the South, causing huge economic losses to enterprises and other institutions.[18] Now, one government strategy is to provide subsidies to power plants with the argument that this keeps energy prices affordable also for poorer social strata. This is far from the truth, however. In Uganda, for instance, only 12 per cent of all households are connected to the national power grid and the biggest beneficiaries of the subsidies are large industrial organizations and middle- and upper-income households, not the poor.[19] For instance, Century Bottling Company (CBC) which produces Coca Cola, made a profit of 9.7 million $ in 2011, but paid only 809,700$ for electrical energy; if it had to pay the true costs, it would have had to pay $3.4 million. In Kenya, Malawi, Zambia and other states the elected representatives of different provinces receive allocations from the national treasury to allow them to streamline the development process; in practice, the funds often are primarily used only for political purposes (Van der Valle 2009: 9).

Ethnically Biased Educational Policies and Resulting Inequalities

Education is of crucial importance for Africa in two regards, as a central factor promoting socio-economic development and equality, but also as an agent who reproduces social and economic inequality. In this case, we can see again the close interaction between class stratification and ethnic differentiation.

The role of the modern educational system in regard to inequality is Janus-faced: on the one side, it is a central factor promoting equality based on individual talent and achievement as against inheritance of social positions and privileges and – in this way – to socio-economic development. In this regard, Africa lies behind all other continents. Table 6.1 (pp. 164–5) shows that the mean years of schooling attended today are only about 5 to 7 years, in some countries even less. The primary school enrolment rate is still only about 80 per cent in many countries, illiteracy among adults 20 to 40 per cent (in Ethiopia even 70 per cent).[20]

On the other side, education is itself a factor contributing to the reproduction of inequality. A society based on an extended, comprehensive system of education is a much more systematically stratified society than one in which only a small fraction of the population is able to read and write (Haller 1986). Social inequality

---

18   One reason for this problem is also that governments prescribe low energy prices which then make it impossible for energy firms to make necessary investments to the maintenance of the existing, and the acquisition of new, equipment.

19   Andrew M. Mwenda, 'Uganda's $200m electricity subsidy gravy train', *The East African*, 16–22 January 2012, pp. 8,9,11; see also *The East African*, 30 January–5 February 2012, p. 14: 'Uganda's energy experts back move to cut subsidies amid tariff wars'.

20   See World Development Report 2012, The World Bank, Tables 2.12 and 2.14.

is inherent in modern societies wherein the educational system plays a significant role in the allocation of young people to occupational positions (Bourdieu and Passeron 1977). In this regard, African societies were faced with two challenges not present to this degree in other parts of the world: first, the whole system of education had to be built up anew in societies which had only oral traditions of cultural transmission and learning; second, the immense ethnic-linguistic diversity of many countries made it imperative to establish a new *lingua franca* as language of instruction in most countries. In both aspects, some of the basic principles for the present situation have been laid by the colonial powers. Let us first have a short look at the educational policies and structures established by them.

There existed significant differences between the main colonizing European powers in regard to educational policies (Basu 1982). The first colonizers, Catholic Spain and Portugal, fostered some education of the indigenous population. The reason was that Pope Alexander VI. (1492–1503) allowed their colonization venture and the enslavement of the natives only if it went together with their evangelization (Reader 1998: 333). British colonization, in contrast, was mainly interested in the economic advantages they could take out of the new territories. The French were eager to prevent the development of an autonomous, indigenous educated elite which could have challenged their domination. In structural terms, however, the main strategies and outcomes of these different colonizing powers were similar: their efforts bringing education to the local people was confined to a small segment of the population, mainly the higher strata, in order to get educated people for colonial administration and indigenous priests and teachers. In India, the British focused upon the children of the hereditary aristocracy, in Sub-Saharan Africa specific ethnic groups were preferred over others. The youth of lower classes was provided only with limited vocational and craft training. For all children entering the colonial educational system, learning the language of their colonizers (English, French, Portuguese and Spanish) was the first task. The use of European textbooks led to manifold contradictions between the content of education and African reality; pupils learned about northern seasons, about European mountains, states and kings, but nothing about Africa (Reader 1998: 621). As a consequence, the main purpose of education often was missed. The following statement still has considerable validity today:

> What most students picked up was a smattering of English and a tendency towards repetition of half-understood sentences. This encouraged memorizing and did not train a student to think for himself. Lessons were imported in a mechanical way, learned by heart and reproduced in examinations by students. Examinations in fact dominated high schools and universities (Basu 1982: 65f.).

In most of the many recently established universities in Sub-Saharan Africa, lectures are taking place in extremely large classes and examination processes dominate several weeks of the academic year. Another consequential effect was that education became an important factor in class formation, tending to separate the Western-educated elite from the masses often dispraised as 'illiterate' or 'unlettered' (Habte and Wagaw 1981: 679). Such an attitude can be observed still today among university students who try to separate themselves from ordinary people, for instance in public transport (Müller and Haller 2012).

Here, also the language problem is highly relevant. African languages were looked upon from the beginning as having only limited social and cultural scope (Sow and Abdulaziz 1981: 530). In spite of the fact that the 2,000 African languages constitute nearly one-third of all world languages, they are neglected in general works on the topic.[21] In the last decades, African language departments have been established in African universities and African studies departments in Europe, America and Asia. A considerable split is emerging, however, because the majority of Africans continue to utilize their own language in daily communications and transactions, but in higher education, government and business the European languages became dominant. This difference increases the split between the mass of the population and the professional, managerial and governmental elites (Habte and Wagaw 1981: 696). Kasozi (1994: 11) writes about Uganda in this regard: 'English is a stratifying agent separating society into two groups: the privileged, who speak it, and the deprived, who don't' (see also Habte and Wagaw 1981: 679). In the same vein, Wangari Mathai (2009:

---

21 An example is the informative handbook of Bodmer (1989) 'The Languages of the World', in Bodmer (1989), *Die Sprachen der Welt*, Herrsching: M. Pawlak (English ed: The Loom of Language, Allein & Unwin).

220) sees in this linguistic split an indication of a deep social gulf which has negative consequences for the quality of political leadership:

> Most elites speak and manage in a foreign language that's spoken and read only by a tiny minority and not understood at all by the large majority of their peoples. The elites communicate with each other in official languages [...] Their grammar pronunciation, and sentence structure are not on the level of a native speaker. However, since those they speak with are also speaking imperfectly, they don't know they are making mistakes. By and large, neither the elites nor the masses know each other's mother tongues and rarely we do make an effort to learn them. As a result, we have a very limited reach in being able to spread our ideas, or listen to others.

Since the gaining of political independence in the 1960s and 1970s, the new African states have invested huge effort in building up and extending their school systems. They have also made impressive advances in this regard. According to Habte and Wagaw (1981: 690), already around 1980 education was the most important government expenditure in Africa (around 25–35 per cent of total expenditure). However, comparing their educational expenses pro child or youth, it turns out that the African countries spend relatively less for pupils in elementary education and more for those in higher education than European and American countries.[22] Thus, educational policy favours the middle and higher social strata. Universal primary education between 1999 and 2010 increased from 54 per cent to 67 per cent in Sub-Saharan Africa; however, with these figures, this region was still lying behind all others around the word (World Development Report 2012: 96; see also UNESCO 2009: 1ff.): half of all the 75 million children worldwide who were not in a school in 2006 lived in Sub-Saharan Africa.[23] The youth (15–24) illiteracy rate in 2005–10 was 23 per cent In SSA, that among the whole adult population 38 per cent (World Development Report 2012: 96). What is most evident and relevant for this study is that there were large gaps between the poor and wealthy segments of the population in all countries. Large differences exist in the mean years of schooling between persons from the lowest and highest income quintiles; in most Sub-Saharan African states it is 4 to 5 years, in Ethiopia and Nigeria even about 6 years.[24] However, there exist also significant differences within Sub-Saharan Africa (Lloyd and Hewitt 2009). The rate of children who completed primary school in 2010 was 67 per cent in SSA as a whole (compared with 86 per cent in South Asia), but only 33 per cent in Cameroon and Chad, 45 per cent to 60 per cent in Uganda, Mali, Niger and Senegal, 70 per cent in Ethiopia and Rwanda, 84 per cent in Namibia and over 90 per cent in Ghana and Tanzania (World Development Report 2012: 94–6). These differences are clearly related to general levels of development, but also some poor countries were able to achieve considerable improvements. It is evident that these include also the most egalitarian countries.

An additional, serious problem relates to the occupational perspectives of graduates from the higher schools. Given the weak development of industry and private economy, they aspire mainly to get jobs in the public sector which is, however, possible only for a small fraction. As Adogamhe (2010: 59) has observed for Nigeria in this regard: 'Thus, in its effort to provide education for all Nigerians, the government has inadvertently created a new economic class of educated but unemployed Nigerians'. This tendency is strengthened by the fact that most students in higher education come from middle- and upper-class families (Müller and Haller 2012).

Since ethnicity is of central importance in Sub-Saharan Africa, it is obvious that it will be relevant also for the schooling system and for educational opportunities. There are very few studies which have investigated directly this issue, probably also because it is highly contested. Since ethnic groups are settling in specific regions, membership in such groups is closely interrelated with region. As an approximation to data on inequalities between ethnic groups, we can look, therefore, on countries in which data on education systems by regions are available.

An interesting case in point is Nigeria, which is, with its 150 million inhabitants, the most populous and internally one of the most heterogeneous countries of Sub-Saharan Africa. In the sequel of a new

---

22   See World Bank, 'Indicators on Education' (http://data.worldbank.org/indicator/SE.XPD.TOTL).

23   UNESCO (2009), *Overcoming Inequality: Why Governance Matters*, p. 27.

24   UNESCO (2009), *Overcoming Inequality*, p. 28.

regionalization of the country whose declared intent was to give more power and resources to the regional and local ethnic groups, since 2002 about half of federal revenue (primarily from oil and gas) has been allocated to states and local governments. Of this share, a third is reserved for the oil-producing states in the Niger delta and the remainder is distributed among all states according to a complex formula. The results are large regional inequalities.[25] Regional disparities within Nigeria are enormous. Igbo and Yoruba, dominated states in the south and southwest near the sea, had a GDP per head between 3,500 and 4,000 Dollars. North and northwest states located near the Chad and Niger borders and inhabited mainly by the Muslim Hausa and Fulani had a GDP per head between 1,000 and 1,200 Dollars.[26] Corresponding inequalities in education exist also between ethnic groups. Table 10.4 shows that public spending in the Yoruba-inhabited southwest regions, including the capital Lagos and the state of Kwara, received nearly double the sum of public spending for education than the Hausa-dominated northern states Kano and Jigawa and the Kanuri-inhabited north-eastern state of Borno. The expenditure per capita for a primary age child in the capital Lagos is six times as high as in Borno; the reverse relation exists in regard to the student class ratios; significant differences exists also in teachers' salaries.

A similar situation exists in East Africa. Alwy and Schech (2004; see also Gakuru 1998: 46–7) show that in the regions inhabited by the political dominant Kikuyu group in central Kenya and the capital Nairobi, the qualification of teachers in primary schools was better and primary school enrolment much higher than in the peripheral regions in the north and east. These authors conclude: 'The results suggest a close correspondence of differentials between inequalities in education and ethnic affiliation to the ruling elite. Relatively small, clearly defined ethnic groups have accumulated an advantage over the majority in the national population in terms of educational infrastructure and resources' (Alwy and Schech 2004: 266). In their comprehensive analysis of data from 18 African countries, Frank and Rainer (2012) found that the attainment of primary education was strongly influenced by the ethnicity of the country's leaders during the last decades.

Table 10.4   Regional (ethnic) inequalities in educational spending and school structures in Nigeria (around 2005)

Region/state	Situated in region of ...	Per capita state education expenditure (Nairas)	Public spending per primary school-age child (in 2006 US-$)	Student class ratios in public primary schools	Average annual pay for teachers in prim. and sec. schools (in 1000 Nairas)	
Southwest						
Lagos	Yoruba	3945	132	32	518	609
Kwara	Yoruba	3814	65	52	201	333
Southeast						
Cross River	Bokyi, Tiv	2322	28	52	196	396
Enuyu	Yoruba	2698	34	36	304	595
Central Region						
Abjua, FCT**	mixed	4618	63	73	307	345
Kaduna	Gbagyi	1902	28	70	151	317
North						
Kano	Hausa	1406	26	93	153	284
Jigawa	Hausa	1755	28	67	155	310
Borno	Kanuri	1618	21	145	266	398

Sources: Paul Bennell et al. (2007); UNESCO 2009, p. 149.
**FCT – Federal Capital Territory

25   See the comprehensive UNESCO report, *Overcoming Inequality*. 2009.
26   See http://www.skyscrapercity.com/archive/index.phptt-699568.html

A policy of regional decentralization along ethnic lines must not necessarily lead toward a consolidation or even an increase of regional and ethnic inequalities. I will come back to a different policy which was carried out in Ethiopia in Chapter 13.

African Leaders, Political Movements and Parties Today. Persistence of the Autocratic Ethno-class Domination or Democratic Take-off?

It was already noted before that political leaders often played a decisive role in the history of the young African states. There were a few enlightened men among the former independence leaders who became first presidents of their countries. However, many of the leaders, particularly those who later usurped power through political and military cups, played a fateful, negative role. For the biologist and Peace Nobel Prize winner Wangari Mathai (2009: 25–7), one of the 'major tragedies' of postcolonial Africa lies in the fact that 'African peoples have trusted their leaders, but only a few of those leaders have honoured that trust'. The reasons for the failure of African leadership are, in her view, the legacy of colonialism (which often installed only local collaborators), the Cold War which provided foreign political protection to corrupt leaders and cultural destruction of the African spiritual inheritance. Given this legacy it is of high relevance to have a closer look at the composition of present-day African leaders.

Systematic data on the size and role of the behaviour of the political elites of dominant ethno-classes, their networks and privileges are not available today; to collect such data would be a research task of its own. It is possible, however, to look at some characteristics of the leading elite personalities, the heads of governments and states. This information is highly relevant here because most African states have presidential constitutions and the presidents have extremely strong influence and power. Nicolas van der Walle (2003: 310) wrote in this regard: 'Regardless of their constitutional arrangements … power is personalized around the figure of the president … He is literally above the law, controls in many cases a large proportion of state finance with little accountability, and delegates remarkably little of his authority on important matters'; little influence is left for the parliaments and the political parties; even ministers are 'relegated to an executants' role'.[27] In Kenya, the office of the president had an incredibly large staff of 43,230 persons in 1990.[28] It is quite understandable that the presidents are reluctant to disclose these figures.[29]

In this regard, we can rely on an annual report by the independent weekly magazine *The East African*, edited by the Nation Media Group in Nairobi, Kenya.[30] In their regular annual reports about 'Africa Leadership Scorecard', the magazine investigates how actual presidents 'fared on governance, democracy, press freedom, corruption, and human development in the past year'.

The magazine classifies all presidents in terms of their leadership behaviour, summing up five internationally known indicators for good government into one comprehensive index. The values of this index vary between 39 and 75; they were classified into seven categories of good or bad governance.[31] In addition, each president was shortly characterized, including his background and some of his main achievements and failures. Here, I analyse the report on the situation in 2011.[32] Four questions are relevant in this regard:

---

27   See also *The Nigerian Voice*, 19 June 2011.

28   According to a World Bank Report on Kenya in 1992 quoted in van der Walle 2003, p. 318. I was unable to fine more data on the staff of presidential offices.

29   The president of Ghana, John Mahama, was accused of failing to submit this information to his parliament as prescribed by law. See 'Mahama Denies Violating Ghana's Presidential Office Act'. *Premium Times* (Abuja, Nigeria), 21 August 2013.

30   See http://www.theeastafrican.co.ke/

31   The single indices used were: the Mo Ibrahim Index which assesses the quality of governance in Africa; the Democracy Index of the Economist Intelligence Unit; the Freedom of Press Index, published by Freedom House; the Corruption Perception Index, published by Transparency International; the Human Development Index, published by the United Nations; and the NMG Political Index, developed by the judgements of journalists of the Nation Media Group.

32   Published in *The East African*, 6–12 February 2012. Some of the presidents contained in this list are not in office today, some have passed away (such as Meles Zenawi of Ethiopia or John E. Atta Mills of Ghana) and some have been dethroned and executed (such as Muammar Gaddafi of Libya). This is no problem for the analysis presented, since its aim is that of a structural analysis, not of an accurate description of a specific historical constellation.

the duration of their terms in office, their typical educational background, the ethnic membership and their relevance of their behaviour regarding the respect for democratic procedures.

As regards of the length of time in office, one phenomenon is conspicuous and unique for Africa: once in power, political leaders are very reluctant to give it up again. Some use their political influence to change the constitution in a way that allows them to stay longer in office. However, if we look at Table 10.5, the findings are surprising and raise some hope: the large majority – two-thirds – of all leaders are at most eight years in office. It can be assumed that most of them came to power in regular elections. However, about one-fifth of the presidents are in power 13 years and longer. At the top – with 32 years in power – we find the presidents of Angola, José E. Dos Santos, and of Equatorial Guinea, Teodoro O.N. Mbasogo. The latter is described as 'one of Africa's few totalitarians, a brutal dictator' who once claimed to be a god; he is considered to be one of the wealthiest heads of state in the world. Four presidents are in office between 24 and 26 years. They include Yoweri Museveni of Uganda who has been considered by the West in the late 1990s as a promising 'leader of a new type'. In recent times, a widespread dissatisfaction with his long regime has grown due to the fact that – besides political stability – it has brought little in the stated aims of restoring democracy, eliminating sectarianism and corruption and consolidating national unity.[33] Another one in this group is Blaise Campaore, the president of Burkina Faso. A former military leader, he is described as the 'Classic African Big Man'; he holds regular elections denounced by many as shams and he is also known for his ostentatious wealth which offends many considering that he rules one of the poorest countries in the world. Then we find here the

Table 10.5 Characteristics of the presidents of the 54 African states in 2011

a. Years in office				n	%
1–8 years				37	69
9–12 years				7	13
13–19 years				3	5
20–32 years				7	13
Total				**54**	**100**
b. Educational/occupational background, former career				n	%
Political activist, leader of independence movement and/or liberation army				25	50
Army commander, police officer				14	28
Economists, employee of IWF etc., medical doctor, jurist, university professor				11	22
Total				**50***	**100**

c. Overall performance	Points	Grade	Designation	n	%
Good performers	70–73	A	Outstanding	4	
	62–4	B	Good	3	
	50–59	C	Passable	9	
(Sub-total)				(16)	33
Below standard	45–9	D		4	
	41–4	F		7	
(Sub-total)				(11)	22
Bad performers	29–39	ICU	Intensive care unit	11	
	18–28		The morgue	11	
(Sub-total)				(22)	45
Total				**49****	**100**

*Data missing for 4 presidents; **Not classified: 5 presidents.
Source: *The East African*, 6–12 February 2012, 'Africa Leadership Scorecard', pp. I–XV.

---

33 'Fundamental change still a dream in Uganda', *The East African*, 30 January —5 February 2012, p. 10.

infamous 89-year-old Robert Mugabe of Zimbabwe; in his early career, as a fighter against British colonialism in Rhodesia and for many years a political prisoner, he was considered as a hero all over Africa; later on, he became an authoritarian leader and purveyor of a rigid and violent form of State Socialism; he was also accused of racist attitudes toward Whites and homosexuals. Thus, advanced age or serious health disabilities are no hindrance in trying to remain in office for such men.

The tendency to adhere to political offices as long as possible cannot be explained only by a need for influence and power; this need is strong in political leaders everywhere in the world. In the background to the theory of ethno-political classes developed here we are able to understand why this striving is translated successfully into action only in Africa. An African political leader does not think of himself alone when he tries to gain and to preserve top political office and the extensive privileges associated with it: he thinks of a very large circle of persons whose situation depends on his readiness to share his income with them. This begins with his immediate kin people who might include several wives and concubines and many children thereof.[34] The next circle is that of the extended family and kinship, including parents, brothers and sisters, aunts and uncles and grandparents and grandchildren. This circle includes also the new family and kinship members the leading politicians gain through the intermarriage of their children with other influential and wealthy persons; all in all, it might well comprise some several hundred, if not some thousand persons. Then comes the widest circle which includes the close political affiliates and supporters, first from his own ethnic group and clan, but then also from allied clans and political groups; the size of this group might go from a few thousand up to tens of thousands of people. It is quite evident that the satisfaction of the high expectations of all these people concerning support from their patron will involve huge sums of money and the awarding of nearly an unlimited number of state and semi-state offices, appointments and jobs. As a consequence, the leader must use all available sources to increase and to retain his income. The high concentration of power in the hands of the president allows him widespread use of clientelistic procedures. This explains why in most African states one larger party, once it has won the majority of votes, is regularly re-elected and all other parties remain small and without influence. In this way, political clientelism in Africa

> … overwhelmingly favoured a relatively small number of people who were critical to regime stability. Clientelistic resource did not descend the social pyramid very far, despite much legitimating rhetoric to the contrary. Instead, it served the purposes of cross-ethnic elite accommodation, in which the president sought to build a national elite coalition on behalf of his rule, by including key elites from different regions, ethnic groups, classes and so on in the presidential coalition (Van der Walle 2009: 7).

The second characteristic of the leading political personalities in Africa concerns their education and former occupation and career. Here, Table 10.5 gives a less promising picture. Half of all presidents have been active at the beginning of their careers in independence movements, many of them as military leaders. An additional 28 per cent have been army commanders. Many of the latter came to power through a military coup.[35] Less than one-quarter of the incumbent presidents in 2011 have had civilian occupations which can be seen as good preparation of such a high political office, as jurists, economists, employees of international organizations and the like. The only sign of hope here is that the generation of independence fighters will die off in foreseeable time.

The third question pertains to the connection between ethnic origin and membership of these Big Men and their political careers, strategies and behaviour. It is obvious that this aspect plays a significant role in all countries where one or a few ethnic groups are dominating. Examples include the presidents of Burkino Faso, Burundi, the Central African Republic, Kenya, Niger and several others. As a consequence, in many countries (for example, Nigeria and Kenya) the members of the smaller ethnic groups feel politically disadvantaged

---

34   An example is the present African president Jacob Zuma who is a polygamist, married five times, and is reported to have 20 children from liaisons with several wives.

35   Examples are Sudan's Omar Hassan Al-Bashir who is looked for by the International Court of Justice because of genocide; Mohamed O. Abdelaziz of Mauritania who is accused of suppressing the Blacks of the country; Y. Jammeh of Gambia, and James A. Michel of the Seychelles.

precisely because they were never able to supply a president. I will come back to this issue in the next section and in the final Chapter 13 I will discuss how this problem could be solved in constitutional terms.

How do these African leaders perform in terms of respect for the law, democratic procedures and their attitudes and actions concerning clientelism and corruption? Here, the role model of Big Man seems to inspire also many present-day presidents. I already mentioned Joseph Mobutu Sese Seko, president of Zaire for 32 years (1965–97), a most infamous African 'Big Man'. He used to justify his power with remarks like this: 'Nowhere in this continent have there been two chiefs in a village, a majority chief and an opposition chief. Dating back to ancestral times, there has been only one chief ...' (quoted in Pitcher et al. 2009: 128). It is evident that Mobutu here misinterprets the traditional African past in his sense; *de facto*, most chiefs were not monocrats (see above).

Finally, how does the overall evaluation of the political performance of these heads of state in terms of civic and democratic norms look like? Here, the picture is again more disturbing than raising hope: no less than 45 per cent of the presidents are characterized as 'bad performers', designated as presiding over a state which needs 'intensive care' or even can be called a 'morgue'. If we look at the individual characteristics of these men – there is only one woman in the group, President Ellen Johnson-Sirleaf of Liberia – we find plenty of evidence that the strategies of Big-Man politics, which include clientelism and corruption on a large scale, are still widespread in Africa today. It can also be supposed that most of these men are strongly favouring their own ethnic groups. Thus, a central problem of politics and economic development in Africa is closely correlated to the quality of political leadership, namely the pervasive influence of clientelism and corruption (see also Mathai 2009: 25ff.). Most African countries perform very poorly in this regard.[36] An outstanding negative example is Nigeria with its huge incomes from crude oil.[37] It is widely accepted today that corruption is a serious obstacle to economic growth, directly and indirectly, leading to political instability (Mo 2001).

The analysis of this section can be summarized as follows. Looking at the background and behaviour of the present political leaders of Africa, a sign of hope is that democratically elected and responsible leaders have already become more prominent in the last decade. Present-day examples include the presidents of Angola, Cape Verde, Ghana and Mauritius who got 'A' grades in the evaluation; it is no accident that some of these countries (Ghana, Mauritius) also rank high both in terms of democracy and human development. A foreseeable positive trend is also that the old independence fighters turned into autocratic political leaders will die out. There are, however, also less positive signs. One is that many presidents, often former military officers, came into power through *coups d'état* (Lamb 1984: 109).

When looking at the misuse of political power by so many of these presidents one could ask why Western governments often supported them over decades with money and weapons. Here again the reference to social structures and behaviour patterns in traditional African societies is relevant. It was mentioned above (p. 262) that a peculiar ability of chiefs and leaders were rhetorical skills and the ability to persuade others. When African leaders met with Western politicians, they appeared as cultivated, kind and benign personalities; usually they were also quite ready to accept verbally all obligations with Western donors tied to their support. When at home again, however, they cared little about their promises abroad.

When discussing the relations between political power and economic privileges, the role of political parties is very important. Although this is a topic investigated systematically by political science, it must nevertheless be dealt with here in a brief way. This is so because parties are the main instruments at the level of polity which formulate problems, articulate political aims and programs and recruit political personalities (Beyme 1982). Thus, they are also highly relevant for processes of distribution and the emergence and modification of inequalities. In fact, a main dimension along which parties have been classified by political scientists – the left–right dimension – is closely related to this role; right (conservative, bourgeois) parties are usually in favour of the existing structure of power and privilege, while leftist (Communist, Socialist, social-democratic parties and so on) parties are challenging it in favour of redistribution to benefit the weaker and less privileged groups and classes. Now, a main thesis about party systems in Africa is that they are often ethnically based and this inhibits their function of organizing interests along class lines. In fact, parties in Africa are characterized

---

36 See: http://www.transparency.org/Cpi2012/results/#myanchor1
37 Victor E. Dike, *Corruption in Nigeria: A New Paradigm for Effective Control*, http://www.africaeconomicanalysis. org/

by features which distinguish them significantly from European parties (Erdmann 2004: 37; Basedau et al. 2007): they have barely distinguishable programmes; informal relations and personalism predominate over bureaucratic organization; they are characterized by high factionalism, a weak funding base and little importance of formal membership. In fact, one study found that the quality of democracy is lower in countries with ethnically dominated party systems. (Dowd and Driessen 2008) Yet, the issue is, by far, not that simple.

From the perspective developed in this book, an ethnically based party system can also have positive functions. Several facts are relevant in this regard. First, it is not even true that most African party systems are ethnically based. Basedau and Stroh (2009) show that in four Francophone African countries (Benin, Burkina Faso, Mali and Niger) ethnic parties in the strict sense are almost completely absent; where they did exist, ethnicity matters somewhat as a determinant of party preference, but its impact is weak. Second, if ethnicity matters in party mobilization, it is usually a coalition of several ethnic groups of different sizes which is relevant but not the dominance of one single ethnic group (Erdmann 2004). Such dominance is often impossible given the high number of small ethnic groups (Tanzania is a good example). Third, parties seemingly organized along ethnic lines often reflect regional divisions, including the distinction between centre and periphery, which is a basic cleavage in all African countries, as outlined before. Finally, one can say that 'the very relevance of ethnic identity in political Africa is in part linked to the weakness of socio-economic and class stratification on the continent' (Carbone 2007: 23). Thus, it is erroneous to see in the fact that many parties in Africa are closely linked with ethnic membership an expression of an anti-modern tribalization of politics. Rather, we must admit that the formulation of political interests and the distribution of political and social power and – in its sequel – of socio-economic privilege and discrimination in the African context is impossible without taking into account ethnic differentiation. Wangari Mathai (2009: 217) has expressed this aspect clearly when she argues that the elites 'ought to be in touch with the genuine wishes of the 80 per cent who perceive themselves as Igbo or Yoruba first, and Nigerian second; or Luo or Kikuyu or Maasai first, and Kenyan second; or Dinka and Fur first, and Sudanese second'. And she rightly adds that 'Africans, too, can remain both loyal members of a micro-nation [their ethnic groups] and loyal citizens of a nation-state'. Maybe, the European Union could be an example for Africa in the effort to represent the micro-nations in the governance structures of the macro-nation.[38] There are many different ways how this can be achieved. Social science should not neglect or devalue from the beginning this central dimension of the social structure and political systems of African societies. The inclusion of ethnicity into political processes can contribute to positive developments; if this happens, it depends (a) on the kind of political parties and the way they incorporate ethnic structures, and (b) on the political constitutions of a country. I will come back to this issue in Chapter 13.

Political Attitudes and the Perception of Ethno-class Privilege and Discrimination

The privilege of particular ethno-classes and elite groups and the discrimination of many ethnic groups within Sub-Saharan African countries are more than evident. However, a sociological analysis would be incomplete if we do not ask how people in Africa see this situation, how people perceive their privilege or discrimination and what they think about democracy. As Langer and Ukiwo (2007: 3) rightly note, these perceptions are critical for the understanding of group behaviour and collective actions, including violent mobilization. In this section, two kinds of evidence are presented: first, some findings about general attitudes and perceptions in seven SSA countries; and, second, findings for these attitudes among a few ethnic groups within two countries, Kenya and Nigeria.

The source of the data is the Afrobarometer, Round 2005. The Afrobarometer is a regular comparative opinion survey established in 1999; today, it is carried out in over 30 African countries. It is organized jointly by the Institute for Democracy in South Africa (IDASA), the Ghana Center for Democratic Development (CDD) and the Department of Political Science at Michigan State University. In each country, a national probability sample is interviewed (1,000 to 1,500 respondents) which allows analyses by ethnic sub-groups. In the first analysis, seven countries have been selected because they are of particular interest, and in order to

---

38   How national and European identities can be reconciled in Europe is shown in Haller and Ressler 2006.

cover West, East and South Africa. In the second part, the two cases Kenya and Nigeria have been selected because they have a fractionalized ethnic structure, that is, there are one or a few larger ethnic groups which were able to dominate the political process, thus establishing themselves as dominant ethno-classes.

Democratic Attitudes and Ethnic Identity in Seven Sub-Saharan African Countries

First, let us first have a look at the general attitudes of people in the seven selected countries concerning democracy, the role of political leaders and the attachment to one's own ethnic group and to the nation. Given the fact that most African political systems can at best be called half-democracies, it is of utmost interest to see if people accept this situation or see it critically. These democratic attitudes are highly relevant also for the question of economic inequality: if there is only little attachment to democratic principles, the perspectives for the realization of more equality are also modest given the fact that more equality usually can only be hard-won through political organization and contest.

The findings show that a clear majority of people in Sub-Saharan Africa support democracy (see the first two lines in Table 10.6): between 70 per cent and 90 per cent of the respondents see democracy as preferable to any other form of government, and similar high proportions reject the one-party-rule which was realized in many countries for considerable time (see also Table 8.1, p. 223) A strong exception in this latter aspect are the Tanzanians who had one governing party (the Socialist Chama Cha Mapinzu, CCM) between 1965 and 1992 which still has a broad base among the population; its charismatic founder and first leader, Julius K. Nyerere, is highly adored today (Müller 2012; Aminzade 2013). Results on other statements (not reported here) concerning the freedom of press, the freedom to establish and to join political organizations and the like confirm the democratic attitude of most respondents. As far as the actual democratic situation is concerned, quite a critical

Table 10.6   Social and political attitudes about democracy, ethnicity and nation in seven Sub-Saharan African countries (2005)

(N)	Nigeria (2341)	Ghana (1168)	Uganda (2359)	Kenya (1251)	Tanzania (1167)	Botswana (1186)	South Africa (2289)
Democracy is preferable to any other kind of government	69	84	83	85	91	77	72
Reject one-party-rule	84	84	70	77	44	83	68
[Country] is a democracy with minor problems	27	80	48	56	44	78	67
The government's economic policies have hurt most people and only benefitted a few	79	70	63	73	65	63	48
Once in office, leaders are obliged to help their home community	40	32	31	18	17	13	21
No or just a little trust in president/prime minister	75	22	23	40	5	31	39
Feel attached mainly to ethnic group	33	18	19	15	6	12	12
Feel attached equally to ethnic group, land, nation	50	42	49	44	6	49	27
Respondents ethnic group …							
… is never treated unfairly	18	52	32	24	54	71	49
… has more or same influence as other groups	24	27	20	26	22	21	24

Source: Afrobarometer, Round 3 (2005) (figures: per cent in favour).

attitude prevails: only in Ghana and Botswana, a strong majority (about 80 per cent) believe that their political system can be called a democracy, in South Africa 67 per cent believe that this is true. In the three East African countries, however, only about half of the respondents think this way and in Nigeria even only 27 per cent. A very critical picture emerges also in a statement which captures the central thesis of this chapter, namely that 'the governments' economic policies have hurt most people and only benefitted a few' (the alternative statement was 'The governments' economic policies have helped most people; only a few have suffered'). In six out of the seven countries a clear majority – between 63 per cent and 73 per cent of the respondents – agree with this statement. Only in South Africa, the agreement is considerably lower (48 per cent).

Several items in the survey captured the question how well the political persons/groups – the president, the deputies in the parliament, the judiciary – represented their citizens and if they are prone to clientelism and corruption. Table 10.6 includes two of these items: the question was, if a politician in office should help his family and community; such a stance can be seen as an indicator for a traditional clientelistic 'tribal attitude' irreconcilable with a true democracy. The findings show that the majority of Africans do not think this way; in most countries less than one-quarter support the statement. Only in Nigeria, Ghana and Uganda, the proportion goes up to 30 per cent to 40 per cent. Asked about corruption, quite a large proportion – between one-third and 50 per cent – think that the government, public officials and so on are quite corrupt. It is not surprising, then, that trust in political leaders and institutions is low. We can also see that trust in the president is rather low, only about 20 per cent to 40 per cent in most countries. Table 6.1 (p. 165) shows that also in the external objective estimation, Sub-Saharan African countries receive the lowest scores (as captured by the Corruption Perception Score). Again, Tanzania is an exception on the positive, and Nigeria on the negative pole: in the former only 6 per cent have no trust, in the latter 75 per cent have no trust in their president. Similar results emerge concerning trust in other political leading groups and institutions (not reported in the table).

Finally, it is of interest how important the ethnic groups are for the respondents in terms of personal affiliation to them, compared with national identity, and if the respondents feel some discrimination of their own ethnic group. Findings show that ethnic identity is the most important dimension of identity or is at least as important as national identity: only in Tanzania and to some degree in South Africa is the affiliation with the nation-state stronger than that with the ethnic group. Large differences between countries emerge, finally, concerning the question as to whether people feel that their own ethnic group has been treated unfairly and if the influence of one's own ethnic group is strong enough. In Botswana, a large majority, and in Ghana, Tanzania and South Africa, half of the respondents think so; in Kenya and Nigeria, however, the majority think otherwise, that is, see a discrimination of one's own group. Similar findings emerge in regard to the statement if one's own ethnic group has a similar political influence to other groups; this statement is supported by only one-fifth of the respondents in all of the seven countries.

Political Attitudes and Feelings of Discrimination among Ethnic Groups in Kenya and Nigeria

Now let us have a short look on the variations of these perceptions among the different ethnic groups within two countries, Nigeria and Kenya. The foregoing results have already indicated that particularly in these two countries ethno-class domination may be at work. Before looking at the results, a short overview on the ethnic differentiation within these two countries is in order.

Nigeria has the largest number of ethnic groups among all African states, maybe up to 400 (Ungar 1989: 121–61; Schicho 2001:75–101; Salih 2001: 42, 128–48).[39] However, three among them clearly predominate over all others, the Hausa-Fulani, the Yoruba and the Igbo, the first encompassing about 50, the latter two 25–30 million people each. Thus they are much larger than tribes. In fact, they may be considered as sub-nations integrated mainly by a common language and (in part) religion. The *Hausa-Fulani* are Muslims, living in the north and northeast of the country. They have been predominant in Nigerian politics, and were able to establish Sharia law in several states of their region; their social organization is patrilineal and patriarchal. The *Yoruba* are settling in the economically most prosperous south and southwestern regions, including the Niger delta and the largest city Lagos. In pre-colonial times they had established powerful kingdoms, such us the Oyo Empire, based on their outstanding organizational skills and an efficient cavalry; they also played an important role in British

---

39   See also en.wikipedia.org/wiki/Nigeria

colonial administration. The *Igbo* are residing in the southwest of Nigeria; in former times, they were mainly craftsmen, farmers and traders and lived in dispersed small communities with quasi-democratic constitutions. An important negative heritage of Nigeria was – like that of all West African countries – that slavery had taken a large toll on its societies and cultures (Ungar 1989: 125). After Nigeria became independent, the Igbo tried to secede and established the independent Republic of Biafra but were defeated by central government in a bloody war (1967–70). Afterwards, they lost their influence in Nigerian central government in spite of their economic achievements.[40] Both the Igbo and Yoruba are mainly Christians. As mentioned before, there are many other ethnic groups in Nigeria; since the absolute number of the respondents from them in the sample is too small, we must be content with collapsing them into one heterogeneous category 'others'.

Table 10.7 shows that that there exist significant differences both in the objective situation and in the subjective perceptions and evaluations by the members of these three ethnic groups. The Hausa-Fulani turn out as having the lowest level of education and they believe that they are living in worse conditions than the other ethnic groups. At the same time, however, they are more satisfied with the existing situation of democracy and the influence of their own group in politics. Both the Igbo and the Yoruba are much less satisfied with democracy and the Igbo are most dissatisfied with the influence of their own group in politics. Both findings clearly correspond to the higher levels of education among these two groups, the substantial exclusion of the Igbos from Nigerian national politics and the proportionately higher influence of the Hausa-Fulani in this regard. The latter were clearly overrepresented among the presidents and the various Nigerian national cabinets between 1983 and 2005 (Langer and Ukiwo 2007: 7). After the presidential election of 2011, which was won by Jonathan Goodluck from the southern Christian dominated Ijaw ethnic group, massive and violent protests and terrorism broke out in Northern Nigeria, led by the Islamic sect *Boko Haram* (meaning 'Western education is sin').[41]

In Kenya, there are five ethnic groups, each of which constitutes between 11 per cent and 20 per cent of the population (Ungar 1989: 162–209; Schicho 2004: 260–285).[42] The largest and politically most influential group is the *Kikuyu* (about 20 per cent or 8 million people), settling in central Kenya around the capital city Nairobi. They established their political organization (KAU) already in 1944; in the early 1950s, they led the famous Mau-Mau uprising against the British colonial power. They are overrepresented in higher education,

Table 10.7   Characteristics and attitudes of ethnic groups in Nigeria (2005)

(N)	Ethnic group				All
	Hansa/ Fulani (613)	Igbo (372)	Yoruba (493)	Other (846)	(2324)
	%	%	%	%	%
No completed elementary education	40	6	13	10	18
Last year, many times gone without cash income	21	19	14	22	20
Own ethnic groups' living conditions considered worse than those of other groups	38	27	18	25	28
Not satisfied with democracy	30	50	45	35	38
Influence of own ethnic group less than that of others	18	45	20	32	28
No trust in the ruling party	23	44	38	30	32

Source: Afrobarometer Round 3 (2005).

---

40   See: Sabella O. Abide, 'The Nigerian Presidency and the Igbo nation', http://www.gamji.com/article3000/NEWS3755.htm

41   Olakunle Olowojolu, *Ethnic politics and voting patterns in Nigeria*, 2013; see http://www.academia.edu/1553235/Ethnicity_and_Voting_Patterns_in_Nigerian_Elections

42   See also http://www.africa.upenn.edu/NEH/kethnic.htm (African Studies Center, University of Pennsylvania).

and have dominated Kenyan politics since its independence in 1964; three of the four presidents of Kenya were Kikuyus. A second, at times influential ethnic group in Kenya were the *Luo*, settling in the northwest near the border to Sudan and on the shores of Lake Victoria. They are about 5 million (14 per cent of the population). The Luo cooperated with the Kikuyu leaders in the first phase of the independent Kenya. Later on, when the presidents concentrated power in their hands, they lost their influence. The three further ethnic groups, each with about 4 to 5 million people (11 per cent to 13 per cent of the population), include: the *Luhya*, living in west Kenya, who in earlier times had little consciousness of being one group and had also suffered seriously from the slave trade; the *Kamba*, living in east Kenya, originally gatherers and hunters and later traditional intermediaries between the Arabs along the coast and the hinterland; and the *Kalenjin*, living on the highlands of the Rift Valley (they are called the 'running tribe' because they supply the world's most successful cross-country runners). While not particularly influential in national politics (although they were often engaged in conflicts with their Kikuyu and Luo neighours), they were able to supply one of the presidents, the longest serving Daniel arap Moi.

Table 10.8 presents a few socio-economic characteristics and attitudes of respondents from these ethnic groups. The data show no significant differences in the educational level and socio-economic situation, due to the fact that Kenya is more homogeneous than Nigeria (it is also only about half as large). About 40 per cent to 45 per cent of the respondents in all groups feel attached to their ethnic groups. Significant differences emerge, however, in the subjective evaluation of the relative position of one's own ethnic group and in the trust toward the president: 29 per cent of the Luo and the Kalenjin say that their group is often treated unfairly, while this is more seldom seen in this way among the Kikuyu and the Lubya. Very large differences emerge concerning trust in the president: among the Luo and Lubya, nearly 60 per cent have no or very little trust in the president, among the other groups 31 per cent to 40 per cent, but among the Kikuyus only 24 per cent. Thus, we can see the effect of ethnic membership very clearly here.

Interim Résumé

These results have shown that the attitudes of people in Sub-Saharan Africa are far from being of a tribal-traditional character. Rather, the majority supports democracy and is very critical about the present state of their country in regard to democratic standards. At the same time, the affiliation to one's own ethnic group is also strong. In countries, where we know that one or a few specific ethnic groups are dominant, this is also clearly reflected in the minds of the people. A highly critical political situation seems to emerge particularly in those cases where an ethnic group, which is strong in socio-economic and cultural terms, is rather excluded from the political process; this seems to be the case particularly in Kenya and Nigeria. Recurring ethnic unrest, violence and riots, often connected with political elections (as in repeated Kenyan presidential elections) are a consequence. In Nigeria, alone since its return to civil rule in 1999, there have been 40 violent conflicts (Akinwumi et al. 2007: 37). It would be a big mistake, however, to attribute these conflicts to widening frontiers of primordial consciousness at the expense of civic consciousness as is done in

Table 10.8   Characteristics and attitudes of ethnic groups in Kenya (2005)

(N)	Kikuyu (480) %	Luo (297) %	Lubya (352) %	Kamba (256) %	Kalonjin (204) %	Other (771) %	All %
No elementary education completed	44	43	42	54	45	41	44
Many times gone without cash income	7	14	12	17	3	17	13
Attached to ethnic group*	40	43	42	43	42	45	43
Own ethnic group often treated unfairly	21	29	13	13	14	33	23
No or just a little trust in president	24	58	59	25	40	31	37

*Feel equally or more as a member of [my ethnic group] than as Kenyan.
Source: Afrobarometer, Round 5 (2011).

this publication (and others). Rather, two processes did unfold in Nigeria (and Kenya) and probably in many other countries: first, the new political organizations did not reflect the manifold existing ethnic divisions but only a few of them; and second, the political systems, although federalistic, were not constructed in a way which could lead to a balancing out of the different interests. Here, it is particularly the extreme power vested in the president which over and over again heats up reciprocal distrust and violent conflicts which are evident also in the high level of civil violence in the form of homicides (see Table 6.1, pp. 164–5). Another important finding which clearly came out of this small analysis was that there exist significant differences between the Sub-Saharan African countries in all these regards. An ethno-class domination and an undemocratic political process do not persist everywhere. In some countries, political reforms have been embraced which seem to have established quite well-anchored democratic standards. Tanzania and the Republic of South Africa are two positive examples in this regard.

Summary and Conclusions

Sub-Saharan Africa is probably the most challenging case in point when it comes to investigate the relationships between class stratification and ethnic differentiation. The latter is higher than in any other macroregion in the world and so is economic inequality. There are less relevant data and empirical researches on this issue in Africa than elsewhere. Even so, however, was it possible to show in this chapter that both aspects are clearly interrelated, leading to a unique form of ethnic stratification? It became evident, in particular, that both the experiences of slavery and of colonialism have made a deep impact on African societies. A short overview on African societies before colonialism has shown, however, that many of the present-day ethnic and class differentiations must also be seen as transformations of traditional patterns of African economics, societies and politics. This applies particularly to conflicts between tribes and the roles of chiefs and the 'Big Man' therein, to the importance of personal clientelistic relationships, and the role of incredible violence and human suffering elicited by African leaders in the civil wars after the gaining of political independence. It was shown that ethnic fractionalization and the role of individual elites and leaders hungry for power played a decisive role in these wars. The main thesis of the chapter was that we can speak of a specific form of ethnic stratification in Africa, namely ethno-classes (or political ethno-classes), because the leading elites base their power and privileges primarily on the domination of the state apparatuses and the revenues emanating from this. They also cooperate closely with indigenous and with foreign (European, American and Asian) political and business elites. Several facts have resulted: an over-proportional employment in the state sector; much higher incomes in this sector compared to the rest of the population (who mostly work in marginal self-employment jobs); the preference in public spending for the capitals and large cities and, thus, for the areas where the members of the dominant ethno-classes reside; the emergence of a specific new upper class separated from the rest of the population in living conditions and lifestyles. A short analysis of the characteristics of present-day political leaders in Africa showed that democratic procedures have gained ground but ethnic favouritism and a readiness to use office resources for personal and ethno-class enrichment have not disappeared. The question is how the persisting ethnic differentiations in Sub-Saharan Africa can be aligned with transparent and democratic political processes, how widespread clientelism and corruption can be eliminated, how pervasive inequalities can be reduced and economic growth and human development be fostered. I will come back to this difficult, but urgent question in Chapter 13.

References

Abusabib, Mohamed (2004), *Art, Politics and Cultural Identification in Sudan*, Uppsala: Uppsala Universitet

Adam, Heribert and Kogila Moodley (1993), *The Opening of the Apartheid Mind. Options for the New South Africa*, Berkeley, CA, etc.: University of California Press

Adogamhe, Paul G. (2010), 'Economic policy reform & poverty alleviation: A critique of Nigeria's strategic plan for poverty reduction', *Poverty & Public Policy* 2: 49–79

Akinwumi, Olayemi et al., eds (2007), *Historical Perspectives on Nigeria's Post-Colonial Conflicts*, Lagos, Nigeria: Historical Society of Nigeria

Albertini, Rudolf von (1976), *Europäische Kolonialherrschaft 1880–1940*, Zürich/Freiburg: Atlantis

Ali, Ali Abdel Gadir (2010), 'Demography, Growth, Income Distribution and Poverty: A Survey of Interrelationships', in Olu Ajakaiye, Germano Mwabu, eds, *Reproductive Health, Economic Growth and Poverty Reduction in Africa. Frameworks of Analysis*, Nairobi: The University of Nairobi Press, pp. 191–215

Ali, Taisier M. and Robert O. Matthews, eds (1999), *Civil Wars in Africa. Roots and Resolution*, Montreal etc.: McGill-Queen's University Press

Alwy Alwiya and Susanne Schech (2004), 'Ethnic inequalities in education in Kenya', *International Education Journal* 5: 266–74

Amin, Samir (1980), *Class and Nation. Historically and in the Current Crisis*, New York: Monthly Review Press

Aminzade, Ron (2013), *Race, Nation and Citizenship in Postcolonial Africa. The Case of Tanzania*, New York: Cambridge University Press

Anugwom, Edlyne E. (2006), 'Ethnic conflict and democracy in Nigeria: The marginalisation question', *Journal of Social Development in Africa* 15: 61–78

Atkinson, Ronald R. (2010), *The Roots of Ethnicity. Origins of the Acholi of Uganda Before 1800*, Kampala: Fountain Publishers/Oxford: African Books

Balsvik, Randi Ronning (2005), *Haile Sellassie's Students: The Intellectuals and Social Background to Revolution*, Addis Ababa, Ethiopia: Addis Ababa University Press/Michigan State University, African Studies Centre

Basedau, Matthias and Alexander Stroh (2009), Ethnicity and Party Systems in Francophone Sub-Saharan Africa, Hamburg: GIGA Research (Working Paper)

Basedau, Matthias et al., eds (2007), *Votes, Money and Violence. Political Parties and Elections in Sub-Saharan Africa*, Stockholm: Nordiska Afrikainstitutet

Basu, Aparna (1982), 'Colonial educational policies: A comparative approach', in A. Basu, *Essays in the History of Indian Education*, New Delhi: Concept, pp. 60–77

Benell, Paul et al. (2007), *Nigeria: Education Public Expenditure Review*, Brighton/UK, University of Sussex, Centre for International Education

Beyme, Klaus von (1982), *Parteien in westlichen Demokratien*, München: Beck

Bircan, Cagatay et al. (2010), Violent Conflict and Inequality, DIW, Humboldt University Berlin, Discussion Paper 1013

Blimes, Randall J. (2006), 'The Indirect Effect of Ethnic Heterogeneity on the Likelihood of Civil War', *The Journal of Conflict Resolution* 50: 536–47

Bloom, David E. et al. (2010), 'Realising the Demographic Dividend: Is Africa Any Different?' in Olu Ajakaiye and Germano Mwabu, eds, *Reproductive Health, Economic Growth and Poverty Reduction in Africa*, Nairobi: The University of Nairobi Press, pp. 235–49

Bodmer, Frederick (1989), *Die Sprachen der Welt*, Herrsching: M. Pawlak (English ed: The Loom of Language, Allen & Unwin)

Bourdieu, Pierre and Jean C. Passeron (1977), *Reproduction in Education, Society and Culture*, London/Beverly Hills: Sage

Bozeman, Adda B. (1976), *Conflict in Africa. Concepts and Realities*, Princeton, NJ: Princeton University Press

Bratton, Michael and Nicolas van der Valle (1994), 'Neopatrimonial regimes and political transitions in Africa', *World Politics* 46: 453–89

Carbone, Giovanni M. (2007), 'Political Parties and Party Systems in Africa: Themes and Research Perspectives', *World Political Science Review*, Vol. 3, No. 3, (Online)

Cohen, Robin (1972), 'Class in Africa: Analytical problems and perspectives', *The Socialist Register* 9: 231–55

Collier, Paul and Anke Hoeffler (2002), Greed and grievance in civil war, Center for the Study of African Economies (CSAE), Paper WPS/2002–01

Collier, Paul and Jan W. Gunning (1999), 'Explaining African economic performance', *Journal of Economic Literature* 37: 64–111

Davidson, Basil (1992), *The Black Man's Burden. Africa and the Curse of the Nation-State*, New York: Three Rivers Press

De Grassi, Aaron (2008), 'Neopatrimonialism and agricultural development in Africa: Contributions and limitations of a contested concept', *African Studies Review* 51: 107–33

Dowd, Robert A. and Michael Driessen (2008), Ethnically dominated party systems and the quality of democracy: Evidence from Sub-Saharan Africa, Working Paper No. 92, Capetown: The Institute for Democracy

Dumont, René (1969), *False Start in Africa*, London: Deutsch

Dzimbiri, Lewis B. et al. (2000), 'Multipartism and People's Participation', in L. Dzimbiri et al., *Multipartism and National Integration*, Dar es Salaam, Tanzania: TEMA Publishers

Easterly, William and Ross Levine (1997), 'Africa's Growth Tragedy: Policies and Ethnic Divisions', *The Quarterly Journal of Economics* 112: 1203–50

Elaigwu, J. Isawa and Ali A. Mazrui (1981), 'Nation-building and changing political structures', in *UNESCO, General History of Africa Series*, Vol. 8 pp. 435–67

Erdmann, Gero (2004), 'Party Research: Western European Bias and the "African Labyrinth"', *Democratization* 11: 68–87

Evans-Pritchard, E.E. (1969 [1940]), *The Nuer. A Description of the Modes of Livelyhood and Political Institutions of a Nilotic People*, New York/Oxford: Oxford University Press

Fallers, Lloyd A. (1966), *Class, Status, and Power. Social Stratification in Comparative Perspective*, New York/London: The Free Press/Collier Macmillan

First, Ruth (1970), *Power in Africa*, New York: Pantheon

Flaig, Egon (2009), *Weltgeschichte der Sklaverei*, München: C.H. Beck

Forsyth, Frederick (1976), *The Biafra Story*, London: Penguin Books

Frank, Raphael and Ilia Rainer (2012), 'Does the Leader's Ethnicity Matter? Ethnic Favoritism, Education, and Health in Sub-Saharan Africa', *American Political Science Review* 106: 294–325

Freund, Bill (1998), *The Making of Contemporary Africa. The Development of African Society since 1800*, Boulder, CO: William Mark Freund

Fried, Morton H. (1975), *The Notion of Tribe*, Menlo Park, CA: Cummings

Gakuru, Octavian N. (1998), 'Education Inequality and Poverty in Kenya', in J. Bahemuka et al., eds, *Poverty Revisited: The Case of Kenya*, Nairobi: Acton Publication, pp. 37–53

Goldscheid, Rudolf and Joseph Schumpeter (1976), *Die Finanzkrise des Steuerstaaates, Frankfurt*: Suhrkamp

Gramsci, Antonio (1975), *Quaderni del Carcere*, ed. critica dell'Istituto Gramsci, Torino: Einaudi (5 vols)

Habte, Aklilu and Teshome Wagaw (1981), 'Education and socialchange', in *UNESCO, General History of Africa*, pp. 678–701

Haller, Max (1986), 'Sozialstruktur und Schichtungshierarchie im Wohlfahrtsstaat. Zur Aktualität des vertikalen Paradigmas der Ungleichheitsforschung', *Zeitschrift für Soziologie* 15: 167–87

Haller, Max and Regina Ressler (2006), 'National and European Identity. A study of their meanings and interrelationships', *Revue Francaise de Sociologie* 47: 817–50

Hannum, Hurst (1990), *Autonomy, Sovereignity, and Self-Determination*, Philadelphia, PA: University of Pennsylvania Press

Herbst, Jeffrey (2000), *States and Power in Africa*, Princeton, NJ: Princeton University Press

Hoeffler, Anke (2008), Dealing with the Consequences of Violent Conflicts in Africa, Centre for the Study of African Economies, University of Oxford

Huntington, Samuel P. (1996), *The Clash of Civilizations and the Remaking of World Order*, New York: Simon & Schuster

Hyden, Goran (2006), *African Politics in Comparative Perspective*, Cambridge: Cambridge University Press

Illife, John (1997), *Geschichte Afrikas*, München: C.H. Beck

Kasozi, A.B.K. (1994), *The Social Origins of Violence in Uganda*, 1964–1985, Kampala: Fountain Publ.

Kerbo, Harold R. (2006), *World Poverty. Global Inequality and the Modern World System*, Boston etc.: McGraw-Hill

Kiiza, Julius, Sabiti Makara and Lise Rakner, eds (2008), *Electoral Democracy in Uganda*, Kampala: Fountain Publishers

Ki-Zerbo, Joseph et al. (1981), 'Nation-building and changing political values', in UNESCO, *General History of Africa*, pp. 468–98

Lai, Brian and Clayton Thyne (2011), 'The Effect of Civil War on Education, 1980–97', *Journal of Conflict Resolution* 55: 181–95

Lamb, David (1984), *The Africans*, New York: Vintage Books

Langer, Arnim and Ukoha Ukiwo (2007), Ethnicity, religion and the state in Ghana and Nigeria: Perceptions from the street, CRISE Working Paper No. 34, University of Oxford

Lloyd, Cynthia B. and Paul C. Hewitt (2009), Educational inequalities in the midst of persistent poverty: Diversity across Africa in educational outcomes, New York, Population Council, Working Paper 14

Lloyd, Peter, ed.(1966), *The New Elites of Tropical Africa*, London: Oxford University Press

Lobban Richard (1985), 'Sudanese class formation and the demography of urban migration', in S. E. Ibrahim and N.S. Hopkins, eds, *Arab Society. Social Science Perspectives*, Kairo: The American University in Cairo Press, pp. 163–75

Mafeje, A. (1998), *Kingdoms of the Great Lakes Region. Ethnography of African Social Formations*, Kampala: Fountain Publishers

Mamdani, Mahmood (1996), *Citizen and Subject. Contemporary Africa and the Legacy of Late Colonialism*, Princeton, NJ: Princeton University Press

Manghezi, Alpheus (1976), *Class, Elite, and Community Development in Africa*, Uppsala: The Scandinavian Institute of African Studies

Markovitz, Irving L. (1977), *Class and Power in Africa*, Englewood Cliffs, NJ: Prentice Hall

Marx, Karl (1974 [1848]), *The Communist Manifesto*, Belmont, MA: American Opinion

Mathai, Wangari (2009), *The Challenge for Africa. A New Vision*, London: W. Heinemann

Mathok, Dhieu Diing Wol (2009), *Politics of Ethnic Discrimination in Sudan. A Justification for the Secession of South Sudan*, Kampala: Netmedia Publishers

Mbaku, John M. (2004), 'The state, macroeconomic performance and development in Africa', in K.A. Kalu, ed., *Agenda Setting and Public Policy in Africa*, Aldershot, Hants.: Ashgate, pp. 45–68

Meditz, Sandra W., ed. (1994), *Zaire. A Country Study*, Washington, DC: American University

Michler, Walter (1988), *Weißbuch Afrika*, Berlin/Bonn: J.H.W. Dietz

Miers, Suzanne and Igor Kopytoff, eds (1977), *Slavery in Africa. Historical and Anthropological Perspectives*, Madison, WI: The University of Wisconsin Press

Mo, Pak Hung (2001), 'Corruption and economic growth', *Journal of Comparative Economics* 29: 66–79

Moradi, Alexander (2005), Ernährung, wirtschaftliche Entwicklung und Bürgerkriege in Afrika südlich der Sahara (1950–2000), Dissertation, Universität Tübingen

Mosca, Gaetano (1950 [1896]), *Die herrschende Klasse*, Bern: Francke

Müller, Bernadette (2012), 'A success-story of creating national identity in Tanzania: The vision of Julius Kambarage Nyerere', in Franz Hoellinger and Markus Hadler, eds, *Crossing Borders, Shifting Boundaries. National and Transnational Identities in Europe and Beyond*, Frankfurt/New York: Campus, pp. 145–8

Bernadette Müller and Max Haller (2012), 'The Situation of Students in Sub-Saharan Africa: A Case Study of St. Augustine University of Tanzania', in *International Studies in Sociology of Education*, 22: 169–89

Mwijage, Jovitus F. Kamara (2004), *Major Events in African History*, Morogoro: Salvatorianum

N'Diaye, Tidiane (2010), *Der verschleierte Völkermord. Die Geschichte des muslimischen Sklavenhandels in Afrika*, Reinbek: Rowohlt (French ed. Paris 2008)

Njogu, Kimani, Kabiri Ngeta & Mary Wanjau, eds. (2009), *Ethnic Diversity in Eastern Africa. Opportunities and Challenges*, Nairobi: Twaweza House

Nugent, Paul (2004), *Africa Since Independence. A Comparative History*, Houndmills, Basingstoke/New York: Palgrave MacMillan

Ogwumike, Fidelis O. et al. (2006), Labour force participation, earnings and inequality in Nigeria, Paper presented at the workshop 'Poverty and Inequality in Nigeria', African Economic Research Consortium (AERC), Nairobi, Kenya

Peil, Margaret and Olatunji Oyeneye (1998), *Consensus, Conflict and Change. A Sociological Introduction to African Societies*, Nairobi etc.: East African Educational Publishers

Reader, John (1998), *Africa. Biography of a Continent*, London: Penguin Books

Salih, M.A. Mohamed (2001), *African Democracies and African Politics*, London/Sterling, Virginia: Pluto Press

Schicho, Walter, ed. (1999), *Handbuch Afrika. Vol. 1: Zentralafrika, Südliches Afrika und die Staaten im Indischen Ozean*, Frankfurt: Brandes & Apsel/Südwind

Schicho, Walter (2001), *Handbuch Afrika, Vol. 2: Westafrika und die Inseln im Atlantik*, Frankfurt: Brandes & Apsel

Schicho, Walter (2004), *Handbuch Afrika, Vol. 3: Nord- und Ostafrika, östliches Zentralafrika*, Frankfurt: Brandes & Apsel

Shils, Edward (2000), 'The intellectuals in the political development of the new states', in Jon Hutchinson and Anthony D. Smith, eds, *Nationalism. Critical Concepts in Political Science*, London/New York: Routledge, pp. 767–804

Sigrist, Christian (1967), *Regulierte Anarchie*, Olten/Freiburg: Walter Verlag

Sklar, R. (1967) 'Political Science and Political Integration', *Journal of Modern African Studies* V: 6–7

Sow, Alfa I. and Mohamed H. Abdulaziz (1981), 'Language and social change', in *UNESCO, General History of Africa*, pp. 522–52

Teal, Francis (2010), Higher Education and Economic Development in Africa: A review of channels and Interactions, Centre for the Study of African Economies, University of Oxford

Theobald, Robin (1982), 'Patriomonialism', *World Politics* 34: 548–59

Therborn, Göran (2006b), 'Meaning, mechanisms, patterns, and forces: An introduction', in G. Therborn, ed., *Inequalities of the World*, London/New Yrok: Verso: pp. 1–60

UNESCO (2009), *Overcoming Inequality. Why Governance Matters*, Oxford University Press

Ungar, Sanford J. (1989), *Africa. The People and Politics of an Emerging Continent*, New York etc.: Simon & Schuster

Van der Valle, Nicolas (2003), 'Presidentialism and clientelism in Africa's emerging party systems', *Journal of Modern African Studies* 41: 297–321

Van der Valle, Nicolas (2009), The democratization of political clientelism in Sub-Saharan Africa, Paper presented at the 3rd European Conference on African Studies, Leipzig, June 4–7, 2009

Warioba, Joseph (1996), Corruption and the State. The Warioba Report (Summary), Soundings, Issue 7

Weber, Max (1947), *The Theory of Social and Economic Organization*, translated by A.M. Henderson and Talcott Parsons, New York: Free Press

Weber, Max (1964/I+II), *Wirtschaft und Gesellschaft*, 2 vols, Köln/Berlin: Kiepenheuer & Witsch

Welsh, David (2000), 'Ethnicity in Sub-Saharan Africa', *International Affairs* 72: 477–91

World Development Report (2012), Washington: The World Bank

Yates, Douglas A. (1996), *The Rentier State in Africa: Oil Rent Dependency & Neocolonialism in the Republic of Gabon*, Ternon, NJ/Asmara, Eritrea: Africa World Press

Young, Crawford (1994), *The African Colonial State in Comparative Perspective*, New Haven/London: Yale University Press

Ziegler, Jean (1992), *Die Schweiz wäscht weisser. Die Finanzdrehscheibe des internationalen Verbrechens*, München: Knaur

Ziltener, Patrick and Hans-Peter Müller (2007), 'The weight of the past. Traditional agriculture, socio-political differentiation and modern development in Africa and Asia: A cross-national analysis', *International Journal of Comparative Sociology* 48: 371–415

Ziltener, Patrick (2013a), 'Impacts of colonialism. A research survey', *Journal of World System Research* 19: 290–311

Zoubir, Yahia, ed. (1999), *North Africa in Transition: State, Society, and Economic Transformation in the 1990s*, Gainesville etc.: University of Florida Press

'Separate, but Equal'. The Characteristics, Origins, and Aftermaths of Apartheid Systems

Introduction

In this and the following chapter, three societies shall be compared which are unique in regard to the topic of this book, ethnic stratification, exploitation and exclusion. Although they are extremely different in their constitutional, socio-economic and political make-up, they also show astonishing similarities. All of them are ethnically highly differentiated societies and in all of them, Apartheid, a peculiar system of ethnic exclusion and exploitation, did exist or does still exist today. In the United States and in the Republic of South Africa, this system came into being after centuries of brutal slavery. In Israel, military and state violence against the native population has played a central role in the establishment of this singular ethno-national state after the Second World War and its system of ethnic stratification which certainly cannot be called 'Apartheid' in the strict sense. These facts are reflected in high levels of economic inequality today in all these societies; South Africa has one of the highest Gini coefficient worldwide and is in 'good' company in this regard with a dozen countries in Sub-Saharan Africa and Latin America (see Table 1.1); inequality in the United States is higher than in any other 'new' Anglo-Saxon country around the world (and much higher than in most European societies); in Israel, inequality has increased massively in the last decades, as will be shown below and now is on a level comparable to the USA. In all three countries, levels of poverty are higher than anywhere in the West and the same is true for civil violence. In the frequency of homicides, South Africa again shows the highest value worldwide, and it is quite high also in the USA and Israel. In all these regards, these three societies are worlds apart from well-integrated and egalitarian countries like Sweden and Japan which have been described in Chapter 6.

Yet, the three countries are unique also insofar as their level of development is significantly higher than that of all other countries in their respective macro-regional neighbourhoods, that is, in Latin America, Sub-Saharan Africa and the Near East. The United States is one of the richest countries around the globe, and is in third place in the world also in the level of Human Development; Israel is 16th; even the Republic of South Africa, which is 121nd, fares much better in relative terms than its African neighbour states. This relative advantaged position is also proven by the fact that all three countries experience strong immigration from their less developed neighbour countries or from a worldwide diaspora. They are also paradigmatic insofar as their internal ethnic diversity and inequality brings into particularly sharp focus the general problems of race relations, of the living together of people of very different ethnic groups.

Apartheid has been defined in Chapter 5 as a specific system of ethno-class discrimination and exclusion, significantly different from the brute ethno-class exploitation through slavery, but also far away from a situation of equality between the ethnic groups. The word Apartheid (deriving from *Afrikaans*) was coined in South Africa to characterize this system as it existed there between the early 20th century a multiplicity of laws concerning civil and political rights were enacted whose aim was to enable cooperation between the racial groups in the world of work, but to inhibit close private intercourse and political participation. A similar system did exist also in other places and times around the world. It was particularly important in the United States between the end of the 19th century and the 1950s/1960s, and it is hard to deny that it has been introduced in a modified form today in Israel/Palestine, given the striking similarities between some aspects of the situation in this country with that of South Africa during Apartheid. It seems essential, therefore, to characterize and investigate also in this book this paradigmatic system and its effects on economic inequality. These three countries are particularly significant cases to test the central theses of this book, namely, that ethnic diversity will lead to pervasive economic inequality if it is connected with asymmetric and unequal power relations between ethnic groups. This chapter also ties in with the theory of ethnic stratification developed in this book. Since this theory has been elaborated in detail in Chapters 3 and 5, I limit myself here to sketch out only the central theses.

First, it is evident that neither economic nor class-related theories, or theories of ethnic group formation alone are able to account for the emergence, unfolding and consequences of ethnic stratification in the form of Apartheid, although some of the insights of these theories are clearly important. Economic theories, for instance, posit that Apartheid in South Africa was no irrational system of racist exploitation, but a rational response of political actors, given a hostile environment and the necessity of cooperation between immigrants and natives. The ruling elite in a predatory state had to select the appropriate level of enforcement of control so that white capitalists could employ Black labour without being constrained to grant them full civic and political rights (Lowenberg 1984; Hazlett 2008). A related, Marxist-inspired class theory argues that White workers and their unions had the interest to preserve skilled and foreman positions to themselves – an interest which contradicted that of capitalists in a free labour market. A primordial explanation says that the Afrikaners forged a powerful ethnic identity through the 300 years of their presence in Africa, and pushed to its ultimate conclusions the logic of settler colonialism; thus, Apartheid guaranteed their survival and constituted 'the best possible program for the maximization of their genes' (van den Berghe 1981: 174). It is evident that the first of these theories provides only a partial explanation while the second is far too general to explain the specific system of Apartheid. I start from three general basic assumptions: first, also the specific Apartheid model of ethnic exploitation and exclusion and its consequences for economic inequality can only be understood as an outcome of the interaction between economic and class interests on the one side, and ethnic interests in the preservation of one's social and cultural identity and community on the other side. It is particularly the division of the working classes in ethnic terms, and the unity of the dominant classes in this regard which leads to extreme high levels of economic inequality. The Apartheid form of domination, exclusion and exploitation cannot be understood, however, without taking into consideration the ideological and political level. It is typical for all three societies considered in this and the following chapter that there was a strong religious foundation of the strict segregation between the races; and it was also essential for the implementation of this system that the Blacks were more or less deprived of political rights. These ideological and political forces also contribute to the fact that a very high level of economic inequality persists for quite a long time after the abolishment of Apartheid.

Three questions shall be in the centre of the following analyses: (1) How did the respective systems come into existence? What were their precursors and preconditions? (2) How did these systems correlate with economic inequality? Can we see the consequences still today? (3) How could these systems be overthrown in the United States and in South Africa? What are the prospects for Israel/Palestine to achieve a similar revolution? Certainly, I can give only a few hints toward the answer to this last question. Also in regard to the issues of ethnic relations and related economic inequalities I can provide here only the most basic facts and a few specific, new analyses, given the fact that an immense literature exists already about all three countries. Yet, I think the framework developed in this work provides us with some specific and new insights.

United States: the Long Shadows of Slavery and Apartheid

Racial segregation was practiced in 15 and permitted in four additional Southern US states between the end of the 19th century till about 1950/60.[1] While not called Apartheid proper, as in South Africa, many characteristics were similar (see, for instance, Myrdal 1962 [1944]; Massey and Denton 1993; Goldberg 2009: 70–79). The practice of racial segregation was a reaction to the abolishment of slavery in 1865, after the American Civil War (1861–65) which broke out because the Southern States had declared their secession from the Union, but also because of the issue of slavery. The Southern States wanted to extend slavery into the new territories won in the US Mexican war in the South and West and feared that the emigration of slaves toward the North would undermine slavery in their own states. The Northern States, dominated by the Republicans, wanted to abolish slavery; their main reason to enter into a war with the secessionist states, however, was not slavery but the aim to preserve national unity. In fact, the American Civil War was also an example of a highly problematic war initiated by the dominant national group in a country in order to preserve national unity.

---

1   See Table 11.3 for a listing of the US slave states.

In this section, I will analyse briefly the segregation and economic discrimination as they exist in the present-day United States. Before doing this, it is necessary to have a short look at the origins and forms of Apartheid in the US-South. Three issues are relevant in this regard: former slavery as the basis of racial segregation; the legal-constitutional segregation, corresponding to racial thinking of the late 19th, early 20th centuries as well as an ostensible adherence to human rights; and the factual massive socio-economic segregation and discrimination.

'Separate, but Equal' – Racial Segregation in the US-South, 1876–1964

The system of Apartheid in the US-South cannot be understood without the prior history of slavery in this region (see also Duve 1965; Bilger 1976; Adam and Moodley 1977; Cornevin 1980; Louw 2004; Löwstedt 2012). The first slaves came to the USA in 1619 in the state of Virginia; later on, slaves were mainly brought to regions where soil and climate were adapted for the plantation of cotton and sugar, that is, to the Southern regions. In this early time, there was some overlap between servile work (indentured servitude) and slavery, and also Indians and some Whites were enslaved. In the 18th century, slavery was *de facto* racialized by colonial courts and legislatures insofar as from now on only Blacks and people of African descent were enslaved. The fatal consequences of this step have been clearly foreseen by Alexis de Tocqueville when he wrote that the human and changeable institution of slavery has been linked in a fatal way with the bodily and unchangeable differences between 'races': 'The memory of slavery dishonors the race and in the race the memory of slavery lives on' (Tocqueville 1976 [1835]: 396). By 1860, the census showed that about four million slaves were living in the USA, mainly in the South. But slavery remained a contentious issue since this institution evidently contradicted the spirit of the constitution and basic human rights, adjured in the Bill of Rights Amendments to the US Constitution in 1789. In fact, the Constitution itself did not abolish slavery, but instead included several provisions allowing its continuation. In the North, however, abolitionists were active and were successful in their endeavour in most states already till the early 19th century. In the South, a massive south- and westward migration of slaves took place after the need for their labour had decreased in Maryland, Virginia, and Carolina, and increased in the Southern States Kentucky, Tennessee, Georgia, Alabama, Mississippi, Louisiana and Texas. This was a forced people's movement (slaves were sold from the North to the South) which caused extreme hardships since the slaves were usually separated from their families and had to march on foot long distances from one state to another and to submit to extreme harsh working conditions in the new frontier regions. The treatment of the slaves in the South was characterized by degradation and inhumanity, including extremely harsh punishments and executions, rape and sexual abuse and also by denial of education, although there were significant variations between places and slave owners in this regard. 'Slave codes' regulated their treatment and tried to exclude its most arbitrary and inhumane forms. The ideology of racial purity was behind the relations between masters and slaves in the Southern States (Moon 2004): in the patriarchal culture of the South, women generally were seen as property; sexual relations between Whites and Blacks were strongly forbidden, although exploitative sexual relations between White men and Black women were widely practiced and their offspring not recognized as legal.

Slavery was abolished throughout the United States in the wake of the Civil War (1861–65), lost by the South, in a series of laws enacted in the 1870s. The rights of the Blacks in the South to vote could be assured, however, only through the protection of Union troops. Soon thereafter, however, violent opposition against the freedom of the Blacks emerged; this protest could also knock on the strong federalism in the US Constitution which provided legislative power to the single states. Then, more and more Southern States reintroduced open social and legal discrimination of Blacks. In 1877, the federal troops withdrew from the South and in 1896 the US Supreme Court admitted the constitutionality of the new system of Apartheid, when it recognized a Louisiana state law which required railroad companies to provide 'equal but separate' accommodations for White and Black passengers. A series of such laws – the famous Jim Crow Laws – were soon enacted throughout the South. They dictated segregation between Whites and Blacks in public places and transportation, restaurants and restrooms, in public schools and in the civil service and military. It also undermined severely suffrage of Blacks by imposing strict rules for voter registration, poll taxes, literacy and comprehension tests and residency requirements.

The ideology that all races have the same rights and are provided with the same facilities, although in separate institutions, however, was not realized. In practice, the provision of separate facilities and services implied significant inequalities: those provided for Blacks were of much inferior quality than those for Whites. Ruef and Fletcher (2003) have shown by analysing life histories that the antebellum distinction between free Blacks and slaves had effects also on individuals after the abolition of slavery. Residential segregation was a central mechanism by which the inequality between Whites and Blacks was solidified. This began already in the early 20th century when many Afro-Americans in search of jobs moved to the growing cities in the North, and settled in their inner districts where they could find work in industrial and other plants. But since the Whites soon moved out, also employment opportunities were shrinking, and many Blacks unable to leave the inner city became unemployed and poor. Recent analyses of this form of residential separation call it 'hyper-segregation' since it is all-encompassing for the Blacks in the inner-city ghettos (Massey and Denton 1989).

The 'Diversity Paradox': Slavery and Apartheid as Historical Causes Why Afro-Americans Drop Behind Most Other Ethnic Minorities in the USA

The election of Barack Obama, son of a White American mother and a Black father from Kenya, to the 44th president of the United States in 2009 was seen by many as a watershed in American race relations. It seemed to mark the triumph of the civil rights movement and the final realization of a new 'post-ethnic America' (Hollinger 1995). However, one other fact in the development of socio-economic inequality between ethnic groups in the United States is not in accord with such an interpretation. While practically all new ethnic minorities emerging as a consequence of the several waves of immigration in the last century have been quite successful in terms of integration, success and advancement, this has not been the case for Blacks (Afro-Americans). This 'diversity paradox' (Lee and Bean 2010) is a conspicuous fact and has induced a series of studies. During the last decades, a huge immigration into the USA took place, raising the number of first-generation immigrants from about 10 to about 40 million between 1970 and 2010; alone between 2000 and 2010, 14 million people immigrated, mainly from Mexico and other Latin American countries, and from South and South East Asia, boosting the proportion of first-generation immigrants among the US population to 15 per cent. But most of these immigrants – or at least their children – even if they arrived illegally and had only low qualifications, such as most of the Hispanic immigrants, were able to integrate quite well into American society.

Let us have a short look at this important fact as indicated by official statistics of the US Census Bureau. Table 11.1 shows significant and in some regards very surprising results:

- *Whites* perform very well in most regards: their educational attainment is high, they have the lowest high school dropout rate and proportion of poor people; their income is certainly above average.
- *Asian immigrants*, however, fare better than Whites in some regards: they have the best education and earn even more than Whites.
- *Blacks* are clearly below the average in terms of education and income and they have a high rate of poor households. There is also evidence of discrimination: Blacks with a Master's degree earn less than all other groups with the same degree.
- *Hispanic immigrants* perform much worse in terms of education; in terms of income, they can be compared to Blacks.
- *American Indians* are in a situation comparable to Blacks, that is, they are clearly deprived.

The difference between immigrants from Latin America and Asia can easily be explained: many of the Hispanic immigrants came illegally to the US, or were hired for less skilled, low-paid work in the Southern and Eastern US states (for instance, to carry out seasonal work in Californian agriculture). Immigrants from Asia, however, had to pass through an efficient and selective screening procedure; mostly higher educated immigrants from those countries are accepted. In addition, the high evaluation of education and achievement in the South and East Asian societies and cultures from where those immigrants come may be relevant.

In general, it is obvious, however, that the situation of Blacks or Afro-Americans, who are residing in the USA now for centuries, must be considered as clearly disadvantaged and as a specific problem. Lee and Bean (2010: 18) write in this regard:

Table 11.1   Indicators of the socio-economic situation of the five large ethnic groups in the United States (2005–09)

	White %	Black %	Asian %	American Indian %	Hispanic %
Education (2009)					
No high school completed	9.0	18.1	12.5	20.5	38.8
College graduate or more	30.3	19.8	52.4	*	13.9
Personal income					
Full-time workers, 25+, with Master's degree (Median, in 1,000 $)	52.3	48.2	61.4	*	50.9
Household income (2004)					
Lowest fifth	18.2	32.4	15.1	*	23.5
Highest fifth	21.2	9.3	30.5	*	9.4
Living in poverty (2009)					
Adults 18 yrs+	8.4	20.6	11.4	20.4	22.0

Source: US Census Bureau: Census of Population, Current Population Survey, Survey of Income and Participation (SIPP), (Integrated Public Use Microdata Series, Statistical Abstract of the United States).

> [...] group boundaries are fading more rapidly for Latinos and even more rapidly for Asians than for Blacks, signaling that today's new nonWhite immigrants are not incorporating as racialized minorities whose experiences and situations are more akin to those of Blacks than of Whites [...] Asians and to a lesser degree Latinos are more closely following the pattern of European immigrants, which places them closer to Whites at this point in time than to Blacks. Thus, a new Black-nonBlack color line appears to be emerging that places the new nonWhite immigrants on the nonBlack side of the line and continues to separate African Americans from all other groups.

I think that the basic theoretical assumptions developed in this book provide an excellent interpretation of this conspicuous fact. In Chapter 3, I have specified three factors leading to ethnic discrimination and exploitation and these are also responsible for the upsetting fact that the Blacks continue to be discriminated against much more than most other ethnic minorities in the USA: one is the experience of slavery which affected thinking and behaving of both slave holders and slaves in a fundamental way; the second is the societal and cultural characteristics which the Blacks inherited from their African ancestors; and the third is the continuing discrimination of Blacks which today works in an indirect way, namely through residential segregation and a ghettoization of a considerable part of them. It seems that all these facts have not been recognized adequately in recent American sociological research on this topic. Some recent books in my view are very ambiguous in their concepts and blur basic differences between the Blacks and other groups of immigrants.

Only Afro-Americans have experienced over 200 years of slavery and nearly 70 years of Apartheid. Such a long and devastating experience cannot be equated with the exclusion or short-term exploitation or discrimination of other immigrant groups. This is done, however, by Lee and Bean (2010: 24) or by the authors whom they have in mind in the following passage: 'Blacks, Asians and Latinos have all faced severe de jure and de facto discrimination in the United States in the form of enslavement, exclusion, incarceration, confinement, or deportation'. As examples of immigrating groups with similar discriminations like Afro-Americans they mention, for instance, the Chinese who 'were barred from immigrating to the United States for ten years'; 110,000 Japanese Americans who were detained between 1941 and 1947; and Mexicans who in 1954 were deported by force. Lee and Bean (2010: 54) conclude: Thus, 'for much of U.S. history Blacks, Asians, and Latinos have had more in common with one another in terms of their status than with Whites, and all faced severe discrimination'. However, the discriminations which the Chinese or the Japanese – or better: small groups of them – experienced can in no way compared to those which Afro-Americans had to suffer. In fact, the non-Black groups had to suffer mainly processes of exclusion, but not of exploitation – two very different things between which sociology must carefully distinguish. A conflation of the fundamental differences between Blacks and other ethnic minorities happened also in US civil rights legislation from the 1960s onwards when all non-Whites were considered as belonging to one large group of discriminated 'Blacks'. Some sociologists denote the specific deprivation of Blacks as an African-American 'exception' (Gans 2005). This conceptual ambiguity is also evident in the conclusion of Lee and Bean (2010: 184):

> '... cultural differences appear more surmountable and fade with time and across generations, whereas racial divides are more formidable. Thus, in the marriage market the color line that remains the most relevant is the one that defines Black. This leaves Blacks more maritally isolated than other groups (including other nonWhite groups) and points to a pattern of Black exceptionalism in the marriage market.

In my view, such an interpretation naturalizes skin colour, or 'Blackness' as a biological criterion. In Chapter 3 (pp. 31–2) I have argued that also 'race' in the bio-social sense (connected with physical, body-related aspects) must be considered as a socio-cultural characteristic, not less than that of having a particular mother tongue or religion. Five facts clearly indicate that 'Blackness' in the USA is a historical-cultural category in this sense and that its characteristics can be traced back to the specific experiences of the Black Afro-Americans as former slaves and – in the Apartheid system – as people of inferior social status.

First, racist prejudices and behavioural discriminations exist in regard to Blacks which do not exist in regard to other minorities (Goldberg 2009: 70–102). The prejudices which are involved here came out already in the foregoing quotation. Such prejudices become socially and politically important and consequential if they are ingrained in public institutions and in the behaviour of their officers. Discriminative behaviour is also experienced by Black multiracials, that is, Blacks with a non-Black parent or other ancestor. In the USA, such persons as a routine are categorized as Blacks by teachers; police and security officers see them with suspicion and often treat them in unproportionally harsh ways (Lee and Bean 2010: 130–132).

Second, Blacks themselves have an ambivalent attitude toward ethnic intermarriage and view it even 'as a sign of racial disloyalty or inauthenticity' (Lee and Bean 2010: 89). African Americans mentioned in the interviews, carried out by these authors, that co-ethnic Blacks had accused them of being 'race traitors' when they choose to date and marriage across ethnic lines; through stares and offensive comments, the costs of interracial marriage are driven up. This attitude increased during the Civil Rights movement. The reason was that Black Nationalism in the 1960s had a deeply ambivalent attitude to Africa, admiring its rich cultural heritage and scenic beauty, but also embarrassed by its poverty-stricken and war-torn condition (Goldberg 2009: 82–3). It is in line with such sentiments that multiracial Blacks are often not welcomed within the Black community. Therefore, some Blacks (but also some conservative politicians) have charged that Barack Obama is not really Black because he is not a descendant of slaves (Lee and Bean 2010: 132–4).

Third, the self-ascription of multiracial Blacks as Blacks must be seen as a consequence of the aforementioned political-legal one-drop rule in the United States which presupposes only two distinct categories of Black versus White. The underlying assumption that most Blacks (and only Blacks) are discriminated is then internalized also by Blacks. Therefore, also Blacks with mixed ancestry consider themselves to be Blacks only. This self-ascription is surprising given the fact that three-quarters of the Blacks have in fact multiracial ancestry, and only about 6 per cent chose to identify themselves as multiracial in 2008; Black-White couples identify their children mostly as Black (Lee and Bean 2010: 108, 121).

Fourth, the disadvantaged situation of the Blacks is the result of intra-ethnic favouritism among the Whites. In her in-depth study on perceptions of class and racial discrimination among Whites in New Jersey, Ohio and Tennessee, Nancy DiTomaso (2013) concludes that for the Whites the obvious persistence of racial discrimination constitutes no ethical-moral problem because they do not discriminate Blacks directly. The Whites adhere to an individualistic world-view which ascribes success to individual talent, willingness to take risks, hard work and effort which attributes failure to the absence of such characteristics, but not to structural and institutional factors. Similarly, James R. Kluegel and Eliot P. Smith (1986) found that this dominant conservative and individualistic American ideology was supported among all groups, including poor classes and Blacks. According to DiTomaso, the main mechanism to preserve the privileged situation is favouritism among Whites, the hoarding of opportunities and the reliance on White social networks. This is possible because Whites are segregated in work and neighbourhoods from Blacks: therefore, 'Whites can believe themselves to be fully supportive of civil rights and equal opportunity even though they benefit from unequal opportunity – that is the privileges of being White. Thus, one can speak here – paraphrasing the famous study of Gunnar Myrdal – of an "American Non-Dilemma"' (DiTomaso 2013: 315–20).

We can prove these facts also with data from the ISSP-survey on Social Inequality of 2009. Table 11.2 shows that Americans, and in particular the Whites, ascribe success in life (chances for getting ahead) much more frequently to individual factors such as having ambition and working hard than to assistance from social networks and to support coming from a wealthy family background or knowing the right people. However, there exist clear differences between Blacks and Whites in this regard. Only 25 per cent of the Whites consider race as a relevant factor, but more than half of the Blacks; worldwide, the proportion is in-between (36 per cent). This individualistic ethos and world-view reflects itself also in the much lower proportion of Americans who consider income differences as too high; also Blacks have adopted this American creed. As far as government intervention is concerned, again the difference between Whites and Blacks is obvious: while only one-quarter among the former agrees with this aim, among the latter it is 46 per cent. Thus, the conclusion from these data corresponds to that of Kluegel and Smith (1986; see also Verba and Orren 1985): Blacks more frequently see discrimination at work and are more in favour of concrete political measures, but do not challenge the system and its individualistic bias as a whole.

Nancy DiTomaso found, as reported before, that favouritism is a major mechanism of status attainment among Whites; this finding is well complemented by an in-depth ethnographic study among jobless Black people in the USA. In her study *Lone Pursuit. Distrust and Defense Individualism Among the Black Poor*, Sandra S. Smith (2007) found that persistent joblessness among Blacks (particularly males) was connected with a reluctance among them to seek out help among people in positions which would have enabled them to provide assistance. 'Psychologies of distrust' existed both among job-holders and job seekers in poor

Table 11.2   Beliefs about factors for getting ahead and about income inequality among different ethnic groups in the United States and South Africa

	Factors important for getting ahead				Income differences are too high[*]	Government should reduce income differences[**]
	Hard work[*]	Coming from wealthy family[**]	Knowing the right people[**]	One's own race[***]		
United States						
Whites (1,058)	47	25	38	25	31	27
Blacks (153)	42	50	70	54	25	46
Latinos (138)	32	45	64	35	25	49
All (1,383)	44	30	45	30	29	32
South Africa						
Blacks (1,473)	34	63	67	73	44	29
Whites (393)	44	48	51	61	39	20
Asians (224)	44	47	50	58	58	29
Mixed (307)	40	45	63	67	45	28
All (2,397)	37	56	66	69	45	28
Total sample of 38 nations (abt. 52,200)	32	33	55	36	46	33

[*]Essential/strongly agree (%); [**]Essential + very important/strongly agree + agree (%); [***]Essential + very important + fairly important (%)
Source: ISSP-2009 'Social Inequality'.

neighbourhoods; the first were worried that providing help to persons who later could be unreliable in their jobs could have negative effects on themselves; the latter were reluctant to seek assistance because they feared that they would not be able to fulfil the expected obligations. Also employment and training centre specialists were discouraged by their supervisors and employers from helping those who had gone particularly long without a job.

Fifth, if my theorems mentioned before are valid it should turn out that discrimination and racism against Blacks should be most evident in the US-South, in the former slave and Apartheid states. In fact, in the in-depth interviews of Lee and Bean (2010) and of DiTomaso (2013), the strongest prejudices against Blacks were expressed in the US-South. In this regard, Nancy DiTomaso refers to a very important political trend in American politics since the 1964 election (Johnson vs. Goldwater). This was the capture of White, working-class, low-income voters in the South by the Republicans and the loss of ground by Democrats in this region where they had been dominant for decades. The reason for this far-reaching change was exactly the race versus class issue. The Democrats became the party supporting civil rights in the 1960s but as a consequence they lost the votes of the White working (and often racist) classes in the South. Thus, by an appeal to populism, presidents Reagan, Bush and other conservative Republican politicians 'endeavored, using common folks rhetoric, to attract blue-collar, White, working-class voters from the Democratic Party by appealing to their anti-elitism and anti-intellectualism, even while the Republican Party has primarily supported the interests of business and the very wealthy' (DiTomaso 2013: 150). Also the move of the Republicans toward a new religious fundamentalism is closely related to the race issue. By focusing upon the supposed decay of public schooling and by supporting the establishment of Christian academies, they appealed to the White middle and upper classes.

In this new tension between race and class, also the unions played a significant and contradictory role corresponding to their relevance as been accentuated in Chapter 4 (p. 65). During the period of race segregation, Blacks were often used as strike-breakers against unions. With the rise of the Civil Rights Movement in the 1960s, splits and conflicts between and within unions emerged, for instance, about the admission of Black youth to apprenticeship training which traditionally had been reserved for the sons and acquaintances of union members. According to Nancy DiTomaso, Gunnar Myrdal did make one significant error[2] in his famous work of 1944, when he argued that the Blacks had a forceful weapon in the legal-constitutional foundations of the United States and in the consciousness of the Whites, particularly in the North, for whom it was evident that a gulf existed between the egalitarian constitutional principles and the reality of race discrimination. The error of Myrdal was to underestimate the resistance power of the South in regard to the emancipation of the Blacks. In fact, however,

> [...] the South has continued, contrary to Myrdal's expectations, to have substantial political influence in the country, and it sparked the new right-wing social movements that have influenced politics across the country. Instead of the North forcing the South to leave its conservative politics behind, the South has extended its conservative politics, albeit in new guises, to the rest of the country (DiTomaso 2013: 335).

In the next section, I will show that the US-South is in fact significantly different from the rest of the USA today also in terms of its higher economic inequality.

The African Heritage and Ghettoization as Actual Causes of Black (and Indian) Discrimination

A second group of factors that helps to understand the under-achievement of Blacks in the United States is their African origin and their concentration in urban ghettos today. I think that two kinds of evidence cannot be neglected here although my first thesis in this regard might be controversial.

First, it comes out clearly from the in-depth interviews reported in Lee and Bean (2010: 91) that White-Black intermarriage is opposed by non-Blacks because of the presumed *socio-cultural* characteristics of Blacks. For Asian-White or Latino-White couples in the USA, race is rather unimportant, 'a non-issue' in their relationship; Black-White partnerships are seen quite differently, however. A White woman married to a

---

2   Myrdal was also accused of many other shortcomings which are not true, however, as DiTomaso (2013: 310–311) argues; one of them was that he reduced the discrimination of Blacks to individual factors.

Japanese man said, for instance: 'Well, our whole culture is much more prejudiced against African Americans than Asians. Asians are perceived as hardworking, ambitious, scholastically inclined, strong family, and the African American culture is the opposite' (Lee and Bean 2010: 91). That this is not only pure prejudice, but grounded in objective facts, is beyond question. Immigrant Asians and their children fare extremely well in the US school and employment system as we have seen before. Also more recent data (of 2012) show that people of Asian origin had the highest level of educational attainment of all ethnic groups: 58.5 per cent from the age 25 and over had a college degree or more; the corresponding figures among Whites were 41.1 per cent, among Blacks 30.5 per cent and among Hispanics 21.3 per cent; 5.9 per cent of the Asians had a professional or doctoral degree, the corresponding figures for Whites were 3.1 per cent, for Blacks 1.8 per cent and for Hispanics 1.0 per cent.[3] Enrolment rates in secondary and tertiary education in South East Asia are among the highest in the world today (World Development Report 2012). The relevance of the very rich cultural background – both the existence of an old high-culture and the prevalence of an ethos of achievement – is also evident in the high rates of growth in South East Asia. Contrary to those societies and cultures, most African cultures from which the Afro-Americans descend were rather small societies without a scripture, based on simple technologies.

This characteristic of the origins of the Afro-Americans is closely related to a similar and equally persistent discrimination which is experienced by Native Americans, the Indians. It is quite remarkable that this group is rather neglected among discussions of the situation of ethnic groups in the United States (but see Waters and Eschbach 1995: 429f.). This is understandable, given their relatively small number (5.2 million or 1.7 per cent of the total US population in 2010),[4] but it is justified neither from the sociological point of view nor from the view point of human rights and social justice. American Indians were not departed to another continent and enslaved on a massive scale. However, many of them were killed by military and civil violence after the Europeans discovered the Americas, and all of them were displaced from their vast original territories into small and remote reservations. Although estimates of their number at the time of the Europeans vary greatly (from two up to 20 million), it is clear that by the end of the 19th century only 250,000 Native Americans were left at the present territory of the USA.[5] Most of them died because of contagious diseases, but in many instances the term genocide might be appropriate. In fact, if we look at the statistical data today, the situation of Indians appears clearly similar to, if not as more deprived than, that of Blacks (see also Table 11.1). The unemployment rate in 2010 among them was over 20 per cent, the rate of poverty 20 per cent to 28 per cent, the median income only 70 per cent of that of all Americans. Indians have higher rates of disease and death, one-quarter lacks medical coverage, and problematic behaviours like alcoholism, smoking and consumption of drugs are more frequent.[6] There is one significant difference and one similarity between Indians and Blacks. First, it is remarkable that the number of American Indians more than doubled between 1970 and 1990 (from 827,000 to 1.96 million). This fact can only be explained by the possibility that in the later censuses the Indians could place themselves into this category (while in former times the enumerators had put them mostly into the White category) (Lee and Bean 2010: 43f.). This fact shows a greater self-confidence of Indian Americans who in fact can consider themselves as the original inhabitants of the country and have never been enslaved by the Whites. Second, many Indians live in special territories called reservations; these reservations have their own administration. However, it is particularly the situation on these reservations which is connected with the disadvantaged situation and the discrimination of the Indians. Most of them are far away from places where good educational and job opportunities are available. This fact is highly relevant also for understanding the persistent discrimination of Blacks in the United States.

---

3   Calculated from the Tables provided by the US Census Bureau, Current Population Survey, 2012 Annual Social and Economic Supplement (http://www.census.gov/hhes/socdemo/education/data/cps/2012/tables.html). See also Sue and Okazaki (1990).

4   This number includes also Indians with mixed ancestry; Indians only were 2.9 million. See Profile America Facts, US Bureau of Census: http://www.census.gov/newsroom/releases/archives/facts_for_features_special_editions/cb11-ff22.html

5   See Guenter Levy, *Where American Indians the Victims of Genocide?* George Mason University, History News Network (http://hnn.us/article/7302).

6   See https://www.google.at/#q=modern+social+statistics+of+native+Indians

By far, not all Blacks are in a deprived economic situation in the USA. The full data from Table 11.1 shows that 43 per cent of the Blacks are in the 3rd to 5th highest income quintile, that is, they earn as much or more than the average American. However, they are deprived particularly when living in urban ghettos (Wilson 1987). Long-term residence in very poor neighbourhoods is particularly typical for Black Americans; many of them, in fact, are 'trapped' in them (Quillian 2003).[7] I think that the widely discussed work of William J. Wilson (1978, 2011) has rightly pointed out this fact. He did not argue, as critics wrote, that the discrimination of Blacks had been overcome as a whole. Rather, the title of his book *The Declining Significance of Race* suggested that industrialization and economic growth enabled also many Blacks to advance and led to the emergence of a Black middle class. In general, class became more important than race in determining life chances for African Americans, a thesis which was confirmed with statistical analyses by Hout (1984). However, within the Black community a new schism appeared between lower-income and higher-income families, indicating a growing deprivation and discrimination of the first. A main reason, according to Wilson, is the segregation of these groups into deprived Black inner cities, where the number of very low-skilled individuals vastly exceeds the number of low-skilled jobs (Wilson 2011: 66). This 'ghettozation' of a part of the Black population has been a result of residential segregation patterns which have evolved in the large US cities in the South and Northeast during the course of the 20th century and as a reaction to the success of the Civil Rights Movement.[8] I will come back to the policy implications of this important fact in the previous chapter.

The Variation of Economic Inequality within the United States Today as a Consequence of Slavery and Apartheid

In the multivariate analysis of the determinants of economic inequality in Chapter 4, the United States has been assigned *en bloc* as a country formerly characterized by slavery. This was necessary for the possibility to make international comparisons at the level of countries. It is certainly incorrect, however, since only in 12 of the 49 US states was slavery practiced. A detailed analysis would have to distinguish, in fact, at least four different 'Americas': the East with metropolitan cities similar to Europe (New York, Boston) and old industrial towns and districts (Chicago, Detroit); central, conservative, mainly 'White' America; the thriving West, particularly California where immigration was high in the last decades, not only from Mexico, but also many other parts of the world; it is here, that 'Postethnic America' (Höllinger 1995) seems to come into existence; and, finally, the former slave states in the South. Here, I will focus only on the latter where still 54 per cent of all 36 million Blacks were living in 2000.[9] I will investigate if the degree of income inequality in the former slave states is higher than in the other states of the USA.

Table 11.3 presents the data for income inequality in the US states. The states are ordered along the continuum of economic inequality, as measured by the Gini index. We can see that this index varies from a relatively low value of 40 in Alaska till the high value of 53 in the District of Columbia (Washington, DC) and Puerto Rico. It is evident that the former status as a slave society has a significant impact on present-day economic inequality. Most of the states which had no slavery in history have a lower level of economic inequality today; most of them are situated in the Northeast of the USA, far away from the former slave states in the South: this is true in particular for Alaska, Utah, Idaho and Wyoming which have Gini indices of 43 and less. This fact turns out to be also observable in Figure 11.1, a map of the USA.[10]

The former slave societies (marked by words in bold), on the other side, are all in the higher inequality groups of countries, with Gini coefficients of 45 and more. With these degrees of inequality, they are similar to states like Venezuela or Ecuador in Latin America, to Cameroon or Côte d'Ivoire in Sub-Saharan Africa and to Nepal and the Philippines in Asia. Also some former non-slave states have rather high levels of economic inequality, but

---

7   See also Ed Glaeser, 'Ghettos: The changing consequences of ethnic isolation', *Regional Review* 7 (1997); http://www.bostonfed.org/economic/nerr/rr1997/spring/rgrv97_2.htm

8   Arnold E. Hirsch, *Black Ghettos, Houghton Mifflin Companion to US History*, http://www.answers.com/topic/Black-ghettos

9   See 'The Black Population. Census 2000 Brief', US Census Bureau, August 2001.

10   These findings are corroborated by the recent analysis of Fox et al. (2013) who find that the proportion of Black residents in a US state has a negative impact on redistributive outcomes.

Table 11.3   Income distribution in the states of the USA (2000)

Gini index	States (% Blacks, if 10% +); bold letters: former slave states
40	Alaska
41	Utah
42	Idaho, Wyoming
43	**Delaware**, Hawaii, Indiana, Iowa, Maine, Montana, Nevada, New Hampshire, Vermont, Wisconsin
44	Kansas, Minnesota, Nebraska, Oregon, Washington
45	**Missouri** (11.7), Arizona, Colorado, **Maryland** (28.8), Michigan (14.8), New Mexico, Ohio (12.1), South Dakota
46	**Arkansas** (16.0), **North Carolina** (22.1), **South Carolina** (29.9), **Virginia** (20.4), **Kentucky**, North Dakota, Oklahoma, Pennsylvania (10.5), Rhode Island, West Virginia
47	**Alabama** (26.3), **Florida** (15.5), **Georgia** (29.2), **Louisiana** (32.9), **Mississippi** (36.6), **Tennessee** (16.8), **Texas** (12.0), California, Illinois (15.6), Massachusetts, New Jersey (14.4)
48	Connecticut (10.0)
50	New York (17.0)
53	District of Columbia (61.3), Puerto Rico (10.9)

Sources: % Blacks: US Census Bureau 2000, data reported in http://www.census.gov/prod/2001pubs/c2kbr01-5.pdf; GINI coefficients: US Census Bureau, reported in http://en.wikipedia.org/wiki/List_of_U.S._states_by_Gini_coefficient; former slave states: http://de.widipedia.org/wiki/suedstaaten.

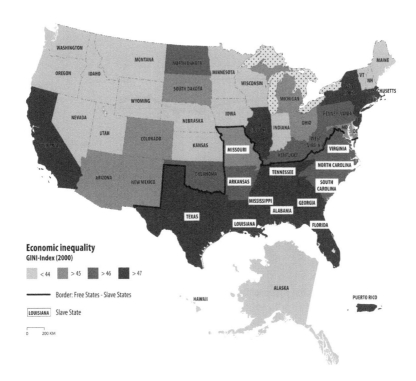

Figure 11.1   Income distribution in the states of the USA
Source: See Table 11.4.

their situation can in most cases be explained by their high proportion of Black population today (for all countries with 20 per cent or more Blacks, this is indicated within parentheses in Table 11.3). We can assume that attitudes and behaviour toward the Blacks throughout the United States and the self-image and behaviour of the Blacks themselves will be influenced by their history of slavery. From this view, the levels of inequality in countries which never were slave states, such as Virginia, Mississippi, Illinois, New Jersey, Connecticut, New York, and in particular Washington DC (with an extremely high level of 61 per cent Blacks), becomes fully comprehensible. The same is true for the high level of economic inequality in Puerto Rico. This state is very different from all other US states: it is situated far away from mainland USA in the Caribbean, its population is Catholic and the language spoken is Spanish. Puerto Rico also had slavery in former times, although it was introduced quite late, in the 19th century, and was never very extensive (covering about 10 per cent of the population).[11] With its Gini coefficient of 53, Puerto Rico is situated perfectly within other independent states of the Caribbean, such as the Dominican Republic (51) and Haiti (54) (see Table 1.1, pp. 5–6).

Immigration and the Increase of Economic Inequality since 1985

A final consideration is necessary concerning the changes in economic inequality in the USA in the last decades. Figure 11.2 shows that income inequality has decreased between 1960 from a Gini coefficient of 34 to one of 30–31 between 1971 and 1984; since then, inequality increased continuously till 2008. There are several reasons for this increase, although it has also been contested.[12] One factor which could have lead to an increase in income inequality is a possible increase of residential segregation of the most deprived group of Afro-Americans which was discussed in the previous section. Another is a change in politics in connection with the rise to power of Republican presidents. Under Ronald Reagan, the top marginal tax rate was reduced from over 70 per cent to 28 per cent (Bartels 2008).[13]

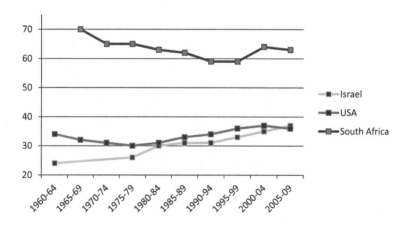

(a) Gini coefficients (mean values for five-year periods)

<hr />

11   Katherine Bowman, Slavery in Puerto Rico, Puerto Rican Culture, Pimentel, 2002, available at: http://maxweber.hunter.cuny.edu/pub/eres/BLPR243_PIMENTEL/slavery.pdf

12   The argument that little or no increase took place is based on facts like changes in book-keeping and reporting of business; in tax system changes; and in a conflation of individual and statistical tax units: see Alan Reynolds, 'Has U.S. income inequality really increased?' *Policy Analysis*, 8 January 2007 (No. 586).

13   See also http://en.wikipedia.org/wiki/Income_Inequality_in_the_United_States

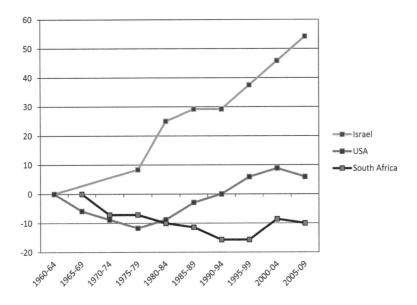

(b) Relative changes (per cent increase or decrease, 1960–64 = 100)

Figure 11.2   Changes in economic inequality in Israel, South Africa and the United States, 1960-64 to 2005-09
Source: Standardized World Income Inequality Database (SWIID) (Solt 2009).

A third factor which probably has contributed to increasing inequality is of general importance for the argument developed in this book. This was the strong immigration to the USA which I have mentioned already before. The increase of immigration was also a consequence of the removal of national immigration quotas in 1965 and the Immigration Act of 1990. Since the mid-1990s, about a million persons have immigrated legally each year. In 1970, there were 9.6 million immigrants living in the USA, and in 2007, 38 million; those of European origin dropped from 60 per cent to 15 per cent.[14] Latin America in general and Mexico and Puerto Rico in particular provided a large proportion of immigrants, and particularly illegal immigrants who are employed mostly in low-paid, unqualified jobs. Thus, it can be assumed that this form of immigration contributed significantly to an increase of overall income inequality (see also Waters and Eschbach 1995). Immigration is a process which is highly relevant for all richer countries around the world and it can significantly change the ethnic composition of a country. We will see this also in the next section on Israel and I will come back to the general question of the effects of immigration on inequality in the next chapter.

The Republic of South Africa: Pervasive Inequality in a Post-Apartheid Society

The Republic of South Africa is also a very interesting and important case from the viewpoint of the problem of this book, ethno-class stratification and income inequality. For nearly a century it exhibited a paradigmatic case of an Apartheid system, a racial segregation and discrimination of Blacks enforced by law (see also Chapter 6). Thus it was not ethnic membership in the more narrow bio-social or cultural sense which was relevant, but the overall distinction between Whites and Blacks. In fact among both Whites and Blacks significant differentiations existed. The two White groups – the British and the Boers, descendants from Dutch immigrants – historically were enemies and had fought two wars against each other in 1810 and 1900 about the abolishment of slavery and the control of the newly detected diamond and gold fields. The Blacks

---

14   Source: US Census Bureau; data summarized in http://en.wikipedia.org/wiki/Immigration_to_the_United_States

were differentiated even more between Zulu, Xhosa, Basotho and other smaller groups; nine different Black languages are recognized as official languages, besides Afrikaans and English. Moreover, a sizable group of coloured people existed; descendants from imported slaves and immigrants from Malaysia, Madagascar and India.

The differences between the several non-White groups, however, lost much of their importance after the establishment of the South African Union in 1909/10 (which was still a part of the British Empire) and the gaining of full political independence in 1931.[15] The first constitutional elements of the Apartheid system were already established in the late 19th/early 20th centuries (Native Location Act and Pass Laws 1879, Natives Land Act 1913). The reason for this unique development was that the White settlers in Cape Town needed labour power, first, for their farms and, later, for the exploitation of the gold mines. In their early period of settlement around the Cape of Good Hope, the Boers had lived in much the same way as the native population as hunters, farmers and cattle herders (Reader 1998: 479–90). Soon, however, they chose a destiny that made them 'the epitome of racism on the African continent' (for an overview see Ross 1983). Several events and facts were decisive in this: one was their need for labour power which they could satisfy by enslaving natives or raping Black children; another was British pressure to abandon slavery which after 1833 (the year of the formal abolition of slavery throughout the British Empire) led the Boers to their Great Trek toward the inland (Terreblanche 2002: 219–38). In the course of this trek, they encountered violent resistance by local tribes and kingdoms similar to that of the Zulus. In this period, they developed the myth of a 'chosen people' in which they resumed an older Dutch national myth of the 16th and 17th centuries when the Netherlands switched over to Protestantism and Calvinism and which exposed the Netherlands to attack by their powerful overlords in Catholic Austria and Spain (Mann 2007: 72). In the wake of the harsh experiences during their trek, the Boers (or Afrikaners, as they later called themselves) became convinced that their unique and hard lot was a God-given destiny, comparable to that of the Jewish people who were also expelled from their original homeland and persecuted throughout the centuries in the countries into which they were dispersed (Thompson 1985): but 'when the cause of a people is conceived to be the very will of God, the collectivity is infused with a powerful sense of purpose that transcends mundane considerations of social organization' (Cauthen 2000: 1000; Smith 1992). Also inspired by their Christian, and particularly Calvinist, background, the Boers adopted a racist ideology which posits that races are fundamentally distinct from each other; that Whites are superior and have to preserve their distinction and must civilize the lower (pagan) races. This was rightly called a 'political theology of race' (Goldberg 2009: 254–64). In fact, racial inequality was 'a cardinal point in the doctrine of the Dutch Reformed Church in South Africa'; it even produced a schism between this and Protestant Churches since it evidently isolated some fundamental ethical principles of Christianity (Dvorin 1951). Religion is still today an important base of social identity of White South Africans; 43 per cent mention it as important, according the 2003 ISSP survey on National Identity. Due to the fact that the Boers had to survive in a hostile environment and were supported by nobody from outside (the Dutch refused to do so), they developed a strong sense of independence and national identity (Cauthen 2000).

From 1948 on, when the Boer-dominated National Party came to power, the Apartheid system was fully developed, classifying all peoples into four racial groups and establishing specific rights and obligations for them.[16] This was an exceptional success of a nationalist movement in comparative terms since the Boers had been a subordinated ethnic group thus far (Adam and Moodley 1977: 54ff.). From now on, sexual contact between Whites and non-Whites was prohibited by law. They also occupied very different positions with Whites monopolizing top positions, Blacks filling the lowest ranks and the coloured population in the middle. There was also a White working class but it was privileged under Apartheid through job reservations. Pierre van den Berghe (1970) therefore has called it a colour or racial caste system (see also Gilliomee and Schlemmer 1985; Terreblanche 2002). We have seen the outcome of this system clearly in Table 1.1 (pp. 5–6) where the Republic of South Africa appears among the group of countries with the highest degree of economic inequality around the world. In 1990, however, the Apartheid system was abolished after decades of national protests and uprisings (often suppressed violently by the dominant Whites) and international critiques and

---

15   For a systematic historical overview see Terreblanche 2002.

16   On the Apartheid system see Ungar 1989: 210–317; Illife 1997: 380–384; Terreblanche 2002; Mwijage 2004: 231–44; Löwstedt 2012.

trade embargos. Negotiations between President Frederick W. de Klerk and the leader of the African National Congress (ANC), Nelson Mandela, led to a true political revolution which was welcomed throughout the world and made Nelson Mandela one of the most admired political personalities of the 20th century. In 1994, the first nationwide multiracial elections were held which resulted in an ANC victory, securing 62 per cent of the votes.

The Abolishment of the Apartheid System and its Immediate Impacts

Since the mid-1990s, the South African governments dominated by Blacks have set in motion a policy of Black Economic Empowerment.[17] This imposes, for instance, Employment Equity Targets on companies and allows for positive discrimination, that is, a preference for Blacks over Whites when filling new jobs. This policy was most successful in the public service where in earlier times the majority of positions and nearly all senior posts were occupied by Whites. By 2006, nearly 75 per cent of all public servants and 60 per cent of senior managers were Blacks.[18] This was quite near to their proportion among the population as a whole (79.2 per cent in the 2011 Census); the proportion of Whites was 8.9 per cent, of coloured 8.8 per cent and Indians or Asians 2.6 per cent.[19] Reforms were also enacted in the educational system (aggregation of the former ethnically divided departments into a single ministry, creation of non-discriminatory school environments and so on) and in the provision of housing. The promotion of racial equality in the educational system became one of the central aims of the new government.[20] However, among the three main pillars of this policy, only in regard to equal treatment has a significant achievement been attained, including equal funding of schools all over the country and abolition of formal access barriers for Black and coloured students (Fiske and Ladd 2005). Less success was attained in regard to the goals of equal educational opportunity and outcomes in terms of students' factual knowledge. In spite of some improvements, 'the majority of African students continue to attend schools that have under qualified teachers and inadequate facilities [...]' (Fiske and Ladd 2005). South African Black students scored lower in international comparative tests of mathematical and other abilities than youths in many other Sub-Saharan African countries.

    Also the political-territorial map was redrawn by abolishing the old provinces and homelands and creating nine new provinces. All these measures were enacted in view of the fact that the factual socio-economic discrimination of the native Black population would not disappear overnight as a consequence of the legal and constitutional reforms. One could see an analogy here to the abolishment of colonialism: independence deracialized the state, but not civil society in Sub-Saharan Africa (Mamdani 1996: 20). Strengths of South Africa in comparison with all other African countries, however, are its developed economy, a strong civil society with forceful unions also among the Blacks and a real democracy (Mamdani 1996: 29–31). However, deep inequalities between Whites and Blacks still exist, and Black people constitute the bulk of the poor population.[21]

    Structural factors which contribute to this persistence of economic inequality are the pervasive inequalities in the ownership of land and of productive enterprises. The first is also a consequence of the Apartheid policy to resettle the indigenous Black population by force on their presumed *homelands* which usually were the most unproductive areas. Eighty per cent of farming land still is in the hands of White farmers[22] – a fact which is resented by many Blacks as indicated in the continuous murdering of White farmers. The economic change in the post-Apartheid era has accentuated prevailing social and spatial disparities; in the former homelands, unemployment and absolute poverty rates increased (Stock 2013). A second important factor is that the abolition

---

17 Partial concessions to possibilities for political participation of Indians and coloured were already made in the early 1980s in granting access to the Tricameral Parliament; Blacks, however, were not included (Adam and Moodley 1977: 19–36).

18 National Planning Commission, The Presidency of the Republic of South Africa, 'Building a representative public service'. (http://www.online-co.za/pebble.asp?relid=62).

19 See www.stat.ssa.gov.za/Census/

20 For an overview on the educational system and opportunities before 1994 see Adam and Moodley 1977: 274–80.

21 A growing inequality in South Africa was reported the *South African Human Development Report* (2013), ed. by the United Nations.

22 'Legacies of Apartheid', https://en.wikipedia.org/wiki/Legacies_of_apartheid (11.7.2013).

of Apartheid led to the loss of a docile and exploitable work force for the White enterprises; as a consequence, they forced the substitution of capital for labour. This process contributed to a massive unemployment increase between 1970 and 1995, from 24 per cent to 46 per cent among Africans and from 20 per cent to 36 per cent among the whole population. As a consequence, economic inequality also increased (Terreblanche 2002: 33, 373, 420). Thus, we can observe here a similar paradoxical trend to that which appeared after the abolition of slavery in America, which also led to a deterioration in the life circumstances of many Blacks in the first period after the liberation. Other factors, such as the HIV/AIDS pandemic, which had infected 20 per cent of adult Black South Africans in 2000 (Stock 2004: 434), as well as a rapidly increasing crime rate, have contributed to a shortening in life expectancy. Nevertheless, South Africa's Human Development Index (HDI) rose from .57 to .62 between 1980 and 2012.[23] GNP per capita in PPP terms was around 9,500 US-$ in 2005. This places the country In position 121 of 187 countries, which is still low, but significantly higher than the mean value for Sub-Saharan Africa (See Table 6.1, pp. 164–5). South Africa is also a country of immigration from other African countries. Inequality of net income declined slightly from a Gini of 61 in 1990 to 59 in 1995, rising again to 63 in 2005 (Solt 2009; see Figure 11.2); unemployment is over 20 per cent.

Fortunately, South Africa is a member of the International Social Survey Program (ISSP) and has participated in the 2009 survey on inequality. Thus, we can use these data here to describe the present pattern of ethnic stratification and inequality in the country in more detail and also present some data on the perception of inequality. This shall be done in three steps: first, descriptive findings are presented concerning the differences in the situation of the main ethnic groups; second, a regression analysis is carried out to investigate if a pattern of ethnic stratification still exists; and third, a few hints toward the perception of inequality by the population are given.

The Persistence of Ethno-class Stratification

Two questions shall be answered here: first, how large is the effect of ethnic membership on income, controlling for other relevant factors? Second, can we find an indication for ethno-class stratification, that is, specific advantages or disadvantages connected with ethnic membership?

Four ethnic groups are distinguished, following the classification of the South African ISSP-researchers and the distinctions introduced by Apartheid: Blacks (Africans), Mixed (coloured), Indians and other Asians, Whites.[24] What are the income chances of these four ethnic groups?

Table 11.4 shows a pattern of sharp differences in the socio-economic situation of these groups: the Whites are at the top, followed by Indians and other Asians; the mixed groups and Blacks are quite similar to each other, both are at the bottom in all indicators. About one-third of these two latter groups have no formal education, only about one-tenth of them have a higher (secondary or university) education; among Indians, these proportions are 14 per cent and 19 per cent respectively, and among Whites the corresponding percentages are 3 per cent and 48 per cent. Large differences exist also in terms of occupational position and income: about half of the Blacks and coloured population work in manual and unskilled jobs, but only one-third of the Indians and 17 per cent of the Whites; the reverse is true for the highest group (professionals, managers) in which we find 57 per cent of the Whites, 39 per cent of Indians, but only 16 per cent of Blacks. Given these facts it is not surprising that Whites are also overrepresented among state employees (given the political revolution it is astonishing). Further, it is evident that the class and status differences between the four ethnic groups are closely related to patterns of residence: Black people are living much more frequently in rural and tribal areas (44 per cent) than all three other groups. According to Sampie Terreblanche (2002: 41), the lifestyle of members of the lower strata (which overwhelmingly are Black) 'constitutes a state of chronic community poverty. People living under these conditions are uneducated, come from broken homes, are in poor health, have poor housing, have few aspirations, and are emotionally confused'. These strata may include 25 per cent, if not more, of the population. Taking all these differences into account, it is not surprising

---

23   See UN International Human Development Indicators: http://hdrstats.undp.org/en/countries/profiles/ZAF.html

24   In fact, the Blacks are not a single 'ethnic group' in terms of Chapter 2. They are composed of different tribes and groups, including the Zulu, Xhosa, Ndebele, Pedi, Sotho and Swazi, as well as recent immigrants from other Sub-Saharan African countries.

Table 11.4   Characteristics of the socio-economic situation of the four ethnic groups in the Republic of South Africa (in %)

	Ethnic groups			
	Blacks (1977)	Mixed (580)	Indians (377)	Whites (580)
Highest education attained				
No formal qualification	34	32	16	3
Lowest formal qualification	6	8	5	3
Above lowest qualification	13	17	15	12
Higher secondary education completed	38	34	45	35
Above higher secondary level	5	5	8	17
University degree completed	4	5	11	31
Unemployed	36	30	18	8
Occupational Position				
Professionals, managers	16	20	39	57
Clerks, sales	30	30	30	27
Skilled and craft workers	17	23	14	13
Operators, elementary occupations	37	26	18	4
Works for government	13	13	9	19
Monthly earnings				
• 1000 ZAR*	42	29	15	6
• 10.000 ZAR	4	9	16	40
Type of community of residence**				
Urban, big city	41	84	100	96
Suburban, outskirt of big city	15	2	0	1
Country village	31	0	0	0
Farm or home in the country	13	14	0	4
Subjective social status***				
Low status (1–3)	37	12	26	2
Lower middle (4–5)	41	39	31	26
Higher middle (6–7)	18	39	39	44
High status (8–10)	4	10	28	29

*1 ZAR (South African Rand) = 0.10 US-$ (10.7.2013)
**Self-assessment
***Self-placement on a scale from 1 (bottom, lowest) to 10 (highest)
Source: International Social Survey Program (ISSP), Survey 2009 Inequality; South Africa.

that also social status self-placement differs fundamentally: three-quarters of the Blacks assign themselves to the lowest two categories; among the coloured population and Indians this proportion is a little bit more than half, among Whites it is only 28 per cent; in the three highest status groups, we find 28–29 per cent of Whites and Indians, but only 4 per cent of the Blacks and 10 per cent of the coloured population.

Let us now look at the determinants of income. Here, the question is if the income differences between the ethnic groups are only due to their different composition in terms of education and occupational position, or if Blacks are discriminated also on the basis of their ethnicity as such. A regression analysis of personal and family income was carried out which enables us to answer this question. In this analysis also other variables relevant for income have been included (gender, age, education, employment status and occupational position). Non-metric variables were entered as dummies (level of education, employment status, occupational position, ethnic group). We calculated separate regressions for individual earnings and for household income. In the first analysis, the overall effect of class-related variables is estimated (education, occupational position versus ethnic membership). The results can be summarized as follows (see Table 11.5):

Table 11.5   Linear regression analysis of earnings and incomes in the Republic of South Africa I. Basic effects of class variables and ethnic membership

Variables	Personal earnings Beta	Household income Beta
Gender	-.18**	-.04*
Age (centred)	.06*	.03
Education (reference group: no formal education)		
Lowest formal education	.01	.04*
Above lowest formal education	.09**	.11**
Higher secondary education	.21**	.25**
Above higher secondary education	.29**	.25**
University degree	.39**	.35**
Occupation (reference group: elementary occupation)		
Professionals, managers	.20**	.18**
Clerks, sales	.07*	.10**
Skilled, craft workers	-.03	-.03
Household size (number of persons)	-.02	.07**
Ethnic groups (reference group: Blacks, African)		
Indian, Asian	.13**	.22**
Whites	.19**	.25**
Mixed, coloured	.10**	.16**
Employment status (reference group: employed)		
Unemployed	X	-.24**
Student, retired etc.	X	-.13**
Observations	1.271	1.434
R² (adjusted)	.45	.52
S.D. of the estimate	.38	0.36

Significance: **p<0.01; *p<0.05

First, we can see that gender has a very strong effect on personal income: women earn much less than men; the same is true to a lesser degree for younger compared with older people. Household income is determined only weakly by gender; women live also in households with lower incomes than men. Then we can see that the two variables related to class position have a strong and significant effect: higher educated people and persons in higher-status occupations (managers, professionals, and clerks) earn more than the less educated and those in manual or unskilled jobs. Also family incomes are differentiated in this way. The unemployed have also lower incomes. Finally, ethnic group membership has significant and strong effects: all three non-Black groups earn more than the Blacks, with the Whites on top and the Indians on second place.

What about the interaction between class position and ethnic group membership? Such an interaction should turn out if our thesis about the formation of ethno-classes is correct. Table 11.6 shows that this is in fact the case. In order to estimate the interaction effects, dummies have been formed combining occupational position with ethnic group membership. If we take Black professionals as a reference group, we can see that all the three other ethnic groups of managers earn more than a Black manager; at the top are the White managers, followed by Indian and coloured managers. If we compare household incomes, the deprivation of the Blacks is even more pronounced: nearly all groups of Whites (except those in elementary occupations) have higher incomes than the family of a Black manager; the same is true for families of Indian clerks and craft workers, and of coloured clerks. If we take the income of a Black person in an elementary, unskilled job as a reference group, we see again that all other occupational-ethnic groups have higher incomes (the only exception is skilled coloured workers who do not earn less than a Black elementary worker). Thus, the

Table 11.6 Linear regression analysis of earnings and incomes in the Republic of South Africa I. Interaction effects between occupational status and ethnic membership

Variables	Personal earnings Beta	Household income Beta	Personal earnings Beta	Household income Beta
	A: Ethnicity and occupation (reference group: Black professionals, managers)		B: Ethnicity and occupation (reference group: Black elementary occupation)	
Black professionals, managers	X	X	.17**	.16**
Black clerks, sales	-.14**	-.13**	.07*	.07*
Black skilled, craft workers	-.21**	-.20**	-.03	-.03
Black elementary occupation	-.23**	-.22**	X	X
Indian professionals, managers	.05*	.11**	.17**	.23**
Indian clerks, sales	-.03	.05*	.07*	.15**
Indian skilled, craft workers	.00	.02	.08**	.10**
Indian elementary occupation	-.01	.02	.08**	.11**
White professionals, managers	.10**	.12**	.25**	.25**
White clerks, sales	.04	.12**	.13**	.22**
White skilled, craft workers	.04	.05*	.11**	.12**
White elementary occupation	.04	.02	.09**	.06*
Coloured professionals, managers	.05*	.06*	.16**	.17**
Coloured clerks, sales	-.00	.03	.11**	.15**
Coloured skilled, craft workers	-.09**	-.07*	.02	.05*
Coloured elementary occupation	-.07*	-.04	.05*	.09**
Observations	1.271	1.434	1.271	1.434
R² (adjusted)	.46	.53	.46	.53
S.D. of the estimate	0.38	0.35	0.38	0.35

Significance: **$p<0.01$; *$p<0.05$
Source: International Social Survey Programme (ISSP), Survey Inequality IV (2009).

answer to the second question posed before is unambiguous: in present-day South Africa, not only do the large income differences between the races persist, but there is also evidence that Blacks continue to suffer from ethnic-class discrimination. I think that we cannot say, as Terreblanche (2002: 399) writes, that the income distribution has shifted from a race-based to class-based structure. The trend is similar to that in the United States: the class character of inequalities has gained in strength (Terreblanche 2002: 29), but ethnic deprivation also persists.

Perceptions of Ethno-class Privilege and Discrimination

How do the people in the Republic of South Africa perceive these patterns of economic and social inequality in their country? Here, we can look at results from ISSP survey 2009 concerning the perceptions and attitudes toward inequality. We can clearly see that the objective patterns of extreme inequality are present in the minds of the individuals: 51 per cent of South Africans see society structured as an elite-mass society – a proportion which is far higher than the average of the other 37 countries around the world (see Table 6.1, pp. 164–5). The same applies to the item 'Race is important for getting ahead in life'; this statement is accepted by 50 per cent in South Africa, compared with only 16 per cent in all other countries (Table 6.2, p. 168; see also Table 8.1, p. 223). South Africans also more frequently perceive strong conflicts between the rich and the poor. It is somewhat surprising, in view of these facts, that the proportion of those who think that income differences are too large and that the government should reduce them is not particularly high. This finding might be seen both as a reflection of an individualistic ideology (maybe inherited from the UK) and (as in the case of Argentina and Chile) as an adaptation of norms and beliefs to the existing objective structure.

How do the members of the different ethnic groups perceive their situation? Some findings in this regard are presented in Table 11.2 (p. 293). Here, we see that people are well aware of the pervasive patterns of relative privilege and deprivation. Blacks ascribe social success much more frequently to factors such as coming from a wealthy family or knowing the right people and less to individual factors (hard work, ambition). The same is true for 'race', although White South Africans are more ready to recognize this as a significant aspect for advancement than White Americans. No great differences between ethnic groups emerge, however, in regard to the general perception of economic inequality and the role of government in its reduction. Evidently, in this regard also the Black and coloured South Africans have internalized an individualistic and liberalistic world-view which does not provide for a very active role of the state.

Some highly relevant facts and observations in this regard are reported in the comprehensive study by Sampie Terreblanche (2002: ff.) on historical and present-day South Africa. She finds an increasing gap between the well-to-do and the elites, including the Black and the poor masses. In her view, the socio-economic problems facing South Africa since the political transition are not only economic, but also problems of social recognition, racial prejudices and political inclusion. While the new members of the upper classes profit from mainstream economic activity, the mainly Black *Lumpenproletariat* is increasingly pauperized. In the old system, the majority of people were impoverished through systematic exploitation, in the new system this happens through social exclusion and neglect (Terreblanche 2002: 423ff.): 55 per cent of the Africans have no job in the formal sector; they are relegated to casual and contract labour. This *casualization of labour* is a fact evident throughout Sub-Saharan Africa. It can be seen as the analogy of the spread of precarious forms of employment in the advanced countries (Dörre et al. 2009). Behind the structural deprivation of the Blacks, however, are also unsympathetic attitudes of both White and Black elites toward the poor, which ultimately are based on racial and class differences deeply embedded in South African history. Thus, a fundamental change in the way in which South Africans view their fellow compatriots is a *sine qua non* for building a better South Africa. It is important that 'every South African – and especially White South Africans – should cleanse himself/herself of any residual racial class, and group prejudices' (Terreblanche 2002: 443).

We can summarize and conclude this section by saying that a clear and significant economic discrimination of Black people persists in post-Apartheid South Africa. Blacks earn less, even if we control for other important determinants of income, such as education and occupational position. In addition, we found a class-ethnicity interaction effect, meaning that Blacks earn less even if they occupy the same positions as the members of all other ethnic groups. The Whites appear as the most privileged group, followed by Indians and other Asians; the situation of coloured people may not be much better than that of the Blacks; they both are located at the lowest levels of the societal hierarchy.

Summary

In this chapter, I have investigated economic inequality in general and the situation of the Blacks, in particular in two former Apartheid societies, the United States and the Republic of South Africa. The segregation of the races in the US-South was clearly less exploitative than that in South Africa, but it also implied a discrimination of the Blacks in many regards. In a short historical retrospect it was shown that this system came into being as a reaction to the abolishment of slavery after the American Civil War. I argued that only such a retrospect enables us to understand the 'diversity paradox' in present-day America, the fact that most ethnic minorities and immigrants were able to integrate themselves into American society and to advance in the social ladder, but not the Blacks. Statistical data were presented which clearly confirmed this fact in terms of educational outcomes. Referring to relevant research, it was argued that it is particularly the concentration in urban ghettos which is responsible for the present-day discrimination of a significant sub-group of Blacks. Their situation in this regard is comparable to that of the American Natives, the Indians who are also strongly deprived. Intra-ethnic favouritism among the Whites, as well as a demoralization of the Blacks themselves, as a reaction to continuing racist attitudes also contributes to their deprivation. The persistent effects of slavery and Apartheid were shown, finally, in the fact that economic inequality is higher in the former US southern slave states than in the other US states. The persistent aftermaths of slavery and of Apartheid were then also shown in the case of South Africa. The abolishment of this system had significant impacts at the institutional and political level; however, in objective social-structural terms, many deprivations of the Blacks did persist. Using recent data it was shown that Blacks earn less even if they are in comparable positions with those of Whites. It was also shown that Blacks, but also the general population, are well aware of these inequalities and discriminations. In the next chapter, the experiences of racial segregation in the US and in South Africa shall be compared with those in a new ethno-national state, in Israel. At the end I will come back to the question of what we can learn for a full understanding of these forms of ethnic discrimination and segregation and for adequate ways out of them.

References

Adam, Heribert and Kogila Moodley (1977), *Südafrika ohne Apartheid?* Frankfurt/Main: Suhrkamp

Bilger, Harold (1976), *Südafrika in Geschichte und Gegenwart*, Konstanz: Universitätsverlag

Cauthen, Bruce (2000), 'The myth of divine election and Afrikaner ethnogenesis', in John Hutchinson and Anthony D. Smith, eds, *Nationalism. Critical Concepts in Political Science*, vol. III, London/New York: Routledge, pp. 1000–1024

Cornevin, Marianne (1980), *Apartheid: Power and Historical Falsification*, Paris: UNESCO

DiTomaso, Nancy (2013), *The American Non-Dilemma. Racial Inequality without Racism*, New York: Russel Sage Foundation

Dörre, Klaus, Stephan Lessenich and Hartmut Rosa (2009), *Soziologie – Kapitalismus – Kritik. Eine Debatte*, Frankfurt: Suhrkamp

Duve, Freimut (1965), *Kap ohne Hoffnung oder die Politik der Apartheid*, Reinbek: Rowohlt

Dvorin, Eugene P. (1951), 'The theory of Apartheid: Nationalist racial policy in the Union of South Africa', *The Western Political Quarterly* 4: 32–47

Fiske, Edward B. and Helen F. Ladd (2005), Racial equity in education: How far has South Africa gone? Terry Sanford Institute of Public Policy, Duke University, Working Paper SANO05-03

Fox, Cybelle et al. (2013), 'Immigration and redistributive social policy', in D. Card and S. Raphael, *Immigration, Poverty, and Socioeconomic Inequality*, New York: Russell Sage Foundation, pp. 381–420

Gans, Herbert (2005), 'Race as class', *Contexts* 4: 17–21

Gilliomee, Hermann and Lawrence Schlemmer, eds (1985), *Up Against the Fences. Poverty, Passes and Privilege in South Africa*, New York: St Martin's Press

Goldberg, David T. (2009), *The Threat of Race. Reflections on Racial Neoliberalism*, Malden, MA: Wiley-Blackwell

Hazlett, Thomas W. (2008), 'Apartheid', in *The Concise Encyclopedia of Economics*, Indianapolis: Liberty Fund

Hollinger, David A. (1995), *Postethnic America: Beyond Multiculturalism*, New York: Basic Books

Hout, Michael (1984), 'Occupational mobility of Black men: 1962 to 1972', *American Sociological Review* 49: 308–22

Illife, John (1997), *Geschichte Afrikas*, München: C.H. Beck (*Africans: The History of a Continent*, Cambridge University Press)

Kluegel, James R. and Eliot R. Smith (1986), *Beliefs About Inequality. Americans' Views of What Is and What Ought to Be*, New York: Aldine de Gruyter

Lee, Jennifer and Frank D. Bean (2010), *The Diversity Paradox. Immigration and the Color Line in Twenty-First Century America*, New York: Russel Sage Foundation

Louw, P. Eric (2004), *The Rise, Fall and Legacy of Apartheid*, New York: Praeger

Lowenberg, Anton D. (1984), Towards an Economic Theory of the Apartheid State, Phil. Dissertation, University of Natal, Durban, South Africa

Löwstedt, Anthony (2012), Apartheid. Ancient, Past and Present, Habilitation thesis, University of Vienna

Mamdani, Mahmood (1996), *Citizen and Subject. Contemporary Africa and the Legacy of Late Colonialism*, Princeton, NJ: Princeton University Press

Mann, Michael (2007), *Die dunkle Seite der Demokratie. Eine Theorie der ethnischen Säuberung*, Hamburg: Hamburger edition (*The Dark Side of Democracy*, New York 2005)

Massey, Douglas and Nancy Denton (1993), *American Apartheid: Segregation and the Making of the Underclass*, Cambridge, MA: Harvard University Press

Moon, Dannell (2004), 'Slavery', in Merril D. Smith, ed., *Encyclopedia of Rape*, Westport, CT: Greenwood Press, pp. 234–5

Mwijage, Jovitus F. Kamara (2004), *Major Events in African History*, Morogoro: Salvatorianum

Myrdal, Gunnar (1962 [1944]), *An American Dilemma. The Negro Problem and Modern Democracy*, New York: Harper & Row

Quillian, Lincoln (2003), 'How long are exposures to poor neighbourhoods? The long-term dynamics of entry and exit from poor neighborhoods', *Population Research and Policy Review* 22: 221–49

Reader, John (1998), *Africa. Biography of a Continent*, London: Penguin Books

Ruef, Martin and Ben Fletcher (2003), 'Legacies of slavery: Status attainment among Southern Blacks after emancipation', *Social Forces* 82: 445–80

Smith, Anthony D. (1992), 'Chosen Peoples: Why ethnic groups survive', *Ethnic and Racial Studies* 15(3): 436–56

Smith, Sandra S. (2007), *Lone Pursuit. Distrust and Defensive Individualism Among The Black Poor*, New York: Russel Sage Foundation

Solt, Frederick (2009), 'Standardizing World Income Inequality Database', *Social Science Quarterly* 90: 231–42

Stock Robert F. (2013), *Africa South of the Sahara. A geographical Interpretation*, New York: The Guilford Press

Sue, Stanley and Sumie Okazaki (1990), 'Asian-American educational achievements. A phenomenon in search of an explanation', *American Psychologist* 45: 913–20

Terreblanche, Sampie (2002), *A History of Inequality in South Africa, 1652–2002*, University of Natal Press, Pietermaritzburg

Thompson, Leonard (1985), *The Political Mythology of Apartheid*, New Haven, CT: Yale University Press

Tocqueville, Alexis de (1976 [1835]), *Über die Demokratie in Amerika*, München: dtv

Ungar, Sanford J. (1989), *Africa. The People and Politics of an Emerging Continent*, New York etc.: Simon & Schuster

Van den Berghe, Pierre L. (1970), 'Race, class, and ethnicity in South Africa', in Arthur Tuden and Leonard Ploticov, eds, *Social Stratification in Africa*, New York/London: Free Press/Collier-Macmillan, pp. 345–71

Van den Berghe, Pierre L. (1981), *The Ethnic Phenomenon*, New York etc.: Praeger

Verba, Sidney and Gary R. Orren (1985), *Equality in America. The View from the Top*, Cambridge, MA/ London: Harvard University Press

Waters, Mary C. and Karl Eschbach (1995), 'Immigration and Ethnic and Racial Inequality in the United States', *Annual Review of Sociology*, 21: 419–46 (reprinted in M. Cross, ed., *The Sociology of Race and Ethnicity I*, Cheltenham/Northampton, MA: E. Elgar)

Wilson, William J. (1978), *The Declining Significance of Race. Blacks and the Changing American Institutions*, Chicago/London: The University of Chicago Press

Wilson, William J. (1987), *The Truly Disadvantaged: The Inner City, the Underclass, and Public Policy*, Chicago, IL: The University of Chicago Press

Wilson, William J. (2011), 'The declining significance of race: Revisited & Revised', *Daedalus* 140: 55–69

World Development Report (2012), Washington: The World Bank

Chapter 12

Israel:
Surge of Inequality in a Young Ethno-nation

In this chapter, I will investigate the last of the three cases where a pattern of ethnic segregation and stratification has been established in modern times and persists still today. This case is Israel – a nation state which was established in 1948 on the explicit basis of ethnic criteria. If we look at socio-economic development, the comparatively young history of this state was a big success:[1] in 2012, Israel's per capita was 31,000 $ (PPP), 27th in the world; it had a diversified, open and competitive economy; it had experienced (with some interruptions) high economic growth since 1952; its population increased from 800,000 at the time of the foundation of the state in 1948 to nearly 8 million in 2012; and it also has a strong democracy with free press and elections. Yet, Israel is also a state which, since the Second World War, has been involved, more often than any other country around the world, in violent conflicts (including seven recognized wars) with its internal minorities and with its neighbour states; and it transgresses continuously internationally recognized human rights and has neglected several hundred UN resolutions to better treat its minorities and the populations of the occupied territories and (today) the autonomous Palestinian regions, the West Bank and Gaza.

The aim of this section cannot be to give an exhaustive overview on the highly complex situation as it exists in Israel/Palestine today. There are libraries of books written on this problem already, which is of global importance given the fact that the continuing tensions and violent conflicts between Israel, the Palestinians and the neighbouring Arab nations are seriously threatening peace in the Near East and beyond. The aim, however, is focused similarly as in all the other chapters of this book: I will present data on recent changes in patterns of socio-economic inequality; and I will show that these inequalities are closely related to the specific patterns of ethnic stratification as well as to the institutional characteristics of the State of Israel and the unclear status of the Palestinians under international law. In all these regards, the findings clearly confirm the general theses developed in Chapter 3 about the relevance of ethnic domination and stratification for patterns of income inequality. When presenting and discussing these facts in the case of Israel, I will try to follow scientific objectivity (Weber 1973) as far as possible. As far as my own position and values are concerned, I think that they correspond to that evident in the work of Adam and Moodley (2005: ix), and to the paradigm of the broad Israeli-Palestinian peace movement (see, for example, Avneri 2003).

The Astonishing Increase of Economic Inequality Since 1961

The data of the changes in the pattern of inequality in Israeli society over the last decades show a very significant change: between 1961 and 2009 we can observe a continuous and strong increase of inequality. In 1961, Israel had a Gini coefficient of 24 and was among the most equal countries of the world, comparable to Denmark, Sweden and Slovenia. From the late 1970s on, inequality began to increase continuously: in

---

1   For a summary see The State of Israel, Ministry of Finance, The Israeli Economy. Fundamentals, Characteristics and Historic Overview, Fall 2012 (available in Internet: http://www.financeisrael.mof.gov.il/FinanceIsrael/Docs/En/The_Israeli_Economy_2012.pdf); see also Klein 2005. Data on economic inequality in Israel are already reported in the SWIID dataset (Solt 2009) for 1961 and then for every year between 1975 and 2005. Since the values for 1961 and those for the mid-1970s are rather similar, we can assume that the single value for 1961 is a valid indicator of the earlier situation. This assumption is also corroborated by a short look at the changes in the political-economic constitution of Israel over this half century which will be presented below.

1980, the Gini was 30, in 1995, 33 and in 2005, it was 37 (see Figure 11.2, pp. 298–9). Thus, in recent times Israel belongs to a group of rather unequal countries, including, for instance, Russia, Portugal, Morocco, the United States and Cambodia. This increase of economic inequality was one of the most marked in any country around the world. Maybe the only comparable case was Russia – and in fact there are some similarities and connections between the USSR/Russia and Israel. In contrast to Israel, all comparable small countries in Europe were able to retain their moderate levels of economic inequality, including most East European countries which underwent the transition from State Socialism to market economies. In some countries (for example Australia, France, Tunisia and Turkey) inequality even dropped. That the inequality increase in Israel was exceptional is also evident in comparison to the other two cases analysed in this chapter, the United States and South Africa (see Figure 11.2). In the USA, inequality declined between 1960 and 1980, and then rose again, but not very steeply. In South Africa, where inequality in general has been extremely high for a long time, over the whole period a slight decrease is observable.

The results presented in Figure 11.2 are corroborated by other economic studies and data. A recent comprehensive OECD report on income inequality trends in the developed countries (2011) showed that in 2010 Israel was 30th among 34 OECD countries in regard to income inequality, outmatched only slightly by the USA, Turkey, Mexico and Chile. This study also showed that Israel was one of those countries in which household income increased since 1980.[2] The proportion of people in relative income poverty was highest in Israel among all 34 OECD countries and it had increased since 1995 more than in most others. According to the Bank of Israel, unemployment was at 24 per cent in 2012,[3] one of the highest rates around the world. The same institution also found an increase in economic inequality over the last 20 years.[4] The conclusion of the Adva Center in Tel Aviv in a study about socio-economic development from 1948 till 2011 seems quite to the point:

> Israel is a classic case of a country whose macro-economic indicators are good but most households are not invited to the end-of-year-celebration, because the country suffers of high poverty compared to other OECD-countries, high inequality, eroding social benefits and a minority business, political and professional class benefitting at the expense of Israeli workers.[5]

The high and rising income inequality is clearly perceived by the population: 54 per cent of Israelis strongly agree with the statement that income differences are too large and 45 per cent want the government to reduce them; both values are higher than the mean of the 24 countries compared (see Table 6.3, p. 169). In July–August 2011, hundreds of thousands from many diverse backgrounds took part in demonstrations against the decline of living standards, the deterioration of public services and government corruption; in these 'social justice protests' also rising poverty rates and the widening gap between the poor and rich played an important role.[6]

Causes and Concomitants of the Rise of Inequality

Why did this dramatic increase of inequality in Israel happen? I think that the framework developed in this book, focusing upon the interaction between ethnic differentiation and stratification, offers an excellent interpretation. Three factors must be mentioned here. The first and second relate to demographic changes – immigration and territorial expansion – the third to a change of the institutional set-up, and a correlated change of the class structure of Israeli society. Let us have a closer look at each of them.

---

2   See also the summary of results at http://www.oecd-library.org/social-issues-migration-health/the-causes-of-growing-inequalities-in-oecd-countries_9789264119536-en

3   See http://www.jta.org/2012/04/20/news-opinion/israel-middle-east/bank-of-israel-chief-inequality-poverty-are-key-long-term-challenges

4   See the report in the Israeli newspaper *Haaretz*, 28 March 2012, and Dahan (n.d.).

5   Quoted in Stephen Lendman, *Social and Economic Inequality in Israel*, http://sjlendman.blogspot.co.at/2011/07/social-and-economic-inequality-in.html; see also the *Adva* homepage at www.adva.org/

6   http://en.wikipedia.org/wiki/2011_Israeli_social_justice_protests

Table 12.1 Gross monthly income in Shekel (NIS) of employed men and women in Israel (2011)

	Men	Women	All
Jews born in Israel			
Father born in Israel	10,227	6,240	8,179
Father born in Europe-America	13,837	8,355	11,062
Father born in Asia-Africa	10,939	7,034	8,903
Born in Europe-America			
Immigrated up to 1989	8,924	13,804	11,506
Immigrated 1990 +	8,899	5,945	7,286
Born in Asia-Africa			
Immigrated up to 1989	6,330	10,819	8,805
Immigrated 1990 +	5,749	4,158	4,717
Arabs	5,894	4,711	5,538
Total	**9,976**	**6,600**	**8,325**

Source: Income Survey 2011 (Table 25) Israel Central Bureau of Statistics, Jerusalem/Tel Aviv (see www.cbs.gov.il/).

Immigration and its Side-effects on Economic Inequality, Public Opinion and Politics

In 1950, two years after its foundation, Israel had 1.37 million inhabitants; the census of 1961 showed 2.16 million inhabitants, 166,000 people were living in Jerusalem at this time. In these early decades, Israeli society was very distinct from that at the beginning of the 21st century. In 2005, Israel had about 7 million inhabitants,[7] that is, its population had more than doubled; Jerusalem increased to over 700,000 people. Two demographic processes were responsible for this massive population increase. The first was a large immigration. In the period 1961–91, between 10,000 and 60,000 persons immigrated each year to Israel, altogether about 850,000. In 1990 and 1991, the number jumped as a consequence of the break-down of the Soviet Union; in just these two years, about 375,000 persons immigrated from the Ukraine, Russia and Belorussia (Goldscheider 1996: 51ff.). Since then, the number has declined continuously to 21,000 in 2005.[8] Overall, about 1.3 million people had immigrated to Israel between 1961 and 2005.

The strong immigration to Israel and the integration of the immigrants was doubtless a big achievement given the fundamental aim of the new state to provide a home country for the Jews around the world (Eisenstadt 1992: 203ff.). Despite the big problems of integrating the newly arrived people, immigration certainly contributed to the economic growth and development of Israeli society. However, it also had negative side-effects, one concerning the increase of inequality, and another one related to the development of negative attitudes toward immigration and a strengthening of the political right in Israeli politics.

The effect of immigration on economic inequality is obvious. Immigration not only led to an increase of ethnic heterogeneity in terms of language, but also of socio-economic differentiation and inequality. One reason for this was the massive immigration from the former Soviet Union, as mentioned before (see also Al-Haj 1993). Although around 80,000 of the immigrants from the former Soviet Union were highly educated scientists and engineers (Karsh 2002: 182), but most were not highly educated. There were also problems in recognizing those with educational degrees. Very few of these immigrants, however, spoke Hebrew at the time of arrival. In addition, many of them settled down in (or were sent to) places where already other immigrants from Russia were concentrated. All these factors contributed to the fact that many of these immigrants may be seriously deprived in socio-economic terms still today.[9]

---

7   The census of 2000 reported 6.3 million, the 2010 census 7.6 million people.

8   Immigration to Israel: total immigration by year; reported at http://www.jewishvirtuallibrary.org/jsource/Immigration/Immigration_to_Israel.html

9   Haberfeldt et al. (2000) differentiated between immigrants from the European Republics of the former Soviet Union and those from the less developed Asian Republics and found that the latter were even more deprived in 1994.

Table 12.1 in fact shows that recently immigrated people earn much less than those born in Israel; particularly low is the income of those who immigrated since 1990 from Asia or Africa. The thesis that the recently immigrated are discriminated is confirmed also by data from the International Social Survey of 2009 on 'Inequality' (see Table 12.2). Here, we can see that the period of immigration correlates closely with subjective class placement and perceptions to inequality and social justice. Compared with Jews born in Israel or living longer in the country, those who immigrated only in 1990 or later (the majority of them coming from the former USSR) place themselves much more frequently into the lower or working class; three-quarters think that they earn less than they deserve. Also economic studies have shown that the more recent Jewish immigrants to Israel have been discriminated. They argue that the main mechanism through which this occurred was unemployment; this trend 'aggravated the erosion of the bargaining power of non-immigrant Israeli workers in low income deciles' (Ben-Bassat 2002: 494). Overall, Jewish Israelis had significantly higher incomes than non-Jews (Arabs and Druze Christians) throughout the period 1980 to 1996, controlling for other relevant factors, like gender, education and occupational position. However, not only immigrants but also native Israelis were negatively affected by immigration insofar as it led to an increase in unemployment and a depression of the lower wages. According to Kovel (2007: 105), the consequence of the large immigration of African and Asian Jews was that 'inferior states and associated racist treatment became their lot' and a solidification of 'a class structure of Ashkenazi overlords and Sephardi/Mizrahi (African Jews) proletarians' took place (see also Wild 2013: 73ff.). In addition, a considerable number of recent immigrants (9 per cent of the workforce) were non-Jewish foreign workers who have to face poor working conditions, low pay, unpaid overtime work and limited job security.[10]

It is surprising at first sight, however, that the new immigrants do not believe that economic inequality is too high in Israel and that the government should reduce income differences (see Table 12.2) They also see Israel less as an elite-mass model, and more as a pyramid. These findings can be clearly understood, however, when looking at the background of the Soviet society from which they came. This society in fact had a clear elite-mass structure, equality was high among the population at large, but chances to improve one's living standard by mobility were also low. So, the newly arrived post-Soviet immigrants do not criticize the competitive and stratified structure of Israel but complain only about their own discrimination. These findings only in part confirm the thesis that the pioneering spirit of the early immigrants has disappeared among the more recent immigrants (Eisenstadt 1992: 433).

Thus, as a consequence of immigration, ethnic differentiation and socio-economic inequality increased significantly in Israel. In this regard, also socio-cultural issues are relevant, such as that of language. Hebrew was institutionalized as the new national language of Israel and this has never been questioned by any Jewish group (Ben-Rafael 1994: 221). In this endeavour, the Zionists followed the example of nation-building in Europe with one significant difference: while in all European nations emerging in the 17th and 18th centuries the new national language was based on a living local language (usually that of the dominant ethnic group), Hebrew was not used as a living language anywhere in the world.[11] However, the continuity of the use of Hebrew by scribes and in worship encouraged the Zionists to establish it as the new state language (Bodmer 1989: 228). Today, Hebrew is generally used in schools, public communications and private life. However, several additional languages are relevant in present-day Israel and their spread and use is closely related to ethnic stratification (Ben-Rafael 1994: 223–31) Three aspects are relevant here.

The first is an aspect which I have shown also in the case of Sub-Saharan Africa (see Chapter 10, p. 269): It concerns English which has acquired the status of the most important second language in Israel, particularly among the well-educated middle and upper classes. These groups are also composed overproportionately of Ashkenazi Jews, originating from West and Central-East Europe (particularly France and Germany, and, recently from the UK and the USA). Table 12.1 shows that immigrants with fathers born in Europe or America get the highest incomes, even higher than persons born in Israel. The use of English has become 'a marker of the strongest strata of society' and it plays a significant role in the formation of the boundaries of the higher social classes and strata, 'expressing their cosmopolitan cultural orientations. The privileged class as a whole considers its allegiance to English an assertion of its social distinction on the basis of symbols valued by

10   OECD, Review of Labor Market and Social Policies: Israel, Paris 2010; see also OECD Outlook 2010.
11   On the role of language in nation building see Gardt 2000; Joseph 2004.

Table 12.2 Perceptions and attitudes concerning inequality among different groups in Israel (2009)

Questions/statements	Jewish Israelis			Arab Israelis	Worldwide ISSP-sample
	Born in Israel	Immigrated			
		pre-1989	post-1990		
	(623)	(240)	(173)	(145)	(53,000)*
	%	%	%	%	%
Respondent's subjective social class: lower or working class	20	28	36	12	35
I earn less/much less than I deserve	58	62	73	60	54
Differences in income are too large**	57	62	44	33	45
It is the responsibility of the government to reduce income differences***	49	47	39	29	32
Israeli society is structured according to …					
… an elite-mass model	18	18	28	12	27
… a pyramid	55	55	51	65	34

Source: ISSP-2009 'Inequality IV' (38 countries). *Rounded figure (variations due to different missing values); **Agree strongly; ***Agree/agree strongly.

society as a whole' (Ben-Rafael 1994: 230). Second, there are two languages whose dispersion is declining but which still are used by significant fractions of the population, Yiddish and Russian. Yiddish was mainly used by Ashkenazi Jews originating from Eastern Europe; in Israel, it was considered more as a marker of lower status.[12] Russian is still used by immigrants from the former Soviet Union; since this is no official language in Israel, it certainly will impede integration into Israeli society and career prospects to some degree.[13] However, since recently also many wealthy Russian businessmen (even non-Jews) immigrated to Israel not the least due to the manifold opportunities for investing money of dubious origin, Russian has gained in relevance and status (Kovel 2007: 107; see also Turner 1984: 128). Third, Arabic is an important language in Israel whose use is also connected with socio-economic inequality because of two reasons. One is that it has depreciated because it is the language of the Palestinians (Israeli Arabs) who are eager to retain their mother tongue (Lewin-Epstein and Semjonow 1994: 624); in higher education, Arab students are discriminated because entrance interviews and all university courses are in Hebrew.[14] Another reason is that Arab is still used by the Mizrahi Jews who emigrated from the North African and Middle East Muslim countries. Since the bulk of all these groups belongs to the lower and middle classes of Israeli society, their use of Arabic strengthens their lower class affiliation or ascription. This depreciating tendency could be offset by the fact that Arabic is the second official language of Israel. However, this does not happen because for the Jews Arabic is associated with their hostile neighbours. Thus, the privileged 'disregard Arabic – in contradiction to the declared attitude of the dominant culture' (Ben-Rafael 1994: 231).

The second effect of immigration was an increase of negative attitudes toward immigration among the Arabs in Israel and Palestine. Such attitudes did not exist in all periods of Palestine history. The earliest Jewish immigrants to Palestine in the late 19th/early 20th centuries (for detailed figures see Eisenstadt 1992: 168ff.) were not received in an unfriendly manner by the local Palestinian population; often they were even supported by them (Pappé 2011: 1). This attitude might have changed in the course of the 20th century, when it was no longer only single families or small groups of Jews arriving in Palestine, but instead large and organized groups. This was particularly the case from 1933 on when Jews were persecuted and murdered by the Nazis in Germany

---

12 Only in recent times, it regained some prestige as a consequence of efforts by ultra-Orthodox Jews (Ben-Rafael 1994: 231).

13 For the relevance of language as a factor of integration of immigrants see Esser 2006.

14 Yarden Skop in *Haaretz*, 19 June 2013.

and, after the outbreak of the Second World War, in East Europe. In this period, opposition to Jewish mass immigration awakened among Arabs which led to a British embargo on Jewish immigration and the sale of Palestinian land to Jewish people. It is quite probable that an increase of negative attitudes toward immigration has taken place also as a consequence of the massive immigration from the former USSR around 1990.

For the situation in recent times, we can look at findings from the International Social Survey Programme on 'National Identity' in 2003. Table 12.3 shows the attitudes toward immigration among Jewish and Arab Israelis, and compares both to the worldwide ISSP-sample. These attitudes are very polarized in Israel: Jewish Israelis have more positive attitudes toward immigration, and Arab Israelis much more negative ones than the people in all 33 countries around the world. The large majority of Israeli Arabs (about 85 per cent) believe that immigrants increase crime rates; that they take jobs away from people born in Israel; that government spends too much on immigrants; and that the number of immigrants should be reduced. In all these issues, there is a much less negative and restrictive stance around the world. Among Israelis, the reverse is true; most of them support immigration and see no negative effects. De facto, Israel has spent probably much more on immigrants than any other government around the world. However, it is quite remarkable that also 39 per cent of the Jews think that immigration to Israel should be reduced and 47 per cent believe that immigrants take jobs away from people born in Israel. Considering the high level of unemployment in Israel this assumption seems not unfounded.

Territorial Expansion and the Discrimination of the Arab Minority

Immigration and the increment of internal ethnic differentiation alone cannot explain the rise of inequality in Israel. A small country like Switzerland too has had strong immigration since the 1960s. Today, about one-quarter of the Swiss population are foreigners, and maybe more than one-third are foreign-born; most of them were speaking different languages and many belong also to religions (such as the Orthodox Christians from former Yugoslavia and the Muslims from Turkey) different from the Swiss majority. Yet, Switzerland was able to retain a moderate level of economic inequality over the last decades; in fact, it had a Gini of 31 in 1980–81, and 30 in 2006–09.

I would like to argue here that a second factor contributing to the increase of economic inequality was due to the expansion of the Israeli territory as a result of several wars, and of the higher fertility of the Arab population. Particularly after the Six-Day War of 1967, when Israeli occupied East Jerusalem, the West Bank and the Gaza Strip, the proportion of the Arab (Muslim) population increased, although the Arabs living in the newly captured territories did not become Israeli citizens (the West Bank and Gaza Strip got the status of occupied territories for about 40 years). Many of the residents in these areas fled before the Israeli invasion; today, the number of Palestinian refugees in camps in Gaza, the West Bank and Arab States is over four million (Löwstedt 2012: 118). Over the whole period, however, the proportion of Arab population within the territory of the State of Israel doubled from about 8 per cent to 16 per cent and that of Jews declined correspondingly from about 88 per cent to 76 per cent in 2005. Also the Christian (Druze) population increased more, but it

Table 12.3   **Attitudes of Jewish and Arab Israelis toward immigration (2003)**

Questions/statement	Jewish Israelis (1.066)	Arab Israelis (152)	Worldwide ISSP-sample (43.009)[*]
	% agree strongly/agree		
Immigrants increase crime rates	45	86	50
Immigrants are generally good for [Israel's] economy	52	28	38
Immigrants take jobs away from people born in [Israel]	47	86	42
Government spends too much assisting immigrants	33	84	47
The number of immigrants coming to [Israel] should be reduced	39	83	56

Source: ISSP-2003 'National Identity' (33 countries).
[*]Rounded figure (small variations due to varying missing values).

is still a small minority (less than 2 per cent).[15] The territorial expansion of Israel led to a general increase of inequality since the lower, disadvantaged groups increased disproportionately. But also the ultra-Orthodox Jewish population groups are disadvantaged economically, for similar reasons as the Israeli Arabs, because of their high birth rates and low rates of labour force participation,[16] and because of indirect discrimination due to the fact that they refuse military service.

These changes in the composition of the population have been of great concern also for political leaders in Israel. The Arabs were often seen and treated by the Jews in a patronizing and dismissive way, not the least because most of them were only small farmers and shop keepers. The new state recognized them, but had also an attitude of distrust (seeing them as a 'fourth column' of the Arabs) and ignorance and blindness in regard to their problems (Eisenstadt 1992: 485ff.; Peleg 2004). Government coalitions with Arab political parties are nearly impossible because an Arab member of the government would not be accepted (Gorenberg 2012: 186). Recently, the increase of the Arab (and Muslim) population in Israel is more and more seen as a big problem – as demographic shifts are always considered as highly important by chauvinist and militant ethnic and national leaders[17] (see also Wild 2013: 94ff.). Flanked by statements of right-wing Jewish intellectuals who saw a 'time bomb' at work in the higher increase of the Arab population, Prime Minister Benjamin Netanjahu, a hard-line Likud politician, adopted this term in 2003. He argued that a proportion of more than the present 20 per cent of Arabs would threaten the Jewish majority of Israel. The massive influx of new immigrants from the former Soviet Union was therefore welcomed by right-wing politicians (Goldscheider 1996: 5–21). In fact, the Russian immigrants and the ultra-Orthodox and the Mizrahi Jews became the main supporters of the right-wing constituency in Israel. Particularly the *Charedim*, the community of the ultra-Orthodox Jews, who now number nearly half a million, have won strategic influence in Israeli politics because they are the main supporters of and actors in the illegal settlements in the West Bank (Gorenberg 2012: 179ff.). Cathrine Thoreifson argues, based on an ethnographic study, in full accord with the central argument of this book, that the interplay between ethnicity, class and Israel's space policy was decisive for this move of Israeli politics toward the right in 1977, when Labour lost and Likud won the elections for the first time.[18] The Jewish and Israeli identity of the Russian and Mizrahi Jews was often questioned. It was felt that the Arab Jews had to be re-nationalized and 'zionized'; 'they continue to occupy an ambivalent, even anxious status in Israel' and they constitute a 'necessary' but significantly poorer and less powerful minority (Goldberg 2009: 177). The more recently arrived Jews were settled down particularly in the border towns to Gaza and the Lebanon which were frequently attacked by Palestinian-fired rockets. This exposed situation, particularly in wartime, offered a possibility to these Jews to move from the margins to the centre of the national frontier; a typical statement they used to describe their situation was: 'We have learned to live with conflict; we have grown strong'. Thus, their socio-economic deprivation was countered to some degree by an enhanced feeling of national strength.

The Arab population in Israel can be called a co-opted ethnic group, comparable to the coloured persons and Indians in South Africa (Adam and Moodley 2005: 23). They enjoy most (but not all) of the basic social and political rights but remain disadvantaged in socio-economic terms. This is clear from statistical data collected regularly by the Israeli Central Bureau of Statistics. Okun and Friedlander (2005) have shown that the educational disadvantages of Arabs have narrowed in the lower levels of schooling but have increased at higher levels.[19] Recent data from the Labor Force Survey 2011 show that significant lower proportions of non-Jews (most of them Muslim Arabs) are employed, and when employed, occupy less qualified occupations (see Table 12.4). Although the number of households with an employed person is similar among all groups (78 per cent), the proportion of employed persons is only about 19 per cent among non-Jewish households (among Arabs only 14 per cent), while it is 39 per cent among the Jewish households.[20] The divergence between these

---

15   http://en.wikipedia.org/wiki/Israeli_Jews
16   Reported in the study of the Bank of Israeli; see Footnote 3 before, and Gorenberg 2012.
17   See 'Perceived Arab demographic threat' at http://en.wikipedia.org/wiki/Israeli_Jews
18   'Israel's internal frontier: The enduring power of ethno-nationalism', Swiss Federal Institute of Technology, Zurich (see http://www.isn.ethz.ch/Digital-Library/articles/Detail/?id=168103).
19   An extended summary of all aspects of the situation of the Arabs and other minorities is presented in Goldscheider 1996; a more recent analysis is given in Peleg 2011.
20   This fact is certainly also connected to the more negative attitude toward female employment among the Muslims.

Table 12.4   Employment and occupational structure of Jews and non-Jews in Israel (2011)

	Jews	Non-Jews	Total
(a) Households by labour force participation			
Total households (in 1,000)	(1,830.5)	(373.6)	(2,204.1)
Household with	%	%	%
... employed persons	76.8	78.2 (76.7)*	77.0
... unemployed persons	38.9	19.4 (14.3)*	35.2
(b) Employed persons by occupational groups			
(Total in 1,000)	(2,553.8)	(470.9)	(3,024,7)
Academic professionals	15.7	9.3	14.7
Other professionals and technicians	16.5	11.2	15.7
Managers	7.9	1.8	7.0
(Sub-total)	(40.1)	(22.3)	(37.4)
Clerical workers	17.2	8.0	15.7
Sales and service workers	20.7	17.7	20.2
(Sub-total)	(37.9)	(25.7)	(35.9)
Skilled workers	13.5	37.1	17.2
Unskilled workers	6.2	13.3	7.3
(Sub-total)	(19.7)	(50.4)	(24.5)
Total	**97.7**"	**98.4**"	**97.8**"

*Values for Arabs alone; **Missing values: Occupation unknown
Source: Labour Force Survey 2011, Tables 1.6 and 2.27; Central Bureau of Statistics, Israel (www.cbs.gov.il).

two proportions can be explained by the fact that the non-Jewish households have more children; however, even the household heads often only get salaries inadequate for escaping poverty; thus as many family members as possible must try to contribute to household income.[21] The occupational distribution shows large differences: 40 per cent of the Jews work in highly skilled and managerial occupations (professions, technicians, managers), but only 22 per cent of the non-Jews; on the other side, 19.7 per cent of Jews, but 50.4 per cent of the non-Jews work in manual, skilled or unskilled work in trade and industry, construction and agriculture. A similar discrimination of the Arabs in Israel emerges in terms of income (see Table 12.1). Their income is only 66 per cent (5,538 NIS) of the overall income (8,325 NIS about 1,748 € in 2013); it corresponds to that of Jewish women who immigrated since 1990.

Israel was among the first members of the International Social Survey Programme (ISSP) which allows us to investigate again the effects of ethnicity on income. The Israeli dataset of 2003 (National Identity) distinguished two categories: Jewish and Arab Israelis. It is possible, therefore, to investigate directly if Israeli Arabs, controlling for all other relevant variables, are also disadvantaged in terms of income chances, although the sub-group of Arab Israelis was not large (n=152) and probably not representative.[22] We control for the following relecant variables: socio-demographic age and gender; educational level; occupational position (here, we combine the ISCO categories into five large groupings which are ordered roughly from higher to lower groups; these are entered as dummies into the regression analysis); employment status; and household size. The findings for both individual earnings and household incomes are reported in Table 12.5 and Table 12.6.

All variables exert significant effects on income in the expected direction: women earn less than men – an effect which of course is much stronger on individual earnings than on household incomes; older people earn more; income increases strongly with the level of education; persons in professional and managerial jobs earn

21   S. Lenman, 'Social and economic inequality in Israel' (http://rense.com/general94/soc.htm).
22   The Arabs in the higher social strata were over-represented in the Arab sub-sample. In terms of education, the Jewish Israelis only somewhat more frequently held a university degree (28 per cent vs. 15 per cent), but in the lower levels, the education of the Arab Israelis was not any worse. In terms of occupational positions and income, the differences were not large.

Table 12.5 Linear regression analysis of personal earnings and household incomes in Israel: basic effects of socio-demographic and class variables and of ethnic group membership

Independent variables	Personal earnings	Household income
Socio-demographic characteristics	**Beta**	**Beta**
Gender	-.33**	-.10*
Age (centr.)	.08*	.05
Education (Reference group: no formal education)		
Lowest formal education	.04	.08
Above lowest formal education	.23*	.24*
Secondary education	.30*	.38**
Above secondary education	.26*	.31**
University degree	.37*	.44**
Occupational group (Reference group: operators and unskilled occupations)		
Professionals and managers	.35**	.22**
Clerks and sales	.08	.00
Skilled and craft workers	.05	.01
Employment Status (Reference group: employed)		
Unemployed	X	-.14**
Student, retired etc.	X	-.12*
Household size (number of persons)	-.00	.14**
Ethnic group (0 = Jews, 1 = Arabs)	-.08*	-.07*
Observations	727	981
R² (adjusted)	.23	.19
S.D. of the estimate	2898,111	4167,97

Statistical significance: **p<0.01; *p<0.05

Table 12.6 Linear regression analysis of personal earnings and household incomes in Israel: interaction effects of occupational status and ethnic group

Occupational and ethnic groups	Personal earnings	Household income	Personal earnings	Household income
	Beta			
	Reference group: Jewish professionals and managers		*Reference group: Jewish operators and unskilled workers*	
Jewish professionals, managers	X	X	.33**	.38**
Jewish clerks, sales	-.31**	-.27**	-.05	.04
Jewish skilled, craft workers	-.11*	-.16**	-.07	.05
Jewish elementary occupation	-.21**	-.23**	X	X
Arab professionals and managers	-.09*	-.14**	.03	.00
Arab clerks and sales	-.15**	-.10*	-.02	.04
Arab skilled and craft workers	-.12*	-.10*	-.01	.02
Arab operators and unskilled workers	-.06	-.07*	.04	.03
Observations	668	804	668	804
R² (adjusted)	.11	.10	.11	.10
S.D. of the estimate	3107,12	4475,31	3107,12	4475,31

Statistical significance: **p<0.01; *p<0.05

significantly more than all other groups; the unemployed and students have smaller incomes; and household income increases with rising number of household members. Ethnic membership also exerts a significant effect, although it is not strong: Arab Israelis earn less than Jews.

What about the income opportunities of Arab Israelis compared with Jewish Israelis if we control for all other variables? Here, we can also see a significant difference: if we take Arab professionals and managers as the group of comparison, all other groups of Jews earn less (which was to be expected); but also Arab professionals and managers earn significantly less than Jewish Israelis in the same occupational positions. If we take Jews in the lowest occupational groups as a comparison group, the disadvantage of the Arabs is clearer: only Arabs in professional and managerial jobs earn more than Jews in unskilled work; all other groups of Arabs do not earn more. Thus, we have here a statistical proof of the thesis that 'Jews of North African and Middle Eastern origin, who were, and still are, found in large members in the lowest echelons of Israeli society, found that an even lower class had come into existence. Certain occupations acquired the nickname "Arab jobs", referring to the manual jobs rejected by Jews' (Cohen-Almagor 2002: 127). Even employers said of some jobs that they 'were not suitable for Jews but were only appropriate for Arabs' (Ibidem).

Evidence for a discrimination of Arab Israelis can also be found in the allocation of public spending. State budgets are a mirror of the social forces in a society and political community (Goldscheid and Schumpeter 1976; see also Peleg 2004: 421–5). How are the expenses of the State of Israel allocated to Jews and Arabs?[23] Since Israelis and Arabs settle predominately in different areas, towns and city districts, discrimination through state expenditures is often, albeit indirect, connected with differential places. Discriminations faced by the Arab Israelis in this regard include: less funding for Arab schools (for each Jewish student, 1.100 $ are spent per year, for each Arab student 192 $); fewer loans and grants for the Arab households, due also to the fact that the size of the loans is connected to the length of army service and most Arabs do not serve; much lower expenses for urban road building and transport for the Arab regions and towns than for Jewish ones; smaller expenses (just 13 per cent) for Palestinian areas in the budget for house construction (2008); this is also related to the discrimination of the Arabs in the ownership of land (they own merely 3.5 per cent of the state land); less spending for social welfare (fewer social workers per 1,000 inhabitants in Arab than in Jewish settlements);[24] provision of most of the welfare support for the Arab Israeli population (which has a much higher rate of poverty) is only by local, community-based philanthropic organizations; a much smaller proportion of Arabs (just 5 per cent) are employed in the Israeli Civil Service (while 20 per cent of the total population are Arabs).[25] One important reason for the discrimination of Arabs in the working world and in public expenditures is certainly the fact that Arab and Israeli workers are not united in common interest organizations. In accordance with the thesis proposed in Chapter 1 (pp. 62, 65), rather the reverse is true: Jewish workers often opposed the employment of Arab workers in certain firms and sectors (Eisenstadt 1992: 358). Those Arabs, however, who were able to enter the public sector are able to attain higher jobs and earnings (Lewin-Epstein and Semjonov 1994).

A careful quantitative analysis about labour market discrimination and income inequality in Israeli society found a clear hierarchy in the stratification system with Ashkenazim (Jews from Europa and America) at the top of the socio-economic ladder, Mizrahim (Jews from Asia and Africa) in the middle and Arab citizens at the bottom echelons of the hierarchy (Cohen and Haberfeld 2003). Only for Arab workers did labour market discrimination increase between 1975 and 2001.

A Fundamental Change of the Economic-political System and the Rise of a Tight Elite Network

The third significant change in the young history of Israel concerned its political-economic constitution. At the time of the foundation of the State of Israel, Socialist ideas had played a significant role. Moses

---

23   The Adva Center in Tel Aviv regularly publishes relevant reports. See, for instance, Shlomo Swirski and Yaron Yecheskel, *How the 2000 Israel State Budget Affects Arab Citizens*, December 1999 (www.adva.org). See also Shazia Arshad, *The Impoverishment of Palestinian Arabs in Israel, Middle East Monitor* (MEM), March 2011 (website: www.monitor.org.uk).

24   Shlomo Swirski and Yaron Yecheskel, *How the 2000 Israel State Budget Affects Arab Citizens* (see footnote 23 above).

25   Shlomo Swirski and Yaron Yecheskel, *How the 2000 Israel State Budget Affects Arab Citizens*, and Shazia Arshad, *The impoverishment of Palestinian Arabs in Israel* (see Footnote 23 above).

Hess, the Socialist German-Jewish philosopher and writer, in his 1862 published book *Rome and Jerusalem*, had designed quite a different project for a new Jewish state than that foreseen in the nationalist plan of Theodor Herzl. In his view, the new Jewish state had to be built from the bottom up by cooperative rural communities and urban workers (see also Eisenstadt 1992: 143). Labour Zionism, building on these ideas, was very influential among the founders and first leaders of the new state (such as Ben Gurion, Golda Meir, Shimon Peres and others) until 1977, when the left lost its parliamentary majority. The Kibbutzim, agricultural cooperatives based on Socialist principles, were an invention admired among leftist students and intellectuals in the West in the 1960s and 1970s. In the first decade of the existence of Israel, massive state investments were also preponderant, made possible also because of large reparation payments from Germany. Another important characteristic akin to Socialism is that the bulk of Israeli land (93 per cent) is owned by the state – a situation totally unknown among any other modern state. A basic law of 1960 determines that stated-owned land must always remain property of the state; it is only leased to the farmers and users.[26] Until 2000, land was not leased to Arab Israeli citizens, a regulation which was cancelled by a decision of the Supreme Court as discriminatory.[27] According to Yakir Plessner (1994), Israel's economy in the first decades was the most strongly socialized of any free country; he argues that this was the main reason why the country slipped into great economic problems in the late 1970s and 1980s. The economist Momi Dahan sees an ebbing of the old Socialist values and a 'process of atomization' of Israeli society since then:

> In the 1980s, values such as cooperation, mutual assurance, and economic egalitarianism did not always pass the test in leading institutions, such as kibbutzim, moshavim [the cooperative settlement movement], and the Histadrut [the Jewish trade union]. The erosion of these values seems to have 'rewritten' rules that formerly imposed wage restraint. In the absence of these rules, executives at the top of the pyramid were able to secure mammoth salaries (quoted in Ben-Bassat 2002: 498).

The early Socialist heritage of Israel may have been idealized and overstated for reasons of legitimating the young state (Sternhell 1998). Moreover, it was narrow-minded in ethnic terms; from the late 19th century on, 'two separate worlds took shape in Palestine, with very different visions of labor'; the local Palestinians were excluded from the egalitarian world of the Jewish settlers. The former were even discriminated and exploited the latter, for instance, by denying local sheep herds the use of common pasturelands and by lending money to the peasants only at high interest rates (Kovel 2007: 51). Later on, however, the egalitarian impetus faded away also from the Jewish community proper. The Kibbutzim themselves changed (Goldscheider 1996: 103–26). Today, there are still 270 Kibbutzims, producing 40 per cent of agricultural output of Israel,[28] but their organization is much less 'Socialist' than it was in earlier times. An official text summarizes all these changes in a succinct way:

> Israel's economy had changed drastically over the decades. In its roots, the Jewish national movement and the first pioneer communities were mainly socialist. Since then, the Israeli economy had become a liberalized and open economy, with strong tenants of capitalism while keeping some aspects of social welfare. Major privatizations had been executed since the 1980's, a trend that expanded during the 1990s.[29]

In fact, overall government expenditure as percentage of GDP decreased from 56 per cent in 1988 to 42 per cent in 2010[30] (see also Klein 2005). In 2010, Israel was accepted as a member of OECD which included 31 of the most developed countries with a free market society and democratic political systems. The OECD praised Israel's scientific and technological proposes, but has also called Israel to improve levels of education and

---

26 To be more precise: the state itself owns only 75 per cent, the rest is owned by the Jewish National Fund (a non-profit, worldwide organization) and by the Development Authority.

27 See 'Israel Lands-Privatization or National Ownership?' (2013) (see www.jewishvirtuallibrary.org/).

28 See http://en.wikipedia.org/wiki/Kibbutz

29 State of Israel, Ministry of Finance, The Israeli Economy. Fundamentals, Characteristics and Historic Overview, Fall 2012.

30 Ibidem. See also the Israel Economy. Footnote 1 above.

to reduce poverty and inequality, particularly among its ultra-Orthodox Jewish and the Arab communities.[31] Thus, Israel's recent history presents also a highly interest case for studying the effects of Socialism on equality and growth. The cases of Russia and China have already been discussed in Chapter 7; comparable cases in Africa are discussed in Chapters 10 and 13.

The increase of economic inequality in Israel over the last decades as shown before was connected closely with the emergence of a new tightly knit, privileged power elite and upper class. In fact, this upper class might be one of the most paradigmatic examples of a homogeneous elite in an ethnically heterogeneous society, as mentioned in Chapter 3. Corresponding to Hypothesis 3 (p. 66), it was able to increase its share of the national income significantly in the last decades. In his careful analysis of the components and determinants of changes in income distribution between 1965 and 1997, Momi Dahan (n.d.) reports two relevant findings. First, the returns to higher education increased more strongly than overall income and this was parallel with an increase of the proportion of higher educated people; second, managers profited from a dramatic increase in real wages. Data of the Ministry of Finance show that the income share of the top percentile of the national income increased from 10 per cent in 2005 to 14.1 per cent in 2010. This was a share considerably higher than in most West European countries and Japan (in most of them, it is below 10 per cent); it was similar to Great Britain and not far below Argentina and the USA (with 17 per cent).[32] Stanley Fisher, the governor of the Bank of Israel in 2010, warned in a public speech that the high concentration of bank capital might constitute a 'systemic risk' for the financial system. According to the Annual Report of the Bank of Israel, the richest 20 families control 25 per cent of the listed companies and own 50 per cent of the total market share in the Tel Aviv Stock Exchange.[33] Also the sociologist Shmuel Eisenstadt (1992: 297ff.) recognized tendencies toward power concentration and the emergence of a new oligarchy since 1977. According to Cohen and Sussex (2000), a winner-take-all strategy has become more and more dominant. Some authors argue that the right-wing shift in Israeli politics and the increasing racism are not mainly due to the Russian immigrants but that it was the strategy of the rich to defend their privileges which evoked resistance and violence.[34] Corresponding to these diagnoses, Daniel Maman (1997) has shown that economic policy forum networks are particularly tight in Israel and he indicates also some of the reasons why this is so. Comparable to other Western countries, state organizations, big business and other interest group organizations are the main actors in these networks. In Israel, however, the state is the most important actor for three reasons: first, state organizations are generally more involved in the management of the economy; second, the Israeli state possesses a vast array of resources, some of the most important of them coming from foreign aid and donors; and third, 'the burden of maintaining a democratic society in the face of continuous military conflict and periodic waves of immigration has led to an unusual concentration of power in the state' (Maman 1997: 271).

A central aspect of the elite network in Israel is the overwhelming importance of the issues of security and defence (Ben-Eliezer 1998; Tyler 2012). An extremely high proportion of state expenditures are going into the military sector. Israel is in 17th place among all states of the world in regard to its absolute level of military and defence expenditures and among the top group in regard to their relative size; military expenditures constituted over 6 per cent of the GDP in 2012.[35] The USA spent 4.4 per cent, France and the UK between 2 per cent and 3 per cent, and most other European countries less than 2 per cent of their GNP for military purposes. Now, it is of utmost importance that a large proportion of these expenditures in Israel are based on external sources. Before 1967, there were two important sources of such support: the large and continuous transfers of liquid capital from the world Jewry through private donations and *Independence Bonds*, and West German reparation payments to the victims and families persecuted by the Nazis, most of which were channelled through the state (Barnett 2008: 549). Later on, an important new external provider of massive financial support emerged,

---

31   *BBC News*, 10 May 2010.

32   Shlomo Swriski and Etty Konor-Attias, Workers, Employers and the National Distribution of Israel's Income, Annual Report of the Adva Center, Tel Aviv 2012.

33   Bloomberg Businessweek Magazine, 7 October 2010; see http://www.businessweek.com/magazine/content/10_42/b4199010761878.htm

34   Gabriel Ash in: *Mondoweis*, 22 November 2010, http://mondoweis.net/

35   According to the data of the Stockholm International Peace Research Institute (SIPRI), reported in http://en.wikipedia.org/wiki/List_of_countries_by_military_expenditures

the United States. A catalyst was the Yom Kippur War of 1973 which was a shock for Israel after the initial lost battles. This event caused a dramatic change in Israel's financial strategy, namely to abandon its concern for independence and to rely increasingly on foreign sources. This change was also due to increasing internal opposition against the high military expenses and taxation. In addition, the French embargo on the export of weapons to Israel reinforced the belief that Israel should develop its own arms industry; the maturation of the economy and of advanced industrial sectors (electronics, chemicals and engineering) made large-scale arms production possible. Supporting political measures included economic decentralization and market liberalization. Today, Israel is among the top exporters of weapons around the world.[36] Private weapon manufacturers proudly advertise that they produce the most efficient weapons, for instance, assault rifles,[37] or war- and occupation-related machinery, such as a highly efficient, unmanned robot bulldozer (also called the 'satanic Killdozer')[38] (see also Ben-Eliezer 1998). Israel is known to be one of the fame nuclear-armed countries not recognized by the Nuclear Non-Proliferation Treaty (NPT); Israel has not signed this treaty.[39] The historian Ilan Pappé (2011: 264ff.) calls Israel a 'state of oppression' and compares it to the Arab *Mukhabarat* state which is 'a state run by an all-pervasive bureaucracy and ruled by a military and security apparatus'.

Oren Barak and Gabriel Sheffer (2007) have scrutinized the civil-military relations in Israel; they conclude that in this country a 'Security Network' came into existence which has no parallel in other democratic societies; military values penetrate and influence most civilian spheres. For David T. Goldberg (2009: 137), 'Israel is not so much a state that has a military; rather, it is a leading example of a militarily fuelled society that codifies and mobilizes a state in its image'. The reason is the incomplete process of state formation (particularly the undefined borders) and the real and imagined existential threats from Palestinians and supposed hostile Arab neighbour countries. Particularly the Likud leaders since 1977 play on the Jewish self-image of vulnerability which reflects itself in a 'paranoid tone', exploiting not only Israel's fears for survival but also Sephardi resentment of Ashkenazim Jews (Elizur 2002). The consequences are serious democratic deficits, including only

> ... nominal separation between its national-security realm and its cultural political, social and economic spheres and a high level of stress in Israeli society. What has emerged is, in effect a tightly knit policy network characterized by intimate ties between acting of retired security officials – including officers who serve in the army's reserves, politicians on the national and local levels, civilian bureaucrats, private entrepreneurs and journalists (Barak and Sheffer 2007: 16; see also Sheffer and Barak 2013).

Within the military, the status distinctions between the different Jewish groups in Israeli society are clearly reflected: the highest ranks are occupied by Ashkanazi, the Jews from other regions predominate in the lower ranks (Gorenberg 2012: 140–141).

According to Patrick Tyler (2012) the military elite has not only dominated in wartime, but has at times also overpowered Israeli's democracy. As a consequence, Israelis are missing opportunities to make peace even when it would be possible to do so. A further indication of this is the preponderance of retired military officers in the political life of Israel which is evident also in the careers of the twelve prime ministers since 1948. No less than half of them had been former military leaders and five of them even led terrorist organizations.[40] Sub-Saharan Africa might be the only other world-region where a similar high proportion of political leaders formerly were military men (see Chapter 10, p. 273). This fact also proves the thesis that 'Israel's political society has turned into a lodestone for retired security officials' (Barak and Sheffer 2007: 5).

---

36   SIPRI Institute Stockholm: http://www.sipri.org/yearbook/2013/05
37   See, for instance, the homepage of IWI (Israel Weapon Industries).
38   See http://www.theregister.co.uk/2009/03/31/idf_robot_d9_revelations/
39   This fact was disclosed, among others, by a former Israeli nuclear technician. See 'Revealed: The Secrets of Israel's Nuclear Arsenal', *Sunday Times*, 5 October 1986. See also https//en.wikipedia.org/Nuclear_weapons_and_Israel
40   Menachem Begin and Yitzhak Schamir were leaders of the terrorist organization Irgun from the 1940s until the mid-1950s (see also Hart 1984: 53–4); Ariel Sharon was accused of war crimes by Israel's own justice system for massacres in 1982; Ehud Barak was leader of secret forces which operated in a terroristic way in foreign countries after the massacre at the Munich Olympic Games 1972. See also Carter 2010: 76ff.; Flapan 1988: 39ff.; Kovel 2007: 150ff.

In this regard, an issue of utmost importance is the financial dependence of Israel and its military expenditures on US aid. In a widely discussed book, John Mearsheimer and Stephen Walt (2007) show that US aid for Israel is by far larger than aid by the USA to any other country. Total aid until 2005 was $154 billion, today, it is around $3 billion each year in direct, and about $1.4 billion in indirect aid. This aid constitutes 2 per cent of Israel's GDP or $500 for each Israeli per year. This aid is given unconditionally as a lump sum; its use is not controlled by the US as it is done in all other forms of international aid. It is evident that Israel would have been incapable of sustaining its large army and carrying out so many wars without this massive support. It is surprising for the writer of this book that no author so far has designated Israel as a *rentier state* from this point of view. This concept is usually applied to those Arab states where incomes from oil constitute a large fraction of national income. However, in one of the first works on this topic it was argued that the effects of such a rentier income are not confined to the natural gifts (such as oil), but can also emerge out of massive foreign development or military assistance (Luciani 1990; Schwarz 2004: 14). I have discussed the characteristics of rentier states in Chapter 5, when considering briefly the stratification systems in Arab societies (p. 154) and in Chapter 10 when discussing Sub-Saharan African countries (p. 260; see also Ismael 1993; Yates 1996; Schwarz 2004). The US financial support certainly constitutes a much lower proportion of Israel's budget than does oil in the case of many Arab states. However, some side-effects may be at work also in Israel.

One significant side-effect of large external rents is that in the struggle for their distribution those who are sitting in powerful political positions will be privileged and illegitimate means become important. This might particularly be the case in Israel where the main donor (the USA) does not control the use of this support. In fact, Israel rates highest in 2013 among the OECD member states in its level of corruption, according to the Transparency International Global Corruption Barometer; this fact was reported widely in Israeli newspapers.[41] The high level of corruption and the emergence of a new kind of 'Casino Capitalism' (Kovel 2007: 107) is clearly perceived by Israel's population. The statement 'This country is run by a few big entities acting in their own best interest' was answered positively by 73 per cent of the respondents in a representative survey; only in Greece was the proportion a little bit higher, but it was lower even in corruption-ridden Italy; in Germany and France, about 55 per cent said so, in Switzerland only 19 per cent. Half of those interviewed believed that corruption had increased, and 81 per cent believed that it was a specific public sector problem; the political parties and religious bodies were the institutions seen by most frequently as corrupt; the universities (23 per cent) and the Israeli Defense Forces (IDF) were considered least as corrupt (by about 20 per cent).[42] These figures are confirmed by the fact that quite a number of top-level politicians, including former state presidents and prime ministers, have been accused of corrupt practices such as tax evasion, breach of trust, bribery and illegal bank accounts, and were subject to investigations or had to leave office after such accusations in the media.[43] Police Commissioner Yohanan Danino said at a Herzlyia Conference, Israel's centre stage for the articulation of national policy by its most prominent leaders,[44] that the major threats to Israeli society today are violence, particularly among teens, and corruption among public figures; in his view, organized crime has gone beyond the pale and became intertwined with government operations.[45] Problems related to violence include the proliferation of firearms, everyday violence in streets and behind the steering wheel and political-military violence against Palestinian terrorists and citizens (Medding 2002: 139).

---

41   See, for instance: 'Israel among most corrupt of OEDC countries', *The Jerusalem Post*, 9.7.2013; 'Government corrupt, run by narrow interests, Israelis say', *The Time of Israel*, 9.7.2013.

42   As far as IDF are concerned, the objectivity of public opinion might be questioned.

43   They include former Prime Ministers Benjamin Netanjahu, Ehud Olmert, Yitzhak Rabin, Ehud Barak and Ariel Sharon, as well as former presidents Ezer Weizman and Moshe Katsav; the latter was sentenced to seven years in prison in 2011, because of indecent acts, sexual harassment, rape and obstruction of justice. See 'A nation under investigation', *Newsweek Magazine*, 31.8.2009; 'Israel faces corruption "epidemic"', *BBC News* 24.9.207 (http://en.wikipedia.org/wiki/Moshe_Katsav)

44   http://en.wikipedia.org/wiki/Herzliya_Conference

45   Adiv Sterman, 'Israel beset by violence and corruption, says police chief'; *The Times of Israel*, 13.3.2013.

Palestine: a Residual State in Israeli Bondage

In the context of this chapter it is essential to have also a look at the Palestinian Territories which today are not part of the state of Israel any more but *de facto* continue to depend on Israel to an extremely strong degree. Israel had occupied (among other regions) East Jerusalem, the West Bank and the Gaza Strip in the Six-Days War of 1967. East Jerusalem was later declared (against international protests) an integral part of the state of Israel. The four-decades long occupation of these Palestinian territories by Israel was itself a situation highly problematic from the viewpoint of international law; Israeli governments preferred to call the West Bank 'disputed territories'.[46] The governors in these territories were Israeli military commanders and the Palestinians living there

> ... are actually cast as noncitizens of the Israeli state. They have been ruled for more than four decades by a power that denies their political rights and too often violates their basic human rights under the protest of an indefinite state of exception justified by Israel's 'belligerent occupation' that has become part of the framing and justifications of the annual renewal of a formal state of emergency (Ophir et al. 2009: 18).

According to these authors, one can speak here of 'submission without rights', of the normalization of a state of exception, even colonization and neglect of humanitarian concerns (see also Finkelstein 2007, Ben-Eliezer 2012).

The West Bank and the Gaza Strip gained some independence in 1993/94 when Israel recognized the PLO as the representative of the 'Palestinian people' and the Palestinian National Authority was established as a 'government'; in the early 2000s the United Nations granted Palestine observer status and UNESCO affiliated it as a member. Thus, Palestine is on the way to become its own state. Its autonomy and capacity to act are still extremely restricted, however, for three reasons: because the state administration is not really able to control and administrate its territory, given the interference of Israel; because of the extremely low level of revenues from the population, given their poverty; and, as a consequence, because of its dependence from foreign donors. It can also be called a 'shadow state' (Goldberg 2009: 131). The autonomy of the political authorities and of economy and society in Palestine is restricted massively in two forms by Israel: in the West Bank by the building and development of new Israeli settlements which are connected with special streets and highways with Jerusalem; these streets dismember the territory of the West Bank and constitute extreme handicaps for the Palestinian population through hundreds of road-blocks and about a dozen military check points (Ophir et al. 2009; Kaletsch 2010; Löwstedt 2012: 118; Wild 2013: 97ff.). Today, more than 300,000 Israeli Jews are living in the settlements spread over the West Bank, besides the 2.3 million Palestinians. The establishment of these settlements contradicts international law concerning occupied territories (Ophir et al. 2009: 47, Gorenberg 2012). The Gaza Strip from which Israel has withdrawn its occupying forces in 2005 is handicapped massively by a factual military encircling and isolation: all the border-lines, as well as the sea and air, are closely controlled and supervised by Israel. The UN and other international organizations, therefore, still consider Israel to be the occupying power in Gaza.[47] Here, in a territory of only 360 km^2, 1.7 million people are living under incredibly restricted circumstances – a higher population density than in many large world cities.[48] Most of the Palestinians living here have never been outside of this territory (Finkelstein 2007: 294).

The economic situation of these two main Palestinian territories reflects their territorial fragmentation and political dependence. Before looking at the present-day situation, one should also keep in mind that throughout the last decades, many people – particularly better educated and qualified – left these territories, particularly the Gaza Strip. In this way, they caused a significant brain drain (Abu-Shokor 1995) which bereft Palestine of its political leadership (Peretz 1977; see also Pappé 2011). Table 12.7 shows some basic indicators for Palestine as a whole, comparing it with Israel and with the neighbour states Lebanon, Jordan and Egypt. The comparison with these countries is of interest because one could assume that Palestine's situation today would be similar, if all other conditions had also been the same. We can see that Palestine performs quite well

---

46 See http://en.wikipedia.org/wiki/Israeli-occupied_territories
47 http://en.wikipedia.org/wiki/Israeli-occupied_territories
48 See, for instance, the overviews at http://de.wikipedia.org/wiki/Pal%C3%A4stinensische_Autonomiegebiete

Table 12.7   Socio-economic indicators for Palestine (West Bank and Gaza) in comparison to the neighbour countries (2010)

	Palestine	Egypt	Jordan	Lebanon	Israel
Population 2010 (Mio)	4.2	81.1	6.0	4.2	7.6
Population growth (2000–10) (%)	3.2	1.8	2.3	0.6	1.9
GNP/capita (Int.$)* (ca 2005–12)	1.679	6.723	6.148	14.610	28.809
Life expectations at birth (2010)	73	73	73	72	82
Gross enrolment rates (% of relevant age group)					
• primary	91	106	97	105	113
• secondary	86	…	91	81	91
• tertiary	50	30	42	54	62
Employment to population ratio (15 and older)	31	44	36	42	54
Youth unemployment					
• males	39	17	23	22	15
• females	47	48	46	22	13
Population below national poverty line	22–31**	22	13	…	…

Source: World Bank, World Development Indicators 2012, Washington.
*World Bank: Gaza 876$; West Bank 1.924$
**Palestinian Central Bureau of Statistics (2012)

in a few, but very badly in other indicators. In terms of GDP per capita, it is at the bottom of all five countries; with an income of about US$1,600 per capita Palestine belongs to very poor countries like India or Nigeria; in Egypt and Jordan, GDP per capita is four times higher, in Lebanon nine times and in Israel 18 times. One reason for the low GDP/capita of Palestine is the extremely high population growth (one of the highest in the world). In terms of life expectancy and educational levels, the Palestinians are comparable to the other Arab states. A big gulf, however, exists in regard to the employment situation: the employment level is clearly lower than in any neighbouring country; and particularly youth employment is very high. The nearly hopeless work and life prospects for young Palestinians are certainly one of the factors why a considerable number of them are ready to use violence against Israel or even to sacrifice their own lives as suicide bombers (see also Heinsohn 2008). In Palestine, also the proportion of poor people is very high, at least one-third; in the Gaza Strip it might be as high as 70 per cent (Carter 2010: 241). Up to 80 per cent of the population are dependent to some extent on food aid (Goldberg 2009: 125). More detailed studies show an extremely dismal picture of Palestine in general and of the Gaza Strip in particular:

> … the deterioration of the Palestinian economy, a humanitarian crisis characterized in large parts by levels of impoverishment and social decline that have no parallel during Israel's 36-year occupation of the West Bank and Gaza, and the destruction of ordinary life. Not since 1948, perhaps, have Palestinians faced such conditions of loss and dispersion (Roy 2004: 365).

When Israel did care about the socio-economic situation of the Palestinian population, it did so primarily in order to prevent dangerous developments. In the area of public health, for instance, the aim was not to develop a comprehensive healthcare system but mainly to control and prevent epidemics and vaccine-preventable diseases; thus, it was mainly a strategy of surveillance (Ophir et al. 2009: 462–3).

Given the fact that this extremely poor economic situation in the Palestinian territories is the direct consequence of the establishment of the State of Israel, and its further expansion since 1948 – particularly to the Gaza Strip, where a large proportion of people are 1948-refugees and their descendants – we must in some way consider Israel and Palestine as one unit. If we were to calculate a Gini index for this whole unit, the degree of economic inequality in Israel/Palestine would certainly be among the highest around the world.

In order to avoid a one-sided picture about Israeli politics concerning the Palestinians, a brief remark is necessary here also concerning the situation of Palestinian refugees in other countries where their situation is also quite deprived. The largest group of relocated Palestinians – over two million – live in Jordan where most of them have become Jordanian citizens. However, even as such they are strongly underrepresented in politics and confronted with discrimination in private and state sector employment; a quota system limits university admission for Palestinian youth. The unaffable, even hostile treatment of Palestinians by the Jordanian king and government is paralleled by an ambivalent attitude by the Palestinians toward Jordan; this attitude emerged already in 1948 when Jordan reached a secret agreement with the Zionists to partition the territory of Palestine and attach the West Bank to Jordan.[49] Even worse may be the situation of the Palestinians in Lebanon, where a new 'foreign underclass' was created; they were not allowed 'to put down roots, acquire citizenships, and improve their life chances' (Adam and Moodley 2005: 25). Thus, their situation might be comparable to many of the foreign workers in Saudi-Arabia and the Gulf states.

Interim Considerations

Israel as an Apartheid Society – Or What Else?

The formation of the State of Israel and its changes through the first half century of its existence are a paradigmatic example of the persistent power of ethno-national identifications, and their effects on political processes and conflicts in the modern world. Israel grew out of the idea that a people dispersed over, and discriminated in, many countries of the world should form its own state: hence the Jews claimed it as having been the homeland of their ancestors, based on texts several thousand years old. Based on a clear, long-term plan and due to a series of favourable conditions (Pappé 2011: 15ff.), the Jews were able to establish a state which today far outperforms in most regards all its Arabic-Islamic neighbour states. On the other side, it is obvious that something basic went wrong in the course of this process. How else can it be interpreted that the State of Israel has to live in a kind of continuous state of war; that the UN and global non-governmental human rights organizations have convicted Israel over and over again as having transgressed human rights principles and international laws; and that the image of Israel around the world is extremely negative, comparable only to that of Pakistan and Iran?[50]

In concluding this section, I would like to discuss if and how we can interpret both this phenomenal success of Israel and its depressing side-effects in terms of the theorems proposed in this book. This makes it necessary to answer three specific questions: (1) Can we say that one specific aspect of ethnicity among its three dimensions – bio-social ethnicity ('race'), language or religion – was the decisive driving force in this endeavour or must it be understood more as a political process of the building of a new nation-state? (2) How were the settlement of the Jews in present-day Israel and the foundation of the new state achieved? How can this be interpreted from the viewpoint of ethnic differentiation and stratification, exploitation and exclusion? (3) How did state and society of Israel develop since then? Can we consider present-day ethnic stratification in Israel as an Apartheid system or – if not – as what else?

First, which aspects of ethnicity were the most basic in the idea of Zionism and the establishment of the State of Israel? Can they be regarded in some way as primordial or were they also to a large degree 'invented' and constructed in terms of ideology and politics, as in all other cases of national reawakening around the world as documented widely by historians and sociologists of nationalism? (Lemberg 1964; Kohn 1967; Smith 1986; Anderson 1998; Hutchinson and Smith 2000). It seems out of question that also in the case of Israel the latter is true and that the reference to the old biblical texts contains mythological aspects. The idea of the Jews as the people chosen by God must also be considered as an invented national myth (see also p. 300

---

49   See http://refworld.org/docid/49749cfcc.html; and http://en.wikipedia.org/wiki/Palestinians_in_Jordan

50   In representative surveys in 21 countries, a BBC poll found that only 21 per cent of all interviewed 13,000 persons had a positive view of Israel; about Russia, 30 per cent had a positive view, about Germany, the UK, Canada and Japan about 60 per cent. See 'Views of China and Russia decline in Global Poll', BBC World Service Poll 2009. Available at http://www.globescan.com/news_archives/bbccntryview09/BBC_Country_Release_09.pdf

above; Smith 1992; Cauthen 2000). The recognized, devout Jewish scientist and theologian Yeshayahu Leibowitz wrote in 1959 that it is an idolization if the religious right considers the territory of Israel and the state of Israel as sacred (quoted in Gorenberg 2012: 20). This applies also to the first element, that of 'race' or bio-social ethnicity in the narrow sense, the thesis that all Jews are descendents from a common ancestry. This view has become institutionalized in the basic Israel immigration and citizenship laws which say that every person on the globe with a Jewish mother is entitled to immigrate and to attain Israeli citizenship (see also Wild 2013: 2). The common ancestry, that is, the bio-social community of all Jews around the world is a highly contested issue, however. First, it can hardly be proved in a definite way that present-day Jews really are descendents from the ancient Jewish tribes; in addition, this argument ultimately is based on a highly problematic race-biological thinking (Lipphardt 2008). In recent years, results from studies on the transmission of human genomes have been quoted in favour of it. These studies show in fact, for instance, that Jews from a particular European region are more similar to each other in genetic terms than to the non-Jewish people in this region.[51] However, this can easily be explained by the fact that within Jewish Diasporas (as also among others) a high level of inbreeding did exist. On the other side, DNA studies also show that Jews share many characteristics with their Arab neighbours. Historical evidence is not in favour of the thesis that Jews emigrated from Palestine to different parts of Europe and the world and reproduced themselves there, but rather suggest that in many cases the local people converted to Judaism (Sand 2010).

A similar argument is valid for Hebrew as the language of ancient Israel. The old Hebraic disappeared after the siege of Jerusalem in the 6th century B.C. and did persist only as a language of scribes and religious rites. At the time of Jesus, vernacular language in present-day Israel was Aramaic; also the Evangelists wrote in this language (Bodmer 1989: 228). Thus, in the thousands of years of Jewish history, Hebrew was used for only a few centuries.

The most important base for ethnic-national identity of Jews is doubtless religion (see also Turner 1984: 141; Eisenstadt 1992: 187ff.). As outlined in Chapter 2 (p. 33) this is the dimension of ethnicity which fuelled some of the most fervent nationalisms in history. However, even religion is far from providing an unequivocal base for Jewish national identity. There exists an extremely wide variation in adherence to the Mosaic religion among the Jews both within Israel as within the worldwide Jewish Diaspora. The spectrum runs from the sizable group of Jews (particularly in the West) who are more or less convinced atheists, over those who are lukewarm adherents to Judaism, to the point of extreme and ultra-Orthodox Jews; all these groups have very different visions of Jewish people; many of them reject Zionism and some even the State of Israel (for the Jewish diaspora see Goldscheider 1996: 227–48; for differences in historical symbolisms Smith 1986: 204–5). The same was true for many highly prominent Jewish scientists and writers at the end of the 19th to the start of the 20th century, such as Albert Einstein or Franz Kafka. For more recent examples see Kolsky 1990). Sigmund Freud wrote about Zionism in 1930:

> I certainly sympathize with its goals, am proud of our University in Jerusalem and delighted with our settlement's prosperity. But, on the other hand, I do not think that Palestine could ever become a Jewish state [...] It would have seemed more sensible to me to establish a Jewish homeland on a less historically-burdened land. But I know that such a rational viewpoint would never have gained the enthusiasm of the masses and the financial support of the wealthy. I concede with sorrow that the baseless fanaticism of our people is in part to be blamed for the awakening of Arab distrust.[52]

In 2010, 43 per cent of Israelis declared themselves as 'secular', an additional 23 per cent as 'traditional not so religious'.[53] Table 12.8 shows that only one-third of the Jewish Israelis say that religion is an important element of their identity. When, in the same ISSP-survey on national identity, 84 per cent also agree that 'to be a Jew' is an important characteristic of a 'true Israeli', they understood this evidently in a very broad sense, not only in the bio-social or religious sense. From this point of view, Mark Tessler (2009: 7) is right when he states that 'Jews are not at all a religious group' but 'a national community of believers' like the Muslims.

---

51   See, for instance, 'Genetic Ancestry', Jewish Virtual Library (www.jewishvirtuallibrary.org).

52   Edward C. Corrigan, *Jewish Critics of Zionism and of Israel's Treatment of the Palestinians, Dissident Voice*, 16 April 2010 (dissidentvoice.org).

53   The Social Survey Israel, 2009–2010, carried out by the Central Bureau of Statistics; see www.1.cbs.gov.il/

Table 12.8   National and political attitudes among Jewish and Arab Israelis

Question/statement	%	Jewish Israelis (1066)	Arab Israelis (152)	Worldwide ISSP-sample (43.000)*
Important unit of identification**				
... ethnic background	%	11	59	19
... religion	%	32	53	20
... nation(ality)	%	44	49	31
Feeling toward [Israel] is ...				
... very close	%	80	26	48
... close	%	15	43	40
It is very important/important for being truly [Israeli] to ...				
... speak [Hebrew]	%	92	51	88
... respect [Israeli] political institutions and laws	%	84	93	88
... have [Israeli] ancestry	%	52	40	64
... to be [a Jew]	%	84	24	XX
I would rather be a citizen of [Israel] than of any other country of the world	%	79	69	76
There are some things in [Israel] that make me ashamed of Israel	%	65	54	59
People should support their country even if it is wrong	%	60	28	38
Very/somewhat proud about ...				
... how democracy works	%	41	65	54
... fair and equal treatment of all groups	%	26	51	46

Source: ISSP-2003 'National Identity' (43 countries). *43 countries; the total N varies because of differing missing values in different questions; **Mentioned as 1st, 2nd or 3rd important unit.

An attempt to base the state of Israel on the religion of Judaism would have to come to grips also with principal problems. It is a characteristic of democratic nation-states that they are fully impartial about the religion of their citizens and make a strict distinction between the public, political and the civic and private sphere. Joel Kovel (2007: 6) has expressed the problematic of a religious foundation of a nation-state bluntly in this way: 'Nationalism is bad enough, but it can be sublimated by devices like the World Cup. Nationalism by divine decree – whether Judaic, Islamic, Christian or Hindu – and exercised with violent state power, is a living nightmare'. In fact, if religion were the main base of the State of Israel, it could be called a 'theocracy' (Kovel 2007: 169). This would be the case if the country would be governed by Jewish religious law, *halakha*; such a proposal, made in 2009 by Justice Minister Yaakov Neeman, caused a storm of protest.[54] The fact that the majority of Israelis observe religious customs and practices in their daily life (for example, Passover, Seders, a *Mezuzah* on the doorpost, fasting on Yom Kippur) does not qualify Israel as a theocracy.

Thus, the answer to the first question is clear: there are no primordial bases of the Jewish 'people' which alone could explain (and justify) the way the State of Israel has been founded and enlarged. This process is the result of the deliberate political action of the Zionists; the establishment of the State of Israel has to be considered as a project of nation formation which has to be judged by the same criteria as other similar projects around the world. Out of these considerations, I do not believe that the Israeli-Palestinian conflict is one about fundamentally different values (as suggested by Adam and Moodley 1977: 290), but one of different identities and socio-economic and political interests. Such conflicts, however, can be solved through improved communication, understanding and peaceful bargaining.

---

54   Gideon Levy, 'Let's face the facts, Israel is a semi-theocracy', *Haaretz*, 10 December 2009.

The second question to be answered relates to the way the State of Israel was established and how this process can be characterized in terms of ethno-national class and state formation. A central 'foundational myth' of Israel is that the settlement of the Palestinian lands took place in a more or less peaceful way, since they were rather thinly populated and the local Palestinians left their places more or less freely after the advent of the Jews (Flapan 1988). Historical facts tell a different story: during the war of 'independence' in 1947/48, about 700,000 Palestinians were expelled from their villages and towns violently, by terror and by planned military force. Systematic violence was used in the displacement of the resident Arab-Palestinian population, including banishment of people, destruction of houses and villages and massacres among civilians (Hart 1994: 48–63; Gorenberg 2012; Löwstedt 2012: 116–7; Wild 2013: 17). Former US president Jimmy Carter (2010: 61) compared these processes with the forced relocation of Cherokee Indians from his own home state of Georgia in the *Trail of Tears* in 1838 which led to the death of over 4,000 Cherokees. The atrocities carried out by the Israeli military and by private armed groups executed in several Palestinians villages had the intended effect, namely, that many other Palestinians living in these regions or nearby were frightened. This fact is hardly mentioned in official Israeli historical textbooks. Even such an internationally recognized sociologist like Shmuel Eisenstadt does not mention the Palestinian victims when he writes about the wars of 1947/48: 'But all these wars required a high price. About 6,000 [Israli] soldiers ... died' (Eisenstadt 1992: 244) Thus, the seizing of the 'holy lands' (Erez Israel) was by far no peaceful process but based on systematic and well-developed plans which involved both non-violent and violent means. It can hardly be denied that the violence, the disproportionate attacks and retaliations committed in 1947/48 and later were also motivated by a drive for revenge (Kovel 2007: 8ff.; Pappé 2011; Wild 2013: 104ff.). Hatred of Nazis and other violent anti-Semites were deflected onto Palestinians and Arabs, putting into action the later passages of the beautiful Bible Psalm 137 ('By the rivers of Babylon, there we sat down and wept, when we remembered Zion') which praise revenge (Kovel 2007: 13). Thus, violence has been a central element in the foundation and development of the State of Israel – contrary to the old image of Jews as a 'timid and passive' people (Medding 2002: vii). Overall, it began already in the early 20th century with non-violent means when the Jewish Agency collected money to acquire land in Palestine; this land, then, was bought from large Arab land owners with contracts which were not made known to the people living and working on the land.

Later on, the strategy of violent expulsion of Arabs was abandoned. However, the aim to convince the Arab people to leave the territories claimed by Israel as their historic land (Jerusalem, the West Bank, the ancient Judaea and Samaria) has persisted in two forms. One is by applying brutal forms of retaliation and oppression against the places in which it is suspected that Palestinian terrorists reside. In these military retribution acts, the number of Palestinian victims is usually high and includes not only potential (male) terrorists, but also wives, children and elderly people. Since the second Intifada in 2000, the number of Palestinian casualties has increased massively; between 1967 and September 2000, more than 2,000 Palestinians (most of them civilians) were killed, between September 2002 and December 2006 about 3,000 Palestinians (and 1,000 Israelis) were killed (Ophir et al. 2009: 241; Finkelstein 2007: 153f.). Arabs suspected of terrorism living within Israel or within the occupied territories have an extremely high risk of being sent to prison. With a prison inmate rate of 223 per 100,000 people, Israel fares better than the leaders in this classification (1st place, USA 717, 10th place, Russia 475), but much worse than all European countries.[55] The Israeli rate of inmates is also significantly higher than in the neighbouring Arab states.[56] In line with the increase of economic inequality during the last decades in Israel, the prison population has also increased massively; in the early 1990s, there were about 10,000 prisoners; since the early 2000s, it has doubled to 20,000 in 2010.[57] This increase was also connected with the second Intifada (literally: Insurrection) which broke out in 2000 after Ariel Sharon's provocative visit to the Temple Mount in September 2000 (see also Baumgarten 2002: 215ff.). Palestinian men (mainly from the West Bank) comprise at least half of prison inmates in Israel. Looking at the risks of Palestinian men to be imprisoned in Israel, the figures look even more spectacular:

55   Data reported by ICPS – The International Centre for Prison Studies (affiliated to the University of Essex), London; see http://www.prisonstudies.org/info/worldbrief/wpb_stats.php?area=all&category=wb_poprate
56   In the Lebanon and Jordan, the rate was about 120 around 2010, in Egypt 97 that is only about one-third of that in Israel. See ICPS, Footnote 55 above.
57   See ICPS, Footnote 55 above.

Since 1967, 800,000 Palestinians, roughly 20 per cent of the whole population or 40 per cent of the male population, had been imprisoned by Israel at one point in time.[58] This extremely high level of criminalization constitutes a close parallel to the other two countries discussed in this section, the United States and South Africa (Wild 2013: 104ff.).

If we try to get at an adequate interpretation of the way how the State of Israel was established after the Second World War and how it has behaved since then, it must be seen as a form of *settler colonialism* (Veracini 2010; Löwstedt 2012; Adam and Moodley 1993: 15–23; Adam 2013). The essence of such a form is that the colonialists – the settlers – immigrate to the new place and want to settle down there forever; in this process, they take over the land inhabited by the original populations and develop their own economy. In the course of this process, the natives are often expelled or even exterminated if they do not die out because of imported diseases and drugs. Land is the key resource in settler colonies because the new immigrants and invaders want to establish themselves forever in the occupied territory – they have no options of returning to a 'homeland'. Thus, the appropriation of the land was a central aim also for the Jews who settled down in Palestine (Carter 2010: 258). Their immigration and settlement was legitimized by ethnic-national, ideological and racist arguments saying, for instance, that the original inhabitants were unable to develop the resources of the country (Veracini 2010; Wild 2013).[59] Australia, Canada, the United States and South Africa are examples of such colonialism. In fact, the founders of the Zionist movement, including Herzl, had written and spoken explicitly of a 'colonial project'; plans for a 'population transfer' were developed already in the 1930s. At the *Settler Colonial Studies* homepage, established by two respectable researchers on the subject (Lorenzo Veracini and Edward Cavanagh), a clear distinction is made between colonialism in general and settler colonialism; while the first makes wide use of the indigenous population as labour force, 'settlers want indigenous people to vanish (but can make use of their labour before they are made to disappear)'.[60]

This in fact seems to have happened also in Israel/Palestine. In the first decades of its existence, and particularly after the annexation of the West Bank and the Gaza Strip, the Arab workers were welcome in Israeli enterprises as cheap labour power – comparable to the Blacks in Apartheid South Africa (see also Löwstedt 2012: 115ff.). The geographer Oren Yiftachel (2012) calls the relation between Israel and the occupied territories in this era a 'creeping Apartheid' – an undeclared, structurally based process which was partly Apartheid, partly political-military oppression. Later on, however, this policy was abandoned and there were even conscious efforts made to 'import' temporary workers from other countries to replace the Palestinian workers. In 2012, about 109,000 foreign non-Jewish people with a work permit arrived in Israel; the largest group came from former Soviet Union countries, the Philippines, Thailand and India.[61] Thus, Israel is no longer dependent on Palestinian labour; 'the presence of Filipinos and Thais likewise makes it possible for Israelis to think of Israel as cosmopolitan, as an ethnically heterogeneous late modern state evidenced by the ready availability of Asian food' (Goldberg 2009: 114).

The present strategy followed by the conservative leaders of Israel is to extend Israeli settlements in the West Bank and make living there for the local Arab population more and more troublesome and uncomfortable. One aspect of this strategy is rather unique in comparative terms: it is to encircle the Israeli state territory sharply and to restrict movement over this border as far as possible. The main instrument and symbol of this is the new wall which Israel has been building since 1994 in the West Bank along the 1949 'Green Line' between Israel and Palestine. It is planned to be 700 kilometres long, 440 km have already been built.[62] It consists partly of an extremely high concrete wall, flanked on both sides by a 60-metre-wide exclusion area and highly guarded control transition posts; in all these regards, it is comparable to other 'Iron curtains' which have existed in Europe and elsewhere (Haller 2015). Israel claims that the intent of the wall – to reduce terroristic attacks by Palestinians within Israel – has been fulfilled. Statistics in fact show that the number of Palestinian

---

58   Information by the Palestinian Prime Minister, reported in http://en.wikipedia.org/wiki/Palestinian_prisoners_in_ Israel. See also Carter 2010: 267.

59   See also http://en.wikipedia.org/wiki/Settler_colonialism

60   See http://settlercolonialstudies.org/about-this-blog/

61   Data of the Central Bureau of Statistics, reported in www.ynetnews.com/articles/0,7340,L-4412537.html

62   See http://en.wikipedia.org/wiki/Israeli_West_Bank_barrier. For an extensive documentation, including pictures, see Ophir et al. 2009.

infiltrations, suicide bombings and other attacks on civilians in Israel went down significantly. Critics of the wall point to facts like the following: it has partly been built within Palestinian territory; it restricts the movement of Palestinians living nearby massively, including their travel to work, to schools and hospitals in Israel; many Jerusalem Palestinians who were living outside the barrier moved to Jerusalem, causing housing shortages and other problems. The building of the wall has also been criticized by international human rights organizations as well as by the UN and the International Court of Justice. It also makes the hope for a two-state solution more and more unrealistic (Finkelstein 2007: 19).

What can we conclude concerning the question of the changing character of Israeli nationalism and its methods of ethnic exploitation and exclusion during the last decades? The answer might be that all three basic forms, as outlined in Chapter 4, have been employed: first, a settler colonialism applying the violent expulsion of the native population; in the following period an Apartheid system with an exploitation of the labour power of the Arabs/Palestinians; and, recently, a continuation of settler colonialism in the West Bank, avoiding direct use of violence. In addition, a new form of exclusion is being applied concerning the Gaza Strip; we could call it the putting into quarantine of the dangerous adversary, its more or less complete foreclosure. Israel itself has been described as an 'open civilian fortress' (Eisenstadt 1992: 288). In terms of the relevance of the ethnic aspect, Israel can certainly be called an ethno-nation or an ethnocracy (see also Yiftachel 2006). In this state, also Apartheid mechanisms continue to be practised, albeit not in the form of exploitation but of exclusion: first, by excluding the Arab Israeli citizens within the state of Israel from full social and political participation, and second, by locking out Palestinians from interactions with Israel and by confirming and restricting them within their own territory.

Perspectives for a New, Democratic and Peaceful Israel

What about the future prospects of the State of Israel, its internal Arab minority of the Palestinians and its relations with the Arab neighbour states? Today, Israel is really locked in a situation which seems as unchangeable as well as unsatisfying and disturbing. Right-wing people and leaders might definitely not want peace because this would also imply the abandonment of the most far-reaching Zionist plans. In order to answer the question about the future prospects for a peaceful Israel and Palestine, we have to make again a short look at the ideological and political roots of Israel. As already mentioned, the present-day state of Israel can be traced back to the Zionist movements of the late 19th century, established in ideological terms by Theodor Herzl in his influential book *Der Judenstaat*. This book was published in 1896 under the impression of massive anti-Semitic events in Europe (The Dreyfuss-affaire in France, pogroms against Jews in Tsarist Russia), and it proposed the establishment of a nation-state of the Jews in the land called *Eretz Israel* (the Promised Land, the Holy Land) in the Old Testament, that is, the territory of Palestine. In this state, the Jews should once and forever be free of persecution and be able to cultivate their specific, unique culture. The World Zionist Movement, established in 1897 as the Zionist Organization, an umbrella organization of many related movements, was a decisive force in this endeavour. It has laid down five principles in its 1968 Congress in Jerusalem: establish the unity of the Jewish people around the world with the State of Israel in the centre; bringing together all Jews in this state; strengthening the State of Israel, based on principles of justice and peace; preservation of Jewish (Hebrew) cultural identity; protection of Jews everywhere in the world.[63] One can certainly say that these principles are not merely written on paper, but are followed by the actions of the State of Israel and of Zionist organizations around the world.

The State of Israel is unique in historical and comparative terms in its ideological foundation and its institutional set-up: on the one side, it is certainly a democratic state with all attributes relevant in this regard (free press, competitive elections, division of political powers and so on); on the other side it contains an ethnic foundation, alien to the modern, Western concept of a democratic state. It is a principle of the concept of democracy that racial and cultural attributes of citizens – such as their language or religion – should be irrelevant before the state. All people living permanently on the territory of a state should have the same rights and duties (see also Weber 1964/II: 657–60). To be accepted as a member of a state is certainly a basic human right. Article 2 of the UN Declaration of Human rights of 1948 states: 'Everyone is entitled to all the

---

63   See http://en.wikipedia.org/wiki/Zionism

rights and freedoms set forth in this Declaration, without distinction of any kind, such as race, colour, sex, language, religion, political or other opinion, national or social origin, property, birth or other status'. These principles have been confirmed in the Declaration of Independence of 1948 which declares: 'Israel [...] will foster the development of the country for the benefit of all its inhabitants; [...] it will ensure complete equality of social and political rights to all its inhabitants irrespective of religion, race or sex [...]'. It is evident that these universal human and national rights are not respected fully in Israel/Palestine today. Brian Turner (1984: 120) denotes Zionism in this regard as a racialist ideology. Steven Salaita (2011) has argued (based on an intricate analysis of texts of present-day Zionist organizations) that Zionism ascribes a soul to the State of Israel – an endeavour highly dangerous because it implies many features which typically are associated with anti-Semitism. Here, the question arises if the Jews need their own 'pure' Jewish state in order to be safe or if there is a possibility for a peaceful and equal living together with the internal Arab minority, and – maybe in the future – with all Palestinians within and outside of Israel and with the Arab neighbour states.

In this context, we should again have a short look on the attitudes of the population of Israel. An important question here is if Arab Israeli citizens identify themselves with the State of Israel and what the relative importance of this identification is in comparison with ethnic identification. The answers to these questions are of utmost importance for the fundamental question of a lasting solution of the Israeli-Palestinian problem. We can again rely here on the International Social Survey Programme which in 2003 had the topic 'National Identity'. This survey, collected in 43 countries around the world, covered a wide variety of questions about the main sources of personal identity (family, occupation, gender and so on), including ethnic and national identity; questions about the main dimensions for belonging to a nation; and national pride and shame (related questions about attitudes to immigrants have already been analysed). The question about the main sources of personal identity mentioned ten different dimensions, and the respondent had to indicate with which one he identifies in the first, second and third place. If all are summed up, at the top are family and occupation, followed by age and gender; also nation, ethnic background and religion were mentioned, but only by 20 to 30 per cent of the respondents. This situation looks quite different in Israel and among its two main ethnic sub-groups, the Jews and Arabs (see Table 12.8). First, identification with one's own ethnic group is much stronger among the Arabs than among the Jews: 59 per cent of the first consider their ethnic background as an important component of their personal identity, much more than among Jews (11 per cent) or in worldwide comparison (19 per cent). A similar finding emerges concerning the relevance of the language Hebrew as a central characteristic of an Israeli: nearly all Jews, but only half of the Arabs think this way. These results are not very surprising.

The most important question, however, is if the Arabs identify themselves with the state of Israel. Here the findings are very clear: they show that this is in fact so. The Israeli nation is a central identity component for 44 per cent of the Jews and for 49 per cent of the Arabs; Jews feel themselves much more frequently very close to Israel than Arabs; but if we sum up the answers in detail, 69 per cent of Arabs have also a positive attitude in this regard. Respecting the political institutions and laws of Israel is even more important for Arabs than for Jews (93 per cent vs. 84 per cent); the somewhat chauvinistic statement 'I would rather be a citizen of Israel than of any other country in the world' is supported by large majorities of both groups; Arabs are also more proud about the way how democracy works in Israel than Jews (65 per cent vs. 41 per cent). There are only three statements in which Arabs are less supportive and more critical of Israel than Jews. Only 28 per cent agree to the openly nationalistic statement 'People should support their country even if it is wrong' while 60 per cent of Jews support it. This is a proportion much higher than in the worldwide sample (38 per cent) and it is quite easy to understand why this is so. It was already mentioned that UN Security Council issued hundreds of resolutions, convicting the State of Israel because of producing threats, breach of peace or acts of aggression against Palestinians; the sanctions proposed in many cases were not realized only because of the veto of the USA.[64] These resolutions have been questioned by many as having been the result of effective international Arab propaganda, supported by the Soviet Union; it may also be true that many other violations of human rights around the world were not condemned.[65] Nevertheless, one must say that in regard to present-day globally accepted standards of ethical behaviour in politics, Israel has very often acted in a way which

---

64   See http://en.wikipedia.org/wiki/List_of_the_UN_resolutions_concerning_Israel_and_Palestine

65   This argument, however, is hardly tenable given the fact that often also European and other states around the world, unaffiliated to the Arab world or the USSR, supported these resolutions.

was wrong. It is highly surprising, given these facts, that Arab Israelis nevertheless seem to be attached quite closely to the State of Israel as seen before. Thus the deeply anchored view in Israel that Arabs will never accept the right of existence of the State of Israel (Flapan 1988: 145) is not true – as it was not true that the PLO wanted the destruction of Israel (Carter 2010: 100). In fact, also the high level of disaccord among the different Arab states toward Israel and Palestine indicates that the existence of an enemy of several hundred millions of hostile Arabs is a chimera. The ISSP-data show, furthermore, that Arab citizens of Israel are more proud of Israel than Jews concerning Israeli democracy (65 per cent vs. 41 per cent) and its fair and equal treatment of all groups (51 per cent vs. 26 per cent).[66] The latter surprising result could also be interpreted in another way: it shows that even among Jewish Israelis the policy of the state concerning minorities is seen as quite critical; the respondents probably had in mind here mainly the Arabs, but maybe also the less privileged, recent Jewish immigrants from the former Soviet Union and from Africa. Another statement which shows a surprising higher level of self-criticism of Israeli Jews is as follows: 'There are some things which make me ashamed of Israel'; 54 per cent of Arabs, but 65 per cent – that is, two-thirds – of all Jewish Israelis agree with this statement. This interpretation is confirmed by the fact that in recent times there were repeated public demonstrations of thousands of Israelis demanding a fairer division of the economic and military burden, but also reforms to allow a better integration of the Arab-Israelis.[67]

The conclusion from these findings seems to be rather clear: there is no general distrust of Israeli Arabs against the State of Israel, rather the reverse is true. We could deduce from this surprising result that also among Palestinians and Arabs the present high level of distrust and of hostile attitudes would vanish if a serious and acceptable-for-all solution of the Israel-Palestinian problem emerged. Thus, I am much more optimistic in this regard than some authors who have compared Apartheid in South Africa with Israel (see, for example, Adam and Moodley 1977). I will come back to the political and institutional preconditions of such a solution in the following chapter.

Conclusions and Outlook: the United States, South Africa and Israel in a Comparative Perspective

The United States, South Africa and Israel are three societies characterized historically or at present in one way or another by systems of Apartheid, in former times by ethnic exploitation and still today by a high degree of ethnic segregation and exclusion. The aim of the previous and this chapter was to investigate the extent and character of economic inequality in these three societies from a comparative perspective. In the USA and in South Africa, the question was if the former exploited and excluded ethnic minorities are still discriminated today, that is, receiving lower incomes than comparable other groups with similar characteristics. Israel is a new state established in 1948 and its development since then is of extreme importance from the perspective of this book because it shows both the extreme positive power of ethnic-national identification and action, but also because some of its negative concomitants; in fact, this unique, new ethno-national state has used and still uses practices and strategies of ethnic expulsion, segregation and exclusion. The comparison between these three cases is highly instructive because the first two have been able to overcome the systems of race segregation and Apartheid which was an immense political achievement considered as impossible by many contemporaries in former times. Thus, it is of extreme scientific and political-practical interest that we learn from the experiences of the United States and the Republic of South Africa for the case of Israel.

Both for the USA and South Africa, significant achievements can be noted: in the USA, the Afro-Americans have attained full civil and political rights, and the majority of them have been able to rise in educational, occupational and income terms. In South Africa, the Blacks today not only have full rights in every sphere of life, they even dominate government and are advancing strongly in public service; we could also observe a weak decrease in overall economic inequality. In contrast to these two cases, but in full accordance with the theory proposed in this book, economic inequality has increased continuously and strongly in the new ethno-national state of Israel throughout the last decades, connected with the emergence of new minorities

---

66   In this regard, however, the overrepresentation of Arabs in middle and higher strata could have distorted the findings somewhat.

67   Yossi Mekelberg, 'Minority report: On equality and inequality in Israel', *Al Arabiya News*, 9 June 2013.

in the course of martial territorial expansion, huge processes of promoted immigration and the rise of a tight, privileged and often corrupt economic-political-military elite network.

Three elements were defined as constitutive for Apartheid systems: a racist ideology positing essential differences between ethnic groups, a legal and constitutional distinction between them and a social and territorial segregation. In the United States and South Africa, the official racist ideology as well as its embodiment in law and state constitution has been abandoned; Blacks are now considered as citizens with full and equal rights in all spheres of life. Yet, the abolishment of race segregation and Apartheid has not been, and will not be in the future, a smooth and fully accomplished process. The abolition of slavery in the US-South after the end of the Civil War in 1865 was followed by a reactionary process which led to a new form of racial segregation which was practiced for nearly a century. A comparable restorative process occurred after the victory of the Civil Rights Movement in the 1960s and 1970s; in the last decades, conservative, right-wing forces originating in the US-South have been able to get an upper hand in US politics. Moreover, a significant number of Blacks are still discriminated strongly in socio-economic terms through processes of residential segregation and ghettoization. Both in the USA and the Republic of South Africa, a discrimination of Blacks persists; in the US-South and eastern large cities with high numbers of Blacks (such as New York), economic inequality is significantly higher; in South Africa, Blacks with educational degrees and occupational levels comparable to other ethnic groups earn less. Among Whites, there exists some resistance to the new order on the factual and ideological level, by exaggerating White victimhood and the new problems of the country (Steyn and Foster 2008).

How does the situation look in Israel and what are the perspectives for an improvement here if we take into consideration the historical and recent revolutionary experiences in America and in South Africa? A decisive fact in this regard is that ethnicity, in this case Jewishness, defined in bio-social, religious and linguistic terms, is still the base for the granting of citizenship. The preservation of a clear Jewish majority in the State of Israel is seen as an absolute necessity by the dominant political elites. The sizable Palestinian minority within Israel has citizenship rights, but the persistence of some direct and indirect legal and political discrimination is also evident. Palestinians living in the West Bank and the Gaza Strip had 'rights' defined only within the limits of Israeli occupation for many decades. The state of autonomy granted to the Palestinian authorities in recent times hardly gives them the effective power to govern, administrate and care for the welfare of the citizens; it may rather be compared to the administration of a refugee camp. Territorial and social segregation strongly impedes social, cultural and political life and independence of the people living here. In the United States, the Indian reserves still exist but Indians are not constrained to live there; in addition, these reserves also have their own rights in terms of self-administration and new sources of income. In South Africa, the former 'homelands' ('Bantustans') in which the Black population was constrained to live under ignoble conditions have been dissolved and a new administrative division of the country was established. Contrary to these two cases, territorial and social segregation persists and is even enforced continuously in Israel/Palestine in an extremely strong form: Palestinians in the West Bank are more and more restricted in their freedom to move, to work and to live within this area; those in the Gaza Strip are living in a kind of prison, and there is practically no movement possible between these two areas. Thus, these areas together do not exhibit one of the main criteria of an independent political community, a territory which they control, and it is hard to see how they could do it in the future (see also Adam and Moodley 2005: 175).

The three cases of the USA, the Republic of South Africa and Israel/Palestine can also be compared concerning the origins and concomitants of their systems of ethnic-racial domination, segregation and exclusion. It certainly true that in all of them violence was involved in the occupation of the territory and in the expulsion of the native populations. A similarity exists between the United States and Israel also in regard to changes in the influence of right-wing political leaders. In the United States, the abolishment of slavery in the 1860s has been followed by a counter-revolutionary restoration which led to race segregation; the civil rights movement in the 1950s/1960s, which achieved the abolishment of race segregation, later on induced a strengthening of right-wing Republican and other political forces in the US-South and beyond. Also in Israel, since 1977 a sharp turn of politics toward an increasing influence of ultra-Orthodox and right-wing political parties took place.

Finally, it has been shown that a particular socio-economic deprivation of the ethnic minorities, the main topic of this book, persists in all three societies. In the United States and South Africa, however, there are clear signs of its decrease, and sizable numbers of Blacks have been able to rise up the social ladder and take over top administrative and political positions. The same is true in Israel/Palestine to a limited degree, at the most for the Arab Israeli citizens, but in no way for the Palestinians living outside the borders of the State of Israel. If we consider the whole territory Israel/Palestine as a unit, the degree of consolidated economic inequality is doubtless much higher than in the United States and probably as high as in the Republic of South Africa, if not higher.

Adam and Moodley (2005: 59–101) have elaborated in detail the differences between South Africa and Israel. These include, among other factors, less economic interdependence between Jews and Arab Palestinians in Israel than in South Africa, a decisive (instead of a unifying) religious split, massive third party intervention and a military political culture. Yet, I believe that in spite of all the massive problems that presently afflict Israel/Palestine, including the extreme violence and the threats for the civilian Jewish and Arab populations both in Israel and Palestine, the revolutionary reforms in the USA and South Africa show the way for a solution for Israel. Two forces can be mentioned in this regard. One is the incredible strength of ethnic-national identification and organization both from the side of the Israelis and from the Palestinians. In this regard, one has to mention the continued resistance of the Palestinians and their organizations (PLO, Fatah, Hamas and so on) and leaders, above all the deceased Yassir Arafat,[68] in their fight against Israeli occupation. This resistance had begun in 1920, and outlasted the military suppression by the British (1936–38), and, since 1948, Israeli military actions as well as continued subversive assaults by several Arab regimes (Hart 1994). Another indication were the two Intifadas (1987–93, 2000–05) broadly based, unplanned and unanticipated, first peaceful, but later violent riots of the Palestinians against Israeli occupation. A second force which contributes toward a solution of the Israeli-Palestinian problem is the power of universal ideas of human dignity and equality, particularly when they are adopted and proposed by important social and political groups within Israel/Palestine and worldwide. I have mentioned clear trends in this direction in this chapter.

I think that there is no doubt whatsoever that the basic requirement for a lasting solution to the peaceful living together of Jews and Arabs in the territory of Palestine would be to step away from the definition of Israel as a 'Jewish' state, even if this idea may appear incomprehensible to the majority of Jews today. The realization of such a deep-going reorientation could be supported by the recognition – for which some evidence was presented here – that the Palestinians and Arab neighbours of Israel as well as their leaders (for the position of the decade-long PLO-leader Yassir Arafat see Baumgarten 2002) are ready to recognize the right to existence of the State of Israel and do not continue to be prone to perpetual revenge for the injustices suffered. They would also have to redefine their deeply entrenched anti-Zionist and often anti-Semitic attitudes (Adam and Moodley 2005: 177). This is also proven by the experience of South Africa where 4.5 million Whites live rather safely side-by-side with a majority of 42 million Black Africans. Given the present-day extreme fragmentation and dispersion of the Arab-Palestinian population over three different territories, a two-state solution appears as impossible and only a one-state solution as feasible. In the following, final, chapter I will outline some indications for a suitable constitution for such a state.

As far as the power of universal ideas of human rights is concerned, we can see at least three factors or forces which could in fact support this now seemingly utopian perspective. The first are the open-minded and peace-oriented Jewish citizens living within the State of Israel itself. In this chapter, we found clear evidence that they recognize the huge problems associated with the present situation and would like very much to see a peaceful solution. They may now even constitute a 'silent majority'. The second force is the Diaspora Jews worldwide. Several studies have shown that their backing of the continuation of the violent occupation of Palestinian lands, the harsh treatment of suspected terrorists and of the civilian Palestinians in general is accepted less and less and support for present-day Israeli politics may become significantly weaker (Tal 2010). The third factor is world-wide public opinion which is very critical of Israeli politics, as has also been alluded to before. In this regard, the attitudes of the five million Jews living in the United States, the most important ally of Israel, is of crucial importance.

Three additional essential pre-conditions for the realization of a real breakthrough in the Israeli-Palestinian problem must also be mentioned here. The first is that new, charismatic political personalities must come to power in Israel which are ready to turn toward entirely new solutions and to argue forcefully and in a credible

---

68 For a comprehensive biography of Arafat see Hart (1984).

way toward novel ways out of the problem. Charismatic personalities (Weber 1964/I: 179–82, II: 832–73) have always played an extremely important role in history, and particularly so in revolutionary periods when a new order is created (Grinin 2010). The rise and action of such personalities has been of decisive importance also in the non-violent overcoming of Apartheid in the United States and South Africa; one could mention here personalities such as Martin Luther King, whose famous speech in Washington in 1963 ('I have a dream') gave a strong impetus to the American Civil Rights Movement; and the South African politicians Nelson Mandela and W.W. de Klerk who concluded the peaceful agreements finishing Apartheid in the early 1990s. Mandela was celebrated worldwide as a hero since he was ready to shake hands peacefully with the Whites in spite of the fact that he was imprisoned by them for 27 years. His funeral on 11 December 2013 was attended by about 90 heads of states from all over the world.

The second is that also the Palestinians must change their ways of thinking and acting. They must not only depart from resorting to violence and terror against military personnel and civilians, but also change their basic identity and attitudes. These are characterized by a fundamental distrust against Israel, an inferiority complex, and a feeling to be martyrs condemned to endless suffering. Based on her in-depth study, Helena L. Schulz (1999: 164f.) writes that the Palestinians are trapped 'in a mystification and romanticisation of a victimized self'; in some way their identities are a mirror image of the Israeli self-image of a struggling hero. In addition, one must mention here also the negative side-effects of the high dependency of Palestine on international donors. These are well comparable to the effects of US support for Israel. In Palestine, civil society organizations which receive and distribute the money from the donor countries emerged as the most important new form of societal steering which led to a deep crisis in the political parties, a shift from politics to service delivery and allowed the emergence of a new political elite which, in turn, led to a new process of polarization:

> The middle class [...] was rapidly fading, falling into lower strata. On the other hand, a small group of senior officials in the public administration, security apparatus and the elite surrounding the President accumulated wealth through dubious deals, corruption and mismanagement and monopolizing certain economic activities at the expense of the private sector. All this, combined with restrictive Israeli economic and security measures, led to a fast drop in income levels and an increase in unemployment rates as compared to the pre-Oslo period (Shafi 2004: 10).[69]

A consequence of these trends was the fatal split of the Palestinian political elites between El Fatah, the official representation of Palestine, and Hamas, the leading power in the Gaza Strip.

Third, also the international community, first of all the United States, but also the European Union and other important actors in international relations, must change their attitude and behaviour toward Israel in a fundamental way. There is not much comment necessary here in regard to the necessary changes in US politics after the demonstration above which showed how deeply American politics was involved in the development of militarism in Israel. But also the European Union, which fortunately also has very close relationships with Israel and, at the same time, a much more critical attitude toward Israel's politics concerning the Palestinians. It would have to change their politics in several regards: first, toward a more definitive repudiation of the Israeli politics concerning the continuous settlements in the West Bank and the encircling of the Gaza Strip. In this regard; it is also questionable why it still considers Hamas, the victory in the election in the Gaza Strip in 2006, as a terroristic organization. Second, it has to consider seriously the negative side-effects of its huge financial support of the Palestinians. This support changed the national agenda in Palestine from a national agenda to service delivery through NGOs. These 'became an industry providing thousands of attractive jobs for the local economy' (Shafi 2004: 11f.). The aim of the donors, to separate between development and political agendas, failed because the development of the last decade has 'proved beyond any doubt that political stability is a necessary pre-condition for sustainable development' (ibidem). Because of their dependency on foreign funding, the new professionalized Palestinian elites lost their reputation among the public.

---

69 In December 2013, the US$5.6 billion support of Palestinians by the EU was criticized because the money was used to employ public employees who in effect did not work. See *Die Presse* (Vienna), 11 December 2013.

Several authors also propose that the international community should seriously consider sanctions against Israel as a means to exert pressure, as it did against South Africa for decades (Lim 2012); it is questionable, however, if those sanctions had a significant effect (Adam 2013). It is beyond question that a peaceful and widely accepted solution of the Israeli-Palestinian conflict would give free reign to a new era of socio-economic prosperity, political peace and security for all the peoples in Israel, Palestine and the Near East as a whole.

Summary

In this chapter, a unique case in regard to the central topic of this paper – ethnic stratification – has been analysed. The state of Israel has been founded in 1948 explicitly as the homeland for all Jews around the world and its constitution still defines it in this way. Also the development of economic inequality since then was unique: Only in a few countries of the world, a similar significant increase took place in the last half century. Three reasons have been found for this change: the strong immigration, which in the more recent time brought mainly immigrants of post-Soviet countries to Israel, allocating them into the lower strata of society; the territorial expansion through several wars, doubling the proportion of the Arab population within the state of Israel; and the changes in the economic and political system which transformed Israel from a socialist-egalitarian society into a highly unequal capitalist society. In this society a tight network of political, military and economic elites controls economic and political power; in connection with massive financial support from external sources, a high level of corruption has developed. How can we characterize Israel in terms of the typology of ethno-class systems developed in Chapter 5? In the first, formative stage, Israel could be denoted as a settler colonialist system; the present-day Israeli actions in the West Bank may still be of this sort; elements of an Apartheid system have been in force during the period when the Arab population was employed in Israeli enterprises; today, the Palestinian problem overshadows everything else; Palestine, particularly the Gaza strip, can be seen as a residual state in Israeli bondage. In the last part of the chapter, the prospects for a positive development in this region have been discussed. I mentioned several factors which raise well-founded hopes in this regard: The fact that Israel has a well-functioning democracy and a thriving economy with a solid scientific-technological base; that many Israeli Jews themselves as well as members of the world Jewish diaspora are becoming more and more critical about the politics of the elites in Israel; and that the Arab Israelis identify strongly with the state of Israel. It was argued that a long-lasting peaceful solution of the problems would require a change of the definition of Israel from that of an ethnic state to that of a modern secular state which would be able to provide a home for all peoples living on the territory of Israel and Palestine.

References

Abu-Shokor, Abdelfatta (1995), Review of Labour and Employment Trends in the West Bank and the Gaza Strip, UNCTAD-Paper, EDC/SEU/9

Adam, Heribert and Kogila Moodley (1977), *Südafrika ohne Apartheid?* Frankfurt/Main: Suhrkamp

Adam, Heribert and Kogila Moodley (1993), *The Opening of the Apartheid Mind. Options for the New South Africa*, Berkeley etc.: University of California Press

Adam, Heribert and Kogila Moodley (2005), *Seeking Mandela. Peacemaking between Israelis and Palestinians*, Philadelphia, PA: Temple University Press

Adam, Heribert (2013), 'Siedlungskolonialismus: Ökonomische und ideologische Motive in der Konfliktlösung in Apartheid-Südafrika und Palästina' in Daniela Klimke and Aldo Legnaro, eds, *Politische Ökonomie und Sicherheit*, Weinheim/Basel: Beltz, pp. 62–73

Al-Haj, Majid (1993), Ethnicity and immigration: The case of Soviet immigration to Israel, *Humboldt Journal of Social Relations* 19: 279–305

Anderson, Benedict (1998), *Die Erfindung der Nation*, Berlin: Ullstein (*Imagined Communities*, 1983)

Barak, Oren and Gabriel Sheffer (2007), 'The study of civil-military relations in Israel: A new perspective', *Israel Studies* 12: 1–27

Barnett, Michael (2008), 'High politics is low politics. The domestic and systemic sources of Israeli security policy, 1967–1977', *World Politics* 42: 529–62

Ben-Eliezer, Uri (1998), *The Making of Israeli Militarism*, Bloomington, IN: Indiana University Press

Ben-Eliezer, Uri (2012), *Old Conflict, New War: Israel's Politics Toward the Palestinians*, Cambridge, MA: Harvard University Press

Bodmer, Frederick (1989), *Die Sprachen der Welt*, Herrsching: M. Pawlak (English ed.: *The Loom of Language*, Allen & Unwin)

Carter, Jimmy (2010), *Palästina – Freiheit nicht Apartheid*, Neu Isenburg: Melzer Verlag (American ed., *Palestine: Peace not Apartheid*, New York: Simon & Schuster)

Cauthen, Bruce (2000), 'The myth of divine election and Afrikaner ethnogenesis', in John Hutchinson and Anthony D. Smith, eds, *Nationalism. Critical Concepts in Political Science*, vol. III, London/New York: Routledge, pp. 1000–1024

Cohen, Asher and Bernard Susser (2000), *Israel and Jewish Identity. The Secular-Religious Impasse*, Baltimore, MD: Johns Hopkins University Press

Cohen, Yinon and Yitchak Haberfeld (2003), Gender, ethnic, and national earnings gaps in Israel: The role of rising inequality, The Pinhas Sapir Center for Development, Tel-Aviv University

Cohen-Almagor, Raphael (2002), 'The Delicate Framework of Israeli Democracy During the 1980s: Retrospect and Appraisal', in Karsh, Efraim, ed., *Israel: The First Hundred Years*, pp. 118–38

Dahan, Momi (n.d.), The rise of economic inequality, School of Public Policy, Hebrew University of Jerusalem

Eisenstadt, Shmuel (1992), *Die Transformation der israelischen Gesellschaft*, Frankfurt: Suhrkamp

Eliezer, Ben-Rafael, (1994), *Language, Identity, and Social Division. The Case of Israel*, Oxford: Clarendon Press

Elizur, Judith (2002), 'The Fracturing of the Jewish Self-Image: The End of 'We Are One'?' in Karsh, Efraim, ed., *Israel: The First Hundred Years*, pp. 14–30

Esser, Hartmut (2006), *Sprache und Integration. Die sozialen Bedingungen und Folgen des Spracherwerbs von Migranten*, Frankfurt am Main/New York: Campus

Finkelstein, Norman G. (2007), *Antisemitismus als politische Waffe. Israel, Amerika und der Missbrauch der Geschichte*, München/Zürich: Piper (American ed., *Beyond Chutzpah*, University of California Press)

Flapan, Simcha (1988), *Die Geburt Israels. Mythos und Wirklichkeit*, München: Knesebeck & Schuler (American ed., *The Birth of Israel*, New York: Pantheon Books)

Gardt, Andreas (2000), *Nation und Sprache. Die Diskussion ihres Verhältnisses in Geschichte und Gegenwart*, Berlin etc.: de Gruyter

Goldberg, David T. (2009), *The Threat of Race. Reflections on Racial Neoliberalism*, Malden, MA: Wiley-Blackwell

Goldscheider, Calvin (1996), *Israel's Changing Society. Population, Ethnicity, and Development*, Boulder, CO: Westview Press

Goldscheid, Rudolf and Joseph Schumpeter (1976), *Die Finanzkrise des Steuerstaaates*, Frankfurt: Suhrkamp

Gorenberg, Gershom (2012), *Israel schafft sich ab*, Frankfurt/New York: Campus (The Unmaking of Israel, New York 2011)

Grinin, Leonid E. (2010), 'The role of an individual in history: A reconsideration', *Social Evolution and History* 9: 95–136

Haberfeld, Yitchak, Moshe Semyonov and Yinon Cohen (2000), 'Ethnicity and Labour Market Performance among Recent Immigrants from the Former Soviet Union to Israel', *European Sociological Review* 16: 287–99

Haller, Max (2015), 'Why empires build walls. A historical-sociological interpretation of the new Iron Curtain between Africa and Europe', in Alberto Gasparini and Eliezer Ben-David, eds, *The Walls Between Conflict and Peace*, Leiden/Boston: Brill

Hart, Alan (1994), *Arafat*, Sidgwick & Jackson

Heinsohn, Gunnar (2008), *Söhne und Weltmacht. Terror im Aufstieg und Fall der Nationen*, München/Zürich: Piper

Herzl, Theodor (1896), *Der Judenstaat. Versuch einer modernen Lösung der Judenfrage*, Leipzig/Wien: Breitenstein

Hutchinson, John and Anthony D. Smith, eds (2000), *Nationalism. Critical Concepts in Political Science*, London/New York: Routledge

Ismael, Jacqueline S. (1993), *Kuwait. Dependency and Class in a Rentier State*, Gainesville, FL: University Press of Florida

Joseph, John E. (2004), *Language and Identity. National, Ethnic, Religious*, Houndmills: Palgrave Macmillan

Kaletsch, Klaus-Peter (2010), *Border Line. Palästina – Israel. Wer zieht die Grenzen?* Gelnhausen: Wagner Verlag

Karsh, Efraim, ed. (2002), *Israel: The First Hundred Years*, London/Portland, OR: Frank Cass

Klein, Michael W. (2005), 'Studying texts: A gemara of the Israeli economy', *Israel Economic Review* 3: 121–47

Kohn, Hans (1967), *The Idea of Nationalism*, New York: Collier-Macmillan

Kolsky, Thomas A. (1990), *Jews Against Zionism: The American Council for Judaism, 1942–1948*, Philadelphia, PA: Temple University Press

Kovel, Joel (2007), *Overcoming Zionism. Creating a Single Democratic State in Israel/Palestine*, Toronto: Pluto Press

Lemberg, Eugen (1964), *Nationalismus*, 2 vols, Reinbek: Rowohlt

Lewin-Epstein, Noah and Moshe Semjonov (1994), 'Sheltered labor markets. Public sector employment, and socioeconomic returns to education of Arabs in Israel', *American Journal of Sociology* 100: 622–51

Lim, Andrea, ed.(2012), *The Case for Sanctions Against Israel*, London: Verso

Lipphardt, Veronika (2008), *Biologie der Juden. Jüdische Wissenschaftler über ‚Rasse‘ und Vererbung 1900–1935*, Göttingen: Vandenhoek & Ruprecht

Löwstedt, Anthony (2012), Apartheid. Ancient, Past and Present, Habilitation thesis, University of Vienna

Luciani, Giacomo, ed. (1990), *The Arab State*, London: Routledge

Maman, Daniel (1997), 'The power lies in the structure: economic policy forum networks in Israel', *British Journal of Sociology* 48: 267–85

Mearsheimer, John J. and Stephen M. Walt (2007), *The Israel Lobby and the U.S. Foreign Policy*, New York: Farrar, Straus and Giroux

Medding, Peter Y. (2002), *Jews and Violence. Images, Ideologies, Realities*, Oxford/New York: Oxford University Press

Okun, Barbara S. and Dov Friedlander (2005), 'Educational stratification among Arabs and Jews in Israel: Historical disadvantage, discrimination, and opportunity', *Population Studies* 59: 163–80

Ophir, Adi, Michal Givoni and Sara Hanaif, eds (2009), *The Power of Inclusive Exclusion. Anatomy of Israeli Rule in the Occupied Palestinian Territories*, New York: Zone Books

Pappé, Ilan (2011), *The Forgotten Palestinians. A History of the Palestinians in Israel*, New Haven/London: Yale University Press

Peleg, Ilan (2004), 'Jewish-Palestinian relations in Israel: From hegemony to equality?' *International Journal of Politics, Culture and Society* 17: 415–37

Peleg, Ilan (2011), *Israel's Palestinians. The Conflict Within*, Cambridge/New York: Cambridge University Press

Peretz, Don (1977), 'Palestinian social stratification; The political implications', *Journal of Palestine Studies* 7: 48–74

Plessner, Yakir (1994), *Israel. From Ideology to Stagnation*, Albany: State University of New York Press

Roy, Sarah (2004), 'The Palestinian-Israeli conflict and Palestinian socioeconomic decline: A place denied', *International Journal of Politics, Culture and Society* 17: 365–403b

Salaita, Steven (2011), *Israel's Dead Soul*, Philadelphia: Temple University Press

Sand, Shlomo (2010), *Die Erfindung des jüdischen Volkes. Israels Gründungsmythos auf dem Prüfstand*, Berlin: Progylaen (English ed., *The Invention of the Jewish People*, New York: Verso)

Schulz, Helena Lindhom (1999), *The Reconstruction of Palestinian Nationalism. Between Revolution and Statehood*, Manchester/New York: Manchester University Press

Schwarz, Rolf (2004), State formation processes in rentier states: The Middle Eastern case, Paper presented at the 5th Pan-European Conference on International Relations of the ECPR, The Hague

Shafi, Salah Abdel (2004), Civil society and political elites in Palestine and the role of international donors: A Palestinian view, EuroMeSCopaper 33, Instituto De Estudios Estratégicos E Internacionais (IEEI), Lisboa

Sheffer, Gabriel and Oren Barak (2013), *Israels Security Networks. A Theoretical and Comparative Perspective*, Cambridge: Cambridge University Press

Smith, Anthony D. (1986), *The Ethnic Origins of Nations*, Oxford etc.: Blackwell

Smith, Anthony D. (1992), 'Chosen Peoples: Why ethnic groups survive', *Ethnic and Racial Studies* 15: 436–56

Solt, Frederick (2009), 'Standardizing World Income Inequality Database', *Social Science Quarterly* 90: 231–42

Sternhell, Zeev (1998), *The Founding Myths of Israel: Nationalism, Socialism and the Making of the Jewish State*, Princeton, NJ: Princeton University Press

Steyn, Melissa and Don Foster (2008), 'Repertoires for talking white: Resistant whiteness in post-apartheid South Africa', *Ethnic and Racial Studies* 31: 25–51

Tal, Rami, ed. (2010), Annual Assessment 2010. Executive Report No.7, Jerusalem: The Jewish People Policy Institute

Tessler, Mark, (2009), *A History of the Israeli-Palestinian Conflict*, Bloomington, IN: Indiana University Press

Turner, Brian S. (1984), *Capitalism and Class in the Middle East*, Atlantic Highlands, NJ: Humanities Press

Tyler, Patrick (2012), *Fortress Israel. The Inside Story of the Military Elite who run the Country and Why They Can't Make Peace*, New York: Farrar, Straus and Giroux

Veracini, Lorenzo (2010), *Settler Colonialism. A Theoretical Overview*, Hampshire, UK: Palgrave Macmillan

Weber, Max (1964/I+II), *Wirtschaft und Gesellschaft*, 2 vols, Köln/Berlin: Kiepenheuer & Witsch

Weber, Max (1973), *Soziologie. Weltgeschichtliche Analysen*. Politik, Stuttgart: A. Kröner

Wild, Petra (2013), *Apartheid und ethnische Säuberung in Palästina. Der zionistische Siedlerkolonialismus in Wort und Tat*, Wien: ProMedia

Yates, Douglas A. (1996), *The Rentier State in Africa: Oil Rent Dependency & Neocolonialism in the Republic of Gabon*, Ternon, NJ/Asmara, Eritrea: Africa World Press

Yiftachel, Oren (2006), *Ethnocracy. Land and Identity Politics in Israel/Palestine*, Philadelphia, PA: University of Pennsylvania Press

Yiftachel, Oren (2012), 'Between colonialism and ethnocracy: "Creeping apartheid" in Israel/Palestine', *MERIP* 27: 7–37

Chapter 13

Pre-conditions and Perspectives for Peace and Equality in Ethnically Differentiated Societies. Political Implications and Conclusions

Introduction

The aim of this concluding chapter is to discuss positive ways toward peaceful and equal relations between different ethnic groups, both within and between nation-states. In this sense, it attempts to show alternatives to the strategies of ethnic exploitation and exclusion sketched out in Chapter 5 and elaborated in Chapters 6 to 12. The following considerations include normative, theoretical-explanatory and empirical elements and facts.

Four processes and strategies of coming to terms with ethnic encountering, differentiation and stratification are discussed: secession of ethnic-regional sub-units from a state; federalisation of the political system; policies empowering deprived ethno-classes and international migration. Which of these strategies is feasible and commendable depends on the size, character and territorial localization of the ethnic sub-groups within a state: (1) if a sub-group is large enough and settling on a relatively compact territory on the edge of a state, its people can consider the secession from this state and establish its own, new state. It is a form that also affects the other parts of a state and the secession may produce second-order minorities within the emerging new state (Kolsto 2001); (2) if a state includes sizeable ethnic sub-groups which are settling in a relatively compact way, but dispersed over the whole territory of the state, a federalization of the political system is a good solution, providing all ethnic groups with considerable economic, socio-cultural and political autonomy. Also in such a case, complex problems may arise covering the size of the federal sub-units, and their composition in ethnic terms; (3) again a different situation exists if there are clearly deprived larger or smaller ethnic minorities within a state, either territorially concentrated or dispersed. My proposal is not to focus on affirmative action but on strategies and measures to empower them so that they can participate and work actively to improve their situation. Three areas are elaborated on in which empowerment appears as most promising: educational policy, community and town planning and the development of welfare state models suited for poor countries. The last section takes up the question as to what the effects of global migration are in the advanced countries concerning the emergence of new minorities and the increase of inequality. Here, different models of immigration and integration politics are sketched out, ranging from exclusion of poor people toward an active recruitment of highly skilled people. Rationales and problems of these different strategies both from the normative and social-structural perspective are discussed.

In Chapters 3 to 5, I argued that economic inequality in ethnically differentiated societies is higher if a system of ethnic stratification exists, that is, if certain ethnic groups as a whole occupy a privileged or deprived position in society. Inequality will be the highest, if systems of ethnic domination, exploitation and exclusion have existed in the past or are re-emerging today. The complementary thesis is that different ethnic groups will be able to live peacefully side by side if societal and political institutions are structured in a way which ensures equal opportunities and conditions for participation in political processes for all ethnic groups. I start from three central assumptions in this regard: (1) we have to look at strategies for reducing inequality, privilege and discrimination not only at the individual, but also at the collective level; (2) a direct support for or preferential treatment of an ethnic sub-group or minority is recommendable, however, only in specific situations; (3) in order to produce a long-lasting impact on the improvement of the socio-economic situation of a deprived group, its members must be involved directly in all decision and implementation processes, that is, they must be empowered to take matters into their own hands. Empowerment means an extension of individual and collective capacities to act in a self-determined way, to pursue the goals and values which one regards as important (Seve 1968; World Bank 2002: 10–18; Sen 1999; Ibrahim and Alkire 2007; Stockmann et al. 2010). The opposite is vulnerability which is an endemic situation in which poor people find themselves (Stockmann et al. 2010:240). Empowerment has an intrinsic value: because it implies more freedom, it increases happiness (Haller and Hadler 2004). It has also an instrumental value, permitting the expansion of assets and capabilities of poor people to participate in, negotiate with and control accountable institutions that affect their lives (World Bank 2002: 11). In this regard, also social movements are of utmost importance (Diani and McAdam 2003; Tilly 2004). Legislative measures alone are often without effect because they are vaguely formulated and because the dominant groups find ways to prevent their implementation (Mohanty 2001).

A fourth type of processes and strategies which affect ethnic stratification is related to international migration. In Chapter 5, I have sketched out some basic mechanisms which particularly the rich countries of the North employ in this regard; the prevention of mass immigration from South as well as selective immigration and integration policies were identified as relevant political strategies. In this chapter a typology of different immigration and integration policies of the states in the North is developed and their implications for the emergence of new ethno-class differentiations and inequality are indicated.

Secession and the Foundation of new Nation-states

If an ethnic-national minority is living more or less concentrated on a certain territory within a larger, heterogeneous state, secession from this state is an option which will provide it with full political autonomy. Secession will also have effects in regard to socio-economic development and inequality for the new nation; it will be an advantage in general because a new state is better integrated; and it should also eliminate exploitation by the dominant ethnie in the centre. In this section, I will discuss first the reasons for secession from the viewpoint of political philosophy and the main stages of its historical enforcement; then, an overview on historical attempts at secession is given, and the reasons for their success or failure; finally, some pre-conditions and rules are outlined which should be respected so that a secession process occurs peacefully and increases the welfare of all parties involved.

Self-determination and Secession as Basic and Powerful Human Rights

Secession is based, in principle, on the right of self-determination. While there exists no general recognized, universal right of secession, several political philosophers have argued that such a right emerges under specific conditions, particularly in the case of the oppression of a minority.[1] Even more important is that the right to secession has been established politically *de facto* already two centuries ago, when the United States declared their independence from England; another cornerstone was the French Declaration of Human and Citizen's rights of 1789. At this time, self-determination was a moral and revolutionary principle; since then, and particularly after the Second World War it has been developed to a generally recognized norm of international relations (Hannum 1990). The right to secession follows from the principle of the sovereignty of people, which implies that political power can only be exerted in consent with the governed, and that it is the right of citizens to change the form and agents of power if a government behaves in an unjust way. Thus, the idea that also a whole people or nation has certain rights was a new important element, added by the French Revolution. Individual and collective freedom are dependent on each other. A further strong impulse for the development of the idea of self-determination was provided during the First World War and the breakdown of the multi-national Habsburg and Ottoman Empires because many of their peoples successfully asked for their own nation-states after they had lost the war. US President Woodrow Wilson declared in his Fourteen Points that self-determination should be allowed to all peoples. A further affirmation of the principle of self-determination was given in the Atlantic Charter of 1941, in which President Roosevelt and Prime Minister Churchill stated that territorial adjustments after the war should be in accord with the wishes of the peoples concerned.[2] The United Nations confirmed these principles in several declarations in the 1960s and 1970s,

---

1 For an overview see http://en.wikipedia.org/wiki/Secession

2 http://en.wikipedia.org/wiki/Atlantic_Charter. For an extensive discussion see Hannum 1990.

particularly in connection with the abolition of colonialism. A UN Declaration of 1970[3] states that every nation has the right to establish its own state or to unite with another one. In Anglo-American political philosophy, a vivid discussion is going on about the rights and the conditions under which secession can be legitimized.[4] It is argued that such rights particularly exist when an ethnic group has been conquered by another people. Arguments against secession are if anarchy is threatening, if the secessionists claim rights to a territory inhabited by other people, and – a quite interesting argument related to distributive justice – if the renegade regions are wealthier than the others (Buchanan 1991).

In fact, since the beginning of the 20th century, a series of successful secession processes have taken place all over the world: 1904 Norway seceded from the Union with Sweden; 1916 Ireland from the UK; 1947 Pakistan from India; 1949 Taiwan from China; 1970 Bangladesh from Pakistan; in the early 1990s the Baltic states, Belorussia, Ukraine and other former Republics from the USSR and Slovenia and Croatia and other Republics from Yugoslavia; 1993 Slovakia from Czechoslovakia and Eritrea from Ethiopia. The last secession took place in 2011 when South Sudan split up from Sudan. In this case, most of the normative pre-conditions for secession were given: 20 years of suppression and human right violations by the northern central government; linguistic and religious differences; little economic exchange (Mathok 2009).[5] However, many historical efforts at secession were suppressed by military force. Again, the United States provides one of the earliest examples. The main reason for the outbreak of the Civil War in 1861 was the declaration of independence by the Confederate States of America, seven Southern slave states. The resulting Civil War might have been the only war in history made between two democratic nation-states (Rauch 2005). Later defeated secession efforts include those of two Southern Republics from Brazil in 1845; the secession of Katanga from the Republic of Congo in 1960; and of South-East Nigeria, called Biafra in 1967–70, from Nigeria. All these attempted secessions were abolished by brutal military interventions leading to hundreds of thousands of deaths and millions of refugees. Probably the largest number of affected people was the process of separation of Pakistan and India in 1947 which took place after a series of violent clashes and massacres between Hindus, Sikhs and Muslims all over India. In his novel *Train to Pakistan*, Khushwant Singh (1988) has described vividly the panic which captured the people during these terrible events.

Power and Deprivation as Factors Affecting the Success or Failure of Secession Movements

What are the factors leading to secessions and determining their success or failure? As I have outlined elsewhere (Haller 1996), in such a process a complex interaction is involved between elites and the population at large both in the seceding and in the mother states; issues of the preservation and/or enlargement of socio-economic rights and privileges of the different ethnic groups and their leaders play a definite role. The political elites in the central state will in principle oppose secession because it reduces their sphere of influence. For the elites in the renegade provinces, the situation looks complementary: they can gain in power and status and also in terms of socio-economic privileges through an upgrading from provincial governors to leaders of an independent state. Complaints about factual or believed ethnic domination are widely used by them as arguments for secession. For the population in the renegade provinces, the relative economic position is relevant: usually, efforts at secession are strongest in economically more developed provinces because people believe that the central government takes away too much and inhibits development; people in the poorer regions are less prone to secession since they often profit from central redistribution in the existing state. This 'power game' between the elites of the centre and the renegade region will only be overruled if – in addition to a working democratic system – the elites are prepared to trust each other, and to negotiate as long as necessary in order to arrive at commonly acceptable solutions; that is, if a consociational inter-elite accommodation takes place (Lijphart 1984).

---

3   'The Declaration on Principles of International Law Concerning Friendly Relations and Cooperation among States in Accordance with the Charter of the UN', Res. 2625 (XXV); see Kristan 1993.

4   For an overview see http://en.wikipedia.org/wiki/Secession. An extensive discussion is presented by Hurst Hannum (1990).

5   One must admit, however, that also the Southern Liberation Army (SPLA) has committed many human right violations in its fight for independence, including forced recruitment of child soldiers.

Thus, the Southern US elites who wanted to secede from the Union in 1861 feared that their way of life would be threatened and the abolition of slavery would deprive them of their cheap labour power. The Northern elites did not want that slavery would be extended to the new US territories and feared unfair competition from the South. The resulting Civil War was the deadliest in American history (with over 600,000 dead soldiers). When the Eastern Igbo-dominated province of Nigeria (Biafra) wanted to secede in 1967, General Yakubu Gowon issued the famous statement, 'To keep Nigeria as one is a task that must be done'; he and his Hausa and Fulani Muslim allies in the North were certainly motivated by the wish to preserve their privileges as leaders of this huge country which soon got huge external incomes from the export of oil. During this Nigerian civil war, hundreds of thousands of soldiers and over a million civilians died (mainly of starvation in the secessionist Eastern province) and terrible atrocities were committed. In historical retrospect, it seems tragic today that the Northern militaries who overthrew the central government and brought Gowon to power first had the intention to split the Northern from the two Southern states. They refrained from it because several advisers, including emissaries of the British and American governments, dissuaded them from this plan[6] (Forsyth 1976).

After 1989/90 a third phase of the establishment of new states out of multi-national empires started. The comparatively well-developed Baltic states and the Croats and Slovenes were the first who instigated secession because they believed that their membership in the USSR and Yugoslavia, respectively, deprived them of further developmental opportunities. The secession of Slovakia from Czechoslovakia which was only weakly based on ethnic differentiations can even be considered as the achievement of a single person, the authoritarian Slovak politician Vladimir Meciar, who pulled it through. Opinion polls showed that the majority of the Slovak population did not want the secession. Several examples of successful historical secessions clearly show that the political elites of the central governments consented mainly because they had lost power and support. The defeat of the multi-national Austria-Hungarian and Ottoman Empires in the First World War released the largest secession movement; before the war, not even the Czechs had moved toward securing their own state. It is significant in this regard that the multi-national Russian Empire did not break apart only because a new, determined elite, greedy for power – the Bolsheviks led by Lenin – took over the leadership of the country. They suppressed by force counter-revolutionary military forces (the *White Army*) which had a strong base among non-Russian nations (particular among the Ukrainians). Similarly, in the 1980s the Soviet and Yugoslav leaders and their Communist parties had lost support as a consequence of catastrophic economic decline (see Chapter 7).

Today, secession is by far not outdated as a way to solve ethnic-national conflict to provide more power and to reduce economic deprivation of ethnic minorities. Even in some large, multi-national Western countries which guarantee considerable autonomy to their different nationalities strong secession movements are active. It is quite possible that before the end of the 21st century, Quebec will have seceded from Canada, the Basque country and Catalonia from Spain, Scotland from the United Kingdom, and Belgium has broken apart into a Flemish and Wallonian state. In theory, although not in practice, it is hard to see why the Kurds – a people of nearly 30 million, with its own language and culture, and spread over four countries (Turkey, Iraq, Iran and Armenia) – should not establish their own state. In fact, they aimed to political autonomy already in the late 19th century. In the new Republic of Turkey, after Atatürk had established a modern, secular Republic in 1923, a massive program of ethnic regrouping took place which led to the deportation of hundreds of thousands of Kurds to other areas. The denial of the status of an ethnic minority later on provoked repeated insurgences against the assimilation policy of the Turkish governments, which – as a consequence – led to brutal counter-actions by Turkish military, imprisonment and torture of Kurdish leaders (Strohmeier and Yalcin-Heckmann, 2000: 92–114). This suppression of an ethnic minority confirms Mann's provocative but hardly refutable thesis (2005) that ethnic cleansing is a concomitant of modern democracy. In this case, however, already the precursor of Turkey, the Ottoman Empire, had practiced ethnic cleansing during the First World War. Then, over a million Armenian males were killed and women, children and the elderly were deported from their home regions.[7] That Turkey has followed such a harsh policy against this large minority – about 18–20

---

6   See also http://en.wikipedia.org/wiki/Yakubu_Gowon. It must be added, however, that Gowon after the surrender of Biafra followed a rather wise policy of 'no victor, no vanquished', including an amnesty to the participants in the Biafran uprising, and reconstruction and rehabilitation programs for the extensively damaged Region.

7   See http://en.wikipedia.org/wiki/Armenian_Genocide

per cent of the population – is no accident. It is certainly related to the socio-economic structure of Turkish society, which is the most unequal country at the intersection of Europe and Asia (see Table 1.1), and to some deficiencies of its democratic institutions and practices. In recent decades, however, reforms were enacted by Turkey to provide basic human rights and in some spheres (private schools, media and so on) the use of the Kurdish language is allowed. Finally, new secession movements could emerge in the vast border Republics and provinces of Russia and China which are inhabited by dozens of populous ethnic-national sub-groups with a culture very different from the dominant one; they include Muslims in several Russian Republics, Buddhists in Tibet, and Muslims (the Uyghur in the Xingjian province) in China.

Interim Conclusion: Pre-conditions for Peaceful Processes of Secession

Under which conditions can we consider secession as a realistic alternative for an ethnic-national sub-group, legitimate from the normative perspective and viable from the political-practical point of view? The most important of them include: a self-consciousness as an ethnic-national minority; a high level of political organization and unity; an adequate economic strength; the democratic character of the state from which a group or region wants to secede; support from a neighbouring 'mother' country and by the international community.

An important question here is what the value-based normative conditions are which legitimate a secession.[8] Five aspects can be mentioned in this regard: (1) first, an ethnic-national group must be sufficiently large and live on a more or less clearly delineated territory, situated in a border region of the country; (2) in practice, the population within such a territory is never fully homogeneous in ethnic terms. It is therefore essential that the dominant group of the renegade region explicitly provides full rights of the new (second-order) minorities after the establishment of the new state. In the case of the Baltic States, for instance, this has not been granted to the new large Russian minorities (Kolsto 2001); (3) very important is the procedure that has to be followed during the process of secession. Here the majority principle cannot be applied since it would imply a steamrolling of the minorities. A general principle could be that at least two separate referenda should be held before secession can take place: first, one among the prospective new minorities, asking them if they agree with the carrying through of referendum at all; then, one among the whole population about the secession itself. We can learn here also from historical examples, particularly that of Switzerland, where, after 1945, efforts were going on to split a new French-speaking Canton Jura from the mainly German-speaking Canton Bern. After a first attempt in 1957 failed, a more concerted and democratic procedure was followed in 1970, when votes at three levels were made about the decision[9]; (4) also the majority population of the seceding ethnic regional group must be fully included in a democratic process, leading eventually to secession. It was already indicated that in some cases simple leaders pushed a single through the process without asking for a proper vote on it. In these cases (Ireland, Basque country) small and self-appointed 'liberation fighters' have acted, terrorizing not only the central state, but also their own population; (5) a final condition for a peaceful process of secession is related to its point in time and speed: it seems absolutely necessary that the whole process takes enough time and is not pursued too quickly or at all costs by the province which wants to secede. If this happens, mutual misunderstandings and distrust between the centre and the renegade region will increase massively and eventually lead to a violent reaction of the centre. In fact, it seems highly probable that the war in Yugoslavia would have been avoided if Slovenia and Croatia had not declared their independence so swiftly and one-sidedly. Since the authoritarian Milosevic regime would have been overthrown at some time anyway, a later and slower approach could have brought independence to these countries without bloodshed; but it is also possible that they then would not have pursued this aim further. Thus, the violent break-up of Yugoslavia does not prove that secession is not a solution to ethnic-national conflicts;[10] the peaceful secession of many states from the former Soviet Union has already been positive for some, such as the Baltic states.

---

8   See also Buchanan 1991, Gordon 1998; for an overview http://en.wikipedia.org/wiki/Secession

9   First, there was a vote among the whole population of the relevant sub-region; second, the inhabitants of the single Communes voted to which Canton they would like to belong; third and fourth, there were ballots of all Swiss voters and of the representatives of all Cantons. See Fiseha 2006, p. 209f.

10   This thesis seems to be proposed by J. Marko (2012:268) in an article which otherwise is very informative.

Federalism

Federalism is an obvious alternative solution for ethnically differentiated societies if the ethnic groups are concentrated territorially, that is, living on more or less clearly circumscribed geographic areas within a nation-state. In this section, I will discuss the question how federalism might contribute to economic equality within a pluriethnic or multi-national state in four steps: first, federalism is defined and it's actual relevance is shown; then the relation between federalism and economic equality is sketched out; in the next section three models of federalism are discussed, one very positive (Switzerland), one partly positive (Ethiopia) and one negative (Nigeria); and finally, some interim conclusions are drawn.

Definition and Relevance of Federalism Today

Federalism is called vertical separation of state powers. In such a political system, the jurisdictions of the central government are limited by the granting of competences to lower-level regional (called variously states, regions, provinces, cantons) or local units (municipalities, towns). Seven elements are characteristic of a federal system: the existence of two or more orders of government directly acting on behalf of their citizens; a formal constitutional distribution of legislative and executive authority; a representation of the distinct regions within the federal (central) policy-making institutions (for instance, a second chamber of parliament); a supreme written constitution, amendable only by common consent of federal and regional representatives; a supreme court which rules definitely on the interpretation of the constitution; and processes and institutions which facilitate inter-governmental collaboration (Blindenbacher and Watts 2003; Scott 2011; Heinemann-Grüder 2012; Härtel 2012). Federalism plays a significant and increasing role in modern societies. Most of the largest world countries – including Brazil, Canada, India, Russia, the United States and to some degree also China – have federal constitutions. This is obvious given their size and high level of internal differentiation which preclude a central steering of every sphere of social life (Kohr 1983). However, also some small or medium-sized states have strong federal systems; Switzerland is a paradigmatic case in point. In a recent study on 42 democratic countries, Hooghe et.al. (2010) found that only eight of them had no federal structure with an appreciable degree of political autonomy of the lower-level units; 17 have one, 16 have two and one country (Germany) has even three sub-national levels of government and administration. In addition, 31 states enacted constitutional reforms between 1950 and 2006 and in 29 of them the federal structure was strengthened. A related development showing that the principle of homogeneous, fully independent nation-states is losing ground is that more and more states around the world are engaged in establishing macro-regional associations or federations; here, the European Union is a paradigmatic example (Elazar 1996; Haller 2012).

Pre-conditions for an Equalizing Effect of Federalism

The quantitative analysis in Chapter 3 has indicated that economic inequality is significantly lower in countries with a federal structure. A look at Table 1.1 (pp. 5–6) also shows that there are in fact several ethnically heterogeneous countries with a federal system and a surprising egalitarian structure; they include Belgium, Switzerland, Canada, Ethiopia and India. Federalism can be an effective instrument for a more equal distribution of the resources of states which include territorially concentrated ethnic minorities for at least five reasons: (1) regional and local problems have a higher chance to be recognized and articulated; (2) regional governments can enforce their specific interests; (3) they can push in particular a financial adjustment and equalization between the different regions of a state; (4) regional self-government creates and offers jobs of different qualifications at many levels; (5) the existence of a regional government and administration attracts also private enterprises and firms.

Federalism is no guarantee for economic equality, however. It is only one among a number of other determinants. There exist very different types of federalism depending on the degree to which the aforementioned criteria are fulfilled. In fact, we have seen that quite a number of highly unequal countries also have a federal structure, including the Latin American countries Brazil and Mexico, the United States and Russia and Sub-Saharan African states like Nigeria. Thus, it is evident that some additional conditions must be present in order for federalism to work as a political framework furthering economic equality. Two aspects are particularly relevant: the democratic character of a federal system and the degree of 'consolidation' between the ethnic and political structure.

A first and obvious condition for federalism to act in favour of ethnic-national minorities in a society is that the political system as a whole must be truly democratic, political bargaining must occur openly and the constitution must be respected by all (Blindenbacher and Watts 2003). These characteristics did not exist in the State Socialist societies in East Europe (Kolsto 2001), and they still do not really exist in many Sub-Saharan African countries. In Chapter 7 (pp. 198–200) I have shown that in the Soviet Union and Yugoslavia a 'pseudo-federalism' existed which on paper granted far-reaching autonomy to the Republics. In reality, however, the administrative and governmental authorities were dominated and tightly controlled by the vast central party apparatus (the *Nomenclatura*). When the autonomy of the Republics was threatened, as it happened in Yugoslavia under Milosevic, the political and party elites of Slovenia and Croatia united themselves and began to initiate a process of secession. Similar problems exist today in the two large African countries Nigeria and Ethiopia. I will come back to these two cases later in this section.

A second important aspect is the relation between the ethnic diversity and the constitutional structure of a federal state. The question is: What are the pre-conditions which make sure that federalism works toward more equality between ethnic groups? Here we can tie in with the useful distinction between different types of social differentiation and social structure developed by Peter M. Blau (1977) who generalizes ideas of Georg Simmel (1923; see also Haller 2008a: 20–28). Blau argues that the degree of social structural heterogeneity is determined by the number and types of parameters relevant in a society. Two types of parameters are distinguished: nominal parameters include different groups without a ranking between them, such as gender, age and ethnicity; vertical parameters, such as education or income, constitute a rank order. The more parameters are relevant in a society and the more categories each one has, the more differentiated it is. If the characteristics of a group in one parameter are highly correlated with those in other parameters, it is called a consolidated social structure, if this is not the case, a multi-form heterogeneous structure.

This idea has direct implications for the relation between ethnic differentiation and the constitutional structure of a state. If the ethnic sub-groups within a state are territorially dispersed, as is typically the case in immigrant societies, or for the Blacks in the United States, territorially based federalism certainly cannot be an instrument for granting them political autonomy and power. If the ethnic groups are living concentrated on certain areas, federalism can be a solution. It can take two forms: one is that the ethnic territories as a whole are considered as units and granted political autonomy in their own regional government; the other is that the federal sub-units are not strictly related to the ethnic divisions. Both types exist presently around the world and we can deduce some plausible hypotheses about the consequences of these two forms for social integration and stability and for economic inequality. If the ethnic and territorial-political divisions coincide, the probability that ethnic conflicts are reinforced is much higher because membership in a federal sub-unit is correlated with other social characteristics. As a consequence, regional redistribution will become more difficult because they intensify inter-regional and inter-ethnic competition and conflicts. If ethnic division and regional divisions do not coincide, the probability is reduced that conflicts arise between ethnic groups about a certain issue.

The paradigmatic case for the partial dissociation of ethnic differentiation and federal structure is Switzerland; also the present-day constitution of Nigeria corresponds to this type. An impressive example for such a type is (at least in part) also India. Examples where the two dimensions coincide include Belgium, Canada, Spain and Ethiopia. Another one was Communist Yugoslavia. In this multi-national state, established in 1918 as the United Kingdom of Serbs, Croats and Slovenes, in 1946 a strong federal system was established, constituting six Republics and two autonomous provinces. There was a high level of correspondence between social-structural and ethnic divisions and the political sub-division. The two northern Republics, Slovenia and Croatia, were distinguished from all others by their religion (Catholicism as against Orthodoxy in Serbia and Montenegro and Islam in parts of Bosnia-Herzegovina, Kosovo, and Macedonia), and by their higher level of socio-economic development; Slovenia has also its own language. After the founder of Yugoslavia, the former successful military leader Josip B. Tito, died in 1980, the animosities and conflicts between these Republics escalated to a civil war after the secession of Slovenia and Croatia in 1991. Resentments in the northern Republics about redistribution, mismanagement and corruption at the level of central government in Serbia and in the southern Republics were also nourished by ethnic-national prejudices. In Chapter 7 (p. 198ff.) I have shown that the breakdown of Yugoslavia was caused to a large degree by its hidden political-authoritarian centralism. But let us have a closer look at two of the more successful among these cases, Switzerland and Ethiopia, and on one of the less successful, Nigeria, which shows that federalism is no guarantee for equality.

Switzerland: the Strength of Democratic and Dissociated Federalism

Switzerland, although a small country (about 8 million people), is highly differentiated internally by language (four groups) and by religion (Catholics and Protestants, and recently also immigrated Muslims from Bosnia and Turkey).[11] The federal division into 26 Cantons, however, is not related directly to these divisions; there exists not one Canton for the German-, the French- and Italian-speaking communities, but the first two large groups are split over several Cantons. However, the single Cantons, most of them rather small, are homogeneous internally, each with an officially dominant language. The Swiss Confederation, established as early as 1291 by three small rural communities, has grown over the centuries by the voluntary accession of all other territories. Today, it constitutes a very complex federal system which solves the problem of preserving unity and diversity in a unique way. First, majorities both of the Cantons and the citizens' votes are necessary when general decisions (such as about a change of the constitution) have to be made; in this way, the interests of small Cantons are preserved even if a majority of the population thinks otherwise.[12] Second, Switzerland has developed a paradigmatic type of a *consociational democracy* in which extensive discussions and negotiations precede political decisions which then are usually made by consensus (Lehmbruch 1967; Lijphart 1984). Third, the instrument of direct democracy, popular decisions (referenda) about single issues, plays an important role; the outcomes of referenda often contradict the aims and plans of the elites. These are constrained, therefore, to seek widely acceptable solutions right from the start of a political discussion. Swiss federalism, although quite expensive, enjoys large support among the population. There was never any serious discussion about the secession of the French or Italian Cantons, or of restricting the autonomy of the Cantons in a significant way.

This extremely well-balanced political system has been able to preserve Swiss unity and political independence in spite of a short civil war in 1848, persistent and deep-going conflicts between religious and political factions (Catholics vs. Protestants, Conservatives vs. Liberals) throughout the 19th century, and military threats from outside during the World Wars. Federalism has certainly contributed to make this country and its economy one of the strongest and richest worldwide with a very high level of immigration and a moderate level of economic inequality[13] (see Table 1.1). Today, Switzerland is among the top three countries around the world in all relevant positive development indicators and shows the lowest values in social and political problems (see Table 6.1). Together with the Norwegians and Australians, most Swiss think that the middle strata are the largest in their society (see Figure 6.2).

Federalism contributed significantly to economic equality because Switzerland has also an extensive policy of regional redistribution. It operates through several channels: A revenue equalization between the Cantons; extra support for health and social services in the less developed Cantons; extensive assistance of agriculture, particularly in the mountain areas; a comprehensive development of public transport infrastructure (roads, railway lines, bus systems) also into remote and mountainous areas.[14] In this way, huge sums of money are

---

11   Informative descriptions of the Swiss constitutional system and politics are given in Elsasser et al. 1988; Fleiner 2001; Fiseha 2006 (pp. 197–211).

12   A very important split in this regard occurred in several decisions and referenda about the access of Switzerland to the European Union. In 1992, large majorities of both Swiss parliaments were in favour of it, but a narrow majority of the citizens rejected it (see Haller 2008b: 12).

13   The distribution of wealth, however, is very unequal (see Table 6.4).

14   For summaries see Hansjörg Blöchliger, *Baustelle Föderalismus, Buchverlag der Neuen Zürcher Zeitung*, Zürich 2005; *Expertenkommission im Auftrag des Staatssekretariats für Wirtschaft, Überprüfung und Neukonzeption der Regionalpolitik*, Zürich 3003; Markus Schneider, *Umverteilung: Fluss ohne Wiederkehr, Die Weltwoche* (Zürich), 18 November 2013.

transferred from the rich Cantons and cities (Zurich, Basel, Geneva) to the poorer Cantons and Communes. This policy has certainly been successful in many regards: in Switzerland, one will hardly find degenerated urban areas or decaying rural villages as is frequently the case in the French or Italian Alps; the level of regional inequality (as measured by the regional dispersion of the GNP per capita) is lower in Switzerland than in other central European countries of comparable size (Austria, Czech Republic, Denmark) and much lower than in all larger West European countries.[15] However, this strong regional redistribution has also aroused criticism which focused on several negative concomitants: the falling back of Switzerland as a whole in growth of productivity because the support for the weaker regions led to relative neglect of strong centres; lack of transparency of many cash flows; construction and sustenance of too many, little used infrastructures; negative incentives for Cantons and Communes which are induced to spend money but not to act in efficient and economical ways. As a consequence, Switzerland is now redirecting its regional policy to find a new, more efficient balance between the promotion of economic growth centres and support of peripheral regions.

Federalism as an Instrument for the Safeguarding of Power and Privilege: the Case of Nigeria

In Nigeria, the most populous country in Africa (today with over 130 million inhabitants), the federal structure was inherited from British colonial administration; it consisted of a tripartite structure with three large, but very unequal regions which were also loosely related to ethnic differentiations. The North, dominated by the Muslim Hausa-Fulani, constituted the majority of the population (about 40 per cent); the South-Eastern region was dominated by the Igbo, the South-Western region by the Yoruba. The people in these two regions are mainly Christian. Within each of these three regions, many additional, smaller ethnic groups exist, and also many members of the three main ethnic groups live in other territories than those distinguished here. Between 1967 and 1996, federalism was extended continuously by the military governments by creating more and smaller federal units (36 in the end). In this way, they tried to come to grips with the continuous conflicts and violent fights between the different ethnic groups. These conflicts involved not only the three large, but also the several hundred smaller, ethnic groups which make Nigeria, maybe together with India, the ethnically most differentiated country worldwide (Levinson 1998: 156–9; Anugwom 2006; Akinwumi et al. 2007; Olaniyi 2007; Heinemann-Grüder 2012). Today, Nigeria is a formal democracy, but lacks many prerequisites for a well-functioning democracy.[16] The original tripartite federal system was differentiated into more and smaller units because an imbalance existed between the large, politically dominant Muslim North and the two southern provinces which on their side were more developed but had little political influence – a situation containing a blasting force for violent conflicts.[17] The military coup of 1966 led to a concentration of political power in the South; as a consequence, another new military coup in the same year brought again a northern leader, General Yakubu Gowon, to power. The reaction was the secession of the Southeast province where Igbos established their own new state of Biafra; this state was subdued in 1970 after a cruel civil war. In subsequent military coups, the federal system of Nigeria was continuously changed toward more and more regional units; at the same time, a presidential system was introduced.

All in all, the military was 28 years in power in Nigeria between 1960 and 1999 (when the first president was elected); the military 'has ruled by decrees, eroding the independence of the judiciary and trampling on the rule of law, in a profoundly authoritarian way' (Fiseha 2006: 172). It is not only this irksome legacy which limits the potential of the Nigerian federal system to work in a way which observes the interests of all ethnic groups. Today, Nigeria has 36 states which do not coincide with the many ethnic subdivisions; the Muslim Hausa-Fulani area in the North is subdivided into ten states, the Yoruba area into seven, and the Igbo area into five states. However, although ethnicity was explicitly not considered as a criterion for the forming of these states, it played a significant role implicitly; the creation of many new territories and related administrations

---

15   In 2001, the Index of interregional variation of GNP per capita was 14 in Switzerland, 30.6 in Austria, 33 in the Czech Republic, 27 in Denmark, about 26 in Germany and Italy, about 45 in France and the UK; only in the Netherlands, Sweden and Greece it was as low as in Switzerland (see Blöchliger, Baustelle Föderalismus, Footnote 14 above).

16   On Nigeria and its federal system see Fiseha 2006 (165–82); Suberu 2006.

17   A similar situation existed in Uganda and led there to the rise of Idi Amin who led one of the bloodiest regimes in Sub-Saharan Africa (see Chapter 10, p. 261)

also produced tens, if not hundreds of thousands of new posts at the federal, state and local levels. The outcome was no rationally planned structure; rather, the proliferation of states had the function of enabling all ethnic groups to participate in public resources and of stabilizing the existing regimes at the national, state and local levels. A related fundamental problem of Nigeria is that about 80 per cent of all government finances come from the export of oil; the consequence is that both the national and the state governments are strongly dependent on the distribution of these revenues (Suberu 2006). The centre receives the largest amount of them (56 per cent), the rest is divided between the states and localities. This 'fiscal centralism' (Suberu 2006: 77), in connection with the large powers of the president (a characteristic of most African countries, as outlined in Chapter 10, pp. 272–6), has very negative consequences: '... both the revenue allocation system and the federal character concept have focused Nigerian politics corruptly, inefficiently and even explosively around the distribution of centralized economic and political opportunities, thereby undermining genuine federalism, unity, democracy and development' (Suberu 2006: 77). As a consequence, inequality between the regions has increased and Nigeria today is a very unequal country (see Table 1.1).

Historical Federalism and State Socialism as Forces Reducing Inequality: the Cases of Ethiopia and Tanzania

Nevertheless, federalism can also be a viable solution for integration and equality in poor nations of the Global South. In Chapter 8 the case of India was discussed, the most impressive and successful example of such a nation. A few similar examples, however, exist also in Sub-Saharan Africa. Here, Ethiopia and Tanzania stand out by a considerable degree of equality: in fact, with a Gini coefficient around 35 they are similar to the ethnically homogeneous North Africa countries (see Table 1.1) In both cases we can see an effect of federalism and of State Socialism.

Ethiopia seems predestined for a high level of inequality: with about 80 different tribes and languages, this huge, 80-million-inhabitant country is one of the most diversified in terms of ethnic differentiation in Africa (and in the world). Over centuries, it was also a very unequal, feudal society with the three classes of peasants, warrior-rulers and priests; in this society, people were very conscious and respectful of class status (Schicho 2004, vol. 3, pp. 195–217; Markakis and Ayele 2006: 19, 26). However, for most of its history, Ethiopia was a de facto federation (Fiseha 2006: 13). In this country which was one of the oldest continuous African kingdoms, the rulers could never govern in absolute terms because the feudal lords controlled each other and the emperor, fighting over seizure of central power and succession as emperor (Hoben 1973). The power of the Ethiopian rulers was under control because they often needed the support of regional rulers to defend the country against external invaders which threatened the existence of the country repeatedly (Meyer Fortes 1961). Also the Christian Coptic Church was quite independent and had considerable influence (Illife 1997: 78–85). Already in the early 15th century, the Ethiopian kings sought contacts with European rulers. Ethiopia was the only country in Africa which was able to resist invasions and colonialism despite repeated attempts from neighbours in the North, West and East.[18] In the war between Ethiopia and the expansive Muslim Sultanate Adal (1529–43), Portugal assisted Ethiopia in its victorious Battle of Wayna Daga and probably rescued it from demise. In 1875, Ethiopian troops defeated an army of Turkish/Egyptian forces and in 1896 an Italian invasion army at Adwa; particularly the latter victory was and still is a historical event of pride for people throughout Africa (Abraham n.d.: 45–74).

The persistence of the federal structure of Ethiopia was also related to its internal geographical and social structure: the farmers in the fertile high lands (where also – unique for Africa – a simple plough was in use) had their own rights on the land. But these land rights, as in most other parts of Africa (Maathai 2009: 227), applied to the kinship group or community, not to an individual person or family; they had only the right to the use of land (Ziegler 2008: 174). This *rist* system was highly valued and defended against all efforts to abolish it. The members of the aristocracy had the right to *gult*, a tribute of the farmers in the form of labour to their local rulers.[19] However, despite their rights, farmers had to pay a plethora of taxes; so, they were often 'reduced to living on the borderline of subsistence and under the menace of periodic famine' (Markakis

---

18   With the exception of the period 1936–41 when fascist Italy occupied the country; Italy was never able, however, to control the entire territory (see Schicho 2004: 195ff.).

19   A different situation emerged in the huge new territories in Southern Ethiopia which were conquered by emperor Menelik II in the early 20th century. There, land was distributed to members of the Northern aristocracy and the local

and Ayele 2006: 27). But the socio-cultural distance between lords and population at large was never very pronounced (Hoben 1973; Freund 1998). What is most important is that despite the extreme poverty, which characterizes Ethiopia till today, the population was never enslaved on a broad scale. Thus, Ethiopia was already in historic times a relatively equal country; this was reflected also in the violent antagonism to the authoritarian regime established by Haile Selassie from 1939 to 1974 (Markakis and Ayele 2006: 77). This stimulated also protest movements among students and critical intellectuals which in the end led to his downfall (Balsvik 2005; Markakis and Ayele 2006).

The second reason for the comparatively low level of economic inequality of Ethiopia is its recent history of Socialism. The egalitarianism of society and politics was strengthened massively between 1974 and 1987, when the authoritarian 'Communist' DERG regime was in power which radically abolished all aristocratic privileges, nationalized banks and enacted an extensive land reform (Schicho 2004: 208). Ethnic divisions played a decisive role when the DERG military junta was overthrown by a coalition between forces of the largest ethnic group of Ethiopia, the Amhara, and the ethnic group of Tigre who dominated in the Northern Province of Eritrea (their coalition was called Ethiopian People's Revolutionary Democratic Front, EPRDF) because the DERG regime had eliminated their independence. The DERG leader from 1974 to 1987, Mengistu Haile Mariam, was from the ethnic group of the Oromo, settling mainly in Southern Ethiopia and always under the control and exploitation of the dominant ethnic groups and emperors. At the level of the general population, ethnic differences were downplayed by the regime. The reforms of the Communist DERG regime have not been abolished altogether after its overthrow. Use of the farm land in Ethiopia, for instance, remains to a large degree in the hands of small farmers; they produce 95 per cent of the coffee beans, one of the most important export goods of the country (Ziegler 2008: 168). The educational system still includes elements of central planning and development, provides special support for the smaller ethnic groups and their languages and aims to avoid the resurgence of ethnic chauvinism.[20] In 1994, a new constitution was adopted, creating nine autonomous provinces along linguistic-ethnic lines, thus again strengthening regional self-government (Turton 2006; Ziegler 2008: 162ff.).

The effect of Socialism can be also seen in the case of Tanzania. This is a huge country in East Africa localized between the Indian Ocean and the Great Lakes (Küper 1973; Schicho 2004/III: 310–335). The continental part – formerly Tanganyika – is inhabited by many small ethnic groups; it was a former German and British colony and it has significant proportions of Christians. The Muslim-dominated islands Zanzibar and Pemba experienced a second wave of colonization by Arab and Indian rulers in the 19th century who exploited slave labour on a big scale. In Tanganyika, the charismatic leader Julius Nyerere of the Independence Movement, TANU, introduced a moderate form of Socialism, which was extended to Zanzibar after their unification as the Republic of Tanzania in 1964. Equality was propagated as a guiding ideal, a the control of large-scale production, imports, development of educational and health systems as a means toward that end was introduced. In the latter regards, some achievements were attained which last until today (Aminzade 2013). Today Tanzania is a rather equal society in the Sub-Saharan Africa continent (see Table 1.1). A failure of the Socialist politics of Nyerere, however, was the planned large-scale socialization of the rural communes and production in the course of which about five million people were resettled into agricultural communes (*Ujamaas*).

Interim Résumé

We may close this section with four general conclusions concerning the relevance of federalism for the reduction of inequality in ethnic heterogeneous state societies:

1. First, it is beyond question that federalism is an appropriate and powerful institutional mechanism for guaranteeing possibilities for socio-economic, cultural and political autonomy of ethnic sub-groups

---

population (among them many Muslim ethnic groups, such as the Oromo, Somali and others) were reduced to the status of tenants.

20   Ethiopian university students, for instance, are distributed by the central authorities all over the huge country and its provinces.

and minorities in a society. However, federalism is no guarantee in this regard; several additional conditions must be given for its positive effects.

2. A foremost condition is that a country is a real democracy, that its constitution is not only written on paper but determines political processes and is practiced in everyday political life. If this is not the case, federalism can be used as an instrument by the ruling classes to consolidate their hold on power. Also the leaders and elites, and the higher 'service classes' (Goldthorpe et al. 1987) of all ethnic sub-groups and regional sub-units can use federalism as an instrument to preserve and increase privileges by creating myriads of public jobs and unlock many sources of unearned income.

3. If in a country the ethnic-national sub-groups are settling in a more or less compact manner on specific territories of a country, the question arises if the borders of the living spaces of the ethnic groups should coincide with the political-administrative borders of the regional sub-units. The answer seems to be straightforward: it seems much better and conflict-damping if they do not fully coincide. Switzerland can be quoted as a paradigmatic positive example; former Yugoslavia was discussed as a negative one. However, in some countries such a divergence may not be advisable because of historical reasons. Old and well-established Western democracies, like Belgium, Spain and Canada, show that such a kind of federalism may be working, but is also continuously challenged till the present day. The regional units in Ethiopia, devised in the new constitution on purpose along ethnic lines, might provide an additional test as to how such an arrangement will work.

4. One last point not discussed before should be mentioned here at least. In addition to within-nation federalism, also the many newly emerging federations of states around the world might be an instrument for bringing about more equality both between and within the nation-states. The reasons are that the establishment of a federation fosters the opening of the economies of the participant states; thus it leads to an increase of trade between them, which in sequel supports economic growth. Such an opening is particularly important in the case of secessionist states which often are very small. For this reason Slovenia and the Baltic States have sought to get access to the EU as soon as possible. In addition, if the regional association goes so far – as the European Union has done – to implement common economic policies, it will also include sooner or later elements of regional redistribution and equalization. Such macro-regional associations may also be helpful for mitigating ethnic conflicts. Ethnic minorities within a state often have a 'mother state' in which this ethnic group is dominant. In such a case, the relations between the two states are crucial: if they are peaceful, a solution for the autonomy of the minority group in the other state can often be found more easily.

Policies for the Empowerment of Deprived Ethno-classes

There exists a third form of situation in which deprived ethnic minorities may find themselves where neither secession nor federalization are feasible strategies to improve their situation. These are groups which are relatively clearly circumscribed and visible as ethnic groups or even ethno-classes but which are spread over large parts of a state. Examples include for example Blacks and Natives in the USA and the Gypsies in Europe. In other cases (such as Brazil), class and ethnic membership are intertwined in a complex way, producing clearly privileged and disadvantaged ethno-classes without clear boundaries between the groups. Which policies and measures are adequate in such a situation? In this section, I propose a third set of strategies which seem advisable in order to improve the situation of these deprived ethnic minorities and to reduce overall economic inequality.

As outlined in the beginning of this chapter, I start from three central assumptions: (1) we have to look at strategies for reducing inequality, privilege and discrimination not only at the individual, but also at the collective level; (2) a direct preferential treatment of an ethnic sub-group of minority is recommendable, however, only in specific situations. This is so because the different causes of discrimination usually affect not only the members of an ethnic sub-group, but also members of other deprived strata, and because preferential treatment of an ethnically defined sub-group can easily slide into a problematic form of favouritism; then, it is usually very difficult to draw benefits from a group even if its situation has improved and they would no longer be entitled to that benefit. Evidence for the problematic effects of many forms of affirmative action is also provided by the fact that they are strongly opposed by the groups affected negatively by them; (3) the strategies and policies proposed should not be devised by political elites and experts alone and applied from above, but developed by the concerned social groups themselves. Their main aim should be empowerment: assisting the deprived groups to develop by themselves the instruments and strategies most beneficial for them. It is indicative that also authors in the Global South see empowerment as a crucial aspect of development (Mutua 2010: 68). Traditional development aid apparently has only limited effectiveness; the South East Asian countries received much less aid than Africa but developed much better (Kerbo 2012: 503–17; Ziltener 2013). Development aid by government and NGOs has even serious negative side-effects: it does not support, or even impedes, local entrepreneurism and activities; it often destroys regional markets; and it is misused by corrupt leaders and military governments (Stockmann and Gaebe 2003; Nuscheler 2004; Polman 2010). For the Nobel Peace Prize Winner of 2005, the Kenyan Wangari Maathai (2009: 129), disempowerment – the lack of self-confidence, apathy, fear and the inability to take charge of one's life – is the most unrecognized problem of Sub-Saharan Africa today. Four central elements of empowerment are relevant in this regard: improvement of access by poor people to information; inclusion of all persons and groups concerned; accountability, that is the ability to call public officials, and private employers and service providers to account for their actions; and improvement of local organizational capacity, the ability of people to work together, and mobilize resources to solve problems of common interest (World Bank 2002: 14–17; see also Sen 1999, 2010).

Which concrete societal institutions, instruments and measures are most important, when the focus is on empowerment? Certainly, nearly every area of policy affects also the socio-economic situation and opportunities of members of ethnic minorities and deprived ethno-classes. This is certainly so for ethno-policies related to the labour market and direct measures of economic redistribution, but it is also true for policies aiming toward the preservation of the cultures of minorities, their languages and religions (for overviews see Cordell and Wolff 2004; Toggenburg and Rautz 2010). One could mention here also the eight Millennium Development Goals (World Development Report 2012: 18–19). These aims, however, are either very general, focusing on groups not in the centre of interest in this book or on specific issues and problems. I will focus in the following on the discussion of three aspects which are general and very relevant from the perspective of ethno-class discrimination and deprivation: educational policy; community, town and regional planning, and welfare state policy. All these three aspects lie across the Millennium Development Goals but are highly relevant also for their achievement. For each of these areas, I try to justify why they are important; present some empirical facts related to ethno-class deprivation and inequality in the respective area; and sketch out a few basic principles which a self-empowerment policy should follow.

Comprehensive Egalitarian Educational Policy

Education is of utmost importance in the modern world: as human capital, it is the basis for individual achievement in the world of work, and it fosters personal development, independence and self-reliance in every sphere of life; in this regard, it is particularly important for girls and women. At the societal level, a good general and vocational education of a population is the basis for sustained economic growth, but also for civic and political participation (Lutz 2009; Sauer and Zapter 2011; UNESCO 2012; Dreze and Sen 2013). Looking at the global situation, all countries around the world have made significant progress concerning enrolment rates at the elementary level; their rates are now 87 per cent in the developing world, but South Asia and Sub-Saharan Africa still lie behind (World Bank 2012: 4). Even more disturbing is that the quality of schooling often remains very poor. Reasons are that children start too late, attend the schools irregularly and drop out early. What is most important here is that there exist huge differences between the rich and poor strata, particularly in the Global South. Some examples: in Colombia, one of the most unequal countries around the world, 42 per cent of children from poor households started their school career too late, but only 11 per cent from rich households; in Ghana, over half of females and one-third of males 19–29 years old who had attended six years of school could not read afterwards; in Turkey, 64 per cent of boys from poor households, but only 30 per cent of girls attend a lower secondary school; among rich households, gender parity exists (UNESCO 2012: 6–15; see also UNDP 2013). All these countries are characterized by pervasive economic inequality (see Table 1.1). It is certainly the case that the inequalities in education are particularly pronounced for members of lower classes containing large proportions of ethnic minorities. There are five aims toward which educational policy should strive in order to improve the educational situation and opportunities of deprived ethno-classes:

1. A main problem in this regard, particularly in the poor and the developing countries in South Asia, Sub-Saharan Africa and Latin America, is that the school system is often split into a well-developed, high-quality system for the upper class on the one side, and an insufficient system for the poor on the other side; which one of them is private and which one public varies between countries. In Sub-Saharan Africa the public elementary schools are rather poor and cheap; in Brazil, the high-quality tertiary education system is public and supported by the state; it is not expensive, but social selection operates earlier, since only the private lower systems have the quality to prepare their students for university entrance. The overwhelming proportion of families from the poorer social strata can afford only to send their children to the cheap and poor system; in this way the ground is laid for life-long lower opportunities. It is really a scandal that private businesses and entrepreneurs can make huge profits out of the bad educational services they offer and use them also as a means for political clientelism.[21] Thus, a first aim at the elementary level is that the educational system of any country should be of good quality for every child and youth. It seems that this can best be assured if all children can attend an inexpensive public school; it must be assured, however, that the public school system retains high quality throughout a country. Also at the secondary and tertiary levels, at least a significant part should be public, thus assuring both that it has high quality and is affordable for persons from lower ethnic class backgrounds. Empowerment of the concerned people is highly relevant here: the development of a high-quality basic and secondary school system can be furthered and enhanced significantly if all relevant actors at the community level are involved in decision-making, and if teachers, administrators and government officials are made accountable for the workings of the school system (World Bank 2002: 172). School and community pride and morale are raised if a well-designed school development planning takes place, which involves the local community and all relevant issues (Sanoff 2000: 106).

2. The school system should also be comprehensive and integrated; that is, children should be sorted as late as possible into different tracks of education whereby one leads to higher, qualified occupations, the other only to manual and service jobs. However, one should not make these two strategies into an absolute. First, we must keep in mind the limited success of reforms of the education system in the 1970s and 1980s aiming at removing class inequalities; the lesson from them is that 'educational inequalities and their ideological justifications cannot be fought from within education alone' (Williams 1986: 150). Thus, a radical reform of the educational system would entail improving not only its instrumental function for providing human capital and improving mobility chances for lower classes (a function which is supported, for instance in Brazil, also by the dominant classes; see Reis: 1996), but also its function of equalizing society as a whole. In fact, many Sub-Saharan African countries consider the establishment of a more equal society now as a main goal of education (Davies 1986). Second, it is a matter of fact that state intervention must not necessarily be associated with the aim of a reduction of inequality and stratification (as presupposed by Esping-Andersen 1990). That is, the extent and direction of state intervention must be seen as two separate dimensions (Beblavý et al. 2011). In many countries the extended private system of secondary and higher education cannot be transferred as a whole into a public system. In this regard, we can tie in with the recommendations of the World Development Report (2012: 34) that the non-state sector should be recognized as an important provider, funder and innovator in education; it is particularly strong in South Asia, Latin America and the Caribbean. In these countries, public authorities should also support this sector financially and provide educational and didactic know-how, personal and technical resources.

3. The regional distribution of schools at all levels should be well-balanced so that also in remote, peripheral and rural areas children and the youth have access to good schools at the primary and secondary level. Today, the higher schools and universities in poorer countries are strongly concentrated in cities and economically strong regions. In these countries, a high proportion of children end elementary

---

21 T. Fatheuer (1994: 35) shows how this happens in the Brazilian school system. The inhabitants of the big slum Kibera in Nairobi pay each year $40 to 50 million to the owners of their huts living outside the slum (Mutua 2001).

schooling without having acquired a basic literacy (UNESCO 2012: 1–13). Reasons are too large teacher-pupil ratios (they are 26:1 globally, but 40:1 in Sub-Saharan Africa); inadequately trained and paid teachers; absenteeism of pupils, particularly of girls, because they are required to help at home, constrained to marry early and burdened by unplanned pregnancies. Residential segregation within cities was one of the main factors which the famous Coleman Report (Coleman et al. 1966) found responsible for the lower school achievement of Black children in the USA. A similar process today may be at work in European cities where children of immigrant parents are concentrated in specific town districts and types of schools (Wong and Nicotera 2004; Braun and Voss 2014: 59–62).

4. In order to assure an adequate representation of deprived minorities in the higher school system, deliberate quotas may be considered. However, the effects of quota systems are often limited as the Indian experience has shown (see p. 219). Moreover, they can have negative effects on the preferred minorities themselves, by lowering the quality of the graduating cohort of the targeted group and later leading to income discrimination in the labour market (Wydick 2008). A system of special college preparation courses for the youth from discriminated groups might be a better solution; its key would be to improve the ability of parents and teachers to identify gifted children at an early age. Additional support can be provided by courses on computer and information technology skills by nation-wide governmental or charitable organizations; such activities have been organized successfully in Brazil for the youth living in favelas and for Indian villagers (World Bank 2002: 73–84).

5. Parents and communities should be empowered to participate in the establishment and development of educational facilities and in the running of the school system.

A report of the World Bank (2002:173) states in this regard: 'Education is an area in which expanding the involvement of community actors has led to marked improvements – higher enrolments and better quality schools'. One reason is that by such forms of participation, teachers, administrators and government officials are made accountable for their actions and behaviour; another one, that the parents and community members themselves can contribute in various ways to an improvement of the schools.

Community, Town and Regional Development and Planning

The second overall political perspective for coming to grips with the situation of deprived ethno-classes is a comprehensive process of community, town and regional development. The district and house, country and region where one lives is a central determinant of life chances. Two streams of arguments are relevant in this regard; the first relates to patterns of ethno-class segregation and socio-economic discrimination, the second to the phenomenon of local and regional identity and the potential for the emergence of grass-roots movements.

First, ethnic discrimination is correlated highly with countrywide and intra-urban patterns of residential segregation of ethnic groups. These patterns are closely connected with deprivation in many other regards, in the provision of basic social services (education, health, safety), public infrastructures (roads and transport, water and energy) and employment and income opportunities.[22] Patterns of residential segregation, on their side, are connected with a significant grade in power between town and countryside, centre and periphery, both within nation-states and worldwide (Reuber 2012: 103–6). We have encountered sharp patterns of nation-wide segregation and discrimination of deprived classes and ethnic groups throughout this book: in China, the main dividing line between prosperous and poor regions is between the eastern and central areas, where the core ethnic group, the Han, reside, and the vast western rural areas, where most minorities live (Ping 1986). Massive inequalities related to ethnic differentiations within cities also exist in Sub-Saharan Africa and Latin America; both the African slums and Latin American favelas house over-proportional numbers of people from poor ethnic groups or Blacks (Pallier 2010; Dymski 2011). The relatively low level of urbanization of India can only be understood if one knows that millions of 'metro campers', poor communities from the countryside, camp on the brink of the megacities in slum-like cheap accommodations (Farndon 2008: 179ff.). These 'shadow cities' (Neuwirth 2006) are increasing at an extremely rapid rate in the megacities of the South since the millions of migrants from the countryside can afford to live only in such settlements (Münz and Reiterer 2010: 178–82).

---

22 For the effects of residential school segregation on inequality see Logan et al. 2012.

In India it is especially in the countryside where the members of the Scheduled Castes and Tribes are deprived because they do not own their own land (Moharty 2001). Also in Brazil, the regional context and its interactions with skin colour and gender are of decisive importance: '... it has been estimated that if you are a Black female living in the rural north-east you have 95% chance of falling below the poverty line' (Reis 1966: 199). Ethnic segregation over the macro-regions and states of the USA has not changed very much between 1880 and 1960:

> Despite much-touted mass migration of the American population to the West, the regional distribution of the total population in 1960 is quite similar to that in 1880; the Blacks still predominate in the South, European immigrants in the East and Centre, and the Mexicans in the South-West. This pattern is closely related to differential job and income opportunities. Particularly those regions where blacks are concentrated fare less well than others (Katzman 1969).

Table 11.3 (p. 297) shows that in several southern US states, the proportion of Blacks still is between 28 per cent and 36 per cent; in Washington, DC it is 61 per cent. On the other side, in about half of the US states, the proportion of Blacks is below 10 per cent. Similar trends and structures can be observed in regard to intra-urban residential segregation within American cities, as shown before (see also Dicken and Lloyd 1984: 298–316; Massey and Denton 1989, 1990, 1993). In Western Europe, immigrants with ethnic backgrounds other than the natives also often concentrate in suburban towns, although this tendency is stronger in the large French and British cities than in Germany (Meyer 2007; See also Jandly et al. 2003; Fassmann et al. 2009). In many Western cities, processes of gentrification are going on through which wealthier residents and strong businesses return to inner-city areas, often to the detriment of the poorer residents there. An accompanying phenomenon is the 'revanchist city' whereby middle- and upper-class people as well as the media exaggerate the dangers of inner cities inhabited mainly by immigrants, ethnic minorities, homeless people and other problem groups (Smith 1996: 207). These groups are less and less supported by town politics (Reuber 2012: 108–13). In former State Socialist countries, such as the Soviet Union or China, restrictions on immigration of rural people into cities have been relaxed with the consequence of massive immigration. Moscow has grown strongly in the last decades; with over 11 million inhabitants (15 million in the agglomeration) it is now the largest European town. Economic inequality is highest in Moscow compared to other Russian towns and provinces – a fact which is certainly connected with the presence of 15 per cent ethnic non-Russians in the town.[23] In this regard Moscow is very similar to New York (see Chapter 11). In China, a massive rural-urban migration led to an increase of the urban population with permanent residence status from 191 million in 1980 to 455 million in 2000 (Ping 1996).

A second aspect proving the importance of the regional-territorial level for patterns of ethnic discrimination relates to local and regional identity and to the potential for the rise of movements to combat inequalities. The space, the places and regions where one lives have considerable symbolic significance for the residents and arouse regional consciousness and identity (Strassoldo and Tessarin 1992). Most close social relations have a territorial base; the names of places are connected with many common experiences, including ceremonies and feasts which consecrate a place. The French geographer Paul Claval (1998: 155) has emphasized this point most clearly: 'Space is a major factor cementing groups. It gives a very strong sentimental coloration to identities based on territories ... and contributes to encouraging those based on common origins, similar ways of life or shared roles and convictions'. The neglect of this cultural aspect had clearly negative consequences in the agrarian reforms in some Latin American countries where the rural population is mainly Indian. While open racial discrimination disappeared, other problems emerged, including an alienation of the *campesinos* from their way of life (which still is depreciated), leaving them 'with a confused and hybrid identity' (Calderón 1977: 218; for a case study in Uganda see Batungi 2008). Paul Claval (1998: 156) points also to the close connection between territory and ethnicity: 'The strongest argument that geographical groups can advance to justify their coherence is that of being a native: people are born in a place and belong to it. Ancestors sprang from the local ashes and earth and returned there at their death, in an endless cycle renewed within each generation'. Collective memories are often connected with the idea of a promised land and the memory of wanderings which a group had to incur in order to arrive in this land. We found this particularly in the case of the South Africa Boers and of the Jews in Israel.

---

23   See *Ria Novosti*, 8.6.2012 (http://de.ria.ru/society/20110608/259389334.html).

The existence of territorial-regional identity can also be seen as a strong element supporting the organization of deprived ethno-class groupings, the arousal of their consciousness and the strengthening of their cooperation and collective organization. In this way, terrains of resistance may emerge (Reuber 2012: 128–42). What are the possibilities for local-territorial units and the people living there to participate in social and political affairs and to fight for a reduction of deprivation and discrimination? Here, we can tie in with the literature on Community Planning. Three general aspects must be considered in a planning process which really involves the people at the grass-roots (see the comprehensive works of E.D. Kelly and B. Becker 2000, and H. Sanoff 2000): first, all relevant, competent and concerned parties and groups must be involved. These include professional planners (their task, however, finishes after a plan is approved), the representatives of the central government and administration, the local political leaders and public officials and, last but not least, the citizens in the area. Second, the development of a comprehensive plan must include all topics relevant for local, county and regional development. They include: the use of public and private land; designating particular areas for entrepreneurial-industrial, consumer or recreational use; the specification of future development centres, of historic sites and central places; the planning of transportation and circulation; environmental, park and open-space planning; planning of utilities and infrastructure (electricity and gas, telephone and TV, water and sewer services); school and health facilities; housing. Third, a comprehensive planning must consider the question of the appropriate units and levels of planning. Citizens' interests might be focused mainly on local needs and problems; central governmental actors will think in a nation-wide framework. It is important to consider interactions between planning at different levels and include territorial units which are outside the scope of those who first identify a problem. The reliable provision of a poor neighbourhood with clean water may only be possible if a large regional system of water supply is established; the building of an interstate highway cannot ignore local land uses, forms of housing estates or recreation areas. Top-down federal initiatives concerning the role of slums and favelas often unleashed bottom-up organizing energy and participatory voices (Dymski 2011: 31).

Can the situation of deprived ethno-classes be tackled and improved by such a policy? It is beyond doubt that this question can be answered in a positive way: for ethnic groups concentrated on specific, disadvantaged territories – be these ghettos in large towns of the North, slums within the megacities of the South, or remote, underdeveloped rural areas in huge nation-states – an improvement in any one of these aspects would be a definite progress. The reason why the minorities living in such areas have fewer opportunities and face life-long deprivation is exactly that their places of living are insufficiently equipped with good transportation and infrastructure (which causes them continuous waste of time), sanitation and health services (which reduces health and longevity beginning) and scarce educational and employment opportunities.

Will deprived ethnic minorities and social groups be interested in, and be ready and able to participate in processes of community planning? This is an issue which is clearly underexposed in works on the topic. Kelly and Becker (2000), for instance, rightly emphasize that the participation of citizens in all stages of the planning process is essential; most chapters of their book include a box 'The Role of the Individual Citizen'. However, this citizen remains a somewhat pallid figure, there is no hint toward differences in interest and participation by age and gender, levels of education, by occupational skill and responsibility and, alas, by ethnicity. Also in Sanoff's handbook (2000) there is no particular reference to the role of ethnic minorities. There exists a vast literature, however, on political participation which shows that those who are better educated, employed in good positions, and economically well-off are much more interested and active (see for example Schäfer and Schoen 2011). Thus, it would be a first requirement for planners to consider carefully the characteristics of the ethnic groups involved and to provide for specific measures in order to arouse their interest and win their participation. In this regard, we can draw on works of several authors who have advanced alternative and supplementary ways of political participation, variously called 'strong democracy' (Barber 1984), 'real democracy' (Bryan 2004) or 'radical democracy' (Cohen and Fung 2004). An obvious requirement in this regard would be the consideration of the language of the group if this is distinct from that of the larger society.[24] But also a knowledge of and respect for particular religious and cultural traditions if they exist would be necessary. The issues should be closely related to their personal life-world and interests, and the process must lead to some definite results. There are many examples from

---

24   For a case study in Thailand see Reuber 2012, p. 138.

around the world which show that a high participation is possible if these conditions are fulfilled. Positive consequences of such processes are not only better decisions and more appropriate results; the process of working and achieving things together also creates a new sense of community, and develops local people's confidence, skills and ability to cooperate.[25]

What would be the main substantive areas of policy necessary for an improvement of living standards and a reduction of poverty and inequality on the countryside and in peripheral areas? It is not the place to discuss those issues here in detail. The relevance of three measures, however, is evident. The first is a land reform which should provide a basis for self-sufficient work for the landless workers and small farmers. Land is a key asset for poor people in rural areas where a large part of the poor of the world live. In countries with high inequality, land is very unequally distributed (for example in Latin America). In theory, redistribution of land should be a main instrument for increasing equality. In practice, however, many hurdles exist (World Development Band Report 2006: 162–8). After redistribution, productivity may decrease, because the new holders do not have the relevant skills or resources; the reforms are often carried through incompletely; and they are often focused on a few high-productivity areas. However, all this must not happen; the outcomes of land reform depend on the institutional context and the strategies pursued (Ip and Stahl 1978). Thus, all these problems point to the need to include all parties concerned from the beginning into the process of land reform. If it is well-planned and carried through, its positive effects are beyond question. The contrast in the development of East Asia and Latin America is clearly connected with the fact that inequality in land distribution is much higher in the latter region (Kerbo 2012: 481; Frankema 2006). A second important policy area for peripheral areas is investments in technical infrastructure, such as roads and trains, and provision with electricity and clean water. The third is investments in welfare institutions, such as education, health and social services. In the latter two regards, the most peripheral, set-off rural areas which are often inhabited by ethnic minorities are strongly disadvantaged compared with economic centres and cities.

Development of New Models of Democratic Welfare States

The quantitative analysis in Chapter 4 has shown that state social spending is the most important single factor contributing to more economic equality. Tied in with this finding, I would propose here as the final thesis that development of the central elements of a welfare state is a key instrument for achieving more equality also in ethnic heterogeneous societies in the less developed world today. This thesis shall be divided into three sub-theses.

First, a sufficiently strong and well-functioning state as such is already a basic presupposition. It is a myth that the state has lost its power and autonomy as a consequence of globalization (Weiss 1998). If this has happened in part, it did so mainly due to privatization and deregulation processes enacted under the compulsion of the big business and the powerful; when they needed state support (as in the bank crisis) they used the state quite extensively. Those who are affected most adversely by the retreat of the state are the poor. Striking examples are the favelas within and around many large cities in Latin America, where infrastructures and public services are deficient, and the state has delivered the control of violence to drug cartels of organized crime (Fatheuer 1994). In Sub-Saharan Africa the retreat of the state has led to serious problems in many important areas of economy and society. Privatization often implied only the development of a well-developed parallel welfare system and the increasing neglect of the public system.[26]

Second, we can say that the modern welfare state is a universal institution ideally suited to integrate ethnic heterogeneous societies into a political community and to produce socio-economic equality (Wilensky 1975; Alber 1987; Esping-Anderson 1990; Kuhnle 2004; Brooks and Manza 2006; see also Chapter 3, p. 71). The concept of citizenship, developed by Marshall (1950), is of central importance in this regard. Citizenship is a status which confers basic rights to every member of the political community, irrespective of their individual characteristics. It constitutes three sets of rights: civil rights, the individual freedom to decide how one wants to live in regard to marital status, employment and occupation, and territorial living place; political rights to participate fully in the political process; and social rights to enjoy adequate levels of social and economic

---

25   See the homepage of the British Community Planning Network http://www.comunityplanning.net/
26   For the Chilean health system see Witte 1994.

welfare and security, and to participate in the social and cultural life of a community, corresponding to the standards prevailing in a society. The economist Amartya Sen (1999) has developed a strong argument which says that the main aspect of positive development of a nation is to expand the real freedoms that people enjoy: 'Development requires the removal of unfreedom: poverty as well as tyranny, poor economic opportunities as well as systematic deprivation, neglect of public facilities as well as intolerance or overactivity of repressive states' (Sen 1999: 3). It is evident that Sen's concept of freedom as unfolding of the positive capabilities of people corresponds largely to Marshall's basic rights. It was shown that the personal perception to be able to decide freely about one's personal matters contributes significantly to life satisfaction (Haller and Hadler 2004).

Third, the expansion of the welfare state is clearly connected with democracy. Normative theories of democracy as well as empirical research on the evolution of welfare states agree with this thesis. In his famous work *Democracy in America*, already Alexis de Tocqueville (1945[1835]) has argued that public expenditures tend to increase in democracies for several reasons: because the mass of people support public expenditures for which they must not pay directly; the political elites who try to improve everything because in this way they can win elections; and democracies in general are characterized by spirit of continuous reform and improvement.

Today, a basic education, employment and decent work and protection in the case of unemployment, health insurance and old age pensions are considered as the most important social rights in the sense of Marshall. Democracy has been essential to enforce those rights for the whole population. There exists, in fact, a high correlation between the age of the democratic tradition of a country and its level of social spending in these areas (Schmidt 2004; see also Table 4.2, p. 100) The thesis that democracy and a welfare state are associated with more equality is obvious (see also pp. 69–70; in addition Wilensky 1975; Boix 2003). Measured as a proportion of GDP, social expenditure in 2000 was about 25 per cent in Western Europe, 19 per cent in Central and Eastern Europe, 10 per cent to 15 per cent in the CIS states, America and the Middle East and only about 5 per cent or less in Sub-Saharan Africa and Asia (ILO 2010). Particularly in Sub-Saharan Africa social expenditure is very low and often covers only 20 per cent to 30 per cent of the population (see also ILO 2000: 53ff.). From this point of view, the poorer countries around the world – which, by and large, are also the most heterogeneous in ethnic terms – have a long way to go toward effective welfare states. The welfare state has been a phenomenal success; it has been introduced, after the lead of Germany and Britain, everywhere in the world, supported by leftist as well as centrist political parties; its introduction has provided a level of independence and social security for the mass of people which never existed before in history (Dahrendorf 1979). In some way an exception from this pattern is the United States where the ideas of freedom and equality of opportunity was always more important than that of equality of results, that is, of an equal income distribution (Flora and Heidenheimer 1981; Verba and Orren 1985; Hess 2001; Haller et al. 1995). However, even in the USA the role of policies was important; inequality increased more under Republican than under Democratic presidents (Bartels 2008).

To promote generous social security and social benefits in communities like India or Chile to the whole poor population is impossible for the near future (Ping 1996: 238). However, there are trends and forces which make it highly probable that the less developed countries will, by and large, follow the pattern of the developed ones, and extend their welfare state systems significantly. The following four factors and trends support the thesis that also the South will take over the idea and basic principles of the welfare state and extend social spending in the future. First, one of the strongest predictors of the amount of welfare state spending is the level of socio-economic development (Schmidt 2004). Looked at in isolation from other factors, GDP per capita correlates highest with social spending; its effect remains significant also in the regression analysis (see Tables 4.2 and 4.3, pp. 100, 106) Thus, as societies become richer – and this process is much faster in recent times in the Global South – they will also become able and ready to spend more on social affairs.

Second, it has been shown that some of today's developing countries – including Egypt, Tunisia, Sri Lanka, Bolivia and Panama – spend more on social transfers than the advanced OECD countries have spent historically at similar income levels (Lindert 2005). Also some Latin American countries, such as Chile, have a well-established welfare state tradition with high coverage of the population (White 1994).

Third, a vast amount of quantitative and historical political-economic research has shown that social spending and economic growth do not oppose but rather complement each other: a healthier, better educated and skilled population is an asset also for economic productivity and growth (Vobruba 1983, 1989; Lindert 2004; World Bank 2005). This connection will certainly be a motivation for governments in developing countries to increase investments in the welfare state. Fourth, a wave of democratization processes have taken place since the Second World War: they began with the overthrow of authoritarian governments in South Europe and Latin America in the 1970s and 1980s, continued with the fall of Communist regimes in East Europe in 1989/90, and that of authoritarian regimes in East Asia, and led to the Arab Spring revolutions in 2010. Today, about 60 states around the world can be considered as rather well-functioning democracies.[27] The spread of democracy will be a strong force inducing the extension of welfare states. Democracy has a positive effect, because social spending is strongly supported by the population (Haller et al. 1995; Svallfors and Taylor-Gooby 1999; Brooks and Manza 2006).

Fourth, the worldwide spread and assertion of human rights will be a force supporting the extension of welfare spending in the poor countries of the South (Beudel et al. 2007; Pegram 2010). From this point of view the state has a positive obligation to use all its available resources in order to uphold basic economic and social rights, in particular the right to food and water and attending to the health of its citizens (Sternad 2013: 77). In this regard the poor states may have to revise their budgets and to cut less important or even problematic expenses (for example those for military) in favour of social expenditure (see also p. 261 for the case of Sub-Saharan Africa).[28] However, the establishment of welfare states which have a significant effect on more equality is by far not an automatic process – even in countries with a democratic system and a majority of voters belonging to poor social strata. South Africa and Brazil are cases in point. In both countries the elites which strongly determine political priorities do not feel responsible for finding solutions to poverty and inequality in spite of the fact that they recognize the urgency of these problems. The poor masses are so much attuned to this unjust system that they do not question it or support more radical reformers. As shown in Chapter 1, after the transition in 1994 in South Africa, economic policy and socio-political attitudes have not been developed in a way which considers the problem of inclusion of the large poor, mainly Black, masses as a primary political objective. The development model proposed by the neoliberal 'Washington Consensus' is still followed in many countries of the South (for its inapplicability to Africa see Engelhard 1998). Terreblance (2002:417ff.) thus argues that a transition to a social-democratic, 'European' version of Capitalism is urgent for Africa.

On the other side, we can assume that the welfare states in the less developed countries will not exactly be structured in the same way as the comprehensive and strong welfare states now existing in the North. When thinking about a welfare state model suited for the Global South, we must abandon much of the Eurocentric writing in this regard. First, the provision of the welfare state in the South will never be as fully organized and bureaucratized as the European welfare state is. Already between North/Central and South Europe a significant difference exists in this regard – in the North, people want to organize all things in detail, lay big emphasis on being reliable in every transaction, have tight time schedules (Levine 1997; Haller et al. 2013), whereas the model prevalent in South Europe, in Italy in particular, is one of muddling through, of organizing things ad hoc, of improvising creative solutions if unexpected problems arise: it is rather such a procedure which can be a model for the Global South (Willi 1983).

Second, here exists a general difference in the relations between individuals, other persons and the role of formal rules therein. In the African context, for instance, a person is a thoroughly social person, a continuous 'work in progress', a complex, multilayered entity including the elements of gender, generation, class, race and ethnic identity; the regulation of social relations and obligations by contracts is felt as alien, even amoral (Comaroff and Comaroff 2012: 79, 91). In the South, social relations with other people, with the family and extended kin and with members of the village and the town district are much more important and they will remain so in the future (Hyden 2006). The European, and in particular the Scandinavian, model of the welfare state is based on a strong individualism. Welfare state support is directed at individual men and women, children and the elderly, but not toward families. In the South, however, poor and homeless people, sick and the elderly are never left alone as happens frequently in European cities when an old person dies in an apartment building without the knowledge of anybody else living in the same house.[29] Thus, even a well-developed welfare state in the South should not be directed only or mainly at the individual person and to the employed people as is

27 See www.freedomhouse.org
28 It is symptomatic in this regard that there is very little information available on the budgets of these states.
29 In our survey in Ethiopia, the interviewed people could not understand in the first instance the meaning of 'homelessness'; they said that every person without a shelter is accommodated by somebody (Haller and Müller 2010).

the case in the European (particularly the Scandinavian) welfare state. Even the European welfare state has 'grown to limits' (Flora 1986): the burdens for taxpayers and employers are very high, and many argue that interventions should shift from direct subsidies toward an increased reliance on active citizens and the support of autonomous sectors, supporting a 'creative altruism' which is essential for social integration (Matzner 1982).

Dolly Arora (1995) has pointed to a particular third aspect of welfare state development in the South, looking at the case of India. She argues that a considerable number of programs for the poor, the under-developed rural areas and the discriminated tribes have had little effect because they were counteracted by evasive tendencies. This happened through a neglect of the rights of the deprived (for example women); by developing programs available only through formal workplaces so that the masses of poor people are not included; through ambiguous legislation and inadequate provisions for its execution; and through the abdication of state responsibility in favour of the private or volunteer sector. In addition, welfare state programs are often manipulated by the powerful, because they could negatively affect their interests. Additional problematic effects are anti-welfare fallouts from various other crucial political programs: an example was a 'green revolution strategy' in India which furthered the use of high-yielding grains of wheat and chemical fertilizers to the detriment of the poorest people in the countryside.

A fourth important aspect in regard to the development and character of welfare states in the South is directly related to ethnic differentiation within nation-states. As we have seen in several parts of this book, it is undeniable that there exists a strain between an equality-orientated 'orthodox' Socialist welfare state and the aims of economic growth and prosperity. The favouring of extensive social security programs over economic openness and competition was certainly a main force contributing to the downfall of the State Socialist regimes in East Europe; they also contributed to the relative stagnation in southern countries, like India, Ethiopia and Cuba. Now, in the ethnically heterogeneous societies of the South, the pressure toward the preference for comprehensive welfare programs is generally less intense; given the pervasive poverty of these countries, people may feel that a strong economic growth as such will be to their own advantage as well – in particular, it is felt that the government of a country contributes significantly to this growth. In fact, the main aim of welfare state development was always the alleviation of poverty and new social emergencies as they resulted from industrialization and urbanization, but not changes in the overall distribution of income (Matzner 1982: 203; Zijderveld 1986). Thus, it was also a means of legitimizing the new social and political order of industrializing states, and, therefore, it was supported also by conservative political elites and leaders, such as Bismarck in Germany (Alber 1987). Policies and investments which are most conducive for economic growth must not be the most effective for poverty reduction; the social groups which can make use of investment support (for instance of micro-credits) typically are not the poorest of all (World Development Report 2006: 101–4). Some spectacularly successful countries in Africa, however, show that even on this poorest sub-continent of the world a remarkable level of political stability, democracy and economic growth can be achieved. One example is Botswana, rightly called an 'African Miracle' (Samatar 1999). In 1966, this country was one of the poorest around the world, but till 1996 it was able to increase its GDP per capita to $1800, thus joining the group of relatively well-developed Southern countries; the annual growth rate throughout most of this period was 10–11 per cent. This success was not mainly due to the detection of rich diamond occurrences (as we have seen, such mineral resources were rather a developmental handicap in many other nations), but to the existence of a small and united upper class and political leadership, conscious of the importance of building effective public institutions for a prosperous Capitalist economy (Samatar 1999: 67). The traditional land-owning and stock-breeder class was able to retain their power under British rule and, after having gained independence in 1966, entered into an alliance with educated groups such as teachers and modern-minded public officials. Also here an individual leader, the first president Seretse Kama (1966–80), grandson of a Bamangwato king, educated in South Africa and England, played an important positive role.[30] Foreign aid was used to provide water, health and education for the rural masses, while the resources from the state itself and from multi-national capital were used to fuel growth. For its positive political and economic development, Botswana had the advantage that it was a rather homogeneous country in ethnic terms, with the Tswana as the dominant group (Levinson 1998: 112). In spite of all these positive developments, Botswana remains one of the most unequal countries worldwide. This case clearly shows, therefore, the economic equality cannot and should not be made into an absolute,

---

30   See http://de.wikipedia.org/wiki/Seretse_Khama

replacing all other important societal and political goals. Similar constellations – that is, dynamic economic growth and a stable political system, but relatively high economic inequality – exist also in other countries. Another African success story is the island Mauritius in the South Indian Ocean, which is very heterogeneous in ethnic terms (Levinson 1998:255; World Development Report 2006: 116–8). Mauritius experienced strong economic growth and maintained a competitive democratic system since its independence. The reason was that the leadership of the initially dominant party abandoned its earlier radical Socialist programme and began to support foreign investment; later on, it was ready to deliver government to another political party. Similar patterns can be observed in the economically successful countries Singapore and Thailand, where Chinese elites played an important role (Kerbo 2012: 503ff.). Also here, the economic success and political stability of democracy were possible in spite of high ethnic diversity. Here, the main finding of Andrea Schlenker-Fischer (2009: 258–62) on the viability of democracy in ethnically heterogeneous societies is relevant, namely, that the different ethnic groups and their associations must be interconnected by overarching, inter-ethnic relationships which integrate the elites of the different ethnic sub-groups into overall society and politics. Such an integration is easier to achieve in consociational than in competitive democracies.

Economic growth, democratic consolidation and welfare state development will also be the main forces which could contribute to an improvement of the situation of one of the largest and most serious ethnic minorities in Europe, that of the Romas and Sintis. Their number is estimated between 8 and 12 million (about 6 million living within the EU); they live mainly in the post-Communist Central and Southeast European countries Hungary, Slovakia, Romania, Bulgaria, but also in Turkey, Russia and Spain (Scholze 2013). The Roma are differentiated from their host societies at least partly in terms of language, religious and social practices and they recognize themselves and are recognized so as a specific ethnic group. Today, they are strongly deprived and partially also discriminated in terms of education, employment and income and in living conditions; 80 per cent and more of the Roma households are endangered by poverty. This deprivation increased massively after the transition in East Europe as did ethnic hatred and racism from the side of the native populations. As a consequence, many Roma tried to immigrate to West Europe where they also encountered harsh rejection by natives and politics. However, given the widespread poverty of large parts of the general population in many post-Communist South East European countries, the deplorable situation of the Roma is not that unique. It is, however, quite remarkable, that one of the largest groups of the Roma which had lived in the old Romanian state had experienced a harsh form of slavery there. Some of the habits of present-day Roma, for instance, draw on begging in West European towns in order to earn a living, which may be related to that heritage (see also Mappes-Niediek 2012). The effect of economic prosperity, democracy and the welfare state on the situation of the Roma can be seen by comparing their position in the two neighbouring countries Austria and Slovakia. In Austria the position of the few thousand Romas who returned after 1945[31] has improved somewhat also due to the fact that they have been recognized officially as a minority which includes some basic rights in cultural terms.[32] In post-Communist Slovakia, where about half a million Roma are living, they participated less in the country's strong economic growth. Many Roma live in segregated, poor villages, often illegally built simple housing, only 19 per cent of the adults have completed secondary education and more than 90 per cent live below the national poverty line.[33] Thus, in this case, special minority subsistence programmes are needed in order to break through the cycle of low education and unemployment, poverty and dependency. The European Union has provided support (Jandl et al. 2003; Henn 2011) but the national governments often are reluctant to participate efficiently in the programs, due also to pressure from widespread racist, popular attitudes and right-wing political groups.

International Migration: Ethnic Restratification or Pathway to Egalitarian Plural Societies?

International migration is of utmost importance for the topic of this book because it is a process which directly affects ethnic differentiation and stratification both between and within sending and receiving societies.

---

31   Most of the earlier Roma's have been murdered in Hitler's concentration camps.
32   See 'Soziale Ausgrenzung Fokus: Roma in Österreich', *polis aktuell*, Nr.5, 2010.
33   Simona Foltyn, 'Slovakia's forgotten Roma', AL Jazeera America, 20 October 2013.

International migration has increased strongly in recent decades. According UN statistics, in 1990, 143 million people were living in a country other than that of their birth, in 2000, 175 million and in 2013, 232 million.[34] The highly developed countries of the North attracted most immigrants (136 million). In 2011, over 8 million people immigrated to the 35 OECD countries; in addition, nearly half a million asylum seekers were received (OECD 2013). Among the main countries of arrival were the classic 'immigration countries', the USA (with 2.6 million), Australia and Canada (each over half a million). However, also some countries historically quite homogeneous in ethnic terms and restrictive against immigrants experienced massive immigration; the first among them was Germany (with 841,000 immigrants, the second largest immigration country worldwide), but also the two South European countries Spain and Italy, and Korea (all between 300,000 and 400,000 immigrants). As a consequence, about 40 million foreign-born persons were living in the USA, over 10 million in Germany, about 7 million in Canada, France and the UK and 5 to 6 million in Australia, Spain and Italy (see also Jandl et al. 2003; Stockmann et al. 2010: 287–300; for Europe Dustmann and Frattini 2013; Recchi 2013: 125–56; Faist et al 2013). The top countries in relative proportions of immigrants were Canada, Australia, New Zealand and Israel and Switzerland (20 to 26 per cent), followed by Austria, Belgium, Ireland, Spain and Sweden (15–16 per cent); in the USA and Germany, the proportion was 13 per cent.

These data have already indicated the second aspect why international migration is relevant for patterns of ethnic stratification. As a consequence of these huge people movements, the probability increases that people who differ in terms of ethnic-national characteristics will come and live together. This is evidently the case for practically all Southern immigrants into the rich countries in the North, but it is true also for many migrants within the EU which includes countries with over two dozen different languages and four large religious denominations. In the USA, about 50 per cent of resident foreigners came from Canada or Western Europe; in 2009, this proportion had declined to a mere 8 per cent, in favour of immigrants from Latin America, the Middle East and Asia (Card and Rahael 2013: 4).

In this section, I will discuss the question how international migration affects national patterns of ethnic stratification: does it lead toward an increase of national structures of socio-economic inequality within the receiving states or toward more equal, even 'plural societies' where old and new minorities live peacefully together without significant processes of exclusion and discrimination? I will proceed in three steps: starting with a discussion of some theoretical approaches, I will formulate three general theses; then, paradigmatic models of migration and integration policy are sketched out showing the resulting effects on economic inequality; finally, some general conditions favouring or inhibiting the integration of immigrants are discussed.

Theories of Migration and its Effects on Ethnic Stratification

Economic theories are an obvious starting point here because they have been clearly elaborated and include some of the most relevant aspects of international migration. At the micro-level, economic theory assumes that decisions to move to another country are induced by economic reasons, that is, prospects of getting employment and higher wages there (Borjas 1989; Massey and Denton 1993; Jordan and Düvell 2002; Jennissen 2004; Hadler 2006). Neo-classical economic theory postulates, at the macro-level, an equilibrium model assuming that real wage differences between countries give rise to flows of people and capital until a new international equilibrium with equal wages everywhere is reached: lowly skilled and paid or unemployed workers migrate to countries in need of workers and with high wages, and capital investment moves the other way, from high-wage to low-wage regions. Keynesian theory assumes that also nominal, not only real wages are important and that money is not only a medium of exchange but also one of saving; therefore, migrants may also consider to re-migrate after having enough savings, or to send remittances home. In this model, there must not necessarily emerge an international equilibrium in wages but only one in employment since migration is seen as being mainly induced by unemployment. Human capital theory sees migration as an investment in skills and occupational experience and takes into account also potential long-term advantages; migrants (particularly the young) are not only oriented toward immediate high(er) wages. Dual labour market theory distinguishes between primary and secondary economic sectors and labour markets (Doeringer and

---

34   UN press release '232 million international migrants living abroad'; http://www.unis.unvienna.org/unis/en/pressrels/2013/unisinf488.html. See also Münz & Reiterer 2009, pp. 150–159.

Piore 1985). The first sector embraces capital-intensive production with skilled and well-paid workers in stable jobs; the second sector is characterized by mass and labour-intensive production through unskilled work. International mass migration is mainly induced by worker shortages in the second labour market which by itself may be caused by different factors (for example, demographic decline, educational expansion).

These theories, by and large, correspond to the main facts of international migration flows which clearly go from South to North and from poorer to richer regions within and between countries. They also grasp the facts that the mass of migrants are poorly skilled and immigrants in most countries work at the lower levels of the occupational structure and earn less than natives. However, these theories do not include some factors important from the sociological perspective; they neglect, in particular, the aspect of ethnic differentiation and stratification. They have also no immediate explanation for the fact that mobility is much larger within than between nations, even if income differences between the latter are often much higher. Alone in India, there were 309 million internal migrants in 2001 – more than the number of people who were mobile between countries in the world as a whole (Faist et al. 2013: 5). In the following, I would like to propose three theses related to the aspects of ethnicity and inequality:

1. At the micro-level, the hypothesis is obvious that ethnic criteria will influence intentions and decisions to migrate. First of all, it is much easier to migrate to a country and to find employment and work there if one commands its language; this is the most important single factor of integration (Esser 2006; Lewis 2013). Some of the largest and most continuous streams of migration occur between countries with the same language, such as between Ireland and the UK, between all English-speaking countries in Europe and around the world, between Austria, Germany and Switzerland, between Latin America and the Iberian Peninsula. But also religion may be important. The Gulf States, for instance, preferred guest workers from Islamic states. Integration may become difficult if very different religions are involved. Thus, the problem of the integration of the foreigners in Germany is often seen mainly as a problem of immigrants from Turkey and other Muslim countries (Sarrazin 2010). Thus, we can deduce the following hypotheses from these perspectives: international migration and the integration of migrants will not be difficult if they come from similar ethnic-national backgrounds, from countries with comparable levels of development and if the immigrants are highly skilled and needed by the labour market. Immigration and integration will be more difficult if the immigrants come from countries with significantly different ethnic-national backgrounds (in terms of language and religion) and if their migration was motivated mainly by strong economic push and pull factors. Worldwide processes of secularization as well as linguistic globalization (for example, the spread of English as a new world language) will reduce these problems.

2. At the meso-level, the sociological insight is relevant that migration often occurs in 'chains' (see Han 2006; Jandl et al. 2003: 22). In this regard, a distinction between three types of 'transnational social spaces' is useful (Faist et al. (2013: 14): transnational kinship groups, transnational circuits (including persons and organizations or professional groups) and transnational communities, such as cross-border religious groups and churches. Emigrated people motivate and support their kin and friends at home to follow them. In the countries of destination, the migrants often settle in ethnic enclaves and neighbourhoods (the Chinatowns are the best-known example). This form of migration is particularly relevant in the case of legal and illegal mass migration from adjacent countries and regions, which differ strongly in terms of socio-economic development, as is the case between the USA and Mexico and adjacent Latin American countries, and between East Europe and West and South Europe. The settlement in ethnic communities is an advantage in the first phases of residence, providing support and help in many activities. But later on the establishment and maintenance of such ethnic communities may turn out as a handicap when contacts to relevant people and networks in the larger society are not developed (Card and Raphael 2013: 1–2).[35] However, local social ties and networks in the country of origin may also inhibit migration. For Europe, it was found that potential costs of migration included 'loss of social ties, socio-cultural differences and language barriers'; they had strong negative effects on the intention to migrate (Fouarge and Ester 2008: 68). As a consequence, also in Europe migration

---

35   See also the problem of urban ghettos, discussed in Chapter 11, pp. 294–6.

within nation-states is much more frequent than that between states (Hadler 2006). Better educated migrants and those from ethnic backgrounds similar to the receiving country, particularly those of the second and the third generations, will be integrated quite well.

3. At the macro-level, we could distinguish between three types of societies: (a) ethnic homogeneous societies with little immigration in the past; (b) 'multicultural societies' with old, autochthonous ethnic minorities settling on specific territories (such as Belgium, Spain and Canada); (c) immigration societies and 'plural societies' whose population consists to a large proportion of old and new immigrants intermixed and dispersed over the country. In such 'plural societies'[36] they interact mainly in the economic and political sphere, but less in the social and cultural sphere. Examples of 'immigration societies' are the USA and the other Anglo-Saxon countries of the New World; typical of 'plural societies' are some small states such as Mauritius or Singapore with a mixture of many ethnic groups (a 'medley of peoples'); sometimes, also multi-ethnic nation-states such as India or Malaysia are included in this group. We could expect that traditional 'immigration societies'[37] will be better able to integrate immigrants than societies which were rather homogeneous and closed in former times. However, immigration may create new problems and lead to an increase of inequality in any society if it occurs very fast and on a large scale. The integration of immigrants with a different background will be a serious problem for ethnically homogeneous societies; these societies should also in general be less open to immigration. Empirical facts which prove this hypothesis include the historically rather low immigration rates to Scandinavian societies, as well as to Japan. The aforementioned OECD data show that Japan received only about 267,000 immigrants and 2,540 asylum seekers in 2012, far less than most West European countries (see also Chapter 6, pp. 182–3) However, the sociological perspective indicates also trends which reduce the personal and social costs of international migration. One of them is that the character of migration has changed significantly over the 20th century. Before the Second World War, emigration from Europe to America, for instance, implied that the emigrants had to say goodbye to their homeland forever; most did not even return for a short visit. Today, transnational mobility patterns are much more complex and fluid: the change of residence is not in only one direction, but there exists also return migration, networks to the place of origin may be continued and so forth (Glick-Schiller 2006; Faist et al. 2013). Also at the macro-political level, a change toward more openness for other cultures and for sub-cultures of immigrants has taken place. In the present-day world, the international variation in migration and migration politics became narrower also because international human rights norms have been institutionalized (Soysal 1994; Zolberg 1996; Pegram 2010).

Models of Migration Politics and their Effects on Ethnic Stratification

Let us discuss now some policy implications of the aforementioned facts and trends. Here, we have to consider the immigration policies of the different countries and ask if they considered questions of ethnic differentiation and stratification and how they coped with them. Four strategies can be distinguished in this regard, ordered along the continuum from openness to closeness: the model supporting integration of co-ethnics; the laissez-faire market model; the *Gastarbeiter* model; and the selective and exclusionary model. Different countries followed different models but not in all periods and in connection with all types of immigrants.

(a) *To bring home co-ethnics.*   This strategy implies that a nation-state deliberately aims toward supporting and increasing immigration, to bring together the members of an ethnic group in one's own state or even in a new state established for this aim. In Chapter 12, we encountered one highly successful example for

---

36   The concept of 'plural society' was coined by the British-born colonial public servant writer John S. Furnivall (1880–1960) who wrote many informative books about Burma and other South East Asian societies.

37   The United States, Canada, Australia and other 'new' societies in the South are often called 'immigration societies', because the immigrants and their descendants today constitute the majority of the population. However, this term may not be fully appropriate and euphemistic given the fact that immigration and settlement often did not take place peacefully but involved violent expulsion and suppression of the natives (this aspect was indicated to me by Anthony Löwstedt).

such a strategy, namely that of Israel; Israel was able to increase its Jewish population from about 600,000 at the time of the establishment of the state in 1948 to nearly 8 million today. Another state which acted in a similar way, although it did not pursue such an active immigration policy, was Germany which automatically granted citizenship to the refugees from the former German territories in East Europe and to ethnic Germans from Russia and other post-Soviet countries if they could prove their German ancestry. In numerical terms, also this policy was very successful; about 4.4 million *Aussiedler* (resettlers) immigrated to Germany between 1950 and 2005.[38] The question is: how successful were these policies: were they able to manage the problems of integration of the immigrants? How did socio-economic inequality develop as a consequence of immigration?

At first sight one would expect that in such cases the immigrants should be well received and integrated. However, migration and integration processes may not go on very smoothly even in such cases. We have seen in the foregoing Chapter 12 (pp. 311–14) that even in Israel, a new type of ethnic stratification and deprivation emerged, together with a significant increase of overall economic inequality. Fewer problems are reported in regard to the German *Rücksiedler* from the East, maybe not the least because at the same time a higher number of workers from Southeast Europe, particularly Turkey, immigrated to Germany who were ready to occupy the jobs in the secondary labour market. However, even in the case of the German resettlers, of whom two-thirds had not spoken German at home, unemployment was disproportionately high. The conclusion from these cases is clear: even a common ethnic background is no guarantee for successful integration into a new country if immigration occurs within a short period and on a very large scale. It seems necessary in any case to adapt the level of immigration in some degree to the labour market potential of the receiving countries.

(b) *The laissez-faire liberal model.* This strategy implies that a state should not interfere too much into issues of migration and integration, which are considered as individual decision processes, regulated by market forces. Today such a model is pursued partly by the European Union and the USA. The European Union considers an open labour market between the member states as an essential ingredient of a full Common Market and expects positive consequences from migration: first, an increase of levels of employment and reduction of unemployment – an endemic problem of the EU; second, a spread of European identity among citizens in the member countries. Thus, the intra-EU migrants are seen as the vanguard of the open and mobile 'European citizen' (Recchi 2013: 61–89; see also Jordan and Düvell 2002). Therefore, the EU has enacted measures to improve internal migration, particularly among the young and highly skilled. One is the ERASMUS programme which supports exchange of students and teachers. A new European mobility space did in fact emerge partly in the labour market. The integration of migrants from EU member states in terms of education, labour market access and income is clearly better than that of EU migrants from outside (Jandl et al. 2003: 30–33; Dustmann and Frattini 2013). This was certainly due also to the positive measures of the EU in support of internal migration. The first among them was the introduction of European citizenship with the right to settle down and work everywhere in the Union; but also to measures supporting the employment in other nations including the recognition of educational degrees, consideration of insurance entitlements and so on were relevant. The worse integration of the immigrants from outside the EU, however, is certainly also connected with the fact that as a rule they are more different in ethnic terms.

However, in other cases EU internal migration contributed to the emergence of unexpected, serious problems. The countries which adhered most closely to the aim of open labour markets after the admission of ten new member states in East and South Europe were the UK, Spain and other South European countries. As a consequence, a massive wave of immigration to the latter countries started which catapulted their very low proportions of foreigners (1–2 per cent) into very high ones: in 2011, 6.7 million foreigners were living in Spain, constituting 14.6 per cent of the total population. However, a concomitant of this increase was an explosion of unemployment. It is highly probable that this increase was connected with immigration. In 2011, Spain had an unemployment rate of 22 per cent – one of the highest in the OECD area; youth unemployment soared to over 50 per cent. The immigration to Spain had two peculiar characteristics: first, the immigrants came from quite different destinations, from the new EU member countries Bulgaria and Romania, but also

---

38   See 'Aussiedler und Spätaussiedler' in: http://de.wikipedia.org/wiki/Aussiedler_und_Sp%C3%A4taussiedler

from Latin America and Morocco; second, the bulk of immigrants was employed in sectors of low-skilled, poorly paid work, such as agricultural mass production, the building industry and personal services (Agrela 2002). Thus, a kind of 'negative selection' of immigrants occurred: contrary to the traditional immigration countries (USA and so on), not highly skilled, but unskilled workers were attracted (Münz and Reiterer 2009: 162). The absorption of this huge number of people was possible because the Spanish labour market ever since had been split clearly into a primary, protected and well-paid segment, and a secondary, insecure, low-skilled and paid segment (Reichmann 1994): 60 per cent of the immigrants found jobs in the second market, compared with only 30 per cent of the Spaniards (Eltetö 2011). In the wake of the economic crisis, the Spaniards themselves were not ready to resume jobs in the secondary labour market which also explains the massive rise of unemployment. In addition, the immigrants had the lowest labour force participation in Europe (Jandl et al. 2003: 25ff.). Strong immigration, particularly from Poland, occurred also in the UK (Jordan and Düvell 2002). Here, in recent times a reorientation of migration politics toward a more restrictive stance took place in the wake of their problems of finding employment.

(c) *The Gastarbeiter model.*   This kind of migration policy was pursued first in the German-speaking countries. In the course of the labour shortages during the economic miracle of the 1960s and early 1970s, these countries signed bilateral contracts with several South and South East European and North African countries in order to recruit low-skilled workers from there for industry and for a restricted time. This was in line with the *ius sanguinis*-model of citizenship (that is, citizenship to be granted mainly to descendants of ethnic Germans) valid at this time in Germany (Brubaker 1992), and its corresponding designation as 'not-an-immigration' country. As a consequence, millions of Italian, Spanish, Yugoslav and Turkish migrant workers came to central Europe. However, the original idea to send them back in times of recession was not realized for most of them. The 'guest workers' took roots in their countries of destination, some married partners from these countries and many brought their partners and children later to Germany. The German-Turkish agreement, for instance, ended in 1973 but few Turkish workers returned, and by 2010, the number of Turks living in Germany had increased to four million people.[39] Similar policies were pursued in other European countries, such as Belgium, the Netherlands and France. It was practised even in the State Socialist German Democratic Republic which also suffered severe shortages of labour power, not the least due to the strong wave of emigration to West Germany; the workers recruited worldwide from other State Socialist countries had to suffer severe limitations in their freedom to move and live in the GDR.

The outcome of the guest worker policy of migration in the receiving countries certainly was that the bulk of the first-generation immigrants formed a new sub-stratum at the lowest level of the societal hierarchy,[40] thus cementing or even reinforcing existing patterns of socio-economic inequality. It evidently has been a problematic policy, as contemporary observers had noted (see, for example, Castles and Miller 2008) and has obviously failed since the guest workers did not return home. Germany now has adapted its policy of immigration and granting of citizenship, and has accepted a new self-definition as a 'country of immigration'. In fact, however, Germany has never been so exclusivist in its immigration policies as it often has been accused. Skopflin (2000: 25) rightly points to the fact that by far not all Germans living outside the Federal Republic had a right to acquire citizenship automatically and that the huge task of integrating 13 million Germans from the East after the Second World War led to some neglect of other groups of immigrants.

In fact, the German-speaking countries (Austria and Switzerland more than Germany) were able to integrate the immigrants quite well into their labour market. A comparative study of immigration and integration policies in Europe, carried out by Ruud Koopmans (2010), has shown that multicultural policies which grant immigrants easy access to equal rights and do not provide strong incentives for host country language acquisition and interethnic contacts, when combined with a generous welfare state, have produced low levels of labour market participation, high levels of segregation and an overrepresentation of immigrants among those convicted for criminal behaviour. Such countries were Belgium, the Netherlands and Sweden; also the

---

39   See http://en.wikipedia.org/wiki/Gastarbeiter
40   The Swiss sociologist H.J. Hoffmann-Nowotny (1973) has coined the term '*Unterschichtung*' for this process.

UK with its lean welfare state was better able to integrate the immigrants.[41] Further, residential segregation is less pronounced in the German-speaking countries than in France or the UK (Gestring 2007; Meyer 2007). The concept of the emergence of immigrant 'parallel societies' (*Parallelgesellschaften*), proposed recently by a conservative writer (Sarrazin 2010) and right-wing politicians, has no empirical foundation. However, there still remains the problem that today (2012) over seven million people have lived for years in Germany who did not get citizenship or did not apply, even if they had been entitled to do so. This problem is even more serious for their children. In this way, they continue to be excluded from basic political rights.

However, another group of countries still practices a kind of *Gastarbeiterpolitik* which is much harsher than that practised in earlier times in Germany. These are the oil-rich Muslim Gulf states. I have hinted at their immigration policy in Chapter 5 (pp. 153–4). In 1995, there were 25 million foreign workers in the six Gulf Cooperation Council states; they comprised 90 per cent of the UAE labour force, 83 per cent in Qatar, 82 per cent in Kuwait, 69 per cent in Saudi Arabia, and 60 per cent in Bahrain.[42] Migrant workers have a very precarious legal status in these states. They have very few job-related benefits, are usually excluded from social insurance programs designed for natives and often have only short-term labour contracts; when these end, they often must leave the country. A foreign worker needs a sponsor, which usually is the employer; the workers are fully dependent on him; he often takes their documents (making it impossible for them to leave the country) and has to report any breach of the regulations to the authorities. Residence rights are closely linked to work permits and the acquisition of citizenship is very restricted, particularly for migrant workers from non-Arabic states, such as Pakistan, Bangladesh, the Philippines and Thailand.[43] Particularly women, mostly employed as domestic workers, face many forms of open and hidden discrimination and exploitation.[44] The International Labour Organization (ILO) estimates that 600,000 workers in the region can be classified as victims of trafficking.[45] The concepts of bonded labour or new slavery (Bales 2004) may well apply here.

(d) *Selective immigration policy: exclusion of unwanted immigrants, active recruitment of highly skilled labour.* In the rich countries of the North, a fourth model of immigration policy has emerged over a few decades. On the one side, it is a model of excluding unwanted immigrants, particularly from the poor countries of the South as shown in Chapter 5 (pp. 135–40). (Jordan and Düvall 2002: 235ff.) In fact, a new Iron Curtain has been built; it comes to the fore most openly between Africa and Europe, and between Mexico and the Southern border of the USA (Haller 2015; see also Kerbo 2012: 333–7). Complex systems of surveillance have been implemented along these borders; the selective granting of visas excludes the vast majority of people in the South; illegal immigration along the borders is controlled with quasi-military methods; and a virtual new Iron Curtain has been erected on the land borders. Similar instruments and measures are used to keep aloof, unwanted immigrants from Australia's coasts. They have delivered the story of a successful TV series 'Border Security: Australia's Front Line'. The developed countries, and particularly the USA and the EU, cooperate with the border countries in the South so that these take over the duty of preventing illegal immigration; such contracts have been made also with all of the former authoritarian North African leaders. Finally, inside the Northern countries, internal controls of identity and the possession of documents confirming the right to stay in the country have been intensified.

What were the reasons for implementing these measures and what were their effects? At least four reasons can be mentioned: first, the huge differences in economic standards of living; mean incomes in most African countries are only one-tenth of or even less than mean income in Europe and rates of poverty are very high in

---

41   In the early 2000s, however, the labour market for immigrants in the Netherlands and Sweden has improved significantly (see Jandl et al. 2003: 27).

42   *Migration News*, vol. 2, no. 3, March 1995.

43   UNHCR – The UN Refugee Agency, 1 May 1991; see http://www.refworld.org/docid/3ae6a8068.html. Raschid al Amin, *Migrant workers in the Gulf, International Centre for Trade Union Rights*, vol. 5, no. 4, 1998.

44   See ILO, *Gender & Migration in Arab States. The Case of Domestic Workers*, ed. by Simel Esim and Monica Smith, Beirut, ILO Regional Office 2004.

45   'Forget about rights', *The Economist*, 10 August 2013. See also Human Rights Watch, 'Bad dreams. Exploitation and abuse of migrant workers in Saudi Arabia', 14 July 2004.

Sub-Saharan Africa; second, differences in demographic development; the European countries fear that they would be flooded by a massive immigration from Africa where birth rates and population growth are extremely high and employment prospects for young people startlingly bad; third, differences in the political situation; the civil wars in Sub-Saharan Africa, and the revolutionary turmoil in the Arab North African countries have led to high numbers of refugees; fourth, the agitation and activities of political groups and parties, particularly from the right side, in the North which ask for a closing of the frontiers against the South.

What have these measures achieved? On the positive side – given the aim to control and reduce legal immigration from the South – one can surely say that they have achieved their aims, at least in Europe. Immigration from Africa is much below the potential; it is estimated that today about 3.5 million people of African origin are living in Europe.[46] However, negative side-effects of these measures are also obvious. They include the violation of human right principles in the para-military border controls; in the Mediterranean, at least 10,000 people have lost their life, not the least because support was refused to people in distress at the sea; second, an increase of human smuggling and trafficking which has become a vast and profitable business and led to an additional exploitation of illegal migrants; third, an increase of illegal employment in Europe and to the exploitation of these immigrants (Futo and Jandl 2007). In the USA, an estimated number of 2.1 million unauthorized immigrants entered the country as children; even if they attended US public schools, their chances for social mobility remain constrained (Gonzales 2013). An additional, negative side-effect of illegal immigration is that after the experience of the high costs of illegal border crossings, the immigrants do not want to repeat the experience and therefore do not return home (Massey 2013).

The other side of the migration policy of the Northern countries is to facilitate and support the immigration of highly skilled workers from everywhere in the world, corresponding to their needs. Here, the global inequality in the world system (Wallerstein 1974, 1975) reflects itself also in migration patterns. In the United States, for instance, thousands of physicians have been recruited from Latin America to fill the less-well-paid jobs in the hospitals while native physicians could take over the more lucrative private doctor's offices (Portes and Walton 1981). In the countries of the South, this *brain-drain* leads to a severe shortage of highly skilled work. Overall, the skill level of immigrants to the USA rose significantly between 2000 and 2009 (Card and Raphael 2013: 9): this improvement was mainly due to immigration from Asia. Latino immigrants, all in all the largest group, constituting 16 per cent of the US population in 2010 (Mexicans have numbered 31.8 million), were subject to a systematic process of racialization (Massey 2013). The cause of increasing illegal immigration and racialization were several amendments to the Immigration and Nationality Act which placed caps on immigration, giving each country an annual quota of just 20,000 immigrant visas. In parallel with these trends, 'efforts by politicians, academicians, and pundits portray Latin Americans as a threat to American society made considerable headway with the public' (Massey 2013: 263): as a consequence, public opinion also became more critical on immigration. Income inequality which recently was growing in the USA (OECD 2008) probably was also connected with these immigration processes.[47]

Interim Résumé

Following the economic assumptions sketched out at the beginning of this section, international migration should be beneficial for all involved countries. It should contribute to a relief of the tight labour market situation in the sending countries, provide new sources of income through remittances of the expatriates and result in gains in human capital by persons returning from emigrating. For the receiving countries, it should contribute to their economic growth and affluence by providing much-needed labour power. However, sociological considerations point also to obstacles, problems and side-effects in the processes of international migration: people usually do not want to leave their places of birth, the social networks established there and the cultural environment in which they have grown up. In fact, international migration is much less frequent than migration within nation-states. International migration is also correlated in a significant way with new

46   en.wikipedia.org/Schwarze_in_Europa
47   See also Waters and Eschbach 1995; US Census Bureau, 'The Changing Shape of the Nations Income Distribution. 1947–1998', Current Population Reports, June 2000; Bartels 2008; Reynolds (2007), however, questions the thesis of an increase of income inequalities in the USA because of methodological problems of measuring income inequality.

problems and the emergence of socio-economic inequalities related to ethnic discrimination and deprivation. The findings presented in the previous chapters and in this section point to three aspects which are crucial in this regard.

First, the amount and speed of international migration processes is relevant; if large numbers of migrants are entering a country, problems will arise if the labour market cannot absorb them easily; problems of integration will be aggravated if the immigrants lack some relevant social and cultural resources (for example knowledge of the language dominant in the receiving country). It is evident, however, that huge processes of migration occur only or mainly if incomes and standards of living diverge strongly between countries; the incentive to migrate is stronger the nearer two countries are located to each other. Thus, a first, albeit very general, conclusion is that socio-economic development of the poor countries of the world toward a level which excludes mass poverty is crucial for relieving emigration pressure. This thesis is not trivial because it is also the dynamic and perspectives of development which are relevant for people. Even if a country starts from a rather low level, the anticipation of positive changes might induce among its people, and particularly among the brightest of them, optimism and the option of voice instead of exit (Jordan and Düvall 2002). Such a difference might explain the extreme difference in overall optimism and life satisfaction in the post-Communist East European countries and Latin America; standards of living deteriorated massively in several East European countries after the transition and many people are quite depressed today (Haller and Hadler 2004).

Second, the way how migration processes are motivated and which instruments are used in their steering is relevant; if only the interests of the receiving countries predominate, an exclusion of many people in sending countries interested in migration will be the consequence, as well as an increase in illegal migration and all negative correlates of it. In fact, in this regard a new stratified global mobility regime has emerged in which the rich countries and the individuals with relevant assets (skills, knowledge) are clearly privileged (Bauman 1998). The immigration policy of the rich countries should be reoriented in many regards. They should accept also a proportion of less skilled immigrants from the South (maybe selected by a lottery); they should send back high-skilled people after some time to their home countries where they are needed most; and they should contribute to the establishment of high-quality school systems and facilities for vocational training in the South.

Third, the political situation of the immigration countries is relevant. It is evident that adherence to basic human rights requires a democratic political structure. Furthermore, the dominant political orientation in a country is relevant when it comes to accepting international refugees and asylum seekers. The social democratic Scandinavian countries are doubtless leading in this regard, after they changed their historical policies in this regard fundamentally.[48] Integration of immigrants in a way which does not increase economic inequality is easier in societies which have adopted an explicit policy of multiculturalism, that is, tolerate or even support different cultures within a nation-state. The first country which adopted such a policy officially was Canada. Its Multiculturalism Act of 1988 states that Canada recognizes and promotes the understanding 'that multiculturalism reflects the cultural and racial diversity of Canadian society and acknowledges the freedom of all members [...] to preserve, enhance and share their cultural heritage and [...] that multiculturalism is a fundamental characteristic of the Canadian heritage and identity'.[49] One reason why Canada was a pioneer in this regard has certainly been that it is not only a classical immigration society but also a society composed of two sub-nations, with a continuing threat of secession of the French-speaking province of Quebec from the majoritarian English-speaking Canada. This policy which is very different from that of 'White Australia' in former times is certainly one factor explaining the lower economic inequality in Canada than in Australia and the United States. Another important measure providing more fairness toward immigrants is to grant double citizenships to migrants; in 1959, only 5 per cent of all states did so, but in 2005, 50 per cent (Faist et al. 2013: 24).

---

48   For the principles of Sweden in the first half of the 20th century see Chapter 6. Recently, however, the Scandinavian countries are revising their immigration policies again.

49   Quoted in http://en.wikipedia.org/wiki/Canadian_Multiculturalism_Act; see also Momin 2005: 18–20.

Summary and Retrospect

Ethnic membership and class position are closely intertwined in many countries around the world. The way how this occurs, however, varies significantly. In some countries, some ethnic groups are living concentrated on a certain territory, and their deprivation (or privilege) is obvious; in other cases, the two dimensions are so closely intertwined that it is hard to recognize them at all; a case in point is the Brazilian 'coloured class structure'. In this chapter, I have discussed three basic social and political strategies which are available to come to grips with the varying forms of discrimination of ethnic groups and ethno-classes. These strategies include: the secession of a group from the mother state; the introduction of a federal constitution; the strengthening of the autonomy of territorially concentrated groups; and the empowerment of ethnic groups and classes by providing them with high-qualified general and vocational education, by fostering their participation in community, town and regional development, and by developing new models of public social welfare which should take into consideration both the limited financial power of most countries of the Global South as well the strength of their social networks and communal relations. In all these measures and policies, the empowerment of the deprived groups was considered as a strategy much more promising than that of establishing quotas and affirmative actions. In the last section of this chapter, the issue of migration from the poor countries of the South to the rich North was picked up, asking about the role of ethnic diversity and stratification in them. Four different strategies of immigration and integration policy exist: the model to bring home co-ethnics; the laissez-faire, liberal model; the Gastarbeiter model; and the model of a selective immigration policy. The factual achievements and shortcomings as well as the problems of each of these models from the viewpoint of human rights were discussed. Also in this regard, the main conclusion is obvious: international migration which has increased significantly over the last decades will not bring about 'plural societies' everywhere in the world. Rather, the different basic models of ethnic-national integration which exist today – plural societies, multicultural societies, ethnically rather homogeneous societies with a 'dominant culture' (*Leitkultur*) – will continue to exist also tomorrow. Each of these models, however, must come to grips with globalization and the corresponding rise of people movements around the world and try to adhere to basic principles of human rights in their rules of foreclosure and admission of foreigners.

In this book, I started from two basic assumptions: first, that economic inequality within nations is a very important although widely neglected topic for economics and sociology; and second that the interaction between class formation, social stratification and ethnic differentiation explains why some nations are rather equal, while others are characterized by pervasive inequalities. A set of crucial intervening factors and processes were identified which determine if ethnic differentiations will lead to inequality or not: historical experiences of racist violence in slavery and Apartheid systems; the character of the political institutions of a state: its authoritarian or democratic structure, its political centralization and the role of the elites therein and its readiness to spend on social matters; and, finally, secular and religious ideologies of equality and inequality. By focusing upon these factors it is possible to explain the outstanding international variations in this regard, and in particular the striking differences between economic equality in most European nations and glaring inequality in most Sub-Saharan African and Latin American countries. We can identify both a positive path leading toward prosperity and equality, and a negative one connected with circles of violence, leading to economic stagnation and decline, and to persisting or rising inequalities. Both small and large nation-states can follow one or the other path. The power of ethnic-national identifications proved to be beneficial in cases where it helped to integrate and develop very heterogeneous nations; but it was fateful in cases where elites captured state power, using violent means, suppressing democracy and neglecting universal human rights. The power of ethnic and national identifications, relations and conflicts is also evident if we look at political and economic developments at the global level not only in the long century of nationalism (1860–1945), but also in recent decades. The neo-imperialist wars in Korea, Vietnam, Iraq and Afghanistan, the recurring 'permanent revolutions' in China, the bloody civil wars in Sub-Saharan Africa, the overthrow of democratic governments by military regimes in Latin America have not only cost millions of human lives, they have also cemented inherited structures of power and privilege, of deprivation and discrimination. The aim of economic equality cannot be made an absolute at the neglect of ethnic and national cleavages as the Communist and State Socialist regimes around the world had to learn. 'Sustainable' economic equality can be attained only if there are trustful relations between elites, a commitment to democratic procedures involving citizens at large and a readiness to devote significant parts of state budgets for them. All this requires the recognition of the continuing importance of ethnic-national identifications and relations at all levels of a social and political community.

References

Abraham, Kinfe (n.d.), *Adwa. Decolonization, Pan-Africanism and the Struggle of the Black Diaspora*, Addis Ababa: The Ethiopian International Institute

Agrela, Belén (2002), Spain as a recent country of immigration: How immigration became a symbolic, political and cultural problem in the 'New Spain', The Center for Comparative Immigration Studies, University of California, San Diego, Working Paper 57

Akinwumi, Olayemi et al., eds (2007), *Historical Perspectives on Nigeria's Post-Colonial Conflicts*, Lagos, Nigeria: Historical Society of Nigeria

Alber, Jens (1987), *Vom Armenhaus zum Wohlfahrtsstaat. Analysen zur Entwicklung der Sozialversicherung in Westeuropa*, Frankfurt/New York: Campus

Aminzade, Ron (2013), *Race, Nation and Citizenship in Postcolonial Africa: The Case of Tanzania*, New York: Cambridge University Press

Anugwom, Edlyne E. (2006), 'Ethnic conflict and democracy in Nigeria: The marginalisation question', *Journal of Social Development in Africa* 15: 61–78

Arora, Dolly (1995), 'Addressing welfare in Third World contexts. Indian case', *Economic and Political Weekly*, 29 April 1995, pp. 955–62

Bales, Kevin (2004), *Disposable People. New Slavery in the Global Economy*, Berkeley, CA etc.: University of California Press

Balsvik, Randi Ronning (2005), *Haile Sellassie's Students: The Intellectuals and Social Background to Revolution*, Addis Ababa, Ethiopia: Addis Ababa University Press/Michigan State University, African Studies Centre

Barber, Benjamin (1984), *Strong Democracy*, Berkeley, CA: University of California Press

Bartels, Larry M. (2008), *Unequal Democracy: The Political Economy of the New Gilded Age*, Princeton, NJ: Princeton Univeristy Press

Batungi, Nasani (2008), *Land Reform in Uganda: Towards a Harmonised Tenure System*, Kampala: Fountain Publishers

Bauman, Zygmunt (1998), *Globalisation. The Human Consequences*, Oxford: Polity Press

Beblavý, Miroslav et al. (2011), Education Policy and Welfare Regimes in OECD Countries, Brussels: Centre for European Policy Studies, CEPS Working Document No. 357

Blau, Peter M. (1977), *Inequality and Heterogeneity. A Primitive Theory of Social Structure*, New York/London: Free Press/Collier Macmillan

Blindenbacher, Raoul and R.L. Watts (2003), 'Federalism in a changing world. A conceptual framework for the conference', in Raoul Blindenbacher and Arnold Koller, eds, *Federalism in a Changing World: Learning from Each Other*, Toronto: McGill-Queen's University Press

Boix, Carles (2003), *Democracy and Redistribution*, Cambridge: Cambridge University Press

Borjas, George J. (1989), 'Economic theory and international migration', *International Migration Review* 23: 457–85

Braun, Norman and Thomas Voss (2014), *Zur Aktualität von James Coleman. Einleitung in sein Werk*, Wiesbaden: Springer

Brooks, Clem and Jeff Manza (2006), 'Why do welfare states persist?' *The Journal of Politics* 68: 816–27

Brubaker, Rogers (1992), *Citizenship and Nationhood in France and Germany*, Cambridge, MA: Harvard University Press

Bryan Frank (2004), *Real Democracy*, Chicago, IL: University of Chicago Press

Buchanan, Allen (1991), *Secession: The Morality of Political Divorce from Fort Sumter To Lithuania and Quebec*, Boulder, CO: West View Press

Calderón, Fernando G. (1977), 'The Quechiua and Aymará peoples in the formation and development of Bolivian society', in UNESCO (1977), pp. 185–219

Card, David and Steven Raphael, eds (2013), *Immigration, Poverty, and Socioeconomic Inequality*, New York: Russell Sage Foundation

Castles, Stephen and Mark Miller (2003), *The Age of Migration: International Population Movements in the Modern World*, Basingstoke: Palgrave-Macmillan

Claval, Paul (1998), *An Introduction to Regional Geography*, Malden, MA: Blackwell

Cohen, Joshua and Archon Fung (2004), 'Radical democracy', *Swiss Political Science Review* 10: 23–34

Coleman, James et al. (1966), *Equality of Educational Opportunity*, Washington, DC: US Government Printing Office

Comaroff, Jean and John L. Comaroff (2012), *Der Süden als Vorreiter der Globalisierung*, Frankfurt/New York: Campus (American ed. Boulder 2012)

Cordell, Karl and Stefan Wolff, eds (2004), *The Ethnopolitical Encyclopedia of Europe*, Houndsmill, Basingstoke: Palgrave Macmillan

Dahrendorf, Ralf (1979), *Lebenschancen. Anläufe zur sozialen und politischen Theorie*, Frankfurt: Suhrkamp

Davies, Lynn (1986), 'Policies of inequality in the Third World: dependency or autonomy?' *British Journal of the Sociology of Education* 7: 191–204

Diani, Mario and Doug McAdam (2003), *Social Movements and Networks*, Oxford: Oxford University Press

Dicken, Peter and Peter E. Lloyd (1984), *Die moderne westliche Gesellschaft*, New York: Harper & Row

Doeringer, Peter B. and Michael J. Piore (1985), *Internal Labor Markets and Manpower Analysis*, Armonk, NY: M.E. Sharpe

Dreze, Jean and Amartya Sen (2013), *An Uncertain Glory: India and its Contradictions*, Penguin Books: Allen Lane

Dustmann, Christian and Tommaso Frattini (2013), 'Immigration: The European experience', in Card & Raphael, *Immigration, Poverty, and Socioeconomic Inequality*

Dymski, Gary A. (2011), 'Ten ways to see a favely: Notes on the political economy of the new city', *Revista Economica* 13: 7–31

Elazar, Daniel J. (1996), 'From statism to federalism – A paradigm shift', *International Political Science Review* 17: 417–29

Elsasser, Hans et al. (1988), *Die Schweiz*, Stuttgart etc.: Kohlhammer

Éltető Andrea (2011), 'Immigrants in Spain. Their role in the economy and the effects of the crisis', *Romanian Journal of European Affairs* 11: 66–81

Engelhard, Philippe (1994), *L'Afrique – Miroir du Monde? Plaidoyer pour une nouvelle économie*, Paris: arléa

Esping-Andersen, Gøsta (1990), *The Three Worlds of Welfare Capitalism*, Cambridge: Polity Press

Esser, Hartmut (2006), *Sprache und Integration. Die sozialen Bedingungen und Folgen des Spracherwerbs von Migranten*, Frankfurt am Main/New York: Campus

Faist, Thomas, Margit Fauser and Eveline Reisenauer (2013), *Transnational Migration*, Cambridge: Polity Press

Farndon, John (2008), *India Booms*, London: Virgin Books

Fassmann, Heinz, Max Haller and David Lane, eds (2009), *Migration and Mobility in Europe. Trends, Patterns and Control*, Cheltenham, UK/Northampton, MA: E. Elgar

Fatheuer, Thomas (1994), 'Jenseits des staatlichen Gewaltmonopols. Drogenbanden, Todessschwadronen und Profiteure; die andere Privatisierung in Rio de Janeiro', in D. Dirmoser et al., eds, *Jenseits des Staates?* Bad Honnef: Horlemann, pp. 23–38

Fiseha, Assefa (2006), *Federalism and the Accommodation of Diversity in Ethiopia*, Nijmegen: Wolf Legal Publishers

Fleiner, Thomas (2001), 'Federalism: Basic structure and value of Switzerland. Recent Developments in Swiss Federation', *Tijdschrift voor Bestuurswetenschappen en Publiekrecht* 56: 291–303

Flora, Peter and Arnold J. Heidenheimer, eds (1981), *The Development of Welfare States in Europe and America*, New Brunswick, NJ, and London: Transaction Publishers

Flora, Peter, ed. (1986), *Growth to Limits. The Western European Welfare State in Comparative Perspective*, Vol. 1, Berlin and New York: W. de Gruyter

Forsyth, Frederick (1976), *The Biafra Story*, London: Penguin Books

Fouarge, Didier and Peter Ester (2008), 'How willing are European to migrate?' in Peter Ester et al., eds, *Innovating European Labour Markets*, Cheltenham: E. Elgar, pp. 49–71

Frankema, Ewout (2006), The colonial origins of inequality: Exploring the causes and consequences of land distribution, University of Groningen, Groningen Growth and Development Centre, Research Memorandum GD-81

Freund, Bill (1998), *The Making of Contemporary Africa: The Development of African Society since 1800*, Boulder, CO: William Mack Freud

Futo, Peter and Michael Jandl, eds (2007), *2006 Yearbook on Illegal Migration, Human Smuggling and Trafficking in Central and Eastern Europe*, Vienna: International Centre for Migration Policy Development

Gestring, Norbert (2007), 'Ethnische Segregation, Quartierstypen und soziale Netzwerke', in Meyer, *Wohnen – Arbeit – Zuwanderung*, pp. 135–45

Glick-Schiller, Nina, et al. eds (2006), *Nations Unbound: Transnational Projects, Postcolonial Predicaments, and Deterritorialized Nation-States*, Amsterdam: Gordon and Breach

Goldthorpe, John H., C. Llweellyn and C. Payne (1987), *Social Mobility and Class Structure In Modern Britain*, Oxford: Clarendon Press

Gonzales, Roberto G. (2013), 'Reassessing human capital and intergenerational mobility', in Card and Raphael, *Immigration, Poverty, and Socioeconomic Inequality*, pp. 232–54

Gordon, David, ed. (1998), *Secession, State and Liberty*, New Brunswick, NJ: Transaction Publ.

Hadler, Markus (2006) 'Intentions to Migrate within the European Union: A Challenge for Simple Economic Macro-Level Explanations', *European Societies* 8: 111–40

Haller, Max (1996), 'The dissolution and building of new nations as strategy and process between elites and people. Lessons from historical European and recent Yugoslav experience', *International Review of Sociology* 6: 231–47

Haller, Max (2008a), *Die österreichische Gesellschaft. Sozialstruktur und sozialer Wandel*, Frankfurt/New York: Campus

Haller, Max (2008b), *European Integration as an Elite Process. The Failure of a Dream?* New York/London: Routledge

Haller, Max (2012), 'Values and Interests in Processes of Macro-Regional Integration', in Nikolai Genov, ed., *Global Trends and Regional Development*, New York/London: Routledge, pp. 25–44

Haller, Max (2015), 'Why empires build walls. A historical-sociological interpretation of the new Iron Curtain between Africa and Europe', in Alberto Gasparini and Eliezer Ben-David, eds, *The Walls Between Conflict and Peace*, Leiden/Boston: Brill

Haller, Max, Bogdan Mach and Heinrich Zwicky (1995), 'Egalitarismus und Antiegalitarismus zwischen gesellschaftlichen Interessen und kulturellen Leitbildern. Ergebnisse eines internationalen Vergleichs', in Hans-Peter Müller and Bernd Wegener, eds, *Soziale Ungleichheit und soziale Gerechtigkeit*, Opladen: Leske + Budrich, pp. 221–64

Haller, Max and Markus Hadler (2004), 'Happiness as an Expression of Freedom and Self-determination. A Comparative, Multilevel Analysis' in Wolfgang Glatzer, Susanne von Below and Matthias Stoffregen, eds, *Challenges for the Quality of Life in Contemporary Societies*, Dordrecht etc.: Kluwer, pp. 207–31

Haller, Max and Bernadette Müller, eds (2010), Europa in Afrika. Afrika in Europa. Ergebnisse des Forschungspraktikums Global Sociology, Graz: Universität Graz, Department of Sociology

Haller, Max, Markus Hadler and Gerd Kaup (2013), 'Leisure time in modern societies: A new source of boredom and stress?' *Social Indicators Research* 111: 403–34

Han, Petrus (2006), *Theorien zur internationalen Migration. Ausgewählte interdisziplinäre Migrationstheorien und deren zentralen Aussagen*, Stuttgart: Lucius & Lucius

Hannum, Hurst (1990), *Autonomy, Sovereignity, and Self-Determination*, Philadelphia, PA: University of Pennsylvania Press

Härtel, Ines, ed. (2012), *Handbuch Föderalismus*. Vol. IV: *Föderalismus in Europa und der Welt*, Heidelberg etc.: Springer

Heinemann-Grüder, Andreas (2012), *Föderalismus als Konfliktregelung. Indien, Russland, Spanien und Nigeria im Vergleich*, Opladen: B. Budrich

Henn, Jessica (2011), *Minderheitenschutz der Roma in der Europäischen Union*, Berlin: BWV Verlag

Hess, Andreas (2001), *Concepts of Social Stratification. European and American Models*, Houndsmill, Basingstoke: Palgrave

Hoben, Allan (1973), *Land Tenure among the Amhara of Ethiopia: The Dynamics of Cognatic Descent*, Chicago/London: University of Chicago Press

Hoffmann-Nowotny, Hans-Joachim (1973), *Soziologie des Fremdarbeiterproblems*, Stuttgart: Enke

Hooghe, Liesbeth, Gray Marks and Arjan H. Schakel (2010), *The Rise of Regional Authority. A Comparative Study of 42 Democracies*, London/New York: Routledge

Hyden, Goran (2006), *African Politics in Comparative Perspective*, Cambridge: Cambridge University Press

Ibrahim, Solava and Sabina Alkire (2007), Agency & Empowerment: A proposal for internationally comparable indicators, Oxford Poverty and Human Development Initiative (OPHI), University of Oxford, Working Paper

Illife, John (1997), *Geschichte Afrikas*, München: C.H. Beck (*Africans: The History of a Continent*, Cambridge University Press)

ILO (2000), *World Labour Report 2000*, Geneva: International Labour Organization

ILO (2010), *World Social Security Report 2010/11*, Geneva: International Labour Organization

Ip, P.C. and C.W. Stahl (1978), 'Systems of land tenure, allocative efficiency, and economic development', *American Journal of Agricultural Economics* 60: 19–28

Jandl, Michael, Albert Kraler and Anna Stepien (2003), Migrants, Minorities and Employment: Exclusion, Discrimination and Anti-Discrimination in the 15 Member States of the European Union, International Centre for Migration Policy Development (ICMPD), Luxembourg: European Communities

Jennissen, Role P.W. (2004), *Macro-economic Determinants of International Migration in Europe*, Amsterdam: Dutch University Press

Jordan, Bill and Franck Düvell (2002), *Irregular Migration. The Dilemmas of Transnational Mobility*, Cheltenham, UK/Northampton, MA: Edward Elgar

Katzman, Martin T. (1969), 'Ethnic geography and regional economics, 1880–1960', *Economic Geography* 45: 45–52

Kelly, Eric D. and Barbara Becker (2000), *Community Planning. An Introduction to the Comprehensive Plan*, Washington, DC/Covelo, CA: Island Press

Kerbo, Harold R. (2012), *Social Stratification and Inequality. Class Conflict in Historical, Comparative, and Global Perspective*, New York: McGraw Hill

Kohr, Leopold (1983), *Die überentwickelten Nationen*, München: Goldmann

Kolsto, Pal (2001), 'Territorial autonomy as a minority rights regime in post-Communist societies', in Will Kymlicka and Magda Opalski, eds, *Can Liberal Pluralism be Exported? Western Political Theory and Ethnic Relations in Eastern Europe*, Oxford: Oxford University Press, pp. 200–219

Koopmans, Ruud and Paul Statham, eds (2000), *Challenging Immigration and Ethnic Relations Politics: Comparative European Perspectives*, Oxford/New York: Oxford University Press

Kristan, Ivan (1993), 'Das Recht auf Selbstbestimmung als Menschenrecht', in S. Devetak et al., eds, *Kleine Nationen und ethnische Minderheiten im Umbruch Europas*, München: Slavica Verlag Dr. Anton Kovac, pp. 44–50

Kuhnle, Stein (2004), *The Developmental Welfare State in Scandinavia: Lessons for the developing world*, Geneva: United Nations Research Institute for Social Development

Küper, Wolfgang (1973), *Tansania*, Bonn: Deutsche Afrika-Gesellschaft

Lehmbruch, Gerhard (1967), *Proporzdemokratie. Politisches System und politische Kultur in der Schweiz und in Österreich*, Tübingen, Mohr Siebeck

Levine, Robert (1997), *A Geography of Time*, New York: Basic Books

Levinson, David (1998), *Ethnic Groups Worldwide. A Ready Reference Handbook*, Phoenix, Arizona: Oryx Press

Lewis, Ethan (2013), 'Immigrant-native substitutability and the role of language', in Card and Raphael, Immigration, *Poverty, and Socioeconomic Inequality*, pp. 60–97

Lijphart, Arend (1984), *Democracies. Patterns of Majoritarian and Consensus Government in twenty-one Countries*, New Haven, CT: Yale University Press

Lindert, Peter H. (2004), *Growing Public: Social Spending and Economic Growth since the Eighteenth Century*, Cambridge: Cambridge University Press (2 vols)

Logan, John R., Elisabeta Minca and Sinem Adar (2012), 'The geography of inequality: Why separate means unequal in American public schools', *Sociology of Education* 85: 287–301

Lutz, Wolfgang (2009), 'Sola schola et sanitate: Human capital as the root cause and priority for international development?' *Philosophical Transactions of the Royal Society* B 364 pp. 3031–47

Maathai, Wangari (2009), *The Challenge for Africa. A New Vision*, London: W. Heinemann

Mann, Michael (2007), *Die dunkle Seite der Demokratie. Eine Theorie der ethnischen Säuberung*, Hamburg: Hamburger edition (*The Dark Side of Democracy*, New York 2005)

Mappes-Niediek, Norbert (2012), *Arme Roma, böse Zigeuner: Was an den Vorurteilen über die Zuwanderer stimmt*, Berlin: Ch. Links Verlag

Markakis, John and Nega Ayele (2006), *Class and Revolution in Ethiopia*, Addis Ababa: Shama Books

Marko, Josef (2012), 'Ethnopolitics. The challenge for human and minority rights protection', in Claudio Corradetti, ed., *Philosophical Dimensions of Human Rights. Some Contemporary Views*, Dordrecht: Springer, pp. 265–91

Marshall, Thomas H. (1950), *Citizenship and Social Class and other Essays*, Cambridge: Cambridge University Press

Massey, Douglas and Nancy Denton (1993), *American Apartheid: Segregation and the Making of the Underclass*, Cambridge, MA: Harvard University Press

Massey, Douglas S. and Nancy A. Denton (1989), 'Hypersegregation in U.S. Metropolitan areas. Black and Hispanic segregation along five dimensions', *Demography* 26: 373–91

Massey, Douglas S. (2013), 'Immigration enforcement as a race-making institution', in Card and Raphael, *Immigration, Poverty, and Socioeconomic Inequality*, pp. 257–81

Mathok, Dhieu Diing Wol (2009), *Politics of Ethnic Discrimination in Sudan. A Justification for the Secession of South Sudan*, Kampala: Netmedia Publishers

Matzner, Egon (1982), *Der Wohlfahrtsstaat von morgen*, Frankfurt/New York: Campus

Meyer Fortes (1961 [1940]), *African Political Systems*, London: Oxford University Press

Meyer, Frank, ed. (2007), *Wohnen – Arbeit – Zuwanderung. Stand und Perspektiven der Segregationsforschung*, Berlin: LIT

Mohanty, B.B. (2001), 'Land distribution among Scheduled Castes and Tribes', *Economic and Political Weekly* 36: 3857–68

Momin, A.R. (2006), 'India as a model for multiethnic Europe', *Asia Europe Journal* 4: 523–37

Münz, Rainer and Albert Reiterer (2009), *Overcrowded World? Global Population and International Migration*, London: Haus Publishing

Mutua, Alfred (2010), *How To be Rich in Africa & Other Secrets of Success*, Nairobi: GDC Books

Neuwirth, Robert (2006), *Shadow Cities. A Billion Squatters, a New Urban World*, London/New York: Routledge

Nuscheler, Franz (2004), *Entwicklungspolitik*, Bonn: Bundeszentrale für politische Bildung

OECD (2008), *Growing Unequal? Income Distribution and Poverty in OECD Countries*, Paris: OECD

OECD (2013), *International Migration Outlook 2013*, Paris: OECD Publications

Olaniyi, Rasheed (2007), 'Ethnic conflicts and the rise of militarised identities in Nigeria', in Akinwumi, *Historical Perspectives on Nigeria's Post-Colonial Conflicts*, pp. 56–69

Pallier, Verena (2010), Die Favelas von Rio de Janeiro. Eine sozioökonomisch-ökologische Betrachtung, Diploma thesis, Faculty for Natural Sciences, University of Graz

Pegram, Thomas (2010), 'Diffusion Across Political Systems: The Global Spread of National Human Rights Institutions', *Human Rights Quarterly* 32: 729–60

Ping, Huang (1996), 'Globalization and rural inequality in China', in G. Therborn, *Inequalities of the World*, London, New York: Verso, pp. 220–246

Polman, Linda (2010), *Die Mitleidsindustrie. Hinter den Kulissen internationaler Hilfsorganisationen*, Frankfurt/New York: Campus (first Dutch ed. 2008)

Portes, Alejandro and John Walton (1981), *Labour, Class and the International System*, Orlando etc.: Academic Press

Rauch, Carsten (2005), *Die Theorie des demokratischen Friedens*, Frankfurt/New York: Campus

Recchi, Ettore (2013), *Senza Frontiere. La libera circolazione delle persone in Europa*, Bologna: Il Mulino

Reichmann, Thomas (1994), Explaining unemployment in Spain, International Monetary Fund, Working Paper WP/94/201

Reis, Elisa P. (1996),' 'Inequality in Brazil: Facts and Perceptions', in Therborn, *Inequalities of the World*, pp. 193–219

Reynolds, Alan (2007), 'Has U.S. Income Inequality Really Increased?' *Policy Analysis* 586: 1–24

Reuber, Paul (2012), *Politische Geographie*, Paderborn: Ferdinand Schöningh

Samatar, Abdi I. (1999), *An African Miracle. State and Class Leadership and Colonial Legacy in Botswana Development*, Porthmouth, NH: Heinemann

Sanoff, Henry (2000), *Community Participation Methods in Design and Planning*, New York etc.: J. Wiley

Sarrazin, Thilo (2010), *Deutschland schafft sich ab. Wie wir unser Land aufs Spiel setzen*, München: Deutsche Verlags-Anstalt

Sauer, Petra and Martin Zagler (2012), '(In)equality in education and economic development', Wittgenstein Centre, Vienna University of Economics and Business

Schaefer, Armin and Harald Schoen (2011), 'Mehr Demokratie, aber nur für wenige?' *Leviathan* 41: 94–120

Schicho, Walter (2004), *Handbuch Afrika, Vol. 3: Nord- und Ostafrika, östliches Zentralafrika*, Frankfurt: Brandes & Apsel

Schlenker-Fischer, Andrea (2009), *Demokratische Gemeinschaft trotz ethnischer Differenz. Theorien, Institutionen und soziale Dynamiken*, Wiesbaden: VS Verlag

Schmid, Eefje and Jutta Wagner (2004), *Migration in und aus Afrika*, ed. Bundesministerium für wirtschaftliche Zusammenarbeit und Entwicklung, Bonn

Scholze, Markus (2013), Integration der Roma in der EU, Master thesis, Department of Sociology, University of Graz

Schöpflin, George (2000), *Nations Identity Power. The New Politics of Europe*, London: Hurst & Company

Scott, Kyle (2011), *Federalism. A Normative Theory and its Practical Relevance*, New York: Continuum

Sen, Amartya K. (1999), *Development as Freedom*, New York: Knopf

Sen, Amartya K. (2010), *Die Idee der Gerechtigkeit*, München: Beck (English ed. 2009)

Seve, Lucien (1968), *Marxism and the Theory of Human Personality*, London:Lawrence and Wishart

Simmel, Georg (1923), 'Der Streit', in G. Simmel, *Soziologie. Untersuchungen über die Formen der Vergesellschaftung*, München/Leipzig: Duncker & Humblot

Singh, Khushwant (1988), *Train to Pakistan*, New Delhi: Ravi Dayal

Smith, Neil (1996), *The New Urban Frontier. Gentrification and the Revanchist City*, London/New York: Routledge

Soysal, Yasemin (1994), *Limits of Citizenship: Migrants and Postnational Membership in Europe*, Chicago: University of Chicago Press

Sternad, Andrea (2013), The Right to Humanitarian Assistance in International Human Rights Law, Diploma thesis, Department for International Law, University of Graz

Stockmann, Reinhard and Wolf Gaebe, eds (1993), *Hilft die Entwicklungshilfe langfristig?* Opladen: Westdeutscher Verlag

Stockmann, Reinhard, Ulrich Menzel and Franz Nuscheler, eds (2010), *Entwicklungspolitik. Theorien – Probleme – Strategien*, München: Oldenbourg Verlag

Strassoldo, Raimondo and Nicoletta Tessarin (1992), *Le radici del localismo. Idagine sociologica sull'appartenenza territoriale in Friuli*, Trento: Reverdito editore

Strohmeier, Martin and Lale Yalcin-Heckmann (2000), *Die Kurden. Geschichte, Politik, Kultur*, München: C.H. Beck

Suberu, Rotimi T. (2001), *Federalism and Ethnic Conflict in Nigeria, Washington*: United States Institute of Peace Press

Svallfors, Stefan & Peter Taylor-Gooby, eds (1999), *The End of the Welfare State? Responses to State Retrenchment*, London: Routledge

Terreblanche, Sampie (2002), *A history of inequality in South Africa, 1652–2002*, University of Natal Press, Pietermaritzburg

Tilly, Charles (2004), *Social Movements, 1768–2004*, Boulder, CO: Paradigm Publishers

Tocqueville, Alexis de (1945 [1835]), *Democracy in America*, New York: Vintage Books (here quoted after the German ed. 1976: *Über die Demokratie in Amerika*, München: dtv)

Toggenburg, Gabriel N. and Günther Rautz (2010), *ABC des Minderheitenschutzes in Europa*, Wien etc.: Böhlau

Turton, Davic (2006), *Ethnic Federalism. The Experience of Ethiopia*, Oxford, Ohio: Ohio University Press

UNESCO (1977), *Race and Class in Post-Colonial Society: A Study of Ethnic Group Relations in the English-Speaking Caribbean, Bolivia, Chile and Mexico*, Paris: UNESCO

UNESCO (2012), *EFA Global Monitoring Report: Youth and Skills: Putting Education to Work*, Paris: United Nations Educational and Scientific and Cultural Organization

Verba, Sidney and Gary R. Orren (1985), *Equality in America. The View from the Top*, Cambridge, MA/ London: Harvard University Press

Vobruba, Georg (1983), *Politik mit dem Wohlfahrtsstaat*, Frankfurt: Suhrkamp

Vobruba, Georg, ed. (1989), *Der wirtschaftliche Wert der Sozialpolitik*, Berlin: Duncker & Humblot

Wallerstein, Immanuel (1974), *The Modern World-System I. Capitalist Agriculture and the Origins of the European World-Economy in the Sixteenth Century*, New York etc.: Academic Press

Wallerstein, Immanuel (1975), 'Class-formation in the capitalist world-economy', *Politics and Society* 5: 367–75

Waters, Mary C. and Karl Eschbach (1995), 'Immigration and Ethnic and Racial Inequality in the United States', *Annual Review of Sociology*, 21: 419–46 (reprinted in Cross, *The Sociology of Race and Ethnicity I*)

Weiss, Linda (1998), *The Myth of the Powerlessness of the State. Governing the Economy in a Global Era*, Cambridge: Polity Press

Wilensky, Harold (1975), *The Welfare State and Equality*, Berkeley, CA: University of California Press

Willi, Victor (1983), *Überleben auf Italienisch*, Wien: Europaverlag

Williams, Jenny (1986), 'Education and race: the racialisation of class inequalities?' *British Journal of Sociology of Education* 7: 135–54

Witte, Lothar (1994), 'Lateinamerikanische Sozialversicherung zwischen Staat und Privatisierung', in Dirmoser, Dietmar et al., eds, *Lateinamerika – Jenseits des Staates?*, Bad Honnef: Horlemann, pp. 65–105

Wong, Kenneth K. and Anna C. Nicotera (2004), 'Brown vs. Board of Education and the Coleman Report: Social Science Research and the Debate on Educational Equality', *Peabody Journal of Education* 79: 122–35

World Bank (2002), *Empowerment and Poverty Reduction: A Sourcebook*, Washington, DC: World Bank

World Bank (2005), *Equity and Development. World Development Report 2006*, Washington, DC: The World Bank, New York: Oxford University Press

World Development Report (2006), *Equity and Development*, Washington/New York: The World Bank/ Oxford University Press

World Development Report (2012), Washington: The World Bank

Wydick, Bruce (2008), 'Do race-based preferences perpetuate discrimination against marginalized ethnic groups?' *The Journal of Developing Areas* 42: 165–81

Ziegler, Jean (2008), *Das Imperium der Schande. Der Kampf gegen Armut und Unterdrückung*, München: Goldmann

Zijderveld, Anton C. (1986), 'The ethos of the welfare state', *International Sociology* 1: 443–57

Ziltener, Patrick (2013), *Regionale Integration in Ostasien. Eine Untersuchung der historischen und gegenwärtigen Interaktionsweisen einer Weltregion*, Wiesbaden: Springer

Ziltener, Patrick (2013a), 'Impacts of colonialism. A research survey', *Journal of World System Research* 19: 290–311

Zolberg, Aristide R. (1996), 'Immigration and multiculturalism in the industrial democracies', in Rainer Bauböck et al., eds, *The Challenge of Diversity. Integration and Pluralism in Societies of Immigration*, Aldershot: Avebury, pp. 43–65

Index

Index